JOHN BEARD – HANDEL AND GARRICK'S FAVOURITE TENOR

Neil Jenkins O.D.

2012

DEAN CLOSE SCHOOL

LIBRARY

JOHN BEARD – HANDEL AND GARRICK'S FAVOURITE TENOR

Neil Jenkins

Bramber Press

First published in 2012 by
Bramber Press
St. Mary's House
Bramber
West Sussex
BN44 3WE
Email: info@bramberpress.co.uk
www.bramberpress.co.uk

ISBN 978-1-905206-13-1

Front cover: Portrait of John Beard by Thomas Hudson
c.1743, wearing his 'Macheath' costume
(Gerald Coke Handel Collection)

Title page: Portrait of John Beard by John Michael Williams
c. 1735, at the beginning of his career

Printed and bound by CPI Group (UK) Ltd, Croydon, CR0 4YY

CONTENTS

ILLUSTRATIONS

MUSICAL ILLUSTRATIONS

FOREWORD

John Beard has appeared as a footnote in books about Handel and Garrick for too long. Whilst the other major figures in London's artistic life in the mid-eighteenth century have all received a considerable amount of scrutiny, and biographies have recently appeared of leading composers like Handel, actors like Garrick, actresses like Lavinia Fenton and Martha Ray, society hostesses like Mrs Teresa Cornelys, whore-mongers like Jack Harris, and other men-of-letters, painters and suchlike, which have contributed to a fuller and richer understanding of life in, and around, Covent Garden market, John Beard (1715-91) has been consistently overlooked. And yet he walked through these same streets, rubbing shoulders with the rich and the poor, and counting amongst his friends some of the prime movers in this galaxy of stars. Through his membership of the clubs held in London's coffee shops, and particularly his long association with the Beefsteak Club, he was intimate with the likes of the writers Fielding, Boswell, Goldsmith, Bonnell Thornton, Bickerstaffe and Smollett; the poet laureate William Whitehead; the painters Hogarth, Hayman and Hudson; the politicians Wilkes and Lord Sandwich; the composers Handel, Thomas Arne, William Boyce, John Stanley, Charles Burney, and a host of others eminent in the fields of music, medicine and entertainment. His world was the world of London's two patent theatres at Drury Lane and Covent Garden. In his 33 year career he spent 16 years at Drury Lane, 11 of them under Garrick's leadership, and 16 at Covent Garden, for the last 8 of which he was its manager. Beard followed Garrick's lead in modernising the theatre during his time at the head of the Covent Garden company; and, while neither of them was able to do much about the pricing structure which allowed late-comers to enter for half-price after the 3rd Act, or the unwieldy custom of performing a main-piece followed by an after-piece – thus playing to two increasingly different audiences on the same night – they were able to introduce order into an environment where hitherto the public had done very much as they pleased. Despite the set-back of serious riots, their two-pronged approach meant that, by the mid-1760s, the Front Curtain demarcated the two halves of the theatre, with the general public no longer able to roam backstage (or even onstage) freely. Both of these enlightened theatre managers improved the morals of the theatre. They were both men of probity, and endeavoured to run tight ships. Under their leadership the acting profession began to acquire a better reputation, and their theatres were cleared of the worse elements of the Covent Garden neighbourhood. Their book-keeping was orderly, and can still be consulted in libraries today. Until now Garrick has taken all the credit for these improvements and Beard's contribution has not been acknowledged.

The area where Beard has received most attention is as the tenor soloist for whom Handel wrote many of his opera and oratorio roles. This was a major part of the singer's life, since it was Handel who plucked him from the obscurity of the Chapel Royal choir, and placed the nineteen-year-old singer straight into leading operatic roles. He was still singing for Handel on the last occasion that the blind composer supervised a performance of his own music: *Messiah* on April 6 1759. In the years after Handel's death Beard was in demand up and down the length of the country as a soloist in the roles that Handel had written specifically for his voice: the title roles in *Judas Maccabaeus*, *Samson*, *Jephtha*, and – of course – the tenor solos in *Messiah*. He visited the fledgling Music Festivals that were growing up in England's Cathedral cities and provincial music centres, and took part in the annual

1

Foundling Hospital performances of *Messiah*, for which he was rewarded by being made a Governor.

But this work had to be fitted into his principal day-job as a contracted singing-actor at the London theatres. His work with Handel was the icing on the cake, and always required the consent of the theatre managements. In the few years that he was unable to join Handel (1748, 1749 and 1750) it may have been the terms of his current contract which prevented it.

But another, more likely, reason was a personal one. Beard had a fascinating private life, and was the first male theatrical personality to marry into the aristocracy. It had often happened the other way around, of course: various noblemen kept actresses as mistresses, and just occasionally married them. But Beard was the first humble actor/musician to achieve the opposite when he wed Lady Henrietta Herbert (née Waldegrave) in 1739. This brought him into contention with her family. His new father-in-law (the 1st Earl Waldegrave) was a member of Sir Robert Walpole's government and the British Ambassador in Paris, and his brothers-in-law (the 2nd and 3rd Earls) had the ear of the king (George II). In addition, Beard – an Anglican – found himself wed to a catholic descendant of King James II – and therefore a close relation by marriage of Bonny Prince Charlie.

Beard's early life is like something out of a Henry Fielding novel: the young man who comes to London to make good, and finds himself immersed in a world of Pleasure Gardens, Balls and evenings at the theatre, peopled with duplicitous noblemen and ladies, and encumbered with enormous debts to a host of tradesmen. But, of course the difference is that he was the performer at the Pleasure Gardens and the theatre, and the debts were his wife's. Whilst his private life was a tangled mess of protracted court cases, in which his aristocratic catholic wife endeavoured to obtain the jointure which was rightly hers, he gained fame and notoriety as the foremost *Captain Macheath* of his day in John Gay's perennially popular *The Beggar's Opera*; as the performer of Arne's delightful songs in the current staging of Shakespeare's plays; as a singer of Cantatas and ballads in the intervals at the theatre; and as a principal performer in Ballad Operas, Pantomimes, Burlettas and Comedies. In the summer months he was in huge demand as a singer of popular ballads at fashionable Ranelagh Gardens. His wife's story is not so happy. After a marriage of 14 years she seems to have died of the classic 'broken heart' when her daughter by her first marriage to Lord Herbert, Barbara, renounced catholicism, cut herself off from her mother, and married back into the Herbert family – thus denying Henrietta the chance of gaining the proper inheritance to which she was entitled. It was at this time that Beard found it difficult to make himself always available for Handel's performances. The only oratorios which were not originally written for his voice, however, were the ones from these years: *Alexander Balus*, *Susanna*, *Solomon* and *Theodora*. When he rejoined Handel in 1751 the roles were all revised to suit his voice.

For lovers of a good picaresque 18th century novel Beard's life then took a change for the better, and the happy ending was in sight. After nearly 6 years of widowhood he married again. This time he found himself fortuitously allied to the influential Rich family when he married Charlotte Lane, John Rich's widowed daughter. John Rich had made his fortune out of *The Beggar's Opera*, and had built Covent Garden Theatre in 1732 with the profits of its first season. By 1759 he was old and ailing, and so he invited his new son-in-law to be his assistant manager. When he died in 1761 Beard acted for the Rich family as Manager, and achieved the notable success - from which the theatre has subsequently never really deviated - of turning it into an opera house. The operas which Beard commissioned and introduced to the London public were successors to the Ballad Operas which had long been popular as after-pieces, and which were the backbone of his own repertoire: works like *The Devil to Pay*, *The Chaplet*, *The Lottery* and *Damon and Phillida*. But Beard approached the best composers and librettists and produced full-length main-pieces – *Artaxerxes*, *The Maid of the Mill*, *Love in a Village*, *Love in the City*, *Thomas and Sally* and *The Jovial Crew* which rivalled *The Beggar's Opera* in length, tunefulness and popularity. These works were given the nick-name of "sing-song" operas; and the word and style was subsequently exported abroad and transmuted into the term "singspiel", which now describes similar works of late 18th century Vienna, such as Mozart's *The Magic Flute*.

When his singing career was affected by the onset of deafness, Beard supervised the sale of Covent Garden theatre, and its precious royal patent, for the handsome sum of £60,000. This was divided between the five members of the Rich family: Beard's wife, her three sisters and their step-mother. Thus Beard was able to retire in comfort to a new villa close to the River Thames in Hampton, Middlesex, on a parcel of land which he had bought from Hampton's other famous theatrical resident, David Garrick. Here he lived for twenty-four years of well-deserved rest, on a pension provided by one of his greatest admirers. King George III had been a frequent visitor to Covent Garden since the age of six, and as King heard Beard sing two Court Odes to him every year, on his birthday and at New Year. During the early years of his reign, before ill-health affected him, the King attended as many plays, operas and oratorios at Covent Garden as he could. In Beard's last oratorio season, he attended on every night. Beard's reward was to be the only singer ever created 'Vocal Performer in Extraordinary to His Majesty'.

A certain amount of Beard's fascinating life is already known, but some of the earlier information was poorly researched and inaccurate. Thus the Dictionary of National Biography contained the erroneous information that he had been a singer at the Duke of Chandos' palace of Cannons, where Handel wrote the masque *Acis and Galatea* and his first English oratorio *Esther*. True, these pieces were subsequently in Beard's repertoire, but he was too young to have taken part in their first performances (c. 1718-20). None of the Dictionary entries has ever been sure of the date of his birth, and this was the piece of information which I have also had the most difficulty in discovering. Equally problematic was the precise details of his marriage to Lady Henrietta Herbert, which no-one had hitherto been able to prove conclusively had taken place. Fortunately some determined research was successful in turning up the exact location and record of this scandalous liaison, which set all tongues wagging in London's smart society of the 1730s. The precise date of his birth has now been almost certainly discovered as a result of painstaking research into the full gamut of male children born into 'Beard' families in London during the appropriate years of the eighteenth century.

Other inaccuracies in older references are the statement, in the New Grove Dictionary of Music and Musicians, that he had been made a D. Mus. at Oxford in 1759. At the present time there is no evidence that this happened, although he certainly accompanied Thomas Arne there in July 1759, and sang in the oratorio concerts that took place when Arne received his Doctorate.

My researches have taken me far afield, and some of the most useful and pertinent discoveries have been made in the USA. The ability of American Universities to inherit, or purchase, material relating to the British Theatre in the Eighteenth Century means that a lot of ephemera has been saved from destruction. Earlier work done by the editors of *The London Stage 1660 – 1800* in these libraries has been invaluable in opening up this period. The painstaking recreation of the daily performances in the main theatres of the time, together with the accompanying commentary, by the editors of *The London Stage* has revealed rich seams of information. In this manner I came to discover a book at the Folger Shakespeare Library in Washington whose relevance to John Beard's life and career had hardly been recognised. Compiled by his good friend and colleague, the actor and poet William Havard, this collection of letters, poems, and ephemera which he entitled "Jeu d'esprit" has opened a useful window into Beard's domestic life during both of his marriages, to Henrietta and to Charlotte, as well as elucidating his activities at the Beefsteak Club.

I must record my grateful thanks to the Librarians at the many libraries that I have visited in the course of my research: those at the Folger Shakespeare Library, who helped make my various visits there so comfortable and productive; the librarians at the Pendlebury Music Library, Cambridge and at the Cambridge University Library who must have got used to my frequent visits; those at the Bodleian Library, Oxford, who let me peruse all of Boyce's 'Court Odes'; the University of London, the University of Sussex and its useful microfilm reader, and the Gerald Coke Handel Collection – which includes much relevant material, including the *Messiah* vocal and instrumental parts – at the Foundling Hospital. At the Library of the Royal College of Music I discovered manuscript music that had belonged to Beard at one time, and from which he had performed; and at the British Library there were other notable finds, including a song which Beard had composed.

Many individual scholars have given enormous help. Donald Burrows has been unfailingly helpful and enthusiastic, and has given clear pointers to where material relating to Beard's work with Handel can be found. His recent scholarly works on Handel have been consulted with enormous regularity and have assumed the significance – along with Otto Deutsch's *Handel a Documentary Biography* and *The London Stage* – of being my 'bibles'. The works of other notable Handel scholars which have proved invaluable have been those of Winton Dean, Harry Diack Johnstone and Roger Fiske. Winton and Harry have given useful guidance and encouragement; and I am only sorry that I never got to know Roger Fiske early enough to be able to pick his brain: nobody knew so much about London's Theatre Music as he did. Other Handel and Eighteenth Century music scholars who have been happy to help me have been Ruth Smith, Rosamund McGuinness, Graydon Beeks, Susan Wollenburg, Elizabeth Gibson, Olive Baldwin, Thelma Wilson, David Hunter and Simon McVeigh. Jane Clark has also been enthusiastic, and told me about Beard's present of Scarlatti harpsichord music to the young Charles Wesley; while John Greenacombe was able to tell me about the existence of a picture of John Beard's house in St Martin's Lane, as well as providing details about Bernard Gates' Chapel Royal choir school premises in James Street, Westminster.

At Hampton I was helped by the vicar of St Mary's Parish Church, the Rev. Derek Winterburn, to find and photograph Beard's memorial tablet, currently hidden in a dark corner behind the organ; and I was fortunate to visit Beard's home, Rose Hill (now the Hampton Public Library) at the precise moment that a sub-librarian was finishing some research into the grounds and gardens as they had been in Beard's day. Other assistance regarding Beard's retirement years was kindly proffered by the staff at Richmond Library's Local History Collection. Further information about Beard's homes in London, the theatres at Drury Lane and Covent Garden, and London's 18th century coffee houses was provided by the London Metropolitan Archives.

The present head of the Waldegrave family, James Sherbroke the 13th Earl, has been of enormous assistance in allowing me access to the family's papers at Chewton Mendip. These include the manuscript letters of Henrietta, her father James the 1st Earl, and her grandmother Barbara Webb. These have helped to elucidate the negotiations surrounding Henrietta's first marriage to Edward Herbert, and her subsequent attempts to placate her father after her marriage to John Beard. Also of great assistance was the loan of a copy of the 'Waldegrave Family History', which had been prepared in 1975 by Lady Mary Hermione Waldegrave, the wife of Geoffrey Noel the 12th Earl, and mother of the present Earl.

Whilst researching the Waldegrave connection I was intrigued to find that a portrait of Henrietta existed, and had appeared in print in an old copy of *Country Life*, but had since disappeared. The Earl gave me such information as he had, and I set out on a quest to find it. This led me to Canada; and through the kind offices of Lee Dickson it was traced to its present owners. A colour photograph which they have kindly prepared for me appears within these pages, alongside the equally handsome portrait of John in his fine red 'Macheath' coat which hangs on the staircase at the Foundling Hospital Museum in London.

The impetus to do the research for this book was provided by Girton College, Cambridge, when they offered me the *Cummins Harvey Fellowship* in order to take time out from a busy singing career and concentrate on a project which had been a pipe-dream since the moment that I first walked into Beard's retirement villa *Rose Hill* in 1974. At that time I was a Hampton resident, and I was also performing, and recording, much of the repertoire that John Beard had been the first tenor to sing. Some early research led to me giving talks about the London Pleasure Gardens, and singing the music by Arne, Boyce, Stanley and others that was provided for them. This was subsequently broadcast on Radio 3. In the Handel tercentenary year of 1985 I toured a lecture-recital about Beard's work with Handel. But it was through the enthusiasm of my friend Rev. James Hawkey, then an undergraduate at Girton College, that my desire to write Beard's biography reached the ears of Dr Martin Ennis, Director of Music at Girton, and a member of the Cambridge Music Faculty. My profound thanks are due to him, for both believing in my ability to accomplish this project, and for persuading the College authorities to award me the Visiting Fellowship.

I have left my biggest thank you to the end, as this book could not have been completed if it had not been for the completely invaluable assistance that I have received from my brother, Terry Jenkins. What started out as a simple request to assist me by tracking down John Beard's date of birth, turned into a partnership which has made the writing of this book more stimulating and more accurate. Terry's first big success was to discover the details of Beard's marriage to Henrietta in the archives of the Fleet Prison – where the extraordinary event had taken place in a 'cloak and dagger' manner that was not uncommon at the time. Since it appeared that he thrived in the musty atmosphere of the National Archives, Terry was happy to research further abstruse matters, and so free up my time to pursue other avenues of research. He discovered details of Beard's bank account at Coutt's Bank; and to him must be ascribed the excellent explanation of Henrietta's convoluted legal dispute with the Earl of Powis (which took him to the Powis archives at the National Library of Wales), as well as the compilation of the family trees of the Beard, Herbert and Rich families.[1]

The Beard family tree has kept him occupied in seemingly fruitless research for several years, since John Beard's origins prior to the moment when he emerged as one of the choristers at the Chapel Royal are shrouded in mystery. The fact that he had a brother, William, and a sister with the unusual name (for the 18th century) of Catherine, should have revealed his parentage in the parish records. The 'eureka' moment was reached, however, when a chance comment in one of Beard's few extant letters, lying in the Harvard Theatre Collection, referred to a significant event in October 1785. Terry pointed out that this coincided with the birth of a 'John Beard' in October 1715, exactly seventy years earlier. We are confident that we now have the proof that his birth took place at some time in that month.

Terry also made good friends with John Beard of Australia and his wife Pam, who are direct descendants of John Beard's brother William, of Kenton near Exeter. I was happy to meet them in the summer of 2005, and learn of the subsequent history of the family. Unless some wonderful new information comes to light, it seems that we shall never know any more about John and William's parentage or their ancestors. There is a chance that there may be a tenuous connection to the Beards of Cowfold, Sussex, as the family inherited Beard's signet ring, containing a "differenced" version of the Coat of Arms granted to this particular Beard family in the 16th century. John Beard, the singer, also had it carved onto his wife Henrietta's tomb in 1753 (see the illustration below). But the College of Arms has no record of an authority being granted for the use of this design; and one must conclude that Beard simply used an appropriate existing design, in his desire for upward mobility, whilst he was married into the aristocracy.

Neil Jenkins, *Bramber, Sussex. 2012*

Armorial bearings used by John Beard

---

[1] See Appendix 7

ABOUT THE AUTHOR

Neil Jenkins is known as an internationally acclaimed Tenor singer in Opera and Oratorio. He has performed with all of the British orchestras and opera companies, and has appeared regularly in the opera houses of Paris, Berlin, Amsterdam, Chicago, Geneva, Lyon, Tel Aviv, Venice, Santiago and Cardiff. In 1974 he moved to Hampton, Middlesex, where he lived for six years and discovered that the elegant Public Library had been built by John Beard at the end of the eighteenth century as his retirement villa. Coincidentally, at that time Neil had just been singing much Handel music that had been written for this famous English singer. With Dr Paul Steinitz he had just recorded the Handel Wedding Anthem *Sing unto God* (with a spectacular final tenor aria performed by Beard in 1736) for EMI records, and also recorded several of Handel's early Oratorios (*Athaliah, Saul, Esther*) for BBC Invitation Concerts. He recorded the Cannons version of *Acis & Galatea* with both Neville Marriner and Alfred Deller, and also performed Beard's role in the opera *Arminio* in an authentic 18th century staging in Abingdon. In the next few years he was to meet much more of the tenor music that Handel had tailored to Beard's distinctive voice. He recorded *Deborah, Israel in Egypt, Alexander's Feast, Messiah, Judas Maccabaeus, Belshazzar, Saul* and *Solomon* for the BBC under the batons of Roger Norrington, Richard Hickox, Charles Mackerras and Andrew Parrott, and performed them at the Proms and at Festivals in Bath, Edinburgh, Jerusalem, Turin, Swansea, Spitalfields and St. John's Smith Square. His early interest in Beard's life led to him giving illustrated lecture-recitals about English 18th century vocal music. He toured the country with a programme about 'London's 18th century Pleasure Gardens' which he had also presented on Radio 3. In 1985 he devised and performed a tercentenary tribute, which included much music written for Beard's voice, entitled 'Mr Handel of London'. He also performed *Israel in Egypt* at the Handel Tercentenary Festival.

In the 1990s Neil turned his attention to the works of Bach, and spent ten years re-editing and retranslating all of the great choral works (*St. Matthew Passion, St. John Passion, Christmas Oratorio, Easter Oratorio, Ascension Oratorio* etc) for the New Novello Choral Edition. After preparing a new edition of Schutz's *The Christmas Story* he then turned to the works of Haydn and made new editions of both *The Creation* and *The Seasons*, in which he completely revised their English texts in line with discoveries that he had made through his researches. His first book, *The Text of Haydn's Creation* (Haydn Society 2005), was devoted to the origins of these librettos. At the same time he also edited several song albums for Kevin Mayhew Publishing and Oxford University Press.

All the time he was formulating the idea of writing Beard's biography if he should ever get the chance. That chance came in 2002, when he was awarded the *Cummins Harvey* Fellowship at Girton College Cambridge, in order to take time off from his busy singing and editing career to undertake the necessary research in the libraries and museums of Britain and the USA. This book is the result of his labours. In 2011 portions of it appeared in the Ashgate Press volume *Handel* in their Baroque Composers series (ed. David Vickers), having appeared previously in the *Göttinger Händel-Beiträge* (2008). In 2004 Neil was awarded the *Sir Charles Santley Award* by the Worshipful Company of Musicians for his musical achievements.

INTRODUCTION
THE ORIGINS OF JOHN BEARD

Chapel Royal choristers processing across St. James' Park to Chapel

The date and place of John Beard's birth, together with the names of his parents, have always been a mystery. When he died in 1791, the newspaper and magazine obituaries only recorded that he had been "bred up in the King's Chapel". His origins were obviously unknown and of no interest to them. This may come as a surprise to a modern audience, which has grown accustomed to the media's obsession with a celebrity's life. However, it was not unusual in those days, and there are many other examples of famous people whose origins still remain unknown.

The name 'John Beard' proves to be remarkably common in London in the first half of the 18th century. The occupations pursued by other people with this name, and who have so far been identified, shows the wide diversity. The list includes: attorney, barber, carpenter, druggist, distiller, exciseman, gardener, labourer, musician, mariner, ropemaker, soldier, tailor, weaver and woollen draper, together with several apprentices and 'gentlemen'.

At the outset of the research into Beard's origins, it immediately seemed possible that the musician of the same name could be a prime candidate for Beard's father, and explain how and why Beard followed the same profession. This John Beard died in 1742 'on board the King's ship Suffolk'[2]. It seems unlikely that the ship had a band on board, and so he might have been recently impressed. He left a widow, Elizabeth, who was the sole beneficiary of his will. As I shall explain, research can show conclusively that in 1742 the singer John Beard had a mother called 'Ann'. So, on the evidence, this line of research can be abandoned.

---

[2] National Archives: PROB10/1958 (transcript in PROB11/728)

If John Beard's birth was to be identified, then it seemed the only way forward was to follow the dictum of Sherlock Holmes: "When you have eliminated the impossible, whatever remains, however improbable, must be the truth". The date of Beard's birth is generally given as c.1716, and is calculated from one source - the obituaries published in the newspapers. On Tuesday, 8 February 1791, *The Public Advertiser* announced:

> On Friday last [i.e. 4 Feb.], *at four o'clock in the afternoon, died in the 75th year of his age, at his house in Hampton, where he has resided since his retirement from the stage, John Beard, Esq; formerly one of the proprietors and acting manager of Covent-Garden Theatre.*[3]

The details are corroborated by the inscription on his monument in Hampton Parish Church (now hidden by the organ) which states that he died on 4 February 1791 aged 74 years. No other reference has ever been found that mentions either his age, or when and where he was born. Now Beard joined the choir of the Chapel Royal as a boy, and it is therefore reasonable to assume that his parents were church-goers and would have taken their son to be baptised. Unfortunately, church records only show that there were many children who were born in the years around 1716 with this name. There is insufficient evidence to identify him, and it is necessary to search further. *The Morning Chronicle & London Advertiser* for Thursday 14 March 1782[4] contained the following announcement:

> "Died - Mar. 9, aged 89, Mrs Beard, mother of John Beard esq. of Hampton".

The parish records[5] show that this was Mrs *Ann* Beard, who was buried in the church vault on 15 March. This lady was certainly of an age to have been Beard's mother - she would have been around 24 in 1716. However, it is wise to be cautious, and knowing the mortality rate among child-bearing women, she could just as easily have been his step-mother.

Beard's Will[6] is the next source of information about his family, although it raises more questions than it answers. He had no children of his own and, after making provision for his wife, made bequests to a number of relations. It is tempting to think that these must have been his *only* surviving relatives, as there is no evidence to suggest he was alienated from any part of his family. He left bequests to the following:

- Nephew   William Beard of Kenton, Devon; John & Charlotte Beard, children of William
- Niece   Thomasin Jordan, wife of John Jordan of Penryn, Cornwall
- Children of late niece: Elizabeth Withycomb
- Niece   Harriett Crawford, wife of William Crawford, late of High Holborn, cabinet maker
- Sister   Catherine Beard

The nephew and nieces in the West Country were the children of William and Thomasin Beard of Kenton, Devon. (Kenton lies to the south of Exeter, close by the estuary of the River Exe, and next to Powderham Castle, seat of the Earls of Devon.) This William Beard, who died before 1791, was therefore John Beard's brother.

---

[3] British Library: Burney Collection of Early Newspapers
[4] British Library: Burney Collection of Early Newspapers (also in the *Gentleman's Magazine*)
[5] Parish records at London Metropolitan Archives
[6] National Archives: PROB 11/1202/p.208

One's first reaction is that John Beard's origins must also lie in South Devon, although, up to now, it has been assumed that he was probably born in London. There were certainly many Beard families in this area, particularly in the next parish of Dawlish. However, extensive research has failed to link them to either of the two brothers. William seems to have arrived in Kenton out of the blue, and then married the widow, Thomasin Bickford, by Licence, on 3 August 1733 at St Thomas by Exeter[7]. Marriage Licences were generally necessary if one of the parties was remarrying. However, it could also imply that William was not a local man. Perhaps he was returning to a part of the country where earlier generations had lived. The Licence describes him as a 'husbandman', and by 1740 he was a 'yeoman'. The records show that he worked on the land for the Earl of Devon and several of the local Estates. This presupposes that he had some previous experience of such work, which is unlikely if he was born in London. It is also difficult to think of a reason why a man should move from London to a distant rural area: the general trend was in the opposite direction - away from the land and into the cities.

William Beard was buried at Kenton on the 7th August 1772, aged 60 - the inscription on his gravestone is still legible. This means that he must have been born c.1712. His Will was proved at the Court of the Archdeaconry of Exeter in 1775 but its contents remain unknown as, unfortunately, all Devon Wills were destroyed by bombing in World War 2. His son, also called William, and later generations, continued to farm in the West Country.

Another beneficiary of John Beard's will was his niece Harriett Crawford; and this leads to another enigma. Harriot (sic) Beard married William Crawford on 16 May 1765, by Licence[8], at St George's, Hanover Square. The need for a Licence implies that she had not lived all her life in the parish, but she *was* baptised there on 25 May 1743, the daughter of Major and Ann Beard. The Rate Books for the parish list Major Beard at Lancaster Court, off New Bond Street, from 1741 to 1743. However, the St Marylebone burial records show that he was, in fact, buried there on 1 April 1743.[9] His name thus appears in two different parishes as 'Major'. Army records, however, show that there was no-one called Beard with this (senior) rank in 1743. The name has also not been found in the records of other organisations which used military ranks, such as local militia or the East India Company. All one can tell from this source is that John Beard had another brother, but his name remains a mystery. One possibility is that he was an older brother by a different wife, also called John, who used the soubriquet Major to differentiate himself.

Lastly, we come to Beard's sister, Catherine, who he describes in his Will as an 'innocent'. Early dictionaries define one use of this word as 'idiot' - meaning that she must have been mentally retarded in some way. Beard left her an annuity, but it seems likely that Catherine pre-deceased him. Beard made his Will on 14 June 1786, some years before he died, and a Catherine Beard was buried at St Andrew's, Holborn five months later on 15 November 1786. Catherine was not a common name at the time, and this is probably her.

That is all the genealogical information we can glean from Beard's Will, but there is further information to be found in other sources. Beard and Lady Henrietta Herbert were married in January 1739, and then lived in the Holborn area. We know this from advertisements in the papers for the purchase of tickets for

---

[7] All Kenton Records at Devon Record Office, Exeter
[8] Vicar-General Marriage Licence (at Genealogical Society, London)
[9] Parish records at Westminster Archives

Beard's benefit performances at Drury Lane. In both April 1739 and April 1740, the advertisements gave his address as New North Street, Red Lion Square. The street lay in the parish of St. George the Martyr, Queen Square, Bloomsbury, and the parish records[10] show that a Catherine Beard was baptised in this church on 27 July 1740 - the daughter of John and Anne Beard of North St. This would immediately seem to be the sister we are looking for: the address appears to be the same, yet it is clearly not a child of Beard and Henrietta. Moreover, the mother's name was Anne, as expected. It would not be unreasonable to find Beard and his parents living at the same address. So this *must* be his 'innocent' sister. If her mother is the same Mrs Ann Beard who died in 1782, aged 89, she would have given birth at the age of 47. Not impossible, and may have been a contributory factor in Catherine's mental disability. This information now gives a possible name for Beard's father - 'John', like his son.

The 1740 baptismal record for Catherine gives the address, simply, as North St. - but there were two sections to this street: New and Old North St. (They straddle Theobald's Road). This may seem a pedantic point to make, until we examine the parish records more closely. These show that the couple called John & Ann Beard had other children who were baptised in the Church in 1737 and 1738, and their address was given then, more precisely, as *Old* North St.

By some fortuitous chance, we can check exactly who was living in these streets at this time, because the 1739 Scavengers' Rate Books for the parish still exist[11] (there are no others between 1732 and 1750). These Rate Books show the occupier of each house, and were obviously prepared in advance, in ink: any necessary changes were then added in pencil. The books clearly show a John Beard in both parts of the street: Book 4 has the name of J^{no} Beard added, in pencil, to a previously empty house in New North Street, implying that he had only recently arrived there. Book 3, however, already has an entry in ink for John Beard in Old North Street, showing that this person had lived there during the previous year. This all fits together nicely, and one might conclude that John and Henrietta, after their marriage in January that year, merely made their home close to where his parents were already living. But there is a problem.

One of the other children born to John and Ann Beard, baptised on the 14 April 1737, was named John King Beard. The use of the second name 'King' identifies his parents. They must have been John Beard and Ann King, who were granted a Marriage Licence on 16 April 1736[12] – and their first child was predictably born a year later. The Licence application shows that this second John Beard was a bachelor of St Katharine Cree, a druggist aged 27. If the declared age is correct, he must therefore have been born c.1708/9 and cannot possibly be the father of our John Beard! If we assume that the Catherine born in 1740 is indeed John Beard's sister, then we apparently have the extraordinary situation where there are two couples called John and Ann Beard living at the same address. This coincidence would seem to be ridiculous. However, it is unlikely that the marriage licence would get both the status and age of the applicant wrong. The only explanation is that John Beard the musician did have both a father and a brother called John. Is this the reason for the soubriquet 'Major' Beard?

[10] Parish records at London Metropolitan Archives
[11] Camden Archives, Holborn Library, Theobald's Road
[12] Bishop of London Marriage Licences, London Metropolitan Archives

We can deduce, from a different source, that Beard's father must have died before June 1742. On 31 May that year, Beard's wife Henrietta sold part of her joynture. The indenture[13] that was drawn up allowed Beard to draw £25 p.a. to set up a trust fund for his mother Ann. This implies that she no longer had a husband to support her. It may also explain a curious entry in the *London Evening Post* of January 15 1741. Beard and Henrietta must have been abroad at the time, and the paper announced: "We hear that some time since died at Lille in Flanders, Mr Beard the late celebrated singer". This statement was never corrected and therefore remains unexplained. However, it could make sense if it contained one crucial omission, and referred to information from Lille that the *father* of Mr Beard the celebrated singer had died.

Another source which threw up some unexpected information was the Folger Library in the U.S.A.[14] This Library contains an undated manuscript entitled "An Epitaph on the Death of Miss Anna Beard" written by Beard's friend and colleague William Havard. The epitaph refers to the *"Virgin Innocence . . . . centr'd in this Maid"*, and concludes:

> *"Thy griefs with a fond, weeping Brother join,*
> *Lament her Death, and be prepared for thine".*

A literal reading of this suggests that Beard had another, previously unknown, sister who died young.

So we have now established, at the very least, that he had two brothers: William and 'Major'; possibly two sisters: Catherine and Anna; a mother (or stepmother) called Ann, and possibly a father called John. Is this enough to identify the family? The answer, unfortunately, is that there is no obvious family that fulfils *all* these criteria.

More and more parish records are being transcribed and placed on databases where they can be searched online. It is therefore possible to carry out research more thoroughly. This is especially helpful in tracing whether a child died in the first few years of life. It is not enough just to find an appropriate baptism. Several children called John Beard who were born around 1716 can be disqualified for this reason alone. There appears to be just one choice remaining for his birth, and it actually comes from 1715. This would make him a year older than expected, but such a discrepancy is not unusual; it would also make his first appearance as a tenor in 1734 slightly more plausible.

A John Beard was christened at St Botolph Bishopsgate on 6 October 1715[15] to parents John and Jane. No occupation or address were given. However, a couple with the same names had a daughter, Hannah, christened at St Dunstan, Stepney on 1st February 1713. In this entry, the father's occupation was given as 'ropemaker of Wapping'. It seems sensible to assume that they were the same couple. We can then find that a couple called John and Jane Beard had a daughter who was baptised on 8 July 1722 at St Dunstan – and named Anne. As the daughters' names are so similar, this may simply indicate that Hannah had died. This, then, could be the 'Anna' for whom Havard's epitaph was written. What is more worrying for a researcher is that the parish records for this entry list John

---

[13] National Library of Wales – Powis papers: D3/9/11
[14] William Havard, 'Jeu d'esprit', N.a.2. Folger Shakespeare Library, Washington, USA
[15] Records of City of London parishes at London Metropolitan Archives

Beard as a tailor. Are the ropemaker and the tailor the same person? We can also find a tailor named John Beard listed in an earlier entry from 1712 at St John of Wapping. On the 24 April 1712, William Beard, son of John, tailor, and Ann, of Nightingale Lane was baptised there. The year of this birth fits the known details of Beard's brother who lived in Devon. It may also be relevant that Wapping is in the East End of London where the docks are situated. It would not be difficult to make one's way to Devon, by sea, from there.

These three parishes all occur in a tightly-knit area of London's East End, and it is not possible, from the paucity of detail in the parish records, to state conclusively that these children all belong to the same family. It can be argued that Jane and Ann are alternative spellings of the same name. However, it was unusual at this time for a skilled man to change his trade or occupation. Indeed, one technique that can be used to establish the location and identity of people with the same name is to assume a continuity of occupation. Perhaps significantly, the baptism in 1715 is the only one from this period that I have not been able to eliminate from my inquiries. However, the suggestion that this may be the baptism of the famous singer is based on the lack of a negative, rather than the presence of a positive, fact. Nevertheless, it is the closest possible match that has so far been discovered for him (and his siblings).

On 1 December 1785[16] John Beard wrote to Dr Samuel Arnold to thank him for the Dinner which he attended in October. It includes the following remarks:

"...that I have been fortunate beyond my deserts or expectation I own; but be assur'd I should heartily despise myself (and so would you) could I ever be guilty of affecting the least superiority over the humblest of my school-mates, excepting only the painfull pre-eminence of age; and to that alone I ascribe the extreme kindness of my brethren on the happy 21st of October; kindness that has kept my heart warm ever since, and will, as long as my (somewhat impaired) memory lasts."

Contemporary newspaper reports state that the dinner ostensibly celebrated the 100th anniversary of the birth of Bernard Gates, who had been in charge of the Chapel Royal Choristers when Beard joined the choir. But Beard was obviously the guest of honour at this event, and it is likely that it was also a joint celebration of his own 70th birthday; thus confirming his birth in October 1715. It now looks very likely indeed that he can be identified with the John Beard who was baptised at St. Botolph Bishopsgate on 6 October 1715.

If the inference from the 1785 dinner is correct, then the age on his memorial tablet, which states that he died on "4th February 1791 aged 74 years", would then be wrong, implying that his second wife Charlotte was unaware of his correct age. One source that appears to confirm that Beard was, indeed, 75 when he died can be found in a "Collection of Epitaphs"[17] which includes the epitaph *"Satire, be dumb!"* The year of his death was given correctly, if not the day itself, as the entry ends:

"Ob. February 5, 1791, Aetatis suae, 75".

---

[16] Harvard Theatre Library, USA

[17] 'A collection of Epitaphs and Monumental Inscriptions...', London, 1806, British Library Ref. 1568/8945 *See* page 369

CHAPTER 1
JOHN BEARD AT THE CHAPEL ROYAL

1.   1727 – 1734

The first that we ever hear of John Beard is when he is discovered singing in the Chapel Royal Choir, at St James' Palace, under the direction of Maurice Greene.[1] The choral foundation there made provision for ten choristers. They were housed and educated together, and sang two services a day. When the King moved to another of his Palaces, at Windsor or Hampton Court, they duly followed him and carried on with their duties there.

Up until his death in 1727 the choristers were housed, taught and conducted by William Croft. The records show that he received £240 for "keeping, maintaining and teaching 10 children of the Chapel, at 24 pounds per annum". He received an additional £80 "for teaching the children to play on the organ, and compose, read, write and cast accompts."[2] After his death in Bath on August 14 a new appointment had to be made in a hurry as the death of King George I on June 11 had necessitated an autumn coronation for his son, George II.

Maurice Greene was appointed to the position of Organist and Composer of the Chapel Royal on September 4. But the Dean, Edmund Gibson, felt that, together with his important post as Organist of St Paul's Cathedral, he held too many musical positions to be entrusted with the daily care of the boys as well. Consequently a Gentleman of the Choir, Bernard Gates, who had himself been a chorister in the time of John Blow and now held the position of "Tuner of the Organs", was appointed Master of the Children.[3]

Somehow these two new appointees had to bring the choir's numbers back up to capacity. Along with the sudden death of Croft another blow had befallen the choir when 5 choristers – half of the total – had left the choir with broken voices in the previous few months.[4] John Beard would have been 12 when he was recruited into the choir. Where he came from, and how Gates or Greene knew of him, it will be impossible to tell. Greene would have needed his choristers to be already trained, in view of the important Coronation that was looming. One of the servants in St James' Palace was a Samuel Beard, who worked in the Buttery; so perhaps he was a relation. Another Beard – John Beard of Cripplegate – was married at St James' Palace in 1709. As it appears that the only people who were accorded that privilege were the Royal Servants, this could well be another relation working in the Royal Household. It would be very convenient if it could be proved that this John Beard was the singer's father. The dates would work out very neatly as we know that William, the eldest sibling, was born in 1712. For the moment this scenario only appears possible if John the chorister happened to be from a second marriage. (See: the Beard family tree in Appendix 7.) As most choristers were, and still are, taken into choirs at the age of 8 or 9 it is possible that he came from another London choir. But it is very unlikely that the names of the boys in St Margaret's Westminster, or St

---

[1] In John Chamberlayne, *Magnae Britanniae Notitia,* 31st Edition, 1735, National Archives Library
[2] New Cheque Book, 31; Ashbee & Harley, *The Cheque Books of the Chapel Royal*, Aldershot, 2000, vol.2 p.29
[3] Ashbee & Harley, *The Cheque Books of the Chapel Royal*, Aldershot, 2000, i. 220-1
[4] Burrows, 'Handel and the 1727 Coronation', *Musical Times* 118 (1977) p.469 ff. The five boys who left the choir in June 1727 are named in Burrows, 'Handel and the English Chapel Royal', Oxford 2005, p.574 as: Henry Lloyd, Charles Degard, Manly Morgan, Luke Coltman, William Lamb.

James Westminster (now Piccadilly), the nearest and most likely choirs, will ever be known. From existing records[5] it seems unlikely that he was in the Westminster Abbey Choir either.

A study of the choristers at the Chapel Royal provided by Burrows' new book on 'Handel and the English Chapel Royal' reveals that they stayed singing in the choir in the 18th century much later than boys do these days. Whereas boys' voices breaks at about 13 years of age these days, they used to last much longer. Even just before the Second World War it was not uncommon for boys to be still singing treble at the age of 16. In Beard's time it can be seen, from Burrows' research, that boys were being discharged from the choir at 18, 19 and even 20 years of age. Curiously the Chapel Royal never seem to have recorded the date on which a boy entered the choir, although the Palace records for other employees, the Gentlemen of the choir and other servants, are very detailed.

Beard belonged to the first of Gates' intake of choristers. The boys were obviously fond of their master as can be seen by the annual dinner that was given in his memory. As late as 1785 this was still taking place. The event that John Beard attended on 21 October 1785 also celebrated what would have been Gates' 100th birthday. As we have seen, this was almost certainly Beard's own 70th birthday. The list of guests contained in a newspaper report of October 24 indicates that there were three choristers present who had been part of Gates' early intake: John Randall (latterly the Professor of Music at Cambridge University), Thomas Barrow, and Beard himself.[6] Also present were two other singers who had worked with Handel: Samuel Champness who had sung solo roles in oratorios from about 1754, and his son Thomas who had sung in the chorus at the last two Foundling Hospital performances of *Messiah* given by Handel, in 1758 and 1759.

The treble line at the time of the 1727 Coronation probably consisted of the following boys: Thomas Skelton, Henry Brown, Thomas Weldon (who all left in 1729); Jonathan Martin, John Potter, Carleton White (who all left in 1730); James Cleavely, James Nares (who left in 1731); Samuel Howard (who left in 1733) and John Beard. The most reliable way of cross-checking this would be by consulting the *Magnae Britanniae Notitia.* Unfortunately the entries in the 29th edition (1728) and the 30th edition (1729) are hopelessly inaccurate and include boys who had left long before. There is then a six-year gap when the book was not published at all. This corresponds with virtually the whole of Beard's time in the choir. It is only in the 31st edition of 1735 that his name finally appears.

We know from an accurate source – two of the performers – that the ten boys of the 1732 choir all took part in a semi-staged performance of Handel's 'Esther', under the direction of Bernard Gates. This is the choir's line-up for that year: Samuel Howard, John Beard, John Randall, Price Cleavely, John Moore, James Allen, Thomas Barrow, James Butler, Robert Denham and John Brown. Samuel Howard had left, as has been shown, in 1733, and John Brown may have died in office. The new intake to replace these two comprised Thomas Morland and John Wynn.

It is impossible to be absolutely accurate, as the order in which boys joined the choir was not necessarily the order in which they left it. So their respective

---

[5] in the Muniment Room, Westminster Abbey
[6] The Morning Post and Daily Advertiser, Monday 24 October 1785: "Amongst a number of Musical Gentlemen then present were Mess. Beard, Barrow, Abington, Rev. Mr Champnes, S Champnes, Parsons, Taylor, Randal, Smart etc. etc. The stewards on the occasion were Dr Arnold and Mr Dupuis".

seniority cannot be easily deduced. The delay of a year in recording information into the *Magnae Britanniae Notitia* is understandable; but it is a pity that there is no record at all in the important years 1730-34. By 1735 the almanac was back on an even keel and the information it gives about the choir seems reliable. It shows that the composition of the choir, in Beard's last year, was: John Randall, James Allen, John Beard, Thomas Barrow, James Butler, Robert Denham, Price Cleavely, John Moore, Thomas Morland and John Wynn. These, then, were all of the choristers who shared Beard's life between 1727 and 1734.

Their choral duties were outlined in a document prepared by the Dean, Edmund Gibson, in 1726:

'Rules for ye decent and orderly performance of Divine Service'[7]

The behaviour of the choir – and particularly the Gentlemen – must have been getting very lax. Some adult singers were obviously not putting very much effort into their singing. Others spent time during the services wandering around with messages, or arriving late and leaving early. Excerpts that particularly pertain to the choristers are:

- "It is hereby order'd that the several members of ye Quire do joyn in Psalms, Services, and Chorus's with a due application, and with a proper strength and extension of voice.
- And the Master of ye Boys shall take care to chuse only such into their number, as have good voices and suitable capacities, and shall not only instruct them in ye grounds of Musick, but also qualify them in due time to bear their part in the Verse Anthems.
- The Surplices for the use of the Chapel shall be of a due fineness, wideness, and length, and shall always be kept whole and clean. For which end the Children's Surplices shall be wash'd every week.
- And to prevent ye disturbance which is necessarily occasion'd by sending messages backward and forward in ye Chapel during ye performance of divine service, the Subdean or some other appointed by him, shall on every Sunday and Holiday make known to ye Quire, and also to ye Organists, before Prayers begin, what Service and Anthem shall be perform'd for that time; and on all other days he shall make known ye same, during ye voluntary.
- Three several days are appointed as the great Festivals, that is to say, the Feast of St John the Evangelist, Easter Tuesday, & Whitsun Tuesday for ye Priests & Gentlemen who are then in Waiting …to receive the Blessed Sacrament all together, as becomes good Christians, living in Peace and Unity one with Another.
- Also such of ye Boys of ye Chapel as have been confirm'd (which the Master shall take care of as they grow up) and who are arriv'd to ye full age of sixteen years, shall receive ye Holy Sacrament on ye three days before mentioned."

In addition to the normal daily offices of Matins and Evensong the choir took part in various 'special' services. It was on these occasions that the larger, and orchestrally accompanied anthems were performed. For the normal daily service the

---

[7] Lambeth Palace Library, *The Fulham Papers* – Gibson, vol. 2

accompaniment was on the organ. During Beard's time the job of composing such extra music would have been expected to fall to Maurice Greene. But, commencing with the Four Coronation Anthems that were needed for the 1727 Coronation, this was now more likely to be given to the Chapel's other house composer, Handel.[8] The fact that Handel usurped his glory at the 1727 Coronation with his magnificent compositions may have contributed to Greene's animosity towards him. Having formerly been the best of friends when Handel first arrived in England, and used to practise on the organ at St Paul's Cathedral alongside him, they later became very cool with each other. Burney states that "for many years of his life [Handel] never spoke of [Greene] without some injurious epithet".[9] George III annotated his copy of Mainwaring's biography of Handel, in reference to Greene: "…that wretched little crooked illnatured insignificant Writer Player and Musician the late Dr Green Organist and Composer to King George II, who forbad his composing the Anthems at his Coronation …and ordered that G.F. Hendel should …have that great honour. He had but four Weeks for doing this wonderful work."[10]

Although there are not many pictures of the Chapel Royal choir in Beard's day there is a diagrammatic illustration and painting of the children wearing their long white surplices as they process to the 1727 Coronation. They also wore livery coats in this period – forerunners of the ones still worn by the choristers today and which are so distinctive a feature. There is a painting of a crocodile of the ten boys crossing St. James' Park c.1790 (reproduced on p. 8) wearing this outfit with the bicorn hats that must have been their normal day-wear. The dainty shoes that are shown in the watercolour were made of waxed leather, since we learn from the Lord Chamberlain's documents[11] that Gates received 'sixty pairs of waxed leather shoes' in 1735, at a cost of 10 guineas. This bulk-buying must have stood him in good stead for many years to come!

Further information about their daily life comes from Serjeant of the Vestry, William Lovegrove, who wrote this in 1752:

- By the present Establishment, the Children are ten in number, they wear the King's Livery, which is provided them Annually out of the King's Wardrobe. The Master's Duty is to teach them to sing, to play upon the Harpsichord or Organ, Writing, Arithmetic, and compose.
- They are to attend the Service of the Chapel daily throughout the Year, where his Majesty resides, Kensington excepted.
- When their voices break and they become unfit for the Chapel, His Majesty gives thirty pounds to the Parents or friends of each Boy, to place him out Apprentice. If they behave well, and their voices turn out useful, they are frequently admitted Gentlemen of the Chapel Royal.[12]

The place where the boys lived, worked, studied music and had their regular choral rehearsals was Bernard Gates's house, in James Street, Westminster. It was quite close to St. James' Park, so that the twice daily walk across the park, for Matins at 11am and Evensong at 5pm, was not too arduous. But, situated within a short walking distance of Westminster Abbey, it was also ideally placed for Gates' other

[8] Handel had been appointed' Composer for the Chapel Royal' on 25th February 1723
[9] Burney, 'A General History of Music', London 1935, vol. 2, p. 489
[10] William C. Smith "George III, Handel, & Mainwaring", *The Musical Times* 65, Sept. 1924, p. 790
[11] Public Record Office, LC5/47/257
[12] David Baldwin, 'The Chapel Royal Ancient and Modern', London 1990, pp. 306-7

official position as a member of the Abbey choir. After Beard's time in the choir Gates was to take on the additional duties of Master of the Westminster Abbey choristers in 1740. His wife Elizabeth (who died in 1737) must have been an important asset during Beard's time, acting as matron and looking after the boys' diet and daily welfare. There was at least one servant in this household, though probably a cook as well, since we learn from Reginald Spofforth, writing in his *Musical Memoranda* in 1785, that "...the boys have no Pocket Money, except the Christmas Boxes, and what is occasionally given. The Christmas Boxes formerly amounted to £30. When it was £30, after several deductions, the Senior Boys received only £2 7s each. They paid half a guinea to the servant for a Christmas Box, Blacking Shoes and Cleaning; four guineas a year to the Barber for Sunday [hair] dressing, which was flour and Powder, blue-salt sometimes."[13] The sums that Spofforth mentions receiving can be further elucidated by the payments for services that we know were made during Beard's time: 5 shillings to each boy at Christmas, and 5 shillings at the distribution of the Royal Maundy.

Something about the boys' diet can be deduced from a roughly contemporary document relating to the choristers at Westminster Abbey. In view of the fact that Bernard Gates was Master of the Abbey choristers from 1740 – 1757, in addition to the Chapel Royal boys, it gives us a very good idea of what was considered normal for growing boys at this time: "Ordered: That so long as that Custome shall continue there be allowed Twenty pounds per annum for Roots Greens and other Kitchen herbs with their boiled meat five days in the week butter, and vinegar and pepper included. Ordered: That a Crown a Quarter be allowed the Bed-maker of the Dormitory for Fire to air the Room and warm the Boys Beds at the end of each Breaking up."[14] The 'breaking up' refers to what we would now call 'the end of term'. The Chapel Royal *Cheque Book* confirms that the choristers were allowed holiday breaks – though they were nothing like as long as what is considered normal today:

"A play week or week of Vacation from all Choir attendance having been always allow'd after the holydays of Xmas Easter & Whitsuntide 'tis determined for the removal of all doubts and disputes that the first week after ye above three great solemn tides or feasts … shall be reckoned ye play week or week of Vacation above mentioned…"[15]

More can be learned about the daily life of the choristers from a later document of 1804 which ratifies some of the pre-existing customs and usages that must have been around from Beard's time.[16] This conforms very much to the 1726 regulations, and fleshes out the daily routine even more clearly. Regulation 6 is particularly interesting, in light of the extra-mural activities that commenced in Beard's time. Although written by a later Dean, one can imagine that very little had changed in the interim:

1. They shall have proper instructions in *singing* and *playing* for a reasonable time in every Day, four Days for singing and two for playing.

---

[13] David Baldwin, 'The Chapel Royal Ancient and Modern', London 1990, p. 327
[14] 14 December 1736; quoted in Edward Pine, 'The Westminster Abbey Singers', London, 1953, p. 141
[15] Ashbee & Harley, *The Cheque Books of the Chapel Royal*, Aldershot, 2000, vol. 1, p. 144
[16] David Baldwin, 'The Chapel Royal Ancient and Modern', London 1990, p. 327-8

2. They shall have one good instrument to practise on, constantly kept in good Order.
3. They shall have a writing Master, as formerly *three* times a week and to be two Hours with the Boys each time.
4. More attention shall be paid to their Moral and their religious Principles more particularly on *Sunday* when some Instructions shall be given them in the Doctrines and the Duties of Religion.
5. The Senior Boys shall not be suffered to treat the juniors cruelly, and harshly, but shall be punished if they do.
6. The Boys shall not be allowed to sing at either of the play Houses[17] and when they return home from singing at the *Oratories,* the *Antient Music,* or any other Concert public or private, upon the leaving they shall have a coach to carry them home and a good Supper, and in Winter a fire at their return.
7. More attention shall be paid to the cleanliness of their persons, their clothes and the room they principally inhabit; more particularly they shall have *two Towels* and *two Shirts* a week and the Maidservant who waits upon them shall be enjoined carefully to attend to all these things.
8. The Subdean shall attend once in every Quarter at the Master's House and hear the Boys sing and play and read and repeat the Church Catechisms.
9. The Boys shall be furnished with some Bibles and prayer Books, and each a form of Prayer for their own Private use, which they shall be enjoined to use Morning and Evening.
10. A fair copy of these Regulations shall be hung up in the School Room that they may be known to the Boys.

Rule 6 was to have a lasting effect on the development of Handel's oratorios. During the composer's lifetime the boys sang in his oratorios as in a concert, but took no part in any stage representations. After Handel's and Gibson's deaths Beard did manage to persuade the relevant authorities to let the Chapel Royal choristers walk across the Covent Garden stage in a dramatic representation of the 1761 Coronation Service; but it must have been due to his close friendship with their organist, William Boyce, that this temporary lifting of the injunction was made.

The instruction in Rule 6 about having "a coach to carry them home" indicates that transport had to be summoned up on every occasion that they moved off their patch. St James' Palace was within walking distance. But a coach was hired to take them to the outlying Palaces, when their duties demanded that they temporarily relocate. For example, we learn from the records that they were lodged in Kingston-upon-Thames when the King resided at Hampton Court Palace.[18] Although the principal summer residence for the Hanoverians was usually Kensington Palace, Hampton Court was a convenient base for hunting parties. The royal party spent the months of July to October there in 1733, with the choir in attendance. When the royal party moved from Hampton Court to Windsor, transport for the choir was usually by water.

When Gates provided the choristers for Handel's Foundling Hospital performances of *Messiah* in the 1750s there is a revealing entry in the General

---

[17] this was an important ruling by Dean Gibson, which was to have a lasting effect on the development of Handel's oratorios
[18] G.D. Heath, 'The Chapel Royal at Hampton Court', Twickenham Local History Society, 1979

Committee Minutes from which we can learn two interesting things: a) that one day's coach hire in London cost 14 shillings, and b) that Handel was paying Gates seven guineas at this period for the use of the boys in two performances: i.e. at a rate of 3½ guineas - £3 13s 6d - for each performance.

> "The Secretary acquainted the Committee, that Mr Gates the Master of the Children of the King's Chapel, having received, by Mr Handel's order, Seven Guineas for their Performance, in the Chapel of this Hospital on the 1st and 15th May last, had brought to the Secretary Five pounds Nineteen shillings thereof, chusing only to be reimbursed the One Pound Eight shillings he paid for the Two Days Coach hire for the said children to and from the Hospital..."[19]

Sadly the house where Beard lived for seven years under all of these regulations no longer survives. The street has also been renamed. The house was on the south side, eight doors down from, and to the east of, the present no. 22 Buckingham Gate, which in spite of its Victorian front is a late-18th century house built in 1784. It must lie somewhere under the present 23-24 Buckingham Gate. Bernard Gates and the ten choristers occupied this house from 1727 until 1757. It certainly had a room that was large enough to cope with full rehearsals. There is a newspaper report in 1730 that "on Thursday last the Coronation Music (composed by Mr Handel) was perform'd at Mr Gates's, Master of the Children of the Chapel Royal".[20] In 1740 another newspaper, reporting on the rehearsal of Princess Mary's Wedding music, stated: "Yesterday, at Mr Gates's, was a practice of a fine new Anthem compos'd by Mr. Handel, for her Royal Highness the Princess Mary's Marriage; the vocal parts by Mess. Abbott, Chelsum, Beard, Church of Dublin, Gates, Lloyd, and the Boys of the Chapel Royal..."[21] In this same room, eight years earlier in 1732, Gates had mounted the remarkable staging of 'Esther' - in celebration of Handel's 47th birthday - which was to show Handel the direction in which his next compositions should lie.

Beard therefore had a good education, in tiny classes. The experience was to stand him in good stead in later life. The ability to play a keyboard instrument must have been a valuable skill, which would be of enormous assistance to him in learning the vast amounts of new music that he was to encounter. Also, if he needed to make an extra income in the early days of his career he would have been well placed to teach singing. One can imagine that a young musician like him might find many elegant young ladies wishing to gain this accomplishment. To that end we can imagine that his early musical life must have resembled that of the young protégé of 'Don Basilio' who comes to teach 'Rosina' in Act 2 of 'The Barber of Seville'. Perhaps this is how he first encountered his wife Henrietta. His interest in keyboard music remained in later life, too, though he may have purchased much of it for his harpsichord-playing wife. He was a frequent subscriber to contemporary musical publications, and his library included works for the Harpsichord by Scarlatti, Henry Burgess, William Boyce, Thomas Gladwin, John Alcock, George Berg, John Bennett and James Nares. The fact that he also subscribed to copies of solos for violin and keyboard by Joseph Gibbs, Alessandro Bezozzi and William Bates suggests that he may have been competent on that instrument also.

---

[19] Minutes of the General Committee of the Foundling Hospital, 13th June 1750
[20] London Evening Post, 26-8 November 1730
[21] Daily Advertiser, Tuesday 6th May 1740

The Coronation of King George II would have been the first major event in Beard's time in the choir: – quite a way to start, then, with the first performance of 'Zadok the Priest' etc! Handel's pencilled comments in the manuscript of 'The King shall rejoice' shows that he expected there to be 12 trebles on the top line.[22] As the Chapel Royal doubled up with the Westminster Abbey choir for this event he may well have got that number and more. For a full account of the Coronation music, how it was performed and how it was received, Burrows is the best source.[23] Apparently there were several moments of confusion, and the anthem "I was glad" was accidentally omitted at the King's entrance into the Abbey. Handel's new Anthems did not escape unscathed. The Archbishop of Canterbury wrote on his service sheet, at the point where the first one, "The King shall rejoice", was to be performed:

The Anthems in confusion: All irregular in the Music

The performers were widespread, in galleries opposite each other but at a great distance. Keeping the stereophonic music together in these conditions would have been hard enough at the best of times. An added complication was that there were two conflicting orders of service in use – the original one and an emended one. This may have resulted in each side beginning a different piece of music at this point in the ceremony. Another silly mistake was that the Anthem 'Come Holy Ghost' was also accidentally omitted, resulting in 'Zadok the Priest' entering onto the world's stage a trifle too early. Thereafter things must have settled down, as William Wake, the Archbishop, made no further annotations about musical matters.[24]

Other special services that took place during Beard's time as a treble were the Thanksgiving Services for the King's safe return from Hanover.[25] In 1729 and 1732 there were new orchestrally accompanied anthems and Te Deums by Greene,[26] who oversaw the music for these services. A pattern began to emerge during this period to keep the two appointed composers happy, which saw Greene composing for the services that followed the King's return, while Handel was kept in reserve for the bigger, national, celebrations.[27]

One court position that both composers must have wanted badly, as it carried a salary of £200, was that of Master of the King's Musick. Greene was appointed to this in 1735 on the death of John Eccles. The major duty was to compose two annual Odes in partnership with the Poet Laureate, for the court festivals celebrating New Year and the King's birthday. This was generally regarded as a tedious job, and the music that composers like John Eccles and Maurice Greene produced was of a fairly workaday nature. The poetry that they were given to set was similar hack-work. Handel had been lucky when he set the 'Ode for Queen Anne's Birthday' in 1713. Although not the holder of the court position, he seems to have stepped in for John Eccles on this one occasion. The poem provided by Ambrose Philips contained eminently settable verses and attractive pastoral imagery.

---

[22] "C[anto] 12". See: Burrows, 'Handel and the English Chapel Royal', Oxford 2005, p.275
[23] Burrows, 'Handel and the English Chapel Royal', Oxford 2005, pp.251 – 308.
[24] Burrows, 'Handel and the English Chapel Royal', Oxford 2005, pp. 262 - 264
[25] Burrows, 'Handel and the English Chapel Royal', Oxford 2005, Appendix H, pp. 606-7
[26] 2nd November 1729, & 29th October 1732. see: Burrows, 'Handel and the English Chapel Royal', Oxford 2005, p.606
[27] Burrows, 'Handel and the English Chapel Royal', Oxford 2005, p.286

It is interesting to speculate what might have been the artistic result if Handel had been appointed to the post instead of Greene: and one can only wonder whether his odes might not have been of a lasting nature, like the 'Ode for Queen Anne's Birthday' and the magnificent 'Ode to St Cecilia'.

Beard would have sung in these Odes as a boy, when Colly Cibber's inane words would have been set to music by John Eccles. The performances took place in a large chamber of the palace where the monarch was currently residing, usually the Great Presence Chamber at St James', on the morning of the King's birthday[28] and on New Year's morning. Evening Prayer was cancelled on these days "...it being difficult for the Gentlemen and Officers of the Chapel to come to the Gate of the Court by reason of the great Concourse of People on those Publick Days".[29] A group of instrumentalists from the King's Band joined the Chapel Royal singers, who were sometimes not all required, yet on other occasions were supplemented by outside performers. As there were usually solos for each voice, Beard would have gained useful experience in the solos that would have come his way from about 1732 onwards. There was a public rehearsal at one of the London taverns a day or two before the official performance at court[30]; but after that the Odes were consigned to oblivion. Not many of Eccles' still survive.

Beard was closely involved with the performance of these odes for the whole of his singing career. After his voice broke and he became a tenor soloist he returned to sing the tenor solos every year from 1735 until 1768. When he was applying for the position of 'King's Waiter' in 1757 he claimed in his petition that "...he has had the honour to be principally employ'd in the performance of the Birthday and New-years Odes for twenty-four years, for which he has never receiv'd any Allowance or Gratuity whatsoever".[31] Although the maths is a little inaccurate - by 1757 he can have sung tenor solos for only a maximum of 23 years - it does appear that he slipped effortlessly from singing the treble solos to singing the tenor ones immediately on his departure from the choir. Even when the post of Master of the King's Musick passed to William Boyce his services were retained. The very last singing engagement that he ever undertook was at New Year in 1768, eight months after his official retirement, when he joined Boyce for the New Year's Ode "Let the voice of music breathe". His m/s copy, with his name inscribed upon it, is in the complete collection of Boyce odes which still survive in the Bodleian Library.[32]

The choir also participated at the annual Festival of the Sons of the Clergy in St. Paul's Cathedral. Apart from a newly composed anthem, the main musical event was a performance of an orchestrally accompanied Te Deum and Jubilate. This had usually been Purcell's famous setting of the Canticles in D major. But when the mould was broken on 25 February 1731 and a performance of Handel's *Utrecht* Te Deum and Jubilate was given instead, Handel's work (celebrating the 1713 treaty) began to gain in popularity and supplant Purcell's setting.[33]

Bernard Gates was a moving force in London's musical circles at this time, with a finger in a lot of musical pies. As a regular member of the Academy of Vocal

---

[28] at this period it was October 28th

[29] Ashbee & Harley, *The Cheque Books of the Chapel Royal*, Aldershot, 2000, vol. 1, p. 308

[30] The Blackwell History of Music in Britain, 'The Eighteenth Century', Oxford, 1990, p. 88

[31] The Newcastle Papers Vol. CXCI, BL: Add. 32876 f.317

[32] Bodleian MS. Mus. Sch. d. 320b

[33] Burrows states that "there is no evidence for a performance of the Utrecht music at the Sons of the Clergy Festival before 1731: the oft-repeated statement ...that Handel's setting superseded Purcell's at the Festivals from 1713 onwards is not supported by the evidence". Op. cit. p. 98 & 285

Music (later: the Academy of Antient Music) he mounted a performance of Handel's *Utrecht* music on 14 January 1731 – one month earlier than its Festival performance. This would have kept the Chapel Royal children out late in the evening, on a non-ecclesiastical venture. But it was a sign of things to come: for, if it had not been for Gates and his willingness to provide interesting musical opportunities for his talented choristers, the history of Handel's oratorios might have been very different. It has been suggested that the January performance served as a rehearsal for the Sons of the Clergy service a month later.[34] This arrangement seems to have been repeated again during Beard's years in the choir, when the *Utrecht* music was rehearsed at the Crown Tavern on February 16 1734 for a performance at the Festival in St Paul's Cathedral three days later.[35]

Handel had been Bernard Gates' honoured guest at his house on February 23rd 1732. The Master of the Choristers must have felt that he had built up a particularly strong line-up of boys after 5 years in the job. He may have wanted to show them off. As we have seen, he was very happy to loan them out to London's musical gatherings during this period. Consequently he trained them up in an entertainment that Handel had written at Cannons in 1720 for the Duke of Chandos. It seems to have received no other performance in the intervening years.[36] How he came by the score is a mystery, unless he had taken part in the first performance at Cannons, as has been sometimes suggested.[37] According to the cast that was printed in Burney's "Account of the Musical Performances ...in commemoration of Handel" all 10 boys of the current choir were involved. Burney acknowledged that his information came from "Dr. Randall, the musical professor at Cambridge, and Mr Barrow, who were among the original performers when it was dramatically represented".[38] The cast, as given by them, was:

Esther	John Randall
Ahasuerus, & 1st Israelite	James Butler
Haman	John Moore
Mordecai, & Israelite Boy	John Brown
Priest of the Israelites	John Beard
Harbonah	Price Cleavely
Persian Officer, & 2nd Israelite	James Allen
Israelites and Officers:	Samuel Howard
	Thomas Barrow
	Robert Denham

Beard's part, as Priest of the Israelites, was not the star role. In fact there is no 'Priest of the Israelites' mentioned in the libretto, so it is most likely that Beard sang the music for the Israelitish Woman. Her aria, "Praise the Lord with cheerful noise" is a religious invocation, and may have seemed to Gates to be better described as for

---

[34] Burrows, 'Handel and the English Chapel Royal', Oxford 2005, p.285 f/n 83

[35] Deutsch, 'Handel, a documentary Biography', London, 1955, p. 358

[36] "He [Handel] made no attempt to introduce either of the Cannons masques to London". W. Dean, 'Handel's Dramatic Oratorios and Masques', London, 1959, p. 171

[37] Dean says, in 'Handel's Dramatic Oratorios and Masques', London, 1959, p. 204: "He is said to have taken part in the Cannons performance of Esther, but this seems unlikely ...and is not confirmed by documentary evidence".

[38] Burney, "An Account of the Musical Performances ...in commemoration of Handel", London, 1785, p. 100

a 'Priest' than for a 'Woman' in view of the nature of the singer taking the part. Chrysander, moreover, stated that the aria was sung at Cannons by a boy; though Winton Dean has suggested that this information was more likely to have applied to Gates' performance.[39] It was quite a modest role, but contains a lively allegro aria in C major, lying well in the voice and sprinkled with distinctively Handelian runs. It is an aria in which an extrovert performer can make his mark, and it is possibly from this time that Beard's prowess came to the attention of Handel:

> Praise the Lord with cheerful noise,
> Wake my glory, wake my lyre.
> Praise the Lord, each mortal voice,
> Praise the Lord, ye heav'nly choir.
> Sion now her head shall raise,
> Tune your harps to songs of praise.

A libretto, first brought to the attention of scholars by Winton Dean, explains the manner of performance. The boys must be assumed to have acted the story out on a stage, wearing the costumes that had been prepared by a certain Mr Huggins, a member of the Society. In front of them were ranged the instrumentalists and adult chorus members "from the choirs of St James's, and Westminster …after the Manner of the Ancients, being placed between the Stage and the Orchestra; and the Instrument Parts …were performed by the Members of the Philharmonick Society, consisting only of Gentlemen".[40]

The private performance on February 23 led to two further public performances at the Crown and Anchor tavern for the Academy of Ancient Music, on March 1 and 3. Viscount Percival (later the Earl of Egmont) recorded in his diary: "From dinner I went to the Music Club, where the King's Chapel boys acted the *History of Hester*… This *oratoria* or religious opera is exceeding fine, and the company were highly pleased, some of the parts being well performed".[41]

One month later there was a pirated performance by unknown performers – possibly a group led by Thomas Arne – at the Great Room in Villars-Street York Buildings.[42] This must have set Handel thinking. His response was to hire the Haymarket Theatre and mount an 'official' public performance to counter the piracy. For a full evening's entertainment, along the lines of his Italian Operas, he decided to expand the concise Cannons version which had hitherto been performed. Although he took the opportunity to rewrite the recitatives and the finale, most of the new music came from existing works. Some of these were old works from early on in his career (*La Resurrezione* - 1708, & the *Queen Anne Birthday Ode* - 1713),

---

[39] W. Dean, 'Handel's Dramatic Oratorios and Masques', London, 1959, p. 203
[40] W. Dean, 'Handel's Dramatic Oratorios and Masques', London, 1959, p. 204
[41] W. Dean, 'Handel's Dramatic Oratorios and Masques', London, 1959, p. 204, and Deutsch, 'Handel, a documentary Biography', London, 1955, p. 286
[42] W. Dean, 'Handel's Dramatic Oratorios and Masques', London, 1959, p. 205

but he also utilised passages from the 1727 *Coronation Anthems*. There was never any intention to simply mount the version that Gates had staged, with the boys taking the acting roles. Handel clearly had in mind a lucrative performance with his Italian professional singers - who included the legendary Strada and Senesino. They would be taking the lead roles of Esther and Ahasuerus. This performance was clearly going to be a cut above its predecessors. Whether it was intended to stage it with action as the boys had done, and for which its dramatic story was entirely suitable, the reaction of Edmund Gibson - not only Bishop of London but also Dean of the Chapel Royal - suggests that he thought it would be.

Handel realised that he needed a choir to sing the choruses. As his operas never made that demand, and there was no full-time opera-chorus in existence, he turned, logically, to Bernard Gates for help. His boys knew the chorus music. He knew that the Gentlemen of the Chapel Royal choir would be willing to hire themselves out, too. When Gibson learned of this development, according to Charles Burney "...he would not grant permission for its being represented on that stage, even with books in the children's hands".[43] So, Gibson was clearly under the impression that Handel was planning to use his chapel choristers onstage in operatic dress. But, as Winton Dean says: "The singular idea of presenting a dramatic work in the theatre without action would scarcely have occurred to anyone on its own merits."[44] Gibson's embargo, in fact, laid the seeds of a new idea. If the boys couldn't 'act' with books in their hands presumably they could still sing - as long as they weren't actually 'acting'. This last-minute compromise is the whole reason for oratorios being traditionally given as concert performances. To quote Dean again: "What cannot be denied is that the birth of English oratorio, dependent alike on an act of artistic piracy and the moral scruples of a prelate, was casual and unpremeditated, its parentage discreetly veiled, and its legitimacy not above suspicion".[45]

The unique new entertainment in which John Beard and his fellow choristers were privileged to take part was advertised as: "*The Sacred Story* of ESTHER: an *Oratorio* in *English*. Formerly composed by Mr *Handel*, and now revised by him, with several Additions, and to be performed by a great Number of the best Voices and Instruments. N.B. There will be no Action on the Stage, but the House will be fitted up in a decent Manner, for the Audience. The Musick to be disposed after the Manner of the Coronation Service."

The last sentence explains that the audience would expect to see the musicians, not in their usual place in the pit, but arranged in tiers built onstage in the manner that the orchestra had been deployed in purpose-built galleries at the King's recent Coronation. This unusual idea rapidly became the norm for Handel oratorios. When they became an established feature of a particular theatre's season, as at Covent Garden from the 1740s onwards, a tiered construction was built and stored for the purpose in the theatre's scene-dock. A later version of the one that must have been specially constructed in May 1732 can be seen in a contemporary print.[46]

For a description of one audience member's reaction to this novel layout, we can turn to a pamphlet published the same year, "*See and Seem Blind*":

[43] Burney, "An Account of the Musical Performances …in commemoration of Handel", London, 1785, p. 100-1

[44] W. Dean, 'Handel's Dramatic Oratorios and Masques', London, 1959, p. 205

[45] W. Dean, 'Handel's Dramatic Oratorios and Masques', London, 1959, p. 206

[46] *Survey of London,* volume XXXV, The Athlone Press, University of London, 1970, plate 47

"This being a new thing set the whole World a Madding; Han't you be at the *Oratorio*, says one? Oh! If you don't see the *Oratorio* you see nothing, says t'other; so away goes I to the Oratorio, where I saw indeed the finest Assembly of People I ever beheld in my life, but, to my great Surprize, found this sacred *Drama* a mere Consort [i.e. concert], no Scenary, Dress or Action, so necessary to a *Drama*; but H[ande]l was plac'd in Pulpit, (I suppose they call that their Oratory), by him sate *Senesino, Strada, Bertolli,* and *Turner Robinson*, in their own Habits; before him stood sundry sweet singers of this poor *Israel*, [the Chapel Royal contingent] and *Strada* gave us a *Hallelujah* of Half an Hour long…"[47]

Strada's 'Alleluia' aria was one of Handel's additions, and had been imported – presumably to please her by giving her another chance to show off her astonishing vocal roulades and flourishes – from his recent Cantata '*Silete Venti*' of 1729. The first performance of this expanded 'Esther' took place on Tuesday 2 May. It was a huge success and was repeated five times within three weeks. Handel is said to have pocketed £4000 from it. He must have been very gratified to have discovered such an inexpensive way of reutilising old, non-operatic material. Out of the Cannons masques, and the Chapel Royal anthems, a new art-form had been accidentally born. It would be John Beard's great fortune to have arrived on the musical scene at such a propitious time. Although he witnessed the birth of English oratorio in 1732 from the front row of the chorus, he would also have seen that no tenor was yet given a role in this version of the oratorio. Handel had not decided to entrust anything more than incidental verse-lines to the Chapel Royal tenors in his recent anthems. Since the departure of Thomas Gethin[48] in 1731 there was, seemingly, no tenor capable of singing a solo aria. Gethin's replacement was David Cheriton, who never appears to have sung a solo; and the only other tenor to have been given modest solo recitative by Handel in this period was James Chelsum, who had been in the choir since 1718. All of the solo tenor parts in the 1720 Cannons version of *Esther* had now been rewritten for alto or castrato voices. Even Handel's current Italian tenor, Signor Pinacci, was kept out of the production. It is remarkable to think that, within the space of three short years, Beard would find himself standing amongst some of these same soloists at the front of the stage. His role in Handel's 1735 revival was probably the small one of *Habdonah* (now renamed from *Harbonah*). By 1736 he had impressed Handel enough for the composer to have re-transposed the main role of *Ahasuerus* back down into the tenor pitch for him.

A year after these *Esther* performances, in the Spring of 1733, the Chapel Royal choir embarked on a new venture of self-promotion in order to raise the profile of the Fund that had been set up in 1729 to help the widows of its members. In order to accumulate some capital three mid-day concerts were put on at the Banqueting House Chapel in Whitehall. The first featured the works by Handel that were currently in the Chapel Royal repertoire. Burrows speculates that the 'Te Deum, Jubilate and Two Anthems' that were advertised for March 13 were familiar pieces from the repertory that Handel had composed in 1722-6, mostly consisting of

---

[47] From "See and Seem Blind: or a Critical Dissertation on the Publick Diversions, etc." Deutsch, 'Handel, a documentary Biography', London, 1955, p. 300-1

[48] Thomas Gethin was a tenor in the Chapel Royal choir from 1716 – 1731 having previously been a chorister. Handel wrote his name ('Getting' / 'Gething') against solos in *As pants the hart*, c.1722; *Te Deum* in A major, c. 1724; and *I will magnify thee*, c. 1722-6.

26

reworked *Chandos* (Cannons) Anthems. The Te Deum and Jubilate were more than likely to have been the *Utrecht* setting, which was becoming very popular by now. The second concert, on April 3, contained Purcell's Te Deum and Jubilate and Bononcini's Funeral Anthem for the Duke of Marlborough. The third programme showed off Greene's talents as a composer, with performances of a *Te Deum* and *Anthem on His Majesty's Return from Hanover* (probably the most recent ones, performed in October 1732), and his short quasi-oratorio '*The Song of Deborah and Barak*' that had also been given its first performance the previous October at the Apollo Academy.[49] Any solos or verses in these pieces might well have gone to the 17½-year-old Beard, whose treble voice must have been approaching its apogee by now.

Almost the last occasion when Beard would have sung as a member of the Chapel Royal choir would have been the wedding of Anne, Princess Royal to the Prince of Orange. Originally planned for the autumn of 1733, it was delayed and repeatedly postponed since Dutch political business kept Willem in Holland for longer than anticipated. The French Chapel at St James' Palace was prepared for the event and kept mothballed. On the engraving by J. Rigaud of the actual event, which ultimately took place on March 14 1734, one can just detect the gallery that was built above the altar, at the east end, for the musicians. In Burrows comprehensive work on the music of the Chapel Royal choir there is a very helpful enlargement of this portion of the picture, and a key to the musicians that can be identified in it.[50] One thing that strikes a modern musician is that the musicians are very muddled up. The ten choristers are not neatly corralled together in one area, but spread amongst the gentlemen of the choir and the instrumentalists in groups of 2 or 3. One boy appears to be in a very high gallery on his own, surrounded by flutes and violins. There is one, however, right at the front of the lowest gallery, nearly obscured by a large central chandelier. This would be a soloist's position, to judge by the usual concert layout at the theatres. Could this sketchy character be John Beard? It is a delightful thought…

There were difficulties over the preparation of a Wedding Anthem. Greene was initially given the job, and had composed one to the text of "Blessed are all they that fear the Lord" by the middle of October 1733. This was advertised in the press.[51] Then the King must have got to hear about it, and the order went out to commission one from Handel instead. Greene was paid £13 12s 3d for the unperformed work[52] and his resentment against Handel mounted even further. Handel immediately set to work on his rival Wedding Anthem "This is the day that the Lord hath made", and it was completed in time for the Royal family to hear a rehearsal of it in the chapel on November 5. The wedding should have taken place on November 19, but - on November 18 - the Prince was taken ill and the ceremony had to be deferred. Once again the chapel and its decorations went into mothballs.

After an illness of several months, and a trip to Bath to recuperate, the Prince was well enough to return to court. The Chapel was prepared once more, and the specially constructed galleries were extended down the length of the building, as can be seen in Rigaud's engraving.[53] The wedding finally took place a month before

[49] Smither, *A History of the Oratorio*, Vol. 2, Univ. of N. Carolina Press, Chapel Hill, 1977, p. 200
[50] Burrows, 'Handel and the English Chapel Royal', Oxford 2005, Fig. 12.2 and Table 12.3, pp. 334-335
[51] The Daily Post, October 19th 1733
[52] Burrows, 'Handel and the English Chapel Royal', Oxford 2005, p. 611
[53] Burrows, 'Handel and the English Chapel Royal', Oxford 2005, plate V, between p. 312 & 313

Easter, on March 14 "between the hours of Four and Ten in the Evening".[54] Handel's anthem would have no doubt received last-minute rehearsals, since four months had elapsed since it was last sung through; but there are no further press reports of a public rehearsal. The only mention of the music at the ceremony itself is uninformative: "...a fine Anthem, compos'd by Mr Handell, was performed by a great Number of Voices and Instruments".[55]

The anthem betrays signs of having been put together in a hurry, in the fortnight or so that Handel had available after the rejection of Greene's composition. Most of it was lifted out of *Athaliah*, composed earlier in the year and heard at Oxford - but not yet in London. There are many indications in the *Athaliah* conducting score of how the anthem should be constructed; and it appears that Handel would have been prepared to make do without a new conducting score for a performance of this hurried composition. He seems to have considered *Athaliah* as a timely source for both the anthem and the Serenata, *Parnasso in Festa,* which was composed in honour of the happy couple, and heard by them the day before the wedding. Burrows remarks on the extraordinary fact that the two very different works, one sacred and the other secular, had four movements in common - set to different texts of course. Other works that were plundered were *Nisi Dominus* (1707) and the *Caroline* Te Deum (1714) from which the final chorus was constructed.

For a biographer of John Beard the most intriguing aspect of the new anthem is what part he had in it as a soloist. His name ('Bird' / 'Beard') appears in pencil three times in the conducting score of *Athaliah*, from which the anthem aria "Strength and honour" was taken. Originally this was one of Athaliah's arias - "My vengeance awakes me". It was written in the soprano clef and sung by Mrs Wright at the premiere in Oxford. It is the most surprising transfer from *Athaliah* in terms of its text, since the original expressed Athaliah's determination to seek revenge:

> *My vengeance awakes me, compassion forsakes me;*
> *All softness and mercy away, away, away!*

In the wedding anthem the new text describes the virtues of the King's daughter:

> *Strength and Honour are her Clothing, and she shall rejoice in time to come.*
> *She opens her Mouth with Wisdom, and in her Tongue is the Law of Kindness.*

At a later stage Handel's amanuensis J.C. Smith (senior) wrote it in tenor clefs for Handel's new conducting score. The pencil annotations of Beard's name must have

---

[54] The St James's Evening Post, 7-9 March 1734
[55] The London Evening Post, 14-16 March, 1734

been made at differing times, in view of the fact that he was to sing the aria on several later occasions:[56]

- in 1735 when it was transferred to his role of 'Mathan' in the London premiere of *Athaliah*
- also in 1735 when it was transferred to his role of 'Sisera' in *Deborah*[57]
- in Handel's so-called 'Oratorio' of 1738, which included oratorio excerpts
- in Handel's aborted 1743 revival[58]
- in Handel's 1756 revival[59]

One of the clues to the dating lies in the nature of these three pencil-marks. The earliest is presumably the scrawled 'Bird', which must be from a time when Handel was unfamiliar with the young singer's name. Later he wrote it correctly as 'Beard'. Finally, the third one is in the hand of J.C. Smith.

I think that this reveals the unfolding of John Beard's relationship with Handel. According to my speculative timetable the aria is slated for 'Bird' the treble in November 1733, when the hurriedly composed anthem was tried out in the presence of the Royal family. By the time the wedding finally took place four months later J.C. Smith had prepared a proper conducting score for Handel. It would not be improbable that Beard's voice had broken in the interim. This would have meant that, if Beard was to retain the solo, the soprano aria would have to be sung at tenor pitch. Burrows remarks on this transposition that it "… works well enough, though the solo part at times becomes rather entangled with the basso continuo. Nevertheless Handel must have been more or less satisfied with the arrangement, since the aria was also sung in other contexts by a tenor".[60] This performance could, then, have been the occasion on which the young Beard so impressed Handel that he considered employing him as an opera soloist, young and inexperienced as he was, in his forthcoming season at Covent Garden.

The other pencil-marks would relate to the later performances in 1735 when Handel was well acquainted with Beard's skill in the aria, and was prepared to transfer it lock, stock, and barrel into another work; and later still when J.C. Smith was assisting Handel in preparing a miscellaneous programme for his 1738 'Oratorio'. Fortunately this conjectural timetable is supported by Burrows, who agrees with it to a large extent when he says: "…it may be best to consider Beard as a possible treble soloist for 'A good wife is a good portion' [an earlier aria in the anthem that remained a treble solo] …It is, of course, possible that his voice changed between the time that the anthem was composed in autumn 1733 and its eventual performance the following spring".[61]

By March 1734 Beard had worked his way up to a very senior position in the choir. His days as a chorister were very nearly over. One of the earliest written references to him is a letter from Lady Elizabeth Compton which describes Beard as having 'left the Chappel at Easter'.[62] Easter Day was on 14 April, and he would have left after the 'great Festival' which the Chapel Royal establishment celebrated on Easter Tuesday, before they went on holiday for a week. The two performances

---

[56] Burrows, 'Handel and the English Chapel Royal', Oxford 2005, pp. 336-338
[57] Pencil cue in Handel's hand: "Ex Athaliah Mr Bird / My vengeance awakes me" in the Deborah score
[58] W. Dean, 'Handel's Dramatic Oratorios and Masques', London, 1959, p. 261
[59] W. Dean, 'Handel's Dramatic Oratorios and Masques', London, 1959, p. 262
[60] Burrows, 'Handel and the English Chapel Royal', Oxford 2005, p. 327
[61] Burrows, 'Handel and the English Chapel Royal', Oxford 2005, p. 338
[62] "A Scholar of Mr Gates, Beard, who left the Chapell last Easter…" Lady Elizabeth Compton, 21st November 1734, Deutsch *Handel a Documentary Biography* p. 375

of the *Utrecht* Te Deum and Jubilate in February, and the Wedding Anthem on March 14th would have been some of the last occasions on which he would have been heard in public as a member of the Chapel Royal choristers.

On leaving the choir it has been shown earlier that the departing boy was given financial assistance. In 1752 this was £30 "to place him out Apprentice", according to William Lovegrove. When Beard received his dues in 1734 the rate was £20 with the addition of a present of clothing from the Crown worth 10 guineas, viz:

"...the usual allowance of one Suit of plain cloth, one Hat and Band, two Holland shirts, two Cravets, two pairs of Cuffs, two Handkerchiefs, two pairs of Stockings, two pairs of Shoes and two pairs of Gloves."[63]

As Lovegrove added: "...If they behave well, and their voices turn out useful, they are frequently admitted Gentlemen of the Chapel Royal."[64] John Beard may have thought that this would be as much as he could expect of his career. But, as has been shown earlier, his prowess must have been noted by Handel at least since 1732. It may have been his singing of Handelian arias in *Esther* (1732), the *Utrecht* Te Deum (1732-4), and the Wedding Anthem (1734) that led the composer to consider him as a potential opera soloist. It was Beard's good fortune to be in the Chapel Royal choir at a time when the Gentlemen tenors were particularly undistinguished and he could be given a chance to shine. Handel took great delight a decade later in "forming a tenor voice" when he arrived in Dublin without one[65]. Perhaps this was an earlier occasion when he chose to "form" a young soloist for his forthcoming repertoire. John Beard had very little time to gain experience in stage-craft. It seems as though his exciting new career as a fully-fledged opera singer was going to have to be learned "on the hoof".

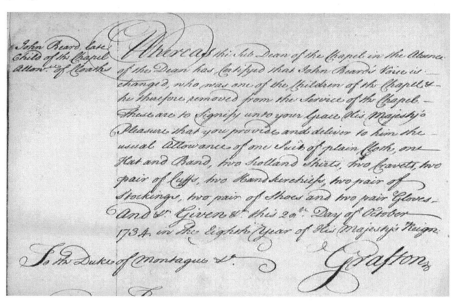

---

[63] PRO LC5/73/122

[64] David Baldwin, 'The Chapel Royal Ancient and Modern', London 1990 pp. 306-7. See also footnote 89

[65] "I have form'd another Tenor Voice which gives great satisfaction..." Handel to Charles Jennens, December 29th 1741, quoted in: Deutsch *Handel a Documentary Biography* p. 530

CHAPTER 2
JOHN BEARD AND THE LONDON THEATRE

1. HANDEL 1734 – 7

Beard's 'broken' voice must have matured remarkably quickly. The letter from Lady Elizabeth Compton which describes Beard as having 'left the Chappel at Easter'[1] may well have been partially correct, even though his discharge papers from the choir, issued by the Lord Chamberlain's Office, are dated 29 October 1734. Beard may have stayed on in the choir after leaving the trebles (and Bernard Gates' choir-school), and sung as a tenor for the next six months "on account of his general usefulness to the choir"[2]. At this early stage the possibility of obtaining a permanent position in the back row of the choir may have seemed his most likely career-prospect. He was 19 years of age, and no English tenor had yet made a successful career as a concert or opera soloist without recourse to a back-up choral post. Any indication that this might be the direction in which his career would develop would have been unthinkable at this stage.[3]

And yet, on November 9, a mere ten days after being honourably dismissed from Royal service, he appeared at Covent Garden Theatre as *Silvio* in Handel's "*Il Pastor Fido*". It was the beginning of a relationship that would last throughout the remaining twenty-five years of Handel's life. Henceforward Beard would always be his tenor of choice. He was, in fact, the only singer who took part in performances of every single one of Handel's English oratorios. Beard was singing for Handel, as tenor soloist in '*Messiah*' on the 6 April 1759 - the last occasion that Handel would ever hear any of his music performed.

The tenor soloists that Handel used prior to Beard's appearance fall into three categories:

    a) English tenors employed by the Chapel Royal choir
    b) Italian opera singers, who sang subsidiary role in his operas
    c) English singing-actors, employed at London theatres in plays & ballad operas

The principal tenor soloist at the Chapel Royal choir between 1716 and 1731 was Thomas Gethin. He had been a boy in the Chapel Royal, and is named as a treble soloist in an anthem by Croft. In a career that could so easily have been mirrored by John Beard he moved straight from Chorister (leaving in March 1716) to Gentleman in Ordinary (on 9 November the same year). During the 1720s he was Handel's tenor soloist whenever his anthems and *Te Deums* required one. Handel did not give him elaborate solos, but mainly employed him in solo 'verses' or trios with the alto and bass soloists. The minutes of a Chapter Meeting of 3 May 1731 record that "Mr Thomas Gethin One of the Gentlemen of his Majesties Chapel Royal, having been frequently Admonished by the Dean of the Chapel, for his frequent Absence and Irregularities …was (as incorrigible) turn'd out of his Place…" He decided to try his luck in the Barbadoes, "having received some encouragement from the Musical

[1] Deutsch *Handel a Documentary Biography* p. 375
[2] Burrows *Handel and the English Chapel Royal* p. 336
[3] A report of the funeral of the tenor John Freeman in the 'Universal Spectator & Weekly Journal' of December 18 1736 states: "we hear he will be succeeded in the Office of Gentleman of the King's Chapel by Mr Beard".

Gentlemen of that Island to come and settle amongst them". His unexpected departure left the field open for Beard.[4]

The singers who had been employed in the opera roles that Beard took over in the years 1734-7 were: Signor Carlo Scalzi, a 'second soprano' according to Winton Dean[5] in *Il Pastor Fido* and *Arianna in Creta*; and Signor Fabri, a tenor, in *Poro* and *Partenope*. The English singers that Handel had used from the London theatres were: Philip Rochetti, who went with Handel to Oxford in 1733 and sang Dorindo (*Acis & Galatea*), Mathan (*Athaliah*) and roles in *Esther* and *Deborah*; Thomas Salway, who also accompanied Handel to Oxford and sang Damon in *Acis & Galatea*, thereafter taking up a place as principal singer in John Rich's theatrical company at his newly built Covent Garden theatre. Meanwhile Charles Stoppelaer, a Drury Lane singer, was taken up by Handel at the same time as Beard, and given small roles in *Ariodante* and *Alcina* - both in 1735, and the even smaller part of 'An Amalekite' in *Saul* (1739).

The first visible sign that Handel had extended an invitation to the nineteen year-old Beard to join his company could be a significant change in the way that Handel composed for one of the characters in the new opera *Ariodante*. "In the autograph score, ... begun in August 1734 and completed on 24 October, Handel wrote the music for the role of Lurcanio in the soprano clef for Acts I & II (which he completed on 9 September), but went over to the tenor clef in Act III".[6] Perhaps Handel originally had other plans for the performer of this role. When he thought of inviting Beard to sing it (the premiere was on January 8 1735) he realised that the young singer could also be useful in the two revivals that preceded it: *Il Pastor Fido* and *Arianna in Creta*. Thus his debut with Handel's company was brought forward to November 9. An effective publicity machine was brought into play, because news of Beard's debut even reached the newspapers in places as far-flung as Ipswich: "We hear ...that Mr Handell has got an extreme fine English voice, who will speedily sing at the Theatre in Covent Garden, and who never sang on any stage".[7]

It was good that he could begin in secondary roles, and acquire the necessary stagecraft by watching and learning from the rest of the cast. Although his early performances must have been wooden in delivery, it probably helped that there was still a great reliance on stock theatrical gesture at this time. The movement towards a 'natural' style of acting would only gain momentum in ten years time, with the arrival of David Garrick on the theatrical scene. It is possible of course, that Handel had made the offer to Beard earlier in the year - presumably some time after Easter - and had given him several months to acquire some stage technique. Who Beard would have gone to for acting lessons is not easy to determine; but there must have been such people available in the theatre world, just as there were dancing-masters around to help teach another essential skill.[8] Bernard Gates, who had produced the staging of *Esther* in 1732, may have given him his initial guidance. As he was on such good terms with Handel a plan could have been concocted between them both.

---

[4] see: Burrows, 'Thomas Gethin: a Handel tenor', *Musical Times* 116, 1975, pp.1003-6

[5] W. Dean, 'Handel's Dramatic Oratorios and Masques', London, 1959, p.659

[6] Burrows *Handel and the English Chapel Royal* p. 337

[7] Ipswich Gazette, 9th November 1734, Deutsch *Handel a Documentary Biography* p. 374

[8] Richard Charke was a singer, actor, composer, and – according to Burney – a dancing-master before he left England in 1735. He had all the right credentials to help Beard, including a great need to earn money. See: Fiske, 'English Theatre Music in the Eighteenth Century', Oxford, 1973, p.124-5

Elizabeth Compton's letter is interesting for another reason. It was written on November 21, by which time Beard would only have appeared a maximum of 4 times in *Il Pastor Fido*.[9] She had presumably not been to see it yet, although she had spoken to Handel. So, after such few performances she was able to report on Beard's surprisingly confident debut: "A scholar of Mr Gates ...shines in the Opera of Covent Garden & Mr Hendell is so full of his Praises that he says he will surprise the Town with his performances before the Winter is over".[10]

Handel had needed to rewrite the role of 'Silvio' for Beard's tenor voice, since it had been sung by castrati in the two previous runs: by Signor Valentini at the first performances in November 1712, and by Signor Scalzi in the performances that had taken place earlier in the year, between 18 May and 15 July. A comparison of the versions of Silvio's arias composed in 1712 and 1734 shows that Handel made no concessions to his new singer's youth and inexperience. He treated the rewrite as a simple logistical exercise of turning the music for one type of voice into something equally satisfying for the other.

Silvio's Act 1 aria "Quel Gelsomino" was replaced with "Non vo' mai seguitar", newly composed for this revival.[11] A lively *Allegro* in C major, it has many semiquaver runs, and takes the voice up to top A. The vocal line has wide leaps, and is very similar in mood to the wedding aria from *Athaliah* with which Beard had caught Handel's attention back in March.

In Act 2 Handel retained the castrato aria "Sol nel mezzo risona del core" in its original key of B flat; but - despite the necessary downward adaptation for a tenor - gave it a bravura vocal line, taking the voice up to top B flat within 4 bars, and repeating this phrase in the manner of a hunting-call. Handel very rarely wrote a top B flat for Beard's voice, and never took him higher than top A in the oratorios which were written for his voice between 1736 and 1752.

The style of this aria is significant, because Beard made a feature of singing extrovert hunting songs during his theatrical career. He first came to popular fame and prominence with his performance of Galliard's hunting song "The early horn".

[9] It was performed on November 9, 13, 16, 20 & 23.
[10] Deutsch *Handel a Documentary Biography* p. 375; and Norfolk Record Office BL/T/5/2/3
[11] Dean and Knapp, 'Handel's Operas', Oxford, 1987, p. 220

As we shall see, it became one of his calling cards, and was frequently requested between the acts. Here, in his first appearance on stage, Handel had sensed this possibility in his voice. He was to use the facility with which Beard could go up to trumpet-like top notes many more times: in "Thou shalt dash them" (*Messiah*) and "Sound an alarm" (*Judas Maccabaeus*) to name but two of many instances.

The Act 3 aria, "Sento nel sen", was a lilting 3/8 ballad, very lightly scored, with a highly decorated passage in unison with the violins. Thus Handel provided Beard with a decent length of role for his first stage-work, which included plenty of Italian recitative, and three very varied arias. Moreover, there was a possibility for his youthful voice to shine in each.

Handel now had no need of the likes of Signor Pinacci, his most recent Italian tenor who had sung with him between 1731 and 1732. Beard had proved himself equal to the task. Handel was sufficiently satisfied to keep him on in his company. In the three years 1734-7 Beard's roles with Handel's opera company not only included secondary roles in revivals of existing operas: Silvio *(Il Pastor Fido)*, Alceste *(Arianna)*, Alessandro *(Poro)*, and Emilio *(Partenope)*; but also new operas in which the roles were specifically tailored to his voice: Lurcanio *(Ariodante)* and Oronte *(Alcina)* in 1735; Amintas *(Atalanta)* in 1736; Varo *(Arminio)*, Vitaliano *(Giustino)*, and Fabio *(Berenice)* all in 1737.

Thus the start of Beard's career coincided with the last period of Handel's career as an opera composer, when success was beginning to desert him. However, the singer was extremely fortunate to have emerged on the scene at the precise moment when Handel began to adapt his style to the composition of oratorios. During these years (1734-7) Handel's programmes swung wildly between opera and oratorio. When Handel engaged Italian soloists and decided to write opera Beard was always given a good subsidiary role. When the Italians left, or went across to the rival opera company, Handel was forced to use the group of English singers that he had begun to build up. The English oratorios that he either revived or composed anew had increasingly important roles for the tenor soloist. Beard was in a win/win situation, whatever the composer decided to do.

At this time Handel was falling back on previously-composed oratorios to make up for a shortfall in his operatic repertoire. This was good for Beard, who appeared in *Esther* (now as a tenor) in March 1735, April 1736 and April 1737. He took part in the revival of *Deborah* in March 1735. Although detailed programmes for these do not exist, Winton Dean has suggested that his roles were likely to have been 'Habdonah' and 'Sisera' respectively. In *Athaliah* (April 1735) he sang the part of 'Mathan'. In both of these last works, as we have already seen, Handel inserted the aria "Strength and Honour" that Beard had first sung at the 1734 Royal Wedding.

Oratorio was such a new concept at this time that the public took a little time to get accustomed to the idea of hearing sacred works, without action, in London's theatres. In February 1732 Viscount Percival referred to *Esther* as an "*oratoria* or religious opera"; but by May2 he was writing the word in his diary as "*oratory*", and on May 6 he finally alighted on the spelling "*oratorio*".[12]

Handel chose the word "*Oratorio*" to describe his miscellaneous programme of sacred music in March 1738 because there was no better word in existence in English at the time. There was a French expression, *Concert Spirituel*, and this was used more frequently as the century progressed (see Gemininani's Benefit Concert on April 11 1750 which was called a 'Concert Spiritual' or 'Spirituale') to describe such miscellaneous programmes. Gradually the word 'oratorio' began to settle down in the English language with the meaning it has now. Towards the end of the century it even began to mean a concert of any kind, especially in country districts. There was always a difficulty when the subject matter was not biblical; and pedants tried to restrict the word to those pieces by Handel and his followers that were on a sacred subject. They used the words 'pastoral', 'masque' and 'serenata' for such secular pieces as Boyce's *Solomon*, Handel's *Acis and Galatea*, and his quasi-opera *Semele*. But this problem is with us still, and the word 'oratorio' is frequently used today to cover the entire spectrum of choral works performed without stage action.[13]

The first oratorio that had a part specifically written for Beard's voice was *Alexander's Feast* (actually a Cecilian *Ode*). The premiere was on February 19 1736, and it gave him his first considerable success. The first night saw a 'capacity' audience of 1300 people crowding into Covent Garden theatre - as many as it could hold at the time - and it "met with general applause".[14] As Sir John Hawkins said: "Instead of airs that required the delicacy of Cuzzoni, or the volubility of Faustina to execute, he (Handel) hoped to please by songs, the beauties whereof were within the comprehension of less fastidious hearers than in general frequent the opera, namely, such as were adapted to a tenor voice, from the natural firmness and inflexibility whereof little more is expected than an articulate utterance of the words, and a just expression of the melody; and he was happy in the assistance of a singer possessed of these and many other valuable qualities.".[15]

One aria that Beard sang was "Happy Pair", containing the famous Dryden line "None but the brave deserves the fair", that was later plagiarised by W.S. Gilbert in the libretto of *Iolanthe*.[16] It can be seen in this excerpt that Handel had changed his style of writing for Beard's voice quite significantly. Instead of the fancy decorative fioritura of "Sento nel sen" there is a robust vocal roulade with less semiquavers and demisemiquavers. The overall 'feel' of the music is simpler and more direct. This was a style that he would use repeatedly in the more jovial music which he provided for Beard. Other examples feature prominently in *L'Allegro ed il Penseroso* and in *Semele*. Charles Dibdin described Beard's voice, when he knew it twenty-five years later, as "sound, male, powerful and extensive. His tones were natural, and he had flexibility enough to execute any passages however difficult, which task indeed frequently fell to his lot in some of Handel's oratorios; but, with these qualifications: where the feelings were most roused, he was, of course, the most excellent. If he failed at all it was in *acquired taste*, which I will venture to pronounce was a most fortunate circumstance for him; for I never knew an instance

---

[12] Deutsch, op. cit. p. 288 & p. 290-1
[13] Orff's *Carmina Burana* is a case in point. But what other word would be suitable: *Ode*, or *Cantata*?
[14] The London Daily Post, 20th February, 1736
[15] Hawkins A General History of the Science and Practice of Music, 1776, Vol. 2 p. 889
[16] in the Act 2 Trio of *Iolanthe* "He who shies at such a prize"

where *acquired taste* did not destroy natural expression; a quality self-evidently as much preferable to the other as nature is to art".[17] This aria - which demonstrates Dibdin's comments about his voice being natural and flexible - quickly entered Beard's miscellaneous repertoire of songs, and was frequently performed by him between the acts at Drury Lane and Covent Garden.[18]

The other tenor aria in *Alexander's Feast*, "The princes applaud with a furious joy", did not lend itself to being taken out of context. But it is another example of the extrovert *Allegro* arias that Handel would write for Beard throughout his career. As in "Non vo' mai seguitar" from *Il Pastor Fido* it is liberally sprinkled with semiquaver runs and top As.

Soon there would be tenor arias like this in *Israel in Egypt*, *Samson*, *Belshazzar*, and *Judas Maccabaeus*. Because of Beard's ease of delivery of the quick passages, and his trumpet-like top notes, Handel could see that his tenor voice was capable of more than a subsidiary role. As this list of oratorios shows, Handel would soon remove the castrato from his traditional position as the male hero: and it would be the tenor who would replace him.

Charles Burney writes frequently about Beard's vocal qualities in his '*A General History of Music*'[19], with the added bonus that he knew and liked Beard the man, who had done much to help him in the early stages of his own career. Although he never heard the young Beard sing, he knew his voice well from about 1750 onwards.[20] Comparing Beard to his closest rival, the tenor Thomas Lowe, he says: "...with the finest tenor voice I ever heard in my life, for want of diligence and cultivation, he (Lowe) never could be safely trusted with any thing better than a ballad, which he constantly learned by his ear; whereas Mr. Beard, with an inferior voice, constantly possessed the favour of the public by his superior conduct, knowledge of music, and intelligence as an actor."

This, then, was the voice for which Handel began to write increasingly important roles. Their music, and the variety of arias and recitatives which Beard undertook in them, is discussed in Chapter 14. A search through the Handelian correspondence will show that once he had discovered Beard, he was remarkably faithful to him - even when the singer had been unwell - and engaged him whenever he could:

---

[17] Charles Dibdin, 'A complete History of The English Stage', London, 1797, p. 362
[18] Although not originally specified in playbills in the 1730s, by April 1739 the titles of songs and ballads were sometimes given. On April 3rd that year Beard was advertised as singing "Happy Fair" from *Alexander's Feast* and "Would you taste the noontide air" from Arne's *Comus*.
[19] Burney *A General History of Music*, 1789
[20] On 13th December 1750 Burney's burletta *Robin Hood* was mounted at Drury Lane with Beard in the title role.

"I have taken the Opera House in the Haymarket. Engaged as singers ... Beard, Reinhold, ... and I have some hopes that Mrs Cibber will sing for me ... I think I can obtain Mr Riches's permission (with whom she is engaged to play in Covent Garden House) since so obligingly he gave leave to Mr Beard and Mr Reinhold."[21]

"I have a good Set of singers ... Mr Beard (who is recovered) [is] *Belshazzar* ..."[22]

"I asked him what singers he had got: he said he was very well provided, having Champness, Beard, Frasi, Cassandra Frederick and Miss Young; upon which I asked him if he was quite full so as to want no other assistance: he answered somewhat hastily, quite full, and that he wanted no more voices. I had intended to mention young Norris[23]; but upon his being so positive, I could not do it."[24]

Another existing role that Beard took on at this stage was 'Acis' in *Acis and Galatea*. Although Handel had written the delightful music for this pastoral character in 1718 for an unspecified tenor, the *serenata* remained unknown until Philip Rochetti undertook it for his Benefit in 1731. It was well written for the tenor voice and for Beard's tessitura. When Handel began writing specifically for him in the oratorios of 1736 onwards, this was the model that he must have kept in mind:

Love in her eyes sits play - ing, and sheds de - li - cious death; love____ on her lips__ is stray - ing,__ and warb - ling in____ her breath; love on her lips is stray - ing, and warb - ling in her breath.

Beard possibly sang Acis's arias more often than those of any other Handelian hero, since the *serenata* was popular with musical gatherings of every type. It was often chosen for Benefit concerts at Hickford's Rooms and Ranelagh Gardens, as well as being popular at the music festivals springing up in the Cathedral cities. Beard was frequently engaged to sing the role throughout London and the provinces. He sang it for Handel for the first time in March 1736, and thereafter excerpts often featured in his miscellaneous programmes.[25]

Handel's operatic success seemed to have deserted him by the end of June 1737. The season had involved Beard in every month since November 1736, and ended with the now very popular *Alexander's Feast*. Handel had given Londoners a mixture of operas and oratorios in one of his longest-ever seasons. But he cannot have grasped that the oratorios, using a cheaper cast of English soloists, were doing better business for him than the operas with the expensive Italians. He must simply have considered the oratorios as stop-gaps - and cheap ones at that, since they required no elaborate costumes, scenery or stage business. They were fitted in amongst the opera performances irregularly. At this point Handel had not realised that they would make suitable material for the Lent Season, when normal theatrical

---

[21] Handel to Jennens, 9th June 1744, quoted in Deutsch *Handel a Documentary Biography* p. 591

[22] Handel to Jennens, 2nd Oct. 1744, quoted in Deutsch *Handel a Documentary Biography* p. 596 The illness from which Beard had recovered was a recurrent problem with his hearing.

[23] Thomas Norris, tenor, 1741-90, who would sing in the Handel Musical Commemorations in 1784-90.

[24] Thomas Harris to James Harris, 7th January 1758, reporting on a meeting with Handel, quoted in Burrows & Dunhill *Music and Theatre in Handel's World*, p. 328

[25] for example, in the items he sang for the Annual Concert in aid of Decayed Musicians

performances were forbidden. That would happen later. Nor did he yet see that his long-term future lay with this repertory.

It was also at this time that Handel's health began to suffer, leading him to take an extended cure at Aix-la-Chapelle during the Summer of 1737. This must have been a blow to Beard: Handel had clearly made no decision about a 1737-38 season by the time he left England. Beard had endured a similar bleak time during the Autumn of 1735 when, once again, Handel's season had started late. It was obvious that he could not totally rely on Handel to provide employment and, with no other singing dates in his diary, he would need to look elsewhere for work. So it was to the theatre impresarios that he took his talent. Without guaranteed work from Handel, Beard knew that he had to find a position as a singer in their farces, pantomimes and after-pieces.

2. *AD HOC* WORK AT COVENT GARDEN THEATRE: 1736-7

At this time, Handel used which ever theatre was available for his seasons. When the King's Theatre Haymarket (the best for sound) was not available, he rented either the Lincoln's Inn Fields Theatre or Covent Garden Theatre from the impresario John Rich. Thus it was that Beard made his operatic debut in the theatre that Rich had built. Rich must have noticed something appealing in Beard's performances of Handel's extrovert arias whilst they were wooing the audiences in his own theatre. Perhaps his ear, too, had caught the strong virile sound of his young tenor voice, which was so rare in those days. Rich's problem was that he was well-provided with a singer for his farces. Thomas Salway was contracted for all the pieces that would have suited Beard. It was one of the unwritten rules of the theatre that a performer hung on to his or her roles unless they wished to relinquish them, or they moved from one theatre to another.

The only possibility for engaging Beard was to give him a new role, if one should come along. And so, at the beginning of 1736, three months after the theatre season had started, he was given a loose invitation to do occasional work in new afterpieces and as an interval singer. This seemed to work well enough. Although Beard's diary became incredibly full, he managed to combine performances for Handel's short oratorio season (February - April 1736) and the even shorter opera season (May - early June) with new afterpieces for Rich.

John Rich - who has a very important role to play in John Beard's story - was himself a pantomime actor. He was the foremost Harlequin of his day, performing under the stage name of 'Lun'. Covent Garden was famous for these spectacles. One suspects that Rich thought they were the most important works on offer in his theatrical repertory. He spent more money on their costumes, scenery and special effects than on any other of his shows.

By tradition there was always a new pantomime early in the New Year. In January 1736 it was *The Royal Chace* with music by John Ernest Galliard. A small role, the 'Royal Chasseur', had a hunting song, but did very little else in the action. There was no spoken dialogue. It was an inspired choice of role for Beard. It also brought him into the regular Covent Garden company, where he would meet the actors who normally had a day off when he was there with Handel. In his first show he not only worked with his future father-in-law (Rich) but his future mother-in-law Mrs Stevens (Rich's third wife) and James Bencraft, his future brother-in-law.

Somewhere in the wings he would have occasionally seen the girl who would one day become his second wife - Rich's daughter Charlotte.

The pantomime *The Royal Chace* was advertised in London's daily press as "…a new dramatic Entertainment. The characters new Drest. With new Scenes, representing the exact views of the Hermitage, and Merlin's Cave, as taken in the Royal Gardens of Richmond".[26] Charles Burney was aware of Beard's unexpected success in it when he wrote in his history of music:

"…This year Mr Beard who had his musical education in the Chapel Royal, first appeared on the stage at Covent Garden in the dramatic entertainment of the Royal Chace or Merlin's Cave, and instantly became a favourite of the town, by the performance of Galliard's most agreeable of all hunting-songs, "With early horn".[27] Hawkins similarly recounts in his History of Music that it was due to this famous song that "…for some hundred nights, Mr Beard first recommended himself to the public".[28]

Whether Beard's performance had anything to do with the pantomime's success or not, the work had staying power. It was given as the afterpiece on most evenings for the rest of the season. Only on June 3 did a vocally tired Beard need to ask his understudy (a Mr Roberts) to go on for him. Meanwhile he had also managed to perform twenty times for Handel. He was assisted in this by reason of Handel's performances being held, once again, in the same theatre. So there was never any danger of Beard being double-booked, as happened later in his career.

The Royal Chace would now become a stock repertory piece at Covent Garden. Beard was still singing the 'Chasseur Royal' in it as late as 1748 - before he changed houses for an 11-year contract at Drury Lane. It was still in the Covent Garden repertoire in Beard's last season as manager there, in 1766-7, by which time he had passed the role on to the next generation of young singers.[29] Also this season John Rich found him a role in another pantomime which would stay for a long time in the repertoire. On March 6, by which time nearly every member of the theatre-going public had seen *The Royal Chace,* Rich decided to resurrect a 1730s pantomime, *Perseus and Andromeda*, that was last seen at Lincoln' Inn Fields theatre. Beard was given a major role as 'Perseus'; although the main protagonist was, as always, taken by Rich in his impersonation of Harlequin. Tom Davies, Garrick's biographer, gives us an idea of what these shows must have been like:

"To retrieve the credit of his theatre, Rich created a species of dramatic composition unknown to this, and, I believe, to any other country, which he called a Pantomime: it consisted of two parts, one serious, the other comic; by the help of gay scenes, fine habits, grand dances, appropriate music, and other decorations, he exhibited a story from Ovid's *Metamorphoses*, or some other fabulous history. Between the pauses of the acts he interwove a comic fable, consisting chiefly of the courtship of Harlequin and Columbine, with a variety of surprising adventures and tricks, which were produced by the magic wand of Harlequin; such as the sudden transformation of palaces and temples to huts and cottages; of men and women into wheelbarrows and

---

[26] The London Stage, ed. Arthur Scouten, Part 3, p.546

[27] Burney, 'A General History of Music', London 1935, vol. 2, p.1003

[28] Sir John Hawkins, 'A General History of the Science and Practice of Music', London 1776

[29] On 25th October 1766, and for the subsequent run, the singer was Squibb, who joined the company in 1764.

joint stools; of trees turned to houses; colonnades to beds of tulips; and mechanics' shops into serpents and ostriches... There was scarce one which failed to please the public, who testified their approbation of them forty or fifty nights successively".[30]

The 1736-7 season was one of Beard's busiest working for Handel. He appeared with him in opera from November till June, and gave 34 performances of leading roles in *Alcina, Atalanta, Poro, Arminio, Partenope, Giustino* and *Berenice*. Handel also mixed in some oratorios amongst this stimulating collection of new works and revivals. Beard sang in performances of *Alexander's Feast, Il Trionfo del Tempo e della Verita* and *Esther* a further 11 times. But he does not seem to have been required for the performances of *Il Parnasso in Festa* on March 9 and 11, or for the pasticcio *Didone Abbandonata* on April 13, 20, 27 and June 1. This is probably just as well, as his diary was further complicated by revivals of the Pantomimes *Perseus and Andromeda* in November and December 1736, and *The Royal Chace* in February and March 1737. Throughout the next two months, April and May, he sang interval songs on every day that he was not loaned out to Handel. One of these was the satirical ballad which had recently been published in Bickham's "The Musical Entertainer": '*The Ladies Lamentation for the loss of Senesino*'[31]:

> I gently requested the cause of her moan,
> She told me her sweet Senesino was flown...
> 'My sweet Senesino for whom I thus cry
> Is sweeter than all the wing'd songsters that fly...'

Beard performed this on most evenings in May 1737. But witty Henry Carey was soon writing his riposte when the next haughty castrato to be taken to the public's heart, Farinelli,[32] left England in the summer. This was entitled '*The Beau's Lament for the loss of Farinelli*', and included these lines, which must have pleased the young English singer who had now made such a significant mark:

> Come, never lament for a singer, said I,
> Can't English performers his absence supply?
> There's *Beard* and there's *Salway*, and smart *Kitty Clive*,
> The pleasantest, merriest mortal alive.

After this thoroughly marvellous season, in which he had skilfully combined the high art of opera with the low art of pantomime, Beard was once again at the mercy of Handel's faltering health and lack of managerial acumen. He could foresee that there would be lean pickings in the coming season of 1737-8. But, at the same time that he approached Rich for a continuation of the *ad hoc* arrangement that he had enjoyed for the previous two years, he must also have been tempted by an improved offer from Charles Fleetwood, the manager of Drury Lane. Fleetwood was keen to poach him as he suddenly found himself without a singer for the musical afterpieces at his theatre. The thing that must have clinched the deal was that

[30] Thomas Davies, 'Memoirs of the Life of David Garrick, Esq', vol. 1, London, 1780, p. 92-3
[31] Senesino (Francesco Bernardi, c. 1690- c. 1750) sang for Handel's Royal Academy from 1720-8, returning to London in 1730 for Handel's revived company. In 1733 he was poached by the Opera of the Nobility. He left England at the end of 1736 and returned to the opera houses of Europe.
[32] Farinelli (Carlo Broschi, 1705 - 1782) was in London from 1734 singing for the rival company to Handel's, the Opera of the Nobility. He left England in the summer of 1737, and took up a position at Court in Spain.

Fleetwood was now offering him the chance to be a real actor, with speaking roles. Beard must have aspired to playing the glamorous role of 'Captain Macheath' in *The Beggar's Opera*. This was the pinnacle of all ambitions for a male singer at the theatre. But 'Macheath' was a real actor's role: there was as much dialogue as there was song, including long soliloquys for which a real talent in acting was required. 'Macheath' had to hold the stage at all times, and slip effortlessly from speech to song and back again. Moreover, it was a 'mainpiece'; so it was customarily undertaken by a leading actor with an adequate singing voice, rather than the other way round. The role had originally been conceived for the legendary tragedian James Quin, who baulked at the amount of singing that was expected. The first interpreter in 1732, therefore, was Thomas Walker, who is seen standing centre stage in leg-irons in Hogarth's famous painting of the Newgate Prison scene.

The possibility of playing this role may have been dangled in front of Beard as a carrot by Fleetwood, to get him to leave the company where he was beginning to put down roots. Initially he would be expected to work his way up to *The Beggar's Opera* by learning his craft in the shorter ballads operas that were the staple fare at Drury Lane, such as *The Devil to Pay*, *The King and the Miller of Mansfield*, and *The Virgin Unmasked*. Fleetwood tied him into a three-year contract. We know this, because - many years later - when Beard was encouraging the young Charles Dibdin at the beginning of <u>his</u> career, he suggested that he would take him on contract for three years at an increasing yearly salary, and: "…if I approved it, order an article to be prepared for three, four, and five pounds a week, which, he assured me, were the terms on which he commenced his own career".[33] Thus, by the time that Handel eventually put together a company to perform *Faramondo* in 1738, Beard had been obliged to secure employment elsewhere, possibly endangering his relationship with Handel. Handel was now performing at the King's Theatre Haymarket with a strong cast of Italians headed by Caffarelli. There were no tenors engaged to replace Beard and no tenor music was written for the opera. Instead, Handel filled Beard's place with William Savage, five years his junior, who had sung in the 1735-6 oratorios as a 'boy' and by now was probably singing as a counter-tenor.[34]

3. THREE-YEAR CONTRACT AT DRURY LANE THEATRE, 1737-40

Beard landed on his feet at Drury Lane. Fleetwood needed a singer, and he had plenty of work to offer. He gave his new acquisition a part in every piece that came along. How Beard learned all this material in time seems quite incredible. There were sixteen shows in which he was employed in the first season, and they were all new to him. The first to come his way was the ballad opera *The Devil to Pay*, which was very stock fare at both theatres. It was a farce, created out of an earlier play *The Devil of a Wife* by Charles Coffey, into which a succession of popular ballads had been inserted. For the first two nights, August 30 and September 1 1737, Beard played it as it had been performed by his predecessor, Thomas Salway, and enjoyed a modest success. The prompter kindly wrote into his record: "the first night of Beard's playing – his success great".[35] This was the first occasion on which Beard

---

[33] Charles Dibdin, 'The Professional Life of Charles Dibdin', vol. 1, 1803, p.46
[34] "There is much confusion over his …vocal compass, soprano, alto, tenor, and bass parts all having been ascribed to him". W. Dean, 'Handel's Dramatic Oratorios and Masques', London, 1959, p.659
[35] from a diary of Benjamin Griffin, BL Egerton 2320. The London Stage , Part 3, p.681

had delivered any lines of spoken dialogue in the theatre, and he was clearly worried. The prompter wrote, after the second performance, "Sir John [Loverule]: Beard - the second time of his appearing on that stage in any speaking character". The speaking role was not particularly arduous - in fact there was probably more singing than speaking involved; and as he was such a likeable character in real life the role of 'Sir John', described in the scenario as 'an honest Country Gentleman, belov'd for his Hospitality', seems to have been a gift. Before his first entry the Butler says: "Our master indeed is the worthiest Gentleman – nothing but Sweetness and Liberality".[36] At Beard's first appearance this description is borne out by the character's affable manner - much like a latter-day Sir Roger de Coverley - of reproving his new and shrewish wife, who has earlier started to beat and berate their servants as they noisily carouse:

"For shame, my Dear. – As this is a time of Mirth and Jollity, it has always been the custom of my house to give my servants Liberty in this season, and to treat my Country Neighbours, that with innocent Sports they may divert themselves". When he was offstage in Act 2, out hunting, there was a music cue for the sounds of a hunt – "*Horns wind without*" - at Jobson's line:

---

[36] All lines taken from Charles Coffey, 'The Devil to Pay, or, the Wives Metamorphosed', London, 1748

"Hark! the Hunters and the merry Horns are abroad. Why Nell, you lazy Jade, 'tis break of day; to work! to work!" - which must have given him a brilliant idea: the public at Covent Garden had clamoured for his performance of "The early horn" all last season. Why not insert it into the action at this point? And so that was what happened at the third performance, September 3, when the playbills advertised the song as 'by particular desire'. The 'desire' could well have been Beard's own, to increase the impact he made in the role. Anyway, it worked. As had previously happened, the song became a favourite of the new public, and Beard's success in the speaking and singing role was now assured. George Bickham included the song in "The Musical Entertainer" (published in 1737) where it is entitled 'The Meeting in the Morning', and subtitled *Sung by Mr Beard with Universal Applause*".

The other roles that Beard had to play before Christmas were 'Quaver' in *The Virgin Unmasked*, Rovewell in *The Contrivances*, Damon in *Damon and Phillida* and Leander in *The Mock Doctor*. After twenty-four performances of these five works Fleetwood felt confident enough to try Beard out in the part he most wanted to play. And so, on 25 October Beard got to play 'Macheath' for the first time.

In all of these pieces he was working with the best players in the Drury Lane company. The leading actress/singer was Kitty Clive who played opposite him in every show, and was the 'Phillida' to his 'Damon', in the ballad opera by Colley Cibber. She was also famous as 'Nell' in *The Devil to Pay*. Beard had to work hard to achieve a success like hers in this piece - which may explain why he inserted his favourite ballad into it. As Burney says, "In this farce Miss Rafter first acquired celebrity, and after she was Mrs Clive, to the end of her theatrical life, she never received more applause, or earned it better in any part she acted, than in that of 'Nell'. Her singing, which was intolerable when she meant it to be fine, in ballad farces and songs of humour was, like her comic acting, every thing it should be".[37] The leading dramatic actor and actress were Charles Macklin and Mrs Hannah Pritchard. All of them came together in Beard's first *Beggar's Opera*, with Charles Macklin as 'Peachum' and Mrs Pritchard and Kitty Clive as the squabbling wives 'Lucy' and 'Polly'. At the climax of the story 'Macheath' has to decide which wife to choose. The music for this ballad is known as 'Lumps of Pudding', and takes the singer up to a high A within the melodic line:

Beard's debut was auspicious, and the piece was played five times in a fortnight. This was unusual. The work was always popular with the public, and could be guaranteed to do well at the box office if it received the customary arrangement of one performance a month. But it was risky to try too many performances in close proximity, as - at 3 hours long - it was normally played without an afterpiece. A long run would have kept the normal repertoire off the stage and a lot of 'straight' actors

[37] Burney, 'A General History of Music', ed. Frank Mercer, London, 1935, p.1000

idle. Beard's success was cut short by the death of Queen Caroline on November 20. This closed the theatres until January 2 1738. When Drury Lane reopened the *Beggar's Opera* resumed its place in the repertory and was played once a month.[38]

With the theatres now open for business again it was time for the traditional pantomimes. These were mounted at Drury Lane in competition with the better-known and more established offerings at Covent Garden. In 1738 Fleetwood was determined to provide even stronger competition by engaging a new Harlequin of his own, Henry Woodward, who proceeded to adopt a version of John Rich's trademark by calling himself 'Lun junior'.[39] Beard was engaged in the musical part of these productions at the beginning of the year, playing 'Poudre' in Woodward's *Ridotto al Fresco or the Harlot's Progress*, the 'Conjuror' in *Harlequin Restored*, and 'Mercury' in *The Fall of Phaeton*. More traditional ballad opera entered his repertoire too, and much of it would be the mainstay of his work in the afterpieces for the rest of his career. Pieces like *The King and the Miller of Mansfield*, in which he played 'Joe', *The Lottery*, in which he played 'Lovemore', and *The Intriguing Chambermaid*, in which he played 'Valentine', would be among his stock works for the next 30 years. Only one other mainpiece came his way in this season, and it was another work that would find a permanent place in the repertoire at both theatres. Thomas Arne was beginning to make a mark in the theatre with incidental music for plays, having had a flop with his first opera *Rosamond* in 1733. When he turned his attention to Milton's masque of *Comus* he wrote his first 'hit'. It opened on March 4th 1738, and Beard had the best music in it as an unnamed 'Bacchanal'. 'Not on beds of fading flowers' and 'Now Phoebus sinketh in the west' are still highly delightful to sing today, and are in many present-day singers' repertoires. Sounding a little like Handel in his best pastoral mode, they are even fresher than that composer's sometimes stilted arias.

As Burney, who always seems to put his finger on it, says: "Arne furnished the whole kingdom with such songs as …improved and polished our national taste".[40] There was also good music in *Comus* for a couple of sopranos too, including a charming 'Echo' aria. In no time at all the songs became enormously popular. Extracts - including the aria 'Would you taste the noontide air'[41] - entered Beard's miscellaneous repertoire and were regularly sung between the intervals. *Comus* had a long run of eleven nights in its first season, and then entered the repertoire, where it stayed successfully for the whole of Arne's life and Beard's career. Fortunately it had some good dramatic roles for the principal actors too. But it was Arne's delightful music that propelled it into the ranks of a 'classic'. Beard programmed it in every season at Covent Garden during his time as manager there in

[38] Jan 25th, Feb 4th, April 27th, May 31st. There was no performance in March as Arne's *Comus* had a long run.
[39] Woodward's first performance in the role of Harlequin was on October 22nd 1737.
[40] Burney, 'A General History of Music', ed. Frank Mercer, London, 1935, p.1015
[41] For example, it is advertised in playbills on April 7, 9, 12, 25, 27, 28, & May 3 1739

the 1760s. The number of performances averaged out at three a year, apart from 1759 when it was played twelve times.

Not all of the plays that were mounted at Drury Lane in Beard's first season enjoyed the same success as these thirteen. The other three pieces that make up the total of sixteen that he played in 1737-8 were more ephemeral. *Sir John Cockle at Court*, in which he played 'Sir Timothy Flash', was a sequel to *The King and the Miller of Mansfield*; and *The Lover's Opera* was a ballad opera from 1729 that was cast in the same mould as the *Beggar's Opera*. But neither were as successful as the originals. *The Coffee-house*, in which he played 'Bawble', was a satirical piece by Henry Carey (author of 'Sally in our Alley') that only lasted one night. Despite using the whole galaxy of Drury Lane stars, and providing the Poet Laureate Colley Cibber with a cameo role playing himself, Carey's star was on the wane. From all accounts it was a witty look at contemporary life as seen from the audience's standpoint - as frequenters of the local coffee-houses. But they missed the point, and thought that Carey was ridiculing their favourite haunts and their popular landladies. The London Evening Post, reviewing the performance and reminding its readers that the Lord Chamberlain's Licensing Act of 1737 had very recently rid the theatre of the worst excesses of political satire, wrote: "It's remarkable that the new farce called "The Coffee-house" - the first performed since the Act of Parliament took place - [was] damned by the Town".[42]

Two other important things happened for Beard towards the end of his first season at Drury Lane. In April he was granted his first Benefit night there, and found himself quite low down in the pecking order at number 20.[43] His programme was an arduous one that was chosen to show off all his skills. Since the artist was entitled to select the repertoire for their individual Benefit Night it is always very revealing to see what they chose. Beard is no exception. He chose his best roles, and played in both halves of the evening: the mainpiece was *The Beggar's Opera*, and the afterpiece was *The Devil to Pay* with "'The Early Horn' introduced into Beard's part". Since *The Beggar's Opera* was normally played without an afterpiece at this period it not only made for a very substantial evening's entertainment, but put a lot of strain on him as the principal personage in both halves. His fellow actors included the principals who had joined him earlier in the season: Mrs Pritchard, Mrs Clive, and Charles Macklin. He would have been bound to make a handsome profit with this cast and this repertoire. Sadly that sort of information is missing from the first few years of his career; but four years later, when the records suddenly become available, it is clear that he was one of the highest grossing artists on Benefit Nights. The first sum that we know of was the £207 that he made in 1742. His repertoire choices on that night were *Comus* and Fielding's *The Mock Doctor* - another couple of popular works - and it is clear from the size of the profit that he drew a full house. In 1737 he seems to have started as he meant to go on.

The second important event for Beard at this time was the invitation from Handel to join him, once again, as tenor soloist in a concert of oratorio music. Beard must have been delighted to learn that he had not queered his pitch with Handel by taking the Drury Lane contract. Handel, for his part, was granted a benefit night by

---

[42] London Evening Post, 28th January 1738
[43] After 6 actors, nos. 7 & 13 in the order were the dancers Nivelon and Lalauze; Thomas Salway, the tenor from whom Beard eventually took over was at no. 15; and Richard Leveridge, the famous bass who had sung for Purcell, was at no. 18. Beard's Benefit was on April 22nd 1737. The London Stage, Part 3, p.661

the managers of the opera company at the King's Theatre Haymarket; and - having failed to put on any oratorio performances in Lent when the theatres were closed - decided to present a mixed programme of excerpts from recent oratorios, Chandos Anthems and Coronation Anthems. As he was without a tenor in his opera company Beard was the logical choice for any tenor solos that might be required. A letter from the 4th Earl of Shaftesbury, written a fortnight before the concert on March 14, is very helpful in outlining the programme and explaining that "Beard [will have] two songs. But I do not know exactly where and what songs…"[44]

Handel's 'Oratorio', as it was called in the press, brought him an estimated £1000 profit[45]. Beard was the soloist in some items from *Deborah*, which included his Handelian party-piece 'Strength and Honour'. The current stars of the Italian opera - Caffarelli, Montagnana and Signora Francesina - sang arias from the operas; and the Chapel Royal singers continued their long association with Handel choral works by singing in the choruses.

The season 1738-9 was to prove an enormously successful one for Beard, in public and in private. Things had worked out well at Drury Lane. As a result of his growing success and reputation there Charles Fleetwood was prepared to make some concessions regarding the time that Beard would need off in order to join Handel again. Handel himself must have let the young tenor know that he would be needing him in some new oratorios - as long as he could make himself available. The two new works that he was composing in the summer and autumn of 1738 were *Saul* and *Israel in Egypt*.[46] Both were composed with Beard's voice in mind for the principal tenor roles; so it was important for Beard to clarify matters with Fleetwood before the new season started at Drury Lane on September 7. Fleetwood could see that Beard's popularity was approaching the sort of status associated nowadays with 'pop-stars'. He was too valuable a commodity to lose. So an arrangement was made whereby Beard would be released for Handel's dates, accompanied by a proportional drop in salary. But he would have to work doubly hard on all of the other days. We can see, from a quick glance at his diary, that he had some very arduous weeks of singing ahead of him. But his new-found fame was also beginning to attract the ladies.

At some time during 1738 he met Lady Henrietta Herbert, a young widow of twenty-one with aristocratic relations. It is not too fanciful to suppose that she first caught sight of Beard onstage at Drury Lane. How their romance was carried on thereafter cannot be satisfactorily explained. Some have suggested that it would have been possible for them to have met, politely, at Court, on the occasion when Beard sang the King's Birthday Ode there.[47] That took place on October 28;[48] but the timing seems rather impractical in view of his documented hunt for a priest willing to marry them during the course of November (see the next chapter for fuller details). It is more likely that Beard was employed by Henrietta as a singing teacher, or even a harpsichord teacher, and had therefore known her for a longer period. The

---

[44] Burrows & Dunhill *Music and Theatre in Handel's World*, p. 44

[45] "In the evening I went to Hendel's Oratorio, where I counted near 1,300 persons besides the Gallery and Upper Gallery. I suppose he got this night £1,000." Earl of Egmont's Diary, 28th March 1738

[46] *Saul* was composed between July 23rd and September 27th. *Israel in Egypt* was begun on October 1st.

[47] Robert Halsband made this suggestion in 'The Noble Lady and the Player', *History Today*, July 1968, p.467

[48] There was an ode "performed before His Majesty in the Great Council Chamber at St James' ", The Daily Gazeteer, 30-31 0ctober 1738.

fact that they both lived in the Red Lion area of Holborn must also have played a part in enabling them to meet without drawing undue attention to themselves.

At the beginning of the new 1738 season he was about to be twenty-three. He was young and fit, and well able to cope with the workload. He was also increasingly famous. His songs were not only being anthologised in collections like "The Musical Entertainer", but were available from ballad-sellers in the street, like the *New Song in praise of Old English Roast Beef* which can be found in the Cambridge University Library's *Madden Collection* of Ballads.

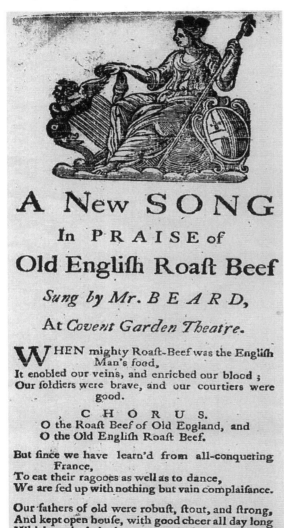

A New SONG

In PRAISE of

Old Englifh Roaft Beef

Sung by Mr. B E A R D,

At *Covent Garden Theatre.*

WHEN mighty Roaft-Beef was the Englifh Man's food,
It enobled our veins, and enriched our blood ;
Our foldiers were brave, and our courtiers were good.

C H O R U S.
O the Roaft Beef of Old England, and
O the Old Englifh Roaft Beef.

But fince we have learn'd from all-conquering France,
To eat their ragooes as well as to dance,
We are fed up with nothing but vain complaifance.

Our fathers of old were robuft, ftout, and ftrong,
And kept open houfe, with good cheer all day long
Which made their plump tenants rejoice in the fong

But now we are dwindled to what fhall I name ;
A fneaking poor race, half begotten and tame,
Who fully thofe honours that once fhone in fame.

When good Queen Elizabeth fat on the throne,
'Ere Coffee and tea and fuch flip-flops were known
The world was in terror, whene'er fhe did frown.

47

Fleetwood was finding it useful to have him singing between the acts on every occasion that he was not otherwise involved on stage. Sometimes he had to combine both jobs, as when he sang Purcell's 'Mad Dialogue' with Kitty Clive on the nights that he was in the new pantomime *Colombine Courtesan.* Other favourite songs that were programmed repeatedly this season, and featured heavily on the playbills, were 'Caelia that I once was blest', 'See from the silent groves', 'Would you taste the noontide air', and 'The Protestation'. There must have been many others that were never recorded on the playbills at all. Occasionally, for a special evening, Beard would fulfil specific requests. Thus, in May 1739, when he had recently joined a local Masonic brotherhood – the Free and Accepted Masons - the entertainment in the interval of their fundraising programme at the theatre was 'On, on, my dear Brethren', 'Thus mighty Eastern Kings' and other songs in Masonry sung by 'Brother Beard'.

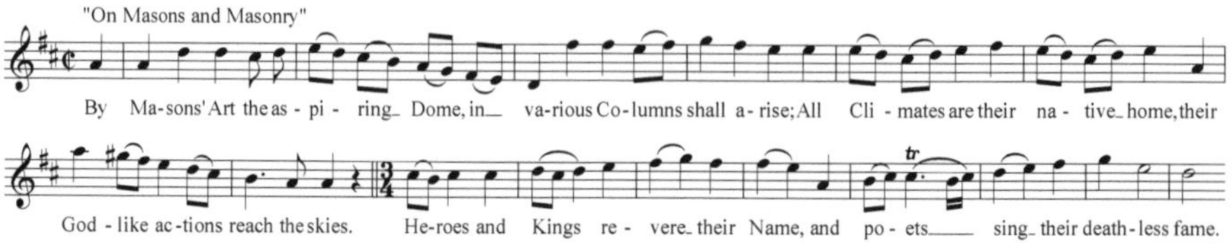

Having learned sixteen shows the previous season Beard was well set up for the current repertoire. Nearly all his pieces were repeated again. He played 'Macheath' a further seven times, at the rate of once a month; but as there were no further performances of *Comus* this season, his other mainpieces were revivals of Shakespeare's *Macbeth* and Sir John Vanbrugh's *The Provok'd Wife*. In the 18th century *Macbeth* was played in a version that would be scarcely recognised today. The scenes for the Witches were extended and elaborated with music playjng an important part. The main witch, 'Hecate', (Beard's role), had extra scenes with some splendid music by Richard Leveridge, especially when "Heckat goes into the Machine to fly". 'Her' lyrics at that point are "O what a dainty Pleasure's this to sail in the air / when the moon shines fair". Another of Hecate's songs is "Let's have a dance upon the Heath, / We gain more life by Duncan's Death", which is beautifully placed in the best part of the tenor's voice, rising naturally to a high G at the climaxes. Burney, in describing this music, which he thought had been composed by Matthew Locke, wrote: "its rude wild excellence cannot be surpassed". Beard had already played opposite the old trouper Richard Leveridge when he worked for Rich at Covent Garden in 1736. Now he was to sing the music which the singer, who had known Henry Purcell and been in the cast of *The Indian Queen* in 1695, had made obligatory in contemporary performances of the play. Mollie Sands, quoting from a contemporary source, says that Beard and his fellow cast-members "appeared as the singing witches, wearing mittens, plaited caps, laced aprons, red stomachers, ruffs, etc".[49] 'Hecate' was a role that Beard played for a further twenty years, and in which he would witness the extraordinarily powerful performances of David Garrick, in the title role.

In the Vanbrugh play *The Provok'd Wife* Beard's role was 'Colonel Bully', whose main reason for being on stage was to sing "the songs proper to the play".

[49] Mollie Sands, 'Invitation to Ranelagh', London, 1946, p. 84

One of these was the ever-popular 'Bumpers 'Squire Jones' - later anthologised in *The Gentleman's Magazine*:

The play was a perennial favourite, and stayed in Beard's repertoire up until the end of his career.[50] This was a type of mainpiece that kept him busy at the theatre, without being terribly arduous. There were other roles that were principally included in a play so that songs could be sung on stage. In a few years Beard would begin his long relationship with the songs that Thomas Arne provided for Shakespeare's comedies. In these Drury Lane performances, for which Arne wrote his evergreen melodies, Beard appeared in the role of 'Amiens', or 'Balthazar', or suchlike, to sing the songs and speak a few lines of dialogue, without being enormously integral to the plot.

There were several new pantomimes this year. *Colombine Courtesan*, in which he played 'the Spaniard' was followed by *Robin Goodfellow* by his old fellow-chorister at the Chapel Royal, Samuel Howard. Fiske writes of Howard that "...he seldom puts himself to the strain of writing anything longer than a simple ballad, and it is strange that he should have given up theatre music so young, when his first attempts had been so auspicious. Of his pantomime *Robin Goodfellow* only

---

[50] His last performance as Colonel Bully, 'with songs in character', was on May 7th 1765.

49

one song survives."[51] Beard's role in this was 'Squire Freehold', the first of a long line of Squires that his avuncular looks and comfortable girth would destine him to play. The song, and others that Howard wrote for Beard to sing at the Pleasure Gardens, owe a large debt to Handel – probably as a result of the good schooling he received in composition from Bernard Gates and Maurice Greene. But they also have the easy fluency of Arne. Burney perceptively noted that Howard "preferred the style of his own country to that of any other so much, that he never staggered his belief of its being the best in the world by listening to foreign artists or their productions".[52]

4. BACK WITH HANDEL AGAIN: 1739

Handel's 1739 oratorio season was presented at the King's Theatre Haymarket. He had finished the two new oratorios with major roles for Beard, who was available for the performances, despite being contracted to Drury Lane theatre. Handel's line-up of soloists included 'La Francesina' (Elisabeth Duparc), Cecilia Young, Savage, Waltz and Reinhold. The Earl of Shaftesbury, reminiscing many years later on the lack of Italians in the company, appears to have been unimpressed by the home-grown talent that Handel was nurturing: "But his singers in general not being capital, nor the town come into a relish of this species of music, he [Handel] had but a disadvantageous season."[53]

The two new oratorios were *Saul*, and *Israel in Egypt*. There was a dress rehearsal for *Saul* on January 8 1739. Mrs Pendarves wrote to her sister on January 7: "Tomorrow I go to hear Mr Handel's Oratorio rehearsed." On January 9 Lord Wentworth wrote to the Earl of Strafford: "Mr Handel rehearsed yesterday a new Oratorio call'd Saul..." So it is indisputably clear that this rehearsal took place on the 8th. But John Beard, rehearsing for the role of *Jonathan*, had other significant matters to attend to on that day as well. As will be shown, in the next chapter, this was the day in which he married his first wife, Lady Henrietta Herbert of Powis (née Waldegrave). The liaison was a scandalous one, and was the talk of the town. Giacomo Zamboni wrote to his employer, Prince Antioch Cantemir, in February 1739 to report on life in London. Having discussed the lack of culture that Europeans would find there, he goes on: "There remain of course the two English theatres, but for some time now the brawls in them have been so numerous and so frequent that one could not go there without some risk of exiting with a battered head. Yet that of Drury Lane is always full, and Beard, who has become a son-in-law of the British Ambassador to France, continues to sing there after having married the daughter of His Excellency, which makes many curious to go there. O tempora! O mores! Oh liberty and property! O che bel mondo!"[54]

And so, on the January 8 1739 John Beard sang the role of *Jonathan* in the morning rehearsal of Handel's *Saul* at the King's Theatre Haymarket; took his customary role in *Colombine Courtesan* at Drury Lane Theatre in the evening; but married Henrietta in the afternoon. This is the recently discovered entry in the Fleet Register:

---

[51] Fiske, 'English Theatre Music in the Eighteenth Century', Oxford, 1973, p.167
[52] Burney, 'A General History of Music', ed. Frank Mercer, London, 1935, p.1014
[53] Earl of Shaftesbury's Memoirs of Handel, 1760, quoted in Deutsch *Handel a Documentary Biography* p. 847
[54] 'The correspondence of Gio. Giacomo Zamboni', RMA Research Chronicle 24, 1991, p.171

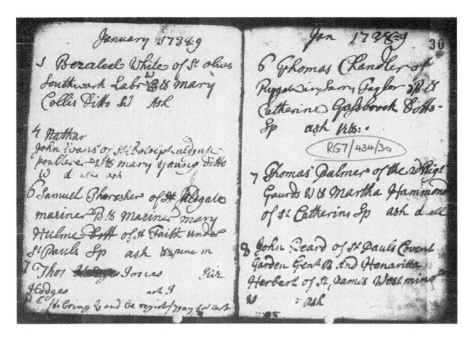

One of his arias in Handel's *Saul* had a most applicable text for a commoner who had just furtively married into the aristocracy:

"Birth and Fortune I despise! From Virtue let my Friendship rise.
No titles proud thy stem adorn; Yet born of God is nobly born.":

Chapter 3 will tell the story of the commoner who wed above his station in more detail.

There was no time for the luxury of a rest or a honeymoon. Beard was busy enough at this point in the season singing just for Handel. He appeared in his concerts thirteen times in four months (*Saul* Jan 16, 23, Feb 3, 7, March 27, April 19; *Alexander's Feast* Feb 17, 24, March 20, *Il Trionfo del Tempo* March 3; *Israel in Egypt* April 4, 11, 17). But this was not his main employment. Fleetwood was still requiring his services. In order to understand the pressures that Beard was under at this time, it has to be remembered that he appeared at Drury Lane on virtually every single day of the week that he had not been given dispensation to work for Handel.

As we can see, from the list of engagements below, he sometimes had to rush from one venue straight to the other. From a useful little book published in 1767, John Brownsmith's 'The Dramatic Time-Piece', it can be discovered that main-pieces [m/p] at Covent Garden and Drury Lane started at 6pm and usually lasted for approximately 2½ - 2¾ hours. Therefore the after-pieces [a/p] started between 8.30pm and 8.45pm. Handel's Oratorio performances started at 6.30pm. With each Act lasting a little under 1 hour Beard would not have exited the

Haymarket much before 8.20pm when he left *Saul* at the end of Act 2. Thus he had very little time in which to reach Drury Lane and prepare himself!

The King's Theatre Haymarket was quite a distance away from Drury Lane, and so this arrangement was far from ideal. But Beard was helped by the fact that 'Jonathan' dies before Act 3 of *Saul,* enabling him to make an early exit from the theatre. On those nights he would not have been able to take a customary obeisance at the end. Here is the period in question:

Jan / Feb 1739	Drury Lane		Haymarket
Mon 15 Jan	The Mock Doctor (a/p)		
Tues16	The King & Miller of Mansfield (a/p)	+	*Saul*
Wed 17	The King & Miller of Mansfield (a/p)		
Thurs 18	The Lottery (a/p)		
Fri 19	The King & Miller of Mansfield (a/p)		
Sat 20	The King & Miller of Mansfield (a/p)		
Mon 22	The Devil to pay (a/p)		
Tues 23	The Virgin unmasked (a/p)	+	*Saul*
Wed 24	The Provok'd Wife (m/p) + The Lottery (a/p)		
Thurs 25	The Intriguing Chambermaid (a/p)		
Fri 26	The Intriguing Chambermaid (a/p)		
Sat 27	Damon and Phillida (a/p)		
Mon 29	The Devil to pay (a/p)		
Tues 30	------ *[presumably expecting to sing for Handel, who moved to Saturday]*		
Wed 31	The Mock Doctor (a/p)		
Thurs 1 Feb.	The King & Miller of Mansfield (a/p) + singing between the acts		
Fri 2	The Intriguing Chambermaid (a/p) + singing between the acts		
Sat 3	Damon and Phillida (a/p)	+	*Saul*

From this it can be seen that, although he valued his work with Handel, it had to be sandwiched in between his other contractual obligations. It was not until April, when his involvement in *Israel in Egypt* would have made a quick dash for the exit less seemly,[55] that he managed to obtain complete clearance from the Drury Lane management on the dates that Handel required him. Thus his April diary, whilst appearing slightly more merciful on the face of it, still required a fit and healthy singer - especially when he followed the arduous role of 'Macheath' in *The Beggar's Opera* with a further role in the afterpiece:

April 1739	Drury Lane	Haymarket
Mon 2	--	
Tues 3	The Devil to pay (a/p) + interval songs: Beard's 'Benefit'	
Wed 4	--	*Israel in Egypt*
Thurs 5	The Beggar's Opera (m/p) + The King & Miller of Mansfield (a/p)	
Fri 6	--	

---

[55] The performers made their bows and curtain calls to the audience at the end of oratorio performances, according to Burney, who describes the blind Handel being "conducted towards the audience to make his accustomed obeisance". Burney, 'An Account of the Musical Performances ...', London, 1785, p.29-30. Also: see William Coxe *Anecdotes of G.F. Handel and J.C. Smith*, 1799, p. 25

Sat 7	The King & Miller of Mansfield (a/p) + singing between the acts
Mon 9	The King & Miller of Mansfield (a/p) + singing between the acts
Tues 10	The King & Miller of Mansfield (a/p) + singing between the acts
Wed 11	-- *Israel in Egypt*
Thurs 12	The Lottery (a/p) + singing between the acts

5. THE 1739 - 40 SEASON

Beard had his most complicated Season yet in 1739-1740. Handel invited him to sing in his Oratorios as usual - this time at the Lincoln's Inn Fields Theatre - and another invitation had arisen, to take part in a regular series of concerts at Hickford's Rooms. After a normal autumn devoted to his standard roles in the mainpieces *Comus* and *Macbeth*, and the afterpieces *The Lottery*, *Colombine Courtesan* and *The Fall of Phaeton*, he somehow contrived to get Charles Fleetwood, the Drury Lane manager, to give him leave of absence in January and February. But he knew he would be required thereafter. Beard was playing a dangerous game by asking for so much time off. But as he was coming to the end of his 3-year contract, he may have indicated his desire to leave the theatre at the end of the season. This was undoubtedly bound up with his marital affairs. Whether he thought that his marriage - once some unresolved financial matters were sorted out - would lead to a comfortable life of luxury and idleness living on his wife's dowry, or whether he foresaw that his wealthy father-in-law, 1st Earl Waldegrave, was terminally ill, he certainly made a decision not to return next year for the 1740-41 season.

Fleetwood prepared for a season without Beard by reallocating some of his smaller roles in the after-pieces as early as January 8 1740: Berry took over the role of 'Joe' in *The King & Miller of Mansfield*; James Raftor (Kitty Clive's brother) sang 'Quaver' in *The Virgin unmasked;* Stoppelaer played 'Valentine' in *The Intriguing Chambermaid;* and Oliver Cashell took over 'Colonel Bully' in the main-piece *The Provok'd Wife*.[56] This was a risky move on Beard's part, because roles were highly prized, and once performed by an actor were held to be their prerogative.[57] By yielding up these roles Beard was making it difficult for himself to retrieve them, if he ever needed to return to Drury Lane in the future. One role which he was determined to cling on to was 'Sir John Loverule' in *The Devil to Pay*. This was the first speaking and singing role that he had ever performed,[58] and was a fine character part with plenty of good arias. He had enjoyed a great success with it now for three seasons. And so, on March 17 1740, it was undertaken by Stoppelaer on the understanding that Beard could return to it later. This he did on March 27, and again - for his annual 'Benefit' - on April 9. *The Beggar's Opera* was another work that was particularly associated with Beard at this time. So Fleetwood simply refrained from slating it for performance until Beard was available to him again. After a performance on January 29 it wasn't in the programme any more until April 12, by which time the Handel and the Hickford's Rooms seasons were both over. Fleetwood also bent over backwards to meet Beard's needs by deliberately holding

---

[56] Information provided by *The London Stage*, Part 3 [1729 – 1747], ed. Arthur H. Scouten
[57] Kitty Clive outlined 'a receiv'd Maxim in the theatre' in her 1736 struggle to retain the role of 'Polly' in *The Beggar's Opera* at Drury Lane: "no Actor or Actress shall be depriv'd of a Part in which they have been well receiv'd. until they are render'd incapable of performing it either by Age or Sickness". BDA entry 'Clive' p.347
[58] 30th August 1737 "… the first night of Beard's playing – his success great." From a diary of Benjamin Griffin [British Library, Egerton 2320]

back some new pieces until he was more available. Thus the revival of Arne's 1733 opera *Rosamond*, in which Beard was going to be required, was delayed until March. The new satirical afterpiece *Lethe* which David Garrick had recently written was similarly withheld until April 15: unbelievably late in the season. *Lethe* would gain a regular slot in the Drury Lane repertoire when Garrick took over as Manager. Beard would sing it regularly from January 1749 onwards. But for this season there would only be the one performance. Into a slim plotline, that has various London society creatures coming to drink the waters of forgetfulness at a bar run by Aesop, Arne had fitted several quite elaborate songs for Beard as 'Mercury' and Mrs Clive as 'Mrs Riot'.[59]

One can see the attraction of these two Spring concert series to Beard. After several years of endeavouring to give good performances for Handel under increasingly trying circumstances, Beard knew that he could now make ends meet, at least temporarily, without the need for his £5 a week salary from Drury Lane. For these few months in the Spring of 1740 he was completely free-lance: - and was possibly the first English tenor to manage to survive in this way. The repertoire that he was asked to perform was all of a highly exciting and challenging nature. At Hickford's Rooms he performed the role of 'Garcia' in J. C. Smith's all-sung opera *Rosalinda*[60] (not to be confused with *Rosamond*) . Cecilia Young, now Mrs Thomas Arne, sang the title role. The lyrics were by John Lockman, who also wrote the text for Smith's oratorio *David's Lamentation over Saul and Jonathan,* which was the next work to be given in the series.[61]

Coincidentally Lockman was the librettist for Thomas Arne's opera *Rosamond,* which he had been continually recomposing since its disastrous performances in 1733. This was now mounted (in a revised version) as an after-piece on March 8. In it Arne had added a long Italianate aria 'Rise, Glory, rise', running to 36 pages of music, for Beard. It is scored for oboes, trumpets, drums and strings and was much admired by musicians like Charles Burney. Stylistically it foreshadowed the opera that he would write for Beard in the 1760s. Beard must have remembered Arne's success in writing opera seria when he commissioned *Artaxerxes* from him twenty-five years later.

Rosamond ran for 13 performances. Quite how Beard always managed to be available to every one in this season is almost impossible to work out! A study of the entries in *The London Stage* would often suggest that he was in two places at the same time. However, on those occasions when it appears from the newspaper advertisements that he should have been singing for both Handel and at the concerts at Hickford's Rooms, it appears that he put in a 'deputy' at the latter. Thus on 14 and 21 March 'Mr Salway'[62] was advertised as his late replacement. Beard obviously considered Handel's engagements as the more important ones.

For Handel he sang *Acis* in *Acis and Galatea* in a season which started late (due to illness) on Thursday 21 February. Perhaps it was Beard himself who was ill: he performed at Hickford's Rooms on 8 February, a time which is known to have been remarkably cold. Handel's own performances on the 4th and 7th were put off "in

---

[59] see: Fiske, 'English Theatre Music in the Eighteenth Century', Oxford, 1973, p.206. Several of the songs are contained in a manuscript at the Royal College of Music, RCM m/s 2232.

[60] January 4, 11, 18, 25, February 1, 8. February 15th was probably cancelled due to a performer's ill-health.

[61] February 22, 29, March 7, [14], [21], [27], April 2, 11

[62] Thomas Salway, c.1706-1743, a singer on contract to Rich at Covent Garden Theatre. He had sung occasionally for Handel in the 1730s before the composer started using Beard regularly.

consideration of the weather continuing so cold".[63] Neither venue was able to go ahead with performances on the 14th or 15th. After only one performance of *Acis and Galatea* Handel produced his newest oratorio. *L'Allegro ed Il Penseroso* was given on February 27, March 6, 10, 14, and April 23. Beard was well for all of these performances, and shared the solos with Elisabeth Duparc, Russell and Reinhold. *Esther* received one performance on March 26 (with Beard back in the role of *Ahasuerus)*[64], and *Acis* was repeated, with the *St. Cecilia Ode* on March 28, as a Benefit Concert for the Fund for the Support of Decayed Musicians (later the Royal Society of Musicians).

The two new oratorios from the previous year were revived for one performance each: *Saul* on March 21, and *Israel in Egypt* on April 1. Thus Beard sang for Handel in a total of ten performances this season.

His full diary was further complicated by returning to his contractual duties at Drury Lane in March, April and early May. This is what he undertook in these four months. It will be seen that he did not appear at Drury Lane at all between January 10 and March 8. On March 27 he was able to appear at Hickford's Rooms and at Drury Lane when the Hickford's Rooms concert was advertised as starting early and lasting from 6pm to 8pm: thus allowing Beard enough time to get back for his starring role in the afterpiece *The Devil to Pay* which would have begun at about 8.45pm. He had a similar rush across town on April 11, 18 and 25. On March 3 and 19 he made time in this mad diary to fit in appearances at two Benefit concerts for musician-friends:

Jan / May 1740	Drury Lane *Afterpieces start at c 8.45pm; Mainpieces at 6pm*	Hickford's Rooms *"to continue for 20 consecutive Fridays" at 6.30pm except for March 27th (6pm)*	Lincoln's Inn Theatre *Handel's oratorios started at 6pm.*[65]
Fri Jan 4		Rosalinda (1)	
Tues Jan 8	[*Edward Berry deputises*]		
Thurs Jan 10	Comus (m/p)		
Fri Jan 11	[*Berry deputises*]	Rosalinda (2)	
Fri Jan 18		Rosalinda (3)	
Fri Jan 25		Rosalinda (4)	
Tues Jan 29	Beggar's Opera (m/p)		
Fri Feb 1		Rosalinda (5)	
Mon Feb 4			[**Acis** *cancelled: too cold*]
Wed Feb 6	[*James Raftor deputises*]		
Thurs Feb 7			[**Acis** *cancelled: too cold*]
Fri Feb 8		Rosalinda (6)	
Thurs Feb 14			[**Acis** *cancelled: singers ill*]
Friday Feb 15		[*Rosalinda cancelled: singers ill*]	
Tues Feb 19	[*Oliver Cashell deputises*]		
Thurs Feb 21			**Acis + St Cecilia Ode**
Fri Feb 22		David's Lamentation over Saul and Jonathan (8)	
Wed Feb 27			**L'Allegro ed Il Penseroso**
Fri Feb 29		David's Lamentation... + songs (9)	
Mon March 3		*Benefit for Brown. 'Vocal by Beard'*	
Thurs Mar 6			**L'Allegro ed Il Penseroso**
Fri Mar 7		David's Lamentation... + songs (10)	
Sat Mar 8	Rosamond (a/p)		

---

[63] London Daily Post, 6th February 1740

[64] Winton Dean *Handel's Dramatic Oratorios and Masques* p. 212

[65] see Deutsch, op. cit. pp 490-1

Mon Mar 10	Rosamond (a/p)	+	**L'Allegro ed Il Penseroso**
Tues Mar 11	Rosamond (a/p)		
Fri Mar 14		[*Salway deputises* (11*)*]	**L'Allegro ed Il Penseroso**
Sat Mar 15	Rosamond (a/p)		
Mon Mar 17	[*Michael Stoppelaer deputises*]		
Tuesday Mar 18	Rosamond (a/p)		
Wed Mar 19		*Benefit for Valentine Snow. 'Vocal by Beard'*	
Fri Mar 21		[*Salway deputises* (12)]	**Saul**
Sat Mar 22	The Mock Doctor (a/p) + interval songs		
Mon Mar 24	Rosamond (a/p)		
Tues Mar 25	interval songs		
Wed Mar 26			**Esther**
Thurs Mar 27	The Devil to Pay (a/p) + David's Lamentation (13) *to begin at 6 & end at 8*		
Fri Mar 28		*Beard doesn't do Hickford's*	**Acis + St Cecilia Ode**
Sat Mar 29	interval songs		
Tues April 1			**Israel in Egypt**
Wed Apr 2		David's Lamentation... (14)	
Mon Apr 7	Rosamond (a/p)		
Tues Apr 8	Comus (m/p)		
Wed Apr 9	The Devil to Pay (a/p) + interval songs: Beard's 'Benefit'		
Thurs Apr 10	The Virgin unmasked (a/p) + interval songs		
Fri Apr 11	Rosamond (a/p) + David's Lamentation... (15)		
Sat Apr 12	Beggar's Opera (m/p)		
Mon Apr 14	The Provok'd Wife (m/p) + The Mock Doctor (a/p) + interval songs		
Tues Apr 15	Lethe (a/p) - first performance of Garrick's satire		
Wed Apr 16	interval songs		
Thurs Apr 17	interval songs		
Fri Apr 18	Columbine Courtesan (a/p) + Rosalinda (16) at 7pm		
Sat Apr 19	interval songs		
Monday Apr 21	interval songs		
Tuesday Apr 22	The Devil to Pay (a/p) + interval songs		
Wed Apr 23			**L'Allegro ed Il Penseroso**
Thurs Apr 24	interval songs		
Fri Apr 25	interval songs + David's Lamentation... (17)		
Sat Apr 26	interval songs		
Mon Apr 28	interval songs		
Thurs May 1	Comus (m/p)		
Fri May 2		*Beard doesn't do Hickford's Rooms*	
Thurs May 8			Handel **Wedding Anthem**
			[*at the Chapel Royal*]

I have included Beard's engagements up to May 8, as that was the last occasion on which he sang prior to taking a year and a half's rest from the theatre and concert hall. It was not that he was tired - although after that daunting schedule he deserved to be. Nor does the list include the numerous rehearsals that he must have undertaken for such a varied and new repertoire. As well as seeing out his Drury Lane contract he must have felt honoured and obliged to sing for Handel, to whom he owed so much, before he could entertain any notions of accompanying his wife on the various urgent visits abroad which she had planned.

As events turned out he was required to sing at the wedding of Princess Mary, George II's fourth daughter on the May 8. The nuptials had been announced in the press in early March,[66] and so Beard would have had some prior warning that he would be required to stay in London at least until they had taken place. The anthem for which Handel required him was a pasticcio of movements from the two previous wedding anthems. He may have sung once more the aria 'Strength and

---

[66] Daily Advertiser, Friday 7th March 1740

Honour' against which his name ('Bird') had been pencilled in the manuscript of the 1734 Wedding Anthem "This is the day which the Lord has made".[67] He would also have been required for the virtuoso concluding section taken from the 1736 Wedding Anthem "Sing unto God" – itself a reworking of a castrato aria in *Parnasso in Festa* - which he had sung on April 27 of that year, and with which Handel now concluded the pasticcio. There was a newspaper report on Tuesday 6 May of a rehearsal taking place at Bernard Gates' house on the previous day. From Beard's diary it can be noted that it was an otherwise free day: "Yesterday, at Mr Gates's, was a practice of a fine new Anthem compos'd by Mr. Handel, for her Royal Highness the Princess Mary's Marriage; the vocal parts by Mess. Abbott, Chelsum, Beard, Church of Dublin, Gates, Lloyd, and the Boys of the Chapel Royal..."[68]

On May 10 Thomas Harris wrote to his brother about the music ("there was nothing new in the anthem...") and gave a most intriguing addendum: "I hear that Beard is gone off together with his lady, who I believe had contracted debts before her marriage."[69]

Beard had indeed gone abroad at the earliest possible moment. Strictly speaking he was obliged to play at Drury Lane until the end of the season, which was not until May 30. But the leeway that he had been given in January and February may have been shown to him once again by a kindly disposed Charles Fleetwood. It was now the benefit season, and actors were free to choose their own repertoire and performers. It was only at this time, and on these limited occasions, that actors could try their talents in roles that were normally the well-guarded province of others. Stoppelaer and Raftor continued to play the roles that they had taken over from Beard, and others such as Ridout and Ray (who may have been the official understudies) were tried out in his other parts. Only the role of *Macheath* really mattered, and this was certainly not going to be given by the management to an untried actor. When *The Beggar's Opera* was performed on May 17 the original interpreter Thomas Walker,[70] who had created the role in 1728 (and is depicted in Hogarth's famous painting), was invited back to replace the absent Beard. This was casting from strength indeed!

---

[67] Burrows *Handel and the English Chapel Royal* p. 358
[68] Daily Advertiser, Tuesday 6th May 1740
[69] Burrows & Dunhill *Music and Theatre in Handel's World*, p. 97
[70] Thomas Walker 1698-1744 created the role of *Macheath* at Lincoln's Inn Fields Theatre, 29 Jan. 1728

CHAPTER 3
FIRST MARRIAGE

Lady Henrietta Herbert must have had plenty of time to question why she had been in such a rush to marry Beard. As was shown in the last chapter he was engaged on a very tight contract at Drury Lane. The earliest that he could expect to be released was at the contract's end. This would be in late May 1740, more than a year after their wedding. She had many pressing matters to attend to, concerning her young daughter Barbara, her complicated finances, and her family relationships. To compound her distress, the liaison with a mere singer - one of the "singers of *Roast Beef* from between the acts at the theatres" in Horace Walpole's evocative words[1] - had shocked the whole town and led to her family shunning her.

It must all have seemed so different at the beginning of their courtship. She was still only twenty-one when she is likely to have first seen Beard at the theatre, or in the Red Lion Square area of Holborn. She was a widow with a three-year-old daughter. She was still impressionable, and the liaison with an actor may have seemed like a daring adventure. For his part, Beard may have thought that his luck was in. To put it in perspective, he may have felt like Tom Rakewell in the series of Hogarth paintings of 1734, *The Rake's Progress,* (issued as etchings a year later) which follows a young man in his quest for riches in the heart of London. Here was John Beard, aged twenty-three, suddenly in the company of the daughter of an Earl, and the widow of a Marquis' son. He could be forgiven for thinking that there might be some fortune in it for him. Perhaps he need never sing again for his supper. In Hogarth's second picture of the series[2] the elegant Tom Rakewell is surrounded by a circle of London types that would have been very well-known to Beard: a dancing instructor, a fencing master, a huntsman with hunting horn, several middle-class tradesmen, tailors and wigmakers. Seated at a harpsichord is someone Beard now knew very well: Handel. He is only seen from behind, but the wig and the pose are very distinctive. On the music stand is a score to be sung by Senesino, Carestini, Cuzzoni, Strada, Negri and Bertolli. Looking at the etching of this painting, which was now easily available on the streets of London, Beard must have felt that he was witnessing his own dream coming true.

Weddings between aristocrats and commoners were not unknown. Whilst it had always been accepted that the male aristocracy made liaisons, both official and unofficial, with popular actresses, it was certainly not the custom for the roles to be reversed. So far, only noblemen had got away with marrying actresses - not the other way round. The best recorded of these was Anastasia Robinson's marriage to the Earl of Peterborough in 1722. She had sung in the first performances of six of Handel's operas before leaving the stage. Another famous singer in her day was Lavinia Fenton, who was the first 'Polly' in *The Beggar's Opera*. The besotted Charles Paulet, Duke of Bolton, went to virtually every performance, and was painted by Hogarth leering at her from the stage box in his famous painting of the Newgate Prison scene. At the end of the first run of the opera, in 1728, she left the cast to become Paulet's mistress. On the death of his wife in 1751 she eventually achieved her goal and became his Duchess.

---

[1] Letter of Horace Walpole, Feb. 24th 1743, quoted in Deutsch *Handel a Documentary Biography* p. 560
[2] 'Engravings by Hogarth', ed. Sean Shesgreen, New York, 1973, 'A Rake's Progress' Plate II, , p. 29

Lady Henrietta's story has to be told now, as it will help to explain how this young widow came to be in London in 1738, without her child, and in a position to begin a liaison with an actor. In order to understand the implications of her subsequent marriage, and the consequences it had for Beard, it will be necessary therefore to describe, in some detail, the life of Henrietta before this date. In so doing, we enter the sometimes shadowy world of the Roman Catholic aristocracy. These were the noble families who had never abandoned the old religion, and continued to support the Jacobite cause. For this reason it can often be difficult to ascertain precise dates, especially of births and marriages which were carried out privately and secretly. We can immediately see an example of this in the confusion surrounding the date of Henrietta's birth.

HENRIETTA WALDEGRAVE

Henrietta Waldegrave – or Harriet as she was often known - was born on the 2nd January 1717, the only daughter of James (later Earl) Waldegrave and his wife Mary Webb. She was probably born in Flanders, like her two brothers, where her Catholic parents were living 'in prudent exile'. The date of Henrietta's birth can be clearly found in several sources, notably in the pedigree kept by The College of Arms. However, other writers have confused the issue and stated that she was born in 1719, and caused the death of her mother[3]. They further claim that this was the cause of her father's later indifference and hostility towards her. This is all untrue: her mother certainly did die in childbirth, but Henrietta was not the child.

On Saturday January 17 1719, The Original Weekly Journal reported that *"The same evening* [January 15]*, the Lord Waldegrave's Lady miscarried, at his Lordship's Lodgings in Bow-Street, Covent-Garden."* A week later, the same newspaper announced *"On Wednesday Night dy'd the Lord Waldegrave's Lady, a Roman Catholick. She was Daughter of Sir John Webb, and Sister to the Dowager Countess of Derwentwater."* [4]

It was a miscarriage that caused her mother's death. The confusion seems to have arisen because both events took place in January; but they were two years apart. Surprisingly, for a Catholic, Mary Waldegrave was buried in Westminster Abbey. The Abbey records show that she 'died in childbirth aged 23' and was buried in the central aisle of the nave. The decision to allow such a burial has always been the prerogative of the Dean of Westminster. At the time, this was Francis Atterbury, who was known to be a Jacobite sympathiser.[5] It also appears that Waldegrave was in London, because he was one of the patriotic Catholic peers who were trying to negotiate a 'modus vivendi' with the Hanoverian regime. Presumably Atterbury was also involved in these negotiations, and permitted the burial as a gesture of goodwill.

---

[3] The correct date is also given in Burke's Peerage. The source of this inaccuracy is the 'Waldegrave Family History' compiled by the then Countess c.1975, and kept in the Waldegrave private papers at Chewton House. It has been quoted many times since, and also appears in the new edition of the DNB. This has now been corrected for the on-line version.

[4] Mary Webb's elder sister, Anna-Maria, had married the 3rd Earl of Derwentwater, James Radclyffe. He was involved in the rebellion of 1715, which intended to install James 2nd's son on the throne, and was beheaded on Tower Hill on 24th February 1716, when all his honours were forfeit.

[5] In 1722 Francis Atterbury, Dean of Westminster & Bishop of Rochester, was committed to the Tower for complicity in an attempt to restore the Stuarts. He was deprived of all his offices, and banished the kingdom. He left England and settled in Paris, where he died in 1732. (see DNB)

James, 1ˢᵗ Earl Waldegrave

Following the death of her mother, Henrietta and her two brothers went to live with their paternal grandmother at the family seat in Navestock, Essex. Her grandmother, who had been a widow for many years, was born Lady Henrietta Fitzjames, an illegitimate daughter of James 2nd by his mistress Arabella Churchill. The Waldegrave family, therefore, were actually very closely related to the deposed monarch. Henrietta's father, for example, was a first cousin of Bonnie Prince Charlie, the Young Pretender, albeit by an illegitimate line.

However, after his wife's death, three years later in February 1722, Waldegrave scandalised his family by renouncing his Catholicism and declaring himself a Protestant: an act that was seen as a betrayal by other Catholic peers. He swore the oath of allegiance to the Hanoverian crown, and was soon rewarded with a post in the household of King George I. Diplomatic appointments in the government of Robert Walpole then followed: as Ambassador in Vienna and Paris. His close Jacobite connections seem not to have compromised his position, and must have been considered of less importance than his potential usefulness and contacts in the Catholic courts of Europe. Consequently he spent most of his life after 1725 abroad, and can have seen virtually nothing of his children. He was created an Earl in 1729, and ensured that his sons followed his example and abandoned Catholicism by sending them both to Eton for an Anglican education.

Lady Waldegrave made no objection to her grandsons being brought up as Protestants, but she did insist that her granddaughter Henrietta should continue to be brought up in the old Faith. Whilst in her care Henrietta had begun to learn the things that a young lady should be accomplished in, playing card games and taking lessons on the spinet.[6] There were probably dancing lessons and French lessons too. When Lady Waldegrave died intestate in April 1730, she left instructions that the 13-year old Henrietta was to be placed in the care of her maternal (and staunch Catholic) grandparents, Sir John & Lady Webb.

Waldegrave's steward at Navestock, Underhill, immediately wrote to him in Vienna: "...as to Lady Harriet, my Lady having left the directions I mentioned in

---

[6] 'Waldegrave Family History' Part 2, compiled by M.H.W. 1975, p. 55

my last, those that had the management of it thought fit to send her with al Speed, accordingly she began her journay yesterday morning attended by her maid & one Hill a Steward of Mr Talbotts who has lived many years in his, and Sir John Webb's Familly. Dr Jernegan orderd me to give the £40 my Lady left for Lady Harriot to the said Mr Hill which I accordingly did. I allsoe paid Lady Harriott's maid a bill of £4. 7s. 4d. which she laid out for her Lady but there was no provision at all made for mourning for her, her friends thinking it better to defer it till she arrives at Paris."[7]

Sir John & Lady Webb of Great Canford, Dorset must therefore have been in Paris at this moment: they were firmly committed to the Jacobite cause, and spent much time abroad in France. Sir John Webb wrote from there to Waldegrave in Vienna on April 23rd 1730:

"My Lord. I truly condole with yr. Lor[p] the loss you have had in Lady Waldegrave's death, wherein you have many that share with you in their grief, but none more than my wife, self and Family who have had great and continuall obligations to her Ladyship. My Lady having left written directions for Lady Henriette to be immediately sent over to my wife after her death, it was accordingly performd having been only a day or two at her Aunt Talbott She arrived last night, and is now with us in perfect health, having had a very favourable journey. My wife, who is very much yr. Lor[p]'s servant, will take all possible care of her, and wee both hope yr Lor[p] will not be against her continuing in this Country it being soe much Lady Waldegrave's desire, and her dying request. Lady Henriette left Lord Chewton and her brother John very well, and at Mrs Dunch's . . . . My wife and I and the rest of our little family join in their Compliments to yr Lor[p] and are very fond of Lady Henriette who is a fine child."[8]

Waldegrave received dispensation to travel back to England to sort out his mother's affairs, but only got as far as Paris. Lady Waldegrave wrote in 1975: "One would have had warmer feelings about Lord Waldegrave if, at this juncture, when he was given the opportunity by the Secretary of State, he had hastened home to cheer up his sad little boys and relieve the worries of his faithful servants. But he didn't; he was so intent on getting securely into his new position [as Ambassador in Paris] that, although he made his mother's death the excuse for departing at speed from Vienna, he came no nearer home than Paris".[9] It is not known how long the Webbs stayed in Paris after Henrietta joined them, but it is possible that she could have met her father there. If so, then this was probably the last time she ever saw him...

A few years later the Webbs started to look for a suitable husband for Henrietta. Their choice fell on Lord Edward Herbert, the younger son of the 2nd Marquis of Powis. Now the Herbert family had been even more closely identified with James 2nd and his abdication: they had helped to smuggle the King's 6-month old son (James Edward Stuart, later known as the Old Pretender) out of the country, and then had joined the deposed monarch at his Court-in-exile in France. James had rewarded the Marquis with the title of Duke of Powis, but this title was never recognised by the Hanoverian regime. For his Jacobite activities, the Marquis had been outlawed and attainted in Britain, and all his estates forfeited to the Crown. He

---

[7] 'Waldegrave Family History' Part 2, compiled by M.H.W. 1975, p. 59
[8] 'Waldegrave Family History' Part 2, compiled by M.H.W. 1975, p. 89

[9] 'Waldegrave Family History' Part 2, compiled by M.H.W. 1975, p. 60

had also served several terms of imprisonment in the Tower of London. However, although his Estates had been restored in 1722, the Powis line was not secure as neither of his sons had yet married and produced an heir.

Lady Webb wrote twice to Waldegrave before receiving a reply (the spelling is as it appears in the letter):

"My Ld. The ocasion of my Giving you this trobel is at the request of my Ld Edward Harbett, who is Desirous of an Alians with Lady Hearriot. the person that Mensoned it to Me telles us that my Lord his Father will Give him twenty thousand pound & five hundered pound a year in fines. the affars of that family are Sayed to be upon a Mutch better foting than they have bin, the Lead Miyens having produsett tene or twelve thouand pound a year." [10]

She then goes on to say that Lord Edward's elder brother doesn't look like marrying, so that very probably Lord Edward will inherit all the Powis estates. Ominously she concludes: *"Lord Edward has had very ill health but is recovered"*. Waldegrave however was not keen on the proposed marriage, perhaps feeling that it might compromise his Anglican status if his daughter married a Catholic, and replied from Paris:

"Madam, I received the honour of both your Ladyship's letters relating to the proposals made to you by Lord Edward Herbert. As my daughter was left by my Mother to your Ladyship's and Sir John's care I am persuaded you will continue your goodness to her and that she will be ruled by you in the present case as well as in all others. I am really no judge in such matters. Your Ladyship knows more of my daughter than I do and can better discern than anybody what she may think best for herself. For my part I own I think there is a very great disproportion of age. Lord Edward is full five and forty, his present income is moderate, his health I know nothing of. There are many chances in the case. His brother may not marry, but he (if he is unhealthy) may die before his brother who is healthy, and of a long-living family. These are my objections but are only so to myself. If your Ladyship and Sir John and my daughter are of a different opinion I am contented ..." [11]

Waldegrave was mistaken. Lord Edward was not 'full five and forty': this was his unmarried elder brother William, Lord Montgomery.[12] Lord Edward was born c.1704, and was thus about 30 years old – a perfectly suitable age to be marrying. Many later writers have taken Waldegrave's statement at face value, and commented on the great disparity between the ages of the groom and bride. This was simply not true.

Negotiations slowly proceeded over the terms of the Marriage Settlement, and Waldegrave became increasingly bored. He wrote to his Steward: *"I am not fond enough of the match to do any extraordinary things for it, and it was meerly out of compliance to Sir John and Lady Webb that I did not declare against it. However, this keep to yourself. tell Mr Strickland and Mr Pigott [his lawyers] to get the matter settled with as little trouble to me as they can."* [13]

By midsummer 1734 the negotiations were complete, and on July 7, the 17-year old Lady Henrietta Waldegrave married Lord Edward Herbert at Odstock

---

[10] 'Waldegrave Family History' Part 2, compiled by M.H.W. 1975, p. 90

[11] 'Waldegrave Family History' Part 2, compiled by M.H.W. 1975, p. 91

[12] William, Lord Montgomery was born c.1689 – the 2nd child of the Marquis of Powis. His parents married in May 1685 (pre-nuptial settlement in Powis papers – NLW). The National Trust Guide to Powis Castle erroneously states that he was born in 1698.

[13] 'Waldegrave Family History' Part 2, compiled by M.H.W. 1975, p. 92

House, Wiltshire in a private ceremony, probably performed by Jesuit priests. Odstock was one of the three English estates owned by the Webbs, and one of the last remaining Catholic enclaves in the County: it is known that the family secretly 'paid the Jesuits for assisting at Odstock' in 1736.[14]

A pre-nuptial Agreement had been signed the previous month, on June 15, which detailed the financial arrangements that were to be made for the newly-wed couple.[15] The groom's father, the 2nd Marquis of Powis, pledged £20,000, and Earl Waldegrave £6000 [16] - although the latter claimed he could only afford to pay half of this down, paying interest on the other half until his eldest son's marriage, or his own death whichever should happen first. These figures would not have come as a surprise to the young couple, as they had been exactly specified many years before in their parents' own Marriage Settlements. Indeed, Lord Edward had already borrowed money against his expected settlement. Henrietta was particularly fortunate, as the £6000 pledged by her father was meant to be split equally amongst all his daughters. As the only daughter, she received it all.

However, this was not a cash gift. The money was to be spent on purchasing "freehold manors, lands, tenements and hereditaments" from which the couple would derive an income by way of the rents paid by the tenants.

What is obvious in retrospect is that the Marquis of Powis could hardly afford to be so generous - although his estates had been restored to him in 1722, his financial affairs were still in a confused mess. Years earlier he had been persuaded by his eldest daughter, Lady Mary Herbert, to invest heavily in South Sea stock, and when the 'bubble' burst in the 'Mississippi year' of 1720, he lost a fortune.[17] In 1729, he was said to be 'in low circumstances, all his real estate greatly encumbered, and sold or disposed of all his personal estate'.[18] Nevertheless, the Marquis had no option other than to honour his own Marriage Settlement. As he did not have £20,000 at his disposal, he simply transferred the title, or a part-share of the title, from a number of estates that he already owned, to the couple.[19]

Further clauses in the 1734 Agreement stipulated that after her husband's death, Henrietta would receive a jointure of £600 per annum; and any dependant children £100.[20] This settlement was not only very generous, it was positively reckless, and should be compared with the £175 a year 'pin-money' that she was to receive while her husband was alive. However, the Powis family must have felt that the young couple could look forward to many years of happy marriage before such a clause might be invoked. They certainly did not foresee that Edward would die four months later. After a short illness, in November of that same year, he died in Bath – leaving his wife already pregnant.

---

[14] 'A History of Wiltshire', vol. 3, ed. Pugh & Crittall, *Institute of Historical Research*, OUP, 1956, p. 88

[15] Powis Castle papers: D3/8/11-12 (NLW)

[16] In order to find this amount, Waldegrave had to settle his mother's affairs. She had died intestate in 1730, and her estate had been legally blocked to prevent claims from a spurious second husband, Lord Galmoye. In 1734 Waldegrave applied for a Grant of Administration, as £1000 of Henrietta's jointure came from a Trust set up by his mother which was payable when she married.

[17] Many records of the ensuing litigation between members of the Powis family and Lady Mary Herbert can be found in NLW. The Hardwicke Papers (British Library Add. 36171 ff. 1-47) contains the Appeal to High Court of Chancery 1766, which summarises all earlier litigation.

[18] Court of Chancery: Town Depositions (C24/1455-18, National Archives)

[19] A full list of these properties appears in the Marriage Settlement; and also in Henrietta's Memo. of 15/11/1745: Powis Castle Papers No. 9653 (NLW)

[20] At the time of writing all these figures should be multiplied by a factor of approximately 90 to give an equivalent modern value.

The news of Lord Edward's death was one of the few occasions when Waldegrave did momentarily show some spontaneous feeling towards his daughter. He wrote to his superiors in London: *"Ld Edward Herbert who married my Daughter is dead, and tho' the marriage was made in a great measure without my Consent and entirely without my approbation the Condition my Daughter is left in cannot but move a father's Compassion."* [21]

On June 24 1735 Henrietta gave birth to a daughter, Barbara. Although she was a widow, Henrietta, at the age of 18, was still a minor; and so her grandfather, Sir John Webb, was appointed guardian both to her and her new-born daughter. The Marquis of Powis thus found himself not only without the hoped-for heir to the title, but legally committed to pay £700 per annum without any immediate benefit either to his family or estate. Nor had any of the money been properly invested, as required by the Marriage Settlement. No wonder he demurred and defaulted on the payments. This was the origin of the dispute which came to dominate the rest of Henrietta's life: it led to continuing litigation with the Powis family, which even continued after her death in 1753.

The Marquis employed all the delaying tactics he could think of, and wrote to his lawyers querying whether he was legally bound to pay any money at all to Henrietta, as she was still a minor. Accordingly, in 1736, Henrietta was obliged to submit the first Bill of Complaint in the Court of Chancery [22] against the Marquis for payment of the jointures due to her and her daughter. As a minor, the application was jointly in her name, and her "best friend", Lord Petre. [23]

The two plaintiffs claimed, in the Bill, that *"the said Marquess of Powis and Lord Montgomery*[24] *will neither pay the said £20000 nor permit the same to be raised by a sale or mortgage . . . nor will they so much as pay your oratrices the interest of the said £20000"*.

The Bill of Complaint also states that *"... the said Marquess of Powis and Lord Montgomery pretending that they cannot with safety pay the interest thereof to your oratrices for that they being infants are therefore incapable of giving a proper discharge for the same..."*

There were then several delays for replies, answers and submissions by the defendants and other interested parties. In one submission, Henrietta's claim is still called 'pin money', which shows how the Powis family were seeking to trivialise her claim. Lord Arundell also complained that any payment would compromise his wife's existing jointure. [25] It is difficult for us nowadays to appreciate the 18th century attitude towards the concept of 'jointure'. The aristocratic society of the day obviously thought it perfectly acceptable for a husband - even a wealthy one - to negotiate and expect an annual payment from his wife's family. At this time however, Henrietta's situation was different - she was now a widow, and did not have a husband to support her.

---

[21] 'Waldegrave Family History' Part 2, compiled by M.H.W. 1975, p. 94

[22] Court of Chancery - Herbert Lady v Powis Marquess (Winter Division) C11/524/33 (National Archives). Copy also in Powis Estate papers (NLW).

[23] Cousin of Henrietta's, by marriage, on the Webb side. In 1732, the 8th Lord Petre married Anna Maria Barbara Radclyffe – daughter of the disgraced James Radclyffe, 3rd Earl of Derwentwater and Anna Maria Webb.

[24] Title of William, the eldest son.

[25] Lord Arundell of Wardour was married to Edward's sister, Anne, and had received a jointure of £8000 from the Marquis of Powis some years previously.

The case was eventually heard by the Lord Chancellor on 22 July 1736, and he made a series of judgments[26] which completely vindicated Henrietta and stated that, as she had *"maintained herself from the death of her sayd husband"* it was proper to pay her the full jointure of £600; and that such payment should be made through her guardian (and grandfather), Sir John Webb, until she was 21. Barbara, who *"from her birth had been maintained by her mother"*, had her entitlement increased to £150 per annum.

From the fragmentary records that still exist, it is clear that the Marquis did make a series of payments to Henrietta following this judgment. The payments came at sporadic intervals, and were for varying amounts - presumably the Marquis paid what he could, when he could.[27] So the arrears were mounting. In 1738 though, he made seven payments which totalled £800. This cleared £200 of the arrears, but meant that £300 was still outstanding.[28]

It appears that Henrietta did not go back abroad to her maternal grandparents after the birth of Barbara in 1735. Or if she did, she returned to England by 1738, leaving Barbara in their care. Where she would have resided cannot now be determined. While she was a respectable widow, she would surely have been welcome at any of her extended family's addresses. These included the Webb's three country estates, her father's estate at Navestock, or Powis Castle. However, eventually she must have come to London.

Her younger brother was residing in London, as Lord Egmont's and Lady Mary Wortley Montague's correspondence proves, and may have been at her father's London house in Albemarle Street. Lord Edward Herbert may have had his own London address but, at this time, the Powis family still had the use of Powis House, in Great Ormond Street. This imposing and palatial house had been built in 1700 for the 2nd Marquis, who was resident there with his eldest son, William, between 1731 and 1739. The Webb family also had a London address in Great Marlborough Street. However, it seems unlikely that she would have been welcome at any of these addresses when word of the liaison with Beard got around. So the important question remains: where would she then have lived?

There was also a relative, Edward Webb, who practised law at Gray's Inn and was Henrietta's lawyer. At this time he lived in Red Lion Square.[29] She may well have preferred to lodge with this relative, who would also be able to pursue her brother-in-law for the jointure which was not being paid by the 2nd Marquis of Powis.

If she was a resident of Red Lion Square it would partially explain why she chose to return to the same area after her wedding to Beard. The earliest address that can be ascribed definitely to the singer is given in handbills for his Benefit night on April 3 1739. This took place three months after his wedding, and states that tickets for the Benefit were available "at Beard's house, New North Street, Red Lion Square".[30]

---

[26] The judgments start in C33/367 p. 206, Records of Court of Chancery (Nat. Arch.)

[27] In 1735, he paid a total of £450; the next year, £350 and in 1737, £500.

[28] Powis Castle papers (4) Doc. 9651 (NLW)

[29] Hugh Phillips, 'Mid-Georgian London', London, 1964, p.292-3

[30] The London Stage Part 3, p.767

MARRIAGE TO JOHN BEARD: January 8 1739

Although Beard and Henrietta had found a way to socialise freely, either in the Red Lion area of London, or at the theatre, or at complaisant friends' houses, the idea of a marriage between an actor and a titled Lady scandalised contemporary Society. Henrietta's family did all they could to stop it. The Earl of Egmont wrote:

"Her brother [John, her younger brother]*, an Ensign in the Guards, told her that her lover had the pox, and that she would be disappointed of the only thing she married him for, which was her lust; for that he would continue to lie every night with the player that brought them together, and give her no solace. But there is no prudence below the girdle."[31]*

Her brother's vitriolic outburst seems to confirm that it was an actress and colleague of Beard's who introduced them to each other, and that this actress was even Beard's mistress. The gossipy Lady Mary Wortley Montagu wrote to a friend in November 1738:

"Lady Harriet Herbert furnished the tea-tables here with fresh tattle for the last fortnight. I was one of the first informed of her adventure by Lady Gage, who was told that morning by a priest, that she had desired him to marry her the next day to Beard, who sings in the farces at Drury-lane. He refused her that good office, and immediately told Lady Gage, who (having been unfortunate in her friends) was frighted at this affair and asked my advice. I told her honestly, that since the lady was capable of such amours, I did not doubt if this was broke off she would bestow her person and fortune on some hackney-coachman or chairman; and that I really saw no method of saving her from ruin, and her family from dishonour, but by poisoning her; and offered to be at the expence of the arsenic, and even to administer it with my own hands, if she would invite her to drink tea with her that evening. But on her not approving that method, she sent to Lady Montacute, Mrs Dunch, and all the relations within the reach of messengers. They carried Lady Harriet to Twickenham; though I told them it was a bad air for girls. She is since returned to London, and some people believe her married; others that he is too much intimidated by Mr Waldegrave's threats to dare to go through the ceremony; but the secret is now publick, and in what manner it will conclude I know not."

It was perhaps just as well that the writer was not called upon to follow through her colourful and illegal solution to the problem! The 'priest' referred to in the letter must have been a Catholic priest, and shows that Beard was even prepared at this time to abandon his Anglican upbringing in order to marry Henrietta. However, when this plan came to nothing, the couple had to try a different approach. Eventually they did what so many other Londoners did: they went to the Fleet Prison. By one of those idiosyncratic quirks of English law, clergymen who were imprisoned for debt in the Fleet Prison were granted 'The Liberties of the Fleet'. This allowed them to perform clandestine marriages without the need for banns or licence. This dispensation was very popular at the time, and a convenient way to circumvent the rules and regulations of the established Church. Another musician who married in this inexpensive and secretive way was the organist and composer John Stanley, who married Sarah Arlond in 1738. Indeed, it may have been Stanley who helped Beard out of his quandary by suggesting this course of action.

---

[31] Diary of the Earl of Egmont: Vol.3, p.4 (Saturday 13th January 1739)

So, on January 8 1739 Beard had a rehearsal in the morning for his role in Handel's new oratorio *Saul*, and in the evening he played 'The Spaniard' in the pantomime *Colombine Courtesan*. But in the afternoon, he and Henrietta were married. After much new research it has been discovered that they were married by the Rev. Edward Ashwell, at that time a resident of the Fleet Prison, in the Fountain Tavern, Fleet Street. The marriage is recorded in the notebooks of John Burnford, clerk and register keeper.[32] As there had been no conclusive proof of this wedding in any of the church records, some had begun to wonder if it had taken place on the date given in newspaper reports - or even if it had taken place at all.[33] It is curious that the place and circumstances of the marriage have hitherto been a secret. The society of the day obviously came to accept that the marriage had taken place; one wonders if these facts were common knowledge at the time?

However, there is a sting in the tail. Edward Ashwell was no priest - he was an impostor: a fact that was presumably never known by either Beard and Henrietta, or any of their relations! The British Library contains a letter from 1725, giving an account of Ashwell's activities before he was imprisoned: "There was lately at Southam, in Warwickshire, one Edward Ashwell, who in my absence got possession of our school and preach'd in several churches in this neighbourhood. I take the liberty to inform you, since I hear he is at Kettering, that he is a most notorious rogue and impostor. I have now certificates on my hand of his having two wives alive at this present time, and he was very near marrying the third in this town, but the fear of a prosecution upon the discovery of the flaming and scandalous immoralities of his life forc'd him away from us in a short time. Afterwards, in a village not far from us, he attempted to ravish a woman, but was prevented by a soldier then in the house. I can assure you that he is in no orders, though the audacious villain preaches when he can get a pulpit... It would be a very kind and Christian office to give some information among the clergy, that they may not be impos'd upon by him..."[34]

Not all of Henrietta's relations were alienated by the marriage, and a month later in February 1739, her grandmother, Lady Barbara Webb, who had brought her up from the age of thirteen, added a codicil to her Will leaving her £100.[35]

Unaware of the doubtful legality of their marriage, Beard and Henrietta moved into a house in New North Street, just off Red Lion Square. This area of London was popular with Catholics because of its proximity to the Sardinian Chapel in Lincoln's Inn Fields, where they were able to worship. Indeed it is possible that Henrietta had resided in New North Street before her first marriage. The Rate Books list a John Webb in the road in 1730, and this may well have been her uncle. As has already been stated, a distant relative, Edward Webb, who acted as her lawyer was a resident of Red Lion Square. Beard and Henrietta moved several times in the ensuing years, but always remained close to the Square, and in 1750 moved back to No. 12 New North Street. It was a fashionable area without being showy. There was a good mix of inhabitants, from minor aristocracy to wealthy merchants. Placed near

---

[32] RG7/434/30 (Nat Arch). Over 250,000 Fleet marriages were performed, and the records have only recently been transcibed. The can now be searched online at www.bmdregisters.co.uk
[33] "After these Nuptials, concerning which, curiously enough, no mention is found in Peerages of authority, Beard retired a while from the stage". DNB. This entry can now be updated: the Wedding did take place, and Beard continued working until 8th May 1740. It was only then that he 'retired a while'.
[34] Letter from W Hodgson, 21st June 1725 in Lansdowne Manuscripts (841.61 - British Library); also quoted in 'The History of the Fleet Marriages' (J.S. Burn) 1833
[35] PROB11/703/190 (Nat Arch)

the Inns of Court it was popular with the legal profession. Famous inhabitants at this time ranged from the painter Thomas Hudson (who painted Beard's portrait) to Admiral Boscawen and John Harrison, the inventor of the marine chronometer. The houses, which had been built soon after 1684, were remarkable for their fine cornices and the keystones over their windows. A picture by Sutton Nicholls of the square and surrounding streets in 1731 made it appear very handsome, and close to open country.

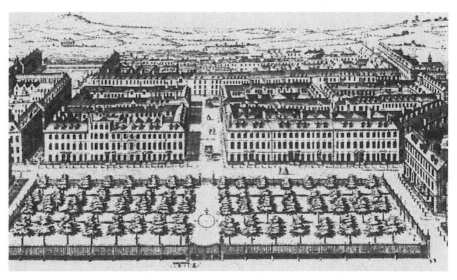

There is a description of a typical interior in an advertisement for a property to let "in Red Lion Square, the corner of Leigh Street, subject to a ground rent of £80 10s 0d per annum". The interior is described as "completely fitted up with mortice locks, carved ornaments over doors and chimneys, new marble chimney-pieces, clean deal floors and stairs with carved brackets."[36] The square is now almost unrecognisable after ugly post-war redevelopment and major improvements to Holborn's one-way traffic scheme, which have destroyed the western end of it. But it still contains one original house from the originally handsome square constructed by "Dr Barebone, the great builder" in 1684. New North Street was completely destroyed by bombs during World War 2. However it is possible to identify the exact house that the couple moved into from a pre-World War 2 photograph in Camden Local Studies Library.[37]

After the marriage, reality soon set in: both Beard and Henrietta had been living beyond their means, and were in debt. The Earl of Egmont commented in his Diary that *"This lady had £600 a year jointure, £200 of which is encumbered by former debts, and £200 she has lately sold to pay his debts. Today it is said her goods have been sold".[38]* The accuracy of this statement is suspect, as later evidence makes no reference to a sale of her jointure at this date; it is also the only mention of the fact that Beard himself had debts. What is certain is that Henrietta did sell part of her jointure in 1741.

[36] Hugh Phillips, 'Mid-Georgian London', London, 1964, p.206
[37] Photo in Camden Local Studies Library, Ref: 89.3 Acc. No. 031566
[38] Diary of the Earl of Egmont: Vol.3, p.4 (Saturday 13th January 1739)

Henrietta

Before that, we have the curious episode of Beard's departure from the stage in May 1740. One explanation for this is that he decided to live the life of a 'gentleman' on his wife's jointure. He may also have hoped to ingratiate himself with Henrietta's father by this action. If so, he did not quite appreciate the reality of the situation. The Marquis of Powis continued to pay sums that fell short of the expected amount.[39] As Beard now had legal control over his wife's financial affairs, these payments were actually made directly to him, and not her. Nevertheless, it seems that the couple could not live within their income, and the debts continued to mount. The Marquis of Powis was also sufficiently embarrassed financially in 1741 to have to mortgage his expensive London home, Powis House. Since 1739, the year of Henrietta's marriage, he had let it to Lord Philip Hardwicke, the Lord Chancellor, for his official residence.[40]

One immediate problem that Henrietta had to sort out was her daughter's care, and this would involve travelling abroad. Lady Barbara Webb, wife of Sir John Webb who was little Barbara's guardian, and who was looking after her great-granddaughter, died on March 28 1740. The 75-year-old Sir John was unable to look after so young a child on his own, although he remained as her guardian; and so the Beards must have decided to place the 5-year-old girl in a convent for her education. Lord Edward Herbert's aunt, Lucy, was Prioress of St. Augustine's Convent in Bruges, and we know that Barbara was certainly educated in that city from about

[39] £337 18s 0d in total in 1739, and £300 in 1740
[40] Hugh Phillips, 'Mid-Georgian London', London, 1964, p.207

1744. This would seem to have been their obvious first destination. As we have seen in the previous chapter, news of her grandmother's death, with the accompanying problem of what to do with Barbara, came at a bad time for Beard. May 9th was absolutely the earliest that he could leave his commitments in London and accompany his wife abroad. Even then he was leaving three weeks before the conclusion of his contract.

While she was abroad, Henrietta also made a last desperate attempt at reconciliation with her father. By 1740 Lord Waldegrave was a sick man - a fact that must have been known to Henrietta; his asthma was getting worse and worse and he was also suffering from 'dropsy'. A later member of the Waldegrave family suggested that people were insinuating that the shame of his daughter's marriage caused these problems. Death was obviously approaching, and this spurred Henrietta to write a preliminary letter to him from Lille, asking for his forgiveness.

She wrote pitifully to her father, once Barbara had been settled into the convent in Bruges, in July:

"My Lord I wont call my Self a troublesome corispondant to your Lordship because I fear my letters have never had the honour of being perus'd by you beyond the first Line, as soone as you found the authur they weer like her Condemnd and thrown from you, or ellce those Vows of Duty and Affectionate Submision I think my Dear father could Never have read without feeling an Emotion in his heart in my favour, but would have Sufferd his angre to have been disarmd by his Kneeling, weeping Child, but I hope this will come in a Luckyer hour to your hands and find you in a Willing Moment to receive my petition, Exert the father over they Judg and forgive your Imploring Daughter, I dont Question (if your Lordship ever permits me to be Named to you) I have enimies who to trample me more on the Earth Exagerate on my follys, and I too well know I have No frind that dares Incounter your Displeasure by endevouring to Soften any part of my past Conduct, thus My Lord if you ever hear of me it only adds to, not decreases my Offences; and perhaps is hightend by Misrepresentation, for faughts I never Committed, Could you My Lord be so Indulgent as to think my Crimes in some sort Magnified and Convince your Self that I frame No other view in Solisiting you then your forgiveness, I belive by degrees the Parant would gain so Much upon you as to Say you pardond; Indeed My Lord I am Sincair in what I say for I wish for Nothing so much as your permission to sine My Self your Lordships Most Dutyfull Daughter and Humble Sert
H: Beard   Lille July ye 9: 1740"

It is not known whether Beard and Henrietta travelled on to Paris from Lille, but Waldegrave was unrelenting. His diplomatic position in Paris was under threat - war with France seemed inevitable and the government were worried about his increasing ill-health; his daughter's social disgrace was the last straw. In the autumn of 1740 he returned to England, and retired to Navestock where he died on April 11 1741.

As Lord Waldegrave lay on his death-bed, Beard returned to the stage. This may be merely a coincidence, but looks significantly as though the two events were related. Beard must have realised that he could not just rely on his wife's income, and that he would not be able to gain any approbation from his father-in-law. He looked for work, and found it at Goodman's Fields, in the East End of London. These pleasure gardens opened on Easter Monday 30 March 1741, and the entertainment included 'singing by Mr Beard'. A week later, trading on his fame for singing a song "in the character of a sea captain of a Man-of-War upon the taking of Porto Bello", which was now also available as a print, he was invited to sing in the pantomime *The Spanish Husband or Harlequin at Porto Bello*.

His name appears, for the last time, in the advertisements for Saturday April 11, the day of Lord Waldegrave's death. Although the show continued for the rest of the summer, Beard's name was never again mentioned in the cast list. Of course, the immediate reason for his absence could have been that he and Henrietta went to Lord Waldegrave's funeral in Essex. Henrietta would have wanted to be seen there, and Beard must have stopped performing so that he could accompany her. Perhaps she felt that her father wouldn't be so cruel as to fail to remember her in his will.

As it was she was gravely disappointed. Waldegrave added a hand-written codicil a month before he died. This reads: '... *and to my daughter heretofore Herbert now Beard I give her five shillings*'. To emphasise his displeasure, Waldegrave then added the words 'worthless' above 'daughter', and 'only' after 'five shillings'. The clerk who copied this for the official records was uncertain how to transcribe this and left a note in the margin: 'if in doubt see original'. Fortunately, the original still remains in the National Archives.[41]

Without any money from her father's Will, Beard and Henrietta's plight became desperate. They were being hounded by creditors who were threatening to take legal action. They turned to their lawyer, Edward Webb,[42] for help. There were eleven named creditors and 'several others' who were not prepared to wait any longer, or accept future payment from her jointure. Several of these creditors were women, from which one concludes that they were probably Henrietta's debts to dressmakers, milliners and the like. Webb drew up an Indenture[43] whereby Henrietta sold £100 of her jointure to him, and in return he advanced them enough cash to pay off their debts. This Indenture also allowed Beard to take £25 a year from the jointure for his own personal use. As her husband, and under the concept of 'coverture', all his wife's money belonged to him; but the Indenture expressly forbade him to 'intermeddle' in his wife's financial affairs. Perhaps he had been using the jointure indiscriminately for his own purposes. However, a further £25 a year was allocated to be paid in Trust to his mother, Mrs Ann Beard, which indicates that, by 1742, she was already a widow and being supported by him.

Having pledged this money from her jointure, it was imperative that the Powis family paid up fully and promptly in order to service the debt the Beards now had with their lawyer. However, Henrietta's situation had radically altered since the earlier Bill of Complaint in 1736, and this affected her legal position: not only had she remarried, but she had also reached 21 and her father had died. Any one of these meant that technically her previous 'cause' was 'abated'.

She would have to start all over again and, from now on, Beard was actively involved as the primary plaintiff. In 1743, he and Henrietta lodged another Bill of Complaint. The new Bill [44] (dated June 3 1743) reflected the changes that were now due to her under her Marriage Settlement. Although her father had

---

[41] National Archives: The official transcript is in PROB11; but the original Will can be found in PROB10/1912.

[42] It is not clear how Edward Webb was related to Henrietta – he also acted as lawyer for her grandfather, Sir John Webb, who merely called him 'kinsman'. Edward was the 2nd son of John Webb of St Andrew's Holborn, and admitted to Gray's Inn on 11/2/1702(3).

[43] Powis Castle papers: D3/9/11 Indenture dated 31/5/1742 – enrolled in Court of King's Bench 21 July 1742 (KB122/191/90 Nat. Arch.)

[44] Records of Court of Chancery: Beard v Powis, C12/733/12 – Nat. Arch.

virtually cut her out of his Will by leaving her a derisory five shillings, nevertheless there were now further payments due from his estate. He had to pay in full the £6000 pledged in her marriage settlement, from which she was entitled "to receive the further yearly sum of £100 over and above the yearly sum of £600" under the terms of the Waldegrave marriage settlement.[45]

The plaintiffs also complained that *"ever since the last decree, the said William Marquis of Powis hath been very dilatory and negligent in payment...and there is now and for four years past has been due and owing the sum of £1000 together with the growing payments since upon the account of the said jointure".* They then allege that *"they have been oblidged to take up that sum* [i.e. borrow] *at interest in order to supply their present occasions* [46] *for want of due payment of the jointure, for which they pay interest after the rate of 5%."*

In conclusion, they ask that the earlier proceedings, orders and decrees may be revived in the same condition as existed before her remarriage and the death of her father; that all the outstanding money should be paid; that her jointure should be paid direct to her, now she was over 21; and that all the capital should be properly invested.

Legal proceedings have always been slow, and the Waldegrave response is dated a year later on July 3 1744. This came from the new Earl Waldegrave, Henrietta's elder brother James, who submitted to the Court that he was eager to pay off the debt of £6000. His actions, though, did not speak as loud as his words. Another year passed, and he had done nothing apart from quibble about how the money should be invested. Finally, on July 17 1746, the Waldegraves transferred £5859 15s 3d worth of South Sea Stock to the Powis estate in full and final settlement of the debt.[47]

The Marquis of Powis' response to this Bill is dated 12 April 1744. It is a tough response, and refutes many of the allegations made by the Beards. He claimed that, at the time of the marriage in 1734, his son, Lord Edward Herbert, had debts which reduced the capital of £20,000 that was available for Henrietta's jointure. The Powis papers confirm this, and show that, as early as 1729, Edward had raised money by borrowing against the security of his future marriage settlement.[48]

The Marquis does acknowledge that there have been delays in payment, but claims this was caused by his tenants not paying their rent on time. He then continues: *"At the time of the exhibiting of the Complainants now Bill there was not half a year due or owing for the maintenance of the said Barbara. This Defendant by his Steward or Agent . . . has since paid and satisfied the said maintenance in full to the 9th January last; and this Defendant saith that several considerable sums have been likewise paid and satisfied to and for the use and on the account of the Complainant Lady Henrietta by this Defendant or his Stewards or Agent for and in respect of her aforesaid jointure after the making of the last mentioned Decree or Order* [i.e. in 1737] *as well before the intermarriage of the Complainant Lady Henrietta with the Complainant John Beard."*

Lord Powis continues that he does not believe that for four years there has been £1000 owing. On the contrary he believes that on the 19 December 1738, a

---

[45] Quoted in 1734 Marriage Settlement – Powis Castle papers D3/8/13 (NLW)
[46] 'occasions' – in the sense 'personal needs or requirements' – OED.
[47] Stated in: Act of Parliament 24 G2 92 (re: Marriage Settlement between Henry Arthur Herbert and Barbara 1751)
[48] Powis Castle papers (3a) Doc. D2/7/8 etc. (NLW)

month before Henrietta's marriage to Beard, there was precisely £36 8s 8d outstanding, which was then paid by his Steward.[49] He does admit that considerable arrears may now be due, but he has no intention of reimbursing the plaintiffs for the costs of any loans they may have made.

He then declares that on 29 March last his Steward "...*did offer to pay to John Beard £600 and desired him to have a receipt for it, and did tender the same to him in Bank Notes, but the Complainant refused to give such a receipt, and his Counsel or Agent then present did alledge that such offer in Bank Notes was not a good tender.*" He states that the Notes remain with his Steward, ready for payment and believes that, if Beard had accepted this sum, then only £200 would be owing on the jointure. This appears extraordinary behaviour on the part of Beard, until we appreciate that these must have been <u>Promissory</u> Notes. All money, at this time, was in the form of coinage. Beard must have been advised that there was no guarantee that these Notes would have been honoured.

The Court records merely list these allegations and counter-allegations, and it is impossible, from this source alone, to get at the truth of how much money was truly paid. However, the Powis papers show that, in August 1744, Edward Webb submitted that the deficit on Henrietta's jointure now amounted to £1769 13s 0d plus interest of £300 'for want of due payment', making £2069 13s in total.[50] The Powis lawyers replied with their own version of the Accounts, which were largely in agreement.[51] But from this second document, we can see that the Powis family had not allowed Henrietta access to any of the capital money. This meant that she was still having to pay the interest on the loans that Lord Edward had taken out before they were married. She had also had to clear other outstanding debts – which included "£70 for coach horses killed by Lord Edward" - and bear the expense of his funeral. Lord Edward died in Bath, but the body had been brought back to Hendon for burial as the Powis family were Lords of the Manor of Hendon, and were traditionally buried in the Parish Church.

There were two events in 1745 which further interrupted the progress of the case. First there was the death of old Sir John Webb, who was still Barbara's guardian. As he was one of the two parties specifically named in the litigation, it meant that the Bill had to be amended. The Beards were obliged to issue a Supplemental Bill and Bill of Revivor in 1746.

1745 was also the year when Bonnie Prince Charlie landed in Scotland. Britain was largely unprepared to defend itself at the time, as most of the army was abroad fighting the French in the war of Austrian Succession. The Jacobites obviously hoped that their supporters throughout the country would rise up and join the rebellion. A letter was intercepted in Poole, close to the Webb's home at Great Canford. It was addressed to a Francis Weild and read "*I thought proper to wish you joy of the success of our friends in the north. When our neighbours arrive in the west, I hope you will be ready to assist them, as promised in your last, but I fear the winds have prevented them as yet. My humble respects to S.J.W. and all friends at Canford...*" [52] Sir John Webb, who had certainly remained a friend of the Jacobite cause, was never required to declare where his patriotic loyalties lay: as it happened he was, conveniently, abroad in France. This was probably not a coincidence, but

---

[49] This payment was made, but the records show that it only reduced the accumulated deficit to £300.
[50] Powis Castle papers (3) Doc. 9661 (NLW)
[51] Powis Castle papers (4) Doc. 9651 (NLW)
[52] Historical Chronicle, Gentleman's Magazine, October 1745

foreknowledge. Somehow he was obviously able to travel with impunity behind enemy lines. At some time in 1745 he remarried in Paris and, within a few months, died in Aix-la-Chapelle (Aachen) in October of the same year. Henrietta's close family connections with the rebels could easily have jeopardised Beard's standing with the Hanoverian Court, which he had been cultivating for many years. It adds another dimension to the reasons behind his keenness to participate in the first performance of the National Anthem (see Chapter 5: *Beef and Liberty*).

The second event which impeded progress on the litigation was the death of the 2nd Marquis of Powis. He died in October 1745 as well, and was succeeded by his son, and Henrietta's erstwhile brother-in-law, William Lord Montgomery. Together with Sir John Webb's death in the same month it meant that Barbara was now without a legal guardian. Diplomatically, Henrietta wrote to the new Marquis in November that she "*should be glad to know what are your Graces sentiments in my regard of my Girle, who at present is without any Guardian but my Self; I don't care for applying at this juncture to Chancery – for the nomination of one – fearing the Court may take cognisance of her education and Principalls as Popery is so great a buggbear, and yet shall be loath to interfere my self – least it should be disagreeable to y' Grace, but my Lord as I refer this, and everything ellce to y' better judgment – and as it is necessary some care should be had for my child – I beg you to determine how I am to proceed.*" [53]

It is interesting that Henrietta did not consider that she and Beard could continue to be legally responsible for Barbara. A new guardian was eventually appointed, and Henrietta must have been reasonably happy with the choice: Anthony, 6th Viscount Montague, who was appointed on 6 August 1746. He was, not surprisingly, also a Catholic and distantly related to the Powis family but, more importantly, he was Henrietta's uncle through the Webb family.[54] He 'placed her at Bruges for her education'; but this looks more like a confirmation of the existing situation, as we also learn that Barbara had been there for 'near two years before'.[55]

William Lord Montgomery may have inherited the title of Marquis of Powis, but all else he received was his father's debts. Many of the family estates were mortgaged up to the hilt, with large arrears of interest outstanding. The new Marquis was aggrieved by this, which appeared to come as a surprise to him. He complained to his lawyers that he now found himself just one of his father's many creditors, and he was especially vexed by the large payments that were due to Henrietta and Barbara. He claimed that he had never been a party to her Marriage Settlement, and saw no reason to continue the payments. This was rather ingenuous a response, and he certainly should have been aware of the terms of his brother's Marriage Settlement: his name - as Lord Montgomery - does appear on all the relevant documents.

Accordingly, the Beards were obliged to issue a separate Bill of Complaint against James Baker, who was acting as the late Marquis's Executor. Baker submitted that he "*doth not know nor can set forth what arrears are now due*", but again admitted that the "*late Marquis might be somewhat dilatory in payment of the jointure*". He then claimed that there were insufficient funds anyway to pay what was owing: - "*...the personal Estate which the late Marquis died possessed of came*

[53] Powis Castle papers, No. 9658 – letter dated 8/11/1745 (NLW)
[54] Henrietta's aunt, Barbara Webb, married Anthony Brown, 6th Viscount Montague on 28th July 1720.
[55] Records of Court of Chancery: C33/391/p.545 (Nat. Arch.)

to the hands custody or power of this Deponent and not sufficient to pay and satisfy as this Deponent conceives what was justly due."

`Henrietta, meanwhile, must have followed the November letter to the new Marquis with another (that is now lost) asking him for money. Her letter of December 13, which flattered the Marquis by referring to his father with the Jacobite title of 'Duke', contains: *"I can never believe your grace would refuse supplying me with a hundred pounds, which tho' of consequence to me – is very triffling to your Grace; I have no resource of friends or credit – those by the usage from the Duke y' father are pretty well draned; and have not upon honour five pounds in the house – this is a melancholy and true State of my Affairs; and I apply to Your Grace for redress; I don't attempt asking for the settling the accounts – all I desire is - till it suits your graces conveniency - I may be supply'd for the necesserys of Life – without being liable to insults..."* [56]

Henrietta wrote again a week later, and her letter contains evidence that the Marquis had at least replied. In this second longer letter, which appears to have been written in great haste, she lists all her grievances in order, and the lack of a satisfactory answer. She states that: *"before your Grace honourd me with your commands for suspending my lawsuit, I had order'd all proceedings to be declined"* but that: *"I see my self reduced to appeal again to Chancery".* She continues: *"I petitiond you for a meer triffle: a Subsistance for my self and child: a Subsistance that has been long cruely with-held by your father, who tho' he did not attain to the absolute starving us, yet plunged me into so menny distresses and difficultyes, that it will require years yet of Penury to extricate me from my distresses: I did not ask for my arriers – I only beg'd for a triffle to inable me to support a Life that he strove to render miserable. You again refuse me – and I was fallsly told, you pitty'd my usage in your fathers time..."*

Later she says: *"I assure you I am without money: or without power to gitt any – have demands on all sides for debts..."* These pathetic appeals were to no avail, and the records show that no money was forthcoming throughout 1746. In reality, the Powis finances were in as much of a mess as the Beard's; and one cannot conjure up money out of thin air. Again they had to turn to Edward Webb for help, and sold a further £200 of the jointure to him for ready cash. [57] This may have paid off their immediate debts, but they had only reduced their creditors from a multitude down to one. And it was not Edward Webb's responsibility to ensure that his share of the jointure payments were made: this was still up to them. The Beards had no option other than to return to the Courts and, in 1747, they issued a further Bill of Complaint. [58]

The Court records make depressing reading, and show how the defendants were able to prevaricate. One can trace the progress of the case, especially at the end of each Law Term, when there is an 'up-date' on unresolved cases. So we read that on October 18 1746 *"It is ordered that ye Defendants have a month's time to plead answer or demurr to the Plaintiffs Bill and that all proofs of Contempt be in the mean time stayed".* A month later, on November 28, nothing had happened and the defendants were given *'three weeks further to answer or demurr'.* On January 25

[56] Powis Castle papers, No. 9659 – letter dated 13/12/1745 (NLW)

[57] Powis castle papers: endorsed on reverse of D3/9/11, 2/6/1746 (NLW). Indenture enrolled in the Court of Common Pleas

[58] One other factor was always included in this litigation, and this was an increase in Barbara's allowance. This increased over the years from £100 p.a. to £500 p.a.

1747 the Plaintiffs were *'advised to amend their Bill, without costs, as defendants have not yet answered'*; on March 25 the defendants were *'given a month to plead'*; on May 13 they were given a further three weeks, and on June 4 a further fortnight. And so it continued.

One wonders what Beard himself thought about this endless litigation. Presumably he supported the actions of his wife, as a matter of principle. Why should the Powis family be allowed to default on a legal contract with impunity? The sums of money involved were also considerable, and greatly exceeded what he himself earned. His yearly Benefit, for example, brought in around £200.[59]

On the other hand, one wonders why Beard and his wife continued to live at such a profligate rate, and incur these debts. Had they learned no lessons since they were married? There is nothing to tell us in the Court records which of them was to blame. However, Henrietta's letters always refer to the debts as hers, and we do know that Beard later managed Covent Garden Theatre in a competent and prudent manner, although he was not personally responsible for the finances. Later, he and his second wife lived a comfortable retirement on their savings and an income of £100 a year. The conclusion would seem to be that these debts can be firmly attributed to Henrietta alone, and that Beard was simply unable to control her spending. Without any evidence, it is also impossible to say what the cost of all this litigation was to them, but it must have been considerable. They were certainly only winning pyrrhic victories.

The 3rd Marquis appears to have done nothing, or little, to stabilise the Powis finances. He was still unmarried, and seems to have led the life of a dissolute rake, According to one witness: 'he never went to bed sober in the last ten years of his life';[60] and, as it turned out, he had not long to live. Perhaps, aware of this, he made his Will on April 28 1747. It seems likely that Henrietta may have had some foreknowledge of its contents, because in May of that year she tried a different tactic. Lord Edward Herbert had died intestate in 1734, and no action had ever been taken with regard to his personal estate. And so, on May 31 1747, 'Lady Henrietta Beard, formerly Herbert, (now wife of John Beard Esq.)' successfully applied for a Grant of Administration for the 'goods, chattels and credits of the Honourable Lord Edward Herbert late of Powis Castle'.[61]

This was more than 12 years after Lord Edward had died, and one wonders why Henrietta had not done anything sooner. Presumably she was prompted into this action by her exasperation at the delays, and wished to establish her legal rights to his personal estate. However, it is not clear whether she did receive any benefit during her own lifetime. Having obtained the Grant of Administration, she did not pursue the matter further, and it was not until 1755 - two year's after her death - that this matter was finally resolved.

On March 8 1748, the 3rd Marquis of Powis, died and left these instructions in his Will:[62]

"Whereas I am greatly dissatisfied with the demand made on me or my estate of twenty thousand pounds for and in respect of the portion of my late brother Lord Edward Herbert deceased now claimed by his daughter or her trustees I

---

[59] 1742 £207; 1747 £197 4s; 1750 £200 5s
[60] Quoted in the National Trust's Powis Castle Guidebook
[61] PROB6/122 – Nat. Arch.
[62] PROB11/762/160 (Nat. Arch.)

therefore desire my said Trustees not to pay the same without first having the directions of the Court of Chancery in that behalf."[63]

The Marquis left all his Estate to a distant 'cousin', Henry Arthur Herbert of Chirbury, which surprised even members of his own family. His sisters were later reported as expressing their astonishment, as Henry Arthur "*was no relation of their family*". The exact relationship is *very* distant, and the two lines had actually diverged nine generations, and over 200 years, earlier. Henry Arthur himself admitted "*he could not set forth how he was related to the Marquis of Powis the Son, but said, there was a Friendship and Correspondence between them ... but admitted he had no Personal Acquaintance with him.*"...[64]

Now that he was in possession of the Powis Estates, Henry Arthur took steps to acquire the title. Unlike the previous Marquis and his family, this branch of the family was no longer Catholic. And so, on April 7 1748, only thirty days after the death of the previous Marquis, he wrote to the Duke of Newcastle "As the late Marquis of Powis, by giving me his estate, has done so much for a Protestant family, I should be very sorry to find that His Majesty with the interposition of my friends, shou'd not be prevail'd upon, to honour me with his approbation of it by granting me his titles". He received the title of Earl of Powis [65] on 27 May.

One of the first things the new Earl had to do was to answer the accusations made by the Beards in the 1748 Bill of Revivor which they had issued following his elevation to the title.[66] He stated, quite understandably, that he had no knowledge of these earlier wranglings, and they were no concern of his. However, his solution to the problem took a different turn. He might have been in his 40's, but he was still unmarried, and so he set in motion a plan to marry the young Barbara. This would unite the families, and legitimise his rights to the title. Barbara, of course was the legitimate heir but - as a woman - could not succeed to the title.

It would also mean that the financial situation could be renegotiated. It is such a neat solution that it might well have been a plan that had been hatched up many years before, and the reason he received the estates in the first place. Up to now, the Powis family appeared to have taken little interest in Barbara's upbringing and education. Maybe they were just biding their time, and now was the time to assert their authority over their only asset. Barbara was only 13 years old, but the new Earl had to move quickly as other potential husbands were already being suggested. One such suitor, who received the approval of Henrietta in 1749, was the son of her current guardian, Lord Montague.

Barbara was still being educated at a convent in Bruges and Lady Mary Herbert, her Aunt who lived in France, heard of this plan and nipped it in the bud. She persuaded the King of France to intervene and avert such a marriage. Obviously, the new Earl needed to remove Barbara from her mother's influence and the protection of Lord Montague, and appoint a new guardian – and one who was to his liking. His choice fell on Lady Herbert of Chirbury. None of the records elaborate further but, with this title, she must surely have been his own mother.

---

[63] The records show that payment of Henrietta's jointure did recommence in 1747. Powis Castle papers No. 21008 (NLW)

[64] The Hardwicke Papers Add. 36171 ff. 1 – 47 (British Library)

[65] The Complete Peerage. The Marquises also held the lesser title of Earl. For this reason, Henry Arthur was sometimes known as the 4th Earl, but was correctly the 1st Earl of the 2nd creation.

[66] Records of Court of Chancery: C12/281/8 (Nat. Arch.)

Barbara was immediately brought back to England, while her future was decided. At this time we have the first evidence that Henrietta's health was beginning to decline. The litigation, and concerns for her daughter, were obviously highly stressful. She did not feel well enough to meet Barbara on her return from France. She wrote to her friend and distant relation, the Honourable Mrs Carryl:

Dear Madam
I have not words enough to express my sensibility of the obligations I am under to yr Ladyship and my cozen Carryl, all I can say is - that as I have (in this unhappy affair) received more marks of goodness and compation from both of you than from all my friends and relations - gratitude and inclination will for ever bind me to you.
If my cozen Carryl would be so good as to be in Westminster hall about 10 o'clock - he might receive my daughter from my Lord Chancelors Hand - for I believe she must be deliverd to some one in Court. I shall have the Honour of wrighting to my Lord and Lady Seaford as soon as ever I hear Miss Herbert has the happyness of being with them - I do ashure yr Ladysp she is a very good humourd inofensive girle and will be as little troublesome as possible to my Lord Seafords family.
Dear Madam - as I fear I shall not be in a condition to stir out today - I intreat you to add one favour more to the manny obligations I have alredy received - which is that you'd see my girle at Lord Seafords, and give her instructions as to her behaviour - I am Madam with true Gratitude and Affection Most Sincerely and Affection.................. [the word tails off as there is no space at the end of the line]
Yours   *H Beard* [67]   *8 o'clock*

To change Barbara's guardian, the Earl not only needed the approval of the Court but, in order to obviate any delay, he also needed the consent of her relatives. The offers and inducements that were made in order to gain the Beards' agreement to the change can be found in the Court records of another action that the new Earl had inherited. This was a separate dispute that had already rumbled on for years, concerning the allowance paid to Lady Mary Herbert,[68] Henrietta's sister-in-law. This litigation was still unresolved in 1766 when Lady Mary made an Appeal to the House of Lords. By this time Barbara had been married - and the Countess of Powis - for 15 years; but, as the dispute had earlier touched on the circumstances leading to her marriage, Beard was cited many times in the submissions, and was eventually called to give evidence to the Appeal in person.

The 1766 preamble describes how Barbara arrived back in England in 1749, still under the guardianship of Lord Montague, and how the Earl *"finding it impractical to accomplish his marriage, while she continued under such Guardianship, prevailed on the executors of the Marquis, to apply to the Court of Chancery to appoint a proper Person to be Guardian"*.

It was then alleged that the Earl - or his Agents - had used strong-arm tactics to gain the approval of Barbara's family: *"...as several of the Relations of Lady Powis professed the Popish religion, the Agents of the said Earl employed on this Occasion, threatned some of them with putting the Penal Laws against Papists in force . . . and to others promised great Rewards and Preferments, particularly to*

---

[67] 'Family of Caryll, Vol. 5, 1748-1755'; British Library Manuscript Collection - Add. 28231 f. 76
[68] An accurate account of the life of Lady Mary Herbert can be found in the new edition of the Oxford DNB. This corrects much erroneous information found in earlier editions.

Lady Henrietta Beard and Mr Beard her husband, to induce them to consent to such Guardianship: And the Respondent, the Earl of Powis, declared he was sorry to see the Husband of the Sister of his Benefactor in so low a Situation of Life, that he would procure Mr Beard a Commission in the Army, or other Preferment, if she would consent to the Appointment of Lady Herbert of Cherbery to be Guardian to her Daughter."[69]

One wonders if Beard was present to hear the insult that he was in 'so low a situation of life'. However it is true that, whatever their popularity, society still regarded actors and singers as no better than rogues and vagabonds. This must have been something that rankled with Beard, and showed how he could never be accepted in the aristocratic circles to which his wife belonged. One also wonders whether she might have still been putting pressure on him to leave the theatre, and obtain employment more fitting to a lady of her rank. If Beard was still tempted by this idea in 1749, it adds another dimension to the possible reasons for his absence from the stage in 1740 and 1741.

The Earl of Powis' Agent, Corbyn Morris, confirmed that the Earl *"endeavoured to procure some Employment for Mr Beard with the Government, whereby he might be enabled to relinquish the Theatre"*, and *"his Lordship more than once about that time mentioned ... that he had made Application to Mr Pelham*[70] *on behalf of Mr Beard."*

We can see that Beard must have given these proposals a certain amount of consideration, in a later statement by Corbyn Morris which is one of the few descriptions we have of Beard away from his professional life:

"Mr Beard, several months after Lady Herbert of Cherbury was appointed Guardian, not having obtained any Office or Employment through the Defendant Lord Powis's Interest, and despairing of obtaining any through that Channel, complained warmly to this Deponent of the ill Usage he received; and Mr Beard and this Deponent thereupon agreed to meet at the Tennis Court Coffee-house ... in order to discourse fully upon this Subject: at such Meeting Mr Beard began warmly to expostulate, and to charge this Deponent with deceiving him, by throwing out fallacious Views of his obtaining Preferment through the Defendant Lord Powis's Interest; and this Deponent thereupon acquainted him, that he had never thrown out any Views of serving him further than what he really believed to have been his Lordship's full Intention, and that instead of acting in any fallacious Manner towards him, he had given him his best Offices, by representing on every Occasion his Services to Lord Powis in the most meritorious Manner; and he then made Mr Beard recollect, that this Deponent, for preventing any Mistakes of his own, and for exonerating himself, had introduced the said Mr Beard to the Earl of Powis, for the express Purpose of his being informed by his Lordship himself of the Favours he was to expect from him, and that Mr Beard had particularly thanked this Deponent for such Introduction, and then declared that he had nothing to charge this Deponent with, for that he rested entirely upon the Assurances he had had from his Lordship himself: And he then further told Mr Beard, that as he could not but remember all these Circumstances, he acted in a very injurious Manner in making such a Charge upon this Deponent; and Mr Beard thereupon feeling this Deponent

---

[69] The Hardwicke Papers Add. 36171 ff. 1 – 47 (British Library)

[70] Henry Pelham became Prime Minister in 1743. He was the younger brother of Thomas Pelham-Holles, the Duke of Newcastle, who succeeded him as Premier in 1754.

firm, and not to be driven to yield to such Accusations, acknowledged what this deponent alledged to be just, but exclaimed in passionate Expressions about the Treatment he had received from the Earl of Powis; in which Manner, after some Time, the Meeting ended:"

The notes that were taken of John Beard's own testimony confirm the substance of these statements and state: *"...that Morris in 1748 or 1749 applied to Lady Henrietta Beard and gave her Intimation of Lord Powis's Intention to Marry her Daughter. That Morris had many Interviews with Lady Heneritta* [sic] *tending to prevail on her to approve such person to be Guardian to her Daughter as should be agreeable to Lord Powis, spoke lavishly of Lord Powis Honour and Generosity and of his kind Intentions to Lady Heneritta, that he would provide as post for Deponent under the Government and put him in such a Sphere of Life that she might appear as the Mother of Miss Herbert".*

Henrietta struggled to maintain some influence over her daughter's future, but matters were slipping from her grasp. She feared for her daughter Barbara, who was still a minor, and for the safety of the catholic religion in which she had been raised. "Suppose Lord Powis should some time hence even have thoughts of marrying you, he cannot do it without your free consent" she wrote to Barbara as early as 1749. In a later letter she wrote:

"I hear Lord Waldegrave [her elder brother] is to come with Lord Powis tomorrow. I judge by that that they are united – and therefore conclude 'twill be the best way for you not to struggle, but to make the best composition for yourself you can. ... Make it one of your articles that your poor Mama may always have free access to you – for I apprehend Lord W. may be for excluding me, tho' I am sure Lord Powis has too much humanity to do it". [71]

She wrote to Lord Hardwicke on June 30 1749 from Chelsea asking for an audience. As Lord Chancellor he was ultimately responsible for Barbara's welfare:

"My Lord
If I am guilty of any seeming Indecorum I beg you'd impute it to my ignorance in matters of form and not to a want of a due respect and submisive confidence in yr Lordships compassion and goodness (espesially) to theose who are peculierly under your protection. My Daughter (Miss Herbert) has that advantage; and I most ernestly intreat the Honour of one quarter of an hours audience in her behalf, when it best suits yr leisure. Besides my Naturall affection to my child - this request is founded on a sinceer desire of conforming my self to your Lordships intentions that I may prove with what respect and sencibility I am
My Lord Your Lordships most humble and most obedient servt   Har. Beard
Chealsea June ye 30th 1749" [72]

This letter was written in the summer, when Beard was singing at Ranelagh Gardens in Chelsea. He and Henrietta obviously took lodgings in the area at that time of the year. However, Beard's address for his benefit on 29 March 1749 does not give a London address, and this is possibly evidence that he and Henrietta were spending

[71] Waldegrave Family Papers, & Countess Waldegrave, 'Waldegrave Family History' Part 2, 1975, p. 96
[72] Correspondence of the 1st Lord Hardwicke 1749 – Add. 35590 f. 315 (British Library)

more time away from the centre of London. The reason for this was probably concerns for Henrietta's health. Perhaps unadvisedly, she sent this letter via Henry Arthur, the new Earl. He forwarded it to the Lord Chancellor, with a note requesting that any reply should be transmitted through his hands.

However, on 22 July 1749 Lord Montague was duly discharged as Barbara's Guardian, and a temporary guardian was appointed until the Court confirmed a new appointment. It was not yet certain that the Court would agree to the choice of Lady Herbert of Chirbury. In the interim the Court forbade Lord Montague or any of his family from having any form of communication with Barbara. This restriction did not apply to Henrietta, and at least one of the letters she wrote to Barbara was delivered by Beard himself. The cover – unfortunately now separated from its letter – reads *"For Miss Herbert, to be deliver'd into her own hands by Mr Beard at the request of Lady Harriot: this she enjoyns him to do – and her to comply with".*[73]

Henrietta wrote to Barbara telling her of "three things you've a right to insist on - first: that your Religion shall not be any ways molested; second: that your inclinations shall never be attempted to be forced; thirdly: that you see your mother as your mother without any restriction".[74]

However, even these conditions were ignored. Beard testified in 1766: *"...that the Evening before Lady Herbert of Cherbury was appointed Guardian Morris* [Corbyn Morris, the Earl's Agent] *told Lady Henrietta that the 2 Arch Bishops would appoint a Chaplain to instruct Miss Herbert in the Religion of the Country and that Lady Heneritta* [sic] *might get at her Jointure and the Maintenance of her Daughter as she could – saith that by these threats she was induced to send her Consent in writing to Lady Herbert of Cherbury's being Guardian, understood and believed that Morris was authorized to make such promises and threats by Lord Powis."*[75]

Preparations for the marriage continued and the Marriage Settlement was ratified by Act of Parliament. Like a lamb to the slaughter the 15 year-old Barbara was married to the 48 year-old Henry Arthur in Bath on 30 March 1751. A letter of William Havard's implies that neither Beard nor Henrietta were able to gain admittance to the ceremony.[76] The date might have proved an awkward one for Beard, coming mid-season. But as it happened, the theatres were closed on account of the death of the Prince of Wales, and it is possible that the couple made the fruitless journey to Bath. If so, Beard was certainly back in London two days later to sing the Funeral Service and an anthem by Boyce for the funeral of Captain Thomas Coram, at the Foundling Hospital on April 3.[77]

As far as we can tell Barbara never tried to see her mother again. Under the terms and conditions, Barbara's maintenance - as defined in 1734 - ceased, and all arrears were wiped out together with the nominal surplus interest on the £20,000 capital. Although this had been calculated at various times, it had never been paid

---

[73] Powis Castle papers No. 1560 (NLW)

[74] Powis Castle papers No. 1550 (NLW)

[75] Appeal to Court of Chancery 1766 - The Hardwicke Papers Add. 36171 ff. 1 – 47 (British Library)

[76] "...I sometimes forget that there are such wretches existing as Lord and Lady P[owis]". Havard, 'Jeu d'esprit', N.a.2. Folger Shakespeare Library, Washington, USA

[77] The Penny London Post, 3 – 5 April 1751, reported that "several gentlemen belonging to St Paul's Choir, as also Mr Beard, and four choristers ...all in surplices ...began to sing the Burial Service, which was composed by Dr Boyce, who played the same on a small organ set on one side of the Chapel..."

and remained merely a figure in the accounts. Furthermore, all the estates that were allotted for Henrietta's jointure were unconditionally returned to the Earl of Powis, 'other than the annuity of £700 for the benefit of Lady Henrietta Beard'. In the four years since payment of her jointure resumed in 1747, Henrietta had received a total of £3471 17s 1d.[78] The Earl made no further payments; but did honour his obligations by purchasing the rights to her jointure, which was for 'life', with a cash sum.

On 15 July 1751, Beard received £2200. Although there is no documentation to show where this money came from, it is such a large sum that it must have been the final payment from the Powis estate.[79] What happened next is quite extraordinary. He opened a bank account at C. Hoare & Co. in Fleet Street with this money and then, within the next 6 weeks, spent it all. The account was closed on 27 August. He withdrew just under £800 in cash, and made a further 16 payments to named individuals. A few of these can be identified - payment of £30 to the lawyer, Isaac Strutt;[80] £88 13s to Robert Lane who was presumably their tailor and who was, at the time, husband to Beard's second wife; £135 17s to James Walmesley, a neighbour in New North Street. Others one can only guess at. However, by consulting the Trade Directories, it appears that many of them were tradesmen. Edward Jernegar, who was paid £32 7s 6d, was a jeweller in Holborn; and Thomas Hodgson who received the enormous sum of £313 18s was a linen-draper and 'chinaman' in Cheapside. If this truly reflects the state of the couple's debts, then it shows what an appalling situation they were in.

With the prospect of no more money coming to them from the Powis family, the couple would now have to rely solely on Beard's earnings. Although he was earning well, they had to face up to the consequences of a savage reduction in their income, and so they left the house in New North Street. We know that, in March 1752 at the time of his benefit, Beard was lodging in Russell Street, Covent Garden. This was undoubtedly convenient for the theatre, not only for Beard, but also for the audience who wished to purchase tickets for his Benefit night.

Other writers have commented on this sudden decline in their life-style, without realising its full reasons.[81] However, it may be an indication that Henrietta was not living there. As her health was still poor, it could be that the couple had down-sized to enable Henrietta to continue to live in Chelsea. Russell Street was not such a terrible address as has been made out. Although there were bagnios and brothels in the area, there were also respectable traders - like Thomas Davies the bookseller, at whose shop Boswell first met Dr Johnson. Many theatre folk found it prudent to live close by: one of the jobs of the call-boy was to make sure that the cast had all arrived for the evening performance. If not, he was sent round to their houses to call them to the theatre. When there was a sudden change of play - as happened occasionally - his job was the 18th century equivalent of a modern telephone-call. With Beard living as far away as Red Lion Square one imagines that

[78] Powis Castle papers No. 21008 (NLW). This document covers the period from the death of the 2nd Marquis (the 'father') in 1745 until 'the same was purchased by Lord Powis' on 12th July 1751.
[79] This is equivalent to @£200,000 in present-day (2005) values
[80] Edward Webb, their lawyer, died in October 1750. Isaac Strutt had been a witness to the 1746 Indenture and must have taken over their legal affairs.
[81] "By May of 1752 they had moved to the poor neighbourhood of Great Russell Street, Covent Garden. There were other indications besides their *déclassé* address that the Beards were now perhaps, in economic straits..." Biographical Dictionary of Actors, Southern Illinois University Press, 1973, 'Beard', p. 404

he was normally left to fend for himself. But Beard had a close friend, a fellow member of the Beefsteak Club, who lived in Russell Street. John [Jack] Armstrong (1709-79) was a local doctor, later appointed the physician to the Hospital for Lame, Maimed, and Sick Soldiers, who particularly looked after the health of actors and musicians. Charles Burney, who was successfully treated by him in 1751, noted that for theatrical people like himself he "constantly refused a fee".[82]

This Jack Armstrong, who wrote poetry and composed music - including amateur cantatas which Beard sang to him, and who loved the company of Beard and his fellow actors - was the most likely person to put him up during the time that Henrietta went to Chelsea.[83] Armstrong may even have been her physician and sent her there for her health. According to Burney the first thing that Armstrong did on his first visit to him was to "lift the sashes, to cool my room, and allow me to breathe pure air". The next thing was to remove him out of the centre of town to "the more elastic air" of a house in the suburbs. Armstrong wrote several medical works, and in "The Art of Preserving Health" he included these lines of poetry:

> *Fly the rank city, shun its turbid air;*
> *Breathe not the chaos of eternal smoke…*
> *It is not Air, but floats a nauseous mass*
> *Of all obscene, corrupt, offensive things.*[84]

Henrietta was ailing, and had been for some time. As early as 12 October 1748 she had written morbidly to her thirteen-year-old daughter "Tho' I am at present thank God in a situation of health that encourages me to hope that I may live to see my dearest daughter - yet - death we all know is uncertain: and I may (for my sins) be denied that satisfaction. I therefore my dearest sit down to make my last and only requests to you, and beseech and beg you by the affection you have ever proffered me … to comply with my desires."[85]

In a state of general decline (though it is not clear what her illness was) Henrietta may not have been seen out and about in society much at this time. But she must have been delighted when her husband was able to take part in the fund-raising *Messiah*s at the Foundling Hospital near their old home in the Red Lion Square area. It is significant that this is the year in which Beard performed 'gratis', rather than returning a portion of his fee as in the previous year. A man with money problems would be unlikely to do that. It is much more likely that the couple had decided to espouse Thomas Coram's noble cause. In 1753 it must have been a troubled man who sang *Messiah* for Handel on May 1. But he managed to mask it, as no sign of his concerns for his wife's health were perceived by the audience. Thomas Harris, who was present, noticed that there was "… no sort of accuracy in the instruments" - possibly because J.C. Smith was at the helm for the first time – but wrote "… the voices did well".[86]

At the end of the month, on May 31, Henrietta died "…at three o'clock in the morning, at her lodgings in Chelsea… A Lady endowed with eminent Accomplishments and every female Virtue; lamented by all who had the Honour of

[82] 'Memoirs of Dr Charles Burney', Univ. of Nebraska Press, 1988, p. 104
[83] [83] "…Dr John Armstrong (d.1779) who lived in Russell Street, Covent Garden, and was a physician to actors" BDA p.100.
[84] 'Memoirs of Dr Charles Burney', Univ. of Nebraska Press, 1988, p. 104-5
[85] Waldegrave Family Papers, Chewton House, Chewton Mendip, Somerset
[86] Rosemary Dunhill & Donald Burrows p. 290

her Friendship; to whom she has left the Example of a well-spent Life, the last Moments of which were attended with a Fortitude, which always accompanies a spotless Conscience and an upright Heart".[87]

William Havard's Epitaph for Lady Henrietta Beard ascribes her death to a heart that had been broken by the treatment she had received from her closest family and relations. Havard had been a great admirer of hers, and wrote affectionately to her, and about her, in his "Jeu d'esprit", from which this previously unpublished m/s poem comes.

Epitaph for Lady Henrietta Beard

This task is mine, I must inscribe this Stone;
And for bad Numbers let the Heart atone.
Nobility adorn'd this virtuous Dame;
Yet not by Birth did she aspire to Fame:
The duties of the Mother and the Wife
Shone strongly forth, and marked a blameless Life.
Yet in her high pursuit of Excellence,
With gent'lest Manners fraught, and clearest Sense...
Kindred Unkindness threw a fatal Dart;
It miss'd her Virtues – but it pierced her Heart.[88]

Henrietta was buried in St Pancras Old Church, a favourite amongst Catholics as it was reputed to be the last church in England where the Latin Mass was still celebrated. Her grave was close to the church, at the south-eastern corner, near the graves of other members of the Webb family. It would not have been disturbed by the building of the railway line into St Pancras Station, but has now been removed. The bulbous shape of this distinctive tomb can be clearly identified on several old prints, and the details of the coats-of-arms on it were drawn and copied in the nineteenth century.[89]

---

[87] Newspaper report, Friday June 1st 1753
[88] William Havard, 'Jeu d'esprit', N.a.2. Folger Shakespeare Library, Washington
[89] B. Lib. Manuscripts - Add. 27488 (p. 81+) - Monumental Inscriptions by Charles Booth

MARRIED LIFE WITH HENRIETTA

During the fourteen years of her marriage to Beard Henrietta learned to live a different life from the one that she was expecting. Many doors were now permanently closed to her. Polite society had decided that she was *persona non grata*. This embarrassing situation continued to be remembered for a long time afterwards. Some thirty years later, a scurrilous poem was published about the Duchess of Manchester. It listed the scandals that had been previously attached to other titled ladies, and includes the lines:

> She's better sure than *Scudamore*
> Who while a Duchess, play'd the whore,
> As all the world has heard;
> Wiser than *Lady Harriet* too,
> Whose foolish match made such a do,
> And ruin'd her and *Beard.* [90]

So Henrietta had to find consolation in her husband's friends, and share his interests. This is a part of Beard's story which is not well chronicled. But certain things emerge. Her name appears in the lists of people subscribing to the publications of music. She was proud enough of her new status to always refer to herself as Lady Henrietta Beard. She is included in the 1743 list of subscribers to William Boyce's Serenata *Solomon*, and the 1747 list for his *Twelve Sonatas* for two violins. Boyce and Beard were close friends. When Boyce took over as Master of the King's Band he wrote fine arias for Beard in the Court Odes. Beard accompanied him to Cambridge when he received his Doctorate. Beard put various theatre commissions his way and took part in their subsequent productions. In this way he helped to establish Boyce as a theatrical composer to rival Thomas Arne in his two popular afterpieces *The Chaplet* (1749) and *The Shepherd's Lottery* (1751). [91] He also persuaded Garrick to commission a *Dirge* from him to rival the one that Arne had inserted into *Romeo and Juliet* at Covent Garden in 1750. Fiske describes Boyce's music as having "far more substance and genuine feeling". [92] It was sung in every production at Drury Lane for the next century. Henrietta would have shared this friendship, and would have been pleased to have accompanied her husband to Court, to hear the Odes that their friend had written. She obviously made many other friends amongst Beard's circle of friends. Her purchase of harpsichord music shows that she continued to take pleasure in the skill she had learned at Navestock as a young girl. Some of these works may have been composed by their musician friends. In 1747 she subscribed to 'Eight setts of lessons for the Harpsichord' by another Chapel Royal musician James Nares; in 1750 to 'Eight lessons for the Harpsichord' by Thomas Gladwin; and also in 1750 to 'Twelve songs with Symphonies' by the female composer Elizabeth Turner. Although this is not likely to be a related matter, but may rather explain some of her medical problems, she

---

[90] Ode by Earl Nugent: Vol. 3, 'The New Foundling Hospital for Wit' (British Library 239 g.27. New Edition in 6 Vols. (1784). Not included in earlier Editions)

[91] "These compositions, with occasional single songs for Vauxhall and Ranelagh, disseminated the fame of Dr Boyce throughout the kingdom, as a dramatic and miscellaneous composer". Charles Burney, 'A General History of Music', New York, 1957, vol. 2, p. 493

[92] Fiske, 'English Theatre Music in the 18th Century', Oxford, 1973, p.217

also subscribed to 'An historical, critical and practical treatise of the gout' by Thomas Thompson.

Amongst the group of actors that Beard worked with every day she may have been reluctant to be too familiar at first. But as time wore on she found some that were respectable, and that she could feel happy to invite into her home. The actor William Havard, Beard's good friend from Drury Lane, who was in the casts of his very first shows there, has left us a glimpse of life in their household. His manuscript collection of odds and ends, 'Jeu d'esprit', contains an assortment of writings that show how much affection he had for her. There is a poem 'On the Birthday of Lady Henrietta Beard' which, in its garbled and envious way, tries to express the love that he saw that the couple had for each other:

> Shall I, dear Jack, address my Lay
> To you, upon this joyous day? –
> Or to the bounteous Dame that gives
> The Happiness my friend receives?...
>
> What starts of Pleasure must she feel! –
> We'll publish what she would conceal;
> Count all her acts of Goodness o'er,
> Try every Art to find her Store.
>
> First then – when Merit she espy'd
> In my Friend's Honesty; - No Pride
> Of titled Birth could make her say
> 'Avaunt! – thou art Plebeian Clay'.
> 'Twas Worth she valued – Worth she saw –
> And Worth to Worth is Reason's Law.
>
> Resolved the married State to prove
> Possest of equal Truth and Love –
> They only to be happy strove...
>
> But I digress: - Say, Johnny, say,
> What didst thou feel upon that Day
> That made her thine? - Was not thy Breast
> Too narrow for its flutt'ring Guest?
> How rapid did the Current move
> Compos'd of Gratitude and Love!
> Yet, to see Thee thus blest all o'er
> Gave her a Joy - just ten times more.
>
> Next, when to smooth the brow of Care,
> And shut the Door against Despair,
> She try'd her lenient, healing Art -
> The Balm soft trickled to the Heart;
> And in restoring Peace to thee -
> She found her Height of Exstasy.

After this idyllic picture of two people happily in love, despite their different social class, and despite some unnamed 'Care' and 'Despair' of Beard's that Henrietta has soothed, Havard then gives us a glimpse of a friendly meal that he has shared with them:

> Say, shall the willing Muse reveal
> What passes at the friendly Meal!
> When, seating thy companions nigh,
> Glad Welcome smiles at either eye?
> Oh! Who can relish other Meat
> When in her looks you find the Treat!

A curious passage then follows. Quite what the 'virtue' was that Havard says he 'stole' is hard to tell. At this point the doggerel verse takes on a metaphysical tone:

> One of her Virtues t'other day
> I slily stole and brought away;
> When I came home, I used it well;
> My bosom was its place to dwell:
> I try'd all Ways its Love to gain -
> I tried all Kindness - but in vain;
> No gentleness could make it stay;
> 'Twas in your Parlour the next Day.

It is possible that, in a roundabout and poetic way, Havard is describing a kitten or cat that Henrietta had given to him. The animal had obviously found its own way back home to her. But the unusual metaphysical tone relieves the doggerel at this point. Henrietta and Beard kept a collection of animals, as we learn from another of Havard's letters, ending: "I will beg the favour of troubling your Ladyship with my Compliments to Captain Baugh (assuring him of my best wishes for his recovery) and to good Mr Pinkard – to Sawney, Coley and all enquiring friends…" 'Mr Pinkard' is mentioned in several other letters, and was obviously a long-lived cat. In 1753 Havard wrote a letter of condolence to Beard after Henrietta's death, and hoped that he would be gaining solace from its company: "I hope my dear Brother has, by this Time, made so happy an Use of …the well-tim'd assistance of Mr Pinkard, as to feel and enjoy the return of his wonted Peace of Mind…"[93]

Havard's unpublished manuscript contains several other writings that will be found elsewhere in this biography.[94] They are the only personal insight into Beard's private life at this time, and chart a long and supportive friendship, which one hopes gave Henrietta pleasure. The couple's mutual love, described in Havard's halting verse, was a long-lasting affection. Henrietta wrote a deeply felt letter, never-before published, to her daughter a few years before Barbara's wedding. At this time her health was beginning to fail. It is immensely touching, in the light of everything that she and Beard had endured since their scandalous secret wedding in 1739.

"My dearest child,   London, 12 of October 1748
…I leave to you, then, my Dearest, my Husband, the dearest kindest best of Husbands - one who has never made me repent my giving up the world for him. I leave him to you - to your generosity - and implore on my knees bread for the

---

[93] William Havard, 'Jeu d'esprit', N.a.2. Folger Shakespeare Library, Washington
[94] including the Epitaphs for 'Anna Beard' and 'Henrietta Beard'; and poems celebrating Beard's second marriage; as well as a response to Beard's suspicion that he could have warned him about the C.G. riot

dearest and best of Men - place him my dear Child above Want for his Life - if you either value y^r Mothers Memmory or blessing. Believe me my dearest Child he truly deserves ev'ry thing you can doe for him: for his behaviour speaks him to all a Man of Meritt - and his affection for me ought to be a recommendation to you - you will heir [*i.e. inherit*] my jointure - and consequently reap the benefit of that which undoes him - therefore my dear Child lett me beg of you to allow him for his Life two hundred pounds a year. ...by that means y^r fortune will not be impaired, he may retire and live happy, and my poor Soul rest in peace in the Grave. - For Oh my Child the thoughts of leaving the Man, the only Man on Earth I love in a State of beggary draws fountains from my Heart and Eyes: pity my distress I conjure you by your hopes of Heaven. I would likewise ask you to see him sometimes - Twill be a kindness to my Memmory - and a comfort to him ... I cannot see to wright for tears - my heart is tender. But when I think of the Miserys he is exposed to - oh my Child - what heart must I have if it did not bleed. Adieu. May God in his Infinitt Mercy bless you in this world and the Next - and Inspire you to perform what I have hear requested of you: pray for me: as I will with my latest breath for you. Your affectionate Mother and petitioner   Har: Beard [95]

Beard, too, expressed his love for Henrietta in a long inscription on her elaborate tomb, which concluded: "On the 8th of January 1739 she became the wife of Mr John Beard; who, during an happy union of 14 years, tenderly loved her person, and admired her virtues; who sincerely feels and laments his loss; and must for ever revere her memory, to which he consecrates this monument". [96]

The monument must have been an expensive one. Beard paid for the biggest tomb in the churchyard, and in the most prominent position. He was not embarrassed by this marriage, which others had thought so unwise. He wanted them to read his inscription, and see that their love had surmounted the social barriers. The tomb has long since disappeared. However, it was sketched many times in the 19th century (see page 84). One such sketch records the two coats-of-arms that were carved on it: one was Henrietta's, and the other was obviously that used by Beard. [97]

Beard's involvement with litigation and the Powis family did not end with Henrietta's death in 1753. [98] Now he found himself on the other side of the fence, and allied with the Earl of Powis as a defendant. As we have seen, as late as 1766 he was still being called on to give evidence in the case of Lady Mary Herbert's protracted dispute over her allowances. In 1755 he had been called to make a deposition in the dispute over the Wills of the 2nd and 3rd Marquises. [99] Although they had been dead for many years, probate of both these Wills had never been settled and the lawyers were still squabbling over whose estate should bear the costs of Henrietta's jointure payments. In this context, Beard declares that, although his wife had been granted Administration of her late husband's affairs, he *"doth not know nor can set forth whether Lady Henrietta possessed any part of the intestate's personal estate - he never having heard or been informed anything concerning the*

---

[95] Private letter in the Waldegrave archive at Chewton House
[96] The Gentleman's Magazine, February 1791
[97] In the 1930s, descendants of Beard's brother William still had possession of Beard's signet ring. This carried the same design, and had come to them as a bequest in Beard's Will. Unfortunately, its present whereabouts is unknown; but copies of the design were made at this time.
[98] The Gentleman's Magazine reported her death on p. 296 of the June 1753 edition: "May 31st: Lady Harriet Beard, wife of Mr Beard... by whose death a jointure of £600 per ann. devolves to E[arl] Powis
[99] Powis Castle papers No. 9204 (NLW)

same". He believed that Lord Edward had died insolvent, and that, if his wife had possessed any part of his estate, that she 'had only administered' them. This is somewhat surprising - one would have expected him to know precisely what his wife was doing. Beard then says that he had procured Letters of Administration for Henrietta's affairs, but had not acted upon them. He, personally, had not therefore acquired any of Lord Edward's personal estate. In consequence of this interrogation, the lawyers reapplied for Letters of Administration of Lord Edward's affairs.[100]

Barbara seems never to have taken any action regarding her mother's tender plea to help Beard financially. She seems to have cut him, and her mother's memory, out of her life altogether. Her husband, the Earl of Powis, in the years after his marriage, took further action to stabilise the family's finances, and sold several of the mortgaged estates. The first to be auctioned, in October 1756, was that of Hendon, near London.[101] There is a certain irony in the fact that the purchaser of the title of 'Lord of the Manor of Hendon' at this auction was a member of the profession that the Earl held in such low esteem. This was Beard's friend and colleague, David Garrick, with whom he was currently working at Drury Lane. David Garrick installed his nephew, Carrington Garrick, as Vicar in the very parish church where Henrietta's first husband, Lord Edward Herbert, lay buried.

EPILOGUE

The Waldegrave association with tenor singers did not end with the death of Henrietta. In the nineteenth century a successor to John Beard's roles on the English stage was John Braham (1774-1856). He sang at Drury Lane and was a favourite at the Three Choirs Festival before enjoying success in France and Italy. His daughter Frances (1821–79) married George Edward, the 7th Earl Waldegrave (1816-46) on September 28 1840. After his death, and her further marriages, she continued to refer to herself as Countess Dowager Waldegrave. In an ironic twist of fate Frances was left in possession of all the Waldegrave estates in Essex and elsewhere on his death. They included 3,000 acres in Navestock. Her husband is buried in St Thomas the Apostle Navestock, near John Beard's first father-in-law, the 1st Earl, and his brother-in-law, the 2nd Earl. The 1st and 2nd Earls share a common memorial on the North Chancel wall. One would never suspect, from the praise lavished on James in the inscription, that he had behaved so badly to his younger sister:

"...He was for many years the chosen Friend and Favourite of a King. He was as a Rock, with many Springs, and his generosity was as the waters that flow from it nourishing the Plains beneath ... He was a stranger to Resentment not to Injuries; ...Thus saith the widow of this incomparable man, his once most happy wife, Maria, Countess Dowager of Waldegrave, who inscribes this tablet to his blessed memory".

Maria was the illegitimate daughter of Sir Edward Walpole, and thus Horace Walpole's niece. She subsequently lost no time in secretly marrying King George III's brother, William Henry, the Duke of Gloucester. So the fulsome inscription on the elaborate monument that she put up when she allied herself with royalty must be taken with a pinch of salt. 'Generosity' was conspicuously not displayed to Henrietta; and 'Resentment' at her alliance with Beard was shown by James and his brother John, the 3rd Earl, for the whole of their lives.

---

[100] Powis Castle papers No. 13466 (NLW)
[101] Catalogue for the 1756 sale of the Hendon Estates (British Lib. 10350.e7). An Act of Parliament authorising this was passed in 1754.

CHAPTER 4
RESUMPTION OF WORK AT THE THEATRE

1. DRURY LANE: SEPTEMBER 1741 – MAY 1743

After his break from the theatre in 1740 Beard was desperate for work. But he didn't sing in the Oratorio season which ran from January 10 until April 8 1741 at Lincoln's Inn Fields theatre. It is a mystery why he didn't go cap in hand to Handel. Perhaps he felt that he had 'queered his pitch' with him; or learned that Handel had made definite arrangements to manage without him. Perhaps he approached him too late. Some works (such as *Deidamia*) no longer required a tenor; and for others (such as *L'Allegro* and *Acis*) a certain 'Mr Corfe'[1] had been engaged. This season was a significant one for Handel as it finally marked his move away from opera to oratorio. *Imeneo* and *Deidamia* were given their final performances. Handel would perform no more operas after this. He was not even certain of his next career move. London was not a place where his music was appreciated anymore. It was with delight that he took up the Lord Lieutenant of Ireland's invitation to visit Dublin.

For Beard there was nothing for it but to eat humble pie and beg for a job at one of the Patent theatres. He must have been desperate to regain his position at Drury Lane. In effect he had lost it utterly, since Fleetwood had replaced him with Thomas Lowe. Lowe had inherited all his roles, from 'Macheath' in the main-piece *Beggar's Opera* down to 'Sir John Loverule' in *The Devil to Pay*, and including the important operatic parts in Arne's *Comus* and *Rosamond*.

Charles Jennens, writing to James Harris on December 5 is the best authority for what was happening at this moment in time: "Beard is come home again, and should have gone with Handel into Ireland, but Fleetwood said he should want him to sing in an English opera. Handel took only Miss Edwards and one Mrs Maclean with him…"[2]

Henrietta would no doubt have preferred to stay in London, and sort out her financial problems. She cannot, at this time, have realised how long and impossible a task it would be. Beard, one suspects, stayed in London and turned down Handel's offer of joining him in Dublin in order to be at her side and support her. Had he gone with Handel he would have sung in the world-premiere of *Messiah*, and would have had the title role in *Imeneo,* besides repeating his roles in *Acis*, *L'Allegro*, *Esther* and *Alexander's Feast*. Handel must have sorely missed him. Donald Burrows explains in the Preface to his edition of the opera how the loss of Beard forced Handel to completely rethink the composition of *Imeneo*: "There is no other opera in which revisions were made on such a comprehensive scale. Handel had to take into account some important differences between the cast of voices that he now had available and the voice-types for which he had prepared the score in 1738 & 1739… In the previous drafts of the score (and possibly at the time of his original plans in 1740) *Imeneo* had been written for the tenor voice, probably with the expectation that John Beard would take the part…"[3]

---

[1] The BDA and Winton Dean give no first name for this singer, but he was probably James, who was born c.1718. From about 1735 he had sung small parts in Handel's oratorios, (Israelite in *Esther* and Abner in *Saul*, both in 1740) but was given bigger roles in 1741 during Beard's absence.
[2] Burrows & Dunhill *Music and Theatre in Handel's World*, p. 129
[3] 'Preface' *Imeneo* ed. D. Burrows, Hallische Händel-Ausgabe, Bärenreiter 2002

Beard's luck turned in September 1741 and he was invited by Fleetwood to come back to Drury Lane for two years. It must have been a very different contract that he signed: Fleetwood had taken him back despite having Thomas Lowe on his roster. Thus he was over-provided with tenors. As a result the work-load was divided between them. Beard found himself with less stage performances than normal[4], but with more singing to do between the Acts. What the 'English Opera' might have been, for which Fleetwood was said to have wanted him, is not at all clear.

Beard and Lowe alternated in the role of *Macheath*, which was played about four times a month. But otherwise there was no remarkable new role for him. It appears that Fleetwood simply took pity on the unfortunate singer (and his sadly disinherited wife) and gave him his old job back, without any real thought for how he could sensibly employ him. With Handel in Dublin there was not even a London oratorio season in which Beard could show off his vocal prowess. He persuaded Fleetwood to let him resume his roles in *Comus*, *The Provok'd Wife* and *The Lottery*; and also returned to the singing witches in *Macbeth*. When Shakespeare's *As You Like It* was revived in May 1742 with music by Arne, he took the role of 'Amiens' and sang 'Under the greenwood tree', 'When Daisies pied' and 'Blow, blow thou winter wind' in settings which quickly became firm national favourites.

As they were both on Fleetwood's books for this short period of their careers it is not surprising to learn of Beard and Thomas Lowe teaming up as a double act. The 'Biographical Dictionary of Actors' refers to Beard's "...'speciality acts', whether *solus* or with Vernon or Lowe or others in comic or pathetic dialogue" which "were the delight of the audiences" – and describes one of these as a "knock-down *duo* rendition of "Bumper Squire Jones".[5] As the playbills reveal, Beard and Lowe alternated each night in their favourite songs, but finally came together for their duo rendition of "Bumper Squire Jones", and a 'Battle Song' by Arne which was advertised as:

'the Representation of a Battle of the two Operatical Generals Per gli Signori Giovanni and Tomasino detti Beard and Lowe'.

Towards the end of the season Beard must have been delighted to be given a couple of choice roles. In the farce *Miss Lucy in Town* he was given the opportunity to make fun of the current stock of Italian singers employed at the King's Theatre. Kitty Clive acted opposite him as the female lead in this sequel to *The Virgin Unmask'd* by Henry Fielding. From Horace Walpole we learn that: "...there is a simple farce at Drury Lane, called Miss Lucy in Town in which Mrs Clive mimics the Muscovita [Signora Panichi] admirably, and Beard, Amorevoli[6] tolerably. But the *run* [i.e. 'vogue'] is now after Garrick, a wine-merchant, who is turned player, at Goodman Fields".[7] The other offering was a role in Buckingham's *The Rehearsal*. This was a popular burletta dating from 1671 which still received an average of eight performances a season. Kitty Clive decided to try out some cross-dressing and play the male lead 'Bayes'. The public was not convinced, and James Winston reported that "she did it most wretchedly". However, it set her thinking; and in time she came up with a farce of her own, *The Rehearsal or Bayes in*

---

[4] At this time – apart from *The Beggar's Opera* - he averaged 2 performances a month. All his other performances were of interval songs. In 1742-3 he added *The Conscious Lovers* to his repertoire.
[5] BDA, 'John Beard', p. 402-3
[6] Angelo Amorevoli (tenor) was in the opera company at the King's Theatre from the autumn of 1741: see Deutsch *Handel a Documentary Biography* pp. 520-528
[7] Horace Walpole to H. Mann, May 26th 1742, quoted in Deutsch *Handel a Documentary Biography* p. 549

Petticoats, in which she would appear on stage in a double role, as the Authoress 'Mrs Hazard' and as herself. (See Chapter 8 'The Garrick Years'.) In this Beard would appear as himself and as 'Corydon', the hero of William Boyce's inserted *Masque*.

2. HANDEL: 1742-1747

Handel was back in London by September 1742, having left Dublin on August 13. He kept his cards close to his chest regarding his next plans for an oratorio season, only telling Charles Jennens "...Whether I shall do something in the Oratorio way (as several of my friends desire) I can not determine as yet".[8] But he spent October finishing the oratorio *Samson*, which he had left incomplete before setting off for his visit to Ireland. The title role was written for a tenor. John Beard's was the voice that he had in mind for the hero. The twenty-seven-year-old singer was soon going to be back in Handel's company. His long absence in 1740-2, which had forced Handel to make some unsatisfactory alternative arrangements, was to be forgotten. Beard was about to get some of the best musical roles of his career.

His theatrical career had now resumed as though there had been no interruption, and he never missed a further season until his retirement in 1767. He remained as busy as ever. After two years back at Drury Lane, sharing roles with Thomas Lowe, the two singers decided to split up and divide the work between them. When a position for a lead singer became available at Covent Garden it was Beard who opted to move, leaving each one free to have the first choice of identical roles at the rival houses.

Thomas Busby described how this friendly rivalry helped the box office takings at both theatres. "Beard gratified the pit and boxes at Covent Garden, and Lowe charmed the galleries at Drury Lane. The managers of each theatre, by way of securing two crowded audiences between them, agreed that these singers should perform one night together at each house, and that, between the acts, both should execute some one song chosen by themselves; but not the same song at both theatres. They began at Drury Lane, where they sang, successively, Galliard's fine hunting song of "The Early Horn"; in which Beard's neatness of execution, and felicity of expression, carried the palm. The air selected for Covent Garden was Arne's noble composition "Rise, Glory, Rise!" a melody that offered full scope to the clear, open, and powerful tones of Lowe, and procured him, in turn, the honour of a victory. On each of these occasions the people began to assemble at the doors three hours before they were opened, and the theatre was crowded to suffocation."[9]

Beard spent five years on the roster at Covent Garden Theatre (Nov. 1743 – May 1748), and this coincided with the period when he did some of his best work for Handel. In these years he created the title role in *Samson* (February 18 1743), *Belshazzar* (27 March 1745) and *Judas Maccabaeus* (April 1 1747). As all of these are virile roles, with a mixture of lyrical and martial vocal writing, it is significant that Handel chose a tenor, rather than a baritone or castrato, for the principal role. It is interesting to compare the arias that were being written for Beard by other composers at this period. In the New Year and Birthday Odes, which he sang annually for Greene and Boyce, he always took the martial and spirited music. Handel himself had first hand experience of how he sang 'The Trumpet's loud

---

[8] Handel to Jennens, September 9th 1742, quoted in Deutsch *Handel a Documentary Biography* p. 554
[9] Thomas Busby, 'Concert Room and Orchestra Anecdotes", London 1825, vol. 2, p. 122

clangour' in the *St Cecilia Ode* and 'The Princes applaud' in *Alexander's Feast*. An added strength must have come into Beard's voice by this time, in addition to the flexibility which had been required in earlier arias such as 'And let all the people say: Alleluia, Amen' in the 1734 *Wedding Anthem*, and many of the arias in *L'Allegro*. When Handel composed *Samson* he gave Beard the challenge of singing both florid music ('Why does the God of Israel sleep') and lyrical airs ('Thus when the Sun', 'Total eclipse'.)[10] In addition, he was able to utilise his undoubted dramatic talents in the more operatic encounters, such as those with 'Delilah' and 'Harapha'. In Winton Dean's words "It was probably the growing success of Beard, who had been singing Handel's tenor parts since 1734, that suggested the revolutionary notion of a tenor 'Samson'. It was a tribute to Beard himself and to English practice, and of some historical importance. *Samson* was Handel's first great tenor part, and one of the earliest in dramatic music outside France".[11]

1743 was also the year that Beard first sang in *Messiah* (March 23, 25 and possibly 29). This was the London premiere of Handel's *New Sacred Oratorio*. From the evidence of the conducting score Burrows has deduced that Beard may have been unwell for one of the three performances.[12] His name is pencilled against *Comfort ye & Every valley* and *How beautiful are the feet* (a recomposition of the 1st version). Thereafter Burrows describes how Avolio's name is pencilled on top of Beard's in various places, suggesting that last minute changes had taken place at some stage. He isn't able to confirm that Beard "fell out from the cast" or that his role in *Samson* was taken by Thomas Lowe on March 31. But he states that Beard "disappears from the advertisements for concerts for a month".

Actually, that is not quite the evidence contained in the 'The London Stage'[13]. The most compelling evidence that he had been ill is an entry in the Winston m/s that he did not sing the arduous role of 'Macheath' on April 5. It is possible that he 'ducked out' of singing ballads in the interval at Drury Lane on April 4. Alternatively he may have been well enough to do a small amount of singing, and simply baulked at doing his most arduous role whilst not fully recovered. Thereafter he resumed his activities on the 6th; and is found singing every day in April. He was in the main-piece *Comus* on April 14 and was well enough to resume *The Beggar's Opera* on April 26. His illness, therefore, was most likely confined to the period 29 March to 5 April. He would have missed two performances with Handel. Here is the relevant timetable:

March / April 1743	Drury Lane	Covent Garden Theatre
Mon 21 March	interval songs	
Tues 22 March	The Beggar's Opera: Beard's 'Benefit'	
Wed 23 March		Messiah [*1ˢᵗ London perf.*]
Thurs 24 March	interval songs	
Fri 25 March		Messiah
Sat 26 March	interval songs	
Mon 28 March	--	
Tues 29 March		Messiah [*Beard ill?*]

---

[10] All of these subsequently entered his repertoire for performance at miscellaneous concerts.
[11] Winton Dean *Handel's Dramatic Oratorios and Masques*, p. 333
[12] Burrows *Handel's performances of 'Messiah': the evidence of the conducting score* ML 56 (1975) p.326
[13] see: The London Stage Part 3 [1729 – 1747], ed. Arthur H. Scouten, pp. 826 ff

Wed 30 March	--	
Thurs 31 March		Samson [*Beard ill?*]
Fri 1 April	--	
Sat 2 April	--	
Mon 4 April	'Song by Beard' [*Was he well enough to sing this?*]	
Tues 5 April	The Beggar's Opera: "*Beard ill and did not act*"[14]	
Wed 6 April	"Stella and Flavia", 'a Ballad by Beard'	

The fact that Beard was so busy at the theatre in the spring season and that he always tried to be free for Handel's oratorios led to other occasions when he was not on his top form. London's notoriously cold weather often prevented performances from taking place. It was the same cold that led to other singers being unwell and failing to sing. Mrs Cibber was notorious for cancelling. However, it is apparent that Beard kept going as long as he could, even when he was smitten. In the prompter's book for a performance in 1750 we read this report on Beard's performance of the title role in *Robin Hood* (Charles Burney's Burletta): "Mr Beard hoarse. Mr Garrick made apology, but he sung very well."[15] Much the same thing may have been happening in 1744 when Beard was repeating his role of *Samson* on February 24. For Mrs Delany wrote to her sister on the next day: "I was last night to hear Samson. …Handel is mightily out of humour… for Beard has no voice at all."[16]

3. CONTRACT AT COVENT GARDEN 1743 - 1748

When Beard transferred to Covent Garden in October 1743 Thomas Lowe did not go to Drury Lane in a complete job-swap, but went instead to Ireland with the Arnes. Drury Lane was not a happy place to be. Fleetwood had by this time withdrawn his attention from the management of his theatre and left the day-to-day arrangements to Pierson, his deputy. Twelve of the principal actors and actresses, led by Macklin and Garrick, left *en masse* and attempted to form a company at the New Theatre in the Haymarket. But they were prevented by the Lord Chamberlain refusing the necessary licence. Fleetwood had replaced the rebel actors by members of the disbanded company at Goodman's Fields Theatre, so it was difficult for them to find work elsewhere. When Garrick realised their predicament and gave in, he and some of the rebels were allowed back into the fold. But they had lost some of their closely guarded rights. Kitty Clive reported that she "yielded so far to the necessity of the time as to act under a much less salary than several other performers on that stage, and submitted to pay a sum of money for [her] benefit, notwithstanding [that she] had had one clear of all expenses for nine years before".[17] Macklin, who had fomented the trouble, was left high and dry and had a disjointed career for the next five years.

    The conflict was given much publicity, and Fleetwood's incompetence became so obvious that he sold out to James Lacy in November 1744. James Lacy was formerly Rich's assistant manager at Covent Garden. In this time of to-ing and fro-ing between the theatres it was not only John Beard who would go where the

---

[14] Winston m/s from Dyer m/s [Folger Shakespeare Library] see: The London Stage Part 3 p. 1046

[15] from the Cross Diaries, December 15th 1750; quoted in *The London Stage*, Part 4, p. 226

[16] quoted in Deutsch *Handel a Documentary Biography* p. 585

[17] Troubridge, 'The Benefit System in the British Theatre', Society for Theatre Research, London, 1967, p. 21

prospects seemed most favourable. Kitty Clive spent the next two seasons at Covent Garden too; and Garrick himself went there from 1746-7, while he was planning his take-over at Drury Lane in joint partnership with Lacy.

Beard may have left his approach to Rich a little late in the day, as there was no work for him at Covent Garden until November. Where he might have been - or why he did not start at the theatre in September - will have to remain a mystery. Rich began his season with a run of performances of *The Beggar's Opera*. Perhaps he was assuming that Beard would have been with him in time for these, or perhaps he had not yet contracted him. At any rate, the role of 'Macheath' was initially taken by Oliver Cashell. Beard may, of course, have been tied up with court cases. This is a time when he was actively involved in Henrietta's affairs as the primary plaintiff. 1743 was the year in which he and Henrietta lodged an important Bill of Complaint. The new Bill[18] was essential to reflect the changes that were now due to her under her Marriage Settlement as a result of her turning 21, and her father dying.

John Rich must have found Beard's presence in his theatre company very agreeable, for this was the moment at which the singer was invited to join Rich's group of cronies in the 'Sublime Society of Beefsteaks'. Membership was very select, and limited to actors and their friends with a good sense of humour and love of fun (see Chapter 5). Work at the theatre began to mount up for him, too. The regular fare was given its usual airing, and he found himself required in the main-pieces *Comus*, *The Provok'd Wife* and *The Beggar's Opera* (from December 23). The farces that he knew from Drury Lane were also staple fare: *The Lottery*, *The Devil to Pay*, and *The Virgin Unmask'd*. With Kitty Clive in the company they were able to put on *Damon and Phillida*, that had not yet been seen in this theatre. Another piece that transferred with them was Shakespeare's *As You Like It*, with Arne's songs. In the intervals Kitty and Beard occasionally sang duets, such as the famous "Together let us range the Fields" from Boyce's recently published serenata "*Solomon*".[19] The pantomime *The Royal Chace* was put on again so that Beard could sing his famous hunting song; and then the new one in the New Year - *The Necromancer* - also involved him as 'The Shade of Leander'.

In the spring of 1744 Beard was fortunate to find that Handel's performances would be at Covent Garden theatre once again. Despite Mrs Delany's reservations about the state of his voice at the *Samson* performance on February 24, he must have recovered quickly, as he made no cancellations this Spring. In fact he completed a very full series of engagements with four performances of the new oratorio *Joseph and his Brethren* (March 2, 7, 9, 14), and two of *Saul* (March 16, 21). Prior to Mrs Delany's comments he had already sung *Jupiter* in the new quasi-oratorio *Semele*, (four performances beginning on February 10). Thus he had leading roles in all of Handel's twelve-night season. Of course this was only the tip of his workload, which – in the same period – included ten performances as 'Orpheus' in Lampe's *Orpheus and Eurydice*, and repeats of his other regular roles. After 25 years as 'Lun', Rich would make *Orpheus and Eurydice* the last show in which he regularly played the Harlequin. He managed to lure Henry Woodward ('Lun junior') away from Drury Lane at this troubled time to assist him. Thereafter Woodward was able to take over the role from Rich in a very smooth way. As a straight actor he was also to become a valuable all-rounder in the company.

---

[18] Records of Court of Chancery: Beard v Powis, C12/733/12 – Nat. Arch.
[19] Both Beard and Henrietta subscribed to the publication of this work, published in the Spring of 1743.

Orpheus and Eurydice had originally landed Rich in a considerable amount of trouble when a certain John Hill claimed that he had made unauthorised use of a libretto on the same theme that he had submitted to him a few years earlier. While this may well have been Rich's starting point, there was not enough of Hill's original left for him to legally claim any authorship. Hill printed his libretto with a detailed Preface, and there was a public reading of extracts from both, read alternately. The audience pronounced in favour of Rich.[20] None of John Frederick Lampe's music survives, not even 'Orpheus's' aria, sung by Beard and addressed to 'Pluto', (played by the 73-year-old Richard Leveridge) over which Hill had a particularly stupid argument about how many minutes it would last. Rich brought his usual stage-tricks into the production, including a huge clockwork serpent which frightened the ladies. The Scots Magazine for March 1740 carried a good description of this amazing attraction, which "…enters, performs its exercise of head, body, and tail in a most surprising manner, and makes behind the curtain with a velocity scarcely credible. It is about a foot and a half in circumference at the thickest part, and far exceeds the former custom of stuffing a bag into such a likeness. It is believed to have cost more than £200, and when the multitude of wings, springs etc. whereof it consists are considered, the charge will not appear extravagant". [21]

Rich had employed the well-known watchmakers Samuel and John Hoole to produce this fore-runner of the serpent which performed a similar function at the opening of Emmanuel Schikaneder's comic opera "The Magic Flute" (1791). There is such a similarity between Schikaneder's requirements for strange beasts, disappearing feasts, flying machines, quick changes of scenery etc. that one cannot help but think that he must have seen a Rich pantomime at some time or another.

In 1744 there were many threats to the stability of the nation. There was the ongoing war with Spain, which had been initially vindicated when British sea-power secured Porto Bello (in present day Panama) in November 1739. Since then Prime Minister Walpole had been discredited, and had been forced out of office in 1742. Earl Waldegrave's attempts, as British Ambassador in Paris, to prevent an escalation of hostilities came to nothing when he came home to die in 1740. George II had allowed the neutral electorate of Hanover to enter the fray, and personally led the 'Pragmatic Army' to victory at Dettingen in 1743. Ever more entangled in these European conflicts, Britain had finally made a formal declaration of war with France in 1744. A new, very real, fear was that the French would foment a new Jacobite uprising at home and supply it with men and armaments.

All of these worries meant that John Beard was very busy at Covent Garden singing patriotic ballads in the intervals. Handel's *Dettingen* Te Deum was performed in honour of the victorious King's return to Court in November 1743. After a lull when London quietened down and enjoyed its New-Year theatrical fare, the mood had changed by mid-March. Thereafter Beard was called upon to sing rousing songs like "To Arms", and "Britons strike home" on most evenings. The theatre searched for a patriotic melody to lift the spirits of their audiences. There was no obvious choice. The works of Purcell and Handel were scoured. Beard sang "The trumpet's loud clangour excites us to arms" from Handel's *St Cecilia's Day* Ode on April 17; and, commencing in March, a fine aria with trumpet obbligato from

[20] Fiske, 'English Theatre Music in the Eighteenth Century', Oxford, 1973, p.165-6
[21] quoted in Fiske, 'English Theatre Music in the Eighteenth Century', Oxford, 1973, p.92

Purcell's *Don Quixote,* with words by Thomas Durfey: "Genius of England" (see next chapter).

But none of these pieces quite answered the current need, although the concluding section of Handel's *Coronation Anthem* 'Zadok the Priest' made a rousing effect when sufficient voices could be gathered together. How the theatres encouraged their house-composers towards the composition of a National Anthem will be explored in the next chapter.

In the autumn of 1744 Handel experimented with a longer season commencing on November 3. He had to move over to the King's Theatre Haymarket since this season was no longer going to be confined to Lent, when he could usually expect to rent Rich's theatre at Covent Garden. Rich was still obliging however. He made Beard (who was now in his second season at Covent Garden) available for Handel[22], and did not require him to rush back for after-pieces as he previously had to do when on contract at Drury Lane. Handel had written two new works: another quasi-oratorio *Hercules*, in which Beard would sing *Hyllus*; and *Belshazzar*, in which the title role had been conceived for his voice. But he began with two performances each of *Deborah* and *Semele*. In *Deborah* the role of *Sisera* was transposed for Beard.[23] Worries about the singer's health surfaced once again in a letter written by the 4th Earl of Radnor to James Harris a few days after the first of the two *Deborah* performances: "Mr Beard, although in great measure come to his hearing, yet is sometimes out of tune..."[24]

But this shrewd judge was satisfied with Beard's performance a few week's later in *Hercules* when he wrote "...Francesina did excellently..., as also Beard."[25] The mention of Beard's 'hearing' is ominous. For a musician it is a desperately important thing to have perfect hearing. This sporadically recurring problem of his was never properly cured. It had the ability to surface at unforeseen times. For the next twenty years Beard would do battle with it, and valiantly continue with his career. But it was ultimately going to triumph and cause him to retire early at the age of 52. Quite when the problems had started in 1744 is hard to pin down. If the Earl of Radnor is writing about Beard having recovered by the *Deborah* performance on November 3 one would expect to see some signs of him having been indisposed prior to this. But there is no evidence that he missed any theatre performances in October. Handel's letter of October 2 to Jennens stating that "Mr Beard ...is recovered" narrows the gap; but Beard was well enough to commence the autumn season on September 26 with a double-bill of *As You Like It* and *The Devil to Pay*. Fortunately for him, the illness must have occurred in the quiet summer months.

After the performances of *Hercules* in January 1745 Handel halted his oratorio programme due to a lack of public interest: "*To what cause I must impute the loss of the publick favour I am ignorant... I beg permission to stop short, before my losses are too great to support.*"[26] He had announced a series of twenty-four performances, and only six had yet taken place. Beard was probably not too bothered, as he had an exceptionally full list of engagements in January and February. All of his usual after-pieces were in the Covent Garden repertoire, and - for main-pieces - in each month he sang one performance of *The Beggar's Opera*

[22] "since so obligingly he gave leave to Mr Beard & Mr Reinhold." Handel to Jennens, 9 June 1744.
[23] Winton Dean *Handel's Dramatic Oratorios and Masques*, p. 238
[24] Burrows & Dunhill *Music and Theatre in Handel's World*, p. 204
[25] January 8th 1745, to James Harris. Burrows & Dunhill *Music and Theatre in Handel's World*, p. 210
[26] Daily Advertiser, 17th January 1745 quoted in Deutsch *Handel a Documentary Biography* p. 602

and four of *Comus*. Lampe's *Orpheus and Eurydice* was still popular and enjoyed thirteen more performances. It was then replaced by his *Pyramus and Thisbe* in which Beard sang *Pyramus* a further thirteen times before Handel was persuaded to resurrect his oratorio season. Handel had made a mistake in starting as early as November. He was still thinking of oratorio as a replacement for opera. Only gradually did it dawn on him that he would do better by concentrating his performances into the Lent season, when other entertainments were curtailed. This pattern only begins to emerge, tentatively, from Lent 1746.

Lampe's *Pyramus and Thisbe* sounds like a lot of fun, and shows that Benjamin Britten, in the 20th century, was not the only composer who could provide a humorous burlesque version of this scene from Shakespeare's *A Midsummer Night's Dream*. There was a sufficient difference between the lofty tones of *opera seria* and the earthy ones of *ballad opera* in this period for Lampe to make great humour out of it. His overture and arias survive in a contemporary publication, without the linking recitatives. But from these it should be possible to mount a modern-day revival. The one-act burletta opens with the composer, 'Mr Semibreve', and the prompter discussing the business of putting the opera on to impress some important friends. 'Semibreve' then enters with the two friends, and remarks:

"One of these Gentlemen having made a tour of Italy, has but little Taste for our home-spun English Entertainments, nor has he yet got the better of his foreign prejudice. But, between you and I, I don't doubt, when he has heard a little of this piece, I shall bring him over to our opinion; and let him see the English Tongue is as fit for Musick as any foreign Language of 'em all."

The opera that follows is all-sung, with many humorous responses to Shakespeare's witty verse. Lampe responds to its 'over-the-top' sentiments much as Britten was to do, two hundred years later. There is a dramatic, Handelian, opera seria aria for Beard - as 'Pyramus' - addressing the Wall: "O wicked, wicked wall!"

His suicide aria is, likewise, a parody of operatic clichés, to the text "Approach, ye furies fell. O Fates, come, come, come, Cut thread and thrum, Quail, crush, conclude, and quell". At the end of the mock-tragedy 'Pyramus' and 'Thisbe' both come back to life, and sing a lively duet "Thus folding, Beholding, Caressing, Possessing" as an *Epilogue*. Beard's ability to slip from popular ballads into the high serious tone of Handel's Italian opera arias, coupled with the ability to parody the contemporary Italian singers, which he had first shown two years earlier in *Miss Lucy in Town*, made this a successful role for him. It received nineteen performances in its first season, and fourteen the next.

When Handel's 1745 season recommenced on March 1 there were two revivals each of *Samson, Saul, Joseph, Messiah* and three of *Belshazzar*. Burrows and Dean outline some alterations to the casting of this last work, occasioned by Mrs Cibber being unavailable (probably for contractual reasons) at one of the performances. It was possibly the last one, which took place at a distance from the others, after the Lent period had ended, on April 23.[27] Because Beard was a good musician and a quick learner he was given some of Gobrias' music to perform[28] as well as his own, when Reinhold shifted from his original role of 'Gobrias' to Mrs Cibber's 'Cyrus'.

At the 1745 performances (9 & 11 April) *Messiah* was also subjected to some alterations that involved Beard. His name is pencilled by the abridged soprano aria 'Rejoice greatly' in its 4/4 tempo version (version B). Larsen states that "Beard must be assumed to have been the first to sing the new form."[29] It appears that Handel did not intend taking the aria away from his soprano soloist (who resumed it at the next performance in 1749) but made the allocation as a stop-gap in an emergency situation. Once again we may assume that Beard stepped into the shoes of an indisposed colleague.[30] In addition, he sang all of the arias that had originally been allocated to the tenor voice at the London premiere in 1743.[31]

4. THE JACOBITE REBELLION: 1745-1746

The autumn of 1745 was a time of great fear throughout England on account of Bonnie Prince Charlie's seemingly unstoppable advance towards London with his Jacobite army. He had planted his standard in Scotland on November 8, and progressed steadily southwards, reaching Derby on December 4. The theatres in London endeavoured to keep open and support the Hanoverian regime with a deluge of patriotic ballads - one of which was written by Handel.[32] A few months earlier Horace Walpole had written: "It is quite the fashion to talk of the French coming here. Nobody sees it in any other light but as a thing to be talked about, not to be precautioned against. ...I am persuaded that when Count Saxe, with ten thousand men, is within a day's march of London, people will be hiring windows to see them pass by". As things turned out, the satirical Walpole got things wrong when the advancing army that he had predicted was composed of Highlanders. The ensuing panic was worst on December 6, 'Black Friday', when there was a run on the Bank of England as news spread that there was no British force between London and Derby to stop the advance. John Beard sang every night, and included all the patriotic numbers that he had sung earlier in the year.

What was wanted was something grand and patriotic, but which could still be performed by the small group that was employed for the theatrical interval music. It was Thomas Arne who would achieve lasting glory by discovering and arranging a suitable tune; whilst John Beard would create a little history by singing it onstage. The next chapter will detail the story of the evolution of the 'National Anthem'.

---

[27] Winton Dean *Handel's Dramatic Oratorios and Masques*, p. 455; Burrows *Handel* Oxford, p. 281
[28] "He reset the movement [no. 55 Air 'To pow'r immortal'] as a recitative for tenor. ... Apart from this the only substantial new movement was a recomposed air for no. 7 ['Oppress'd with never ceasing grief'] in G major, also for Beard as the tenor Gobrias". Burrows *Preface* New Novello Choral Edition of *Belshazzar* 1993
[29] Jens Peter Larsen *Handel's Messiah: Origins - Composition —Sources* London 1957, New York 1972 p. 221
[30] "This is no more than a change enforced by special circumstances". Jens Peter Larsen *ibid.* p. 133
[31] "Beard's entries, often written at the top left-hand corner of the page, seem designed mainly to restore him to his part". Burrows *Handel's performances of 'Messiah': the evidence of the conducting score* ML 56 p.327
[32] see next chapter

The season 1745-6 was also a difficult one for Handel. His health was not good, and he wrote no new works during the autumn. Only when the New Year arrived was he well enough to think about what he could give his public next. About January[33] he compiled a new oratorio - the *Occasional Oratorio* - to meet the current patriotic mood. He only managed to mount three performances of it during Lent.[34] There were also less singers available than usual, as we learn from a letter of William Harris: "He has but three voices for his songs - Francesina, Reinholt and Beard..."[35] As far as Handel was concerned, this was as much as he felt that he could do this season. Any of his subscribers who had felt short-changed after the curtailed previous season were now dealt with, having been given free tickets for these performances. According to the Earl of Shaftesbury: "...He rather gets [i.e. makes a profit] than loses by his Houses. However, as he has obliged his former subscribers without detriment to himself, he is contented".[36]

Meanwhile the London Theatres had survived the Jacobite threat and were doing good business, having retained the loyalty of their clientele. Beard sang at Covent Garden on virtually every night from January to April. When not employed in his usual main- and after-pieces he sang rousing patriotic ballads. As the threat would not be completely eradicated until after the Battle of Culloden (16 April), there was still plenty of scope for him to reprise 'Genius of England', 'God bless our noble King', 'The English Hero's Welcome Home' and other "New Occasional Ballads". From April 25, by which time news of the victory at Culloden had reached London, his repertoire included "An Occasional song on the Defeat of the Rebels" - which may well have been the song 'From scourging Rebellion' [HWV 228] set by Handel. Curiously, the trio from Handel's *Acis and Galatea* became popular as interval music at this time. Could the raging monster 'Polypheme' have been seen as some kind of metaphor for the Jacobites disturbing the settled content of the arcadian landscape in which the 18th century upper classes liked to imagine that they lived?

During the Summer of 1746 Beard added a new ingredient to his usual commitments as Vocalist at Ranelagh Gardens by accepting an invitation from his actor friends William Havard, John Dunstall and James Bencraft to join them in a season of performances at Twickenham and Richmond. Consequently he fitted in performances of 'Macheath' at the new theatres emerging in a corner of the suburbs which was rapidly developing into the playground of the wealthy. Whilst there he would have seen how agreeable the villas were that lined the Thames. Poets and playwrights had joined the aristocracy living there. Pope was famous for his villa at 'Twitnam' [Twickenham] with its Grotto, as was Horace Walpole at his Gothick 'Strawberry Hill'. Handel's librettist Thomas Morell lived there, as well as the painters Thomas Hudson and Samuel Scott. In 1754 this leafy area would also become David Garrick's retreat; and, after him, there was a veritable procession of theatrical types moving in, including Kitty Clive, Hannah Pritchard, Thomas Rosoman (of Sadler's Wells) and Beard himself.

---

[33] Unusually Handel's m/s bears no composition date except 'Anno 1746' at the beginning.
[34] February 14, 19, 26
[35] quoted in Deutsch *Handel a Documentary Biography* p. 629
[36] Burrows & Dunhill *Music and Theatre in Handel's World*, p. 225

5. THEATRE WORK 1746-7

Beard began his performances at Covent Garden late in 1746. As his first appearance appears to be 'Macheath' on December 11 he must either have had a recurrence of his deafness, which was first noted in October 1744, or had been travelling with Henrietta. There are no known references to foreign travel at this time; but it is likely that she visited her daughter Barbara in Bruges from time to time. Beard also had a brother in Devon. The only time when his commitments would allow him to make the arduous 2- or 3-day journey to Kenton would be in the early autumn.

When he returned to work, the cast of *The Beggar's Opera* was a strong one. Several of the usual Drury Lane cast were still at Covent Garden, including the famous tragedians Mrs Cibber and Mrs Pritchard, who took the roles of 'Polly' and 'Lucy'. William Havard, his very close friend, was also in the company.

There were not many new pieces for Beard to add to his standard repertory this season. He had a singing role in Shakespeare's *Henry VIII*, and a more substantial role as the 'Hunter' in Charles Coffey's ballad opera *Phebe or the Beggar's Wedding*. But we learn more about his finances for this year from extant Covent Garden accounts. For his first 9 days performances he was paid £7 10s. This means that his weekly wage had not risen much above the £5 that he had been receiving in 1740. His Benefit night still brought him in a colossal amount which virtually doubled his year's salary. On the 26 March 1747 he received £94 15s from sales at the door, and £102 9s from tickets sold in advance. Out of this total of £197 4s he had to pay the house-charges of £60 (see Chapter 12 for an explanation of these) which left him with a profit of £137 4s.[37]

The Covent Garden accounts also reveal that Handel paid the sum of £210 for the use of Covent Garden on ten nights during Lent 1747. Handel had recovered his health enough to make a considered response to the Jacobite defeat at Culloden. This was an oratorio of more substance than the hurriedly assembled *Occasional Oratorio*. But it came from his pen very quickly, between July 9 and August 11 1746, just three month's after the Duke of Cumberland's victory. The story of the guerilla warfare perpetrated by the sons of Hasmon against the Seleucids is not a very apposite one: but nobody seemed to notice at the time. If the celebratory theme was to be of a small doughty army fighting against the odds for its traditional religion, then the story of *Judas Maccabaeus* might have seemed equally relevant from the other perspective. But Handel's response was in perfect accord with that of his librettist, Thomas Morell, who saw it as an allegory of the Duke of Cumberland's campaign in Scotland. A strong, thrilling voice was required for the military hero *Judas*. This was to be another of Beard's triumphs: a role that he continued to sing with success for the rest of his career, both in London and at the Music Festivals springing up in Cathedral cities.[38] Detailed first-hand comments on his performance are sadly lacking from contemporary diaries and letters: Lord Shaftesbury merely said that it "went off with very great applause",[39] and Catherine Talbot was struck by the effect of the timpani in Beard's aria 'Sound an Alarm' without mentioning him at all.[40] Charles Burney can give us a better idea of the

---

[37] 'The London Stage', Part 3, p. 1299
[38] Worcester 1752, 1758, Gloucester 1754, 1757, Oxford 1754, Birmingham 1760
[39] quoted in Deutsch *Handel a Documentary Biography* p. 848
[40] quoted in Deutsch *Handel a Documentary Biography* p. 640

effect he must have had on the audience when he reported (on a later occasion) "...I entered at the close of an Air of Spirit sung by Beard, which was much applauded".[41] There were six performances in 1747, following three each of the *Occasional Oratorio* and *Joseph and his Brethren*.[42] This Lent season was successful enough to persuade Handel to limit himself to making an annual repeat the basis of his professional career from now on. He also realised that he had a 'winner' in the oratorio *Judas Maccabaeus*, which he subsequently programmed in every season except 1749.

6. THEATRE WORK 1747-50: WHY BEARD DIDN'T SING FOR HANDEL

The work that Beard was doing at Covent Garden in the season 1747-8 was very much a repeat of his usual roles. He must have regretted not moving across to Drury Lane and joining Garrick there in his first season at the helm. Garrick already had Thomas Lowe on the roster, and so Beard must have wanted to avoid a repetition of the lean years when they had shared the work out between them. He stayed tight at Covent Garden and waited. Garrick, who had also just spent the past year in the Covent Garden company, was a frequent visitor to the Beefsteak Club, so Beard would have been on good terms with him. Garrick, for his part, was not particularly musical; in his first season of programming he avoided the repertoire that would have suited Beard. He was also not keen on pantomimes, and replaced them this year with more comic operas (the *Dragon of Wantley* came back into the repertoire) and his own farce *Miss in her Teens*. On many evenings there was no after-piece at all, as he filled out the newly revived Shakespearean repertoire (*Henry V, The Tempest, King Lear, Hamlet, Richard III*) with interludes of ballet.

Handel's 1748 season appears to have been planned in the belief that Beard would still be one of the soloists. A new heroic title role, 'Joshua', was surely conceived with his voice in mind.[43] *Judas Maccabaeus* was slated for more performances (in the event there were five). As things transpired, scholars have deduced from autograph m/s markings, and the names printed in Walsh's 'Songs Selected from the Oratorios', that Beard was not available to Handel in 1748.[44] I have tried to find reasons for this.

There is no evidence that he was ill. As he was on contract to John Rich at Covent Garden it would have been easy for him to take part: Handel rented Rich's theatre on Wednesdays and Fridays during Lent, when the theatres were traditionally 'dark'.[45] Rich was on good terms with Handel, and was happy to house his organ in the theatre for the rest of the year. Donald Burrows also states that "at this period Handel reputedly taught music to John Rich's daughters" - one of whom, Charlotte, would become Beard's second wife in February 1759.[46]

---

[41] *Memoirs of Dr Charles Burney 1726 - 1769*, University of Nebraska Press 1988, p. 100
[42] On the evidence of the manuscript Winton Dean has posited a theory that Beard sang the roles of the two brothers Simeon and Judah in the 1744 and 1747 performances: Winton Dean *Handel's Dramatic Oratorios and Masques*, p. 407-8, 413
[43] Significantly Handel did not revive *Joshua* until 1752, when Beard was firmly back in his company.
[44] "Lowe probably replaced Beard in 1748-51". Dean *Handel's Dramatic Oratorios and Masques*, p. 472 "Beard, for a time, had been replaced by Lowe". Jens Peter Larsen *Handel's Messiah: Origins – Composition – Sources* London 1957, New York 1972 p. 190
[45] Powel: Wednesday 24th February 1748: "Lent now beginning, the House leaves off playing Wednesdays and Fridays". *The London Stage*, Part 4 [1747 1776], ed. George Winchester Stone Jr. Carbondale, Ill. 1960 p. 32
[46] Donald Burrows, 'Handel', *The Master Musicians*, Oxford, 1994, p.294

The tenor who ended up singing for Handel both this season and for the next two was Thomas Lowe. Burney's comments on this singer have already been noted. But the 1748 repertoire was much more designed to show off Beard's vocal brilliance than Lowe's way with a tuneful ballad. Something must have occurred to prevent him taking part. Both Larsen and Pearce wonder whether there had been a falling out: "It is not quite clear why Beard seems not to have appeared in Handel's performances during these years. There may perhaps have been a difference between them".[47] Pearce's suggestion of there having been a quarrel is also unlikely. Beard, as we have seen, owed his entire career to having been discovered and nurtured by Handel. There is no record of him having an awkward or combative temperament: quite the reverse. All of the comments about his personality by his friends and contemporaries refer to his elegant manners and 'clubbable' nature. Since December 1743 he had been a member of the Sublime Society of Beefsteaks. Several writers attest to his charm and good nature during this period. Thomas Davies writes of the club, "with the jolly president John Beard" as "one of the most respectable assemblies of jovial and agreeable companions in this metropolis";[48] and Tobias Smollett likewise writes of "the generous Johnny B[ear]d, respected and beloved by all the world".[49]

If Beard was originally planning to sing, then the reason for his change of mind is much more likely to be associated (as it was in 1740) with his private life. Henrietta's financial affairs were still not settled. Her case was as slow and strength-sapping as Dickens' fictional Jarndyce v. Jarndyce. By 1748 things had hardly progressed at all.

During this unsettling period John Beard must have found it difficult to appear at the theatre, as well as paying frequent visits to lawyers and courtrooms and supporting his sick wife. It would not be unrealistic to find Beard dropping out of *ad hoc* engagements from time to time. And that is what we must assume that Handel's concerts were to him, despite their importance. His theatrical contract was the signed document from which he would have had more difficulty extracting himself. But his theatrical commitments do not preclude the possibility that he <u>could</u> have sung for Handel at some stage. He was certainly free on the relevant days. If further research should ever suggest that he, and not Lowe, did sing some of the oratorios during the period 1748-1750 it would be consistent with his engagement-diary. Let us look in detail at these three seasons, starting with 1748. Could Beard have at least commenced this season with his role in *Judas Maccabaeus* before domestic events caught up with him?

1748	HANDEL	BEARD
Feb 24	*Ash Wednesday*	*LENT starts*
Feb 25		Damon & Phillida
Feb 26	Judas Maccabaeus	
March 2	Judas Maccabaeus	
March 3		Apollo & Daphne
March 4	Judas Maccabaeus	

---

[47] Jens Peter Larsen *Handel's Messiah: Origins – Composition – Sources* London 1957, New York 1972 p. 198, who includes in a footnote a quote from C. E. Pearce, *Polly Peachum* p.213: "When Handel quarrelled with Beard, he intended to engage Lowe for the oratorios, but finding him deficient in the requisite training, was obliged to make peace with Beard, who had both voice and talent".

[48] Thomas Davies, 'Dramatic Miscellanies' vol. 3, 1784, p.167

[49] Tobias Smollett, 'Sir Launcelot Greaves', London 1762, chapter 4

March 5		Apollo & Daphne
March 7		Apollo & Daphne
March 8		Singing: 4th Cantata of John Stanley [50]
March 9	Joshua	
March 10		Apollo & Daphne
March 11	Joshua	
March 12		Apollo & Daphne
March 14		The Muses' Looking Glass
March 15		Apollo & Daphne
March 17		Apollo & Daphne
March 18	Joshua	
March 19		Apollo & Daphne
March 21		Venus & Adonis. *Beard's 'Benefit'*
March 22		Apollo & Daphne
March 23	Alexander Balus	
March 24		Damon & Phillida
March 25	Alexander Balus	
March 26		Apollo & Daphne
March 28		Singing: 'Go lovely rose' [51]
March 30	Alexander Balus	
March 31		Singing: 1st Cantata of John Stanley [52]
April 1	Judas Maccabaeus	
April 2		Apollo & Daphne
April 4	Judas Maccabaeus	
April 6		Singing by Beard, Faulkner & Storer
April 7	Judas Maccabaeus	

In the autumn of 1748 Beard had moved theatres again, and was now with Garrick at Drury Lane. But as this theatre also went 'dark' on Wednesdays and Fridays in Lent there are no known clashes that would have prevented him singing for Handel. Either he was still bound up with legal and domestic matters (the sources quoted in Chapter 3 do not always distinguish clearly between the years 1748 and 1749) or he must have failed to make it clear to the new management that it had been his custom to join Handel in the Lent Oratorio season when Fleetwood had been manager. Garrick was a notorious philistine in musical matters.

<u>1749</u>

The same situation presents itself in 1749. Here the participation of Lowe is reflected more clearly in Handel's new music, suggesting that he had planned the casting around his voice. The new tenor roles in *Susanna* and *Solomon* are light and tuneful but more subsidiary. However, Lowe was obliged to take over Beard's roles in *Hercules*, *Samson*, and *Messiah*. Although *Messiah* was subjected to a thorough revision this year, not having been performed since 1745, it appears that Handel made no significant changes in the tenor arias.[53]

---

[50] Cantata 4, op. 3, '*In the manner of Anacreon*', 'Whilst others barter Ease for State', London 1742
[51] possibly: Maurice Greene 'Go rose, my Chloe's bosom Grace'
[52] Cantata 1, op. 8, '*Imitated from the Italian of Guarini*', "Who'll buy a heart?", London 1748
[53] "It is probable that the small correction [a deletion of 1 bar in the opening and closing ritornelli] in Aria no. 3 ("Every valley") derives from this performance". Jens Peter Larsen *Handel's Messiah: Origins - Composition - Sources* London 1957, New York 1972 pp. 216-7 & 244

1749	HANDEL	BEARD
Feb 8	*Ash Wednesday*	*LENT starts*
Feb 10	Susanna	
Feb 11		Drury Lane plays Dr Johnson's *Mahomet & Irene* on Feb. 6, 7, 9, 11 13, 14, 16, 18. Beard has no role in it. There is no afterpiece until 20th.
Feb 17	Susanna	
Feb 20		The Virgin Unmasked
Feb 21		The Triumph of Peace
Feb 22	Susanna	
Feb 23		The Triumph of Peace
Feb 24	The Choice of Hercules	
Feb 25		The Triumph of Peace
Feb 27		The Triumph of Peace
Feb 28		Much Ado / Triumph of Peace
March 2		The Triumph of Peace
March 3	Samson	
March 4		The Triumph of Peace
March 6		The Triumph of Peace
March 8	Samson	
March 9		The Devil to Pay
March 10	Samson	
March 11		The Lottery
March 14		The Provok'd Wife
March 15	Samson	
March 17	Solomon	
March 20	Solomon	
March 22	Solomon	
March 23	Messiah	
March 27		The Triumph of Peace

1750

Once again a similar situation subsists in 1750, so Handel was obviously still satisfied with Thomas Lowe as his replacement tenor soloist. There was only one new oratorio this season, *Theodora*, in which the solo tenor role is the subsidiary character 'Septimius'. The other music had all been written earlier for Beard's voice.

1750	HANDEL	BEARD
Feb 28	*Ash Wednesday*	*LENT starts*
		Drury Lane plays William Whitehouse's *The Roman Father* in March. Beard has a 'Vocal Part' in it.
March 1		The Roman Father
March 2	Saul	
March 3		The Roman Father
March 5		The Roman Father
March 6		The Roman Father
March 7	Saul	
March 8		The Roman Father
March 9	Judas Maccabaeus	

105

March 12		The Roman Father
March 13		The Chaplet
March 14	Judas Maccabaeus	
March 15		The Rehearsal
March 16	Theodora	
March 20		The Chaplet
March 21	Theodora	
March 23	Theodora	
March 24		The Chaplet. *Beard's 'Benefit'*
March 28	Judas Maccabaeus	*Solomon* (Boyce) for Jones
March 29		Lethe
March 30	Judas Maccabaeus	
March 31		The Chaplet
April 3		The Rehearsal
April 4	Samson	
April 5		Comus
April 6	Samson	
April 7		The Roman Father
April 11		*Concert Spiritual* for Geminiani
April 12	Messiah	

It can be seen from the above that again there were no clashes between Handel's oratorio performances and the Drury Lane theatrical repertoire. Because Handel still performed on Wednesdays and Fridays there was never going to be a clash as that theatre, too, went 'dark' on those days in Lent. At a late stage Beard accepted to sing in two programmes of sacred music that took place in Drury Lane on the 'dark' nights. These were both Benefit performances: one a performance of Boyce's *Serenata* 'Solomon' for the cellist Jones; the other a miscellaneous programme for the violinist Geminiani. Handel moved his *Messiah* to the next day, a Thursday, so that there would not be two sacred concerts competing for the same audience. Only on March 28 do we see a clash between Beard's diary and Handel's oratorios; and that can easily be explained away as Beard taking a late booking. There seems to be absolutely no reason why Beard could not have made himself available to Handel for any of these three seasons if he had wanted to.

Thomas Lowe

CHAPTER 5
BEEF, LIBERTY AND THE NATIONAL ANTHEM

1. THE BEEF-STEAK CLUB.

When Henry Fielding first set his poem *"The Roast beef of old England"* to a catchy well-known air,[1] and the bass singer Richard Leveridge popularised it and added more verses, they somehow caught the mood of the times. This song became an immediate 'hit', and stayed popular for the rest of the century. It was sung on patriotic occasions at feasts and festivals, and was one of the favourite songs at the theatre. But singers and actors did not just sing the praises of British beef in public: they also founded clubs devoted to celebrating it, and the accompanying glories of being British, being beer-drinkers (rather than wine-drinkers), and above all being decidedly not French![2] The first of these seems to have been set up by a group of actors, writers and other notables at the Bumper Tavern in Covent Garden run by the well-known actor and mimic Dick Estcourt. Estcourt kept a written record of all the company's proceedings, bon mots and jokes, and in return was allowed to wear the club badge, a small golden grid-iron, around his neck on a green ribbon. Richard Steele writes about its meetings in several essays for *The Spectator*.[3] A later version of the club, which also chose the grid-iron for its insignia, was named the *Sublime Society of Beefsteaks*. This dates from about 1735 and there are differing tales regarding its origins. Its founding members were John Rich, George Lambert and William Hogarth.

John Rich, the owner and manager of Covent Garden Theatre, was an immensely important theatrical figure of the day, and was later to become Beard's father-in-law. But in 1735 Beard was only a minor star in the Covent Garden firmament. George Lambert was Rich's senior scene painter as well as a landscape artist in his own right. He and Hogarth were good friends who, in this same year, managed to arrange for a copyright bill to be passed which protected the authorship of an artist's original prints - an important achievement that much improved the standing of British artists.

Hogarth himself moved easily in theatrical circles and had already painted several theatrical scenes, including one from "The Beggar's Opera" (1728-9) in which Rich is portrayed watching the scene between 'Macheath' and his rival ladies 'Polly' and 'Lucy' from the side of the stage. Hogarth's satirical narrative cycles "The Rake's Progress" and "The Harlot's Progress" reveal a theatrical flair for arranging his subjects, as though the viewer is watching scenes from a play. Later he was to publicly demonstrate the patriotism which had led to his interest in the idea of a Beefsteak club with the great, mature paintings "The March to Finchley, 1745" and "O The Roast Beef of Old England ('The Gate of Calais')" of 1748.[4]

---

[1] 'The Queen's Old Courtier' in 'The Grub-Street Opera' of 1731. See: Edgar V. Roberts, 'Henry Fielding and Richard Leveridge: Authorship of the "Roast Beef of Old England", Huntingdon Library Quarterly, 27, no.2, February 1964, pp. 175-81

[2] There are many printed ballads in the *Madden collection* of Cambridge University Library which reveal the extent of this repertoire; many stating 'as sung by Mr Beard': e.g. 'A new Song in praise of Old English Roast Beef'; 'The Beer-drinking Britons'; 'Hearts of Oak'; 'Britons' Guardian Angel'.

[3] Robert J. Allen, 'The Clubs of Augustan London', Harvard Studies in English Vol. VII, Harvard University Press, Cambridge 1933, pp.136-40; & Ben Rogers, 'Beef and Liberty', Chatto & Windus, London 2003, p. 79-80

[4] see Matthew Craske, 'William Hogarth', Tate Publishing, London 2000

These three are credited with the origins of the *Sublime Society of Beefsteaks* when one of them, (stories vary as to whether it was Rich or Lambert), not having time for a regular dinner, "contented himself with a beef steak broiled upon the fire in the painting room".[5] An issue of *The Connoisseur*[6] sets the scene vividly when it describes: "the most ingenious artists in the kingdom [who] meet every Saturday in a noble room at the top of Covent-Garden theatre, and never suffer any dish except Beef-steaks to appear".[7]

Membership was restricted to twenty-four, and the initial list shown in Walter Arnold's detailed account of the club[8] includes leading actors, painters and musicians of the day. It was a closely-knit community of workers in the Covent Garden area who shared much in common, including the need for a good meal between the Saturday morning rehearsals (and subsequent visit to the Treasury to collect the week's wages) and the six o'clock start of the evening's entertainment. Meetings were always on Saturdays during Beard's lifetime, and remained at the Covent Garden Theatre until it burnt down in 1808. The rules of the society state:

"that Beef steaks shall be the only meat for dinner, and the broiling begin at two of the clock on each day of the meeting, and the table-cloth be removed at half-an-hour after three".[9]

New members between 1736 and 1743 included the musician and composer William Defesch, the actor Theophilus Cibber, and the artist Francis Hayman. John Beard joined John Rich's Covent Garden company in the autumn of 1743, and was elected a Society member on December 24.

Election to the *Sublime Society of Beefsteaks* was open to anyone who could muster enough votes from existing members when a vacancy in the statutory number of 24 occurred. The candidate was also required to have attended at least three previous meetings as a guest. As an immensely 'clubbable' person Beard is likely to have been to several meetings during the weeks immediately prior to his election. Indeed he was scarcely out of the theatre at all. Between November 25 and December 24 he performed there on fifteen nights. On the day before his election, Friday December 23, he made his first appearance in this new venue as 'Macheath' opposite the 'Polly Peachum' of his lifelong friend Kitty Clive.

Beard remained a member of the Society for all of his life. In fact, he came to embody the spirit and ethos of it during his long tenure. It was fortunate that he took over as manager of Covent Garden Theatre on the death of John Rich in 1761, as he was able to maintain the regularity of the meetings in their usual venue at the top of the backstage area. Several writers attest to his charm and good nature during this period. It was a time when it was run with affection and courtesy by his good friends and relatives. Thomas Davies writes of the club, "with the jolly president John Beard" as "one of the most respectable assemblies of jovial and agreeable companions in this metropolis".[10] Beard was the President in many different years; but certainly held that position in 1784, when the decision was taken to expand the number of members to 25, in order to admit the 22-year-old HRH the Prince of Wales (later King George IV).[11] Almost certainly it was during this period that its

---

[5] Edwards, 'Anecdotes of Painters', 1808
[6] *The Connoisseur*, issue no. 29[sometimes quoted as 19], June 6th, 1754
[7] Robert J. Allen, ibid, p.144
[8] Walter Arnold, 'The Life and Death of the Sublime Society of Beefsteaks', London 1871
[9] Arnold, ibid.
[10] Thomas Davies, 'Dramatic Miscellanies' vol. 3, 1784, p.167
[11] John Timbs, 'Clubs and club life in London', London 1873, p.120-1

satirical customs and quirky laws became entrenched. Tobias Smollett attended as a guest, and wrote in his 1762 novel *"Sir Launcelot Greaves"* of the club's "genial board", where "delicate rumps irresistibly attract the stranger's eye, and, while they seem to cry 'come cut me - come cut me', constrain, by wondrous sympathy, each mouth to overflow. Where the obliging and humorous Jemmy B[encraf]t [*Beard's brother-in-law*], the gentle Billy H[avar]d[12], [*his very close friend*] replete with human kindness, and the generous Johnny B[ear]d, respected and beloved by all the world, attend as priests and ministers of mirth, good cheer, and jollity, and assist with culinary art the raw, unpractised, awkward guest."[13]

Beard was undoubtedly sought out as a member because one of their number, referred to in the rules as *The Bishop*, had to sing the Grace and the Anthem. This, and the singing of stirring ballads, (some of them especially written for the society's sole use) must have frequently fallen to his lot. The rules were an irreverent and humorous parody of Masonry (which was beginning to take hold in London, and to which many of the members also belonged).[14] The 24 members regarded themselves as a Brotherhood and wore a distinctive blue coat and buff waistcoat, with brass buttons impressed with the gridiron and the motto *"Beef and Liberty"*. It was as though these artisans, painters, actors, musicians and writers needed a club in the same way that the medieval world had needed the Lord of Misrule: - to let down their collective hair and replace an ordered society with a temporary world in which all could be equals, and classes could be reversed.

Apart from *The Bishop* there was *The President of the Day, The Vice President, The Recorder* and *The Boots*. These roles were taken in rotation and were a mixed blessing. *The President* had the honour of presiding over the meeting, but also provided the beef at his expense. He had to observe all the ancient forms and customs of the society, and give the customary toasts in strict accordance with the society's specific list. But he had no powers, and was, in fact, closely watched by the other members to see if he made any slight mistakes of protocol, through ignorance or forgetfulness. A certain amount of 'parlour game' mentality crept into all of this, as there were moments when he had to remember to put on one or other of the hats - a Beefeater's hat and a tricorn with a plume - which hung from the back of his chair. Apparently he had to sing 'The Song of the Day' whether he had a voice or not: which renders the duties of the role even more akin to our modern idea of "charades".

The Vice President was the oldest member present and, according to Arnold, "had to carry out the President's directions without responsibility" - whatever that means! *The Recorder* had another role that seems to have come out of the world of the parlour game: he had to rebuke everybody for offences, real or imaginary, and 'record' the witticisms, bon mots and banter that the meeting produced. The archive having been burned in the 1808 fire, we only have a few examples left: such as the time when Garrick was late for a performance at Drury Lane, and on being reprimanded by another of the Patentees that he should "consider

---

[12] Arnold and others have misread this name as 'Howard'. However, it is clear from the papers that the author has consulted in the Folger Shakespeare Library ('Jeu d'esprit' N.a.2) that 'H…d' is the actor & playwright William Havard (1710-1778) and therefore the person who was elected to the society on December 28th 1745, and not William Howard, musician d. 1785.

[13] Tobias Smollett, 'Sir Launcelot Greaves', London 1762, chapter 4

[14] Bencraft was a prominent Mason. His benefit on 10th April 1741 was for the entertainment of the Ancient and Honourable Society of Free and Accepted Masons. Beard was referred to as 'Brother Beard' on May 15th 1739, when he sang "On, on my dear Brethren" at Drury Lane for the same group of Masons.

the stake you and I have in this house" he answered "True, but I was thinking of my steak in the other house!"[15]

The Recorder also had to 'induct' new members. This was a farcical ceremony that always caused great mirth. The newly elected member was brought in blindfolded, accompanied by the Bishop wearing his robes and mitre (old stage props) and bearing a book containing the rules of the society on which he had to swear an oath of loyalty "to support the dignity and welfare of the society, and behave as a worthy member". All the other members were decked out in whatever stage costumes were at hand, one with a sword of state, others as halberdiers accompanying the Bishop, in a parody of the Coronation service. The 'charge' was then delivered by the Recorder. This was by turns serious and lighthearted, but made the point that the brotherhood encouraged a perfect equality between members; but that such an equality should never degenerate into undue familiarity. At the moment after the oath-taking when the new recruit had to kiss the book, a bone of beef was surreptitiously substituted. Practical jokes like this were encouraged, and outrageous toasts were the order of the day.

Quite what the noble members made of this - for there were several from the time of the Earl of Sandwich (elected 1761) onwards - can only be guessed at. When HRH the Prince of Wales sought membership in 1785 he must have been well aware of this dangerous egalitarianism. Whether or not he equated it with the ideals of the French Revolution, brewing at this time, or the American War of Independence which had ended two years previously, or simply dismissed it as the playful rules of a gentleman's club, is not known. But he embraced it warmly when the rules were changed and membership was increased to 25 in order to circumvent the problem that there was actually no vacancy. He was soon joined as a member by HRH the Duke of York (elected 1790) and other brothers and relatives. After Beard's death in 1791 membership of the society became ever more sought-after by members of the aristocracy, wishing to witness royalty in their cups and at play.

There is one extant record of a speech made by the Recorder. Although the society's entire archives were destroyed in the 1808 fire (along with a fine wine-cellar) the Folger Shakespeare Library contains William Havard's scrapbook which he entitled 'Jeu d'esprit'. It contains many letters, poems and writings that illuminate his friendship with John Beard. In his letters he addresses him as 'Brother' - which led some to believe that they were actually related.[16] But Havard had married the actress Elizabeth Kilby in May 1745. So the affectionate term must stem from their joint membership of the 'Free and Accepted Masons' or the 'Sublime Society of Beefsteaks'. His manuscript contains this sketch for a speech made at the admission of T.... F.... Esq:[17] "It has been my good fortune to be appointed to acquaint you that you have this day been unanimously elected a Member of our Society. A Society, as remarkable for the excellency of its Constitution, the Purity of its Manners, and the Sociality of its Members, as for the Sublimity of its situation [a joke about its position at the top of the building]. No member, here, sells his Conscience: no Brother lies in wait for the Fortune of his Friend. – But I will not exalt ourselves by affecting to make comparisons. As to your behaviour here, Sir: - Give me leave to acquaint you, that a Disposition to please and be pleased is the sole Requisite to

[15] John Timbs, 'Clubs and club life in London', London 1873, p.115
[16] "Beard's sister, in turn, married William Havard, who for twenty-two years was the wheelhorse of the profession at Drury Lane". 'The London Stage', Part 4, ed. G. W. Stone, Carbondale Illinois, 1962, p. xci
[17] Theodosius Forrest (January 22nd 1763). Arnold, ibid. p.xix

constitute our mutual Happiness: upon this Green-swerd the wheels of Conviviality will roll pleasantly and without a Rubb".[18]

T... F... was Theodosius Forrest who later wrote 'The Song of the Day' for the society's regular use. This replaced 'The Roast Beef of Old England', with words by Henry Fielding and Richard Leveridge, which had been sung at every previous meeting. It probably continued to be sung for a long time after, as it so embodies the patriotic fervour underlying the spirit of the times, and was firmly in John Beard's repertoire. Later Beard may have introduced the 'New Song in praise of Old English Roast Beef sung by Mr Beard' (see p. 47).

Horace Walpole's comments on Handel hiring "all the singers of *Roast Beef* from between the acts at both theatres"[19] for his *Samson* cast (in which Beard sang the title role) is evidence that he must have been famous for singing it, as well as such other rousing patriotic songs for which there is documentary evidence on the playbills of 1743-5. The bass singer Richard Leveridge himself was on the Covent Garden roster at this time, and Beard and he duetted between the acts in unnamed patriotic songs during the spring of 1744, when, beside the worries of Britain's involvement in the War of Austrian Succession (1740-8) there were the growing fears of a Jacobite invasion as well.

Extracts from the texts reveal the xenophobic content of both songs:

The roast beef of Old England

When mighty roast beef was the Englishman's food,
It ennobled our hearts, and enriched our blood,
Our soldiers were brave, our courtiers were good;
Oh the roast beef of England
And old England's roast beef!

Then, Britons, from all nice dainties refrain,
Which effeminate Italy, France and Spain;
And mighty roast beef shall command on the main;
Oh the roast beef of England
And old England's roast beef!

The Song of the Day

No more shall Fame expand her wings
To sounds of heroes, states and kings;
A nobler flight the Goddess takes,
To praise our British Beef in steaks,
A joyful theme for Britons free,
Happy in Beef and Liberty.

Throughout the realms where despots reign,
What tracks of glory now remain?
Their people, slaves of power and pride,
Fat Beef and Freedom are denied!
What realm, what state can happy be,
Wanting our Beef and Liberty?[20]

[18] Folger Shakespeare Library 'Jeu d'esprit' N.a.2
[19] Letter to Horace Mann, 24th February 1743: Deutsch, p. 560
[20] Ben Rogers, 'Beef and Liberty', Chatto & Windus, London 2003, pp. 77-8, & 82

The last official of the society that needs to be described is *The Boots*. This important position also harks back to medieval traditions, such as the 'Boy-Bishop', where roles were temporarily reversed. *The Boots* was always the newest member. He had to arrive early, collect the wine from the cellar and decant it, and bring the steaks individually from the griddle to the diners. No one was exempted from this duty - not even royalty when it was their turn. Indeed some, such as the Duke of Sussex - George III's 6th son - who held the post in 1808-9, seemed to enjoy the role. A practical joke played regularly by the company was to demand that *Boots* should decant another bottle just as he was about to eat his own long-awaited steak.

Another writer who saw Beard at the club was the young James Boswell, whose great mentor Dr. Johnson became a member on March 4 1780. In his *London Journal* Boswell writes of going there on Saturday 27 November 1762 with Lord Eglinton. *"He carried me to Covent Garden in a coach and bid me wait in the Bedford Coffee House till he sent for me."* Members were entitled to take one guest to the meetings on payment of 10 shillings and sixpence to the Treasurer. So it appears that Boswell was Lord Eglinton's guest for the afternoon; but that he was not allowed to enter until some formality or other had been undertaken. If he was Eglinton's <u>second</u> guest the delay could be more easily explained, since the rules for this were even more complicated: "if he brought a second [guest] he had to borrow a name; in default of obtaining it, the visitor was doomed to retire".[21] Boswell must have observed the niceties of admission, since:

"...In a few minutes the famous Mr Beard of Covent Garden Theatre came for me and carried me up a great many steps to a handsome room above the theatre, in which met the Beefsteak Club, a society which has subsisted these thirty years. The room where it met was once burnt. The Gridiron was almost consumed, but a thin image of it remained entire. That they have fixed in the stucco in the roof. The president sits in a chair under a canopy, above which you have in gold letters, *Beef and Liberty*. We were entertained by the Club. Lord Sandwich was in the chair, a jolly, hearty, lively man. It was very mixed society: Lord Eglinton, Mr Beard, Colonel West of the Guards, Mr Havard the actor, Mr Churchill the poet, Mr Wilkes the author *of The North Briton*, and many more. We had nothing to eat but beefsteaks, and had wine and punch in plenty and freedom. We had a number of songs."[22]

Boswell was present at an interesting time. With Wilkes and Lord Sandwich both dining on the same day the air must have been electric. Having been involved in the notorious orgies of the Hell-Fire Club at Medmenham Abbey both were now at daggers drawn. Wilkes had just published his obscene *Essay on Woman*, and Lord Sandwich was about to take a leading role in condemning it in the House of Lords. Horace Walpole, a notorious gossip but an obviously well-informed one, wrote to Sir Horace Mann:

"... the wicked even affirm, that very lately, at a club with Mr Wilkes, held at the top of the playhouse in Drury Lane [*recte* Covent Garden], Lord Sandwich talked so prophanely that he drove two harlequins out of company".[23]

---

[21] Arnold, ibid. p.4

[22] James Boswell, London Journal, ed. F.A. Pottle, Heinemann 1950, p.56-7

[23] The Letters of Horace Walpole, ed. Mrs Paget Toynbee, Oxford, 1903-5, v, p. 395

A little later he wrote to George Montagu: "He [Lord Sandwich] has impeached Wilkes for a blasphemous poem [the *Essay on Woman*], and has been expelled for blasphemy himself by the Beef-steak Club at Covent Garden".[24]

Beard seemed to have been running a tight ship, and expelled the member for breaking the tenth law of the society, which states that "*every member who shall be found guilty of any crime or misdemeanour in this Society, and shall neglect or refuse to submit to the penalty or censure by him incurred, and duly voted and ordered by the majority ... shall stand expelled this Society.*"[25] In a twist that would have been appreciated by Beard more than most, since he regularly spoke the line in his character of 'Macheath',[26] Lord Sandwich earned the unflattering soubriquet of 'Jemmy Twitcher' (the character in the *Beggar's Opera* who 'impeaches' 'Macheath') for the way in which he turned on his erstwhile friend Wilkes and impeached him. Hogarth drew an unflattering portrait of Wilkes in May 1763 that was soon on sale as an etching.[27] All of this was brewing on the day in November 1762 that the ingenuous 22 year-old Boswell met them.

The gridiron referred to by Boswell, was reputedly the original one used by John Rich in 1735. It had always been given an honourable place amidst their somewhat facetious regalia and was represented on their uniform buttons. It is clear from Boswell's account that it had already suffered in one fire before the awful conflagration that destroyed the whole theatre in 1808. However it had a habit of surviving, and was extracted from the ashes a second time to remain the most significant feature of the rebuilt meeting room.

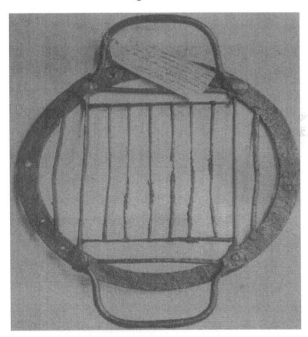

The Beefsteak Club gridiron

---

[24] Ibid. p.396

[25] Walter Arnold, The Life and Death of the Sublime Society of Beefsteaks, London 1871 p. xvi

[26] Scene XIV, Macheath: "That Jemmy Twitcher should 'peach me, I own, surprised me".

[27] 'Engravings by Hogarth', ed. Sean Shesgreen, New York 1973, plate 98

One of the further 'parlour games' that this assembly of theatrically minded members played, towards the end of their meetings, was one that got right under Beard's skin and took him over. It was the requirement to hold a conversation for as long as possible using only quotations from plays, ballad operas, pantomimes etc. Beard was obviously qualified to do well in this; and, indeed, it is possible that it influenced his everyday thought process. For, in the few letters of his which are still extant, the same ease for slipping into quotation is frequently on display. This letter was written to Miss Hull (daughter of his friend the actor Thomas Hull) from his villa in Hampton eighteen years after his retirement from the stage:

Dear Miss Hull,   Rose Hill, 18th Aug. 1785
  "What horrid silence thus invades our ears?" as the King of Brentford says.[28]
Well as I love dumb things, the taciturnity of your pen begins to be alarmingly painful… Let me say with Prior, or somebody prior to him, faith, I don't know who:
                'Let them censure, what care I?
                The herd of critics I defie…'
and there's an end of the matter."

This custom was still prevalent in the Club in 1799 when Thomas Dibdin became a member. In his 'Reminiscences'[29] he describes the parlour-game in more detail:

"I had not been long attached to Covent Garden Theatre before I was elected member of the Covent Garden Beef-Steak Club… It was a most agreeable society, consisting of the principal actors, and every dramatic author, connected with Covent Garden Theatre, as well as several eminent commercial and legal characters… Mr Emery, who was introduced to this joyous assembly the same day with myself, and who was reckoned a very diffident man, was at first much annoyed by these quotations, which, to produce greater effect, were to be given as instantaneously as possible… When, on the first day, it came to Emery's turn to make a quotation he declared that (although an actor) he never could extemporaneously think of an apt extract from a play, nor had he ever made one on any subject. On being pressed, however, without any apparent consciousness of its just applicability to himself, he said: "Indeed, indeed, sirs! But this troubles me."

        Beard spent most days of the week – apart from Sunday – at the theatre, either rehearsing or performing. On performance days he was often in the main show and the afterpiece. It is clear that he liked his comrades and spent much spare time in their company. Being a member of the Beefsteak Club added to the time he was away from home. How did this go down with his wife Henrietta?

        As an aristocratic lady whose marriage had put her into a kind of purdah amongst her own kind, it seems that she transferred much of her social ambition to her husband once the Waldegrave family had abandoned her. Beard's repeated applications for Court positions for which he was not the obvious candidate ('Serjeant Trumpeter' in 1753 and 'King's Waiter' in 1757) may have stemmed from her desire to regain a more visible rank in society. As a prelude she would have supported his membership of any society that brought him into contact with people of rank and consequence. There were aristocrats in the Beefsteak club from the very beginning, even if they only came as guests. The tale is recounted that the Earl of

---

[28] A role in a play based on *Le Roi d'Yvetor*, (later translated by Thackeray as "The King of Brentford")
[29] Thomas Dibdin, 'Reminiscences of Thomas Dibdin', London, 1827, pp. 254-5

Peterborough was present on the occasion in 1735 when John Rich grilled his first steak.[30] His enthusiasm for this informal manner of dining in the upstairs painting room encouraged the formation of the society, to which he brought groups of his titled friends. The records in Arnold's history of the society do not show that many of these were initially elected as members[31]; but the records may be incomplete as a result of the many fires that ravaged the theatre in the late 18th and early 19th centuries. Apart from the obvious advantages of rubbing shoulders with the gentry, Henrietta would probably have seen how membership would also assist Beard in his career. The timing of his election in December 1743, just a few weeks after he had transferred from Drury Lane to Covent Garden, reveals that he was already getting on well with his new employer. John Rich was an astute man of the theatre and could see that he had got hold of a popular and versatile performer. We can see from the confident portrait of Beard in Macheath's famous red coat by Thomas Hudson (dated by experts to this precise period)[32] that, after seven years of hard labour, the singer had really made his mark on London's theatrical world.

Henrietta would not have been particularly discomfited by the times of the meetings either. Two o'clock on a Saturday afternoon merely bridged the gap between morning rehearsal and evening performance. On days when Beard had no evening's singing to worry about he could stay longer, and drink more heavily of the port and porter which flowed freely after the tablecloth had been removed. One such Saturday was soon to arrive, within two years of his election, which would transform British musical life and set the whole nation singing patriotically along with him.

2. PATRIOTIC SONGS

The songs that delighted the *Sublime Society of Beef-Steaks* were the same songs that roused patriotic fervour in the theatre audience. There are many accounts of the audience in the gallery growing restive during some instrumental interlude or high-flown art-song, and calling for the *Roast Beef of Old England* and suchlike popular ballads instead. Sylas Neville, in his diary entry for June 9 1767 - at the very end of Beard's period as Covent Garden Manager - writes:

"Half past 4 went into the Pit at Covent Garden Theatre; after being shut up for the season [it] was opened tonight as a high favour to [Edward] Shuter [1728-76] for whose benefit "The Busybody" with "Love a la Mode", a farce never published, was played... Before it began the Gods, having called for the music to play *Roast Beef,* would not suffer the play to begin till their request was complied with. They pelted Davies and Hull, who appeared first, with orange skins, crying 'Off! Off!'..."[33]

Oliver Goldsmith writes that the lower classes "would find more satisfaction in the *Roast Beef of Old England* than in the finest closes [cadences] of an eunuch [male castrato]".[34] When the management felt that it was prudent to tap

---

[30] John Timbs, 'Clubs and club life in London', London 1873, pp.111-2

[31] Walter Arnold, The Life and Death of the Sublime Society of Beefsteaks, London 1871

[32] "Hudson's striking portrait of the singer and actor John Beard in his red coat trimmed with gold has been dated stylistically by Ellen Miles to about 1743; this was the year when Beard appeared in the first London performance of *Messiah*". Handel: a celebration of his Life and Times, National Portrait Gallery, London, 1985

[33] Tuesday June 9th 1767, The Diary of Sylas Neville 1767-88, ed. B. Cozens-Hardy, London 1950

[34] Oliver Goldsmith, 'The Bee' Number VIII, November 24th, 1759

into the public's loyalty to the House of Hanover they arranged for the last portion of Handel's Coronation Anthem '*Zadok the Priest*' to be performed. This was published in 1743[35] and was therefore suddenly and fortuitously available. The text to the relevant section is:

God save the King, long live the King, may the King live for ever. Alleluia. Amen

Long live the King!   God save the King!   Long live the King!   May the King live,   may the King live   for ev - er,

and it became an unofficial National Anthem at a time when there was no such thing anywhere yet in Europe. But, requiring a choir of skilled voices and an orchestra with trumpets, this piece was not always easy to mount at short notice. Other patriotic ballads had to be found to serve the same purpose.

Therefore the singers found themselves scouring their repertoire of Masques and Oratorios for suitable material, while the house-composers in turn knocked up appropriate trifles. At Drury Lane the chief vocalist was now Thomas Lowe. He had sung in the first performance, at Cliveden in 1740, of Arne's "Masque of Alfred". Throughout 1745 he performed Arne's extracted chorus "Britons never will be slaves" (known to us as '*Rule Britannia*') on most nights. Arne was house composer at Drury Lane, so it is not surprising to find this piece failing to appear on Covent Garden playbills. Beard was not able to sing this rousing song until he was back on the books at Drury Lane (1748-59) three years later.[36] It is likely that, sung with his strong, manly and heroic tones, the piece might well have become popular enough to have taken on the identity of the real National Anthem. But the first recorded occasion on when he sang it, February 23 1751, was long after the Jacobite threat had subsided. Thomas Lowe's milder and more mellifluous performance in 1745 wasn't strong enough to establish it as a serious contender for an important national role. But Handel may have looked on and felt that Arne's tune was sufficiently strong to eclipse any of his martial arias; thus deciding to throw a pot-boiler of his own into the ring.

This was a setting of words by John Lockman '*Stand round, my brave boys*' and was snapped up by Drury Lane. Lowe stepped in front of the curtain to perform it on November 14 in the presence of those volunteering for military service.

> Stand round my brave boys, with heart and with voice,
> And all in full chorus agree,
> We'll fight for our King, and as loyally sing,
> And let the world know we'll be free.
>
> The rebels shall fly, as with shouts we draw nigh,
> And echo shall victory ring:
> Then safe from alarms, we'll rest on our arms,
> And chorus it – Long live the King. *etc*

---

[35] see: G.F. Handel, 'Four Coronation Anthems', ed. C. Bartlett, Oxford 1988, 'Preface'
[36] The Madden Ballad Collection contains 'Rule Britannia' with the variant title 'Britons [sic] Guardian Angel sung by Mr Beard at the Theatre Royal in Drury Lane'

Standround my brave boys, with heart and with voice, And all in full cho-rus a-gree, We'll fight for our King, and as loy-al-ly sing, And let the world know we'll be free, and let the world know we'll be free. The reb-els shall fly, as with shouts we draw nigh, and e - cho shall vic - to - ry ring; Then safe from a-larms, we'll rest on our arms, And cho - rus it'Long live the King,

W. Barclay Squire who researched this little-known piece while Curator of the Music in the Library at Buckingham Palace wrote: "Whether all this stir of patriotism roused Handel, or whether he received a commission from the theatre, it is impossible to say; but on November 14 the *General Advertiser* announced that at Drury Lane that evening there would be sung, at the end of the play of *'The Relapse'*, a Chorus Song set by Mr Handel for the Gentlemen Volunteers of the City of London."[37] The song was advertised for sale the next day, November 15:
"New Musick. This day is published A Song made for the Gentlemen Volunteers of the City of London, and sung by Mr Lowe, at the Theatre Royal in Drury Lane. Set to Musick by Mr Handel."

Thus Drury Lane had strong patriotic music, while Covent Garden was forced to resurrect old favourites from a previous time of conflict. Many years earlier in 1739, during the War of Jenkins's Ear, Beard had found great success with several songs celebrating Admiral Vernon's capture of Porto Bello. During the months of October and November of that year, when Londoners were aware of the hostilities but ignorant of the outcome, Beard sang "To Arms" and "Britons strike home" on most nights. These were two arias from Purcell's incidental music to the play "Bonduca, or The British Heroine"(1695), and their texts were suitably martial and aggressive:

> The oracle for War declares
> Success upon our Hearts and Spears.
>
> Britons strike home, revenge your Country's wrong:
> Strike and record yourselves in Druid songs.

On March 15 1740 London learned of the successful naval action. The theatre was quick to respond, and on the 25th Beard sang 'Nel Pugnar' and 'A Song in the character of a Captain of an English Man-of-War upon the taking of Porto Bello':[38]

> Spain no longer shall assume Boys,
> The true Ocean as their own;
> For at last the time is come Boys,
> We've their Topsails lower'd down:
> Tho' in politics contesting,
> Round to Round they veer about,
> All their shifts and manifesting,
> We will with our Broadsides rout. etc

---

[37] Arthur M. Friedlander, 'Two Patriotic Songs by Handel', Musical Times, May 1st 1925, pp. 416-9
[38] A copy of this is in the Madden Collection, University Library, Cambridge, and is illustrated on page 118

This was something new. Appearing in costume in the interval between the acts he became noted for his little scenes "in character". According to the requirements of the moment, he was happy to don the costume of a common soldier or sailor, or a Captain or Admiral to rouse the audience's spirits. He did it in the theatre, at the Pleasure Gardens, and at private parties in the taverns. Such 'acts' transferred, in time, to the Music Hall. But in the mid-eighteenth century these did not yet exist; and the 'straight' singer of Handel's fine oratorios was just as able to sing florid arias in the guise of the biblical military hero 'Judas Maccabaeus' as to turn his vocal prowess to a ballad in the character of the contemporary hero 'Jack Tar'.

Because of Beard's success at popularising these pieces of propaganda it was possible to read, in the St James Magazine,[39] "...let but *Britons strike home*, or *God save the King*, be sounded in the ears of five thousand brave Englishmen, ...and they'll drive every monsieur into the sea, and make 'em food for mackrel".[40]

The "English Captain's Song" stayed popular through March and April 1740, but at the end of the season it fell out of Beard's repertoire. But in the dark days of 1745, when Bonnie Prince Charlie was expected to arrive in London at any moment[41], Beard dusted off the patriotic songs of 1739-40. To these he added new 'occasional' ballads by the Covent Garden house-composer John Frederick Lampe (composer of the ballad opera *The Dragon of Wantley*). These were not even as successful as Handel's, and quickly faded from view. One of them was called "The English Hero's welcome home", which was rather optimistic as there had been no

---

[39] The St James Magazine, 1762

[40] quoted in: Terence M. Freeman, 'Dramatic Representations of British Soldiers and Sailors on the London Stage', 1660-1800, The Edwin Mellen Press, Lewiston/Queenstown/Lampeter

[41] Horace Walpole, writing to Sir Horace Mann, British Envoy in Florence, on 27th September after the battle of Prestonpans, voiced the dread that all Londoners were feeling: "Prince Charles has called a Parliament in Scotland for the 7th of October; ours does not meet till the 17th, so that even in the show of liberty and laws they are beforehand with us... I have so trained myself to expect this ruin, that I see it approach without any emotion". Scholes, ibid. p. 5-6

battle between the forces by January 8 1746, when it first appears on playbills! The Duke of Cumberland was still pursuing the rebels northwards to Scotland at this time; and a skirmish at Clifton, near Penrith, had been inconclusive. More to Beard's taste was a fine aria with trumpet obbligato from incidental music by Purcell: 'Genius of England' (from 'Don Quixote'). This found a more regular place in his repertoire, beginning with performances throughout October 1745, and remaining there until the end of the season. The text by Thomas Durfey, could not have been better chosen, and may well have helped military recruitment in these troubled times:

> Genius of England
> From thy pleasant Bow'r of Bliss
> Arise and spread thy sacred Wings;
> Guard from foes the British state,
> Thou on whose smile does wait
> Th'uncertain happy Fate
> Of Monarchies and Kings.
> Then follow brave Boys to the Wars;
> The Laurel you know is the prize:
> Who brings home the noblest Scars
> Looks finest in Celia's Eyes.

But what was wanted was something as grand as the extract from Handel's Coronation Anthem, but which could still be performed by as small a group as were employed by the theatres for the interval music. It was Thomas Arne who would achieve lasting glory by discovering and arranging the melody, and John Beard who created history by singing it onstage on Saturday 28 September 1745.

3. THE NATIONAL ANTHEM

Arne was a Catholic - as was John Beard's wife Henrietta - and their personal feelings about the Jacobite invasion must have been very mixed at this time. Beard must have been particularly alarmed as Henrietta had Jacobite blood running through her veins. She was King James II's great-granddaughter by the illegitimate line passing down from his mistress Arabella Churchill. The Young Pretender was almost her age, and was the King's grandson by his second wife Mary of Modena. Thus Henrietta and Bonny Prince Charlie were cousins - though one suspects that she kept this quite quiet at such a delicate moment in time. If it was well-known that Beard was married to *a)* a catholic, and *b)* a relative of the Pretender, then it was very astute of him to make a public show of his loyalty to the House of Hanover by singing hymns for their safety.

Arne played a very clever game. Asked by Drury Lane to produce a ballad in support of the House of Hanover (which his stirring aria 'Rule Britannia' failed to do) he made use of an old <u>catholic</u> anthem tune.[42] This was recognised by some at a very early stage. When Benjamin Victor wrote to the absent Garrick to tell him of the amazing musical innovation in the London theatres he reported that the new loyal words were sung to 'an old anthem tune', and that the song consisted of 'the very words, and music, of an old Anthem that was sung at St. James's Chapel, for King James the Second, when the Prince of Orange was landed, to deliver us from popery and slavery.'[43]

This is also confirmed by Charles Burney in a letter to Sir Joseph Banks of 29th July 1806[44] – which also contains the interesting details of the first performers' names:

'Old Mrs Arne, the mother of Dr. Arne and Mrs Cibber, a bigoted Roman Catholic, assured me at the time, 1746, that God save the King was written and sung for King James, in 1688, when the Prince of Orange was hovering over the coast; she said she had heard it sung, not only at the Playhouse but in the street. Her son, Mr. Arne, composer to Drury Lane Theatre, at the desire of Mr. Fleetwood, the Patentee, harmonised this loyal song for the stage, and he made a trio of it for Mrs Cibber *[his sister]*, Beard, and Reinhold, with instrumental accompaniments without knowing the author of the words or original melody, and it continued to be sung and called for a full year after the suppression of the rebellion.'

As a little digression it is worth noting that the origins of the tune have not been definitively traced by most of the musicologists who have written on the subject.[45] Written in a 'Galliard' style with two distinct halves composed of unequal length - three phrases followed by four phrases - it has a distinctive musical shape. Although there are several 17th century pieces that have been discovered to resemble it closely, and that have musical phrases in common, none make an absolutely perfect fit. There are real similarities with a *Minuet* by Purcell (1696), an Old Song *'Franklin is fled away'*, the carol *'Remember O thou man'* (set in the minor key), and a keyboard piece by the organist John Bull (1562-1628). Frustratingly, the manuscript of the last piece in this list has disappeared, and it is only known from a copy made by Sir George Smart (1776-1867) in the nineteenth century. But it is the only version of the tune to have the unequal shape of three phrases followed by four.

Percy Scholes makes a good case for this being the inspiration behind the old Anthem sung in King James II's time.[46] There is a convincing argument that it was

[42] see Percy A. Scholes, 'God save the Queen', Oxford University Press, London, 1954 pp. 9-13 for a description of the version of the song given in *Thesaurus Musicus*, and published c.1744 (i.e. before its performance at Drury Lane). This appears to be the source for Arne's actual arrangement.
[43] Percy A. Scholes, 'God save the Queen', Oxford University Press, London, 1954, pp. 49-50
[44] W. H. Cummings, 'God save the King', Novello, London 1902, pp. 35-6
[45] including W.H. Cummings, op.cit.
[46] Percy A. Scholes, 'God save the Queen', Oxford University Press, London, 1954, pp. 97-101

performed even earlier for James I in 1607 at the Merchant Taylor Hall, and that the words to Dr Bull's tune were by Ben Jonson, beginning: "God save great James our King".[47] *The Times* newspaper of Wednesday January 30th 1822 carried this report:

"Mr Clark, of the King's Chapel, has, in a work recently published, traced back from the records and books of the Merchant Tailors' Company, that this song was composed and sung on the escape of King James I from the [Gun] Powder Plot, and sung in their Hall by the gentlemen and children of his Majesty's Chapel Royal, on the day when King James dined there, when a grand solemn entertainment, to celebrate the event of the King's escape from the Gunpowder Plot, was given; and it is supposed that the Church Service was performed previous to the entertainment, as the Dean and Sub-Dean were present, and an organ was erected in the Hall upon the occasion, which was on the 16th July, 1607. Dr. John Bull was first Professor of Music to Gresham College in 1596, and was chosen organist to James I in 1607, and played before the King at the above entertainment. It appears by the Merchant Tailors' records, that the Master of the Company conferred with Ben Jonson, who was then Poet Laureate, to write some verses for an anthem, which he accordingly did, beginning with 'God save great James our King,' and Dr. John Bull set them to music, which is the same so universally admired now George is substituted."

Arne's manuscript is interesting for many reasons. It shows what words were sung when it was first performed in 1745, and in what key the music was played. This has traditionally been G major, which is the key of the first publication. But in September of that year he wrote it out in E flat major. The reason was doubtless because his sister - the fine actress who had also been the first singer of Handel's aria 'He was despised' - was a contralto. Beard's tenor part in this trio version is very comfortably written for his range, from low F to high G:

The text published in 1745,[48] though largely based on that penned initially by Ben Jonson in 1607, is actually derived from the version published in 1744 in the *Thesaurus Musicus*. Nobody ever claimed authorship of the lyrics. The *Thesaurus Musicus* version has the usual verse 2 words "O Lord our God arise / Scatter his

---

[47] Andrew Ashbee, 'Records of English Court Music', Snodland, c. 1986
[48] Authorship was claimed on behalf of his father, Henry Carey (author of "Sally in our alley") by George Saville Carey in 1795 on very slender grounds, that have since been discredited. W. H. Cummings, ibid. p.45-

enemies" etc. The *Gentleman's Magazine* added a new verse in its 1745 publication which is still sung today: "Thy choicest gifts in store / On him be pleased to pour...etc." Arne must have been quietly pleased to have foisted on an unsuspecting Protestant nation a tune heavy with Catholic resonance. Even John Beard may have been able to go home to his wife Henrietta and enjoy the subtle joke with her. The actual autograph manuscript of the song is in the British Library.[49]

There is a final mystery to unravel. John Beard was contracted to Covent Garden Theatre between 1743-8. Eye-witness records all show him as singing in the first performance of the anthem at Drury Lane on Saturday September 28 1745. Why?

The answer, although based on speculation, could be as follows. The tenor singer employed at Drury Lane after Beard's removal to Covent Garden was Thomas Lowe, whom we have seen having success with 'Rule Britannia' and Handel's new ballad. He was not a quick learner. Burney described him as having "the finest tenor voice I ever heard in my life", but who "for want of diligence and cultivation could never be safely trusted with anything better than a ballad, which he constantly learned by his ear".[50] In contrast, Beard "... knew as much of music as was necessary to sing a single part at sight, and with a voice that was more powerful than sweet, he became the most useful and favourite singer of his time..."[51]

Lowe was obviously not the man to be entrusted with a harmony part at short notice. Arne knew Beard well; they had worked together at Drury Lane during the 1730s. He now had to prepare something stirring in a hurry, to counter the news of Sir John Cope's defeat at the Battle of Prestonpans, which had just reached London. The Drury Lane management needed to reassure their clientele, many of whom were planning to move out of the capital, with music that was upbeat and patriotic. So Arne cannily took the catholic tune that he had found in the recently published *Thesaurus Musicus* and quickly made a 3-part ballad of it. He probably imagined it would be another occasional piece like all of the others - here today and gone tomorrow. It was a Saturday and he needed good performers. He knew where to find a reliable tenor. One can imagine Beard in the painting room at Covent Garden finishing his steak with the other members of the *Sublime Society of Beefsteaks*; being called outside to address this emergency; learning the new music as he went across the road to his previous home-turf; and finally striding onstage with his colleagues Susanna Cibber and Henry Theodore Reinhold to sing another of Arne's arrangements - little realising what this particular one would lead to.

Its success was so complete that it was in print next day, and being talked about far and wide. Magazines like the *Gentleman's Magazine* were quick to print it, in a show of loyalty, adding new verses of their own. Covent Garden Theatre needed to get onto the bandwagon as well. Their own star singer had been involved in the first performance, after all.

Benjamin Victor's letter to Garrick, which is dated October 10, i.e. a mere twelve days after the first performance, reveals that the custom did indeed spread to both theatres:

"The stage at both houses is the most *pious*, as well as the most *loyal* place in the three kingdoms. Twenty men appear at the end of every play: and one, stepping

---

[49] Add. MS. 29,466
[50] Charles Burney, 'A General History of Music', London 1935, p.1010
[51] 'Memoirs of Dr. Charles Burney', University of Nebraska Press, Lincoln & London 1988, p.131

forward from the rest, with uplifted hands and eyes, begins singing, to an old anthem tune".[52]

The idea of copyright was still in its infancy at this time; but there was an understanding between the theatres that they didn't poach each other's product until a season, or a set number of performances, had passed. No such qualms can have attached to Arne's arrangement of this new loyal song. Obviously the fact that it was only an arrangement - not an original composition - made a significant difference.[53] Charles Burney clarifies matters in his letter of 1806:

"I, then a pupil of Mr Arne, was desired by some of the Covent Garden singers with whom I was acquainted, and who knew that I was a bit of a composer, to set parts to the old tune for the *new house*, as it was then called, which I did utterly ignorant who wrote the words or put them to music."[54]

Beard was likely to be the instigator of this arrangement. As a frequent performer of Arne's music (he had recently been singing in performances of his '*Comus*') and as a colleague of both Arne's wife and sister, he would have been a regular visitor at their household. Here he would have met the teenaged Burney, who had recently arrived from Chester as Arne's apprentice. Initial performances at Covent Garden were not advertised in the press, for the reasons outlined above. But during the course of the autumn there appear references to Beard singing "*the new occasional song*"; and on December 26 the management plucked up the courage to advertise: "*at the end of the play "God save the King".*

It was not clear at this stage that this song was destined to eclipse all the other professions of loyalty being sung onstage. New ones still kept arriving, in tandem with the progress of the fortunes of war. New verses were also added to the existing anthem, whose warmongering lyric was a response to the immediacy of the threat. Without a knowledge of the origins of the National Anthem, lines like "Confound their Politicks, Frustrate their knavish tricks" must seem quite baffling. Understandably this verse is usually omitted in modern performance! But early in 1746, the London public heard verses like this:

> O grant that Cumberland
> May, by his mighty hand,
> Victory bring;
> May he sedition hush,
> And like a torrent rush,
> Rebellious hearts to crush,
> God save the King.

After the Battle of Culloden, on April 16 1746, one could predict that the happy news would be reflected on the daily playbills. While Handel was contemplating a large-scale celebration, with an oratorio on an appropriate theme, (*'Judas Maccabaeus'* in which the heroic leader in the title role would be sung by John

---

[52] Percy A. Scholes, God save the Queen, Oxford University Press, London, 1954, p. 7

[53] According to Scholes (ibid. p.13) the latest date of publication for *Thesaurus Musicus* must be 1744, since it was advertised for sale in the *Daily Advertiser* on 16th November 1744. Therefore the publication of "God save our Lord the King" predates the first recorded performance at Drury Lane by nine months.

[54] Quoted in W. H. Cummings, 'God save the King', Novello, London 1902, p. 36

Beard) the Covent Garden management was offering its public, from April 25 onwards, "an Occasional Song on the defeat of the Rebels, by Beard". This must have been the Handel song 'From scourging Rebellion' or 'A Song on the Victory obtained over the Rebels by His Royal Highness the Duke of Cumberland' that Walsh published a month later on 26 May.

For some time afterwards there was a certain amount of confusion as to which song was being referred to by the title "*God save the King*". This had earlier been applied to the extract from Handel's Coronation Anthem "Zadok the Priest". Now there was an alternative song, much easier for unison singing, with the same title. Gradually the Handel became known as the 'old' version. As late as 1770 it is apparent from the correspondence of the Sharp family - keen amateur music-makers - that these terms were still being employed. One day in 1770 they were making music in their sailing-barge on the river Thames when they encountered King George III and Queen Charlotte, also on an outing by the river.

"They were seated on a bench under a large tree. As soon as we came opposite to them there happened luckily half a bar's rest, in which time the performers pulled off their hats, and went on in time till the watermen had let down the anker and made us fast. The first piece was *God save the King* (to another tune)." [presumably the Arne version]

Later, after the royal party had enjoyed an *al fresco* concert and suffered the interruption of a shower of rain, "we struck up *God save the King* in the old tune [presumably the Handel], and the number of people on the water joined us, and the Hurraugh was noble, and after each time His Majesty moved his hat."

The Sharp family musicians were judicious in the order of their programme. The Arne version of *God save the King* is not exactly jolly, and doesn't encourage an audience to join in with hurrahs. But the lively Handel version that concluded their impromptu concert, with its repeated exclamations of "Long live the King, God save the King!" (see page 116) would have allowed the King time to doff his hat and acknowledge the acclamation each time.

It may appear strange that the British public chose Arne's solemn, catholic, melody as their expression of national solidarity. The text says nothing about being proud to be British - as the jollier *Roast Beef* and *Rule Britannia* type of song had.[55] In fact, reflecting the occasion for which it was first penned, it is little more than a prayer for the safety of the royal family. The impact that this solemnity had on the super-charged feelings of the nation in the perilous days of 1745-6 can be gathered from an eye-witness to the early performances of the original vocal trio version, in which Mrs Cibber sang the melody-line. Lady Lucy Meyrick, discussing the actresses that she had admired in her youth, regarded Mrs Cibber as 'unrivalled' - in comparison to the other leading ladies of the day - in one particular aspect:

"this was in singing *God save the King* in chorus on the stage. She said it was a perfect hymn as *she* sang it; and indeed so it ought always to be, and so we trust it is felt by him for whom with such true British loyalty it is offered up".[56]

[55] Burney's view was that "Rule Britannia" was "the most pleasing air to English words which our national music could boast." 'Memoirs of Dr. Charles Burney', ibid. p.41
[56] Laetitia Hawkins, 'Memoirs, Anecdotes, Facts and Opinions', vol. 1, 1824

After Drury Lane and Covent Garden had established the custom of performing the piece at the end of their evening's entertainments it was not long before the custom was spreading through the kingdom. The Theatre in Goodman's Fields adopted the practice by October 2 1746; and the provincial theatres were soon to follow. Even the chimes of clocks were altered to ring out the new tune. At St Margaret's Church, Westminster, right beside the seat of Government, the bells which had previously rung out the tune of John Beard's popular 'hit' "*Britons, strike home*" since March 1740 were now updated, as we learn from their minute-book:

15 October 1748. The churchwardens are authorised to cause the repair of the chimes, they to be set to the tune of that Loyal Song called 'God save the King'.

The music was also hawked through the streets by ballad-sellers, as can be seen in William Hogarth's famous painting 'The March to Finchley, 1745' that celebrates the volunteer militia sent out to defend London against the Jacobite rebels. In the centre of the picture a guardsman walks along beside a ballad-seller, whose copy of the new national anthem is hanging from her basket. It was called for in the theatre even when there was no pressing military threat, as this poem[57] - showing the theatre from the performer's point of view - reveals:

> The coach below, the clock gone five,
> Now to the theatre we drive:
> Peeping the curtain's eyelet through,
> Behold the house in dreadful view!
> Observe how close the critics sit,
> And not one bonnet in the pit.
> With horror hear the galleries ring,
> Nosy! Black Joke, *God save the King!*[58]

George Anne Bellamy recounts an occasion when the new national anthem interrupted a play. In her unreliable memoirs, written long after the event and usually full of inaccuracies, she tells how the news of the victory at Culloden arrived during a performance of *Macbeth*, whilst the King was in the audience.

"They stopped the play ... and ordering all the singers to unwitch themselves, directed them to sing 'God save great George our King'.[59]

Other popular ballads emerged during Britain's protracted Wars.[60] Handel had success in 1748 with two arias from 'Judas Maccabaeus' - 'Tis liberty' and 'Come ever smiling Liberty' - both of which looked likely to challenge the supremacy of *God save the King* in the audience's affection. They were called for continuously at this time. Now it was the leading ladies, Mrs Storer and Mrs Faulkner, who added lustre to their reputations with the nightly performances.[61]

[57] Robert Lloyd, 'To George Colman Esq: a familiar Epistle, 1761' quoted in Scholes, ibid. p. 30
[58] 'Black Joke' was a popular tune of the day, and 'Nosy' was the theatre musician Giacomo Cervetto
[59] George Ann Bellamy, 'An Apology', vol. 3, p.88
[60] The War of the Austrian Succession lasted from 1740-8. The Jacobite uprising was only one element in it. The death of the Holy Roman Emperor Charles VI in October 1740 sparked off a crisis that led to Spain, Prussia & France all trying to acquire territory at Austria's expense. Peace was negotiated at Aix-la-Chapelle in 1748.
[61] Winton Dean, 'Handel's Dramatic Oratorios and Masques', O.U.P. London, 1959, p. 473

'Tis Li - ber - ty, dear Li - ber - ty a - lone, that gives___ fresh beau - ty to___ the sun, that gives fresh beau - ty to___ the sun.

William Boyce wrote "Heart of Oak" with David Garrick at the time of the Seven Years War (1756-63). This was a huge success at the time, both as a solo number for the male singers, and in the context of its position within Garrick's pantomime "Harlequin's Invasion" (1759):

> Come, cheer up, my lads, 'tis to glory we steer,
> To add something more to this wonderful year,
> To honor we call you, as free men, not slaves,
> For who are so free as the sons of the waves?
> Heart of oak are our ships, Heart of oak are our men:
> We always are ready. Steady, boys, steady.
> We'll fight and we'll conquer again and again.

This recalls the spirit of the songs Beard sang at the time of Admiral Vernon's battle at Porto Bello. Some twenty years after that action Beard was still dressing up as a sailor and doing his patriotic 'act' once again (pictured on page 118). On the 28 November 1760 the 45-year old was creating the role of another sturdy sailor: this time it was 'Thomas', in Covent Garden's new ballad opera "Thomas and Sally". By the 23 April 1761 the playbills featured an additional puff, that he would sing 'by desire, *Heart of Oak*'.

Dibdin would write other stirring nautical songs, to rouse the nation during the French and Napoleonic wars. But the national anthem had taken root. It was often the earliest music that a child would hear. Henry Angelo recounts that: "When not four years old … my nurse took me to St. James's church, when, in the psalms, hearing everyone about me singing, I thought I must join in the chorus, and began to bawl out as loud as I could *God save the King*, the only song I knew. The whole congregation were convulsed with laughter..." [62]

And so the music and words stuck fast. Ordinary people could remember both easily, and felt moved to be able to participate in something that was as loyal as it was solemn. Arne had always worried that Handel's music would eclipse his own. Burney reported that he felt like Marsyas challenging the Sun-God Apollo to a music contest in the old Greek legend. For him Handel, the immigrant German and friend of the Royal Family, was a "tyrant and usurper against whom he frequently rebelled; but with as little effect as Marsyas against Apollo". [63] But in this one respect Arne's music triumphed over Handel's. His version of *God save the King* became the nation's favourite.

---

[62] Henry Angelo, 'Reminiscences', vol. 2, 1828, p. 368
[63] Charles Burney, 'A General History of Music', London 1935, pp.1010-1

CHAPTER 6
THE RISE OF THE CHARITIES

1. THE FUND FOR THE SUPPORT OF DECAYED MUSICIANS

John Beard was still a relative newcomer on the London musical scene in 1738 when the cream of London's musicians joined the violinist Michael Festing, the flautist Charles Weidemann and the bassoonist Thomas Vincent in the *Crown and Anchor* Tavern opposite St Clement Dane's Church on April 23 to try and find a way to help their less successful colleagues. Amongst such distinguished names as Handel, Boyce, Arne, Pepusch, Defesch, Sammartini, Ravenscroft, John Stanley, John Travers and Edward Purcell (Henry's son), it is good to find John Beard amongst the signatories who drew up the original Declaration of Trust. Most of the 228 members who signed up in May were composers, organists and instrumentalists at the theatres. There were very few singers in the list, as there were so few outstanding English singers at this period. Some of the Chapel Royal men are represented - including Samuel Weely and Bernard Gates - but the soloists in the list, apart from the 22 year-old Beard, are Richard Leveridge, Theodore Reinhold and the current *Macheath* of the day, Thomas Salway.[1]

The rules of the Society of Musicians were formalised on August 28 1739, and provided that each subscriber should pay 'at least half a crown a Quarter'. The accruing sum was to be used charitably to help the widows and children of any destitute musician who had been a subscriber for at least a year. It would also cover the cost of a funeral 'not exceeding five pounds'. Since the amount raised by subscriptions would fall short of requirements, the musicians agreed to put on a concert every year to raise funds. In time they also received handsome legacies from musicians' wills. In 1759 Handel left £1000 to the Society; and the Handel Commemoration of 1784 added £6000 to the funds. Handel's strong personal interest in the charity may have stemmed from the initial discovery (prompting Festing into action) that the children of Jean Christian Kytch, his former oboe soloist, were near to destitution and had been spotted driving donkeys through the Haymarket.[2]

Beard was willing to put his talents at the disposal of the society at a very early stage. On the 20 March 1739 Handel put on a performance of *Alexander's Feast* at the Haymarket Theatre 'for the benefit and increase of a Fund Established for the Support of Decay'd Musicians and their Families'. It was an appropriate work to programme in the Society's first-ever charity concert, subtitled as it is *The Power of Music*. Beard and Signora Francesina were the two vocal soloists. The next day the London Daily Post reported:

'On Tuesday Night last *Alexander's Feast* was perform'd at the Opera House in the Haymarket, to a numerous and polite audience... and we hear, several of the Subscribers (tho' they had Tickets sent to them Gratis for this Performance) were so

---

[1] Thomas Salway (c.1706-43) had worked with Handel in 1733 in the Oxford performances of *Esther*, *Deborah* and *Acis and Galatea*. He would have been a more obvious choice for principal tenor in Handel's 1734 season, if the emerging Beard had not attracted the composer's attention.
[2] Donald Burrows, 'Handel', O.U.P. Oxford 1994, p. 201. They had been spotted from the Orange Coffee House driving donkeys through the Haymarket. Richard Crewson, 'Apollo's Swan & Lyre', London, 2000

generous as to pay at the Doors, and others have since sent presents to the Fund: Mr Handel gave the House [*i.e. the takings*] and his performance, upon this Occasion, Gratis, and Mr Heidegger made a present of Twenty Pounds to defray the other incidental Expences".[3]

One year later Handel repeated his generosity to the Fund with a concert at Lincoln's Inn Theatre on 28 March, comprising *Acis and Galatea*, a new Organ Concerto for himself to play, and the *St Cecilia Ode*. This tribute to the Patron Saint of Music was well chosen. The soloists were the same as the previous year - Beard and Signora Francesina - who were familiar with this programme, having performed it already at the beginning of Handel's Lent oratorio season, on February 21.

In 1741 Handel gave the Fund the takings from the performance of '*Parnasso in Festa*' at the King's Theatre on the 14 March. But this was the year of Beard's absence from the stage and he was not in the cast.

The next time that Beard seems to have sung for the Society of Musicians' annual fund-raising concert is on April 10 1745. This took place in his current 'home' territory of Covent Garden Theatre. By now the format for the evening had evolved into a miscellaneous programme, in which a variety of artists were able to give their services. The orchestra performed various overtures and 'Grand Sonatas', and a galaxy of singers performed their favourite arias. Many of these were by Handel. In 1745 the other singers were Signora Francesina, Miss Robinson, and Reinhold. Beard sang 'Total eclipse' and 'Why does the God of Israel sleep' from *Samson*, and the trio 'The flocks shall leave the mountains' from *Acis and Galatea*. In the following years, from 1746 onwards, the concerts regularly took place at the King's Theatre Haymarket, and involved the Italians soloists engaged at the operas there. From 1746 there were regular appearances by a young soprano called Signora Frasi who was later to make her mark in Handel oratorios.[4] According to her vocal coach, Charles Burney, she was 'young and interesting in her person, had a sweet clear voice, and a smooth and chaste style of singing, which ...pleased natural ears, and escaped the censure of critics'.[5] She would become a regular colleague of Beard's in the 1750s, and they would appear together at many concerts in London and at the emerging summer Festivals. Another of her strong features was her excellent diction - "she pronounced our language in singing with a ...distinct articulation"[6] - which complemented Beard's style well.

Beard's next contributions to the Society of Musicians fund-raising recommenced after a six year interval and were to last for many years. On April 16 1751 he chose to sing arias by Handel, and in addition to the *Samson* items from 1745 added 'Tune your harps' from *Esther*, a performance of which he had given on March 15, in Handel's recent oratorio season. In 1752 the concert took place on March 24. Beard was joined by Signora Frasi as usual, and a new bass, Robert Wass from the Choir of the Chapel Royal, who replaced the recently deceased Reinhold.

Extracts from Handel's *Acis and Galatea* were always popular at these concerts. In addition to the trio 'The flocks shall leave the mountains' Beard also performed Acis' graceful aria 'Love in her eyes sits playing'. To this he added two

---

[3] London Daily Post, 22nd March 1739, quoted in Deutsch, p. 478

[4] Handel engaged her for the oratorio season of 1749 as the title role in 'Susanna', and she remained his prima donna until his death in 1759. See her entry in 'New Grove Dictionary of Music', London, 1980

[5] Charles Burney, [see: *Memoirs of Charles Burney*, University of Nebraska Press 1988, p. 93] quoted in Winton Dean, 'Handel's Dramatic Oratorios and Masques', OUP, Oxford 1959, p.655

[6] Daniel Lysons, 'History of the Origin and Progress of the ... Three Choirs Festival', Gloucester 1812

more Handel arias: 'Thro' the land so lovely blooming' and 'The trumpet's loud clangour' from the St Cecilia Ode. The *Acis* trio was called for again on 30 April 1753, and Beard diversified this year by adding to the usual Handel fare an aria by Maurice Greene ('O lovely fair'), the composer of the yearly Court Odes in which Beard sang. The repertoire was even more extraordinary in 1754, when the concert took place unusually early on February 28. The Handel aria which Beard chose was 'Endless Pleasure' from Semele; a curious choice since this is a soprano aria for the diva in the title role. It is certainly strange that he did not choose one of his own arias from the role of 'Jupiter', which he had created in Handel's 1744 season. The obvious choice would certainly have been 'Where'er you walk', which is the best-known tenor aria from the work. But there is no record of him ever singing it as a concert item. He also performed an aria 'O 'tis Elysium all' by Nicolo Pasquali, an Italian composer who had settled in Britain and was working in London and Edinburgh. This was actually a sizeable Cantata entitled 'Celia', which was the first item in Pasquali's *12 English Songs* (published in 1750).

Beard started to become an indispensable feature of the yearly programmes. After the experiment of only using visiting Italian singers was over. he always tried to put in an appearance - even when he had commitments elsewhere. In 1755 he was due to perform the role of 'Prentice' in *The London Prentice* at Drury Lane Theatre on the night of the fund-raiser (March 17). As his show was the Afterpiece, with a start time of around 8pm, he agreed to appear in the first half of the concert at the King's Theatre Haymarket, and then make a dash for Drury Lane. Records do not exist to tell if he was successful: but he was put on the bill in the third place, after an Overture by Dubourg and an aria by Signor Mondini. He offered just one item: a *Cantata* by Thomas Arne. Although not specified in the Programme, this was most probably *Cymon and Iphigenia,* which was in his current repertoire. He had performed it in the interval at Drury Lane twice in the preceding days, on March 13 and 15. The witty libretto describes a country yokel, 'Cymon' [= Simon], falling in love with the sleeping form of 'Iphigenia'. Arne's recitatives and arias gave Beard great scope for some characterful singing:

Several further years elapsed when his commitments at the Theatre prevented him taking part in the fund-raising concerts. Perhaps it was a close-run thing getting back to the theatre in 1755. So it is not until 1759 that his name appears on the playbills once again. On February 2 Arne masterminded an enlarged version of his Masque of *Alfred the Great*, and put it on for the benefit of the fund at Covent Garden. Although Beard was in the last year of his contract at Garrick's Drury Lane, he was released by the management, and therefore joined a cast including Signora Frasi and Miss Charlotte Brent - Arne's new prodigy - with whom Beard would be paired later in the year for performances of *The Beggar's Opera*. His role in this work included, of course, the famous aria 'Rule Britannia'.

From 1761 onwards Beard was too busy assisting the Covent Garden management to be able to take a large part in further concerts for the fund, although it is clear from the letter he wrote on behalf of a colleague's widow (see Appendix 4) that he had its interests at heart. However, he sang for the fund in *Messiah* on April 24 1760. At this time, before John Rich's death, he was only the assistant manager at Covent Garden. He was not required for performance on this particular day. The singing between the intervals was undertaken, according to the playbill, by Lowe, who could not therefore have been the tenor soloist at the King's Theatre Haymarket. In view of the fact that Beard had been the tenor soloist in performances of *Messiah* on 26 and 28 March, and would sing in the Foundling Hospital performance on 2 May, it is more than likely that he was the unnamed soloist on this occasion. He made one last appearance for the fund on 12 March 1761, when he sang a single aria - 'When Bacchus, jolly God' - by his friend, and former fellow-chorister at the Chapel Royal, Samuel Howard.

2. THE FOUNDLING HOSPITAL

The institution of annual performances of *Messiah* at the Foundling Hospital, in April or May, dated back to an occasion in 1749 when Handel first learned of the activities of this new charity. The *Hospital for the Maintenance and Education of Exposed and Deserted Young Children* had been set up ten years previously by the fiercely determined, retired sea-captain, Thomas Coram. Handel came to hear of its ambitious building programme from his publisher John Walsh, who had been elected a Governor in 1748. William Hogarth was also doing a lot of good work publicising it amongst his circle of friends. So John Beard, who met him regularly at the Beef-Steak club, was also bound to know about the ambitious work that was going on at the end of his road. The site was 56 acres of Lamb's Conduit Fields: open country lying at the north end of Red Lyon Street.

Beard would have walked this way often from his house in Red Lyon Square to reach the nearest open and healthy stretch of countryside. If his business had ever been with Charles Jennens, Handel's friend and librettist, he would have also come this way to Jennens' London house in Queen Square. Also close by was Powis House, the palatial mansion built c. 1700 by William Herbert, the 2nd Marquis of Powis and Henrietta Beard's relative by her first marriage. The sight of this opulence must have been galling to the Beards as they fought their legal battles with the Powis family in the 1740s and 1750s. But, having fallen on lean times, the Powis family no longer resided there. The current resident was the Lord Chancellor, Lord Hardwicke (until 1757), followed by Lord Clive and Lord Henley. After a period when it housed first the Spanish, and then the French embassy, it was recovered by the Powis family in 1765. Henrietta's daughter Barbara must have lived in it for some years at this time when she was in London. In 1776 it is marked as 'empty' in the rate books, and it was pulled down a few years later.

By 1749 the Foundling Hospital building was far from complete. The West Wing was the only portion that was finished, and it housed the boys. The East Wing for the girls was yet to be constructed, and took until 1752 to be completed.[7] The chapel, begun in 1747, still needed window glass and furnishings when Handel made a generous offer to the Governors. He offered them a 'Performance of Vocal and Instrumental Musick' in aid of its completion. They were quick to accept, since they were anxious to make their buildings fashionable with wealthy and influential

---

[7] 'The Foundling Museum', London 2004, pp.17-19

classes, as a place to come and view the paintings which Hogarth had assembled,[8] as a place to view the progress of the orphan children, and as a place to worship. The Court Room, elegantly adorned with plasterwork by William Wilton, was a place where potential donors could be entertained and view the art collection: - it was London's very first art gallery in fact. The chapel would be an equally important feature when it was finished. The pulpit was designed and supplied by the architect Henry Keene at his expense. As an organ was also required, Handel's offer of a programme of music was taken up as a way of raising enough money to provide this.

The Hospital Minutes for May 9 1749 thank Handel for his offer. The concert was given, after various changes of date to suit the royalty that were hoping to attend, on May 27 at noon. The unfinished chapel was 'sash'd, and made commodious for the purpose', but there was still no glass in the windows and they had to be covered over with panels of paper instead.[9] The King sent £2000, the Prince and Princess of Wales attended, the tickets were half a guinea each, and more than a thousand people managed to squeeze in. The music comprised selections from the *Fireworks Music, Solomon,* and a new anthem *Blessed are they that considereth the poor and needy* ('The Foundling Hospital Anthem') which had been hurriedly compiled from movements of the 1737 Funeral Anthem together with a chorus from *Susanna* that had been deleted before its first performance. It ended with the *Hallelujah Chorus* from *Messiah* - a work which was still unfamiliar to the audience, but which would be heard in this chapel many more times in the future.

At some time in July 1749 Handel engaged Jonathan Morse of Barnet to provide the organ, which it was hoped would be up and ready for another fund-raising concert in a year's time. The advance newspaper advertisement on April 21 1750 indicated that 'Mr Handel will open the said Organ'.[10] But it soon became apparent that it would not be completed in time. So Morse was pressed 'to have as many stops as he can, for chorus's'.[11] Instead of a mixed programme, in which Handel would have played his organ concertos, it was decided to repeat the last work in his Lent oratorio season. By doing this he would be able to re-use the same performers, and cut down on the need for a serious amount of prior rehearsal. It was an eminently sensible plan, in view of the noon start-time. With a public eager to get good places from mid-morning onwards, (and coming as requested on the printed invitations 'without hoops and swords'[12] in order to be seated more comfortably), there would be precious little time for the performers to get ready. A prior rehearsal on the same day was out of the question.

The work that had concluded Handel's season on Maundy Thursday, April 12 1750, was *Messiah*. Lowe was the tenor, Guadagni the male alto - singing the newly arranged versions of 'But who may abide' and 'Thou art gone up on high' - Caterina Galli the mezzo, Giulia Frasi the soprano and Reinhold the bass. As usual, Bernard Gates provided the Chapel Royal choristers and a group of choirmen. They all duly reappeared at the Foundling Hospital on May 1. The success of the

---

[8] Hogarth decorated the Court Room with a grand scripture-piece: *Moses Brought to Pharaoh's Daughter* 1746; Francis Hayman chose the same theme for *The Finding of the Infant Moses in the Bulrushes*, 1746. Hogarth gave his portrait of Thomas Coram, and Thomas Hudson his portrait of the building's architect Theodore Jacobsen. Hogarth's *The March to Finchley* was won by the Hospital in a Lottery that it organised.
[9] Richard Luckett, 'Handel's Messiah, a celebration', London 1992, p. 163
[10] Donald Burrows, 'Handel', London 1994, p.339
[11] Christopher Hogwood, 'Handel', London, 1984, p. 220
[12] Christopher Hogwood, 'Handel', London, 1984, p. 220

performance was so enormous that a repeat had to be arranged on May 15 for the many people that had been turned away through lack of space. 1386 tickets, at half a guinea, had been sold for May 1, and the unlucky 599 who didn't manage to cram themselves into the building were accommodated at the repeat performance. The Hospital gained a sum of around £1000 after expenses. This event was clearly a crowd-puller - perhaps more so than Handel's performances of the same work in Covent Garden Theatre had been - and an exercise that the Governors of the Hospital were going to try and repeat if they could. Handel finally allowed himself to be elected a Governor, after initially turning down the honour, and an institution - the annual performance of *Messiah* for the benefit of the charity - was founded.

An approach was made before the end of the year for another 'Performance of Sacred Musick'. This time a February date was suggested, but Handel rejected it. It would have taken place before his oratorio season had even started, and would have therefore denied him the opportunity to re-engage a tried and trusted team of musicians. The same pattern as before, of a performance following the conclusion of his season, was much more to his liking, and was eventually adopted. There were two performances of *Messiah* in 1751, on April 18 and May 16. Beard was back working with Handel in this season. Never again would there be a performance of *Messiah* at the Foundling Hospital without him in the line-up of principal singers.

3. BEARD AND THE FOUNDLING HOSPITAL

Henrietta and John Beard would have noted the great crowd of fashionable society drawn to these first two performances. The line of carriages and sedan chairs would have thronged past their door. William Stukely, the antiquary, reported 'an infinite crowd of coaches at our end of the town to hear Handel's music'.[13] It is possible that they went to the concerts as members of the audience. All of the performers were Beard's good colleagues, and we know of several other occasions when he went to hear how his fellow tenors were doing.[14] On this occasion he would have been interested to hear how well Thomas Lowe did in music that had been conceived with his own vocal strengths in mind. None of the music was particularly ballad-like (Lowe's particular *forte*), and most was quite operatically conceived, with rapid runs in 'Every Valley' and 'Thou shalt break them', and intensely-felt emotion in 'Thy rebuke'. The simpler, ballad-like, melodies occurred in the soprano arias, such as 'He shall feed his flock' and 'How beautiful are the feet'.

It is possible that Beard and his wife would have supported this Charity's fund-raising activities because it was one that particularly appealed to the childless couple. Henrietta had a daughter Barbara by her first marriage, certainly. But she did not live with them, and her welfare had been a constant source of sadness to Henrietta, as she gradually lost parental control to a cabal of guardians appointed by her deceased husband's family and her brother, James the 2nd Earl Waldegrave. Henrietta was a young woman - only 22 - when she married Beard. It is curious that there appear to have been no children from this union.

An unpublished poem that the author has discovered in the Folger Shakespeare Library raises the possibility that Beard and Henrietta may have had a

---

[13] Richard Luckett, 'Handel's Messiah, a celebration', London 1992, p. 167

[14] These all date from a later period, but may reveal a regular habit. He heard Dibdin and Harrison in the 1770s & 1780s, and was a regular attender at private Concerts given by the Sharp family in this period: see Brian Crosby 'The Musical Activities of the Sharp family', *RMA Research Chronicle 34*, 2001

daughter. This is *An Epitaph on the Death of Miss Anna Beard* by William Havard. It is a puzzling document that still cannot be satisfactorily explained. Although no date is given on the pencilled page, it could easily date from any period between 1737 and Henrietta's death. Beard and Havard joined the Drury Lane company together in September 1737, and remained close friends, particularly through membership of the Beef-steak Club, well beyond 1753, the year of Henrietta's death. Their friendship only cooled in 1763 at the time of the Covent Garden riots. Although Beard remarried in 1758, any child of this union would surely have been too young to be the subject of this Epitaph:

An Epitaph on the Death of Miss Anna Beard

Reader! When Sorrow stops thy Footsteps here,
An[d] pours the Tribute of an Heart-sent Tear;
Thus reason with thyself – "If blooming Youth,
If Virgin Innocence and spotless Truth;
If filial Piety, and Duty join'd,
The clearest Sense, and most unblemished Mind:
If all these Virtues center'd in this Maid,
And all by Death are blasted and decay'd: -
Taught by Ref[l]ection turn thy Thoughts from Life,
Despise its flatt'ring Pomp, and gilded Strife;
Thy Griefs with a fond, weeping *Brother* join,
Lament her Death, and be prepared for thine."

In the Introduction to this book, the author considered a literal interpretation of the last two lines - conjecturing that Anna could have been a hitherto unknown sister of Beard, and the 'Brother' of the penultimate line was Beard himself.

However, knowing how Havard often referred to himself as Beard's (Beef-steak or Masonic) 'Brother' in their correspondence, this may not be the only explanation. It could well still be a relation, but we must also consider the possibility that Anna could have been a *child* of Beard and Henrietta. If so, Henrietta would have been certain to have raised the child - as she endeavoured to do with her daughter, Barbara - as a strict Catholic. Now Catholic baptismal records are notoriously difficult to find at this time, as all baptisms were performed in secret. Such records as can be found do not show the existence of such a child. There was no secrecy, however, about burials, which were carried out in consecrated ground. As we have seen, Henrietta was buried at St Pancras Old Church - which was also the place where members of her mother's Webbe family were traditionally buried in the 18th century.[15] Although this was nominally an Anglican church, it was the preferred resting-place for many Catholics because of its adherence to the Latin Mass. This would be the obvious place to bury the child, yet the records do not show any such burial. Similarly, there is no record of a burial at St George's, Queen Square - the Beards' parish church. Burials were not permitted at the only nearby Catholic church: the Sardinian Chapel.

---

[15] Henrietta's uncle Sir Thomas Webbe was buried there in June 1763, and his wife Anne in October 1777. Their son, her cousin, Sir John Webbe, was also buried there in April 1797. This Sir John Webbe sold the manor and advowson of Odstock, Wiltshire, to the Earl of Radnor in 1790: see Sir Richard Colt Hoare, 'History of Modern Wiltshire', vol. 3, London 1835, pp. 20-21

And so the identity of Miss Anna Beard, for whom this Epitaph was written, remains a mystery. From the text of the poem it seems likely that the child was young. The presence of a Hospital for young, neglected children up the road must have appealed to the sensitivities of Henrietta, who had never known real paternal or maternal love in her own sad childhood. The day-to-day functioning of the Hospital involved a regular Admission Day, when crowds of poor women would gather at the entrance with their unwanted babies.[16] This became an occasion on which wealthy and respectable ladies would be present to observe the spectacle of the ballot. In Samuel Wale's painting *Admission of Children to the Hospital by Ballot* of this exact period (1749)[17] we can see ladies of Henrietta's age and class in one of the fine rooms supervising just such an occasion. With little to occupy her, apart from her all-consuming legal battles, Henrietta would have had time on her hands to be one of these unnamed ladies.

The charity had to be one of enormous consequence to the Beard household, as he - alone of all the performers - regularly returned his fee. This was no small sum. We can see from the extant records for 1754 and 1758, where there is a blank beside Beard's entry, that Frasi took 6 guineas, and other major soloists 3 or 4 guineas. Five guineas was regarded as a normal amount to pay a soloist at the Three Choirs Festival in this period.[18] This was a week's wage at the Theatre. Even at the height of his fame, in 1760, Beard was only earning a wage of £1 3s 4d a day, or £7 per week (for a six-day week)[19].

Beard would have been delighted to sing for Handel again in 1751. If there had been programme-books as we now know them, containing the performers' names, it would be much clearer if he had taken part in any of his usual roles in the oratorios during the previous 3 years [see Appendix 1]. Without this evidence, much

[16] 'The Foundling Museum', London 2004, pp.26-7
[17] Engraving by N. Parr, published 9th May 1749, see: 'The Foundling Museum', London 2004, p.26
[18] W. Hayes, 'Anecdotes of the Five Music-Meetings at Church Leighton', Oxford, 1768
[19] The London Stage, Part 4, Vol. II, Southern Illinois University Press, Carbondale Ill., 1962, p.816

of the casting of Handel's oratorios has been conjectural.[20] However it is very clear that he took part in the 1751 performance of *Messiah* at the Foundling Hospital on April 18 and May 16, as there is a record in the Minutes that he had returned some of his fee. On May 1 1751 the secretary reported to the General Committee that: "... Mr Smith had returned him, for the Benefit of the Charity, two guineas returned by Beard and one guinea by Mr Corbonelli, two of the said Performers".[21] This custom was repeated again the next year, when, "... Mr Beard agreeing to perform gratis, no distribution was set against his name".[22] Handel played a 'voluntary' on the newly completed organ and Beard sang the arias that are present in the score with his name on it in the Foundling Museum's library.

The 'Messiah' material at the Foundling Hospital is an interesting set of documents. Dating from the time of Handel's bequest, in a codicil to his will,[23] the choral and instrumental parts were presented to the Hospital in time for the 1760 performance. Beard's solo part is very clean and looks hardly used. But it gives us a good idea of the music that Handel, in the last decade of his life, wanted the tenor soloist to perform. Beard must have had another score from which he sang all his previous performances, from the time he made his debut in the work, on March 23 1743, up until Handel's death. This would be the really interesting copy to see, with all its insertions, deletions, and other personal markings! Handel had had such trust in him as a reliable performer that he had often been called on to sing music allotted to other singers when they were suddenly ill or otherwise unavailable. By the time that the Foundling parts were copied out, it appears that the tenor soloist had lost two numbers from the 'Passion' sequence to the soprano soloist. Otherwise, the tenor music was very much as it is performed today.

His part is numbered no. 19, and entitled "Messiah / an Oratorio / Tenore / Principale". The contents are the tenor part to every chorus (single line only) and the following arias (which are shown with both the voice part and continuo bass line):

Page 1-2	Comfort Ye
Page 3-6	Every Valley
Page 18	All they that see him
Page 21	Thy rebuke
Page 22	Behold and see

after which is the statement *Recit & Aria Tacet*; i.e. he did not sing 'He was cut off' & 'But thou didst not leave' in these performances, although he is known to have sung them both on other occasions.[24]

Page 29	He that dwelleth in Heaven
Page 25	Unto which of the Angels
Page 30-1	Thou shalt break them
Page 37	O Death where is thy Sting
	[this contains both vocal lines and bass line]

---

[20] Deutsch (op. cit.) and Winton Dean (op. cit.) do not always agree. Evidence from Handel's own performing material is often the only source of suggestions made by, among others, Donald Burrows, in 'Handel's Performances of 'Messiah': the Evidence of the Conducting Score', *ML*, lvi, 1975
[21] General Committee Minutes, no. 3, pp. 210-211
[22] Wed. April 15th, 1752, from Nichols and Wray, 'A History of the Foundling Hospital', London 1935
[23] "I give a fair copy of the Score and all Parts of my Oratorio called The Messiah to the Foundling Hospital". August 4th 1757
[24] see Watkins Shaw, 'A companion to Handel's Messiah', Novello, Sevenoaks Kent, 1965 & Donald Burrows 'Handel's Performances of 'Messiah': the Evidence of the Conducting Score', ML, lvi, 1975

The intervening pages of the 46-page booklet contain the tenor choral line. There are no markings in any other hand than the original copyist, as there are in some of the other parts that he sang from. The *Court Odes* by William Boyce, which are all in the Bodleian Library, have occasional corrections and pencil marks which must have been put in by Beard, who was the only person to use the part - and only on one solitary occasion at that.

There would have been seven occasions when he could have sung from this *Messiah* part, between 1760 and 1766. Perhaps it is remarkably clean because he knew the part so well by now. Of the 36 performances that Handel had given between 1742 and 1759, Beard had sung in 30. His only absences were from the two premiere performances in Dublin in 1742, and in the period 1749-50 when he was replaced for four performances by Thomas Lowe. Below is a complete list of the performances he undertook, for Handel and other conductors, including known performances between Handel's death and his own retirement. All Covent Garden performances before 1760 would have been directed by Handel, and conducted (from c. 1753) by J. C. Smith, who had returned from France to assist the increasingly infirm Handel in 1751.

4. BEARD'S MESSIAH PERFORMANCES

Beard did not sing in the premiere performances in Fishamble Street, Dublin on April 13 and June 3 1742.[25]   His recorded performances are:

1743   March 23, 25, [29]   Covent Garden (London premiere)

N.B. There is some evidence that Beard may have been ill for one of these three performances. The conducting score contains pencil-markings that imply that Signora Avolio may have taken over some of his music at short notice.[26] Certainly there is a comment in the Winston M/S on April 5 that the Drury Lane performance that night should have been *The Beggar's Opera*: but, as the prompter wrote - "Beard ill and did not act". It is most likely that the performance of *Messiah* that he missed was the one on March 29. The illness was short-lived as there is plenty of evidence on the playbills that he was back at Drury Lane throughout the rest of April and May singing ballads in the Intervals. Burrows is wrong when he says "he disappears from the advertisements for concerts for a month after he had given a performance of *The Beggar's Opera* [22 March] for his own benefit the night before the first performance of *Messiah*".[27] In fact he is advertised on the posters as singing, specifically, 'Stella and Flavia', 'Bumper Squire Jones', 'Was ever Nymph like Rosalind', 'Distracted I turn' and other popular pieces. By April 26 he was well enough to resume the role of *Macheath*. When he returned to the cast of *Messiah* again a year later, in 1745, he resumed singing the whole of his allotted music.

1745   April 9, 11   Covent Garden

---

[25] Beard was originally expected to accompany Handel to Dublin, where it was intended that he would sing in his oratorio season and participate in the first performance of *Messiah*. Instead, Handel had to train up two local tenors to replace him: James Baileys (with whom he had worked in London, December 1737, in the Funeral Anthem for Queen Caroline) and John Church. See Luckett, op. cit. p. 115

[26] Donald Burrows 'Handel's Performances of 'Messiah': the Evidence of the Conducting Score', *ML*, lvi, 1975, p. 326

[27] Donald Burrows, ibid. p. 326

On March 23 1749 when Lowe was the tenor soloist in Handel's Covent Garden *Messiah* Beard was advertised as singing that day at Ranelagh Gardens. He did not sing in the three performances of 1750, on April 12 at Covent Garden, and May 1 & 15 at the Foundling Hospital.

1751   April 18, May 16   Foundling Hospital

N.B. Henry Theodore Reinhold, the bass soloist, died between these two performances, on May 14 1751, leaving a wife and children. Beard immediately arranged for a Benefit Night to be held at Drury Lane Theatre, where the singer had been on the roster. The sudden death of the colleague with whom Beard had sung so many oratorios, and appeared in so many stage shows, stung him into this charitable action for "...a man no less admired for his private character than his publick performance. He has left behind him a wife and four children in great distress; for the relief of whom the managers of Drury Lane, and the actors have agreed to perform a play gratis, some time next week; when it is hoped the good nature of the Publick will favour the intention of the performers. Tickets to be had of Mr Beard, at his house in North St., Red Lion Square".[28]   The performance of *The Conscious Lovers* and *Queen Mab* was tagged on to the end of the Drury Lane season on May 22 and produced the sum of £101 for Reinhold's widow.[29]

1752	March 25, 26	Covent Garden
	April 9	Foundling Hospital
1753	April 13	Covent Garden
	May 1	Foundling Hospital
		N.B. His wife Henrietta died on May 31st
1754	April 5	Covent Garden
	May 15	Foundling Hospital
	July 5	Oxford – conductor Prof. Dr. William Hayes
1755	March 19, 21	Covent Garden
	May 1	Foundling Hospital
1756	April 7, 9	Covent Garden
	May 19	Foundling Hospital
	June 8	Oxford – conductor Prof. Dr. William Hayes
1757	March 30, April 1	Covent Garden
	May 5	Foundling Hospital
	September 16	Gloucester (*Three Choirs Festival*) – conductor . Prof. Dr. William Hayes
1758	March 10, 15, 17	Covent Garden
	April 27	Foundling Hospital
1759	March 30, April 4, 6	Covent Garden

Handel died on April 14 1759. Subsequent London performances were conducted by J. C. Smith, as they had been from the time that Handel's eye-sight had deteriorated, c.1753. But Handel was always present at these latter performances, however, and despite his blindness was still nominally in charge.

---

[28] The London Stage, Part 4, Vol. I, Southern Illinois University Press, Carbondale Ill., 1962, p.254
[29] The London Stage, Part 4, Vol. I, Southern Illinois University Press, Carbondale Ill., 1962, p.255

1759	May 3	Foundling Hospital
		(1st performance after Handel's death)
1760	March 26, 28	Covent Garden
	April 24	King's Theatre, for the *Society of Musicians*
	May 2	Foundling Hospital
	August 3	Gloucester (*Three Choirs Festival*) – conductor Dr. William Hayes
	September 16	Birmingham Festival
1761	March 11, 13	Covent Garden
	April 24	Foundling Hospital
	August 3	Worcester (*Three Choirs Festival*) – conductor Elias Isaac
1762	March 31, April 2	Covent Garden
	May 5	Foundling Hospital
1763	March 23, 25	Covent Garden
	April 29	Foundling Hospital
1764	April 11, 13	Covent Garden
	May 8	Foundling Hospital
1765	March 27, 29	Covent Garden
	April 2	Foundling Hospital
1766	March 19, 21	Covent Garden
	April 15	Foundling Hospital
1767	March 8, 10	Covent Garden

Beard did not take part in the Foundling Hospital performance on April 29 1767. He gave his last stage performance on May 23 at Covent Garden; but his last *Messiah* was on March 10. On April 29 his arias were divided between the castrato Tommaso Guarducci, who was engaged by J.C. Smith for the 1767 season. Guarducci was paid £600 for performing in 12 oratorios - £50 each - which makes Frasi's 6 guineas look very small in comparison, and Beard's generosity even more significant. In order to get good value from his expensive import Smith gave him several tenor arias. He chose to give him the opening solos 'Comfort Ye' and 'Ev'ry Valley'. These must have sounded curious up an octave, but were better served by an experienced and charismatic performer at the opening of the concert than being entrusted (as might otherwise have been the case) to an inexperienced choir singer. Guarducci was also given the intensely emotional 'Thy rebuke' and 'Behold and see'. This left the tenor soloist, a choir singer named Hayes who had been brought in to replace Beard (and may have been one of Dr William Hayes' sons) with very little to do apart from 'Thou shalt break them', some recitatives, and the duet 'O Death, where is thy sting'.[30]

In this catalogue of *Messiah* performances (above) it is worth noting their sudden increase in 1760 and 1761 as musicians around the country scheduled Handel-memorial concerts. These gave an enormous fillip to the infant Music Festivals that were springing up around the country. At a time when Beard was beginning to be enormously involved with his new career in the Covent Garden management it is good to find him making time to visit distant festivals in Gloucester and Worcester (the *Three Choirs Festivals*) and also in the growing

---

[30] Richard Luckett, 'Handel's Messiah, a celebration', London 1992, p. 188-9

metropolis of Birmingham. At a time when this work was still not well known he sang excerpts from it in various miscellaneous concerts. There is a record of him singing 'Comfort Ye' and 'Ev'ry Valley' for the Castle Society, whose meetings took place at Haberdashers Hall. In the same programme, on December 21 1757, Signora Frasi sang the excerpt 'He shall feed his flock'. This could be one of the earliest occasions on which excerpts from *Messiah* were heard in public, since the score and 'songs' had not yet been published, and were not even available to rival groups unless they had acquired manuscript copies directly from the composer.[31] The work would not be published complete until after Handel's death, in 1763, although select arias had been appearing in Walsh's collections of 'Handel's Songs Selected from his Oratorios' since 1749 in versions with keyboard accompaniment. Some scholars have suggested that Handel deliberately kept the work back for personal reasons, despite the fact that the printing plates had been prepared in the mid 1740s.[32]

When we look at this impressive list of *Messiah* performances given by Beard during his career we are not seeing the whole picture. We are not seeing how the Foundling Hospital performances fitted into his busy schedule. Not many scholars have considered this issue. Burrows has pointed out that both Frasi and Beard were the vocal soloists at Ranelagh Gardens during the 1750s, and that there were certain days in May when they would have not been available: "She and Beard were in the habit of performing at Ranelagh House occasionally at noon, the time of the Foundling Hospital performances: it is noteworthy that the Foundling Hospital performances in 1751, 1752 and 1757 were on Thursdays. Frasi and Beard were advertised to sing at Ranelagh on Thursday March 23 1749, Frasi presumably singing in the *Messiah* performance in the evening of the same day. In subsequent years, however, the advertised Ranelagh House performances were not held on the same day as the Foundling Hospital *Messiah*".[33]

But Beard had other commitments as well as the Ranelagh ones. Sometimes the theatrical season lasted well into May. So a charity performance in early April was not a practical proposition. On one of the dates that Burrows mentioned - April 9 1752 - Beard not only sang the *Messiah* at noon, but then returned to Drury Lane, where he took part in both of the evening shows: firstly as Balthazar "with a proper song" *in Much Ado about Nothing* (starring Garrick as 'Benedick' and Mrs Pritchard as 'Beatrice'); and then, in the afterpiece *The Shepherd's Lottery*, singing the role of 'Colin' opposite Miss Norris as 'Phillis'. He must have made a protestation about the Foundling Hospital date being so early, because the next five year's performances are all in May. Only from 1758 do they revert back to a date in April.

He may have thought that a May performance would solve the problem. But in 1754 there was a clash once again, despite the Foundling Hospital date being in mid-May (on the 15th). On this occasion he had another 3-show day. After *Messiah* he returned to Drury Lane for *The Merchant of Venice* where he appeared alongside Mrs Clive's *Portia* as 'Lorenzo', 'with songs in character'; and then

---

[31] William Hayes acquired a score and parts for several early Oxford performances, in July 1754 & June 1756

[32] Richard Luckett, 'Handel's Messiah, a celebration', London 1992, p. 162-3, and Donald Burrows, 'Handel & the Foundling Hospital', *ML*, lviii (1977), p. 277-8

[33] Burrows 'Handel's Performances of 'Messiah': the Evidence of the Conducting Score', *ML*, lvi, 1975, p. 333

concluded a long day with *The King and the Miller of Mansfield*, in which he took his customary role of 'Joe'. Somehow he managed this extraordinary combination of styles over and over again. In 1755 *Messiah* was followed by *Macbeth*, in which his customary role of 'Hecate' required him to sing several arias; and this was followed by the pantomime *Proteus, or Harlequin in China* in which he acted and sang at least two more songs.

1756 was a good year, in which Beard managed to contrive no clash. But in 1757 he had to return to the Drury Lane theatre to sing between the acts and then perform in the afterpiece *The Reprisal; or, the Tars of old England,* by Tobias Smollett. His character was another of his singing sailors, this one with the almost Gilbertian name of 'Haulyard'. In 1758 he was beginning to learn to take things more easily by getting his younger colleague Joseph Vernon to take over his role of 'Damon' in *The Chaplet* 'for the first time' as the playbill says. There was no clash on May 3 1759, on the sad occasion that it was performed after Handel's death. Thereafter, in the years when he was manager at Covent Garden, he made sure that he would never need to rush across London in a hurry again.

But despite the fact that his diary was always pretty full in April and May, with regular theatre commitments, benefits and other charity performances all crowding in on him, the performances at the Foundling Hospital were just one strand in this versatile performer's life. To get a fuller picture it will be useful to map out fully his commitments in some weeks of this period. Then we can see what a strain he was putting on his body - and particularly on his vocal chords. Let us select two typical weeks from years in which he performed at the Foundling Hospital.

Firstly let us look at 1751:

April 1751

Monday 15	D.L. Afterpiece *Lethe* ('Mercury')
Tuesday 16	D.L. Mainpiece *The Provok'd Wife* ('Colonel Bully', with songs);
	Then he went across to King's Theatre Haymarket for the Benefit concert for *The Society of Musicians* and sang the Handel Arias
	'Why does the God of Israel sleep' & 'Tune your harps'.
Wednesday 17	D.L. Mainpiece *The Beggar's Opera* ('Macheath')
Thursday 18	Noon F.H. ***Messiah***. D.L. *The Roman Father* ('Priest')[34]
Friday 19	D.L. Mainpiece *Alfred* (Bard, singing 'Rule Britannia'); Afterpiece *The Chaplet* (Damon)
Saturday 20	free

In this period he had five days of performances in a row, and on three occasions had to perform twice on the same evening - one of them in a theatre some distance away. He also had to perform his longest and most arduous role of 'Macheath' the day before *Messiah*. Fortunately he had a rare day off on the Saturday. A few years later, in 1754, this is the picture:

---

[34] In the evening of the 18th, the prompter Richard Cross wrote in the prompt-book "...this House was hurt by Mr Handel's music at ye Foundling Hospital". The London Stage, Part 4, vol. 1, Southern Illinois University Press, Carbondale Ill., 1962, p.247

May 1754

Monday 13	D.L. Afterpiece *The King and the Miller of Mansfield* ('Joe')
Tuesday 14	D.L. Afterpiece *The London Prentice* (title role)
Wednesday 15	Noon F.H. ***Messiah***; D.L. Mainpiece *The Merchant of Venice* ('Lorenzo'); Afterpiece *The King and the Miller of Mansfield* ('Joe')
Thursday 16	D.L. Afterpiece *The King and the Miller of Mansfield* ('Joe')
Friday 17	D.L. singing between the Acts: 'A Ballad – by Desire'
Saturday 18	D.L. Afterpiece *The King and the Miller of Mansfield* ('Joe')
Monday 20	D.L. Mainpiece *The Beggar's Opera* ('Macheath'); Afterpiece *The King and the Miller of Mansfield* ('Joe')

In this period he performed 6 days in a row, one of which was a 3-show day. After one day off on the Sunday he had to perform the arduous role of 'Macheath' followed by another repetition of the afterpiece that he had been doing in the previous week. *The Beggar's Opera*, lasting well over three hours, was one of the longest pieces performed in the theatre and was not normally given with an afterpiece.[35] Several times in his career this rule was broken and Beard was obliged to play in both halves of the programme.

In the context of this workload it is remarkable that Beard was prepared to do *Messiah* at all. It also makes one aware that he is extremely unlikely to have sung in the choruses. This hotly disputed question has been exercising the minds of Handel scholars for some years now.[36] Burrows is not alone when he propounds this theory in the Preface to his edition of *Belshazzar*: "One difference between the practices of Handel's vocal soloists and those of the present time is of some musical consequence. It seems virtually certain that Handel's soloists sang through the chorus movements: indeed, the 'chorus singers' may have been primarily regarded as supporters for soloists in these movements".[37]

Beard would have never been regarded as a chorus singer. That is a kind of music-making that he had left behind in 1734. His name now adorned many popular ballads that were on sale throughout the capital - "as sung by Mr Beard". If Handel had wanted him to be a chorus singer in addition to taking the solos it would have been akin to a contemporary conductor asking a singer like Placido Domingo to join in with the choruses of the Verdi 'Requiem'. It would be tantamount to admitting that you could not afford the services of sufficient choral singers. But Handel always appears satisfied with the choir singers that he had booked: "I have engaged ...several of the best Chorus Singers from the Choirs". Elsewhere he sets out the disparity between the jobs of soloists and choir singers even more clearly: "I have a good set of Singers ... and a good number of Choir Singers for the Chorus's."[38]

---

[35] Roger Fiske, 'English Theatre Music in the Eighteenth Century', OUP, Oxford, 1973, p. 75

[36] "The soloists may have joined the chorus, however, when not occupied with their own parts". Smither, 'The Oratorio in the Baroque Era' vol. 2, University of North Carolina Press, Chapel Hill 1977, p. 357. "The soloists also sang in the choruses (and could be commended for their excellence in this department)". Richard Luckett, 'Handel's Messiah, a celebration', London 1992, p. 172

[37] Belshazzar ed. Burrows *Preface* New Novello Choral Edition 1993 p. xv

[38] Handel to Jennens, 9th June & 2nd Oct 1744, Deutsch *Handel a Documentary Biography* p. 591 & 596

If one can assume - for a moment - that the grand singers employed by Handel did do what has been suggested by some scholars, then there would have been a distinct and noticeable lack of blend between the female soloists and castrati with highly trained voices and the boy choristers. Handel would not have liked that. One can see in the few extant prints of 18th century concerts that the soloists were right down at the front, well away from the body of the choir.[39] Whereas the soloists at Cannons Park formed themselves into a chorus for certain movements in the works that Handel wrote for the Duke of Chandos during his early years in London, by the time of the mature oratorios Handel had the pick of the London Cathedral choirs at his disposal.[40] If the problem facing the scholars is that Handel's executors only supplied 2 copies of each choral part in the Foundling Hospital material, then the answer to how these were shared out among the six singers[41] must be that further copies were made: not that Beard shared his copy with the choir tenors. The chorus tenor part which is shown in the copy with his name on it - which is cited by the scholars to back up their argument - may simply have been a courteous way of indicating where his arias came in the work: not a confirmation that he, and therefore the other soloists, joined in with the choruses. No one with the kind of workload that Beard was undertaking would have been prepared to do more than was absolutely required of them. To risk the next two paid performances by singing along with the choir, whose job it was, would have been to court disaster. Vocal chords cannot take this kind of punishment. Handel would have been the first to have advised his hard-working soloist - who may well have been doing him a favour by agreeing to take part in the first place - to take it as easy as he could.

In the 1750s Beard's participation in the Foundling Hospital performances became an annual fixture. A further occasion when he sang at the Foundling Hospital must now be mentioned. In 1753 the chapel was finally finished, and the long-delayed opening took place on April 16. Handel was in charge of the music once again, and substantially revised the Anthem that he had written for the 1749 performance. He wrote a new aria for the castrato Gaetano Guadagni who was in the cast. With Beard now back as his tenor soloist he also gave him new music to sing. Burrows supplies the details.[42] It included a new opening aria 'Blessed are they', which Handel inserted by deleting the previous chorus to the same text.

In the solo Part from which Beard sang - which can be consulted at the Royal College of Music [43] - it is clear that the copyist changed the text to the singular third person throughout:

> Blessed is <u>he</u> that considereth the poor and needy;
> The Lord will deliver <u>him</u> in time of trouble:
> The Lord preserve <u>him</u> and comfort <u>him</u>'.

---

[39] "The principal singers were ranged in front of the orchestra, <u>as at Oratorios</u>". Charles Burney, 'An Account of the Musical Performances in Westminster Abbey and the Pantheon in Commemoration of Handel', 1785

[40] 'I have engaged ... Mr Gates with his boys, and several of the best Chorus singers from the choirs'. Handel to Jennens June 9th, 1744.

[41] "...the size of Handel's chorus ... probably never amounted to more than six singers to a part". Winton Dean, 'Handel's Dramatic Oratorios and Masques', OUP Oxford 1959, p. 108

[42] Donald Burrows, 'Handel and the Foundling Hospital', <i>ML</i>, lviii, 1977, pp. 275-8, & Table 1

[43] RCM, M/S 2254

The changes were done at an early stage, and in a similar ink; but the original third person plural of the original chorus-text can still be detected, scratched out or overwritten.[44] The original is a very unsatisfactory text: "Blessed are they that considereth the poor and needy" is poor English. Perhaps it had always been Handel's intention for this to be a solo for a single voice, and it was somehow changed into a chorus when he knew who his 1749 soloists were to be. When the anthem came to be published by Chrysander in the German Handel Society edition of 1872 [45] he used the original text in the replacement Beard aria. This may have been how it was performed in 1759, on May 24, when J. C. Smith put on a concert at the Foundling Hospital in Handel's memory. But Beard would have been certain to have sung in that performance too. He was still in London, performing at Drury Lane on May 21 and 28. If he had used the RCM partbook again he would have repeated the text shown above.

The manuscript (each page containing 5 systems of music) shows evidence of having been sung from. There is a pencilled slur in bar 13 of 'Blessed is he that considereth the poor' showing how the syllables should be fitted to the notes. A different hand to the copyist's (possibly the performer's own) has added a missing rest in a later bar. The duet 'The charitable shall be had in everlasting remembrance' contains corrections to obvious scribal errors which indicate that it was sung from at some time or another. The vocal line is clearly written in a firm hand (now identified as that of William Teede, the elder Smith's son-in-law), but differs in frequent tiny details from Chrysander's 1872 edition,[46] suggesting that it was not consulted by the great Handel scholar.

[44] Burrows describes the alteration to the text: "The tenor part, written by copyist S6 in the 'original' form, has been amended and added to by Smith senior to give the later version of the anthem: over the added tenor aria No. 1 only Mr Beard's name appears, while above No. 2 the headings '3d Part' and 'Mr Lowe' have been crossed out and Mr Beard's name added..." Burrows *Handel and the Foundling Hospital* ML58 (1977) p. 278
[45] Leipzig, 1.5.1872
[46] Handel Gesellschaft, xxxvi. Leipzig, May 1st 1872

The aria 'Blessed is he / are they' must be one of the very last pieces that Handel wrote for Beard's voice. He had already finished his last completely original work, the oratorio *Jephtha* in 1751. Beard sang the title role in it at Covent Garden on February 26 1752. The composition had taken a lot longer than was Handel's custom (from January 21 until July 17 1751) because of his failing eyesight. After the revision of the Foundling Hospital Anthem in 1753 Handel's composition process was restricted to tidying up existing compositions. He wrote nothing entirely new.

At various other times Beard would be seen at the Foundling Hospital. He sang a solo at Captain Coram's Funeral on April 3 1751[47], and attended various functions. His services would have been particularly useful at the annual Feasts, in the singing of Grace, and entertaining the guests with appropriate Ballads afterwards. He is on the guest list for a Feast given at 3pm on Saturday November 5 1757 for 'Dilettante and Virtuosi'. Among the list of famous artists and sculptors present (obviously at the invitation of Hogarth) we find the following actors and musicians: Beard, Bencraft, Vernon, Wilder, and J. C. Smith.[48] The Drury Lane contingent – including Beard - would have had to make their departure in time to reach the theatre for the After-piece, a pantomime called *Harlequin Ranger*, which would have commenced at around 8.30pm.

In 1760 the long period of devoted service that Beard had shown the Foundling Hospital finally received its reward. By this time he had given his services to the charity ten times, and he would still do so another eight more. On Wednesday December 31 he was elected a Governor. By reason of Handel's death a position was vacant. It was very fitting that this honour was done to a singer for whom Handel had so much respect, who had sung the *Messiah* more times under his direction than any other, and for whose voice the arias were originally composed.[49]

The entrance to the Foundling Hospital

---

[47] contemporary newspaper report: "At six o'clock the procession began; ...several Gentlemen belonging to St Paul's Choir, as also Mr Beard, and 4 Choristers two and two, all in surplices" sung the Burial Service and an Anthem composed by Dr Boyce 'If we believe that Jesus died, and rose again'.

[48] John Brownlow, 'Memoranda or Chronicles of the Foundling Hospital', London 1847

[49] Beard was originally expected to accompany Handel to Dublin, (see footnote 25), where it was intended that he would sing in his oratorio season and participate in the first performance of *Messiah*.

5. OTHER CONTEMPORARY CHARITIES

The mid-eighteenth century saw a rise in charitable works of all sorts. Many other funds were established in the wake of the ones for *Decayed Musicians* and the *Deserted Young Children*; and Beard was always approached when fund-raising concerts were planned. With great good nature he was always ready to make himself available. He was known for his compassion, to the extent that other, less fortunate, colleagues almost took advantage of him. Charlotte Charke, Colley Cibber's wayward actress-daughter, was advised to seek help from Beard. "*At length, however, she thought of applying to Mr Beard, whose humanity immediately relieved her...*"[50] She turned up destitute on his doorstep and went away, as she had hoped, with a gift of money.

He could always be relied on to listen sympathetically to a tale of woe. A reading of the advertisements of the newspapers of the time seems to indicate that no Fund-raising concert could be guaranteed of success unless his name was involved with it. A list of events for which we know he sang reveals the breadth of his interests:

Date	Work	Charity
22 April 1752	Miscellaneous arias from Oratorios	The Lock Hospital
2 March 1753	Handel *Alexander's Feast*	The Smallpox Hospital
7 May 1753	Handel *Judas Maccabaeus*	The Lock Hospital
26 April 1754	Sacred Music	The Lying-in Hospital
23 May 1754	Handel *L'Allegro* & *St Cecilia Ode*	The Lock Hospital
24 May 1754	Sacred Music	Middlesex Hospital
10 April 1755	Sacred Music	Westminster Hospital
15 May 1755	Sacred Music	Middlesex Hospital
9 June 1757	Handel *Acis & Galatea*	The Marine Society
26 April 1758	Handel Anthems	Middlesex Hospital
22 June 1758	*The Beggar's Opera*	Distressed Actors
16 May 1759	Miscellaneous arias from Oratorios	The Lying-in Hospital
19 June 1759	*The Beggar's Opera*	Distressed Actors
18 June 1760	Arne *The Judgement of Paris*	Asylum for Orphan Girls
18 May 1762	Miscellaneous arias from Oratorios	The Lock Hospital
15 April 1763	Avison & Giardini *Ruth*	The Lock Hospital
29 Feb 1764	Arne *Judith*	The Lock Hospital
13 Feb 1765	Avison & Giardini *Ruth*	The Lock Hospital

6. DECAYED ACTORS AND THEIR FAMILIES

It will be seen in the above list that Beard took part in two fund-raising events for actors who had fallen on hard times. This was not difficult to do in an age that made no provision for old age or illness. He himself made several attempts to obtain a Royal sinecure so as to avoid possible penury in his old age. Early in his career he had learned that there were musicians in need of urgent assistance; and he had gladly signed up to the founding charter of the Society of Musicians (later to become the Royal Society of Musicians). Rather extraordinarily no one had yet thought of doing the same for actors. Many of Beard's closest colleagues ended their days in financial

---

[50] 'The Life of Mrs Charlotte Charke', reviewed in *Gentleman's Magazine*, November 1755, p.497

distress - notably his fellow tenor Thomas Lowe who, after a financially disastrous period as manager of Marylebone Gardens in 1763-9, was taken on - out of sympathy - as a singer at Sadler's Wells (in 1772) and died destitute in 1783. Charlotte Charke has already been mentioned, but there were many others. Signora Frasi, with whom Beard had enjoyed some of his greatest musical successes, got into serious debt and died destitute in Calais, to which she had fled to avoid her creditors. Caterina Galli, another Handel favourite, emerged from retirement as a result of economic pressure. At the end of her life, according to the *Gentleman's Magazine*, she 'subsisted entirely on the bounty of her friends, and an annual benefaction from the Royal Society of Musicians'.

During his time as manager of Covent Garden John Beard witnessed how easy it was for an actor to fall from favour with the public and lose their livelihood. One case stands out in particular. Mrs Esther Hamilton (formerly Mrs Bland) had been a busy and popular actress. She had acted opposite the young Garrick in a series of famous Shakespeare productions (*King Lear, Richard III, Othello*). Later, in Dublin, she had worked with Thomas Sheridan and become the leading actress at Smock Alley until Peg Woffington had stolen the best parts and left her only with secondary roles. When she returned to London she had a further success at Drury Lane in some sizeable roles; but it was evident that she was no longer able to play juvenile leads.

She was back on the Covent Garden books in the 1761-2 season, when her roles commenced on October 3 1761 with the Queen in *The Spanish Friar*. The Winston Theatrical Record notes her fee at "£1 10s per day, being returned from Ireland that day".[51] Her annual salary worked out at £272: a large amount that she failed to justify when she became arrogant and refused to play opposite certain other actors - particularly the young George Anne Bellamy who had now taken over her previous juvenile roles. She found herself being required to play maturer ladies: Emilia in *Othello*, Ann Lovely in *A Bold Stroke for a Wife*, Mrs Ford in *The Merry Wives of Windsor*, Charlotte Welldon in *Oroonoko*, Flora in *The Country Lasses*, and a host of others. She had a benefit night on March 23, in which she defiantly chose to play the young lead role of Roxana in *The Rival Queens, or the Death of Alexander the Great*.

Unfortunately for her John Rich, who had given her such a comfortable contract, died on 26 November 1761. John Beard, beginning his management with the sweep of a new broom, found her intractable and vulgar. He was determined to improve the moral tone of the theatre, back-stage as well as in the public areas. He would not brook any high-handed behaviour from contracted performers. Mrs Hamilton definitely overplayed her hand when she refused the role of Lady Wronglove in *The Lady's Last Stake* and put her foot down about playing Mrs Conquest instead - a role for which she was no longer suited. She was threatened with the usual penalty: a £20 fine. When she revealed to Beard that she had a special clause in her contract with Rich that did not bind her to any future manager, he saw a way to get rid of her. "This intelligence, instead of meeting the desired and intended effect, had quite contrary consequences; for the knit angry brow and eye of terror changed instantly to features the most placid, smiling and pleasing. He bowed and returned thanks for the unexpected and truly welcome intelligence, and assured

---

[51] The London Stage, Part 4, vol. 2, p. 894

the lady that the article should be cancelled the next day, and she was welcome at the end of May to depart where her fancy pleased best." [52]

Her last role at Covent Garden was Angelica in *Love for Love* on May 21 1762. She was not on any London roster the next season, having returned to Smock Alley in Dublin, where she fancied she would make more money. But her hopes turned to ashes. The Dublin audiences no longer favoured her; she was getting stout and only the role of Mrs Peachum suited her in the theatre's current repertoire. So she set out on a downward spiral of smaller theatrical companies and diminishing financial returns. By 1771 she was reduced to working with strolling players in Yorkshire. Returning to London in 1772 she was pitied by her former colleagues and given small amounts of charity by some. Kitty Clive wrote to a friend about how she had decided to reject a request for assistance from Mrs Hamilton:

"I am really sorry for her. This woman was but a few years ago in possession of nine pounds a week, had all the great characters both in comedy and tragedy and chose to give up an article with five years to run because she had quarrelled with Mr Beard".[53] The tale is taken up by Genest in his history of the English Stage:

"There had been for several years a talk of establishing a fund for the support of such performers as should be obliged through age and infirmities, or accident, to retire from the stage. Various plans had been formed, but none of them took effect; and, indeed, the managers were at first jealous of the undertaking. At length in 1765 the case of Mrs Hamilton, whose income had been considerable, but who was at that time reduced to depend on the contributions of the players, alarmed the whole society.[54] Hull, a judicious actor and a very respectable man, had the honour to be the first who conceived and brought to bear a rational project for the player's fund. To promote this desirable end, he addressed the performers of Covent Garden in a printed letter, in which, after establishing the necessity of some mode of provision, he stated several reasonable propositions as the foundation of his plan. His address produced an immediate good effect. A collection was set forward under the joint efforts of Hull and Mattocks. In this plan they were most liberally assisted by the patronage of Beard and Mrs Rich, then proprietors of Covent Garden."[55]

The *Biographia Dramatica* adds some detail: "The scheme succeeded, and it was agreed that sixpence a pound should be paid out of the weekly salaries towards raising a fund for that purpose."[56]

Thomas Hull was Beard's close friend - the only one to outlive him. In his will Beard left him £50 to buy a memorial ring.[57] While Beard had managed Covent Garden Hull had been invaluable to him as an actor, stage manager, and author. Now this energetic man took hold of the situation, and talked an obliging

---

[52] Tate Wilkinson "The Wandering Patentee" York, 1795, vol. 1 p. 129-

[53] 6th October 1773, quoted in BDA, p. 60

[54] Hull founded the Fund in 1765; but it appears that Mrs Hamilton did not appear in London at her most distressed until 1772, by which time it was well-established, though not yet formalised by Act of Parliament.
According to the BDA Mrs Hamilton was acting in Edinburgh as 'Mrs Bland Hamilton' in 1765-6: p.59

[55] John Genest, 'Some account of the English Stage 1660 – 1830', vol 5, Bath, 1832

[56] Baker, Biographia Dramatica, 1812

[57] There is a collection of 18th century Memorial Rings in the British Museum, Room 46. One of them (no.29) is in memory of John Thornhill, the brother of the painter Sir James Thornhill, who died in 1757 aged 57. The motto 'Beef and Liberty', surrounding the Beefsteak Club's famous grid-iron, is depicted on it in enamel.

management into assisting the establishment of a proper fund that would receive donations, and put on an annual Benefit Night. The first recorded donation came from the playwright Richard Cumberland. In his *Memoirs* he recounts how he came to write the ballad Opera *The Summer's Tale*, which was one of the only two new main-pieces put on in the 1765-6 Covent Garden season.

"Being a vehicle for some songs not despicably written, and some of those very well set, it was carried by my friends to Beard, then manager of the theatre, and accepted for representation... It was performed nine or ten nights to moderate houses without opposition, and very deservedly without much applause, except what the execution of the vocal performers justly obtained... The fund for the support of decayed actors being then recently established by the company of Covent Garden theatre, I appropriated the receipts of my ninth night to that benevolent institution, which the conductors were pleased to receive with much good will; and have honoured me with their remembrance at their annual audits ever since". [58]

Cumberland's ninth night was Monday January 29 1766, and he presented the fund with £74, after which "the Performers returned their sincere thanks ... for his generous donation".[59] The first Benefit Night mounted by the committee itself took place on May 13 1766. Hull wrote a *Prologue* for Beard to speak which was subsequently published.[60]

On December 20 1766 Beard acted for the fund in *The Beggar's Opera*. This was always played at Christmas, and was a sensible choice to get a full house for the fund. The cast was almost the same as for the ground-breaking performances in 1759, with the exception of a replacement for the deceased James Bencraft, and Miss Brent appearing under her married name of Mrs Pinto. The profits to the fund were £159 3s. The next benefit night was a year later, on December 9 1767, after Beard's retirement. The profit of £98 9s, which was disappointing in comparison with the previous year, was passed to the Treasurer, Thomas Hull. If receipts were becoming this variable it would explain the ever more insistent requests for financial support on the daily playbills. This one is from the year 1796:

"Benefit for the fund, established for the relief of those Performers who, through infirmity, shall be obliged to retire from the Stage. The Theatrical Fund was established in 1765, under the auspices of the late Mr Beard and Mrs Rich; and received the sanction of Parliament in 1776. There are now, and have been for more than 20 years, several Annuitants supported by it, chiefly families and widows. Yet notwithstanding it has been so long set on foot, the interest arising from the Funded Capital has never been equal to defraying one half of the annual disbursements. The deficiencies have been continually supplied by progressive weekly contributions from the performers. When this is considered, it is respectfully presumed the generosity of a British Public will be exerted this night in favour of so liberal and beneficial an institution."

Thomas Hull, Treasurer. 7th June 1796 [61]

---

[58] Richard Cumberland, 'Memoirs', London 1806
[59] The London Stage, Part 4, vol. 2, p. 1150
[60] Jester's Magazine, May 1766 – see page 365
[61] The London Stage, Part 4, vol. 2, p. 1868

Thomas Hull comes out of the sorry tale of Mrs Hamilton extremely well. In the managerial position at Covent Garden to which Colman promoted him in 1775 he allowed her to share in benefit nights with minor performers and servants of the house in the years between 1781 and 1784. Through his influence, and probably with the assistance of Beard who was resident nearby, she lived out her last years working backstage at the Richmond Theatre.[62] Tate Wilkinson, who had met her at this sad stage in her life, writes vividly of her tragic fall in his biography "The Wandering Patentee": "Mr and Mrs Hull, her constant friends, were ever glad to let her partake of their friendly board. The last resource (after her various misfortunes, almost the whole of which disasters were occasioned by false pride and consequence) was ... to be Wardrobe-keeper and Dresser at Mr Love's little new theatre at Richmond; her weekly stipend of course was but small... The true reason of the Theatrical Fund being established was owing chiefly to the misfortunes of Mrs Sweeny (Mrs Hamilton's current name after a disastrous late marriage) here recorded. ...Mr Hull was the first proposer of that noble institution, which will be engraven not only on his tomb, but what is better, in the hearts of every brother and sister performer for ages yet to come".[63]

But not all had been plain sailing for the infant fund in the intervening years. Garrick, on returning from his two years of foreign travel felt aggrieved that he and Drury Lane had not been consulted or included in the Covent Garden plans. "The Covent Garden fund was first set on foot at a time when Garrick was on the continent. On his return home he was exceedingly angry and much mortified that a business of such importance should have been carried on without the least communication with him; who, as at the head of his profession... might reasonably have expected to be consulted."[64]

Consequently he set up a rival fund, and used all his contacts to give it a wider publicity and a better financial base. One of the noble Lords that he wrote to was Beard's first wife's younger brother, John, the 3rd Earl Waldegrave. "Mr Garrick presents his duty to Lord Waldegrave and begs his Lordship's pardon for troubling him with the enclosed petition".[65] Beard, one assumes, had been more circumspect and refrained from writing to the aristocratic members of his wife's family who had cut him out of their circle some thirty years earlier. In a letter of January 29 1776 Sir Grey Cooper replied to another of Garrick's invitations: " ...I shall be happy to contribute my assistance to the execution of the plan you propose. Lord North [the Prime Minister] will be much inclined to promote whatever you desire to be done".[66] On an invitation to the Drury Lane Fund's annual dinner, on May 24 1778, the secretary Thomas Holcroft addressed Garrick fulsomely as: "Master of the Corporation and Perpetual President of the Committee for managing the Affairs relative to the Theatrical Fund established at the Theatre Royal Drury Lane". [67] Garrick regularly acted in the Drury Lane benefit nights himself. Genest also tells us that "in January 1776 Garrick paid the expenses of an Act of Parliament for the legal establishment of the fund. It is computed that by donations of one kind

---

[62] according to Fawcett's notebook, now in the Folger Library. See BDA p. 60

[63] Tate Wilkinson "The Wandering Patentee" York, 1795, vol. 1 p. 149-

[64] John Genest, 'Some account of the English Stage 1660 – 1830', vol 5, Bath, 1832

[65] m/s W.b.492, Folger Shakespeare Library, Washington, USA

[66] Garrick letters, vol. 2, pp.131-2

[67] m/s Y.d.262, Folger Shakespeare Library, Washington, USA

or another, and by annually acting in capital parts, he gained the institution near £4500".[68]

Beard and Hull had tried to keep their fund low-key and compassionate. But the new manager at Covent Garden, George Colman, wanted some of the same reflected glory that Garrick was accruing so effortlessly over the road. When he tried to take over the management of the Covent Garden fund he was reprimanded by the Committee, who pointed out that Beard, his predecessor, was a Trustee by virtue of his having contributed to the fund as a performer.

"To George Colman, joint proprietor and manager of Covent Garden Theatre.

October 25th [1774?]

Sir, We are extremely concerned at having any occasion to address you on a subject which has for its basis the most distant supposition of our having been wanting in respect or attention to Mr Colman. When this Institution was first set on foot, it was settled as one of the fundamental and irrevocable rules that no person whatever should be admitted a Member but such as were actually Performers at Covent Garden Theatre, and that the Trustees and Committee should be chosen from them only. Mr Beard, at that time the acting Manager, being also a Performer, was admitted as a weekly contributor, and chosen a Trustee, merely in that situation, totally separated from his other Character. He still continues as a Trustee in consequence of another first rule, that the Trustees should remain unless a very apparent cause appear'd for changing them. This being the situation of the Institution we assure ourselves that Mr Colman on this explanation will no longer entertain the most distant idea of any slight or disrespect by not offering him a part in the direction of this society, and hope that he will not withdraw his usual indulgence of a Benefit."

A footnote to this letter was added by Colman's son, George Colman the younger: "My father was offended at the jealousy of the Committee in rejecting his offer of kindness and interference; and in consequence did, I believe, refuse a Benefit Night". [69] Genest concurs that the players "were deprived of that advantage. Harris also persisted in refusing an annual benefit."[70] When the Fund was formalised by Act of Parliament in 1776 the capital stood at £4,300 as can be seen by the wording in the application:

"And whereas by the profits arising from the voluntary contributions of the performers belonging to the said theatre and others and also by the profits which have arisen from some plays acted for the increase of the said fund a capital to the amount of four thousand three hundred pounds or thereabouts is now in the hands of certain trustees applicable to the purposes aforesaid To the end therefore that the said fund and the growing produce thereof may be effectually secured and duly applied May it please your Majesty that it may be enacted.....etc. etc."[71]

The fund was entirely run by the actors, as can be seen from the final extract from the application:

---

[68] John Genest, 'Some account of the English Stage 1660 – 1830', vol 5, Bath, 1832
[69] 'Posthumous Letters, addressed to F Colman and G Colman the elder' British Library, ref. 10902 h 18
[70] John Genest, 'Some account of the English Stage 1660 – 1830', vol 5, Bath, 1832
[71] House of Lords Records, 16G3n.102 (1776), 'An Act for Securing a Fund belonging to Certain Persons of the Theatre Royal Covent Garden, applicable to charitable uses, and for other purposes'

"And be it further enacted that from and after the passing of this act Thomas Hull, George Mattocks, Thomas Baker, John Dunstall, Frederic Charles Reinhold, Robert Bensley, Matthew Clarke, Richard Rolton, and William Thomas Lewis shall be and they are hereby appointed a committee for the managing of the said fund until the 31st day of December which shall be in the year of our Lord 1776". Colman the elder was not a trustee.

All was smoothed over eventually. According to the younger Colman "Mr Fawcett [Hull's successor as the fund's Treasurer] has greatly advanced its prosperity by his zeal in the conduct of its concerns". The *London Stage* is more explicit: 'As an example of what the Fund was worth the figures of the calendar year 1787 may be cited: £481 4s 8d paid in by the contributors of Covent Garden Theatre, and £362 6s 6d disbursed to various annuitants'.[72] Contributors who had had 6d in the pound deducted from their weekly salary would be able to claim the following amounts, provided that they found themselves indigent in retirement: between £30 and £65 per year, according to the amount of their final salary, and funeral costs of up to £7. Widows' pensions were at a lower rate.

One of the donations that Mr Fawcett would have received would have been the £100 that Beard left the fund in his will. His step-mother-in-law, Priscilla Rich, also bequeathed £100 on her death in February 1783. What would have given him great contentment, though, would have been to learn of the establishment of an actor's rest home in Hampton. The small Thameside town had already acquired a theatrical association with the presence there, in retirement, of the three moguls of mid-Georgian London's theatre world. There was Garrick of Drury Lane, who retired in 1776 with £35,000 (a half share of the patent) to his grand villa with its riverside gardens and Temple of Shakespeare. Then there was Beard, who had retired to Rose Hill on a fifth share (£12,000) of the £60,000 that the Covent Garden patent had realised, and whose new villa commanded a good view of the river from its elevated position just outside the village. Finally there was Thomas Rosoman, living in Jessamine House in Thames Street near the parish church, who had quietly amassed a fortune of £40,000 from the more modest fare set before the public at Sadler's Wells Theatre.

To this delightful spot came Robert Baddeley: "an excellent low comedian, but chiefly distinguished by his representations of comic old men, Jews, and Frenchmen". He bought himself a retirement cottage in the village, too. But he was not destined to use it for long since, as Baker tells us, "he was taken ill when he was nearly dressed for the character of Moses in *The School for Scandal*", and died the next day, November 20 1793.

"By his will he left to the Theatrical Fund his cottage at Hampton; in trust, that they should elect to reside in it four of the fund pensioners as might not object to living sociably under the same roof. In the house are two parlours for their joint indulgence, and four separate bedchambers. This bequest is an instance of his benevolence, and of his respect for his profession. There was also to be a little summerhouse, for the tenants to smoke their pipes in; and it was so situated as to command a view of the Temple of Shakespeare erected by Mr Garrick".[73]

---

[72] The London Stage, Part 5, p. cxxxiv
[73] Baker, Biographia Dramatica, 1812

During Beard's long career the acting and musical professions arrived at a better standing in society than they had enjoyed when he started. Both as a manager, and by his personal example, he contributed much to the improvement in the theatre's moral standards. From the early days of 1738 when the Society of Musicians was founded, to 1765 when, as an elder statesman, he oversaw the founding of the Theatrical Fund, he and his colleagues had taken a significant lead, and acted compassionately in an uncompassionate age. Appendix 4 (p.349) contains a touching letter that he wrote to the Governors of the Society of Musicians seeking extra funds for the widow of Charles Jones, "a worthy Member of our Community". It was a typically generous gesture, and possibly only one of many that he made.

In Genest's words "the institution of these playhouse funds reflects great and lasting honour on the actors who were then on the stage; and every lover of Drama must say of these laudable establishments: 'Floreant!' may they flourish!" [74]

David Garrick, in front of a bust of Shakespeare,
surrounded by a group of Shakespearean actors

---

[74] John Genest, 'Some account of the English Stage 1660 – 1830', vol 5, Bath, 1832

CHAPTER 7
RANELAGH GARDENS

The Ranelagh Gardens season was an easy one for Beard to combine with his work at the theatre. Many of the musicians were the same, as well as the composers. The audience, too, came from the same social strata - from Royalty, via the aristocracy, down to the well-heeled and the nouveau riche: anyone, indeed who could afford the 2s 6d entrance fee.[1] The music that they would have heard would be similar to the interval music at the London theatres, mixed together with even more ephemeral songs and ballads that scarcely outlived one season. So many of these were published subsequently, together with the names of the performer (e.g. 'as sung by Mr Beard at Ranelagh Gardens'), that together they compose a very solid corpus of contemporary music.[2] But, like contemporary pop-songs, they were here today and gone tomorrow. Beard's job of learning all this new material was one of the reasons that he was paid good money by the directors of the Gardens.

Ranelagh had sprung up in the early 1740s as a more up-market version of Vauxhall and Marylebone Gardens. These had been offering food, drink and music in an elaborate garden setting since the mid-1730s. Their one drawback was that most of the entertainment was provided out of doors. Although they each built large supper rooms in which the entertainment could be carried on in bad weather, there are many reports of shoes and expensive clothes being ruined by rain and puddles, despite the management laying down a 'platform entirely covered in' to enable them to circumvent the worst areas.[3] Ranelagh turned the idea of the Pleasure Gardens on its head and made the principal feature an elegant Rotunda of vast proportions. At an internal diameter of 150 feet and an external of 185 it was 'inferior to few publick buildings in Europe'; and at 'near twenty feet more in diameter than the Rotunda at Rome' it was 'covered with a most excellent contriv'd roof'.[4] The rotunda was where the fine assembly gathered for their refreshment, and for the evening concert. Exercise was taken by promenading around in a circle,[5] since the vast expanse of ceiling was supported by an elaborate central construction in the hub of the building, which was originally designated the 'orchestra'.

If it was intended to house the musicians, as in a similar out-door construction at Vauxhall (which can be seen in contemporary views by Rowlandson and others), it was quickly found to be unsatisfactory. As any modern acoustics expert could have predicted, the Rotunda was not a good place to hear well. As with the Royal Albert Hall, which was modelled on the Ranelagh building, it was found that a circular building was a boomy and echoey environment in which to listen to music. In addition, the practice was to keep walking about; sometimes going away from the source of the sound, and sometimes approaching it. Right in front of the musicians, where music-lovers did indeed stop, there were no actual seats for an audience. The only seats were in the two tiers of boxes, where the refreshments were

---

[1] Sir John Fielding said that the Gardens were 'seldom frequented by any below middle rank'. Mollie Sands, 'Invitation to Ranelagh', London, 1946, p.33

[2] See Appendix 5

[3] Mollie Sands, 'The Eighteenth-Century Pleasure Gardens of Marylebone 1737-1777', The Society for Theatre Research, 1987, p. 69

[4] Mollie Sands, 'Invitation to Ranelagh', London, 1946, p. 17

[5] "The numbers of people who are generally assembled here, and who are walking round and round, present a curious sight". Count Frederick Kielmansegge, 'Diary of a Journey to London in the years 1761-2', London, 1902, p.23

served. The *Gentleman's Magazine* set the scene as follows: "Groups of well-dressed persons were disposed in the boxes, numbers covered the area. All manner of refreshments were within call; and music of all kinds echoed (though not intelligibly) from those elegant retreats where Pleasure seemed to beckon her wanton followers". That was written in 1742, the year the gardens opened. Fortunately for the musicians initially hired to provide the musical entertainment, the orchestra was relocated to one of the four entrance porticoes, and the central building - which can also be seen clearly in Canaletto's painting of 1754 and contemporary prints - found a use as a servery.[6]

Although the Rotunda was the main feature, and the Garden's major asset in coping with the British weather, it was surrounded by pleasant gardens with gravelled walks. As at Vauxhall these were enlivened by water-features, lakes, a canal, exotic temples and gazebos. The shady walks, lined with elms and yews, led down to an attractive frontage overlooking the river Thames. Many guests made their way there by boat, rather than risk the traffic jams and footpads that made a journey down 'The King's New Road' a sometimes daunting experience.[7]

The Rotunda at Ranelagh Gardens

On specific occasions there was outdoor music, either from the 'chinese' temple on an island in the lake, or from boats on the canal. It was from this island that fireworks were set off at the conclusion of the evening Balls, Ridottos and Masquerades.[8] The Proprietors did all they could to make a visit to Chelsea a

---

[6] "In the centre is a large open fireplace, serving to give the necessary warmth as well as to supply hot water." Count Frederick Kielmansegge, op. cit., p.23
[7] "To Ranelagh, where saw several friends, saw at Ranelagh Beard's Night, 'L'Allegro and Penseroso'... our two coaches for a good hour and ½ could not get 200 yds". - from 'The Diary of John Baker', London, 1931, p. 125
[8] "The large and pretty garden ...is seldom used except for fireworks; ...but notwithstanding this, you occasionally come across couples there, as it is always lighted up". Count Frederick Kielmansegge, op. cit., p. 24

pleasant experience, and even supplied 'a sufficient Guard within and without the House and Gardens to prevent any Disorders or Indecencies, and to oblige Persons guilty immediately to quit the Place'. More to the point an armed Guard patrolled the badly-lit approach roads.

It is difficult to reconstruct a typical week at Ranelagh, as the information is often lacking. The Gardens customarily announced in the Press when they would be open. At the beginning of the season there would be 'Breakfasts' with live music; but there is very little information on the music that was played. Since it was intended as background music the musicians most probably relied on the staple fare that was played before the plays at Drury Lane and Covent Garden. This consisted of Handel Opera Overtures; the Concerti Grossi of Corelli and Handel; and music by popular Italian composers such as Geminiani and Pasquali. As a competitor to Vauxhall it achieved its aim, and also attracted a better class of client by making its entrance costs higher than at any other garden. Horace Walpole was able to declare: "It has totally beat Vauxhall. My Lord Chesterfield is so fond of it, that he says he has ordered all his letters to be directed thither. If you had never seen it, I would make you a most pompous description of it, and tell you ...that you can't set your foot without treading on a Prince of Wales or Duke of Cumberland. The company is universal; there is from his Grace of Grafton down to Children out of the Foundling Hospital - from my Lady Townshend to the kitten".[9]

Ranelagh opened with a 'Public Breakfast' on April 5 1742. Its evening concerts, which included vocal items, commenced on May 24.[10] This pattern was to suit Beard, who still had commitments at the theatre until mid-May. But it is often clear from his diary that the two contracts of engagement overlapped. Precisely when he first began to be the male vocalist there is not so easy to determine. The newspaper advertisements announced the beginning and end of the season, and highlighted exceptional Balls and Masquerades, but never mentioned the names of the performers. This infomation has had to be extracted from other sources. Thus, we can be sure that Beard was the vocalist by the spring of 1746 as a note in the margin of the Winston m/s for 1744-52[11] itemises what was happening in the months when the London theatres were closed. In 1746 there is a listing for Ranelagh, with the comment 'Beard sung there'. The Winston m/s also indicates that in 1746 the season started on Monday April 20 with Breakfasts, that the evening concerts commenced on May 15 (two days after Beard's last performance). In 1747 the Winston m/s is less detailed; but it appears to indicate that the Ranelagh season was open for Breakfasts (with instrumental music) on Tuesdays, Thursdays and Saturdays; and that Concerts, running from 7pm to 10pm took place on Mondays, Wednesdays and Fridays. This is the first information we have that Beard was only obliged to sing on three evenings a week. The timetable in 1748 is a little different. The Breakfasts now commenced in March, and there was a concert every morning in Passion Week. The evening entertainments commenced on Monday May 2 but were halted between July 6 and August 15. This year it seems that the evening concert was held between 5pm and 9pm, and the season closed on September 10. In 1748 Beard commenced his new contract at Garrick's Drury Lane theatre on September 10. As he was in the after-piece *The Lottery* he would just have had time to make it

[9] Mollie Sands, 'Invitation to Ranelagh', London, 1946, p.42

[10] 'Twice a week there are to be ridottos with tickets price one guinea, which would include supper and music'. Mollie Sands, 'Invitation to Ranelagh', London, 1946, p.39

[11] T. a. 55 (7) at the Folger Shakespeare Library, Washington, USA

from Ranelagh to Drury Lane as long as his vocal items were first in the programme. The mid-summer closure seems to have been something of a custom, because it is repeated in 1749, occurring between July 21 and August 26. In this year the evening concerts began on May 21 (Beard's last theatre appearance was on May 17) and the season closed on September 15. As his first performance at Drury Lane was on September 21 things worked out more conveniently this year.

In this Ranelagh season (1749) Beard negotiated a leave of absence of about a week, from at least July 1 to 4. His good friend William Boyce had been invited to Cambridge to receive a Doctorate, and his colleague Maurice Greene had arranged a three day Boyce Festival at the Senate House and Great St Mary's Church in celebration. Apart from the festival of Handel's music, which accompanied Oxford University's 'Public Act' in July 1733, this was the first-ever one-man festival. Beard went along as guest vocalist, and sang in each of the three concerts. According to the London papers, there were 'near a hundred Vocal and Instrumental Performers' involved, including choral singers from the Chapel Royal, St Paul's Cathedral, Westminster Abbey and St George's Windsor. The two named soloists, who would have the lion's share of the work in the cantata *Solomon*, were Beard and Miss Turner, accompanied by 'upwards of thirty Musicians from the Opera-House'. The other pieces in which there was solo work for Beard were *The Secular Masque*, *Peleus and Thetis*, and the *Ode* 'Here all thy active fires defuse' which was especially composed for the installation of the Duke of Newcastle as Chancellor of the University on July 1. Beard was to remember the potential displayed in *The Secular Masque* when Garrick revived John Fletcher's play *The Pilgrim* in 1750. Boyce had set a text taken from this play, and it was very effectively put back into the new production. The six Gods of the masque are all well characterised musically, and sing some memorable music. Beard's aria, 'The Song of Momus to Mars', is still popular with singers today.

The Winston m/s is helpful in identifying the other singers employed at Ranelagh alongside Beard. There was always a female vocalist - and sometimes more than one. In every season from 1748 - 1752 Beard was joined by Signora Frasi and Mrs Storer. Mrs Storer came in initially to take part in some songs and duets composed by Festing for the 1748 season.[12] Festing had already collaborated with the actor William Havard in 1746, when the latter provided him with the text for an 'Ode upon the return of His Royal Highness the Duke of Cumberland from Scotland". As we know from the Winston m/s that Beard was the vocalist, it must have been he who gave this its one and only performance in August, soon after the victor of Culloden's return.

Another Ode was performed by Beard in 1750.[13] This time the composer was Boyce and the dedicatee was Frederick Louis, the Prince of Wales. 'Strike, strike the lyre' is for a solo voice and an orchestra of trumpet, wind, strings and continuo, and was performed at Ranelagh as a belated birthday tribute. The Prince's birthday was in January. Despite some fulsome phrases predicting a long life...

In George's reign our joys can fear no blast
And Frederick gives assurances they shall last

[12] Festing '6 songs & a dialogue with a Duet, sung at Ranelagh House by Mr Beard & Mrs Storer', London 1748
[13] Although not dated, this Ode was written on paper with the same watermark as Boyce's *Romeo and Juliet* dirge of 1750. Robert J. Bruce, 'William Boyce: some manuscript recoveries', Music & Letters, 55, 1974, p. 440

the Prince disobligingly died on March 20 1751. Nothing daunted, the team of William Havard, poet, and Boyce, composer reassembled to honour the newly created Prince of Wales, George (later George III), who had so recently lost his father. An *Ode* 'Let grief subside' was accordingly performed in honour of his 13th birthday on May 24 1751. A similar tribute was paid the following year, when the same team of poet, composer and singers performed 'Another passing year is flown' on May 25 1752. In both of these odes Boyce added two horns to the instrumentation. A decade later it was the Ranelagh horns that excited the eight-year-old Mozart so much that he wrote parts for them into his very first symphonies.

William Boyce

In 1751 George Harris went to Ranelagh on May 18. Once again he found himself very critical of Beard, not even deigning to mention him by name: "...through the park to Ranelagh Gardens ...very indifferent music, especially as to the vocal.".[14]

    Some of the 'indifferent' music that Beard was singing at this time were the 'Masquerade Song' with a text by Garrick; and various ballads like 'Myrtilla' (illustrated overleaf), and William Boyce's 'On the banks, gentle Stour' which managed to stay in the repertoire from season to season. There was also a taste for regional music. The Welsh harper John Parry, whom Beard invited to perform at his Benefit night in March 1753, came with him to Ranelagh where his harp must have sounded very pleasing in the echoing room. Beard sang the Welsh song 'The Lass of the Mill' with him; and his repertoire at this time also included the Irish ballad 'Aileen Aroon',[15] and the Scottish 'The Highland Laddie'.[16] Some of the most popular Ranelagh songs were soon found in *The Gentleman' Magazine*, or as supplements to such titles as the *London Magazine* and the *Universal Magazine*. Even the most insignificant pieces were quickly anthologised and published. There must have been an enormous appetite for such trifles, perhaps as music to be sung or danced to by the younger generation in their elaborately formal courtship rituals - as can be seen from the instructions appended to 'Bumpers 'Squire Jones' on page 49.

---

[14] Burrows & Dunhill, 'Music and Theatre in Handel's world', Oxford, 2002, p. 277

[15] *Aileen Aroon* appears in Burke Thumoth's *'Twelve Scotch and Twelve Irish Airs With Variations'* (circa 1740). It's original Gaelic title was *Eilionóir a Rúin*

[16] Mollie Sands, 'Invitation to Ranelagh', London, 1946, p.55

A Ranelagh ballad

In 1753 Henrietta died in their Chelsea lodgings during the Ranelagh season. Beard must have been seriously affected by this loss, and obliged to cancel several appearances. It is evident from Havard's letters that he was taking things badly. In one undated letter to Jack Armstrong he writes "...I think Johnny Beard and I are both obliged to you ...for the Solicitude you have shown, in his present situation, to give him relief... ...I have received no answer from Johnny, nor, in his situation, do I greatly expect any: I hope he is in health and that you see him often. I shall write to him again by next post, meantime assure him of my love and warmest regards..." As Henrietta had died on May 31 it is more than likely that Havard had moved out of London and taken employment for the summer months in a provincial theatre - either Jacob's Wells Theatre Bristol, or at Richmond and Twickenham - where he found work most years. This would have prevented him from being at Beard's side, like Armstrong, at this sad time. In another letter, written this time to Beard himself, Havard hopes that he has recovered from the loss sufficiently "...to feel and enjoy the return of his wonted peace of mind. It was the severest trial you could have experienced in this life, and the surmounting it should be esteem'd the greatest triumph. ...I have been favoured with two letters from honest Ben Read: in one of them he acquaints me that the Ranelagh Managers are dispos'd to offer you a Benefit - should the Profits of it amount to what I wish, they will not, however, exceed what you deserve..."[17] Beard did get the Benefit Night at Ranelagh, and Appendix 2 shows what pieces we know were performed and on what dates. The list is sadly incomplete, and only includes the period 1758-1762 because of the lack of detailed advertisements in the daily press. But the quotations from the above letters suggest that the first year in which he would have taken a Benefit there would have been 1753, in the month following Henrietta's death, possibly on June 13. All his subsequent Benefits were taken on Wednesdays in the period June 11 - 14.

1754 was a bad year for Ranelagh, because the Proprietors were refused a music licence. This came about because of the wide remit of a new Act for 'regulating places of entertainment and punishing persons keeping disorderly houses'. Although it was not brought in to interrupt legitimate entertainments at a high class establishment like Ranelagh, it was not until November that the problem could be sorted out and the licence re-obtained. During the earlier period the Gardens remained open for Breakfasts and promenades; but their entertainments of 'Recitations' were a poor substitute for music. The provision of a new Ode on the birthday of the Prince of Wales was also affected. There must have been many out-of-work musicians that Summer.

When the information in the Winston m/s tails off details about later seasons can be traced through the newspaper advertisements. The female singers were subject to change, but Beard was always employed. From at least as early as 1758 the favourite soprano was now Catherine (Kitty) Fourmantel. John Baker was a regular visitor in 1758 and found her to be the only soloist singing there on May 8.[18] This was because the Drury Lane season had not yet ended, and Beard was employed that night in a double bill of Dryden's *Amphitryon* and Arne's *Britannia*. When Baker returned on June 13 1759 he attended Beard's Benefit night and heard *L'Allegro ed il Penseroso*. He had missed Beard's 1758 Benefit, on June 14, which had been the equally popular Handel Masque of *Acis and Galatea*.

Ranelagh became a popular venue for fund-raising concerts during the summer months when the theatres were closed. In June 1757 John Stanley conducted a performance of *Acis and Galatea* for the Benefit of the Marine Society; and in 1758 a concert performance of *The Beggar's Opera* was staged 'for the benefit of some actors who formerly belonged to the theatres'. The takings on that occasion, June 22, were £102 which was subsequently shared out between six recipients. In 1760 the charity was an Asylum for Orphan Girls and the work was a rare outing for Thomas Arne's masque *The Judgement of Paris*. These all had fine roles for Beard. In two successive seasons the entire Ranelagh orchestra and singers

---

[17] 'Jeu d'esprit', N.a.2 pp. 97-99, Folger Shakespeare Library
[18] "...only Miss Fromantel sang". 'The Diary of John Baker', London, 1931, p.109

decamped for the day to Stoke Newington. On July 18 1758, and again on July 19 1759 there was a Benefit Concert at Mrs Butter's Boarding School.[19] The programmes were the easily transportable masques of *Acis and Galatea* and Boyce's *Solomon* that were so frequently called into service at this time. The soloists included Miss Young, Beard and Champness; the concert started at 5pm, and tickets were 5s. Quite how this concert came about, and who the Matthew Hussey was who organised the event has not yet been discovered: but he is likely to have been involved in the London musical scene in some capacity, perhaps as a dancer.[20]

One of Beard's more unusual roles at Ranelagh was in a spoof *Ode to St Cecilia* with a text by Bonnell Thornton. Dr Johnson – according to Boswell – "praised its humour and seemed much diverted with it".[21] Bonnell had written his burlesque 'Ode on St. Cecilia's Day, adapted to the ancient British Musick: the Salt Box, the Jew's Harp, the Marrow Bones and Cleaver, the Hum Strum or Hurdy-Gurdy' in 1749. Johnson heard a performance in 1763, but it was first heard at Ranelagh in about 1758. The date is vague because Charles Burney misremembered the date when he wrote: "In 1769 [recte 1758?] I set, for Smart and Newbery, Thornton's burlesque *Ode on St Cecilia's Day*. It was performed at Ranelagh in masks, to a very crowded audience, as I was told. ...Beard sung the salt-box song, which was admirably accompanied on that instrument by Brent, the Fencing-master, and father of Miss [Charlotte] Brent, the celebrated singer; Skeggs on the broomstick, as bassoon; and a remarkable performer on the Jew's-harp. – "Buzzing twangs the iron lyre". Cleavers were cast in bell-metal for this entertainment. All the performers of *The Old Woman's Oratory*,[22] employed by [Samuel] Foote, were, I believe, employed at Ranelagh on this occasion."[23]

The 18th century audience obviously joined with Dr Johnson in finding this spoof of the usual Purcellian or Handelian St Cecilia Ode hilarious. They would have enjoyed Thornton's Preface, signed (à la Hoffnung) 'Fustian Sackbut', of which this is just a sample:

"If this Ode contributes in the least to lessen our False Taste in admiring that Foreign Musick now so much in vogue, and to recall the ancient British Spirit, together with the ancient British Harmony, I shall not think the pains I employed in the composition entirely flung away on my Countrymen".[24]

The nearest similarity to anything that a modern audience can imagine would be a Gerard Hoffnung concert, a performance of Leopold Mozart's *Toy Symphony* given by 'personalities', or some of the light-hearted shindigs at a Last Night of the Proms.

[19] Information from Simon McVeigh, 'Calendar of London Concerts advertised in the London daily press', Goldsmiths College, University of London, 2003 -

[20] There were several Husseys in London working as dancers in 1757, including T. Hussey and 'Master Hussey'. See 'The London Stage', Part 4, vol. 2, p. 610

[21] Boswell, 'Life of Johnson', London, 1799, ed. G.B. Hill, rev. L.F. Powell, Oxford, 1934, Vol. 1, p. 420

[22] *The Old Woman's Oratory* was a theatrical parody first staged by Smart & Newbery in December 1751, and repeated at the Haymarket Theatre in May & June 1758. It also featured performances on the Salt Box, Jew's Harp, broomstick and other burlesque instruments. It is likely that the performance of Burney's musical setting took place with the same performers in 1758. See: 'Memoirs of Dr. Charles Burney', Univ. of Nebraska Press, 1988, pp. 131

[23] 'Memoirs of Dr. Charles Burney', Univ. of Nebraska Press, 1988, pp. 130

[24] Alan Dugald McKillop, 'Bonnell Thornton's Burlesque Ode', *Notes and Queries*, 23rd July 1949, p. 322

A Bow porcelain figure of Beard playing the saltbox with a marrow-bone[25]

In June 1763 Beard returned to Ranelagh Gardens, where he was now no longer a regular vocalist, for a revival of the famous performance, at the invitation of the current musical director Thomas Arne. This is the one that amused Dr Johnson. The *Monthly Review* entered into the spirit by printing a tongue-in-cheek review, and describing it as "written some years ago in the genuine spirit of true English humour, and lately set to music in as masterly a strain as it was written.

---

[25] Provenance: the Raymond Yarborough Collection, the Henry McGee collection of theatrical figures

...It happened a little unfortunately, indeed, in the late performance of this Ode, that the public ear, vitiated by being so long accustomed to foreign instruments, and foreign music, was not properly affected by the delicate and harmonious sounds of the Jews-harp and the Hum-strum. When this Ode is performed again, therefore, we would advise it to be done in a less tumultuous assembly; or that an additional number of Harp-trillers, and hurdy-gurdy Strummers, may be added to the band".[26] There is just a suspicion, here, that the performance did not project well into Ranelagh's awkward acoustic. Dr Johnson must have been close to the performers to get all the jokes and be much "diverted with it". The music eventually found its way into print sometime in the late 1760s, and was ascribed to 'an eminent master'.[27]

Another humorous work that Beard sang at Ranelagh was the *Medley* that David Garrick wrote for him, for his 1762 Benefit Night. This has fortunately been preserved for us in Tate Wilkinson's autobiography "The Wandering Patentee". Garrick wrote humorous and satirical verses, gently mocking both Beard and his Ranelagh audience, and set them to tunes that the audience would have associated with Beard - such as "Britons strike home", "Nancy Dawson" and other *Beggar's Opera* melodies. One can imagine that audiences were prepared to laugh at themselves on light-hearted occasions like this, when they heard Beard sing

But here they do come, and here they do agree, Sing trolly, lolly, lolly, lolly, lo,
For they can't abide themselves, the company, nor me, Ho, ho! let 'em go, let 'em go

The whole text can be found in Appendix 6 (p.363). Some of the allusions are less comprehensible today than others. But something of the original atmosphere of a company crowded into the hall ready to support their favourite singer at his Benefit can be gleaned from lines like this:

I can only thankful be / You can have nothing at all from me,
But a squeez'd-up seat, and a dish of my tea,
And an olio of speeches and quavers.

At some stage John Beard himself composed songs for the Ranelagh concerts. The British Library contains one song for which he had written the words, and one for which he wrote both words and music. The earlier of the two is the song 'Fairest Creature thou'rt so charming' with music (according to the heading) by the organist Renatus Harris. This has been dated to the 1730s - so it belongs to the beginning stages of Beard's career.[28] It would be very apposite if it could be proved to date from around 1738, when it might have been penned as a love-letter to Henrietta in their courtship:

Fairest Creature thou'rt so charming
none for Beauty can compare[;]
No that Goddess all admiring
was not half so lovely fair.
So bright a Genius none could boast on

---

[26] The *Monthly Review*, XXVIII, 1763, p. 481
[27] Alan Dugald McKillop, 'Bonnell Thornton's Burlesque Ode', *Notes and Queries*, 23rd July 1949, p. 324
[28] There is a problem regarding the likelihood of Beard and the elder Renatus Harris' lives coinciding, as Harris died c. 1724 when Beard would have only been nine. Harris' son John (d. 1743) lived in Red Lion Street c. 1728-9, - also the street in which the Beard family lived, and where this family friendship may have been forged.

mixt with an engaging Air,
Freed from any vile Delusion
Practised oft among the Fair.

The later song is 'Cross Purposes', for which he was entirely responsible. The composition is no more distinguished than that of many other similar songs. But it shows that he put his musical tuition from his days as a chorister at the Chapel Royal to good use, where they were taught "to sing, to play on the harpsichord or Organ ...and compose." As yet it is not known in which season this was first premiered by its author at the Pleasure Gardens for which he remained the principal male vocalist until at least 1762.

CHAPTER 8
THE GARRICK YEARS

1. DRURY LANE: 1748 – 1751

After five years at Covent Garden Beard was tempted back to Drury Lane by the realisation that his talented colleague David Garrick was beginning to do some original work there, and was making constructive improvements to the way that plays were presented. One of the very first changes was to bring in a rule that no member of the public was to stand on, or behind, the stage during a performance. Beard was impressed with the control that Garrick was beginning to impose. He would adopt similar tactics when he took over the management of Covent Garden in the 1760s. Together these two managers would change the whole way that the public enjoyed the theatre, and would transform them into a safer environment for all concerned. Keeping the public one side of the curtain and the performers on the other was a small, but significant, step. For the moment it seemed that Drury Lane was the place to be - with its forward looking manager and his dynamic new approach to programming.[1] In his recent years at Covent Garden Beard had found very little interesting new work coming his way. Only in the realm of pantomime was John Rich keen to develop the repertoire. There had been roles in three new pantomimes for Beard in the past season: 'Mystery' in *Apollo and Daphne*; 'Fortitude' in *The Muses Looking Glass*; and 'Mars' in *Venus and Adonis*. Apart from that there were performances of *The Beggar's Opera* with new leading ladies - Mrs Storer and Mrs Vincent; but his only other appearances in a main-piece was confined to his walk-on singing role 'Colonel Bully' in *The Provok'd Wife*. Rich kept him busy in the after-pieces, of course, with dozens of performances of his trusty roles in *The Royal Chace, Damon and Phillida* and *The Lottery*.

An opportunity for Beard to rejoin his friends Kitty Clive and William Havard in the Drury Lane company emerged when Garrick began to see the virtue of building up a good team of musicians. He had not been satisfied with Thomas Lowe in his first year. Lowe was so bad an actor, by Garrick's own exacting standards, that after one season he felt he had to replace him. Garrick also realised that he had to have pantomimes (which he despised) in his repertory - if only to counteract their popularity at Covent Garden. So the offer of a contract was made to Beard. We can see from his position in the pecking order of Benefit nights that he was considered a valuable addition to the company. At number nine he is the first musician in the list, and closely follows the principal stars, the chief dancer and the Harlequin. This is the descending order, which also reflects their fee-structure: Garrick, Mrs Cibber, Barry, Mrs Pritchard, Mrs Clive, Mlle Auretti (dancer), Yates, Henry Woodward (Harlequin), Beard. Garrick would have brought him into the company to advise him on musical matters, and Beard would have been keen to offer advice on how the musical repertoire could be developed. Garrick was not fond of Thomas Arne, who was the current house composer - and "hardly ever qualified him with any other title in Private, than the Rabscalion".[2] So Beard talked up the alternative abilities of his

---

[1] Samuel Richardson wrote, in 1748, "...now seems to be the time, when an Actor and a Manager, in the same person, is in being, who deservedly engages public favour in all he undertakes, and who owes so much, and is gratefully sensible that he does, to that great master of the human passions [Shakespeare]". Quoted in Alan Kendall, 'Garrick, a biography', London, 1985, p. 54

[2] Roger Lonsdale, 'Dr Charles Burney', London 1965, p.18

friend William Boyce. It is in this period that Boyce began his list of successful stage works for Drury Lane: *The Chaplet* (1749), *The Shepherd's Lottery* (1752), the 'Dirge' in *Romeo and Juliet* (1750), and incidental music for *The Winter's Tale* (1756) and *The Tempest* (1757). In all of these there would be good music for Beard.

Arne remained in charge of the music in Beard's first months at the theatre. In fact, it was a difficult time for both of the composers as, according to Burney, Arne and Boyce "were frequently concurrents at the theatre and in each other's way".[3] Arne produced the songs for Garrick's revival of *Much Ado about Nothing*, which opened in November 1748 and in which 'Balthasar', with 'the proper songs', was the first new role for Beard. He was joined in the musical numbers by Kitty Clive and Henry Reinhold - Handel's principal bass soloist. Arne's other new music this season was *The Triumph of Peace*, written for Drury Lane to celebrate the Peace of Aix-le-Chapelle. Although Handel's offering for the same occasion, the *Royal Fireworks Music*, has remained a classic, Arne's music for this masque, which received a decent run of ten performances, does not survive. Beard, as a 'shepherd', and Kitty Clive as a 'shepherdess' witnessed an elaborate staging which presented "the *Goddess of Peace* descending in a triumphal Car borne upon the Clouds, which, breaking, she is discovered in her Temple, attended by *Justice*, *Liberty*, *Commerce* and *Science*. *War* with his hands fetter'd, stands in a dejected Posture before her..."[4] Curiously Arne seems to have restrained himself from inserting his 'hit' number from the *Masque of Alfred* - "Rule, Britannia" - into the score, although there was plenty of scope for it - since Anne Auretti danced the role of 'Britannia'.

Another mainpiece that required the services of a singer this season was Aaron Hill's *Merope*. This was a new tragedy which was immediately liked, and quickly passed into the theatre repertoire. This was not the case with Dr Johnson's *Mahomet and Irene*. Garrick tried to help his old schoolmaster from Lichfield by mounting the play that he had been working on for so many years. But it failed after being nursed through nine nights.[5] The other interesting work for Beard this season was the afterpiece *Lethe* which Garrick had written several years earlier and which had only received one performance so far.[6] It contained fine arias for Beard as 'Mercury' and Kitty Clive as 'Mrs Riot'. Garrick gave it a make-over, feeling that he had come a long way as a dramatist in the past nine years. The new role 'Lord Chalkstone', that he wrote in for himself, turned the fortunes of this piece right around. Henceforward it was to become stock repertoire, coming second in the list of most performed afterpieces in the entire Garrick period.[7]

Another serious tragedy that required music was William Whitehead's *The Roman Father*. What the music might have been for this is not known; but it involved Beard, Miss Norris, Miss Cole and a chorus of six singers who each received 5 shillings per night. Garrick, who played 'Horatius' in the twelve performances, was skilfully adding to the stock of repertory pieces and finding ways to prevent the fickle public from indulging in the senseless habit of going to new plays simply to hiss and heckle them. A contemporary newspaper printed the following reproof: "Those Gentlemen who borrow'd gold lac'd hats to go to Drury

---

[3] Burney, 'A General History of Music', ed. Frank Mercer, London, 1935, p. 1010

[4] Roger Fiske, 'English Theatre Music in the Eighteenth Century', OUP, Oxford, 1973, p. 208

[5] Harry Pedicord, 'The Theatrical Public in the time of Garrick', Southern Illinois Press, Carbondale, 1954, says that *Merope* received 59 performances in 15 seasons (p. 138). Dr Johnson's only play received 9 performances, despite having Garrick in the cast, and then was forgotten.

[6] on April 15th 1740

[7] Roger Fiske, 'English Theatre Music in the Eighteenth Century', OUP, Oxford, 1973, p. 344

Lane in order to damn the new play are desir'd to return them to the owners, or their names will be publish'd at full length".[8]

Garrick now decided that he needed more musical afterpieces, and asked both of his composers to provide something. It was a clever way of dealing with his dilemma of having both Arne and Boyce on his books. With Beard wishing him to give Boyce a chance, and having a natural aversion to Arne, Garrick gave them both the opportunity to show what they could do. Presumably his decision about who to retain would depend on the relative success of each piece. Arne's *Don Saverio*, in which Beard played the title role, only received three performances and "was much hissed". The prompter, Richard Cross, wrote: "The farce was ill receiv'd that in ye middle I went on and said - Gent[lemen]: we must beg y^r indulgence in permitting this piece to be perform'd once more, for the benefit of Mr Arne who has taken great pains in composing the music - and [then] it shall be play'd no more".[9] The music has long disappeared, but a libretto survives, from which it can be seen that, with five songs, Beard had the biggest singing role but remained curiously outside the actual plot. Involving disguises and love affairs in Naples, this bears an uncanny resemblance to Lorenzo Da Ponte's *Cosi fan tutte*. Through a plot heavy with intrigue passes the foppish and strangely uninvolved character of 'Don Saverio', the brother of the Neapolitan love-interest 'Clarice' (played by Kitty Clive). He is described as 'an affected Imitator of foreign Customs'. A fop is not a character that Beard was often called upon to play, as his physique was more suited to country squires, bluff topers and hearty sailors. But the songs Arne wrote for him were varied and challenging, and required him to sing in French, in praise of Italian Opera, and in praise of his own dancing ability. What actually set the public against the piece has not been recorded. Fiske has suggested that they "disliked seeing men and women in modern dress singing non-stop",[10] as though they would have accepted it better if they had been in period costume. But in the 18th century the concept of performing in 'historically aware' costume was only in its infancy.[11] Even Shakespeare was principally played in a rather more exotic version of contemporary dress. But, since Arne had written his own words as well as music, it is possible that the piece didn't actually hang together and was a self-indulgent jumble. He had written plenty of other unsuccessful works in the past, as Garrick was well aware. After the three disappointing performances Arne took himself off in a huff and went to work at Covent Garden, leaving the field to Boyce.

Boyce's *The Chaplet* fared much better and received a hundred performances in its first eight seasons. By 1767 it had even begun wowing audiences in New York and Philadelphia. The libretto was by Moses Mendez who had provided Drury Lane with an earlier success - *The Double Disappointment*. His creation in that play, the stage Irishman, Phelim O'Blunder, regularly brought the house down. *The Chaplet* was something very different. This was an all-sung Pastoral opera - and its success rather disproves Fiske's earlier judgement about Arne's work, that the contemporary audience disliked the singing being "non-stop". The storyline is much more conventional than Arne's, and would have felt

---

[8] The London Stage, Part 4, vol. 1, Southern Illinois University Press, Carbondale Ill., 1962, p.179
[9] London Stage, Part 4, p.175
[10] Roger Fiske, 'English Theatre Music in the Eighteenth Century', OUP, Oxford, 1973, p. 215
[11] On 13th March 1755 the first comments on proper costuming began to circulate in an article written by Roger Pickering "Reflections upon Theatrical Expression in Tragedy": 'Taste in dress demands that an actor be conversant in the modes of dress ancient and modern, in other countries as well as his own. ....Alexander and Cato were not masters of the snuff box, nor Greek women of French heels...'

comfortably familiar to anyone who liked music in the mould of Handel's *Acis and Galatea*. Two shepherdesses love the world-weary 'Damon' (played by Beard): an innocent one 'Laura' (played by Miss Norris) and an experienced one 'Pastora' played – obviously – by Kitty Clive. Another shepherd, 'Palaemon' (Master Mattocks), is Pastora's spurned lover. This is very much the stuff of the cantatas that Arne, John Stanley and others were writing for Beard to sing at the Pleasure Gardens. Now the audience could see these slight scenarios enacted before them onstage and in attractive sets. It must have been like seeing the paintings of Antoine Watteau (1684 – 1721), or their Dresden china ornaments, coming to life.

The music still survives, as so much of Boyce's output does, and shows that his succession of songs are very much in the light ballad vein that Arne was so adept at writing, and are beautifully scored for flute, oboes, bassoons and strings. Having enjoyed this success, it is strange that Boyce's next collaboration with Mendez should be his last major work for the stage. *The Shepherd's Lottery* must have been commissioned by Garrick hard on the heels of *The Chaplet*'s success, and was premiered in November 1751. Once again its plot is pastoral and quaint. The action revolves around a May-Day ceremony whereby shepherds could choose their partners by drawing their names out of an urn – in the manner of a tombola or a 'keys in the hat' type of wife-swapping. 'Daphne', played with relish by Kitty Clive, is cynically indifferent as to who gets her. 'Phyllis' (Miss Norris) is terrified that the man she loves, Thyrsis, will not be the one to draw her name. 'Colin', played by Beard, is the world-weary 'Damon' of *The Chaplet* all over again, and refuses to draw out any name at all. Fortunately for all concerned 'Thyrsis' (played by Master Vernon) does draw out Phyllis' name. The music is once again highly original, with a fine air for 'Phyllis' that Fiske suggests could have led Boyce to write a good serious opera if he had been minded to. Beard gets his customary martial song, 'The Drum is unbrac'd and the Trumpet no more shall rouse the fierce Soldier to fight', in which Boyce calls up the sounds of a military band, replete with fifes, from his pit orchestra. The most remarkable feature of all was the Finale, which was the first instance in Britain of a type known as "Vaudeville". This was derived from French opera, and consisted of a song, usually strophic, with ensemble refrains and solo verses for each of the main characters. Mozart's *Die Entführung aus dem Serail* concludes with just such a Vaudeville finale. Some of the music from these two Pastorals is still regularly performed today. When Boyce published his *Eight Symphonies* in 1760 he simply repackaged eight overtures from earlier works. Thus Symphony no. 3 is the overture to *The Chaplet*, and no. 4 the overture to *The Shepherd's Lottery*.

During the run of performances of *The Chaplet*, in January 1750, Beard was the victim of a mugging. This must have been all too common in the downtown area of Covent Garden where the theatres, bars and brothels were. Beard was still living in the Red Lion Square area, and must have been in the habit of taking a sedan chair (the eighteenth century equivalent of a taxi) back home after a hard day at the theatre. The Drury Lane prompter wrote in his book, on January 16, "Beard robb'd in his chair at 2 in the morning in Drury Lane."[12]

Beard's house would have been a pleasant walk away from Drury Lane. There was a place in Red Lion Square where chairs were always available for hire - the equivalent of a taxi-rank. In fine weather he would have rarely needed a chair to

---

[12] Winston MS, 7: quoted in The London Stage, Part 4, vol. 1, Southern Illinois University Press, Carbondale Ill., 1962, p.168

go such a short distance. As his walk would have taken him through Holborn, where we know that he had business colleagues and kept accounts with various tradesmen, he may have combined it with some day-to-day shopping activity. But at night things must have been very different. Footpads lurked in dark doorways, and were often reportedly in league with the chairmen, who stood aside during the assault. On another occasion there is a report of the tenor Thomas Lowe being similarly assaulted: "On Friday night last as Mr Lowe, belonging to Drury Lane Playhouse was going down Snow Hill, he was stopped by two fellows, one of whom gave him a violent blow on the temple with a great stick, which stunned him ...As soon as he recovered he felt in his pockets and found they had robbed him only of 11 shillings in silver, being (as he suppose) disturb'd by some people passing by, for they had not taken his watch, nor a guinea and a half which he had also in his pockets".[13]

Beard must have received a similar blow, or blows. The newspaper report implies that he wasn't hurt: "...Tuesday Morning about Two o'Clock as Mr Beard, belonging to the Theatre Royal in Drury-Lane, was going home, his Chair was stopt in Drury-Lane, by four or five Fellows, who took from him his Watch and Money, but did not otherwise treat him ill..."[14] But that is not consistent with subsequent events, since he was off work for several days and didn't return to *The Chaplet* until January 23. In the one performance that he missed, on the 18th, the prompter reports that 'Master Mattocks did his part'. As this young actor was originally cast in the role of 'Palaemon' it would have entailed quite a lot of last minute changes, with an understudy having to come in to replace him. Beard suffered financially from the mugging. With no health insurance available in those days he would have lost his daily salary when he was unavailable, as well as anything the robbers had got away with. It is good, therefore, to see the theatre accounts for this week showing that he was 'lent, by order, £21' to help him out.

At this very time Henry Fielding, by now a Magistrate and Justice of the Peace for Middlesex, was writing his 'Enquiry into the Causes of the late Increase in Robbers' (1751). Both of these attacks had occurred within a stone's throw of the Bow Street Magistrate's Court where he and his brother, Sir John Fielding, dispensed summary justice. Henry Fielding laid the problem fairly and squarely at the door of gin-drinkers: "It removes all sense of fear and shame and emboldens them to commit every wicked and dangerous enterprise".[15] William Hogarth entered the fray and published his twin prints, Gin Lane and Beer Street, in February 1751. Set in a street near St Giles Church, down which Beard would have walked on his route to Drury Lane, the pub in the foreground bears the inscription "Drunk for a Penny - Dead drunk for two pence".[16] At modern prices this would be the equivalent of 36p and 72p!

Another accident which befell Beard the same year turned into a disaster for Charles Burney. He was beginning to make his way in the theatre as a composer and had just written a burletta for Drury Lane called *Robin Hood*. When Beard, in the title role, lost his voice after three performances, the next ones were deferred. Burney would have received payment for his labours on the 3rd night; but authors were always entitled to further payments on the 6th and 9th nights as well. In a document at the Folger Shakespeare Library the process is made very clear:

[13] Monday January 3rd 1743: quoted in The London Stage, Part 3, p. 1025
[14] The Penny London Post or Morning Advertiser, January 17-19 1750
[15] Liza Picard, 'Dr Johnson's London', London, 2000, p. 124
[16] 'Engravings by Hogarth', ed. Shesgreen, New York, 1973, 'Beer Street' & 'Gin Lane', Plates 75 & 76

"When said Dramatic pieces are accepted they shall be prepared for representation and the 3rd, 6th, 9th Nights of such of them as shall have a run or continue to be performed for Nine Nights shall pay or cause to be paid [to the author] whatever shall be remaining of the money which shall be received on the said 3rd, 6th, 9th Nights, after the usual charges[17] are deducted."[18] For reasons which are not clear, and on which Burney does not comment in his Memoirs, the piece was never revived. The prompter's book may give a clue: on all three nights he reported that there was 'noise' in the auditorium - a sign that the audience was restless and voicing its displeasure with the piece.

Before returning to Beard's relationship with Handel, which, in 1751, was about to get back onto a firm footing after a three-year gap, mention must be made of Beard's work at Drury Lane that year. In many ways it was settling down into a very regular pattern. For his main-pieces Garrick was continuing to commission new plays and to revive old plays - including some unknown Shakespeare. Beard was required onstage as 'Lorenzo' in the *Merchant of Venice* this year, and continued as 'Balthazar' in *Much Ado* and 'Amiens' in *As You Like It*. Another mainpiece in which he was involved was a revival of the Masque of *Alfred* by Thomson and Mallet. The work which had been first played at Cliveden in August 1740, was expanded for this revival by David Mallet (his co-author James Thomson having died in 1748). Garrick had persuaded him to turn it into a full-length piece, and develop a meatier title role for him to play. After the rewrite he took the role of 'Alfred' and George Anne Bellamy was his 'Eltruda'. There was some additional dancing put in, and two pieces of Arne's music were reused without any consultation.[19] This added to Arne's list of grievances against Garrick. Fortunately it allowed Beard to sing "Rule Britannia" in its original context, for the first time.

This season also saw a strange rivalry between the two principal theatres when they mounted rival productions of *Romeo and Juliet* on the same days in October. The respective merits of Garrick and George Anne Bellamy versus Spranger Barry and Mrs Cibber in the title roles kept the town agog. "Well-informed connoisseurs took to watching Barry in the first three acts, in which he was reputed to be superior to his competitor, and then rushing to Drury Lane to catch the two final acts, in which Garrick shone".[20] When it was reported that Covent Garden had added a solemn procession, with music by Arne, at the moment that Juliet's supposedly dead body was carried across the stage, Boyce was drafted in to do something similar at Drury Lane. Both scores survive. Arne had composed a *Dirge* with muffled drums, followed by a three-part chorus 'Ah, hapless Maid'. Boyce started his rival music with a tolling bell, and set words hurriedly penned by Garrick himself beginning 'Rise, rise, heart-breaking Sighs'. Baron Kielmansegge was profoundly moved when he saw a performance in 1761:

"In the play an entire funeral is represented, with bells tolling and a choir singing. ...Nothing of the kind could be represented more beautifully or naturally. The

---

[17] At this period the 'charges' were £64 5s 0d
[18] Isaac Bickerstaff's contract, dated May 4th, 1765. Folger Shakespeare Library, Washington, USA
[19] 'As Mr Arne originally composed the Music in the Masque of Alfred, and the town may probably ...imagine the music, as now perform'd, to be all his production, he is advised ...to inform the public that but two of his songs are in that performance, viz: *O Peace thou fairest child of Heaven* and the Ode in Honour of Great Britain, beginning *When Britain first at Heaven's Command...*' *The General Advertiser*, 26 February 1751
[20] 'The *Revels* History of Drama in English', vol. 6, London 1975, p. 101

funeral dirges and the choirs made the whole ceremony solemn ... [which] can be attained more easily here than upon any other stage, owing to the quantity of actors, including dancers and singers, of whom fifty are sometimes to be seen on one night."[21]

Apparently this was still being performed in Fanny Kemble's day, c.1830. Hector Berlioz saw a production of Garrick's version of the play in Paris, starring Harriet Smithson as Juliet, and wrote a similar *Funeral Procession* into his *Romeo and Juliet Symphony* (1839) with strict instructions in the manuscript as to how, and when, it should be played.

In Boyce's *Dirge*, (preserved in manuscript at the Bodleian Library)[22] which had inspired Berlioz, the singers were all the familiar names from the Drury Lane Pastorals: Mrs Clive and Master Mattocks (soprano), Miss Norris and Master Vernon (alto), Beard (tenor) and Reinhold (bass). Beard had a solo in the middle of the opening Largo, to the text:

> *She's gone from Earth, nor leaves behind*
> *So fair a form, so pure a Mind:*
> *How could'st thou Death at once destroy*
> *The Lover's hope, the Parent's Joy.*

In the middle of the season, on March 20 1751, Frederick the Prince of Wales died. The closure of the theatres affected the Benefits, which had just begun. Beard's should have been the next one, on March 21. So everything had to be delayed, and he had to wait until the theatres reopened. The prompter's notebook states: "This Morning we were surpris'd with the unhappy news, that Frederick Prince of Wales dy'd the Night before between ten and eleven. Mr Beard's Benefit was to be on Thursday & many of ye Bills were posted before we heard of this Accident - the Bills were immediately torn down, and the House shut up before my Ld Chamberlain sent orders for so doing. On Friday the 5th April my Lord sent us leave to open on the 8th: being Easter Monday. It is said our having permission to open so soon, and before the Prince was Bury'd, was on account of the actors depending".[23]

Beard's Benefit, rescheduled for April 10, now comprised a mainpiece in which he had no role to play, and the dependable *The Devil to Pay* as the afterpiece. He was fortunate in the cast of Farquhar's *The Stratagem* which preceded it, because, in addition to his friends Havard as 'Aimwell' and Ned Shuter as 'Gibbet', this featured Garrick himself in the role of 'Archer'. In the intervals Beard sang songs, including a *Cantata* by Boyce, and at the end Garrick delivered his *Parody of Shakespeare's Stages of Life*. All in all things had worked out well, despite the delay - and despite the shocking business of Henrietta's daughter Barbara marrying Henry Arthur Herbert, the new Earl of Powis, in Bath on March 30. Beard grossed the same amount at the box office as he had done the previous year: a very respectable £200.

Garrick's *Parody of Shakespeare's Stages of Life* was delivered as the Epilogue. It had been delivered first on March 16, at Woodward's Benefit, when it continued the theme of his afterpiece *A Lick at the Town*. On that occasion it went

[21] Count Frederick Kielmansegge, 'Diary of a Journey to London in the years 1761-2', London 1902, pp.221-2

[22] Wight Bequest. MS. Mus.c.3

[23] The London Stage, Part 4, vol. 1, Southern Illinois University Press, Carbondale Ill., 1962, p.244

down so well that Garrick was urged to repeat it; and he found space at the close of Beard's Benefit. As it is not well known, and is not currently anthologised anywhere, but lies instead forgotten in Garrick's handwritten copy of his *Prologues* and *Epilogues* at the Folger Shakespeare Library, the merits or demerits of his contemporary slant on Jacques' speech (from *As You Like It)* can be consulted in Appendix 6.

2. BACK WITH HANDEL: 1751 - 1759

In 1751 Beard returned as one of Handel's soloists, and he never missed a further Lent season.[24] Winton Dean is not sure whether he sang the in the opening performances of *Belshazzar* on February 22 and 27 and *Alexander's Feast* on March 1, 6, 8 and 13. Beard was free on these nights - as he was for the whole of Handel's short season, which was curtailed by the death of the Prince of Wales. Lowe had been the tenor soloist in recent seasons, but Beard was definitely brought back at some stage during this season. He possibly rejoined halfway through for *Esther* and *Judas*. He certainly sang *Messiah* in April and May. This is his diary:

1751	HANDEL	BEARD
Feb 20	***Ash Wednesday***	***LENT starts***
Fri 22	Belshazzar[*Winton Dean suggests "probably Lowe"*]	
Sat 23		Alfred (m/p)
Mon 25		Alfred (m/p)
Tues 26		Alfred (m/p)
Wed 27	Belshazzar	
Thus 28		Alfred (m/p)
Fri Mar 1	Alexander's Feast + Hercules [*Winton Dean suggests Lowe*]	
Sat 2		Alfred (m/p)
Mon 4		Alfred (m/p)
Tues 5		Alfred (m/p)
Wed 6	Alexander's Feast + Hercules	
Thurs 7	---	
Fri 8	Alexander's Feast + Hercules	
Sat 9		Alfred (m/p)
Mon 11		The Chaplet (a/p)
Tues 12		The Rehearsal (a/p)
Wed 13	Alexander's Feast + Hercules	
Thurs14		Lethe (a/p)
Fri 15	Esther [*Winton Dean can't decide between Beard & Lowe*] [25]	
Sat 16		Romeo & Juliet (m/p)
Mon 18		The Chaplet (a/p)
Tues 19		The Rehearsal (a/p)
Wed 20	Judas Maccabaeus [*No evidence - Winton Dean can't decide*] [26]	
Thurs 21	***Theatres closed until April 8th***	

[24] Apart from performances at the Foundling Hospital Handel was now only performing in Lent.
[25] "The new part was adapted for Lowe, but there is doubt whether he sang it: one of the airs ('Tune your harps') was sung by Beard in public a month later, and another ('Jehovah crowned') was attributed to Beard in Walsh's contemporary edition of the songs." Dean *Handel's Dramatic Oratorios and Masques*, p. 213
[26] "It is not possible to distinguish all the casts" Dean *Handel's Dramatic Oratorios and Masques*, p. 472

When Handel repeated *Messiah* at the Foundling Hospital on April 18 and May 16 Beard was definitely one of the soloists. As we have seen in Chapter 6, this was the year that he returned a proportion of his fee.[27] This custom was repeated again the next year, when: "...Mr Beard agreeing to perform gratis, no distribution was set against his name".[28] Thereafter he always declined a fee.

Beard's annual performances at the Foundling Hospital must have been donated to the charity as a personal act of remembrance, in honour of the wife who had effectively lost her own daughter. If she had valued and assisted Thomas Coram's noble cause when she was a close neighbour (as I have suggested in chapter 6) Beard's generosity would make perfect sense.

Beard's engagement diary now settled into an established pattern. Besides his theatrical work he was required every year for two Odes at Court, one for the New Year and one for the King's birthday. There would be about a dozen performances of Handel's oratorios in Lent, followed by one or two performances at the Foundling Hospital. Other charities were regularly able to call on his services, particularly the Fund for Decayed Musicians and the Lock Hospital. Every year there would be Handel arias sandwiched in between the cantatas that were written for him to perform as interval music in the theatre, or at Ranelagh, by Arne, Boyce, John Stanley and others. His theatrical work included more characters who come on stage principally to sing an interpolated song, both in Garrick's celebrated revivals of Shakespeare plays,[29] and in the usual musical after-pieces and pantomimes. There was always new music too, since every London composer seems to have been Beard's friend. Having him in the cast was almost a guarantee of success for any new piece.

Handel was pleased to have Beard's voice to write for once again. He set to work, despite increasing blindness, on a new oratorio *Jephtha* in which he knew that he could utilise the maturity of musicianship that the 36-year-old singer had now acquired. The singer in the title role is required to sing with great expressiveness and drama, but also with great tenderness and compassion. The six arias, various recitatives and ensembles, cover a wider range of emotions than any yet written for Beard - even including those in *Samson* and *Judas Maccabaeus*. The mastery of the vocal writing in "Deeper and deeper still" and "Waft her angels" has delighted every audience since the time that it was first heard, sung by Beard in February 1752.

The oratorios that had been performed during the three years that Lowe had sung for Handel came back into the repertoire, sometimes significantly altered. Handel was always thinking of how to use his soloists' talents most successfully. With Beard now in the cast of *Theodora* in 1755, for instance, Handel found time to reset the aria 'From virtue springs' - "for Beard" - as the conducting score tells us.[30] A year earlier he had sung 'Jonathan' in *Alexander Balus*. The two final oratorios that he had not yet sung - *Susanna* and *Solomon* which had both been conceived for Lowe's voice - entered his repertoire in Handel's last ever season (1759). In the much revised and altered *Solomon* Beard sang 'Zadok'; but in *Susanna*, where he

---

[27] "... Mr Smith had returned him, for the Benefit of the Charity, two guineas returned by Beard and one guinea by Mr Corbonelli, two of the said Performers". General Committee Minutes, no. 3, pp. 210-211
[28] Wed. April 15th, 1752, from Nichols and Wray, 'A History of the Foundling Hospital', London 1935
[29] He played these new roles in The Winter's Tale (1756), Much Ado about Nothing (1756), The Tempest (1757), Antony & Cleopatra (1759) as well as his previous roles in As You Like It, Macbeth, Romeo and Juliet, The Merchant of Venice etc.
[30] Winton Dean, 'Handel's Dramatic Oratorios and Masques', OUP Oxford 1959, p. 575

sang 'First Elder', not a note of his music was changed, despite severe revisions in the rest of the work.[31]

Another choral work that underwent serious revision when Beard sang it was the Foundling Hospital Anthem, which had been performed in 1749 at the first benefit concert that Handel had given there. It was revived in 1753 for the official opening of the Chapel on April 16. Happily Beard's own vocal part for that still exists at the Royal College of Music.[32] [See also chapter 6].

In these last seasons Handel performed a wide range of his established oratorios, but still had time and energy to refurbish some old ones. As late as 1757 he took the Italian oratorio *Il Trionfo del Tempo e del Disinganno* from 1707, which Beard had last sung twenty or so years previously,[33] and turned it into *The Triumph of Time and Truth*. Beard continued in his previous role of 'Piacere', which was now renamed 'Pleasure'. The works that he sang for Handel between 1752 and 1759 comprise a complete list of all of Handel's own performances in this period. [See Appendix 1]. On account of his blindness these were conducted by J. C. Smith; but it is clear that Handel, who still performed organ concertos between the acts, was in overall charge. One famous anecdote about Beard's singing dates from this season:

"When Smith played the organ at the theatre, during the first year of Handel's blindness, *Samson* was performed, and Beard sung with great feeling
> *Total eclipse – no sun, no moon,*
> *All dark amid the blaze of noon.*
The recollection that Handel had set this air to music, with a view of the blind composer then sitting by the organ, affected the audience so forcibly, that many persons present were moved even to tears."[34] In a letter of 1753 to Elizabeth Harris, her female correspondent, known only as C. Gilbert, similarly wrote "You ask'd me about poor Handel. I paid my devoir to him at the oratorio, and could have cried at the sight of him. He is fallen away, pale, feeble, old, blind, in short everything that could most affect one. ...I was told, at the Total Eclipse in Samson, he cry'd like an infant. Thank God I did not see it".[35]

From the list of performances given in Appendix 1 it will be seen that Handel was rarely performing his secular oratorios (Masques and Serenatas) in these Lent seasons. There were no performances of *Acis and Galatea*, *Semele* or *Hercules* in this period. Only *L'Allegro ed Il Penseroso*, *Alexander's Feast* and *The Choice of Hercules* were given an occasional airing. Otherwise the list of works which Beard performed between 1751 and 1759 includes every one of the English oratorios.

In the years after Handel's death, which occurred on April 14 1759, Beard was more and more occupied with his role as Manager at Covent Garden. He began in that capacity, as John Rich's deputy, only five months after Handel's death, taking over completely when Rich died on November 26 1761. Thus he was well placed to assist J. C. Smith and John Stanley in the continuation of the Lent Oratorio season. During his time as manager the tradition that Handel had started in the mid 1740s was maintained. New oratorios were composed by both conductors[36], and

---

[31] Winton Dean, 'Handel's Dramatic Oratorios and Masques', OUP Oxford 1959, pp. 527-534 & 547
[32] RCM m/s 2254
[33] on 23rd March 1737 and 3rd March 1739
[34] William Coxe *Anecdotes of G.F. Handel and J.C. Smith*, 1799, p. 45
[35] Burrows & Dunhill, 'Music and Theatre in Handel's world', Oxford, 2002, p. 291
[36] J.C. Smith, *Paradise Lost* (1760), *Rebecca* (1761); John Stanley *Zimri* (1760)

others were assembled in a pasticcio fashion out of Handel's other compositions[37]. But it was the actual Handel works themselves that continued to attract the audience. With Beard still in the cast until 1767 it is not surprising to find that the most popular works were those most closely associated with his voice: *Judas Maccabaeus*, *Samson* and *Messiah*. For a complete list of the Oratorios performed at Covent Garden in 1759-67 see Appendix 1.

3. DRURY LANE: 1752 – 1759

Having decided to put Pantomime into his repertoire of after-pieces Garrick decided to do it even better than at Covent Garden. He had already lured Woodward back as his 'Harlequin', causing casting problems at the rival theatre. In 1752 Rich employed the actors Miles and Phillips as replacement Harlequins in two pantomimes, and returned himself, as 'Lun', in a third. Garrick began to spend out the same sort of huge sums on his sets and costumes as Rich was accustomed to do. By December 1752 the *Gentleman's Magazine* was able to report: "This new entertainment [*The Genii*] hath fully decided the controversy and fix'd the superiority of Pantomime to Drury Lane Theatre; ... for beauty of scenery, elegance of dress, propriety of music, and regularity of designs, it exceeds all the boasted grandeur of *Harlequin Sorceror* [at Covent Garden], or of any I have seen either separate or collective. The last scene beggars all description; the most romantic Eastern account of sumptuous palaces are but faint to this beauty, this glow of light, this profusion of glittering gems, which adorn the whole and much exceeds all expectations..."[38] But a year later it printed much less favourable comments, taken from the Gray's Inn Journal, in its October 1753 edition:

"It is surprising that Mr Garrick should ...introduce Pantomime Entertainments, especially as his own universal talents are seconded by a good company of performers. We suppose he does it to gratify the taste of the town; but such Smithfield exhibitions should certainly be banished from all regular theatres; and as Mr Woodward is an excellent comedian, it would be more eligible in him, if he chooses to wear the motley dress any more, to appear in the character of a speaking Harlequin, after the manner of the Italian comedy."[39]

At this period Beard knew that he would spend the first few months of each new year singing some role or other in the Drury Lane pantomimes. They regularly started on December 26, and enjoyed long runs. In 1752 he was in *The Genii*, in 1753 *Fortunatus*, and in 1754 in *Proteus or Harlequin in China*. Sometimes the songs that he sang were published, with a credit for him being the original singer. But mostly the music was as ephemeral as the pieces themselves.[40]

      Two farces now began to hold the attention of the public and provide Beard with opportunities to use his gifts of mimicry. Kitty Clive's *The Rehearsal or Bayes in Petticoats* returned "with alterations and an additional scene". She herself played 'Mrs Hazard' and the singer 'Marcella' that Beard had to act alongside as

---

[37] *The Cure of Saul* (1763), *Nabal* (1764), *Israel in Babylon* (1765)

[38] The *Gentleman's Magazine*, December 1752, p. 582

[39] The *Gentleman's Magazine*, October 1753, p. 493

[40] The songs from the 1754 *Proteus or Harlequin in China* were published by Walsh in 1755 [British Library ref. D. 282. (3.)]

'Corydon'. Kitty's dialogue at his first appearance gives us a delightful insight into his happy demeanour and jovial stage-presence:

"Oh, Mr Beard! Your most Obedient... Sir, I shall be vastly oblig'd to you I am sure; do you know that you sing better than any of 'em? But I hope you'd consider the Part you are to act with *Marcella* is to be done with great scorn. Therefore, as you have such a smiling, good-humoured Face, I beg you'll endeavour to smother as many of your dimples as you can in that scene with her. Come, come, let us begin."[41]

The other farce in which he could let down his hair was *The Englishman in Paris* by Samuel Foote (October 1753) in which he played the cartoon-ish character of a 'Singing-Master, with a favourite French Air".

His Benefits nights did well at this period, bringing him £250 in 1752, £260 in 1753, £280 in 1754 and £300 in 1755.[42] On every occasion he had decided to hitch his star to Garrick, who played the following roles for him in the mainpieces: Duretete in *The Inconstant*, Ranger in *The Suspicious Husband*, Lothario in *The Fair Penitent,* Archer in *The Stratagem,* Don Carlos in *The Mistake* and Marplot in *The Busy Body*. His highest takings were at his Benefit night in 1757 when he grossed £350 in a very strong programme that starred Garrick as Kitely in *Everyman in his Humour*, and Samuel Foote in his own farce *The Englishman in Paris*. Apart from his send-up of a French 'Singing-Master' Beard contributed several songs in the

---

[41] Catherine Clive, *The Rehearsal: or Bays in Petticoats*, London, 1753, Act 2 'Scene: the Playhouse'
[42] "In 1750, two hundred pounds before the curtain [went up], was judged an amazing sum". Tate Wilkinson, 'Memoirs of his own Life', vol. 4, York, 1790, p. 123

intervals and introduced the novelty of Harp solos and accompaniments from Parry, the blind Welsh harper. One year earlier his Benefit night in March 1756 had been affected by the town's nervousness at the approach of another conflict with France. This was declared on May 15, and marked the beginning of the 'Seven Years War'. Beard's interval songs can be seen as a barometer of the nation's preoccupations. Whenever there was conflict in the air (and there had been an unofficial war with France in North America since Edward Braddock's campaign at Fort Duquesne in 1755) Beard would dust off his patriotic ballads. In 1756 he sang a 'Boatswain' and 'Mars' in the Masque of *Britannia*, and the Purcell song with trumpet solo, 'Genius of England', that had last seen service during the Jacobite uprising. Garrick also contributed a Prologue 'in the character of a sailor'. Despite all of these attractions his takings this year slipped a little to £287.

While Garrick was principally using Beard in the pantomimes and afterpieces, the singer was continually striving to get him to support young composers in the creation of English opera. Someone who was featuring strongly in his life at this time was the composer J. C. Smith. He had taken over as Handel's right-hand man, and was now in charge of conducting the oratorios for the blind composer. In February 1755 his opera *The Fairies*, based on Shakespeare's *A Midsummer Night's Dream* was mounted with a cast composed of Handel's singers: Gaetano Guadagni and Joseph Vernon as 'Lysander' and 'Demetrius'; Christina Passerini and Jane Poitier (Mrs Vernon) as 'Hermia' and 'Helena'; Isabella Young as 'Titania', Masters Reinhold and Moore as 'Oberon' and 'Puck'. Beard, with a big rumbustious hunting-song was 'Theseus'. It ran for eleven performances despite being written in a more traditionally Handelian style than the current works of Arne and Boyce. Garrick wrote a Prologue which made the point that *The Fairies* was the first full-length mainpiece opera at either playhouse for many years. It commences with the well-used complaint of those who preferred their opera in Italian:

> An English Opera! 'Tis not to be borne;
> I both my Country and their Music scorn:
> Oh, damn their *Ally Croakers*,[43] and their *Early Horn*.[44]

But then Garrick pleads the case, and lets on that the libretto had been adapted by him:

> Excuse us first, for foolishly supposing,
> Your countryman could please you in composing;
> An op'ra too! - play'd by an English band,
> Wrote in a language which you understand.
> I dare not say "who" wrote it - I could tell ye,
> To soften matters - Signor Shakespearelli:
> This awkward Drama – (I confess th'offence)
> Is guilty too of Poetry and Sense.
> Our last mischance, and worse than all the rest,
> Which turns the whole Performance to a Jest:
> Our singers are all well, and all will do their best.

---

[43] This tune is credited to Larry Grogan, an Irish piper, who wrote it circa 1725. It is said to be based on the rejection of a gentleman's suit by Alicia Croker. In 1753 it was sung in "The Englishman in Paris." It has mistakenly been credited to Samuel Foote, who wrote the play.

[44] Beard's first 'hit' in the theatre: see chapter 2

Referring obliquely to Handel as Smith's mentor, Garrick then encourages the public to appreciate the Handelian tone in which the work is written, with a passing reference to several roles in which the cast have excelled:

> But why would this rash fool, this Englishman,
> Attempt an Op'ra? 'Tis the strangest Plan!
> Struck with the wonders of his Master's Art,
> Whose sacred Dramas shake and melt the heart,
> Whose Heaven-born strains the coldest Breast inspire,
> Whose Chorus-Thunder sets the Soul on Fire!
> Inflam'd, astonish'd! at those magic Airs,
> When *Samson* groans, and frantic *Saul* despairs;
> The Pupil wrote - his Work is now before ye,
> And waits your stamp of Infamy or Glory![45]

The success of this work was enough to encourage Smith to attempt a sequel. His operatic adaptation of *The Tempest* (1756) was probably made without the collaboration of Garrick this time, and didn't have his unqualified support. It only achieved six performances. The cast was composed of Handel singers as in the previous year, with Rosa Curioni in a breeches part as 'Ferdinand', Miss Young as 'Ariel', Mrs Vernon as 'Miranda', Samuel Champness (Handel's new replacement for Reinhold) as 'Caliban', and Beard doubling 'Prospero' and 'Trinculo'. The music is in a lighter style than *The Fairies*, and shows that Smith was responding to well-intentioned advice to copy Arne and Boyce rather than Handel. His songs are shorter and more tuneful in this work. Beard, as 'Prospero', has some big songs as before, in one of which Smith introduces the rhythmic device known as the 'Scotch snap'. He also was given an accompanied recitative full of descriptive touches that foreshadow the work of Haydn.

Years later Smith told his stepson William Coxe, who was compiling his 'Anecdotes of G.F. Handel and J.C. Smith' that it failed "probably because of the negligent manner in which it was staged ... the decorations were indifferent".[46] When Smith complained about this Garrick replied with an argument that Beard was to hear frequently when he was developing English opera at Covent Garden in the 1760s: that "his principal actors threatened to leave him if these musical pieces, in which they had no concern, were so frequently performed".[47] Undaunted, Beard stood beside his composer-friends and continued to lobby on their behalf; while Garrick set about producing a conventional staging of the play with incidental music by Boyce (1757) in which Beard would find himself reduced to singing the role of 'Hymen' in the closing Masque.

Beard stayed at Drury Lane for the longest period that he stayed anywhere - eleven years. In his last four years with Garrick there were still new Shakespeare plays being resurrected after years of neglect. They often required a song or two. Boyce wrote the music for the revival of *The Winter's Tale* in which Beard appeared as a 'Servant' and sang at the sheep-shearing festival. In *Antony and Cleopatra* he sang a 'Bacchanalian Song' with Samuel Champness. Other main-pieces requiring

---

[45] m/s W. b. 467, p.40, Folger Shakespeare Library, Washington, USA. For a complete version see Appendix 6
[46] William Coxe *Anecdotes of G.F. Handel and J.C. Smith*, 1799, p. 47
[47] also quoted in Roger Fiske, 'English Theatre Music in the Eighteenth Century', OUP, Oxford, 1973, p. 244

his services were *The Fair Quaker of Deal* (a 'Sailor' with a new song in character); *The Gamesters* ('Careless' with a proper song); and *Amphityon or the Two Sosias*, "in which will be introduced a new Interlude of Singing and Dancing by Beard, Miss Young, and others". As the Seven Years War progressed - or rather yo-yoed between success and disaster - with victories at Minden and Quebec and frequent set-backs in the North American colonies, so the theatre responded with a suitable repertoire. Once more Beard donned military or naval uniform and sang the role of 'Haulyard' or some other patriotic character. Garrick was kept busy producing a succession of suitable ballads; some of which have subsequently entered the National repertory. Boyce produced the stirring tune to his 'Heart of Oak', and Arne turned this blustering text into a highly successful song for Beard in 1756:

THE

Beer-drinking BRITONS.

Set by Mr. Arne, *and sung by Mr.* Beard,

At the Theatre-Royal in Drury-Lane,

In the Pantomime called Mercury-Harlequin.

YE true honeſt Britons, who love your own
    land,
  Whoſe fires were ſo brave, ſo victorious, and
    free;
Who always beat France, when they took her in
    hand,
  Come join, honeſt Britons, in chorus with me.
    join in chorus, in chorus with me, come
      join, honeſt Britons, in chorus with me.

Let us ſing our own treaſures, old England's good
    cheer,
The profits and pleaſures of ſtout Britiſh Beer.
Your wine-tippling, dram-ſipping fellows retreat,
But your Beer-drinking Britons can never be beat.

The French, with their vineyards, are meagre
    and pale;
  They drink of the ſqueezings of half-ripen'd
    fruit:
But we, who have hop-grounds to mellow our
    ale,
  Are roſy and plump, and have freedom to boot.
Let us ſing our own treaſures, &c.

Should the French dare invade us, thus arm'd
    with our poles,
  We'll bang their bare ribs, make their lanthorn
    jaws ring;
For your Beef-eating, Beer-drinking Britons are
    ſouls,
  Who will ſhed their laſt drop for their country
    and king.
Let us ſing our own treaſures, &c.

Ye true honest Britons who love your own land,
Whose Sires were so brave, so victorious and free,
Who always beat France when they took her in hand,
Come join honest Britons in chorus with me.

Let us sing our own treasures, old England's good cheer,
The profits and pleasures of stout British beer.
Your wine-tippling, dram-sipping fellows retreat,
But your beer-drinking Britons can never be beat.

The French with their vineyards are meagre and pale;
They drink of the squeezing of half-ripened fruit.
But we, who have hop grounds to mellow our ale,
Are rosy and plump and have freedom to boot.

Should the French dare invade us, thus armed with our poles,
We'll bang their bare ribs, make their lantern-jaws ring.
For your beef-eating, beer-drinking Britons are souls
Who will shed their last drop for their country and king.[48]

Garrick was prepared to have Arne back at Drury Lane from time to time, despite his antipathy to the man. With Boyce now concentrating on church music, and with his edition of 'Cathedral Music' taking up so much of his time, Arne was invited to submit music for various main-pieces. In December 1757 he provided music for *The Fatal Marriage* "in which will be introduced an Epithalamium set to music by Dr Arne and sung by Beard"; and in February 1759 *The Ambitious Stepmother* included "the original Hymn to the Sun new set by Dr Arne, and sung by Beard, Miss [Isabella] Young and Miss E[sther] Young".

Arne's English opera *Eliza* had been tried out, too. It "went off with great Applause" according to the prompter Richard Cross.[49] 'Eliza' is Elizabeth 1st, who never appears on stage. Instead, 'Britannia', the 'Genius of England', and some other personifications such as 'Peace', 'Liberty' etc. discuss the subjects of peace and war with shepherds and shepherdesses. Arne was determined to make this masque into a main-piece. It would probably have been better kept short as an after-piece like his *Britannia* of 1755. Fiske is very complimentary about the musical score. Arne had written some old-fashioned - almost Handelian - music, but had scored it attractively. There were fine arias for 'Britannia'; and Beard - doubling the roles of 'Sailor' and 'Shepherd' - had one song, "Come my Lads, form a Ring", with a virtuoso trumpet obbligato, and another in siciliano rhythm, with an unusual obbligato for a 'little flute', describing the valiant lark defending her nest. But the dull libretto by the hack-writer Richard Rolt undermined the music, which was stretched very thinly over three acts. About the only exciting action was a re-enactment of the 1588 Armada, using model ships.

Just before Beard changed theatres for the last and final time, in 1759, he sang some music by Thomas Arne's promising son Michael. Michael Arne is remembered today for some Pleasure Gardens songs, like "The Lass with the delicate air", but is often confused with his father. In May 1759 he was nineteen, and

---

[48] 'David Garrick: selected verse', ed. J.D. Hainsworth, Armidale, Australia, 1981, p.17
[49] The London Stage, Part 4, vol. 2, Southern Illinois University Press, Carbondale Ill., 1962, p.572

just about to be launched into the theatre world with his father's help. He composed the music for *The Heiress, or the Antigallican* which received one performance at its author's Benefit on 21 May. The author was a certain Mr Mozeen who acted in a host of subsidiary roles at Drury Lane, such as 'Waitwell' in *The Way of the World* and 'Cromwell' in *Henry VIII*. He obviously had ambitions as a playwright, and used his joint-benefit with three other jobbing actors to draw attention to himself. Michael Arne would have been a cheap and keen young composer, with a similar desire to make his mark. Beard played the role of 'Worthy' in this obviously unsuccessful show and sang some songs.

At the end of Beard's eleven years at Drury Lane he turned to Garrick for help, when he found his name about to be libelled in a new publication. For some reason he took against having his name used in the translation of Horace's 'Satires' that a Cambridge academic, Thomas Neville, was just about to publish. Fortunately some of the correspondence surrounding this storm in a teacup has survived. Beard wrote to Neville on May 8 1758:

"Sir,

As you have vouchsafed to mention me in your late *Imitation of Horace* ....you will not think me too presuming for rescuing the very little merit I have from the severe lashes of your satire. I am humble enough not to accuse you of injustice for sinking me into the lowest class of my profession; you have an undoubted right to judge of me, and to speak your judgement, however severe, of my public performances. ... If I have merit, I have no vanity, and therefore your good nature might have passed me by, had not my unlucky name been too tempting a bait for your rhyme. In this point I can only tax you with ill-nature; but when you tell the world, speaking of Farinelli and Beard:

> *Press them, you'd think they never would sing more;*
> *Unask'd, no hints can teach them to give o'er –*

this, I say, with regard to me, Sir, is a great calumny. I flatter myself, if you had enquired after my private character, you would have found that as I have not the talents of the great singers, so neither have I the affectation or ill-behaviour which you satirize.... I am, Sir, with a due sense of your favours, your humble servant,

John Beard"

Neville was mortified to have unwittingly upset Beard, and wrote back abjectly:

"Sir,

I had the favour of your letter, which, though written with all the modesty and politeness the occasion would admit, has given me real pain. Had I been aware of your extreme sensibility I should certainly have afforded you no pretence for conceiving the least displeasure against me. As the case now stands, I have nothing left but to assure you that I shall be ready to remove the cause of your complaint at the very first opportunity. I am, Sir, your humble servant,

Thomas Neville"

In order to see how real Beard's fears were that he had been libelled I searched for a first edition of 'Mr Neville's Imitations of Horace' of 1758.[50] It is now a very rare

---

[50] 'Printed for W. Thurlbourn & J. Woodyer in Cambridge & sold by R & J Dodsley in Pall Mall, & J Beecroft in Paternoster Row.'

book and the copy in the Library of Neville's own college, Jesus College Cambridge, had no mention of Beard in the offending passage.[51] Neville must have done a very good job of recalling the original print-run. But a copy does still exist in the British Library.[52] The two variant passages will be found in the extract below. However, it can be learned from a further letter that Garrick got involved in the dispute at an early stage, and made his own enquiries on Beard's behalf. This is a reply to an unknown letter of Garrick's from the Reverend Dr. Warburton, the Bishop of Bristol,[53] written on May 19. It is interesting in many ways - particularly for the extra information it provides about Beard's reputation in society at the time:

"... Mr Neville is a man of worth and family. I am, therefore, much concerned he has given any just cause of complaint to Mr Beard, whom I have never heard anyone speak of but with regard. Nay, I have heard him spoken of much to his honour on the marriage of his Lady's daughter, when a mean, a paltry proposal was made to him. I did not recollect that Mr Neville said anything offensive. But on this occasion, looking into the book, I found the line (the 2nd in the 3rd Satire) which I suppose Mr Beard objects to - and with reason enough, if it be understood, as I suppose he takes it, to insinuate a distance between the merits of himself and Farinelli. But it may only mean the distance in time, from Farinelli's performance here to this day; or the distance in place, in all countries from Italy to England. I would fain suppose Mr Neville (who has lived all his life in a college) meant one of the latter; for he is very inoffensive, as well as a very ingenious man.
I am, dear Sir, with the truest esteem, your most affectionate and obedient humble servant,   W. Warburton"

Beard never realised that - in modern parlance - any publicity is good publicity. The book which caused offence was never going to be a block-buster anyway. One can appreciate that Neville, closeted in his musty hall of academe, was merely trying to make his text sound more modern by using familiar names from the contemporary theatre, rather than the empty ones found in Horace. As Beard pointed out, his own name had been suggested by Neville's choice of rhyme. But the rhyme scheme in the revised version is completely different; as can be seen in this extract:

Horace: extract from Satire III, translated by Thomas Neville M.A

Version 1	*Version 2*
A fault there is, for which the tuneful herd,	A fault there is, save but the modest few,
Are fam'd, from *Farinelli* down to *Beard*.[54]	Which long has guided all the tuneful crew:

Press them, you'd think they never would sing more;
Unask'd, no hints can teach them to give o'er.

---

[51] F. 5. 14, in The Old Library, Jesus College, Cambridge

[52] Thomas Nevile,[sic] 'Imitations of Horace', London 1758. British Library 11385 aaa 32

[53] William Warburton, 1698-1779, the literary executor of Pope and an author of Divine Tracts and a much criticised edition of Shakespeare was, at this moment Bishop of Bristol; & became Bishop of Gloucester in 1759.

[54] The use of Beard's name in this rhyme-scheme opens up the question of how his name was pronounced in the 18th century. "Bird" would rhyme at this point, whereas the conventional pronunciation of "Beard" wouldn't. It may be significant that the earliest mention of his name - and Handel's first recorded spelling of it - are both 'Bird'.

CHAPTER 9
MUSIC AT COURT

THE COURT ODES

A substantial proportion of Beard's working life revolved around engagements at St James's Palace. If he hadn't been plucked from the Chapel Royal choir at a very early stage by Handel, this is the milieu in which he would most probably have remained. As it was, he managed to keep one foot in the Palace door throughout his entire singing career. It is possible that he went back and sang with the Chapel Royal choir in an *ad hoc* way in the early years - though there is no way of finding out more about this as there are no accounts that would show such payments.[1] But it is clear that the organists and composers who were responsible for the choir's performances continued to employ him as a 'guest soloist' on important state occasions. In the earlier chapters it has been seen how Handel wrote the tenor solos in three Wedding Anthems for him. The Master of the Royal Band, Maurice Greene - and later William Boyce - produced two *Odes* per annum for performance at Court. Whereas the Treble, Alto and Bass soloists for these always came from within the ranks of the Chapel Royal choir, Beard returned on nearly every occasion to sing the tenor arias. It appears that there was never a singer of sufficient ability within the choir's own tenor section to be trusted with an extrovert aria during the middle years of the century. Rather than writing an Ode without such a tenor part in it - as had sometimes been done in the time of Henry Purcell - both Greene and Boyce brought Beard in whenever a solo tenor voice was required.[2]

These odes are very little known today. The only significant research into them has been done by Rosamond McGuiness,[3] and there have been no performances of any of them in living memory. Yet the music for all of those produced by William Boyce is to be found at the Bodleian Library in Oxford; and ten of those by Maurice Greene are preserved, either there or at the Royal College of Music.

Providing the text for the odes was a requirement of the office of the poet laureate. During Beard's career this post was held by Colley Cibber from 1731–57; and then by William Whitehead from 1757-85. The poems were often (but not invariably) printed in the *Gentleman's Magazine*; and this can sometimes be the only information about them that still remains. As the century progressed the entries in the *Gentleman's Magazine* expanded, and often included references to the solo singers that were employed, and how the text was divided up into arias, recitatives, and choruses.[4] By consulting all of Boyce's *Odes* in Oxford it has been possible to evaluate the amount of music that the tenor soloist had to sing in each; what the

---

[1] If he had taken part in the Funeral of Queen Caroline, 1737, as a choir tenor, his payment would have been included in the lump sum of £207 18s paid to Mr Christian Smith on February 2nd, 1738. Similarly, if he had sung in the Dettingen Te Deum in 1743 he would have been paid out of the £80 17s paid to Mr Christian Smith "for the hire of extraordinary performers". On neither occasion did Handel specify a solo tenor part for him.

[2] The Gentleman's Magazine for 1741 gives the performers of the Birthday Ode as Mr Bayley, Mr Abbott, and a Boy of the Chapel Royal. This was the year when Beard had left the theatre in order to accompany his wife abroad. In 1744 Beard's name is included with other Chapel Royal soloists in the list given by the Magazine.

[3] Rosamond McGuiness, 'English Court Odes 1660-1820', Oxford, 1971

[4] The entries for 1744, 1754 & 1757 give names of singers and titles of Arias.

mood of his music was; and what were the vocal challenges set him by the composer. These are outlined and discussed in Appendix 3.

There are not many contemporary eye-witness accounts of the quality of the music-making when the Odes were performed, as visitors to Court were much more impressed by the occasion, its sumptuous setting, and the assembled company, than by the actual music they heard. Here is a typical diary entry from the normally garrulous Count Kielmansegge:[5]

"On the 1st of January, 1762, the Court at noon was very full, on account of its being New Year's Day. On these occasions an English Ode, set to music, is played by the Court Band; it did not last half an hour, and was not badly done."

Having failed to comment on the fact that this was a vocal composition, and that there was a soloist taking part in it that he had previously heard sing at Ranelagh Gardens (on various dates in September), and Covent Garden (on November 11), he immediately talks about the things that mattered to him the most: the presence of several striking ladies who were presented to the King. Whether that took place as the music was being performed is not clear. Simon McVeigh avers that "the King conversed with the company during the performance of Court Odes";[6] and this does seem to be the case if Henry Angelo's anecdote is to be believed:

"My father had the honour, for several years, to make his bow at St. James's, at the drawing-room, on the 4th of June, the birthday of our late Sovereign. I, too, had the honour of being introduced, when I made my appearance in my fine French suit.

On the day of my first introduction, being near his Majesty as he walked round the circle conversing with the company, a remark which his Majesty made, whilst the music was performing, made a lasting impression on my memory. This occurred during a sudden storm of thunder and lightning. The trumpets were sounding; and at the moment, a tremendously loud clap of thunder burst, as it were, right over the palace; when the King, addressing himself to Lord Pembroke, exclaimed, "How sublime! What an accompaniment! How this would have delighted Handel!"[7]

As an intriguing post-script Angelo refers to the Court Dress that was obligatory on these occasions and adds "... Strange as it may appear, it is nevertheless true, that some of the motley personages whom I saw there, appeared to have procured their court costume from those repositories of finery, the masquerade shops".

Sometimes a prior rehearsal of the music, normally given at one of the London taverns, was reviewed in the press; but "everyone recognised that these old-fashioned formalities were peripheral to London's essential musical concerns".[8] The quality of the music has been continuously overlooked, even though Maurice Greene and William Boyce are acknowledged to be highly competent musicians - the best native composers and conductors of the day - who simply suffered from the misfortune of living at the same time as Handel.

---

[5] Count Frederick Kielmansegge, 'Diary of a Journey to England in the years 1761-1762', London, 1902, p. 225
[6] Simon McVeigh, 'Concert life in London from Mozart to Haydn', Cambridge, 1993, p. 61
[7] Henry Angelo, 'Reminiscences', vol. 1, London, 1828, p. 445
[8] Simon McVeigh, 'Concert life in London from Mozart to Haydn', Cambridge, 1993, p. 50

There is certainly a problem with the verse that the composer had to turn into satisfactory choruses, recitatives and arias. Colley Cibber invariably turned out doggerel,[9] and justified his reputation as a poor poet. Alexander Pope had made him the anti-hero in his satirical poem "The Dunciad" as long ago as 1743. Another witty epigram went:

> "In merry old England it once was a rule,
> The King had his Poet, and also his Fool:
> But now we're so frugal, I'd have you to know it,
> That Cibber can serve both for Fool and for Poet."

But his verse does, at least, break up into useful sections that lend themselves to musical treatment. Here is an undistinguished passage from the 1757 *New Year Ode* that Beard had to sing:

Recitative   While Britain, in her Monarch blest
                Enjoys her heart's desire,
                Proud to avow that joy confesst, [sic]
                Thus, thus, to her Lord, she strikes her lyre:

Aria   Rude and rural though our lays
                While with hearts sincere we sing,
                Far greater glory gilds our praise
                Than e'er adorn'd the brightest King.

After Cibber's death the laureate appointment was refused by Thomas Gray, and went instead to William Whitehead, who was determined to write better poetry than his predecessor. To most people it seemed more of the same and very little better. Boswell recounts how, at one of his earliest meetings with Johnson in 1763, the Doctor included these remarks:

"Colley Cibber, Sir, was by no means a blockhead; but by arrogating to himself too much, he was in danger of losing that degree of estimation to which he was entitled. His friends gave out that he intended his birth-day Odes should be bad: but that was not the case, Sir; for he kept them many months by him, and a few years before he died he shewed me one of them, with great solicitude to render it as perfect as might be, and I made some corrections, to which he was not very willing to submit. I remember the following couplet in allusion to the King and himself:
> Perch'd on the eagle's soaring wing,
> The lowly linnet loves to sing.
Sir, he had heard something of the fabulous tale of the wren sitting upon the eagle's wing, and he had applied it to a linnet. Cibber's familiar style, however, was better than that which Whitehead has assumed. *Grand* nonsense is insupportable. Whitehead is but a little man to inscribe verses to players."[10]

Charles Churchill wrote equally disparagingly about Whitehead in *The Ghost* (1762):

> Dullness and Method still are one,
> And Whitehead is their darling Son".

---

[9] In the 20th century, D.B. Wyndham-Lewis and Charles Lee considered some of Cibber's laureate poems funny enough to be included in their classic "anthology of bad verse", *The Stuffed Owl* (1930).
[10] James Boswell, 'Life of Johnson', London, 1799

It was Whitehead who really courted fame as the Laureate, and wanted his verse to be available in wide circulation; so he proudly had all his offerings printed by the *Gentleman's Magazine*. But Boyce must have been distraught to find himself obliged to set abstruse and convoluted sentences like this, taken almost at random from the passages given to Beard to sing in the 1766 *Birthday Ode*. Boyce's response to the intractable style was to set the text in a constantly changing sequence of arioso, recitative and chorus: an extremely original and modern approach that was forced upon him by the lack of opportunity to construct a typical 18th century aria or chorus in which the music and text could be repeated as was customary.

Solo, Allegro ma non troppo	So Edward fought on Cressy's bleeding plain
	A blooming hero great beyond his years.
Recit.	But cease the strain
	A loss so recent bathes the Muse in tears.
Vivace	So shall hereafter ev'ry Son who now with prattling
	Infancy relieves those anxious cares
	Which wait upon a Throne.
Recit.	Where, ah too oft, amidst the myrtles
	Weaves the thorn its pointed anguish.
Vivace	So shall ev'ry youth his duty know
	To guard the Monarch's right
	And people's weal.
Larghetto	And thou Great George with just regard to Heav'n
	Shalt own the Hebrew Bard but sung the truths you feel.
Solo & Chorus	By slender ties our Kings of old
	Their fabled Right divine would vainly hold;
	Thy juster claim ev'n Freedom's Sons can love.
	The King who bends to Heav'n must Heav'n
	itself approve.
Chorus	*Blest be the day which gave thee birth.*

Rosamond McGuinness agrees with Simon McVeigh that King George would have listened to the music only cursorily. As his particular taste was for the music of Handel[11] she suggests that he would have found Boyce's music but a pale imitation:

"Posterity has not suffered deprivation by the neglect of these songs. Yet, it may be conjectured that they satisfied the King in spite of the fact that they were often only feeble imitations of the musician whom he so much admired and of whose works he was, apparently, such an excellent and accurate judge. Probably he accepted these songs in the spirit of the occasion and listened to them with an ear different from that with which he would have heard one of Handel's works, but in any case, they possessed two musical virtues which, for him, may have outweighed the absence of a particularly exciting melody and an effective climax: their dramatic portrayal of the texts and their instrumental introductions, obbligati, interludes, and conclusions".[12]

---

[11] At private concerts at Court Mrs Delany noted that "the King generally directs them [the orchestra] what pieces to play, chiefly Handel". Letter of November 9th, 1785, 'The Autobiography and Correspondence of Mary Delany', ed. Lady Llanover, London, 1861-2

[12] Rosamond McGuinness, 'English Court Odes 1660-1820', Oxford, 1971, pp. 207-8

Poor John Beard! According to McGuinness the one element that the King would have failed to appreciate would have been the vocal writing! Fortunately we know from other records that George III was something of a fan of Beard's, and had been enjoying his performances since the age of six. His father, Frederick Lewis, the Prince of Wales, had also been a regular supporter of Beard's, and had 'commanded' Beard's Benefit night on three successive occasions, in the years 1743, 1744 and 1745. The young Prince George was brought to the theatre on March 28 1745 with his father, mother, elder sister Augusta and younger brother Edward to see Beard for the first time in his striking red coat as Macheath, in a production of *The Beggar's Opera* that also starred Mrs Vincent and Mrs Pritchard. In addition the royal party heard "the Song made on the famous Sea-fight at La Hogue, sung by Beard in the character of a sailor". Prior to becoming Prince of Wales on the death of his father in 1751 it has been discovered that he visited the London Theatres twenty-six times, and saw *The Beggar's Opera* twice.[13] His attendance was also quite regular during the nine years that he remained the Prince of Wales whilst he was in his teens. His widowed mother, Augusta, the Dowager Princess of Wales continued to bring her young son to the theatre, once she had observed a suitably lengthy period of mourning.

In a curious twist of fate the young Prince of Wales's life now began to be even more intertwined with that of the singer he so admired. For, in the years 1752-5, his new Governor was none other than Beard's brother-in-law, James 2nd Earl Waldegrave. In that same year the Earl had become a member of King George II's Privy Council. He was currently high in favour with the King, who overlooked the fact that the family was originally of Jacobite persuasion, and that some members (including Beard's wife Henrietta) remained staunchly catholic to the end. Horace Walpole, whose niece the 2nd Earl married in 1759, described him as "a man of pleasure, [who] understood the Court, was firm in the King's favour, and at once undesirous of rising and afraid to fall ...A man of stricter honour, or of more reasonable sense, could not have been selected for the employment".[14] When he came to be King the Prince of Wales was to see his erstwhile Governor in a different light, describing him as a "depraved worthless man". One hopes that he knew how the Earl had been treating his sister Henrietta - just at the time that he was gaining his great reputation at Court; and how she had died of grief for the cruel way her own flesh and blood had treated her.

Writing in 1758 the 2nd Earl Waldegrave described his approach to bringing up the young Prince. He sounds a very hard man to please. One is left with the impression that George would have had an uncooperative and unsympathetic Governor looking after him between the ages of fourteen and seventeen:

"I found his Royal Highness uncommonly full of Princely prejudices, contracted in the nursery, and improved by the society of bedchamber women, and pages of the back-stairs.[15] As a right system of education seemed impracticable, the best which could be hoped for was to give him true notions of common things; to instruct him

---

[13] Harry W. Pedicord, 'By Their Majesties' Command', The Society for Theatre Research, London, 1991, p. 20
[14] quoted in: John Brooke, 'King George III', London, 1972, p.39-40
[15] In an interesting quirk of fate, the position of 'Page of the Back-stairs' was held during this exact period, 1752-8, by George Voelcker who became Beard's brother-in-law when he married Charlotte Rich's sister Sarah. One of the Page's duties was to arrange the King's visits to the theatre; so it is almost certain that this is how he first encountered his future wife.

by conversation, rather than by books; and sometimes, under the disguise of amusement, to entice him to the pursuit of more laborious studies. ...I was a very useful apologist whenever His Majesty was displeased with his grandson's shyness or want of attention; and never failed to notify even the most minute circumstance of the young Prince's behaviour which was likely to give satisfaction".

In fact, the Prince turned into a fine, caring King. The indolent boy whose "parts" were described by Waldegrave as "not excellent, though tolerable if ever they are properly exercised"[16] became a cultured monarch with wide interests. Apart from his devotion to the works of Handel - which brought him into frequent contact with Beard, J.C. Smith, Charles Burney, and their musical circle - he built up a huge library of 65,000 books and a fine collection of paintings. He supported the newly founded Royal Academy of Art, and the scientific researches of William Herschel - originally a musician[17] - who pursued his interest in astronomy as a side-line until his discovery of the planet Uranus made him famous. King George then gave him a pension and built him an observatory at Windsor. It was George who ultimately persuaded the Longitude Commissioners to give John Harrison the well-deserved payment for designing the Marine Chronometer that allowed sailors to deal with the problem of finding Longitude at sea.[18]

Beard would have approved of the King's famous generosity. It is said that he always carried a purse with which to quietly dispense largesse to the needy subjects he encountered on his frequent walkabouts. In 1782, when Parliament was about to regulate the Civil List payments, the King was determined that there should be no diminution of his private income - the Privy Purse. As he said, this was "the only fund from which I pay every act of private benevolence - those acts of benevolence which alone make the station [of Kingship] bearable".[19] There are various references to Beard being similarly prepared to assist friends and colleagues financially, albeit in a more modest way, as has been shown in earlier chapters.

When Prince George came of age in June 1759 Beard was just about to become Deputy Manager to John Rich at Covent Garden. The Prince soon graced this theatre with two Command Performances in close succession: on February 2 1760 he heard Beard as a 'Bacchanal' in *Comus* singing 'Not on beds of fading flowers' and 'Now Phoebus sinketh in the West'; and a few months later, on April 26, he saw him as 'Hearty' in the new ballad opera *The Jovial Crew*, with music by Beard's protégé William Bates. Covent Garden was to remain the Prince's favourite theatre. When he mounted the throne in 1761 he was to visit it 10 or 11 times a season, compared with 4 or 5 visits to its neighbour at Drury Lane.

On September 8 1761 George III married Charlotte-Sophia of Mecklenburg-Strelitz in the Chapel Royal. William Boyce composed the new Wedding Anthem *The King shall rejoice,* and Beard was temporarily drafted into the choir to sing the final aria in it: *Hearken O daughter*. The full rehearsal which took

---

[16] quoted in: John Brooke, 'King George III', London, 1972, p.55

[17] His career in music began when he was employed at Richmond in the orchestra of the Earl of Darlington. In 1762 he moved to Leeds, where he stayed for four years. In 1766 he moved again, now to Bath as a military bandmaster, music teacher and organist at the Octagon Chapel in Bath. He also composed and gave concerts.

[18] "The King is reported to have muttered under his breath, 'These people have been cruelly treated'. Aloud he promised ... 'By God, Harrison, I will see you righted!'" Dava Sobel, 'Longitude', London, 1995

[19] quoted in: John Brooke, 'King George III', London, 1972, p.215

place the previous day[20] must have occurred well before 6pm: at that time he was singing 'Macheath' at Covent Garden in a performance of *The Beggar's Opera* co-starring Charlotte Brent and Mrs Vernon.[21]

It has to be admitted that the reason the King preferred Covent Garden was on account of the Oratorio season that was held there every Lent. He was indefatigably loyal to this legacy of Handel, and would frequently hear the same work twice in the same season. Before he began to suffer from bad health he would attend, on average, 6 or 7 performances out of a season of 10 or 11. In all of these he would have heard Beard singing the principal tenor roles. We know from Fanny Burney of the King's unquenchable love for Handel's music, and she touchingly writes about meeting him at Windsor after his recovery from an early dose of his recurrent disease, in February 1789, when: "...he told me innumerable anecdotes of [Handel], and particularly that celebrated tale of Handel's saying of himself, when a boy, 'While that boy lives, my music will never want a protector'.... Then he ran over most of his oratorios, attempting to sing the subject of several airs and choruses, but so dreadfully hoarse that the sound was terrible".[22]

King George III at a Covent Garden performance of Handel's 'Solomon'

---

[20] reported in *The Ipswich Journal* of September 12th 1761
[21] see: Matthias Range, 'William Boyce's anthem for the wedding of King George III', *The Musical Times*, Summer 2006, pp. 59 - 66
[22] 'Fanny Burney's Diary', The Folio Society, 1961, p. 218

This is a complete list of the King's attendances at the Oratorios during Beard's time as manager of Covent Garden theatre:

Lent Season	Total performances	Number of times the King attended [23]	
1762:	10	5:	Samson
			Alexander's Feast (twice)
			Judas Maccabaeus
			Messiah
1763	10	6:	Occasional Oratorio
			Alexander's Feast
			Judas Maccabaeus
			Jephtha
			Acis and Galatea
			Messiah
1764	11	6:	Deborah
			Nabal (a Handelian pastiche)
			Samson
			L'Allegro ed il Penseroso
			Judas Maccabaeus
			Messiah
1765	11	1:	Judas Maccabaeus

[This year the King was "intermittently ill between January and April"] [24]

1766	11	7:	Deborah
			Alexander's Feast
			Acis and Galatea
			Israel in Egypt
			Samson
			Judas Maccabaeus
			Messiah
1767	11	11:	Esther
			Deborah
			Israel in Egypt
			Samson
			Judas Maccabaeus (twice)
			Theodora
			Acis and Galatea (twice)
			Messiah (twice)

It is intriguing to see that in the last season that Beard sang - 1767 - the King commanded the performance on every single night. He was obviously determined to hear his favourite tenor as much as possible before he was to retire for ever.

In these years, when the Oratorios account for so many of his visits to the Royal Box at Covent Garden, the King did not neglect the theatre's other fare. He heard Beard in his most demanding mainpieces of *Artaxerxes* (Arne's recent opera

---

[23] Information from The London Stage, Part 4
[24] John Brooke, 'King George III', London, 1972, p.109

seria) and *The Beggar's Opera*, as well as in the lighter English ballad operas for which Beard had been responsible: *The Maid of the Mill*, *Love in a Village*, *The Accomplish'd Maid*, and *The Jovial Crew* - which seems to have been a personal favourite as he saw it four times in about as many years. On every visit Beard, as Manager, would have been required to attend on the King and see him settled into the Royal Box. He would have also had to supervise the payment to the Yeomen of the Guard of their customary fee of 2 guineas for accompanying the King to the theatre. We know this from the newspaper reports of a later visit to a London theatre (Drury Lane, in May 1800) when the King survived an assassination attempt. The manager of the theatre at that time was the playwright Richard Brinsley Sheridan. He was on duty that night to escort the royal party to their box. His biographers aver "that, on the shooting, it was he who delayed the entrance of the Queen and Princesses until the disturbance was under control".[25]

With the King visiting Covent Garden a total of 78 times during his years as manager, Beard would have become a very familiar figure to him. In addition to his theatrical work, the King heard him sing thirteen Court Odes, and his wedding anthem. The last occasion on which Beard appeared in front of him seems to have been nine months after he had officially retired. Beard sang at Covent Garden for the last time on May 23 1767, as 'Hawthorne' in *Love in a Village*. But his name appears on the music parts of Boyce's next two Odes: the Birthday Ode 'Friend to the poor' performed on June 4, and 'Let the voice of Music breathe' performed at New Year 1768. It is only in June 1768 that the tenor solos are given to another singer. This is 'Mr Hayes' - presumably the same Mr Hayes who took over from him at the Foundling Hospital performance of *Messiah* in April 1767. In view of the fact that Beard retired due to increasing deafness it is curious to see him still prepared to sing in the Court Odes. The only conclusion that I can draw from this is that the King had specifically requested it.

George III granted Beard a unique honour in March 1764. After years of fruitless petitioning for a Court appointment during the reign of George II, the singer was finally granted what had been denied him by the previous monarch. Starting in 1752 Beard had looked for a position that might carry a salary or pension with it, and made an unlikely bid for the post of '*Serjeant Trumpeter*'.[26] But that was more than a sinecure, and was traditionally undertaken by a real virtuoso on the instrument, since the duties involved the supervision of the State trumpeters.[27] The post was sensibly given to Valentine Snow, a distinguished trumpeter and member of the King's Band. If Beard had been appointed he would have been obliged to use up most of his emolument in supplying suitable deputies. His next attempt came in 1757, when he petitioned the Duke of Newcastle for "the employment in his

[25] Harry W. Pedicord, 'By Their Majesties' Command', The Society for Theatre Research, London, 1991, p.67

[26] "We hear great interest is being made to succeed Mr Serjeant Shore, deceased, as Serjeant Trumpeter to his Majesty, which is in the gift of his Grace the Duke of Grafton as Lord Chamberlain; and that the contest lies chiefly between that excellent performer Mr Valentine Snow, Trumpet to the First Troop of Horseguards; Mr Debourg, [Dubourg] the violin; and Mr Beard, of the Theatre Royal in Drury Lane". Public Advertiser 2.12.1752

[27] "The Serjeant Trumpeter had in 1685 been given wide powers for regulating trumpeters, drummers and fifers throughout the country. ...In the early eighteenth century [he] was responsible for twelve trumpeters, and in the middle of the century for sixteen." John Harley, 'Music at the English Court...' *Music & Letters* 50 (1969), p.340

Majesty's Customs of a *King's Waiter* now vacant by the Death of Mr Newton". In this petition he stated that he had been "principally employed in the performance of the Birthday and New Year's Day Odes for 24 years, for which he has never receiv'd any Allowance or Gratuity whatsoever". The petition goes on, rather pathetically, "your Grace's Petitioner is now approaching towards that time of life which must necessarily render any advantages from his public Performances precarious".[28] In fact, he was only 42 years-of-age, and some of his most interesting times in the theatre and concert hall were still ahead of him. This petition, likewise, fell on stony ground. One of the reasons may have been that his first wife's relatives held important positions at Court and would have been glad to foil his attempts. James, 2nd Earl Waldegrave, (Beard's brother-in-law) was, as we have seen, a Lord of the Bedchamber to King George II in the 1750s, Governor to the Prince of Wales until he handed this role over to the 3rd Earl of Bute in 1755, and - for a short while - First Lord of the Treasury. Henry Arthur Herbert, the Earl of Powis, husband to Beard's step-daughter Barbara, was also in a position of authority at Court, as a Privy Councillor and Comptroller of the Household, having succeeded Lord Edgcumbe.

George III was his own person and was not going to be influenced by his grandfather's advisers. After three years on the throne it seems as though the matter of Beard's long service in the performance of the Court Odes did come to his attention. On March 1 1764 the 'Court Kalendar' announced that Beard had been made *Vocal Performer in Extraordinary to his Majesty*, and would receive an annual pension of £100. The title was a unique one, and had not been used before. Bearing in mind that the Gentlemen of the Chapel Royal choir were known as *Gentlemen in Ordinary* this was a logical extension of that official nomenclature, and clearly reflected Beard's position as a frequent additional performer (as at the Royal Wedding of 1761), on the fringes of the vocal group, yet not sworn in as a salaried member.

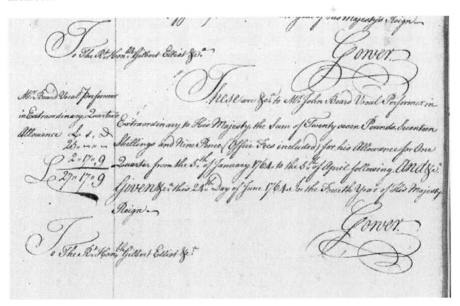

[28] British Library: the Newcastle Papers, vol. CXC1, Add. 32876 f. 317

This was the sinecure he had always been hoping for. But it was an extremely appropriate one to have come his way. At this period there had never been a knighthood awarded to any practitioner of the Arts - and it would not happen until a later reign.[29] This, therefore, was the highest honour that the Court could bestow. It was also rather better than a knighthood (had the post been awarded to a singer in those days) since the real benefit lay in its monetary value. Beard attended Court on March 1 1764 to receive his appointment from the Earl of Gower, the Lord Chamberlain. The warrant states that he was '*to have hold and exercise and enjoy the said place together with all rights Profits Privileges and advantages thereunto belonging.*'[30] Although this was a standard form of words, there seems to have been no actual duties involved as there were for other royal appointments. A search of the royal accounts reveals that Beard received his £100 pension, together with 11 guineas of expenses, every year up until his death. In 1782 an Act of Parliament changed the way in which the Civil List payments were made, and they were transferred to the Audit Office Accounts. At this point the *Vocal Performer in Extraordinary to his Majesty* title disappears from the records, leading some scholars to assume that payments had ceased.[31] But in fact they were continued as a Civil List pension. The last payment was £8 6s 6d, representing one month's pension pro rata; and it was made to Charlotte for the one month that her husband had lived during 1791.[32]

King George III was very much involved with the Handel Commemoration of 1784. We know from the 'Anecdotes' of William Coxe that the King endeavoured to bring J.C. Smith to London from retirement in Bath to be present:

"When the Commemoration of Handel was celebrated with such wonderful effect in Westminster Abbey, under the direction of Joah Bates, Esq. the King was desirous that Smith should be present at the performance, and sent him a gracious and pressing invitation to come to London for that purpose. His Majesty assured him that he should be admitted without difficulty into a commodious seat in the Abbey, and that he should receive every accommodation during his residence in town. Smith was fully sensible of this gracious mark of condescension; but declined the honour with reluctance, apprehensive that from his advanced age, so exquisitely powerful a performance of the works of his great master, would excite such emotions as might too much affect his feeble frame".[33]

It must be assumed that Beard was accorded the same privilege. Living considerably nearer to London he is likely to have taken advantage of the King's invitation. Counting among his close circle of friends both Samuel Arnold and

---

[29] Henry Bishop, the composer, was knighted by Queen Victoria in 1842. William Parsons, the Master of His Majesty's Band, is the first musician that I can trace to have been knighted. But this was performed by the Lord Lieutenant of Ireland in 1795. I cannot trace any singer who was knighted earlier than Charles Santley in 1907, although he was beaten to this honour by an actor, Henry Irving, who was knighted in 1895. King George IV is said to have been restrained from knighting the tenor John Braham 'on the spot' after a particularly fine piece of singing.

[30] Public Record Office – Lord Chamberlain's papers : LC3/58/353. Also LC5/168/311 & 320 for payments

[31] "... he was still carried on the list of musicians there as "Vocal Performer Extraordinary" at a yearly salary of £100, until at least 1782." BDA, p. 402

[32] Payment was made on 5th January 1792. Public Record Office – Audit Office Accounts: AO1/423/208; AO1/426/218; AO1/430/10

[33] William Coxe, 'Anecdotes of G.F. Handel and J.C. Smith', London, 1799, p. 57

Thomas Dupuis, two of the sub-conductors of the enormous choir and orchestra, he was more than likely to have received an invitation from them as well as from the King. Sadly, none of this correspondence still exists. We know from other anecdotes that Beard was seen at performances in London as late as 1789;[34] and Arnold and Dupuis managed to persuade him to attend a Chapel Royal choir dinner in 1785, despite Beard complaining that a further trip to London would be dependant on his health.[35] He was also present at later Handel Commemorations when he heard the tenor Samuel Harrison sing 'Oft on a plat of rising ground' from *L'Allegro ed Il Penseroso*.[36] Afterwards he was heard to remark "*I* never sung it half so well."[37]

The King took a great interest in the book that Charles Burney produced after the 1784 Commemoration,[38] and even made editorial suggestions.[39] He read the book "in MS, sheet by sheet, in fact as it was written'.[40] One of these suggestions was to include the names of the three Handelian performers still alive in 1784 who had sung in Handel's *Alcina* when it was first performed in 1735. This was added as a footnote to the Aria from *Alcina* sung by Madame Mara at the second performance: "Though nearly fifty years are elapsed since [1735], yet there are three of the original performers of that Drama still living: Mrs Arne, widow of the late Dr. Arne, who was at that time a scholar of Geminiani, and is called Mrs Young in the printed books; Mr Savage, late sub-almoner and vicar-choral of St. Paul's [Cathedral], who in the printed copy of the Music is called *the boy*, and in the book of the Words, *young Mr. Savage*; and Mr. Beard, so long the favourite singer, and afterwards, manager in one of our theatres..."[41]

Handel

[34] at Drury Lane for a performance of Stephen Storace's *The Haunted Tower* featuring Michael Kelly.
[35] "..unless call'd by unexpected business [I] shall hardly think of revisiting the Capital on this side of C[hris]tmas..." Harvard Theatre Library, Autographs: Musical & Dramatic, vol. 1, (TS990.1F)
[36] I have traced performances from newspaper advertisements to May 8th & 22nd 1789, & March 3rd 1790.
[37] Laetitia Matilda Hawkins, *Anecdotes of Sir John Hawkins*, 1822, vol. 1 p.13
[38] Charles Burney, 'An Account of the Musical Performances... in Commemoration of Handel', London, 1785.
[39] see: Percy A. Scholes, 'The Great Dr Burney', Oxford, 1948
[40] quoted in 'HANDEL: a celebration of his Life and Times', National Portrait Gallery, London, 1985
[41] Charles Burney, 'An Account of the Musical Performances in Westminster Abbey, and the Pantheon ... in Commemoration of Handel', London, 1785, p. 68

CHAPTER 10
WIDOWHOOD AND REMARRIAGE

1. MUSIC FESTIVALS OUTSIDE LONDON

When Henrietta died in 1753 Beard threw himself wholeheartedly into his work, and returned to live - at least temporarily - in the Red Lion area. In a period of flux, when he may have been unsure about his future, he lodged with Sarah Coleman in East Street. She could have been known to him through the theatre, as well as being a near neighbour from his time as a resident of New North Street, since a 'Mrs Colman' was paid 18 guineas for tailoring 'a purple and silver gown' on January 26 1760.[1] Whether she was related to George Colman, the playwright and co-partner at Drury Lane with Garrick is not known.

The summer months now commenced with a long season as vocalist at Ranelagh Gardens: (he never appears to have been on the 'books' at London's other pleasure gardens at Marylebone or Vauxhall[2] - see Chapter 7). After that he would visit the out-lying music festivals. This lucrative work began with visits to the Three Choirs Festivals through his friendship with their conductors Dr William Boyce and Dr William Hayes. Festivals were still in their infancy and records are sparse; but Beard does not seem to have visited the other musical meeting which assisted the growth of the amateur choral society: the *St Cecilia Festival* at Salisbury. The Harris family members, whose pet project it was, were never particular fans of Beard – as we can see in the extracts from their correspondence quoted in this book – and spent a lot of time promoting their local tenor Thomas Norris. The beginning of the new season in September came around so soon that one wonders when Beard had time to visit his brother and family in Devon, as well as the Beef-Steak club friends who invited him for holidays on their estates.[3]

In a curious way it was good for Beard when Ranelagh lost its music licence in 1754. Without the comfortable summer contract that he had come to depend upon, he had to look elsewhere for work. As a widower there was no reason why he should not venture further afield now. His friends came to the rescue and made some attractive propositions. Dr William Hayes, the Professor of Music at Oxford, invited him to sing three oratorios in the Sheldonian Theatre. This was for the same occasion that had attracted Handel there in 1733: the Commemoration of Founders and Benefactors. The oratorios were all by Handel and ones in which Beard had created the tenor roles. His association with Handel, and fame as an interpreter of his works, was going to be increasingly important for him throughout the rest of the 1750s. On July 3, 4 and 5 1754 he performed *L'Allegro ed Il Penseroso*, *Judas Maccabaeus* and *Messiah* with his fellow soloists from London, Giulia Frasi and Robert Wass. He returned to Oxford for a further three oratorios with Dr Hayes at the Commemoration in July 1759, and sang in *Samson*, *Esther* and *Messiah*. Parson Woodforde went to the *Messiah* on July 5 as an undergraduate, and thought that the 5 shillings he paid for a ticket was rather 'steep'.

---

[1] The London Stage, Part 4, vol. 2, p. 771
[2] As stated by David Coke & Alan Borg in 'Vauxhall Gardens a History' p. 155 fn 64: the inaccurate assertion that he was a singer at Vauxhall occurs in the *Vauxhall Papers, Part 15, 118-19* and regularly thereafter. Lady Mary Wortley Montagu was the first to say that Beard "was a singer at Vauxhall".
[3] Such visits are mentioned in: William Havard, 'Jeu d'esprit', N.a.2. Folger Shakespeare Library. Beard himself writes of making a visit to Hertfordshire. But most of his correspondence is lost.

Since August 1750 some of Beard's city friends had put on a Benefit for him at a small Pleasure Gardens and Spa in Hampstead known as Well Walk.[4] The Assembly Room was known as the Long Room on account of its remarkable length of 80 feet. Initially advertised as the '*Annual Concert for Dorman's Friends*'[5], this became in time '*Mr Beard's Night at the Long Room, Hampstead*'. Beard's appearances there were well enough known to be mentioned in Garrick's poem 'The Fribbleriad'[6]:

> There is a place upon a hill,
> Where cits of pleasure take their fill,
> Where hautboys scream and fiddles squeak,
> To sweat the ditto once a week;
> Where joy of late, unmixed with noise
> Of romping girls and drunken boys –
> Where decency, sweet maid, appeared,
> And in her hand brought *Johnny Beard*.

Beard's visit always took place in August, commencing in 1750 on August 11. Thereafter he made an annual appearance, which was always advertised in the Press.[7] These advertisements sometimes contained the helpful instruction "*there will be moonlight*" as an incentive to those fearful of venturing home in the dark.

This is to acquaint Mr. DORMAN's Friends,

THAT the Annual Concert of Vocal and and Inftrumental

M U S I C K,

Will be performed this Day, being the 24th Inftant, at the LONG-ROOM at Hampftead.
The Vocal Parts by Mr. Beard.
The Firft Violin by Mr. Fefting.
A Concerto on the Harpfichord by Mr. Butler.
A Solo on the Violoncello by Sig. Pafqualino.
A Concerto on the Baffoon by Mr. Baumgartin.
A Concerto on the Trumpet by Mr. Abington.
And all the other Parts by the beft Mafters.
To begin at Half an Hour after Six o'Clock.
☞ Tickets to be had at Tom's Coffee-houfe in Cornhill; at Tom's Coffee-houfe in Covent-Garden.; at Pon's Coffee houfe in Caftle-ftreet, by Leicefter fields; and at the Long Room at Hampftead, at Five Shillings each.
☞ It will be FULL-MOON.

---

[4] The Long Room was constructed in 1735, and a ballroom was put up a little to the east. Hampstead was then ranked, after Scarborough, Bath, and Tunbridge Wells, as one of the politest places in England. The heroine of Fanny Burney's novel *Evelina* endured some ill-bred attentions at a ball in the Long Room, a place 'without any sort of singularity and merely to be marked by its length'. The Long Room was licensed for public entertainment from 1751. It was still used for musical recitals as late as 1800. From: 'Hampstead: Social and Cultural Activities', A History of the County of Middlesex: Volume 9: *Hampstead*, Paddington, 1989, pp. 81-91.
[5] Joseph Dorman, the poet and author of the popular ballad opera *The Woman of Taste: or the Yorkshire Lady* (otherwise known as *The Female Rake*) of 1735, lived in Hampstead, and died there in February 1754. He organised an annual concert for the last 4 years of his life; and his son Ridley and 'friends' carried it on for at least 7 more years, with Beard as soloist.
[6] David Garrick, 'The Fribbleriad', 1761
[7] the following dates have been discovered in newspaper advertisements:Aug. 24th 1751; Aug. 15th 1752; ? 1753; Aug. 31st 1754; Aug. 23rd 1755; ? 1756 / 7 / 8; Aug. 13th 1759; Aug. 25th 1760; Aug. 17th 1761.

During his time as Manager at Covent Garden Theatre, the concerts seem to have ceased. Some of the repertoire is known. It was very much the kind of thing he was singing at Ranelagh and in concerts at the Hickford Rooms in central London. In 1754 he was joined by Elizabeth Turner (soprano) and John Stanley (harpsichord); and in 1755 the repertoire was Boyce's *Solomon*. In 1759 he was joined by Stanley, again as conductor, and by the singers Giulia Frasi, Miss Young and Champness for Handel's *Acis and Galatea*. Copies of the actual Programme Booklet for his 1760 concert still survive at the Folger Shakespeare Library and the Covent Garden Theatre Museum. Once again Beard's devotion to the music of Boyce is revealed. Burney was well aware of this when he wrote; "Mr Beard brought on the stage the secular ode. ...This piece, by the animated performance and friendly zeal of Mr Beard, was many times exhibited before it was wholly laid aside". Accordingly, the second half of this programme comprised just such a performance of the *Secular Masque*. In the first part he sang a Boyce duet "Thou soft invader of the Soul" with Frasi. The programme was completed by a Handel Overture, a violin concerto featuring the leader of the orchestra Abraham Brown, a 'full piece' [probably a symphony] and Beard's performance of the Purcell song "From rosy bowers".[8]

Boyce was the conductor of the Three Choirs Festival during the 1750s. He was at Gloucester at the beginning of September 1754 for a programme of oratorios with which Beard was immensely familiar: *Judas Maccabaeus* and *L'Allegro ed il Penseroso*. There is no evidence that Beard accompanied him; and the timing would have been very awkward if he had gone, as the final performance was at noon on September 13. Beard commenced the autumn season at Drury Lane on Saturday 14 with *The Miller of Mansfield* and the Arne Cantata "The School of Anacreon". At this time the roads were not yet good enough, despite the advent of the turnpikes, to have allowed him to get back to London in that amount of time! However, Boyce must have been disappointed with the soloists that had been provided that year, as he raised the matter with the Festival organisers. The *Gloucester Journal* subsequently reported that " ...the Hon. Mr Edwin Sandys, Prebendary of Worcester and the Dean, Dr Waugh, when they were last Winter in London, in order to induce more company to come to Worcester, used their endeavours to secure the best performers that could be procured; and succeeded so happily that some persons of the greatest eminence in their profession offered to give their assistance for the benefit of the Charity".[9]

Beard was tempted by the fees being offered by the Festival, and was pleased to have the freedom to travel further afield now that he was a widower. Whether he combined his concert tours with a visit to his brother in Devon is not known, but might well have made sense, now that he had acquired more freedom. One of the fastest ways to get anywhere west of London was to go via Bath - which now had the best-kept road to London.[10] Bath was a good centre for making onward journeys, and provided coaches northwards to the Cathedral cities of Gloucester and Worcester, as well as southwards to Taunton and Exeter. The only surviving reference to Beard making his way to the West of England is in an anecdote of the

---

[8] PR 3291 M53 Cage, Folger Shakespeare Library, Washington, USA.

[9] Daniel Lysons, 'History of the Origin and Progress of the Meeting of the Three Choirs...' Gloucester, 1812

[10] "We took two days to make the 108 miles from Bath to London, but the journey can be accomplished in one day by starting a little sooner than we did, especially if you change horses every ten miles; or, better still, if you take four horses, by which means you may accomplish the whole journey without trouble in eleven hours". Count Frederick Kielmansegge, 'Diary of a Journey to London in the years 1761-2', London, 1902, p.134

actress George Anne Bellamy. This places him in Marlborough with a group of actors, including the great tragedian James Quin, at one of the coaching Inns on the way to Bath (to which Quin had retired). Marlborough was at an intersection where coaches could be changed, and new ones taken to west-country towns like Exeter (near his brother's home in Kenton). Perhaps that is why Beard was there. He could have combined Quin's invitation with a journey to see his brother and the nieces and nephews to whom he left money in his will. It is amusing enough to be retold in George-Anne's own highly inaccurate words:

"It being 8 o'clock in the evening, I was apprehensive, from his being in bed, that Mr Quin was indisposed. But I was informed by Mr Beard, who was likewise one of the company, that my worthy friend ...had made a resolution not to go to London again. And as he did not choose to be totally deprived of the society of a few of his particular friends, he had requested them to make a party, and meet him every summer at Smith's. It was agreed that they should remain here till they had drunk a quantity of wine. I cannot now recollect how much that was, - but when Mr Beard mentioned it, I thought it was sufficient to serve them for a year". [11]

The only years in which it would have been logical to find Beard indulging in such junketings would be during the period between Henrietta's death and the beginning of his romance with Charlotte. That would narrow the time-scale to the years 1754-6. That is also the likely period of George Anne's anecdote. Quin had retired from the stage on May 15 1751, after playing 'Horatio' in *The Fair Penitent*, though in the following year he twice played 'Falstaff' for the benefit of friends.

In 1755 Beard managed to get himself released from Ranelagh (which had regained its music licence) for the Worcester Three Choirs Festival performances of Handel's *Samson*, on September 9, and Boyce's *Solomon,* on September 10. The other singers who went with him were Elizabeth Turner, who was something of a favourite at the Festival, having been there the previous year,[12] and three Gentlemen of the Chapel Royal Choir, Robert Wass, Thomas Baildon and Robert Denham. The last of these three had been a Chapel Royal chorister with Beard, and had taken part in the *Esther* performances back in 1732.

There is a reference in a letter of William Fogg to William Havard that Beard was out and about visiting friends in August 1756: "You don't mention our Friend, Johnny Beard, who proposed to set out for your castle as last Tuesday sen'night..."[13]

This was made possible by reason of him not being invited to sing at the Three Choirs Festival at Hereford that year. Having spent time with his friend William Fogg (of whom nothing else is known), it would be good to think that he made use of the time and carried on to his brother in Devon. William Beard was enjoying an equally comfortable life-style as his brother, and was a prosperous yeoman farmer, and probably a land agent for the Earl of Devon at Powderham Castle as well. He had five children between the ages of 6 and 22. There is some evidence that the girls, Elizabeth, Ann and Thomasin (Tamsin) were to spend some

[11] George Anne Bellamy, 'An apology for the life of George Anne Bellamy', London, 1785, vol. 1, p. 256
[12] "She was the daughter of Dr Turner, the organist of Westminster Abbey, and was at that time a favourite singer at the Castle and Swan Concerts in the city". Daniel Lysons, op. cit.
[13] "to Mr William Havard at Thornhill, 18 August 1756 from Wm Fogg". N. A. 2. Folger Shakespeare Library,
Washington, USA. The 'Thornhill' referred to could be in Wiltshire, Sussex or Derbyshire.

time acquiring good manners and 'taste' in their uncle's London home. Elizabeth, 21 in 1756, might well have come back to the St. Martin's Lane address with him. William, the eldest boy, was already following in his father's footsteps, and was employed at Powderham as a 'trusted servant' for many years.[14]

The 1756 Three Choirs Festival took place at Hereford, which has always had a smaller budget than the other two Cathedral cities. They may not have been able to afford so many soloists from London. Although the repertoire was still right up Beard's street (*Samson*, *L'Allegro*, and a repeat of Boyce's *Solomon*) it is presumed that he was not a soloist. But he certainly returned to Gloucester in 1757. The records for this Festival are preserved in part. It was a milestone in a musical sense, because Handel's *Messiah* was given for the very first time at a Three Choirs Festival on September 16. According to Lysons it was "received with rapturous applause, and has been repeated at every succeeding Meeting of the Three Choirs". Prior to that there had been performances of *Judas Maccabaeus* and *Acis and Galatea*.

It is not clear what Beard earned on this visit as the sums in the accounts are misleading and his fee is not separately itemised. But he ran up expenses of £46 5s 9d jointly with Giulia Frasi (£3700 in present-day terms). This amount must have covered their hire of a carriage to and from London and paid their hotel costs. Frasi is credited with a fee of £52 10s (fifty guineas); but, as this looks out of proportion for an engagement of 3 concerts,[15] it probably represents their joint earnings of 25 guineas each [16] (£2100 in present-day terms).

With fees like these on offer Beard was happy to return regularly to the Festival. He returned in 1758 (Worcester), 1760 (Gloucester) and 1761 (Worcester). At Hereford, in 1759, when the conductor was the Hereford Cathedral organist, Rev. Richard Clack,[17] his place was taken by the less expensive singer the Reverend Benjamin Mence.[18] He was a friend and colleague of Beard's, who had sung alongside him in the choir in many of Handel's works at the Chapel Royal. He had also officiated at the funeral of Beard's wife, Henrietta, during the time that he held the position of Vicar of St Pancras Church. Sadly Beard was not able to take part in the historic performance in Hereford on September 14 when *Messiah* was performed in a Cathedral, rather than a concert hall, for the first time.

Once again, as with his Hampstead Benefit night, Beard knew that he would be busy at the theatre once he had taken over the reins of management at Covent Garden in November 1761; so he was never able to return to the Festival thereafter. The oratorios performed during his last three visits were: *Judas Maccabaeus*, *Alexander's Feast*, *Joshua*, the *Dettingen* Te Deum & Jubilate, *Esther*, *L'Allegro ed il Penseroso*, and *Messiah*. At the 1760 Festival the performers were able to pay tribute to the genius of Handel, who had died the previous year. Dr

---

[14] Powderham Castle Servant's ledgers

[15] Frasi asked for 40 guineas and expenses to appear at the Salisbury Festival in 1757, but as this was deemed too high Catherine Fourmantel took her place. Burrows and Dunhill, 'Music and Theatre in Handel's World', Oxford, 2002, p. 326.

[16] William Hayes indicated that a singer of the calibre of Miss Thomas (a leading soprano of the 1760s) would have received 5 guineas per performance and accommodation at an inn. William Hayes, 'Anecdotes of the Five Music-Meetings ...at Church Langton', Oxford, 1768

[17] Organist 1754–79: see Watkins Shaw, 'The Succession of Organists', Oxford, 1991

[18] Benjamin Mence was a Gentleman of the Chapel Royal from 1744 – 53. In 1750 he became Vicar of St Pancras, London, and buried Beard's 1st wife, Henrietta, in the churchyard there in 1753. At this time (1759) he was Rector of All Hallows, London-Wall.

Hayes, the Oxford Professor who had taken over from Boyce as conductor, composed an *Ode to the Memory of Handel* which was performed in Gloucester Cathedral on August 2 1760.

Since Henrietta's death it seems that Beard accepted each and every engagement that came his way in order to keep busy. He cannot have needed the money. There is no evidence that he had debts, and it seems out of character for one who spent so much of his time on charitable work. He was in the enviable position of having three Benefit nights a year: one at the theatre, one at Hampstead, and - as a result of some pressure put on the management by his friends Havard, Ben Read and others – one at Ranelagh Gardens.[19] He should have been comfortable enough to consider leaving his rooms at Mrs Colman's and taking a new home.

2. SECOND MARRIAGE

Beard seems to have simply exchanged one landlady for another. At his Benefit night at Drury Lane on March 30 1756 his address was given in the press as "at Mrs Lane's, next to Old Slaughter's Coffee House, St. Martins Lane". But with this momentous step he had finally moved away from Red Lion Square district which had been his home for the previous twenty years. The area he had moved into was very different. Instead of the quiet roads with terraced Georgian houses, inhabited by lawyers, scholars, minor gentry and the nouveau riche - and men of letters like Jonas Hanway, a noted philanthropist who encouraged the foundation of Sunday Schools and was the first man in London to use an umbrella - he moved into a busy thoroughfare that was also a thriving shopping street lined with coffee houses. The inhabitants were a very different breed: principally self-made men whose business interests were in the arts and crafts: painters, sculptors, architects, cabinet makers. There were many people living nearby that he already knew; and many more came into the area to eat, drink, talk politics, play whist and chess, and read the newspapers at the fashionable coffee house right next door.

Beard would have been well aware of Old Slaughter's, as tickets for Ranelagh Gardens were available there. His connection with the house next door, though, had actually started many years before: in 1742 it appears that another thespian was living in the very house that he would later inhabit. An advertisement in the *Daily Advertiser* for April 10 announced a Benefit for Monsieur Muilmant "with entertainments of Dancing by Monsr: Muilmant, etc, and Singing by Mr Beard. Tickets at Monsr: Muilmant's House, next to Old Slaughter's Coffee House."

Old Slaughter's had been established in 1692 and took its name from the original proprietor, Thomas Slaughter. It was also a meeting place for players of whist and chess, who set up their clubs in the upper rooms. But, in the years that Beard lived next door, it was best known for the concentration of sculptors, painters and engravers who flocked to the house before the Royal Academy of Arts was founded in 1768. London's artistic fraternity mostly congregated in and around St. Martin's Lane at this time. Hogarth was a regular visitor as he had founded a School of Art in the basement of a large house down the road. The exact site of the School has not been identified, but Hugh Phillips places it a few doors down from Old

---

[19] "I have been favoured with two letters from honest Ben Read: in one of them he acquaints me that the Ranelagh managers are dispos'd to offer you a Benefit". Letter from Havard to J.B. Esq. m/s N. a. 2. pp 97-99,
Folger Shakespeare Library, Washington, USA

Slaughter's[20]. It was the precursor of Joshua Reynolds' Royal Academy School, and the directors included Louis Francis Roubiliac (sculptor of Handel's memorial in Westminster Abbey), Francis Hayman the painter (who had already done a fine portrait of Beard) and Gravelot the engraver, who all lived in the area. There are many contemporary diary entries to show how popular the venue was, especially for some one looking for a place to eat before going to the theatre. John Baker went there frequently in 1759: "I to St Martin's Church to hear Mr Kellway[21] - thence Old Slaughter's, where had not been many months". In the following weeks he revisited it every month. James Boswell dined there in March 1763: "I went with Erskine and breakfasted at Slaughter's Coffee-house, and then we walked to Holborn, which did me good". Dr Johnson had also frequented the place during his early years in London "with a view to acquire a habit of speaking French" from the many Frenchmen who resorted there: "but he could never attain to it"[22]. Later, he went there for a drink with Boswell, and witnessed an animated discussion between a similar set of French customers "when a number of them were talking loudly about little matters". As a result, he came out with one of his famous bon mots: "For anything I see, foreigners are fools"[23]. Oliver Goldsmith, writing of various London clubs, and possibly thinking of Dr. Johnson, remarked: "If a man be passionate he may vent his rage among the old orators at Slaughter's Coffee-house and damn the nation because it keeps him from starving".[24] This was certainly a stimulating area for Beard to be living in. All of London's finest regularly passed by his front door.

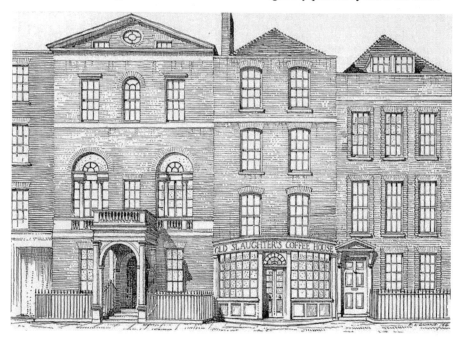

Beard's house in St. Martin's Lane

[20] Hugh Phillips, 'Mid-Georgian London', London 1964, p. 112-3
[21] Joseph Kelway, 1702-82, the famous organist at St. Martin-in-the-Fields, was admired by Handel
[22] James Boswell, 'Life of Johnson', ed. G.B.Hill, rev. L.F.Powell, Oxford, 1934, Vol. 4, p. 115
[23] James Boswell, 'Life of Johnson', ed. G.B.Hill, rev. L.F.Powell, Oxford, 1934, Vol. 4, p. 15
[24] quoted in: Bryant Lillywhite, 'London Coffee Houses', London, 1963, p. 422

Charlotte Lane's handsome brick house is shown at the right-hand side of this drawing from a collection in the British Museum. Four storeys are visible, but there would almost certainly have been a basement as well. In the centre is *Old Slaughter's*, and to the left of that is the house of James Paine (1717-1789), a celebrated architect who built Palladian country houses at Nostell Priory, Kedleston Hall and Wardour Castle, and was responsible for rebuilding Surrey Street - a handsome road running between the Strand and the river Thames. Outside the front door the street was exceptionally broad, well-paved, and referred to colloquially as "the pavement" or "the paved stones" in St Martin's Lane. The bookseller and stationer Samuel Harding advertised the location of his property as "at the Bible and Anchor on the Pavement in St. Martin's Lane". In 1744 the tickets for Defesch's *Serenata* 'Love and Friendship', which was due to be performed at the Crown and Anchor Tavern on March 21, were advertised as for sale "at the Author's lodgings, at Mrs Misaubin's, on the Pav'd Stones, in St. Martin's Lane." [25]

In this fashionable arts-and-crafts area were the homes and workshops of craftsmen like Thomas Chippendale (who lived directly opposite), Peter Channon and Gerrard Johnson (cabinet makers), and well-to-do merchants like Dr Charles Peter and Dr Misaubin. Both of these semi-quack doctors had made a fortune from their pills: the first to counteract 'colic, stone gravel, scurvy and dropsy'; and the other to cure venereal disease. The inside of Dr Misaubin's house is shown in Plate 3 of Hogarth's *Marriage à la Mode*, in which the depraved young husband has come to get himself a cure[26]. The scene gives some idea of the wainscotting and interior elevation that might have been present in Charlotte's house, fifteen doors up on the same side of the street.[27]

It was listed as 'empty' in the Rate Book for 1754, but early in 1755 Robert Lane and his pregnant wife Charlotte moved there from Carey Street (behind the Royal Courts of Justice) in the parish of St Clement Danes: the 1755 Rate Book lists them as 'Laine'.[28] Charlotte was the second daughter of John Rich, and had married Robert Lane on May 6 1749 at St James' Piccadilly. He was a tailor, and obviously someone that Beard had dealings with - and perhaps bought his clothes from. Beard's bank account for 1751 shows a payment of £88 13s to 'Robert Lane' on July 16.

Shortly after this move, however, Robert Lane died. He was buried at St Martin-in-the-Fields on March 16 1755. The parish records give his address as 'next door beyond Old Slaughter's Coffee House'.[29] He was 32 years old. Meanwhile, Charlotte was eight months pregnant, and she gave birth to their third son in April. He was christened George Colecraft Lane on April 25 at St. Martin-in-the-Fields. Two other sons, John Rich and Robert, had been christened in 1750 and 1752 respectively in St Clement Danes church. Other deaths occurred in the house later in 1755. In April, John Restell King died. He was a tailor like Robert Lane, and may well have been his partner. Then, in May, an 82 year-old widow, Esther Clarridge, died. Her address was given as 'Mrs Lane's, next door to Old Slaughter's'. She was presumably a household servant.

---

[25] The London Stage, entry for 21st March 1744.

[26] 'Engravings by Hogarth', ed. Shesgreen, New York, 1973, plate 53

[27] The property was demolished in 1843 when Cranbourne St. was built.

[28] All St. Martin-in-the-Fields Parish Records are at the Westminster Archives

[29] Westminster Archives: F2468 (?). This record of burials gives more personal details of the deceased. It appears to be a day-by-day register of the work done by the parish officers collecting bodies for burial.

Charlotte was also a tailor; and despite being the Proprietor's daughter, was now doing tailoring work for Covent Garden. In the surviving accounts (a m/s list exists in the Folger Shakespeare Library) she is frequently shown as carrying on her husband's business:

- 'paid to Charlotte Lane for the Theatre for Mr Sparks in Dr Wolfe for a superfine full trimm'd black cloth coat and breeches, 14s. Sewing silk & twist 4s. 6d. Buckram stays 2s. 6d. Frilly sleeve lining, pockets, & interlining Cuffs 2s. 6d. Hair Cloth, wadding & Poll Davy 5s. Dimety lining, leather pockets, & silk garters 6s. 6d. 4 doz 2 Coat Death's Head Buttons at 14d. – 4s. 11d. 13 breast ditto at 7d. – 7s. 7d. 5 yds fine black shaloon at 2s. 2d. – 10s. 10d. Making a Camblet Surtout Coat, 7s. 6d. Sewing silk, twist, buskram & stays, 4s. Velvet to line the collar, 1s. 17 Coat, 1 breast black basket buttons, 1s. 8d.' [30]

- 'paid to Charlotte Lane for cleaning for Mr Dyer a white cloth Suit lac'd with silver, 2s. 6d. For altering and mending ditto, silk etc., 6s.'

- 'paid Charlotte Lane for altering and mending a pair of black velvet breeches for Mr Wm Smith, 1s 6d; for making a scarlet camblet frock, 8s; for sewing silk, twist, buckram and stays, 4s 6d; for a velvet fall down collar, 3s 6d; 17 plain gilt buttons at 3d – 4s 3d'.

With such a fine house, in such a prime location, Charlotte would have been glad of a lodger to help with the upkeep. And so, some time before his Benefit in March 1756, Beard moved in. Although he was contracted to Garrick at Drury Lane, Beard would have kept in touch with John Rich through the Beef-steak Club, and known of his daughter's misfortunes. Charlotte must have been very pleased to be able to take in her father's friend as a lodger.

It is curious that once again Beard had taken up with a widow - and, this time, one with three young children. However, very shortly after his arrival, tragedy was to strike again. Charlotte's son, Robert, died and was buried at St. Martin-in-the-Fields on April 28 1756: he was 4 years old. One hopes that Beard's presence was able to comfort Charlotte in her grief.

Although Beard arrived at a time of turmoil, he must, nevertheless, have been pleased to be settled again, after the uncertaincies of the years immediately after Henrietta's death. When he had tried going back to Red Lion Square and renting rooms from Sarah Coleman in East Street, he must have found that area too full of the memories of his sad wife, her declining health, and the interminable lawsuits that were still destined to follow him around. Now he was living close to both theatres and to his recreational addresses. He was a member of several private clubs which met in the local coffee houses. Apart from the *Free and Accepted Masons*, who met in a variety of Covent Garden locations, and the *Sublime Society of Beefsteaks* which met at the Theatre, he was a member of the *Subscription Room Club* at Tom's Coffee House[31] in Russell Street (his erstwhile address in 1752-3). Here he met, drank and played cards with the likes of painters Nicholas Dance and

[30] The London Stage, Part 4, vol. 2, pp. 498, 501 and 508
[31] Bryant Lillywhite, 'London Coffee Houses', London, 1963, p. 148

Samuel Scott, Garrick and other actors; medical men Dr Petit and Dr Schomberg; and Sir Thomas Robinson, the director of Ranelagh Gardens. We learn from one of Havard's letters[32] that he was also a member of the Club at the *Bedford Coffee House*, right beside the main entrance to Covent Garden theatre. Here he met the likes of his friend Dr John Armstrong, the physician who looked after the health of actors, and with whom he had probably resided while Henrietta was ailing at Chelsea. Armstrong was an amateur composer, and Havard writes to him after learning of his own ill-health that "...you cannot conceive how much ye Ran-tan-plan of Johnny Beard will relieve you; and I am convinced that your *Cantata*, sung by him, would soothe even a Paroxysm."[33]

Moving to St Martin's Lane was a new beginning. At this moment in time Beard could not have foreseen just how completely his life was going to change. In time the lodger / landlady relationship developed. The 1756 Rate Book still lists the occupier as 'Charlotte Lane', but in 1758 - the year before their wedding - it is Beard's name that appears. All of this indicates that he was comfortably ensconced with Charlotte before they took the decisive step to marry. The last entry for him is in 1769, where his name is crossed out, and shows that he retained the house for nearly two years after his retirement, in order to have a pied à terre in town.

By 1759, when they married, Beard was 43 and Charlotte was 31. The relationship seems to have been based on common interests, mutual friends, and an affection that was still observable between them in old age. The wedding took place while Beard was still contracted to Garrick and Lacy at Drury Lane. The priest who married them (legally this time!) at the small-scale ceremony at St Martin-in-the-Fields, on Monday February 19 1759, was the curate Stephen Lewis. The witnesses were her father John Rich and Beard's friend Alexander Reid who would be inducted into the *Beef-Steak Society* a few weeks later. Beard reciprocated the favour, and was a witness to Reid's marriage in May 1759 at St Luke's Chelsea. Reid was the Assistant Surgeon at the Royal Chelsea Hospital, and must have met Beard through a mutual friendship with John Armstrong. Beard may even have lodged with Reid when he performed in the summer months at Ranelagh Gardens, which were situated right next door to the grounds of the Royal Hospital.

Now that Charlotte had a new husband any children that she may have had by her first husband might well have taken the surname 'Beard'. As we have seen, her son Robert died in 1756, and the eighteen-year-old John was drowned in a shipwreck off Fort St George, Madras in 1768, having been impressed earlier in that year into an East India Company ship. But no information is forthcoming about the fate of the other son, George Colecraft Lane, born in 1755. No death appears in the records of St Martin-in-the-Fields - either as 'Lane' or 'Beard' - for the whole period that they lived in the Parish. Without any contradictory evidence, we have to assume that this child, at least, survived into adulthood.

Marriage to Charlotte also brought Beard even closer to John Rich and the family that controlled Covent Garden Theatre. Beard had been contracted to Rich for five years in the mid-1740s, but his connection with the theatre dated back even earlier to his operatic debut in November 1734. In the intervening years, Rich had witnessed him grow from a youthful opera singer, with a great public appeal when singing popular ballads, to a versatile all-round performer. As such, he was a valuable commodity to either of the two major theatres. Rich must have persuaded

---

[32] see Appendix 5 for Havard's letter to Beard
[33] William Havard, 'Jeu d'esprit', N.a. 2. p. 62 Folger Shakespeare Library, Washington USA

him to change houses at around the time of his wedding.

And so, in 1759, Beard set out on the last stage in his career by finishing the season at Drury Lane before removing himself permanently to Rich's Covent Garden company. In May he came to the end of a fruitful eleven-year relationship with Garrick; and - even more significantly - the end of a wonderful twenty-five years as Handel's favourite tenor. Even in his last oratorio season, Handel had taken pains to adapt his music to suit Beard's voice: he revised *Solomon* and *Susanna*[34] - two of the oratorios that had not been conceived for him - to show off his strengths. After performances of *Samson, Judas Maccabaeus* and *Messiah,* which had all been designed for Beard, Handel's season - as well as his life - came to a close.

There is little information about Beard's life while he was Charlotte's lodger. Hugh Phillips states that they "entertained extensively in the St. Martin's Lane House. J. T. Smith recalls his father and George Lambert the scene painter having smoked pipes with Beard in this house".[35] No other letters or anecdotes survive from this period. But there is one highly inaccurate story about Charlotte before her relationship with Beard began, from the gossipy pen of George Anne Bellamy. The actress claimed to be a very intimate acquaintance of hers, and described in her memoirs how Charlotte, on one occasion, had got her some tickets for a sold-out Covent Garden performance. This must have been in the early part of 1753. But her memory was erratic as usual:

"During Dinner I was regretting that I could not obtain places to see the new pantomime of *Harlequin Sorceror*. Mr Garrick appearing in *Hamlet* on the Saturday …gave me an opportunity of availing myself of Mrs Lane's interest [i.e. complimentary ticket] at Covent Garden…"[36]

In 1753 George Anne was on the books at Drury Lane and would have needed this assistance in obtaining free tickets. She was not currently performing as a result of having given birth at the very end of January: in the euphemistic words of the Drury Lane prompter, she - "has lain in & is up".[37] *Harlequin Sorceror* was first played on January 13, but, during the run at Covent Garden there were no Drury Lane performances of *Hamlet* at all. In fact, the last time that Garrick had played the role in this season was on November 17 1752.

Our only glimpse of Beard's life together with Charlotte is through the writings, once again, of William Havard. The following text for a song must have been written at some time in the short period between their wedding on February 19 1759 and Rich's death on November 26 1761:

Duette for Mr and Mrs Beard to celebrate the Birthday of John Rich Esq
　　　　　To our's to celebrate this Day: -
　　　　　Many and happy may they rise!
　　　　　May every Minute take a Care away,
　　　　　And drop a Blessing as it flies.

---

[34] Winton Dean catalogues the changes in 'Handel's Dramatic Oratorios and Masques', Oxford, 1959, p. 526-9 and p. 547
[35] Hugh Phillips, 'Mid-Georgian London', London, 1964, p. 107
[36] George Ann Bellamy, 'An apology for the life of George Ann Bellamy', London, 1785, p. 147-9
[37] The London Stage, Part 4, vol. 2, pp. 349

With grateful voice
Let us rejoice,
And raise this fervent Pray'r: –
As Years increase,
May downy Peace
On either Pillow lie!
Soft and serene
Be Life's whole Scene;
And Friendship's Hand hold
Hymen's Torch on high.[38]

From this verse two things can be learned: firstly, that the poem is more a celebration of Beard and Charlotte's union than of her father's birthday; and secondly that Havard is aware that their union is built on "friendship". Some years later, after Rich's death, he writes rather boldly of a loving partnership, based on friendship, in which both parties are beginning to suffer from ill-health:

For Mr and Mrs Beard upon the same occasion - some years afterwards

Again the pleasing Task is ours -
But, tho' we strew your way with Flow'rs,
Some Thorns will still remain:
For see (to sad disease a Prey)
Can aught we sing, or aught we say
Remove the deep-felt pain?
Goddess Hygeia! ever fair
Attend in pity to our Pray'r.
This pair to health restore: -
Then, jocund, shall the bowl go round;
The nimble foot shall beat the Ground,
And Grief be felt no more.
While the dim Torch of Life decays,
Grant them contented, painless Days,
And (if not Pleasure) Ease!
Tumultuous Passions then shall end -
The Lover melt into the Friend;
And all within be Peace.
When Friendship thus unites with Truth,
Age emulates the Joys of Youth: -
Oh! be that Friendship still entire!
Oh! never let that Flame expire!
Let it ascend the heav'nly Dome -
For now (too late to stray from Home)
Your mutual Comforts here you find -
One Heart, and one contented Mind.[39]

This poem is difficult to date, as the content would suggest that it was written quite late, when Beard had retired from the stage. We know from one of his letters that

[38] N. a. 2. f. 106, Folger Shakespeare Library, Washington, USA
[39] N. a. 2. f. 106-7, Folger Shakespeare Library, Washington, USA

Charlotte was suffering from "a severe attack of the gravel" in March 1786;[40] and he himself complained of suffering 'a most painful return of my stranguary complaint' in December 1785.[41]

This would make a dating in 1786 ideal, were it not for the fact that Havard died "of a gentle decay" on February 20 1778.[42] One must assume that these illnesses had come and gone for some years. Quite what the couple made of a poem recounting their illnesses so baldly on a happy, festive, cannot be imagined. The lines about "the Lover melting into the Friend" - while possibly true - are not a very tactful sentiment. But, as with all of these very personal poems, Havard never shrank from calling a spade a spade. In his letters, flowery and obsequious as they can sound, there is usually a bracing message of the 'pull yourself together' variety.

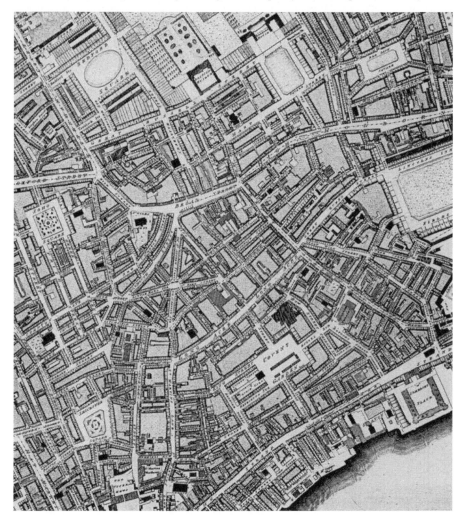

The Covent Garden area

---

[40] Letter to Dr Samuel Arnold, March 9th, 1786
[41] Letter to Dr Samuel Arnold, December 1st, 1785
[42] Biographical Dictionary of Actors, 'William Havard', p. 189

CHAPTER 11
MANAGEMENT OF COVENT GARDEN

BEARD AS DEPUTY MANAGER: 1759 - 61

On Saturday September 22 1759 the Drury Lane prompter, Richard Cross, preparing for the new season, noted in his diary: "Mr Beard is gone to Covent Garden, 'tis said to be Manager".[1] He was right. John Rich had not only persuaded Beard to leave Drury Lane after an uninterrupted period there of eleven years, but he had given him a managerial role for an extra annual salary of £150.

The reason for this is not hard to grasp. Rich was old and ailing. He had a wife and four daughters to leave the business to. But now there was a popular performer who had joined the family as a son-in-law. This was someone he liked, respected, and trusted. He knew the theatre business through and through. In the will that he drew up around this time Beard was named as joint manager with Mrs Priscilla Rich in the event of his death. Priscilla - so long as she remained his widow - had the right to dispose of the Theatre and the Letters Patent by which it had been established. If she remarried she was to be replaced by her brother Edward Wilford, who worked in the theatre's Treasury. If she died, the co-managers were to seek the 'concurrence and approbation' of his four daughters in the running of the theatre.

Rich had married Priscilla as his third wife on November 25 1744. She had formerly been an actress in the company (stage-name Mrs Stevens) before becoming his housekeeper. The daughters had all been the offspring of Amy, his second wife. She had died of 'a hectick fever' in 1737, probably in childbirth, after producing seven children. Two sons and one daughter had died young, leaving only the four daughters Henrietta, Charlotte, Mary and Sarah.

In conversations with his new son-in-law Rich envisaged a plan to meet the challenge that Garrick was currently posing at Drury Lane. Rather than compete for the same audience with the same repertoire, as the two theatres had done so many times before, notably with the famous '*Romeo*' war of 1750 when they had pitted their strongest teams against each other,[2] Beard now came up with a practical suggestion. Since the Covent Garden company contained more singers and musicians than Garrick's, and had a better track record for putting on Ballad Opera and English masques, why not make this a feature of the new season? Why not, in fact, develop an English version of full-length Opera? Rich handed the project over to Beard, and made him his Deputy Manager.

The effect on Garrick's company would be enormous. Thomas Davies, Garrick's biographer, opens his account of Drury Lane's currently fluctuating fortune with this description of Beard's successful campaign:

"The profits of Drury Lane Theatre in 1763 fell very short in their amount to those of preceding years. This was owing to one of those revolutions in the public taste, which we cannot well be surprised at, because it so frequently happens, and is so

---

[1] Cross/Hopkins Diaries, w.a.104 (1) (2) (3) Folger Shakespeare Library, Washington USA. In addition, Ridout, who Genest refers to as 'Rich's Prime Minister' was in bad health, and died in 1761. Beard replaced him.

[2] "Well-informed connoisseurs took to watching Barry in the first three acts, in which he was reputed to be superior to his competitor, and then rushing to Drury Lane to catch the two final acts, in which Garrick shone". 'The *Revels* History of Drama in English', vol. 6, London 1975, p. 101

fairly deducible from the love of novelty and variety. Mr John Beard, a man universally beloved for his many amiable qualities... applied himself with great care to the task assigned him. As he was an excellent singer, and a complete judge of all musical pieces, he was determined to promote, amongst other entertainments of the stage, that which he understood best. He, in a very short time, presented to the public English operas and ballad operas, burlesque operas and dramatic operas etc., particularly *Artaxerxes*, *Thomas and Sally*, *Love in a Village*, *Midas*, & *The Maid of the Mill*; all of which were played successively, and so accommodated by music, as well as acting, to the reigning taste, that they met with uncommon approbation". [3]

By 1764 Beard had succeeded so completely that Benjamin Victor could write:

"Covent Garden appears to be, at this juncture, the Seat of Music and English operas: - under the management of the late Mr Rich it was justly distinguished for Pantomimes - and now, under the direction of his son-in-law Mr Beard, Music must have its reign, and be properly supported by the best English singers". [4]

But all this was in the future. As the season of 1759 approached Beard was determined to make a good start by injecting new life into an old warhorse. *The Beggar's Opera* had been around since 1728 and had received little, if any, updating of its music. Beard now approached Thomas Arne with a request that he should rescore the orchestral accompaniments in a more 'galant' style, using a fuller orchestration. Arne, who was no lover of Garrick, and had had to fight to get his music heard at Drury Lane, accepted with alacrity. He also had his own personal reasons to change houses. Arne had produced a new singer that he felt would astonish the town with her prodigious coloratura soprano voice. Her name was Charlotte Brent.

"Arne made a tender of her abilities to Mr Garrick, at a very moderate income. A taste for music, or even a tolerable ear for a song, was not among Mr Garrick's endowments. Notwithstanding he was strongly pressed by several of his friends to employ Miss Brent, he persisted in refusing... The ensuing Winter he had full leisure to repent his obstinacy; for Mr Beard made Miss Brent his most powerful engine to demolish the success and humble the pride of Drury Lane". [5]

A tale is told of Arne at this time that shows how Garrick's instinct for what would work on the London stage was faltering:

"During his residence at [Thames] Ditton, near Hampton Court, Arne received a visit from Mr Garrick, chiefly with a view of hearing Miss Brent, whose taste the Doctor had cultivated with uncommon pains, and on whose vocal powers he justly set a high value. Garrick readily acquiesced in her superior merit; but at the same time told the Doctor that all his geese were swans. "Tommy", said he, in his usual familiar way, "you should consider that music is, at best, but pickle to my roast beef". "By ---, Davy" replied the Doctor, in a strain of equal jocularity, "your beef shall be well pickled before I have done!" [6]

[3] Thomas Davies, 'Memoirs of the life of David Garrick Esq', London, 1780 & 1808, p. 61-2
[4] Benjamin Victor, 'The History of the Theatres of London from 1760 to the present time', London 1771
[5] Thomas Davies, 'Memoirs of the life of David Garrick Esq', London, 1780 & 1808, p. 63
[6] Baker, 'Biographia Dramatica, 1812

Thomas Davies points out Garrick's error by continuing: "...by his engaging a new singer, rejected by the manager of Drury Lane, [Beard] absolutely turned the scale of public approbation, in spite of all the skill and various abilities of Mr Garrick, in favour of Covent Garden."[7]

Beard not only engaged Arne[8] and Miss Brent, but he also retained the services of Thomas Lowe, who might have thought that his job was on the line. Lowe had been the Covent Garden tenor during Beard's eleven years at Drury Lane. He stayed with Beard for one more season before moving to Drury Lane in 1760. During this time he retained many of his old roles (which they had in common), thus freeing Beard to take part in the new works he was commissioning.

The Covent Garden season started on September 24, and for the first fortnight Beard painstakingly rehearsed his new version of *The Beggar's Opera'* with Arne. Also in the cast were his good friends John Dunstall (whose *Epitaph* he was to write for his gravestone some year's later), James Bencraft - soon to be his brother-in-law,[9] and the popular dancer Nancy Dawson. There is also the possibility that his mother-in-law Priscilla came out of retirement for a short while to take part in this enterprise. The Covent Garden accounts show payments to her on October 13 of £26 5s for five nights, and on October 22 of £31 10s for six nights (i.e. £5 guineas per performance). The only show on stage at the time was *The Beggar's Opera*, so she must have had some kind of role in it. The first night was on October 10, and there was an almost unparalleled run of forty performances from then until December 3. After such a remarkable achievement Rich must have felt that he had been right to place his confidence in Beard. In all there were 53 performances in the first season, and Rich made a profit of £5,000.[10] As Thomas Davies explains:

"A new Polly, or a new Macheath, has successively given such a spirit and lustre to that humorous dramatic satire, that the public has often run in crowds to see it, for twenty or thirty nights successively. Miss Brent was deficient in beauty, as well as form[11], to represent the amiable simplicity of Polly Peachum; but such were the powers of her voice ...that London seemed to be more enamoured with *The Beggar's Opera* than when the principal parts were originally acted [in 1728] by Tom Walker and Miss Lavinia Fenton, afterwards the Duchess of Bolton".[12]

Beard himself was remembered as a fine Macheath. In the Dramatic Censor we read "Mr Beard's appearance and manner of singing [in The Beggar's Opera] were all that could be wished, but, [in] his speaking ...he appeared too much the gentleman".[13] This is a curate's egg of a review - especially in view of the fact that Macheath is a roguish gentleman, known as 'the Captain', looked up to by low-life crooks and doxies. Beard's good breeding from the days of his first marriage would have been a great advantage in the role. Charles Dibdin was an eye-witness to these performances and his verdict was that he "considered Beard, taken altogether, as the best English singer. He did not mouth it, but his words came trippingly on the

---

[7] Thomas Davies, 'Memoirs of the life of David Garrick Esq', London, 1780 & 1808, p. 62

[8] Arne was paid £12 12s on 3rd November 'for composing': Covent Garden MS Cash Book, W.b.2, Folger Shakespeare Library, Washington USA

[9] He married Henrietta, Rich's eldest daughter and Charlotte's elder sister, on 23rd January 1760.

[10] "Rich has cleared £5000 besides his expenses by the run of The Beggar's Opera". Winston ms 8

[11] She had bad breath according to some

[12] Thomas Davies, 'Memoirs of the life of David Garrick Esq', London, 1780 & 1808, p. 64

[13] Francis Gentleman, 'The Dramatic Censor', 1770

tongue; he did not out Herod Herod, but he begot a temperance that gave his exertions smoothness..."[14] The amateur poets were compelled into verse to praise the beauties of this production. After acknowledging the singing of its stars, the object of their universal admiration seems to have been the pretty figure of the female dancer Nancy Dawson (a protegée of Ned Shuter), who had taken over dancing the hornpipe for 'a prisoner in chains' on the indisposition of a certain Mr Miles. Her name quickly passed into legend[15], and the hornpipe was always referred to henceforward by her name:

> See how the Op'ra takes a run
> Exceeding Hamlet, Lear or Lun,
> Tho' in it there would be no fun,
> Was't not for Nancy Dawson.
> Tho' Beard and Brent charm every night,
> And female Peachum's justly right,
> And Filch and Lockit please the sight,
> 'Tis crowned by Nancy Dawson.
>
> See little Davy strut and puff;
> "Pox on the op'ra and such stuff,
> My house is never full enough;
> A curse on Nancy Dawson!"
> Tho' Garrick he has had his day,
> And forced the town his laws t'obey,
> Now Johnny Rich is come in play
> With help of Nancy Dawson.[16]

After the initial success of his first venture Beard looked for a good follow-up. Whilst he was performing the role of the 'Recruiting Sergeant' in Rich's new pantomime *The Fair* by night, he was making arrangements with Arne and house-composer William Bates for new versions of other trusty war-horses by day. Arne revived *Comus* [17] for his star pupil Charlotte Brent, in which - as Sabrina - she sang the favourite air 'Sweet Echo'; and he began to think about a new ballad opera for the next season in partnership with a young man just arrived from Ireland: Isaac Bickerstaffe. Bates was a minor composer at the theatre and the pleasure gardens whose songs Beard had occasionally sung, and whose compositions he was supporting with his patronage: he had recently bought some of his chamber music.[18] Together they brushed the dust off an old piece called *The Jovial Crew* and premiered it on February 14 1760. This was an old play by Richard Brome dating from 1641. It had already been turned into a ballad opera once, at Drury Lane in 1731 and was in the repertoire there when Beard joined the company as a young man in 1738. The story concerns some middle-class girls who escape from their

---

[14] Charles Dibdin, 'A Complete History of the English Stage', London, 1797, vol.5, p.363
[15] 'Nancy Dawson' became the name of the tune to which she danced, and is mentioned in the Epilogue to Goldsmith's 'She stoops to conquer' where 'Madame''Pretends to taste, at operas cries caro / and quits her *Nancy Dawson* for *Che Faro*'. The tune is now known as 'Here we go round the mulberry bush'.
[16] quoted in C.E.Pearce, 'Polly Peachum', London, p. 189
[17] 18-23 January 1760. "Masque not performed these ten years". The London Stage, Part 4, vol 2, p.770
[18] Beard's name appears amongst the subscribers to Bates' 'Six sonatas for two violins'

home and find freedom wandering through the countryside in beggars' disguise.[19] Bates rejuvenated it with some accompaniments in the new style, and Beard gave it a strong cast, with himself and Lowe joining Miss Brent and his new protegé George Mattocks. Mattocks had already had a career as 'Master' Mattocks at Drury Lane between 1749-51 when Beard was on the roster there. Now, at the age of twenty, he reappeared at Covent Garden and his developing voice was nurtured with suitable roles by the older singer. Beard sang the role of 'Hearty', and there was strong support from company principals like Shuter, Dunstall, Mrs Vincent and Miss Young. Fiske consulted the published score and pronounced "some of the songs delightful, notably 'Lovely Nancy'".[20] Apparently Miss Brent was not satisfied with her music and had new arias written by her mentor Thomas Arne.[21] It was quite common for Ballad operas to evolve in this sort of piece-meal way, and during Beard's time as Manager there were very few 'one composer' works of this nature.

Despite Charlotte Brent's prima-donna-ish reservations about his ability, Bates' work on the score was sufficiently creditable for Beard to invite him to revise another old Ballad opera for this season. John Hippisley's *Flora; or The Country Wake* (based on a 1729 comedy by Colley Cibber - *Hob; or the Country Wake*) had been in Beard's repertoire in May 1745. It was performed in the new version on April 9 1760, and stayed in the repertoire as an afterpiece. Beard did not sing in it, but gave the main character of 'Friendly' (which had been his role in 1745) to Lowe. After Lowe's removal to Drury Lane Mattocks took it over.

Meanwhile Isaac Bickerstaffe had provided Arne with a short libretto on a modern theme. *Thomas and Sally* was only intended as a short after-piece; but it broke new ground by being an all-sung mini-opera. Fiske enthuses about the direction in which Arne appeared to be taking English opera in Beard's second season as deputy manager. "It took Arne some months to realise that, with a sympathetic manager and a superlative singer on the premises, Covent Garden would repay the most careful work of which he was capable. His first opera under the new regime was small in scale, but it proved more successful than anything he had written for over twenty years. *Thomas and Sally* ... received more performances in the Garrick era than any other afterpiece, musical or otherwise, and it continued to be repeated at all the patent theatres until the end of the century."

Beard, or possibly Arne, had encouraged Bickerstaffe to look for suitable material in the forgotten repertoire of an earlier age. He certainly was to do so again very succesfully a few years later with *Love in a Village.*[22] The nautical story he now concocted was not unlike Henry Carey's *Nancy*,[23] in that it concerned a sailor - and this was the role that Beard understandably took for himself - who returns home on leave just in time to save his girlfriend from the approaches of a wicked squire (sung by Mattocks). Sally was sung by Miss Brent and Dorcas by Mrs Vernon [Miss Poitier], a colourful personality who went through many husbands, was currently the ex-wife of Joseph Vernon (another tenor), and who was 'the liveliest baggage on the modern stage'.[24]

---

[19] Roger Fiske, 'English Theatre Music in the Eighteenth Century', Oxford, 1973, p. 105
[20] Roger Fiske, 'English Theatre Music in the Eighteenth Century', Oxford, 1973, p. 398
[21] published in his 'Ninth Song Collection'
[22] Beard had sung in *The Villagers*, extracted from an old piece - *Ye Village Opera* - on March 23rd 1756.
[23] Covent Garden, 1st December 1739. A young man, True Blue, in love with Nancy is 'pressed' into the Navy by Dreadnought, a lieutenant of a Man-of-War, in a story curiously foreshadowing 'Billy Budd'.
[24] Hugh Kelly, 'Thespis', 1766, quoted in Roger Fiske, 'English Theatre Music in the Eighteenth Century', Oxford, 1973, p. 639

The music of *Thomas and Sally* is original for many reasons. It was an all-sung musical score with recitatives between the short airs. The last time that Arne had dispensed with spoken dialogue, in *Don Saverio* (February 1750), it had been a failure. Now that the public was beginning to take to Covent Garden as an opera house it had become acceptable. A contemporary writer enthused that the theatre was "so well stored with excellent singers that our fine connoisseurs will have an opportunity of feasting their ears without being obliged to gape at the nonsensical quality of a silly Eunuch, and of a whimsical Signora".[25]

The show started well with an overture whose main tune - played unusually on cellos and bassoon - caught the audience's imagination, and was soon being whistled in the street and sung to the doggerel words 'To ease his heart'. Arne's instrumentation also included clarinets. This was their first appearance in a London theatre. Arne knew that the players were available - (Karl Barbandt and Karl Weichsel were both German oboists who had recently settled in London) - and he persuaded Beard to pay them a special fee of 10s 6d each night for doubling on the clarinet as well as the oboe..

The libretto was published anonymously. It is one of the first things that Isaac Bickerstaffe wrote, and Beard must be congratulated for having snapped up this useful and original writer at the beginning of his career. As will be seen, Garrick tried to poach him. But the contract that Beard had drawn up was so watertight that Bickerstaffe was unable to wriggle out of it; nor was the management prepared to release him. He was contacted to produce one piece a year for five years, with a penalty of a £1000 fine if he should infringe the terms.

"Garrick approached Bickerstaffe; but that gentleman was pleased with the prospect of a connection with Garrick, and therefore indulged him with a little piece he had prepared for this season called *Incle and Yarico*. The music was frequently played over at Hampton,[26] and the latter part of the summer was passed in billing and cooing between the two geniuses. In short, matters were settled as far as lay in Mr Bickerstaffe's power. He wished it, but was unfortunately under articles to Mr Beard etc. for a certain term of years, to supply so many pieces every season... Alas! He had pawned his brains, if I may so call it, with Mr Beard, for something under a hundred pounds".[27]

Bickerstaffe stayed on at Covent Garden, working with a series of composers. These included Beard's 'discoveries' Charles Dibdin and Dr Samuel Arnold. Although tied by his contract to the house he was treated well and produced some of the most original pieces of the decade. These included *Love in a Village*, *The Maid of the Mill* and *Love in the City*, which were all produced during the period after Rich's death when Beard was completely in charge. One last piece, *Lionel and Clarissa*, was set in train during Beard's time and was the most successful of all when it was premiered under Colman's new regime in 1768. Isaac Bickerstaffe went to Drury Lane as soon as his contract would permit, and produced three more musical plays there for Garrick before disappearing abroad in 1772. *Incle and Yarico* appears not to have been one of them. The younger Colman took up the abandoned plot, and brought it out under his own name in 1787, with music by Dr Arnold.

---

[25] *The Gazetteer*, 26th September 1766
[26] Garrick's villa by the Thames in Hampton
[27] 'Universal Museum' vol. 3, 1767, pp. 557-8

Bickerstaffe's contract with Beard, dated May 4 1765, is preserved in a document at the Folger Shakespeare Library. In it we learn that:

"...he would deliver the managers before the 1st September 1766 a complete copy of a new Comic Opera or Dramatic performance by him and called *Love in the City* or by whatsoever title together with the Score of the Music properly adapted thereto and therewith to be performed at the said Theatre; and also before the 1st September 1768 another new Comic Opera[28] and score of Music etc. etc. and before the 1st September 1770 another Opera and score[29] etc. etc. and that the said Isaac Bickerstaffe shall and will attend all Rehearsals or practice of said operas and assist in properly preparing the same for the first public representation on the stage of the said Theatre. Said Isaac Bickerstaffe shall not within said 5 years from 1st September next Introduce produce or deliver directly or indirectly any play opera or other Dramatic piece or performance or any part thereof he is or shall be composer or Compiler of to any person concerned in the direction or Management of any other Theatre or cause any of them to be publicly exhibited or represented at any other Theatre except as thereafter mentioned without Licence or writing first obtained. When the said Dramatic pieces are accepted they shall be prepared for representation and the 3rd – 6th – 9th Nights of public representation of such of them as shall have a run or continue to be performed for Nine Nights - pay or cause to be paid to said Isaac Bickerstaffe whatever shall be remaining of the money which shall be received on the said 3rd – 6th – 9th nights after the usual charges are deducted.[30] Should the Managers reject or decline performance of any Comic Opera by said Isaac Bickerstaffe it shall be lawful for him to get the same represented at any other Theatre in Great Britain or Ireland - When any of the said Operas have been represented Nine Nights it shall be lawful for said Isaac Bickerstaffe to get them acted in any Theatre in the Kingdom of Ireland only - in the penalty of £1000". [31]

When Garrick could not get hold of the services of Bickerstaffe, Beard's 'secret weapon', he began to see the sense in building up a comparable team of singers. In the autumn of 1760 he attracted Lowe back, and set up a rival set of performances for him of *The Beggar's Opera,* with a new singer, Mrs Vincent, as Polly, commencing on September 23. He also got hold of the dancer Nancy Dawson, whose famous hornpipe as 'a prisoner in chains' had so appealed to the previous year's audience. Covent Garden retaliated with 'a new Hornpipe compos'd by Dr Arne and perform'd by Mrs Vernon' a day later on September 24. For some days the two companies alternated their performances. By October 11 they were scheduling them on the same nights. The rivalry was enjoyed by *The London Chronicle*, which previewed the performances by saying:

"There is likely to be as warm a contest between *The Beggar's Opera* at both houses as there was some years ago with the two *Romeo*s. Mr Lowe is to do Macheath at Drury Lane and Mrs Vincent Polly. She has already rehearsed it upon the stage, and in the opinion of the connoisseurs who heard her will form a most formidable competitor for the theatric laurel with the Covent Garden heroine".

---

[28] presumably this was the work that would become *Lionel and Clarissa*
[29] presumably this was the work that would become *The Padlock*
[30] £64 5s were the usual charges at this period.
[31] m/s T. a. 66, ff. 1-3: James Winston's notes from Arthur Murphy's papers, Folger Shakespeare Library, Washington USA. The spelling has been modernised.

Then on September 30 1760, it wrote:

"There seems to be as great an emulation reigning between the two hornpipe dancers (Mrs Vernon and Miss Dawson) as the two Pollies. Disputes run high amongst the dancing connoisseurs, some preferring the one and some the other. Encore is the word to both, and on Friday night the applause was so loud and general to Mrs Vernon during her performance that neither she nor the audience could hear a note of the music".

Despite this temporary popularity Mrs Vernon did not obtain Nancy's celebrity. The poems still kept coming the other's way:

> Come all ye bucks and bloods so gim,
> Who love the rowling hornpipe trim,
> Behold how Nancy moves each limb –
> The charming Nancy Dawson.
>
> How easily she trips the stage!
> Her heaving breasts all eyes engage,
> Love's fire she can best assuage –
> Oh charming Nancy Dawson.[32]

There was much discussion about the relative merits of the two Pollies. Their physical charms were compared as well as their voices and techniques. Oliver Goldsmith wrote an Essay in Smollett's *British Magazine* entirely devoted to this subject. In the end it all came down to this: Mrs Vincent was the better looking; but Miss Brent had the finer voice. [33]

The war was short-lived. Covent Garden's receipts were always greater, ranging from a respectable £100 8s 6d to a good £131 2s 6d. Garrick decided to counter the strength of Arne and Bates at Covent Garden by hiring John Stanley and J. C. Smith - better known for their oratorios - to write original English operas for him. Smith's *The Enchanter* had a 'turkish' plot featuring a heroine called 'Zaida', which curiously foreshadowed a work by Mozart. Stanley's *Arcadia or The Shepherd's Wedding* had little plot, displayed no dramatic instinct, and (according to Fiske) must have been hurriedly composed.[34] After only one season, in which they found their work continually overshadowed by the superior Covent Garden offerings, both composers turned their backs on Garrick for good.

By the beginning of the 1761 season Covent Garden was all set for another run of original English operas, and was gearing up for another battle with Drury Lane. Arne had produced a full-length serious opera that would not only outclass those recently produced at Drury Lane, but also throw down the gauntlet to the Italian companies that visited the King's Theatre Haymarket.

But this was not the way the expected competition turned out. George II had died in October 1760, and the Coronation of George III was scheduled for September 22 1761. Garrick, knowing that the aging Rich would schedule something topical, as he had done on previous Royal occasions, tried to preempt him on September 30 with an afterpiece called *The Coronation*. Rich, though unwell

---

[32] quoted in C.E.Pearce, 'Polly Peachum', London, p. 191
[33] quoted at length in C.E.Pearce, 'Polly Peachum', London, pp. 192-5
[34] Roger Fiske, 'English Theatre Music in the Eighteenth Century', Oxford, 1973, pp. 246-7

with "stone and gravel" took his time and produced a more elaborate show, also called *The Coronation*, some six weeks later on November 13. Davies is an ideally impartial critic when he writes of Garrick's attempt to upstage Rich:

"Garrick knew that Rich would spare no expense in the presentation of his show; he knew too that he had a taste in the ordering, dressing, and setting out these pompous processions, superior to his own. He therefore was contented with the old dresses which had been occasionally used from 1721... The exhibition was the meanest, and the most unworthy of a theatre, that I ever saw. The stage was opened into Drury Lane; and a new and unexpected sight surprised the audience, of a real bonfire... The stage in the meantime, amidst the parading of Dukes, duchesses, archbishops, peeresses, heralds etc. was covered with a thick fog from the smoke of the fire, which served to hide the tawdry dresses of the processionalists. During this idle piece of mockery, the actors, being exposed to the suffocations of smoke, and the raw air from the open street, were seized with colds, rheumatisms, and swelled faces. At length the indignation of the audience delivered the comedians from this wretched badge of nightly slavery, which gained nothing to the managers but disgrace and empty benches... Rich fully satisfied [the public's] warmest imaginations".[35]

John Rich

---

[35] Thomas Davies, 'Memoirs of the Life of David Garrick Esq.', vol. 1, London 1798, pp.365ff.

Rich had begun his preparations early and had laid in large amounts of clothing, fabric and ribbon. The sums spent out were vast. One estimate was that it cost him £3000. In the accounts there are frequent payments for such things as:

'Haberdasher's Bill for Coronation £4 16s 4d; Ribbons for Coronation £2 16s 5d; to Richards for painting a scene $5 5s; for a crimson velvet coat £12 12s; a side drum £1 1s; a white and silver gown and coat £10; paid Richard Vincent for the trumpeters' clothing to be used in Coronation £105; 8 trumpet banners and 2 kettle drum banners £73 10s; white waistcoat embroidered with gold £13 13s; 7 full bottomed wigs, 3 fly wigs, 2 tye wigs, & 1 short fly wig for the Coronation £12 12s.[36]

Whilst preparing this spectacle - which looked set to be as grand as the real thing in Westminster Abbey - Rich contented himself with repeating his spectacular pantomime of 1759, *The Fair*, in which Beard sang three arias by Arne.

When Rich's *Coronation* was finally put before the public on November 13 it was destined to make a huge impact. It lasted until the end of the season, and enjoyed an unbroken run of 44 nights in the season's total of 65 performances. Beard achieved one important scoop, which made it a particularly attractive show for Londoners, and a great draw for visitors from outside the City: he was able to secure the services of the very musicians who had sung at the real Coronation.

The choirs had regularly appeared at Covent Garden in the Lent oratorio series, of course. But they had not taken to the stage in anything of this nature before. Indeed, as we have seen in Chapter 1, the Dean's rules precluded the Chapel Royal choristers singing "at either of the play houses". Beard must have been assisted in obtaining their services by his long relationship with the choirs of the Chapel Royal and Westminster Abbey, and by his friendship with William Boyce (the organist at the Chapel Royal). He must also have been aided by the fact that his current harpsichord player, Jonathan Battishill, was Boyce's assistant organist. Rich was prepared to pay the going rate, and each choir member earned 5s a night. Some eleven 'extras' were drafted in, amongst whom was a very young Charles Dibdin, who has given us an eye-witness account of a budding actor's life in this period. The choir performed some of Handel's 'Coronation Anthems' nightly at the theatre, including the ever-popular 'Zadok the Priest'. The stage set was painted to look like the interior of Westminster Abbey. For the public, it was the nearest that they would ever come to being able to attend such a spectacular event. Although the first night's expenses were £44 17s 8d, the show took a healthy £244 7s at the box office. It continued to bring in over £200 nightly, with average expenses of around £46 3s 8d, up until the death of Rich on November 26, when the Winston Theatrical Record ceases.[37] Baron Kielmansegge went to see it on November 14, and was so taken by the splendour on show that he waxed unusually lyrical about it in his journal:

"The quantity of people forming the procession, the richness and splendour of the costumes, the accurate copy of the festivities, so far as this can be accomplished on the stage, and the inclusion of the principal features of the Abbey, combined to make the whole a wonderful sight. ...The whole of the Westminster Choir sang all the time

---

[36] Winston Theatrical Record, quoted in 'The London Stage', Part 4, vol 2, pp. 892-903
[37] 'The London Stage', Part 4, vol 2, p.903-5

that the procession was passing across the stage, in exact imitation of the real procession. The same number of cymbals and trumpets were there; the bells were rung; and the guns and regimental bands in lines, through which the procession continually passed, were painted on the scenery. ...The dresses, all of which are of velvet, gold, and silver, are said to have cost the owner of Covent Garden theatre £3000. This is the famous old Rich, formerly the best Harlequin who ever appeared on the stage, and whose last act was the arrangement at this theatre of the coronation... I can say without exaggeration that there can hardly be anyone in London ...who will not have seen the play at least once."[38]

But it was to be Rich's final triumph. He had wanted to be able to walk across the stage in his own magnificent procession. But his complaint had gone to his knee and leg. William Havard's letter to his friend B[en] R[ead] explains that: "… they cannot settle whether it is rheumatic or gouty. Be it whichever it may, it has had a very bad effect upon his spirits. He is excessive low; they endeavour to rouse him, to rumble him about, and now and then make him drink a bottle of claret." [39] At his death the effective day-to-day running of the theatre passed into Beard's hands. The stipulation that Rich had made in his will was that Beard and Priscilla should be joint managers. But it must have been decided at an early stage that Beard would be the spokesperson for the new proprietors. The last entry in the Winston Theatrical Record shows that they inherited a favourable balance of £715 9s 9d.

BEARD AS MANAGER: PART 1, 1761 - 1763

"Rich died during the run of The Coronation, having accomplished the sum of his glory, and left the Theatre in equal shares between his widow and Mrs Beard, Mrs Bencraft, and Mrs Morris his three daughters. [*recte* also Sarah Voelcker, the fourth daughter]. Beard was very sensibly appointed manager; who, dreading, perhaps the superior power and ability of Garrick, whom he both loved and feared, determined to raise as formidable an opposition as possible upon the only ground on which he was able to make anything like an effectual stand". [40]

Tate Wilkinson makes an interesting comment in his history of Covent Garden that at Rich's death "Mr Beard became joint manager with the widow and Mr Bencraft".[41] This would have made sense. At the time it was important for someone with a good knowledge of the straight theatre to carry on running the actors and the repertoire of straight plays. It was better for Bencraft to look after this side of things, of which he had a better understanding. Although Beard and Priscilla Rich drew up and signed the contracts[42] there was also a certain amount of responsibility taken in the early days by Edward Wilford, her brother who worked in the Treasury (the theatre's accounts department). Only gradually, and as a result of the 1763 riots and

[38] Count Frederick Kielmansegge, 'Diary of a Journey to London in the years 1761-2', London, 1902
[39] m/s N.a.2. Folger Shakespeare Library, Washington, USA
[40] Charles Dibdin, 'A Complete History of the English Stage', London, 1797, vol. 5, p. 130
[41] Tate Wilkinson, 'The Wandering Patentee', York, 1795, vol. 1, p. 129
[42] In 1761the actor John Palmer was persuaded to forgo signing a contract with Beard, as Garrick had decided that he needed him at Drury Lane. " 'What can Beard do with you? He has young men enough, he does not want you, and I do.' Mr Beard - with a liberality becoming a gentleman, his acknowledged character, at once released him from the engagement, and accompanied this generous compliance with the most cordial wishes for his success." 'Memoirs of John Palmer', *The General Magazine & Impartial Review*, Feb. 1788 p. 62. Garrick then only paid him 25/- a week, whereas Beard had promised him £3.

Bencraft's death in 1765, did Beard begin to accumulate all the power into his hands and come to be perceived as the sole manager. At this early stage his interest was still predominantly with the musical side of the company.

Priscilla Rich

One of the first actions that the new Management took at Covent Garden was to pay off John Rich's brother, Christopher Mosyer, who had been a 'sleeping partner' in the business. Rich had stipulated, in his Will, that his brother was to receive £4000 when the Covent Garden patent was sold, and interest on this sum until such date. Beard, Bencraft and Priscilla decided to clear this matter up immediately, and personally pledged half the amount: Priscilla contributed £1000, and Beard and Bencraft £500 each. The remaining £2000 came from the theatre's coffers, and Christopher Mosyer Rich was duly paid off. The husbands of Rich's other two daughters later joined in, and partially reimbursed the others, so that the debt was spread evenly at £400 each. However, none of the parties actually had this money to hand, so each of them took out a loan, and the 5% interest was put down as a charge against the estate.[43] When the patent was eventually sold, each party was then able to take a clear one fifth of the proceeds.

With Garrick then at his zenith, Beard quickly realised that Drury Lane's dramatic offerings could not be equalled at Covent Garden. Bencraft had a job on his hands countering the strength of the opposition. At this period Garrick was playing the whole range of his formidable repertoire. In the opening months of the 1761 season, between September and November, he played Scrub in *The Stratagem*, Sir John Brute in *The Provoked Wife*, Lusignan in *Zara*, Don Felix in *The Wonder*,

---

[43] *The Will of John Rich – Probate and Problems,* Terry Jenkins, Theatre Notebook Vol. 64, No.1 (2010)

Kitely in *Every Man in his Humour*, Oakly in *The Jealous Wife*, Leon in *Rule a wife and Have a wife*, Posthumus in *Cymbeline*, together with his famous Benedick in *Much ado about Nothing*, and three other Shakespearean roles: Richard III, Macbeth, and Romeo. All these in a three-month period: it was a veritable tour-de-force.

Bencraft did what he could with a group of actors that included Mrs Hamilton, Miss George Anne Bellamy, Ross, Shuter, and Smith. They were all capable actors, but none of the men were as outstanding or as popular as the ladies. Yet, on the occasions when they were in direct competition with Drury Lane (Ross and Garrick both played Don Felix in *The Wonder* on the same day, October 7) Covent Garden still managed to be in profit. The presence of two high-profile leading ladies, who courted publicity, were vain, and disliked each other, made for some interesting evenings - especially when they were cast opposite each other in the same play.

Beard concentrated instead on making Covent Garden musically distinguished. Dibdin, who will so often be our guide during these years, writes that "Beard at the head of his phalanx was irresistible, and certainly at no period has the real excellence and true character of English music been so well understood or so highly relished".[44] The work with which he now challenged Garrick's attempts at English opera was Arne's *Artaxerxes*. But this had to wait until *The Coronation* was well established before it could be heard. Although slated for the autumn, it was not seen on the stage until February 2 1762. Arne had been given the chance of a lifetime by Beard. He had been offered a main-piece, rather than the afterpiece that *Thomas and Sally* had been. He was also allowed complete freedom in his choice of story. Surprisingly he took an existing libretto by Metastasio and translated it into English himself.

One cannot help feeling that Beard must have been disappointed to receive it. An antiquated story (albeit in English), on the theme of an oriental power struggle, was exactly the kind of thing he was trying to avoid. *Artaxerxes* was by now a very old libretto. Since 1730 it had been set over and over again by famous composers.[45] It had been seen and heard in most of the great European opera houses. It was scarcely the exciting new direction in which Beard wanted to take English opera. In addition, it required two castrato singers - the sort of 'eunuchs' referred to by the writer in the *Gazetteer* [46] who did not want to be 'obliged to gape at the nonsensical quality of a silly Eunuch, and of a whimsical Signora'. The *Gazetteer*'s author was destined to see a lot of these particularly singular personages if he went to Arne's new opera. Charles Churchill also complained of the retrogressive step in his satirical poem 'The Rosciad':

> But never shall a truly British Age
> Bear a vile race of Eunuchs on the stage.
> The boasted work's called National in vain,
> If one Italian voice pollutes the strain.[47]

---

[44] Charles Dibdin, 'A Complete History of the English Stage', London, 1797, vol. 5, p. 128

[45] Galuppi set it twice, in 1749 & 1751; J.C. Bach set it in 1761 for Turin; a version by Hasse had been performed at the King's Theatre Haymarket in 1754 and revived there in 1766.

[46] *The Gazetteer*, 26th September 1766

[47] Charles Churchill, 'The Rosciad' lines 721-4, 1761, quoted in Roger Fiske, p. 307

Arne had a lot of work to do to convince an English public that his new piece was not going to be like an Italian opera. All the characters had exotic foreign names that were confusingly similar: Artaxerxes – Artabanes – Arbaces; and the ladies names didn't sound particularly feminine: Mandane and Semira. Like Handel's operas, which hadn't been heard in London for some twenty years, the plot was of rivalries between noble families. Did Arne learn nothing from Handel's experience? Beard must have been hoping for the sailors, squires, country lasses, servants and maidservants to which his contemporary audience could relate. As it was, he had to wait a little while longer for them.

Beard cast this retro-opera from strength. Miss Brent sang Mandane, and had a huge success in the arias that were deliberately written to show off the accomplishment of her coloratura. Her first aria, after the curtain rose, was very long and difficult. Her last, 'The soldier tired of war's alarms', was more difficult still. It became a showpiece for sopranos throughout the next century, and well into the 20th. Arne deliberately chose to write on the same scale as Handel, Hasse, Galuppi and J.C. Bach, as though to prove that he was their equal. Beard sang the role of Artabanes, and for him Arne wrote an aria, 'Behold on Lethe's dismal strand', that Fiske claims "showed a technical ability and an emotional depth he seldom bothered to reveal in his other works".[48]

The two castrati were Tenducci and Peretti. This was Peretti's first appearance on an English stage. Tenducci had arrived in England the previous year and immediately attracted attention with his performance at the King's Theatre in Cocchi's *La Clemenza di Tito*. Peretti was the first to move on from the cast, and his role of the hero Artaxerxes was taken in 1764 by 'a gentleman who never appeared on any stage' - later identified as Mr Squibb - and then by Dibdin, who presumably sang it down an octave. Tenducci had what was agreed to be the best aria in the work: 'Water parted from the Sea'. His voice sent some of the ladies into raptures, and Smollett puts these words into the mouth of one of his characters in '*Humphrey Clinker*':

"The voice, to be sure, is neither man's nor woman's; but it is more melodious than either; and it warbled so divinely, that, while I listened, I really thought myself in Paradise".[49]

Artaxerxes had nine performances in the first season and twelve in the second. Later in the century the castrato roles were taken by other voices. Mattocks sang the title role as a baritone, and his wife sang Arbaces. She later swapped to the title-role when Mrs Barthelemon came into the cast. Another of Arne's pupils, Mrs Farrell, sang the part of Artaxerxes in 1777 and had a new aria composed for her by the very aged composer. Somehow the work, which had seemed such an unlikely success in February 1762, hung on in the repertoire until the end of the century. Haydn 'was delighted' with it in the 1790s, and told Mrs Barthelemon that 'he had no idea we had such an opera in the English language'. He was especially delighted by the Duet 'For thee I live, my dearest'.[50] Even in 1814 Jane Austen could write in a letter that she was 'very tired of Artaxerxes'.[51]

---

[48] Roger Fiske, 'English Theatre Music in the Eighteenth Century', Oxford, 1973, p. 309

[49] Tobias Smollett, 'The Expedition of Humphrey Clinker', Letter of May 31st, London 1771

[50] J. Cradock, 'Literary and Miscellaneous Memoirs', vol. 4, 1828, pp. 127 & 133

[51] Letter of March 5th, 1814.

A performance of *Artaxerxes* on February 24 1763 was the occasion of a famous riot. This will be discussed more fully in the context of Beard's attempts to modernise the running of Covent Garden Theatre. The prints that were produced at the time show all of the principal singers in their costumes, with Beard coming forward to address the rioters. They also give a good idea of the appearance of the theatre during the time that he was its manager.

For the 1762-3 season Beard wanted to build on the success of *Thomas and Sally* rather than allow Arne to take any more risks with the irrational entertainment that Dr Johnson[52] and Goldsmith - like many others - perceived Italian opera to be. For them Arne had already gone too far down that particular road. Goldsmith wrote an article in which he wondered whether Italian operas would continue to be given in England, because they seemed 'entirely exotic'.[53] Peretti and Tenducci went back to the Italian Opera company at the King's Theatre. There they performed leading roles in operas by Galuppi, Vento and Piccinni. Perretti stayed with the Italian company until 1764, and Tenducci appeared with them until June 1766. But the English singers were involved in something that was much more to the average Londoner's taste when Bickerstaffe produced his second offering.

Encouraged by the reception of Bates' *The Jovial Crew* and his own *Thomas and Sally* he had followed Beard's suggestion and searched out something from the past. He had alighted on Charles Johnson's old libretto for *The Village Opera*, dating from 1729. The basic outline of the plot was retained, as were the main characters (although he renamed them). Once again the audience was relieved to see real people like themselves on stage, not foreign Kings and Queens. It was a work that was hard to categorise at the time, as the terminology had not yet evolved for it. We would call it a 'musical'. They had to call it a comic opera or a musical

---

[52] '… an exotick and irrational entertainment, which has always been combated, and has always prevailed'. Dr Johnson, 'Lives of the English Poets', ed. G.B. Hill, Oxford, 1905, vol. 2, p.160
[53] Oliver Goldsmith, Collected Works, ed. Friedman, Oxford 1966, vol. 1, pp. 506-8

entertainment. Scholars these days prefer to be absolutely precise and call it a 'pastiche opera'. Instead of recitative it had spoken dialogue and lots of songs - at least 41 of them. But they were not all old ballads, as in *The Beggar's Opera*. Some were newly composed: six by Arne and two by Samuel Howard. Others had been pinched from other composers' recent works, and had new texts put to them. Twelve had been taken from works by Arne himself. Therefore he was the composer of just under a half of the whole piece. Fiske has described it as a 'transitional work'[54]; but it set a new style all of its own, which was assiduously copied in the next series of 'comic operas' that Beard commissioned.

The story of Bickerstaffe's *Love in a Village* is about recognisably ordinary 18th century people: the people that were being read about in the novels of Fielding, Richardson and Smollett. Young Meadows is in love with Rosetta. She is in disguise as Lucinda's maid, in the household of Lucinda's father, Justice Woodcock. His crony, Hawthorn, has very little to do with the plot, but was a vehicle for Beard to sing some fine songs. These included the first appearance of 'The Miller of Dee' (set to a tune called 'The Budgeon is a fine trade'), and new text to Handel's 'Let me wander not unseen' from *L'Allegro ed il Penseroso*. On the playbills the composers were listed as Handel, Boyce, Arne, Howard, Baildon, Festing, Geminiani, Galluppi, Giardini, Paradies, Agus and Abos, with a new overture by Mr Abel.

Playbill for the original production

---

[54] Fiske, op. cit. p. 328

There is a bucolic courtship between two genuine servants, Hodge and Margery, to complement the wooing of Young Meadows and Rosetta, with overtones of Shakespeare's Touchstone and Audrey in *As You Like It*. Act 1 ends with a fair on the village green. In the famous painting by Zoffany of a scene from the play, Beard, in the role of Hawthorn, is seen at the moment that he tells Justice Woodcock that he is eager to go to the fair. Woodcock's reply is "I wish I could teach you to be a little more sedate". In the background Hodge is shown hovering servilely.

At the Fair there is a 'Servants Medley' for singers described as 'the Housemaid, the Footman, the Cookmaid, and the Carter'. The tunes include 'Nancy Dawson' - now truly established as a favourite - and Leveridge's 'Roast Beef of Old England'. There was certainly something in it for everyone. It was deservedly popular, and ran for 40 nights between December 8 1762 and May 28 1763.

Mattocks was Young Meadows, and Miss Hallam (soon to be Mrs Mattocks) was Lucinda. As the older lovers Dunstall was Hodge and Miss Davies Margery. Charlotte Brent, with eleven songs, was Rosetta, the disguised heroine. Justice Woodcock was played by the company's best comedian Ned Shuter. Although not a great singer he was a splendid comic and ad-libber, and was allowed one ballad, in which he was not expected to sing well: in fact, just the opposite. The way his song is brought into the storyline is reminiscent of Dr Bartolo's Aria in *The Barber of Seville*, where he recalls - and attempts to sing - an aria that he recalled hearing the great Farinelli sing in his youth:

"I once had a little notion of music myself, and learned upon the fiddle; I could play the 'Trumpet Minuet', and 'Buttered Peas', and two or three tunes. I remember, when I was in London, about thirty years ago, there was a song, a great favourite at our club at Nando's Coffee-House. Jack Pickle used to sing it for us, a droll fish! But 'tis an old thing; - I dare swear you have heard it often". He then sings a boring old ballad called 'When I followed a Lass'. One wonders whether there is any real-life memory of Beard's own entertainment at the coffee-house clubs hidden away in that dialogue! Hawthorn remained a favourite part of Beard's, and was the role in which he took his leave of the British stage, on May 23 1767. The *Dramatic Censor* praised him highly in this role: 'Hawthorn, as he lived, so may we say he died with that truly great intelligent English singer Mr Beard, who expressed open-hearted glee with amazing pleasantness and propriety. Every person in this light of comparison appears to great disadvantage'.[55]

By the end of the 1762/3 season it is possible to see just how completely Musical entertainments had come to dominate the Covent Garden repertoire. To take the month of April 1763 as an example: English operas, Ballad operas and Masques appear as mainpeces or afterpieces on most days. [*Artaxerxes* and *Love in a Village* were usually considered too long to be followed by an afterpiece].

COVENT GARDEN REPERTOIRE, APRIL 1763
[straight plays and farces in italics – musical entertainments, including pantomimes, in bold ,]

	Mainpiece	Afterpiece [incl. Farces]
4	**Love in a Village**	-
5	*A Bold Stroke for a Wife*	**The Chaplet**
6	*The Busy Body*	*The Apprentice*
7	**Artaxerxes**	-
8	*Love's last Shift*	**The Dragon of Wantley**
9	**Artaxerxes**	-
11	**The Jovial Crew**	*The Apprentice*
12	*The Refusal*	*Love-a-la-Mode*
13	*Every Man in his Humour*	**Lethe**
14	**Artaxerxes**	-
15	*The Constant Couple*	**Thomas and Sally**
16	*The Careless Husband*	*The Citizen*
18	**The Beggar's Opera**	*The Citizen*
19	**Love in a Village**	-
20	*She wou'd and she wou'd not*	*Love-a-la-Mode*
21	**Artaxerxes**	-
22	**Comus**	*The Apprentice*
23	*Love's Last Shift*	**The Dragon of Wantley**
25	*The Relapse*	**The Rape of Proserpine**
26	*Love makes a Man*	**Thomas and Sally**
27	*The Busy Body*	**Harlequin Statue**
28	**Artaxerxes**	-
29	*All's Well that ends Well*	*The Old Maid*
30	**The Jovial Crew**	*Catherine and Petruchio*

[55] Francis Gentleman, "The Dramatic Censor", York, 1770, vol. 2, p. 169

After the end of this season Garrick had to admit to defeat. It was generally accepted that he had no answer to Covent Garden's musical superiority. He referred to Beard's 'Comic Operas' as mere 'sing-song'. Even though this was meant as a disparaging criticism it was taken up in common parlance as an adequate description of the art-form. In fact it is not so different from the term that arose in Germany and Austria ('singspiel') to describe comic opera with dialogue. Many great works of art came to be written in this form, of which Beethoven's *Fidelio*, Mozart's *The Seraglio (Die Entführung aus dem Serail)* and *The Magic Flute (Die Zauberflöte)* are perhaps the best known. Garrick's attempts at producing 'sing-song' entertainments at Drury Lane foundered through the lack of anyone with the vision to mastermind the project. Fiske outlines a few attempts in the 1764 –5 season - whilst Garrick was out of the country – composed by the minor composers George Rush, Michael Arne, Jonathan Battishill and William Bates. But the three that he describes - *The Royal Shepherd*, *Almena* and *Pharnaces* - all disappeared after a handful of performances each.[56]

In the Summer of 1763 Garrick went to the Continent for a two-year break. He left his part in the management of Drury Lane to George Colman - who later headed the consortium that bought the Covent Garden patent from the Rich family. Dibdin was one of those who saw Garrick's departure as evidence of Covent Garden's supremacy at the box office:

"Thus we find the unremitting success of this theatre was the sole cause of Garrick's retirement to Italy. He had no novelty to produce that could stem this. Host as he was, he was almost alone. There were scarcely any authors to support him… Thus the literal fact is, that the public were no longer Garrick-mad…. and this very naturally made him so sick that he retired to Italy that the public might feel his loss; which they did most completely by the management of his partner; who, finding *Artaxerxes* had grown into high celebrity instantly brought out a string of serious operas, without considering that to produce pieces of that description it is necessary to have writers, composers, and singers".[57]

The same point was made in *A Dialogue in the Shades, between the celebrated Mrs Cibber, and the no less celebrated Mrs Woffington*:

Woffington: And is this all the entertainment the town has had for nine years?

Cibber: No, they have been mostly amused with comic operas, consisting of very indifferent poetry put to old tunes, without character, and scarcely any sentiment.

Woffington: Astonishing!

Cibber: And more so, when you consider that these harmonious pieces would fill houses, when Garrick and myself, in Shakespeare's best plays, could scarce pay expenses. This indeed was the principal reason of the Manager's going abroad…[58]

---

[56] Fiske op. cit. pp. 311-4

[57] Charles Dibdin, 'A Complete History of the English Stage', London, 1797, vol. 5, p. 131-2

[58] 'A Dialogue in the Shades, between the celebrated Mrs Cibber, and the no less celebrated Mrs Woffington', 1766, p.14

With Garrick away in Europe and with Beard planning more comic operas from Isaac Bickerstaffe it is time to stop for a moment and consider how successful both managers had been in trying to change the ways in which the theatres operated. There had been no real changes imposed on their day to day running for many years. Perhaps the last major upheaval had been the introduction of the Lord Chamberlain's licensing act as long ago as 1737, which had slapped a rigorous censorship on new plays. But that had not seriously affected the way that playgoers attended the theatre. Over the years many habits and customs had arisen that were not conducive to the good running of a company. It was these that both managers tried to reform.

First of all, they tried to separate the performing area from the audience. We take this for granted nowadays. No-one thinks that he can sit on the stage with the actors. It is accepted that the audience sit on one side of the curtain, and that the performers act on the other. The proscenium arch acts as a barrier between reality and illusion. When Beard and Garrick had commenced their stage careers (Beard in 1734[59] and Garrick in 1741[60]) this was not the case. The stage thrust forward into the body of the theatre, and there were stage boxes on either side of the principal acting area in which men and women of fashion sat, both to see and be seen. There was also a continual traffic between the pit and the backstage area, principally by young men wanting to chat up the actresses. The author of *The D[ru]ry L[a]ne P[la]yh[ou]se Broke Open[61]* remarked on how they 'pop in and out with as little Opposition as Modesty; and have made so absolute a Burrow of the Stage, that unless they are ferreted out by some means or other, we may bid farewell to Theatrical Entertainments". Garrick has one of the characters in *Lethe* (in which Beard sang the role of Mercury) say:

"I dress in the Evening, and go generally behind the Scenes of both Playhouses; not ... to be diverted with the Play, but to intrigue, and shew myself - I stand upon the Stage, talk loud, and stare about - which confounds the Actors..."

It was all very disturbing: even more so on those nights when extra seating was allowed on the stage area itself, to allow for a larger capacity of audience. This principally happened on benefit nights; but there are accounts of members of the audience being there on other occasions, and generally impeding the progress of the play. [62] 'Mr Bramstone being drunk ran across the stage twice - fell down and was taken off like a dead hero'.[63] The improvement took many years to implement, because the problem lay with the wealthier and more influential patrons. Managements did not want to antagonise them. In fact they treated them very obsequiously. Beard, writing in the Public Advertiser in February 1763 about the cause of the riot, appears exceptionally deferential: "... in Gratitude for the many Favours and Indulgencies received from *the* PUBLICK, and from an earnest Desire to promote that Order and Decorum so essential in all Public Assemblies, the

---

[59] as Silvio in *Il Pastor Fido* (Handel) at Covent Garden, on November 9th 1734
[60] as Richard III (Shakespeare) at Goodman's Fields, on October 19th 1741
[61] 1748, p.18
[62] see: Harry W. Pedicord, 'The Theatrical Public in the time of Garrick', New York, 1954; and Cecil Price, 'Theatre in the age of Garrick', Oxford, 1973
[63] December 14th 1752, London Stage, Part 4, vol. 1, p. 339

Proprietors have now jointly authorized Mr BEARD to declare, that they shall think themselves equally bound with the *Managers* of the other *Theatre*, to an Observance of those Limitations which *they* have agreed to."

Quite early on in the careers of both Beard and Garrick there were notices added to the playbills that 'admissions would no longer be taken behind the scenes'. The Drury Lane prompter Richard Cross wrote in his book, on February 22 1748, that the reason for the vehement behaviour of a party of theatre-goers led by Lord Hubbard - which had led to violent hissing, "one catcall, and an apple thrown at Macklin, and some efforts made by a few but without effect" - was "their being refused admittance behind the Scenes".[64] Garrick had only taken over the management in the previous September; so it is clear that he made a determined effort to improve things at a very early stage. But a year later matters were not much improved, because we learn from Richard Cross that groups of dandies were still being allowed to watch from the stage. "Some Gentlemen crowding behind the scenes, the audience resented it and the farce was stopped for half an hour. I drew lines with chalk, but Miss Norris applying publickly to Capt. Johnson, desiring he would retire, he did and the farce went on with great applause".[65]

Beard was present on this occasion. It happened to be the first performance of *The Chaplet* (with music by William Boyce) in which he sang Damon to the Laura of Miss Norris. Also in the cast was Master Mattocks, whom we have seen returning to Covent Garden in 1760 as Beard's young protegé. Beard would have seen how useless it was to try and keep rowdy young 'bucks', intent on mischief, behind a chalk line on the ground. The only way to prevent further recurrences of the problem was to ban them from the back-stage area altogether. In the early days it was customary to give a specific reason. At *Pantomimes* the excuse was that there was so much equipment in the wings that it was quite impractical:

No money can be returned after the curtain is drawn up, and on account of the machines it is hoped no gentleman will take offence that he cannot possibly be admitted into the orchestra or behind the scenes.

But the problem of the benefit nights still remained. Beard himself profited enormously by having extra seating built onstage for his yearly benefits. Rather than force the elegant society that came to support their favourite thespians on these occasions to have to overflow into the first Gallery, where decorum would normally prevent them from sitting, extra seating had to be laid on in a better area of the theatre. Elaborate temporary constructions were built as an extension of the stage boxes. In 1748, at the very time when Garrick was trying to make his reformation, there is this announcement on the bills for Beard's benefit:

Servants will be allowed to keep places on the Stage, which (for the better accommodation of the Ladies) will be form'd into an Amphitheatre, illuminated and enclos'd, as at an Oratorio....[66]

That accidents could happen if the audience were sitting too close to the action is proved by the following report from Cross:

---

[64] London Stage, Part 4, vol. 1, p. 31
[65] London Stage, Part 4, vol. 1, p.158
[66] 21st March 1748; London Stage, Part 4, vol. 1, p.38

"As the curtain was rising for the farce a Gentleman's sword was taken out of the scabbard and carried up with the curtain and there hung to the terror of those under it (lest it should fall) and the mirth of the rest of the audience. A scene man fetched it down."[67]

This happened on Mrs Woffington's Benefit night, when the stage had been 'formed into front and side boxes'. The performers themselves didn't help the stage illusion on these occasions, when - surrounded by their patrons and friends - they threw realism out of the window. At a *Hamlet* performance one spectator was disgusted when Mrs Cibber 'rose up three several times, and made as many courtesies, and those very low ones, to some ladies in the boxes'.[68]

On other occasions there are reports of members of this select - and very visible - audience foolishly involving themselves in the action by handing back fallen articles of clothing to the performers, whether they had been dropped intentionally or otherwise. Cross reports that, at a performance of Hamlet, "while he was speaking his first speech to the Ghost an ignorant man took up [Holland's] hat and clapped it on his head. Holland unconcern'd play'd with it so, and went off with it" - to which he adds the amusing afterthought: "great prudence"![69] Garrick's biographer Thomas Davies declared that "the battle of Bosworth Field has been fought in a less space than that which is commonly allotted to a cock-match".[70] Another biographer recounts an occasion when an actor had to escape over a balcony, and had to push his way through the audience on stage, politely apologising as he went - 'a practice that put an end to stage illusion for some minutes'.[71]

In 1762 Garrick altered the seating capacity in his pit, and, as a result of the space gained, was finally able to ban spectators from sitting on stage at the next benefit nights. Beard followed suit. Garrick announced, on February 21 1763:

"As frequenters of the Theatre have often complained of the interruptions in the performances occasioned by a crowded stage at the Benefits - the Performers will have no building on the stage... for the sake of rendering the representations more agreeable to the Public".[72]

Beard's notice came three weeks later, when the playbill for the first of the benefit nights announced:

"That there may be no interruption in the Performance, Mrs Cibber begs leave to assure those Ladies and Gentlemen who shall please to honour her with their company, that there will be no building upon the Stage, nor any admittance behind the scenes".[73]

Similar notices appeared on all the subsequent playbills, and the problem of unruly spectators began to abate. But there were other occasions when an entire audience could become a serious problem. And this same year, 1763, saw the worst riot that Covent Garden had hitherto endured.

---

[67] London Stage, Part 4, vol. 1, p.36
[68] Theatrical Review, 1763, quoted in 'The *Revels* History of Drama in English', vol. 6, London 1975, p. 103
[69] April 20th 1756; London Stage, Part 4, vol. 2, p.539
[70] Thomas Davies, 'Memoirs of the life of David Garrick Esq', London, 1781, vol. 1, p.339
[71] P. Fitzgerald, 'Life of David Garrick', 1868, vol. 2, pp. 22-4
[72] A front page notice in the *Public Advertiser*, February 21st 1763.
[73] London Stage, Part 4, vol. 2, p.984

THE HALF-PRICE RIOTS

In order to fully understand the reasons for the 1763 riot it is important to remember that the Patent Theatres were performing two shows nightly, to two different types of audience. If there had only ever been one play or musical piece performed per night it is unlikely that the situation would have arisen. But the custom of presenting an afterpiece as well as a mainpiece had become hallowed by custom. Only a few of the mainpieces were so long that there was no time for an afterpiece. *The Beggar's Opera* was one, and the new opera of *Artaxerxes* was another. The Table on page 224 shows that the brand new comic opera *Love in a Village* was yet a third.

It has been shown in a book by Harry Pedicord that the only people that could be at the theatre when the doors opened were the rich, the idle, tourists, foreign visitors, businessmen who could arrange their own timetables, lawyers (who often made up a large proportion of the pit), members of the Army or Navy who were on furlough, ladies of the night, together with anyone from the lower classes who had been granted time off or otherwise bilked their duties. The performances started at 6pm; but the diaries of James Harris, James Boswell and Sylas Neville prove time and again that late-comers rarely got a good seat, and often had trouble getting a seat at all. The custom was to arrive early.[74] Pedicord's research shows at what time most workers were released from their duties. A sample reveals that few would have been in the queue between 3pm and 6pm:

Tailors - 7pm; Bookbinders - 8pm; Handicrafts - 8pm; Building trades - 6pm; Shopkeepers - 8pm / 10pm[75]

He also works out how much disposable income they had, and compares the ticket prices with the cost of everyday living expenses. One rapidly comes to realise that the cost of a first or second gallery seat, at the rates of either 1 shilling or a sixpence, was a considerable amount to this class of people. A journey-man earned between 12 shillings and one guinea a week. His weekly expenses consumed approximately 8 shillings and sixpence of that if he were single, or nineteen shillings if he were married with children.[76]

And so the reason behind the 'two shows per night' becomes clearer. The afterpieces were generally the only portion of the evening's entertainment that some categories of the potential audience could get to. Their taste was also catered for, by providing a selection of afterpieces that were either Farces, comic operas, Pastorals or - best of all - Pantomimes. These were elaborate spectacles, on which a considerable amount of money had been lavished, with a large cast including dancers and singers; and featuring a favourite and well-loved Harlequin. There was never anything serious played as an afterpiece.

The audience at the 6pm show saw Shakespeare, Ben Jonson, Restoration drama, modern tragedies and comedies, masques, ballad operas and pastiche operas; and so were often ready to leave at the end of the mainpiece in order to make their way to suppers and balls.

---

[74] "At three I called on Blair, as we were engaged to go together to the English Opera of *Artaxerxes...* The house at Covent Garden was much crowded". Boswell's 'London Journal', Saturday 9th April 1763
[75] Harry W. Pedicord, 'The Theatrical Public in the time of Garrick', New York, 1954, p.37
[76] Harry W. Pedicord, 'The Theatrical Public in the time of Garrick', New York, 1954, pp.22-3

In order to handle the *two audiences / one theatre* situation a tradition had arisen of letting the audience in after the third act of the mainpiece at half-price. It is hard to be precise about exactly when this would have occurred as it would have varied from one evening to the next. But the audience managed to cope. In 1767 the Covent Garden prompter John Brownsmith published a useful handbook - *The Dramatic Timepiece* - which "…will likewise be infinitely serviceable to all those whom Business may prevent attending a Play till after the Third Act, which is commonly called "The latter account of it". For by only allowing seven minutes between each Act, for the intervening Music, they will always be certain of the time any Act will be over".[77]

Probably there was some queuing involved; and if the theatre was already full there was the likelihood of a terrible crush. On more than one occasion there was a tragedy when playgoers were crushed to death in a stampede at the entrance. Somehow it never occurred to the theatre managements to let the changeover happen at the end of the mainpiece - which was the whole point of the exercise in the first place. The audience arriving to see the afterpiece (and the last acts of the mainpiece one assumes) were allowed to enter for half-price, which put the tickets within their reach. This tradition was jealously guarded, and any alterations to it caused an immediate uproar. Over the years the managements had been able to claw back one valuable exception to the rule. For the first run of a brand-new pantomime - which was usually the most expensive outlay of the season - full price was charged all evening.

In 1763 Thaddeus Fitzpatrick, a serious critic of Garrick's style of acting who had attacked him in print for his "false and absurd speaking",[78] became incensed when Garrick replied with a satirical poem about him and his followers called *The Fribbleriad*.[79] Garrick had probably thought that he had dealt with the mischief that this thorn in his flesh could do him by making him the laughing stock of London. He had called him *Fitzgig* in the poem, and for his followers he had adapted the name of *Fribble* - one of the characters in his own play *Miss in her Teens*. It was intended as a slight. In the poem he describes the 'wriggling, fribbling race, / The curse of Nature and disgrace'. He goes on, in splenetic form, to describe them in mock-heroic verse that recalls Pope's *The Dunciad*:

> Whose rancour knows no bounds nor measure,
> Feels every passion, tastes no pleasure;
> The want of power all peace destroying,
> For ever wishing, ne'er enjoying –
> So smiling, smirking, soft in feature,
> You'd swear it was the gentlest creature –
> But touch its pride, the lady-fellow
> From sickly pale turns deadly yellow…

---

[77] John Brownsmith, 'The Dramatic Timepiece', London 1767. See Chapter 11 for some examples.
[78] "In my letter of the 20th instant [May 20th 1760] I asserted that Mr G[arric]k never did, nor ever could speak ten successive lines of Shakespeare with grammatical, and I should have added, oratorial propriety…. I therefore challenge him, and the warmest of his friends, to exculpate him from the charge of false and absurd speaking… I am, sir, your humble servant, X.Y.Z. *Bedford Coffee House*." *The Craftsman*, May 28th 1760.
[79] David Garrick, 'The Fribbleriad', 1761

Into this vicious text Garrick adds some light relief, when he describes the *Fribbles* convened in *Panfribblerium* [also quoted on p.195]

> There is a place upon a hill,
> Where cits of pleasure take their fill,
> Where hautboys scream and fiddles squeak,
> To sweat the ditto once a week;
> Where joy of late, unmixed with noise
> Of romping girls and drunken boys –
> Where decency, sweet maid, appeared,
> And in her hand brought *Johnny Beard.*
> 'Twas here, for public rooms are free,
> They met to plot and drink their tea.

It is good to see that Beard comes off so well in the poem. Garrick and Beard were good friends, and Garrick had absolutely no quarrel with him, despite the fact that he had recently changed Houses. Within a few years Garrick would be selling him a parcel of land in Hampton in order to build a retirement home near his own villa. Garrick is here describing one of the Pleasure Gardens where Beard was the vocalist during the summer months. His description of it being 'a place upon a hill' rather rules out Ranelagh, which was beside the Thames. So he must be referring to the 'Long Room at Hampstead', where Beard came every August to sing at the Spa *'Well Walk'* for a short season. There was an Assembly Room for dances and concerts, and an adjoining Pump Room where visitors came to drink the waters - and tea, according to the poem. After a period of being fashionable, when visitors included Dr Johnson, Garrick, Fielding and Fanny Burney, it began to acquire a more insalubrious reputation as undesirable visitors crowded in for gambling sessions. Fitzpatrick and his cronies may have begun the rot!

Neither Beard nor Garrick were to come off lightly once Fitzpatrick realised how effectively he had been savaged by the 'Fribbleriad'. Garrick must have come to rue the day that he gave his arch-enemy such ideas about how to get his revenge. In the closing lines of the poem he writes - all too prophetically:

> Now, Garrick, for the future know
> Where most you have deserved a foe.
> Can you their rage with justice blame?
> To you they owe their public shame.
> Though long they slept, they were not dead;
> Their malice wakes in XYZ.[80]
> And now bursts forth their treasured gall
> Through him, Cock Fribble of them all.

Fitzpatrick took the cue that Garrick had so unwisely given him and let his 'treasured gall' burst forth. This time he determined to attack him in an area that would have the support of some of the theatre-going public. This was the questionable area of whether managements should be allowed to withdraw the half-price discount whenever they chose to. Soon there was an announcement on Garrick's playbills that "Nothing under Full Price will be taken" - and Fitzpatrick

---

[80] Fitzpatrick had attacked Garrick in the pages of *The Craftsman* in 1760, using the pseudonym XYZ.

went to work. On January 25 1763 he issued a challenge in the press. Writing to 'The Frequenters of the Theatres' his open letter announced that there was no historical reason for Half Prices being denied.

"The Public, for a long Time past, though dissatisfied, submitted to an additional Tax, upon producing entertainments evidently attended with extraordinary expence ... Perhaps you may have been told ... that it has been always customary to insist on the Full Price, during the run of a new Performance, of every species. This I deny, and insist ... that, until within a very modern Period, this Privilege was confined to a new Pantomime ... It is impossible to draw the line, and determine where the imposition will end ... nor can any reasonable man take upon him to insure that our Lords and Masters will not require Opera Prices of the Public, when they have fully established the present insult on our forebearance. One way only is left us to obtain redress, which is, to assemble at the Playhouses, and demand, with Decency and Temper, an explanation on this grievance..."

Later that day Fitzpatrick and his followers called for Garrick at the beginning of the performance of *The Two Gentlemen of Verona*, (which was a benefit for Tate Wilkinson) and asked him: "Will you, or will you not, admit the public after the third act at half-price, to all entertainments except the first Winter of a new pantomime?"[81] Fitzpatrick wanted an immediate reply. When Garrick, stalling for time, decided that he could not answer that question until he had consulted Beard at the other house, a riot broke out 'with the usual destruction of property following.'

Charles Dibdin is a fairly reliable eye-witness of events at this time. He drew attention to the fact that managements were introducing 'full-prices only' a little too liberally.

"It is necessary that I should notice by what means the question came to be decided in relation to full price; which, having been originally established to reimburse the expense of new pantomimes, had grown so enormously into an abuse, that managers announced it when they thought proper. This at length produced a riot, which began at Drury Lane, where Garrick, with great good sense, redressed the grievance. Covent Garden however resisted, under an idea that such performances as *Artaxerxes* were even more expensive than Pantomime, considerable sums being upon those occasions laid out for extra vocal and instrumental performers."[82]

Garrick seems to have given in to Fitzpatrick at the first hurdle, even before consulting Beard, in order to prevent any more serious damage to his theatre. On January 25 Cross reports that 'the mob broke the Chandeliers etc' and that the play was cancelled. On the next day 'Garrick appeared and agreed to take half-price at the end of the third act to all performances except the first Winter of a new Pantomime'.[83]

Fitzpatrick was on a high, and, having won his first battle, took the war to Covent Garden as soon as the 'Full Prices only' were advertised there. This did not happen until February 24. Beard had seen what had happened at Drury Lane, but innocently

---

[81] Letter II, Tuesday 25th of January, 'Three Original Letters on the Riots at Drury Lane in 1763', quoted in David Garrick, Dramatist, p. 10-11
[82] Charles Dibdin, 'A Complete History of the English Stage', London, 1797, vol. 5, p. 382-3
[83] London Stage, Part 4, vol. 2, pp. 974-5

thought that, because he had no afterpiece on an *Artaxerxes* night, and because it had been performed all last season for full price only, he would be spared. He also thought that he would be able to use the increased costs of mounting a full-scale opera as an argument. If he was thinking of the 'Pantomime' exception to the rule, he should have realised that this had recently been confirmed - by the fracas at Drury Lane - as only applying to the first run of performances. *Artaxerxes* was now about to set out on its second run. When the playbills reappeared with the offending words 'Nothing under FULL PRICE can be taken' emphasised in capital letters, Fitzpatrick determined on the same retraction from Beard that he had obtained from Garrick. This time there was not the personal animosity between Beard and Fitzpatrick as there had been in the other case. Beard was merely an innocent victim of circumstances beyond his control. But it was he who bore the brunt of all the managerial response. It was he that had to approach the rioters as they stormed the stage, and try to appease them. It was he who put his name to the two letters in the *Public Advertiser* that tried to reason with the public.[84] In a biography of John Beard it would be good to hear his side of the story. So here are some extracts from the published letters. Complete texts will be found in Appendix 4.

'Mr Beard received some private Hints the Evening before the intended Representation, tho' not till after the Bill was sent to the Press, that an Opposition was intended by some particular persons, but flattered himself that the Candour and Justice of the PUBLIC *in* GENERAL would distinguish in a case so particularly circumstanced; and when he was called upon the Stage, would have humbly offered such Reasons, as had they been calmly and dispassionately heard, might possibly have prevented the Violence which ensued. In this he was constantly prevented by an incessant and clamorous Demand of a general and decisive YES or NO.'

'As MANAGER only, and TRUSTEE for other *Proprietors*[85], he thought himself totally unimpowered to resign up their Rights by so sudden and concise a Conveyance; and as the Point in Dispute was an essential Matter of *Property*, conceiv'd their concurrence absolutely necessary to any Determination on his Part, which at this juncture was impossible to be obtained.'

'Mr Beard had at that Time received several anonymous Threatening Letters and Notices concerning many other Branches of what they called Reformation. - He was ordered by *one* to add a *Farce* to LOVE *in a* VILLAGE, or the House should be pulled about his Ears. - By *another*, he was commanded to put a Stop to the farther Representation of that *Opera*, upon the Penalty of enforcing his Compliance, by a Riot the next Night of Performance; and very lately received certain Information of Meetings which have already been held, and an Association forming, to reduce the *Prices* at the Theatre to what they were forty Years since, - though it is *notorious* the Expence of Theatrical Entertainments[86] are more than doubled.'[87]

---

[84] see Appendix 5

[85] The *proprietors* were John Rich's widow Priscilla, and his four surviving daughters Henrietta, Charlotte (Beard's wife), Mary and Sarah. Beard was co-manager with Priscilla, who was something of a 'sleeping partner' in the running of the business.

[86] "... the extraordinary nightly expence attending this performance amounts to upwards of *Fifty Pounds*"; Beard's letter to the *Public Advertiser,* February 25th 1763

[87] Extracts from John Beard's letter to the *Public Advertiser*, March 1st and 3rd 1763.

Beard addressing the audience at Covent Garden [88]

Dibdin takes up the narrative again:

"Covent Garden however resisted, under an idea that such performances as *Artaxerxes* were even more expensive than pantomimes, considerable sums being upon those occasions laid out for extra vocal and instrumental performers. The public however persisted, and, upon Beard's obstinacy, who was very ill advised,[89] they completely gutted the house. The repairs took a fortnight out of the season; and, after a few of the ringleaders had been imprisoned, and the manager had reflected on his folly, it was agreed that full price should only be allowed during the run of a new pantomime. This stipulated, the house opened with the play of *All's Well that Ends Well*, and nothing has disturbed this question since".[90]

Beard and the other co-managers suffered a severe blow. One wonders which of them - the consortium of daughters, Priscilla Rich, Beard or Bencraft - had felt that it was worth taking on the trouble-makers that had forced the mighty Garrick to capitulate.[91] Financially it was not worth it, as the damage done to the interior of the theatre was estimated at £2000.

"The mischief done was the greatest ever known on any occasion of the like kind; all the benches of the Boxes and Pit being entirely torn up, the glasses and chandeliers broken, and the linings of the Boxes cut to pieces. The rashness of the rioters was so great, that they cut away the wooden pillars between the Boxes, so

---

[88] Raymond Mander and Joe Mitchenson Theatre Collection; also Bristol University Theatre Collection
[89] See footnote 16 of Appendix 4 as to whether Beard was 'ill advised'
[90] Charles Dibdin, 'A Complete History of the English Stage', London, 1797, vol. 5, p. 383. See the spoof ballad 'Fitzgiggo, or All's Well that Ends Well' beneath the picture of Beard, referring to the events of March 3rd (Beard's 2nd letter to the *Public Advertiser)*
[91] see William Havard's letter to Beard, and footnote, in Appendix 4

that if the inside of them had not been iron, they would have brought down the Galleries upon their heads".[92]

Both Beard and Garrick must have rued this loss of an opportunity to sort out the anomaly of the admissions policy. It was the last of the major problems to do with the day-to-day running that they had faced, and neither would see it improved. There appeared to be no way that they could now proceed in mounting more elaborate spectacles. Raising ticket prices was out of the question. Ultimately the inability to charge this limited and occasional higher price must have had an effect on their ability to create new pieces of entertainment.

The extra income that 'Full Prices only' would have generated would have not, in itself, been significant. But when it was applied to a work such as *Artaxerxes* that was too long to be followed by an afterpiece, it made sense. It must also be pointed out that the ring-leaders of the riots - Fitzpatrick and his 'Fribblers' - were habitués of the pit. They were well able to pay the full price to see the whole show; but maintained, on a misplaced point of principle, that an audience member had a traditional and inalienable right to see half of the evening's entertainment for half of the price. The logic behind this is hard for us to understand at the distance of some two hundred and fifty years. It might have had some force if it had been the occupants of the Galleries who had fomented the riot. But they seemed to have looked on in stupefaction as hot-headed 'bucks' fought for a discount that would only be of any service to poorer members of the audience.

Meanwhile there had been a quiet and continuous attempt to clean up the morals of the theatres; and Beard was credited with having improved matters enormously in this area. There was more vigilance over the activities of pickpockets and Ladies of Pleasure, although they were not totally eradicated from carrying on their professions within the theatre's four walls. Dibdin records that:

"...instead of the indecency, profligacy, and debauchery, that had been known at different periods to characterise the green rooms, the dressing rooms, and the avenues of the play-house, the manners of the actors and actresses were unoffending, polite, and elegant; and nothing appeared in the conduct of the theatre but might have graced a drawing room. It is but justice ... to say, that during Beard's management of Covent Garden, every possible attention was paid to propriety and decorum."[93]

With the theatre rebuilt Beard finished the rest of the Spring season in style. *Artaxerxes* got eleven uninterrupted performances, and music continued to dominate the repertoire. This was also the colourful time that saw the rows between Wilkes and Lord Sandwich at the meetings of the Beef-steak Club (see Chapter 5). After his Ranelagh season had ended he must have been glad to get away from London in the late summer for some peace and quiet. As there is no evidence of him singing at any summer music festivals this year, and not even any mention of his customary short season at the 'Long Room, Hampstead', it is hoped that he and his wife enjoyed some relaxation in Devon with his brother William and his nephews and nieces.

---

[92] *The Gentleman's Magazine*, February 1763
[93] Charles Dibdin, 'A Complete History of the English Stage', London, 1797, vol. 5, p. 232

The next two years were the most successful period of Beard's management. He had day-to-day troubles with actors and actresses, it is true. But he seemed to be totally on top of the job, and the rioters left him alone. Dibdin reports that "everything that had a fair claim to public favour was warmly felt and rationally admired. It was Beard's business to encourage this taste, which reflected credit on all those who cherished it. He, therefore, was indefatigable to feed it with every variety he could procure, and to place the stage as high as possible..."[94]

His new commissions were all successful, and he scored repeatedly better houses and higher profits than Drury Lane. At the instigation of his friend Thomas Hull the Theatrical Fund was inaugurated. And to cap it all he was soon to receive a remarkable compliment from King George III, who was one of his admirers.

At the beginning of the Autumn of 1763 Beard was still implementing the new ruling with which Drury Lane had led the way earlier in the year. Thus, on the first night of his season, and for the next three months, he placed the following special instruction on all his playbills:

"No money to be returned after the curtain is drawn up. To begin at 6 o'clock. No persons to be admitted behind Scenes. Whereas many complaints have been made of Interruptions, in the performances at this theatre, occasioned by the Admission of Persons behind the Scenes; in Order to prevent the Like for the Future, it is humbly hoped no Nobleman or Gentleman will insist on a Privilege so displeasing to the AUDIENCE in General; whose APPROBATION it is the duty, as well as the INTEREST, of the Managers, to endeavour, on all Occasions, to deserve."

Without Garrick on the roster the best actors at Drury Lane were now Holland and Garrick's new protégé William Powell, who he had trained up before his departure in some of his own parts - including the role of 'Philaster' with which he made a spectacular debut on October 8 1763. The leading ladies were Mrs Pritchard, Mrs Clive and Mrs Yates. This meant that there was something of a level playing field between the two theatres. Consequently Covent Garden was able to resume a healthy diet of straight plays. The cast at Covent Garden had changed little from the previous season, and this experienced repertory company were able to perform Shakespeare, Ben Jonson and modern authors without the shadow of Garrick hanging over them. By the end of the year, after only four months of the season had elapsed, four Shakespeare plays had been presented,[95] with more to come in the new year. The company had also performed 26 other straight plays - most of them more than once. The only musical mainpieces presented so far were: *Love in a Village* (7 times), *Artaxerxes* (5 times), *The Beggar's Opera* (4 times), *The Jovial Crew* (twice) and *Comus* (once). These all had parts for Beard, who also kept himself busy in the afterpieces. His role as a singing 'Witch' in the pantomime *Harlequin Sorcerer* kept him busy on 24 nights, and *Thomas and Sally* was given 8 times. He also had songs to sing in *The Royal Convert*, *The Provok'd Wife*, and *Romeo and Juliet*, for which he had persuaded William Boyce to compose a solemn 'Dirge' for Juliet's funeral procession. In all, he performed at least an average of twenty nights each month.

---

[94] Charles Dibdin, 'The Professional Life of Mr Dibdin', London, 1803, vol. 2, p.28
[95] Romeo & Juliet, Henry IV part 1, The Merry Wives of Windsor, Richard III

So far this season Thomas Arne had not been persuaded to write anything new. In fact he was unlikely to have been available for anything major as the success of *Artaxerxes* had gone to his head. He was now engaged on writing a full-length Italian opera, in Italian, for the King's Theatre company. Believing himself to be the equal of the European composers whose works they regularly performed, he offered the company his *L'Olimpiade*, in which he used another old libretto by Metastasio. It was given two performances. Burney relishes the opportunity to be critical of his unloved master and erstwhile teacher in his 'General History of Music':

"The common playhouse and ballad passages, which occurred in almost every air in his opera, made the audience wonder how they got there. A different language, different singers, and a different audience and style of music from his own, carried him out of his usual element, where he mangled the Italian poetry, ...and accents."[96]

Fiske makes the pertinent remark: "It is sad that Arne never followed up *Artaxerxes* with another English opera". All that Beard could achieve was to tempt him away from *L'Olimpiade* long enough to write the music for an all-sung masque - *The Arcadian Nuptials* - which was presented as an afterpiece to commemorate the wedding of Princess Augusta (the King's elder sister) to the Prince of Brunswick. The royal family were present at the first performance, on January 19 1764 when Beard sang Colin to Miss Hallam's Phillis. There were twenty-four consecutive performances, which out-classed the Drury Lane's wedding offering (*Hymen* - written by a Mr Allen and composed by Arne's son Michael). Arne (senior) liked some of his own pieces well enough to publish them in his collection of songs: 'Vocal Melody xiv'. Perhaps it was this performance that reminded the King to do something for Beard, the singer who gave him such pleasure in the Handel oratorios, and who twice a year performed *Court Odes* for him. The title of *Vocal Performer in Extraordinary to his Majesty* was created especially to honour this favourite singer.

In a month's time the King would be hearing him again in the new mainpiece that Beard had obtained from another Irishman, Kane O'Hara. *Midas* was a 'burletta' - a spoof of classical mythology - not unlike the stories of Gods and Goddesses on Mount Olympus that Offenbach set a century later in *La Belle Helène* and *Orphée aux Enfers*. It had already delighted audiences in Dublin. Perhaps Isaac Bickerstaffe, who was not to produce anything new for Beard for another year, suggested this piece by his countryman as a stopgap. It received a respectable nine performances between February 22 and March 2, thus guaranteeing the author the profits of the 3rd, 6th and 9th nights. The songs, as in other similar pastiches, were by a ragbag of composers. Fiske has identified some as being taken from a volume of Venetian airs by 'celebrated Italian Masters', and the overture was by a London theatre violinist called Richard Collet.[97] He also makes a case for some of the original pieces being by the amateur composer Lord Mornington, the Duke of Wellington's father. Shuter played the title role, Beard sang the role of 'Sileno', and other parts were played by his usual team of Mattocks, Dunstall, Miss Hallam and Miss Poitier. After its original run *Midas* stayed in the repertoire, and received some 75 performances in its first four seasons.

Its popularity can be gauged by this complimentary little poem *in The Jester's Magazine,* composed by an anonymous 'Bumpkin of the Upper Gallery':

[96] Charles Burney, 'A General History of Music', 1789
[97] Fiske, op. cit., p. 319

On seeing 'Midas'

To *Midas* invited
And greatly delighted,
They all sung and acted so clever;
That in rapture I cry'd, a,
To the folk on each side, a,
Burlettas and sing-song forever!

For tho' Justice Midas
Turns out but a Try'd Ass,
In preferring horse Pan to Apollo,
The Airs are so pretty,
And so sweet the Duetti,
They beat all your Operas hollow.[98]

Pastiches were currently all the rage. Even during the oratorio season, in which Beard sang *Judas Maccabaeus, Samson* and *Messiah* as usual, the new work was *Nabal* by J.C. Smith, which reused 'some old genuine performances of Handel'.[99] The new libretto had been set to these old airs and choruses by the librettist of *Judas* and *Jephtha*, Dr Thomas Morell.

In the middle of these performances an event took place that would have reawakened old memories in Beard. For only the second time in the century a noble lady had taken an actor for a husband. On April 9 1764 Lady Susannah Fox-Strangways (1744-1827), the daughter of the Earl of Ilchester, married William O'Brien (d.1815), a popular actor at Drury Lane. The circumstances of her marriage are not unlike those of Beard and Lady Henrietta, except for the ease with which they were able to find a clergyman to take the service. This is how Elizabeth Harris reported it in a letter to James Harris jr. immediately after the event:

"The Court & assembly talk yesterday was all of the match of Lady Susan Strangways & Obrien the player. It is said she went out Saturday with a servant & said she had forgot something and sent her back for it: and said she would wait in the street [for] her return. Obrien was waiting in a hackney coach which she got into & they went to Covent [Garden] Church & were married. It is a most surprising event as Lady Susan was everything that was good & amiable, and how she ever got acquainted with that man is not to be accounted for. They say she sent him two hundred pound a little time since. Everybody is concern'd for Lord & Lady Ilchester who no doubt are made miserable by this rash step."[100]

O'Brien had played 'Squire Richard' in *The Provok'd Husband* on April 3, and was Fribble in *Miss in her Teens* two days later. He should have been at the theatre again on April 9 for the role of 'Lovel' in the farce *High Life below Stairs*. Hopkins the prompter writes in his diary on this day: "After the play Mr Powell made apology that Mr O'Brien had sent word he was not able to do his part, and that Mr King had

---

[98] The London Stage, Part 4, vol. 2, p.1160
[99] The London Stage, Part 4, vol. 2, p. 1045
[100] Dunhill / Burrows, 'Music and Theatre in Handel's World', Oxford, 2002, p.421

undertaken it at very short notice, and hop'd for their indulgence".[101]   In fact O'Brien had just married Lady Susannah at nearby St Paul's Church, Covent Garden as Elizabeth Harris had accurately reported. There was the inevitable scandal, which Charles Burney censoriously called "a great Hubbub and Noise"; and - reminiscent of the reaction of Beard's father-in-law - the Earl was "most terribly afflicted with it". But ultimately the Earl of Ilchester was more humane than 1st Earl Waldegrave had been in 1739. Unlike that unloving parent he had "doated" on his daughter "and was the most indulgent of fathers".[102] Unlike Beard, who went straight back to work the same day, and rode out the storm, O'Brien and his bride fled to New York. Strangely, he wrote back to the Garrick at Drury Lane to say how much he was missing the place; but he didn't enquire whether his services would be required again. Meanwhile Garrick was heard to exclaim "we want a second O'Brien most dreadfully".

In time the Earl relented, and found his son-in-law political appointments that would enable Lady Susannah to retain her station in life. William O'Brien became Provost-Master-General of Bermuda and, on returning to England, Receiver-General of Dorset. Thus his story has a happier ending that that of Beard and Lady Henrietta.

Later in life O'Brien had one more fling with the theatre. In March 1770 he came back to the Haymarket Theatre in the title role of *Douglas* with a 'set of Gentlemen and Ladies who never appeared on any stage'. Soon afterwards he tried his hand at writing plays. His comedy *The Duel* (1772) was immediately damned at his old house in Drury Lane. Hopkins wrote "It was very much hiss'd... and with the greatest difficulty we got thro' the play amidst groans and hisses. After many altercations between the audience and Mr G[arrick]... by the author's consent the play was withdrawn".[103] But O'Brien's short comedy *Cross Purposes* (played as an afterpiece) had better luck at Covent Garden, and retained a place in the repertory right into the nineteenth century.

To return to Covent Garden and Dibdin:

"Never had there been a period when the theatre was more honourably or judiciously managed than when it was under the direction of Beard. He was perfectly an honest man, and his delight was to encourage rising merit... As Nature had taught me music, so music now began to teach me poetry. This propensity Beard very kindly encouraged; and after he had seen some specimens of songs, and other things which I had written and set to music, he advised me to try my hand at something for the Stage, which he assured me, if it proved anything tolerable, he would bring out for me at my Benefit. I now thought my fortune made, went heartily to work, and very soon completed a Pastoral."[104]

Beard's furtherance of Charles Dibdin's career was of some consequence for Covent Garden Theatre. He had been aware of his promise ever since he had been accepted into the company's chorus for *The Coronation* in 1761. The young lad was addicted to the theatre, and - reading between the lines of his autobiography (which illuminates Beard's activity at this period) - was probably rather bumptious

---

[101] The London Stage, Part 4, vol. 2, p. 1051
[102] according to Horace Walpole. See: BDA, p. 90
[103] The London Stage, Part 4, vol. 3, p. 1678
[104] Charles Dibdin, 'The Professional Life of Mr Dibdin', London, 1803, vol. 2, p.29

and 'pushy'. But Beard recognised his promise, and encouraged the young singer's interest in composition by subscribing to his opus 1 'Collection of English Songs'. By 1764 Dibdin was nineteen, and he had been picking up ideas about theatre music and stage-craft for four years. Beard gave him his first big opportunity - as Dibdin explains above - by allowing him to present his own Pastoral *The Shepherd's Artifice* on the benefit night that he shared with Holtom, Buck, and Miss Sledge.[105] Dibdin sang the hero 'Strephon' himself. He obviously regarded the occasion as an opportunity to 'audition' to Beard for bigger roles, as well as showing off the current state of his compositional skill.

Dibdin revived it once more on his next Benefit Night in 1765, but Beard did not feel able to put it into the company's regular repertoire. However, he did give him bigger roles to sing, and eventually entrusted him with the composition of some arias and ensembles in Bickerstaffe's *Love in a City*. Before that saw the light of day, however, there was a sudden new impetus to Dibdin's career. The new pastiche opera this season was Bickerstaffe's *The Maid of the Mill*. It was loosely based on Richardson's novel 'Pamela', and the music had been compiled by another new protegé of Beard's - a young man from the Chapel Royal who would eventually succeed Boyce as organist - called Samuel Arnold. The cast was full of the kind of characters that were working so well for this theatre. There was a miller's daughter called 'Patty', a young man in love with her - 'Lord Aimworth', and a subsidiary character with lots of songs called Farmer Giles. Beard took the role of Giles, Miss Brent and Mattocks played the lovers and the rest of the characters were filled by the usual singers. The role of Ralph was assigned to Dunstall, who had originally performed Hodge in *Love in a Village*.

"Nothing could be so ridiculous, for he was pretty well advanced in life, and totally incapable of singing any one of the songs, and, in every other respect totally unfit for the character. The matter was almost at a stand when Beard mentioned me. I wished to perform the part; but as I saw a great deal of envy in embryo I determined to appear perfectly indifferent about it.... The author was told I should damn his piece; and nothing was unattempted to prevent me from appearing in it. I enjoyed all this, and no persuasion could induce me to rehearse it in earnest... Beard asked me, in the most friendly manner, if I found myself equal to it. With him it was impossible to feign. My regard for him was too great to put on any such conduct. I repeated to him a scene as I intended to perform it, and he applauded my spirit...

I came out in the character. I was encored in all the songs... The first Saturday I paid a visit to the treasurer after the piece came out, I found my salary increased ten shillings a week; the next Saturday it was advanced ten shillings more; and the same additional compliment was paid on the Saturday afterward..."[106]

There were 29 performances between January 31 and May 21 1765. The public loved it. Elizabeth Harris, who was not particularly fond of anything other than Italian Opera & Handel's music, wrote to James Harris jr. on 27 February: "We were at *The Maid of the Mill* last night & were much entertained both with the music & acting. I think 'tis top of all the 'sing-song' plays, or whatever you call them."[107]

---

[105] 21st May 1764; see The London Stage, Part 4, vol. 2, p. 1061
[106] Dibdin the younger, 'Memoirs of Charles Dibdin', STR 1956
[107] Dunhill / Burrows, 'Music and Theatre in Handel's World', Oxford, 2002, p. 440

Dibdin recounts in his autobiography how Beard raised the topic of putting him onto a long-term contract as a result of his success in the role of 'Ralph'. It is fascinating, as it gives us a first-hand account of how Beard started his own three-year contract at Drury Lane with Charles Fleetwood in 1737.

"Beard sent for me to his dressing-room, very cordially took me by the hand, and told me that my salary would continue for a few weeks as it then was; when he should, if I approved it, order an article to be prepared for three, four, and five pounds a week, which, he assured me, were the terms on which he commenced his own career".[108]

Samuel Arnold and Dibdin both won their spurs in this production.[109] Both went on to greater things; and the next period of Covent Garden's success in English opera is largely their story. But Thomas Arne must not be forgotten. Beard was always loyal to him. He had been singing his music since 1738, the year of Arne's first big success with *Comus*. He had been the first tenor to sing Arne's arrangement of the National Anthem in 1745. He had gone to Oxford with him when he had received his Doctorate in July 1759. He was also grateful to him for re-orchestrating *The Beggar's Opera* and giving such a good start to his period of management. Beard must have been one of the few colleagues of Arne's who actually liked him, and wanted to help his faltering career. The piece that Arne now produced was premiered in December 1764, and was intended to be the Christmas 'hit'. Arne wrote both the libretto and music for *The Guardian Outwitted*. It should have been a success. The basic storyline recurs in numbers of later operas that were hugely successful, such as *The Duenna* and *The Barber of Seville*. But it needed the deft hand of a Bickerstaffe - a Garrick even, or a Sheridan - to turn it into sure-fire hit.

      Arne was mortified when it only achieved a paltry six performances. Brooding deeply on his failure he wrote an anonymous 'Elegy on the Death of the *Guardian Outwitted*', which was a parody of Gray's 'Elegy'; and then he retired from the theatre to lick his wounds. Beard was unable to tempt him back to write for him again. If only Arne could have realised where his strengths really lay…

Arne's fate, in this sense, is reminiscent of Sir Arthur Sullivan's: neither composer was proud of the good work they had done in comedy - and both wished to be principally remembered for their 'serious' compositions. In partnership with a good writer Arne could have been the first English composer to write a real comic opera of stature, in the Mozartian mould. His melodies and orchestrations were the best that England could boast of at the time, and his adventurous style was moving from the late baroque (Handelian) manner into the 'galant' style that was being forged across Europe by composers like Stamitz, Haydn, C. P. E and J. C. Bach. He had a good talent for finding, and training, budding new singers. It would be left to Thomas Linley (the younger) and Richard Sheridan to do, a decade later, what Arne could have achieved in the 1760s, when their musical comedy *The Duenna* took the theatrical world by storm.[110]

---

[108] Charles Dibdin, 'The Professional Life of Charles Dibdin', London, 1803, vol. 1, p.46
[109] According to Thomas Busby ('Concert Room and Orchestra Anecdotes', 1825) Arnold was paid £12 for his compositions, which would be similar to the amount that Arne got some years earlier
[110] Covent Garden, 21st November, 1775

Between the abject failure of *The Guardian Outwitted* and the sure-fire success of *The Maid of the Mill* tragedy was to strike the management of Covent Garden when James Bencraft died on January 10 1765.[111] He had stopped acting in order to concentrate on the needs of the actors and actresses in the straight plays. His roles were never big ones. The list of parts he played in the early 1760s included Gibbett in *The Stratagem*, Pantaloon in *The Fair*, a Recruit in *The Recruiting Officer* and the 'Dragon' in *The Dragon of Wantley*. This curious role, in which he was presumably completely disguised, was his last. But the actors he managed had been contented, despite the prominence given to music. He was a good colleague and liked by all. *The Gazetteer* called him 'that truly honest amiable and benevolent man [with] a perpetual pleasantry and delectable vein of humour'. William Havard, who had been as close to him as Beard through their joint membership of the Beefsteak Club, wrote that 'he was master of a peculiar (indeed an original) vein of humour, which rendered him irresistably agreeable... This endeared him to many, and rendered him acceptable to all'.[112]

After Bencraft's death Beard must have felt sufficiently well equipped, with six years of management experience under his belt, to handle the extra workload. It was not going to be easy, and there must have been many moments when he felt that the responsibility of looking after a host of temperamental actors and actresses was too much for him. He had to acquire new skills. There were new plays to read through and select for the coming season. This was one element of the job that he did not get on top of, to his cost.

He was able to get some assistance from old-stagers like William Gibson, who had been in the company for a long time. And there was his friend Thomas Hull, who had joined the Covent Garden company along with himself in the autumn of 1759. Hull's roles were - like his character - honest and dependable, men: such as Horatio in *Hamlet*, Edgar in *King Lear*, and Friar Lawrence in *Romeo and Juliet*. Beard would need his dependable, quiet advice on the choice of repertoire and casting over the next two years. Meanwhile Beard also nurtured Hull's playwriting skill. He had written a farce for the company - *The Absent Man* - the previous year, and he was now entrusted with another - *All in the Right* - which was one of only three new pieces tried out this season. Another was a full-length play *The Double Mistake* by Mrs Griffith, which was played a respectable fifteen times. The only other new piece was one in which Beard paired the up-and-coming Samuel Arnold with the playwright Richard Cumberland. They produced a pastiche opera, much in the style of *Love in a Village*, called *The Summer's Tale*. Like that piece it had a country setting and disguised heroines. It was given the December slot that Arne's *The Guardian Outwitted* had occupied a year earlier. But it did very little better, although Beard gave it the nine nights that would allow Cumberland to make his full fee. As we have seen in a previous chapter (Chapter 6) Cumberland generously gave his profit from the ninth night to the newly established Theatrical Fund. The cast was, fairly predictably, Miss Brent and Miss Hallam as the leading ladies, Mattocks as the leading man, and Shuter in the obligatory comic role of Sir Anthony Withers. Beard played the lusty, yet ageing, bluff lover 'Bellafont' that had become his trade-mark type of role. He was now fifty years old and spreading round the waist. His dialogue had been tailor-made especially for him:

---

[111] He was buried at St. Paul's Covent Garden, 'under the communion table', on January 20th 1765
[112] quoted in BDA, pp. 28-29

"The dance you have led me over hedge and ditch … might be good sport to a slender, well-breath'd stripling of a lover; but to your adorer, who is somewhat corpulent, it is actually intolerable."

By now Garrick was back in England and was once more setting about returning Drury Lane to its position of theatrical pre-eminence. With himself at the helm in his old roles he was determined to turn it back into a strong opposition to Covent Garden. He had come back from Europe with plenty of ideas about improving the stage lighting and costuming. He reappeared on November 14 1765 as 'Benedick' *in Much Ado about Nothing*. Beard's actors began to feel jittery at the competition. David Ross, who had been playing all their starry roles recently - Hamlet, King Lear, Romeo, Macbeth, Othello, Ford (in *The Merry Wives of Windsor*), Felix (in *The Wonder*), First Spirit (in *Comus*), to name only a few - wondered about moving away from London altogether. He wrote to Colman within days of Garrick's reappearance, to enquire about the position of Manager at the new theatre in Bath. In his letter he also over-eggs the pudding in his criticism of Beard. After all, he had already been given the choicest roles any actor could desire. His main rival in the repertoire of straight plays was William Smith; but their roles did not overlap, and each closely guarded his own. However, Ross did play all of the roles for which Garrick was famous at Drury Lane. He had played them 23 times between September and the end of November. Knowing this, his letter appears merely petulant:

"My present situation is most irksome to me and must be to any gentleman or man of merit in his profession to have such an ignorant and now ill-bred fellow as B[eard] presume to conduct the business of a Theatre Royal, of which he is totally ignorant, and oblig'd to apply to the great Gibson[113], who naturally wishes to lower every man to his own standard, while the other despises every degree of merit that is not compris'd in *sol fa* and wishes the theatre only to substitute as an opera house".[114]

In the event Ross did not move away from Covent Garden yet, and did not take up the managerial position in Bath. Colman may have indicated that he was hoping to acquire the Covent Garden patent in due time. Ross was still on the roster, still performing his usual roles, until Beard's retirement. He departed at the same time as Beard, in 1767, to try his luck as manager in Edinburgh. Colman, who was in the consortium that bought the Covent Garden patent, brought William Powell with him from Drury Lane to play Ross' roles. After Powell's death in 1769 Colman offered Ross all of his old roles again "on his old terms". He stayed with the company until about 1778, when ill-health finally forced him to retire.[115] At his Benefit in March 1767, just weeks before Beard's last performance, he earned a profit of £133 1s from

---

[113] Gibson had been in the Covent Garden company since 1753, and - since the death of Bencraft - was now regarded as one of the most senior actors. In 1760, when there is a complete list of actors and their fees, Smith is on the highest rate with £1 8s; Shuter is next with £1 6s 8d, Ross is third with £1 6s 6d per day. Beard is on £1 3s 4d; Bencraft is on 12s; Gibson is on 10s; & Hull is on 6s 8d. BM Egerton m/s 2271. All this might have changed by 1765, but was probably in a similar proportion. Ross's chief rival for principal parts was William Smith; but in 1765 he tended to do the more recent repertoire, leaving Ross the classical parts.

[114] The London Stage, Part 4, vol. 2, p. 1141

[115] During Beard's management Ross always had the 4th Benefit, after Woodward (the Harlequin), Shuter & Smith. In later years he slipped down the pecking order.

playing the title role in *Cato*. The afterpiece was *Thomas and Sally* with Beard still in the cast. Clearly his disagreement with Beard had all been a storm in a teacup.

There were actresses who made problems for Beard to resolve, too. The dancer Miss Poitier had caused a scandal during a performance of her hornpipe in *Love in a Village* by wearing a dress that was cut so low that "her breasts hung flabbing over a pair of stays... like a couple of empty bladders in an oil-shop". What was worse was that "in the course of Miss Poitier's hornpipe, one of her shoes happening to slip down at the heel, she lifted the other till she had drawn it up. This - had she worn drawers - would have been the more excusable; but unhappily, there was little occasion for standing in the pit to see that she was not provided with so much as a fig-leaf... The Pit was astonished..."[116] The King also happened to be in the audience that night, which made it even more shocking. Miss Poitier tried to justify her behaviour in the press, and the correspondence dragged on until March, when it was dropped in favour of the greater scandal of the Covent Garden riot.

Beard also had problems with George Anne Bellamy. These were long and protracted, as the lady had a great idea of her own worth, and behaved continuously like a 'diva'. She had not been on the roster for several seasons when she suddenly erupted on the Covent Garden scene as a result of the efforts of several forceful admirers.[117] She was seriously in debt - to the tune of £4,000 - and these admirers both wanted her to be seen onstage in her old roles as well as being in a position to repay her creditors (to which they belonged). A certain Lord Eglinton was asked to use his influence with Beard to help her regain her contract at the theatre. At first Beard was reluctant. He had been building up a happier company of players in the interim, and George Anne Bellamy's roles had been divided amongst the younger actresses. At the instigation of Priscilla Rich he had also decided to develop the acting abilities of Mary Wilford, her niece. Miss Wilford had been performing up until this time as one of the troupe of dancers that Michael Poitier provided for the entr'acte dances.

Lord Eglinton was not able to give Mrs Bellamy the news that she wanted to hear. Beard informed him that her old parts had been given to Mrs Ward and Miss Macklin. (Miss Wilford would be given others later). "There was consequently no room for another tragic actress, especially as musical pieces were now the staple at Covent Garden."[118] George Anne ascribed her rejection to the fact that she was more expensive than the other actresses. But the admirers were not to be shrugged off. Several of them went to the management and demanded that Mrs Bellamy should be engaged within twenty-four hours, or else they would be "obliged to compel them to a compliance".[119] Beard knew what this meant, and did not relish another riot. Bellamy's admirers, the Brudenell brothers, had plenty of friends with a reputation for violence. Beard capitulated; but it is clear that he tried to give Bellamy parts that would not stir up strife with the younger actresses whose careers he was developing. In her autobiography she recalls the event like this:

"Miss Wordley came running into my bed-chamber, and desired I would make haste and rise, as Johnny Beard was coming to see me. I could not entertain the most

---

[116] quoted in 'The London Stage', Part 4, vol. 2, p. 970

[117] Sir George Metham, Colonel Brudenell & James Brudenell among others.

[118] C. H. Hartmann, 'Enchanting Bellamy', London 1956, p.242

[119] C. H. Hartmann, 'Enchanting Bellamy', London 1956, p.244

distant idea that the manager of Covent Garden would so far lessen his consequence, as to visit a performer whom he had so recently rejected... I found it, however, to my great surprise, to be the patentee himself. Having saluted me with his usual civility he informed me, laughing, that he was come ambassador from the junto, and had the happiness to be deputed by them to engage me."[120]

George Anne came back into the company with the title role in Robert Dodsley's tragedy *Cleone* on December 10 1764. She reclaimed her roles of Constance in *King John*, Cordelia in *Lear* and Desdemona in *Othello* without too much trouble. But she still wanted to play the role that had brought her original fame: Juliet in *Romeo and Juliet*. This had been given to Miss Macklin on September 21, and to Miss Hallam on September 27. She browbeat the management into letting her perform it on January 21 1765, but lost it next season to Miss Macklin, and regained it in February 1767.

The 'Miss Wordley' that she refers to above was about to cause further dispute with the management. At her benefit night on March 25 1765 Bellamy, who was allowed to select her programme, decided to stamp her mark on the role of Juliet by repeating the performance she had given on January 21. As an afterpiece she selected the Garrick farce *Miss in her Teens*. She wanted Miss Wordley, her maid and companion, to take the comic role of the maid 'Tag'. But Beard did not consider that the unknown and untried Miss Wordley was up to the part, which had formerly been performed with great distinction by his friend Kitty Clive. In the end Bellamy had her way - as usual - and the role of Tag was advertised on the playbills as by "a Gentlewoman - 1st appearance".[121] From this point on she felt that Beard started to be openly hostile to her.

One can see why. Her behaviour continued to be unreasonable. On the occasion when she was requested to undertake her former role of Veturia in *Coriolanus* for a Royal Command Performance[122] "I immediately pointed out the impracticability of my recovering such a part in a day. He [Beard] answered me very short that I must positively play it, as I had been expressly named; and consequently it must be so. Indeed... I verily believe that no performer could so completely have massacred a Roman matron as I did that night".[123]

After this refreshing honesty it is interesting to see Bellamy trying to account for the manager's change in attitude towards her. She doesn't suppose that she was an awkward actress, with ideas above herself, who had been foisted on to the company's books by threats. She doesn't admit that she should have been grateful to be given the opportunity to earn the money to repay her vast debts. She isn't even thankful to have retained so many of the parts that she had abandoned when she left the company in March 1762. Instead, she recalls some slight between herself and Beard's wife Charlotte: "The manager had married Mr Rich's daughter, with whom, as I have informed you, I was some years back so intimate. This lady, however, having indiscreetly repeated some conversation which passed at Mr Calcraft's table, he desired I would decline receiving her visits. A great coolness was the result, and we never after were on friendly terms. I can account no other way for this alteration in the behaviour of the manager, which had always been

[120] George Anne Bellamy, 'An apology for the life of George Anne Bellamy', London, 1785, p. 103
[121] 'The London Stage', Part 4, vol. 2, p. 1105
[122] February 18 1765
[123] George Anne Bellamy, 'An apology for the life of George Anne Bellamy', London, 1785, p. 103

cordial till that event took place."[124] George Anne Bellamy's behaviour did not improve in later seasons. She was resentful that Mary Wilford was gaining both the public's affection and some of her younger roles. It must have hurt her to have seen such verses being penned to her young rival as these:

> Her eyes are rolling suns, which dart a ray,
> Bright as the splendor of a Summer Day;
> Her arms are as the foam of ocean white,
> Like waves her breasts heave slowly to the sight...
>
> Her speech the songs of other nymphs excels,
> And on her lips persuasion blushing dwells:
> Her smiles are as the streaming pow'rs of Light,
> Which cheer and gild the rugged front of Night...[125]

George Anne had been unavailable to play in her usual roles at the beginning of the 1766 season as she was in hiding from her creditors. After a court case and a partial settlement of her debts she returned to Covent Garden in November "but found my service was not needful". Once again Beard had been obliged to replace her in the Shakespearean roles. Miss Macklin had resumed the role of Juliet that she had tried out first in September 1764. Mrs Ward had now been given the role of Constance in *King John*. Most galling of all was the discovery that the beautiful and popular Miss Wilford was cast in her role of Cordelia in *King Lear*. Reluctantly Beard took her back in the maturer roles of Queen Mary in *The Albion Queens*, Athenais in *Theodosius*, Indiana in *The Conscious Lovers* and Alicia in *Jane Shore*.

But things came to a head the next time that King Lear was advertised on the playbills. Beard and his mother-in-law (towards whom Bellamy was now hostile) were determined that Mary Wilford should retain the role of 'Cordelia'. "The manager alone appeared to be indifferent about it, having been influenced by his co-partner, Mrs Rich, who had resolved that her cousin should supersede me." Gibson, who was acting as deputy manager, insisted that Miss Wilford would play the role, and that Bellamy should refrain from trying to claim it back. "George Anne flatly refused. She said that she was an indulged servant of the public, and that, whatever happened, she would play the character. Gibson was aghast and pointed out to her that she would inevitably draw on her the hatred of the Rich family."[126] Bellamy took matters into her own hands. She had new handbills printed and distributed to the audience as they entered the theatre in which she explained that she would be prepared to appear if they so requested it. She also mobilised her supporters.

"When the curtain went up, there was an universal cry for your humble servant; and upon Cordelia's appearance, notwithstanding she was the favoured child of the families of the Rich's and the Wilford's, she was obliged to withdraw and give place to me. Being ready dressed for the character, I immediately made my entry, amidst an universal applause."[127]

---

[124] George Anne Bellamy, 'An apology for the life of George Anne Bellamy', London, 1785, p. 110

[125] A Tribute to Miss Wilford, the *Public Advertiser*, February 3rd, 1767

[126] C. H. Hartmann, 'Enchanting Bellamy', London 1956, p.255

[127] George Anne Bellamy, 'An apology for the life of George Anne Bellamy', London, 1785, vol. 2, p. 134

The furious Miss Wilford confronted Bellamy in the Green Room, but "I held the little Cordelia's speech in too much contempt to make any reply to it." Had Priscilla Rich and Beard continued to run the theatre for a further season there is little doubt that Bellamy would have found herself without employment once again. As it was, she fell on her feet. The theatre was sold in the summer of 1767 to the Harris / Colman consortium. She was soon up to her old tricks again though, and was demanding the unheard of luxury of a private dressing-room. But fortunately Beard was no longer the one who had to bow to her demands.

THE BEARD / SHEBBEARE DISPUTE

The biggest problem that Beard encountered at this time was one which determined him to retire from the stage as soon as he decently could. It was a vindictive and spiteful war of words with a rejected author. Try as he might to calm the situation, his opponent would not let the matter drop. In the end, retirement from such tiresome quarrels must have come as an enormous relief. The troublesome author was John Shebbeare (1709-1788), a failed Doctor who used a spurious medical degree.[128] His real name actually appears to have been Joseph Pittard.[129] Garrick, whose acting he had criticised in print,[130] had a run-in with him at about the same time as Beard:

Mr J. Shebbeare to Mr Garrick   November 10th 1766
"Sir, Regarding the Tragedy which accompanies this letter... the person to whom you delivered it, when it was returned, told me that it was your opinion that it must receive some alteration before it could be proper for the stage... Be kind enough to consider this Tragedy so that I may have it returned before Christmas, unless you should not have leisure for it in that time. I am, Sir, your very humble servant,
                                                                    J. Shebbeare"

Mr Garrick to Dr Shebbeare   May 9th 1767
"Sir, I have read and considered the tragedy [*Dion*] with great care, and I am sorry to say that I think it not calculated for representation, and for the following reasons. The chief defect appears to be... that it wants that dramatic force, that raising of the passions, by which alone a Tragedy can be supported on the stage...
I am, Sir, your most obedient humble servant,   David Garrick"[131]

Garrick had received unsolicited plays before, and was clever at deflecting them. He had also taken risks with works that he had wished to help. Dr Johnson's *Irene* must have always come to mind in these circumstances. Although the result of many years labour, this work could not be made fit for performance by the famous actor who had accompanied its pre-eminent author to London from Lichfield. Despite enormous efforts at Drury Lane, even Garrick could not salvage the indifferent, moralistic tragedy. Despite receiving nine performances in February 1749, and earning Johnson £300, it was never revived.

---

[128] He professed to have taken a medical degree in Paris. Fanny Burney described him as "the most morose, rude, gross, and ill-mannered man I was ever in company with" in her '*Early Diary*' (ed. Annie R. Ellis, 1907)

[129] see The London Stage, Part 4, vol. 2, p. 1225

[130] John Shebbeare, 'Observations on Mr Garrick's acting', London 1758

[131] 'The letters of David Garrick', ed. Little and Kahrl, London 1963, vol. 2, p. 573-4

Beard's correspondence with Shebbeare started in a similar vein when he, too, received an unsolicited play that had been written many years previously. But there was a poor system in place at Covent Garden for dealing with these things. There are many anecdotes about Rich's cavalier treatment of such plays. Tobias Smollett satirises him in his novel 'Roderick Random' (1748), in which there is a scene that must certainly be drawn from life:

"... I demanded my manuscript, with some expressions of resentment. "Ay" said he, in a theatrical tone, "with all my heart". Then pulling out the drawer of the bureau at which he sat, he took out a bundle, and threw it on the table that was near him, pronouncing the word "There!" with great disdain. I took it up, and perceiving, with some surprise, that it was a comedy, told him it did not belong to me; on which he offered me another, which I also disclaimed... At length he pulled out a whole handful, and spread them before me, saying, "There are seven - take which you please - or take them all". I singled out my own, and went away, struck dumb with admiration at what I had seen: - not so much on account of his insolence, as of the number of new plays which, from this circumstance, I concluded were yearly offered to the stage".[132]

Shebbeare was an unlikeable man who had recently been imprisoned for a series of outspoken pamphlets against the Government that the trial judge had regarded as being very close to high treason. He was obviously a writer who would go as far as he could to make his point. He was also put in the pillory at Charing Cross for declaring that the 'calamities of this Nation are owing to the influence of Hanover on the councils of England'. It was remarked - by Horace Walpole, who had seen yet another of his scurrilous pamphlets attacking the Whig administration - "we do not ransack Newgate and the pillory for writers".

In Shebbeare's first unsolicited approach to Beard, at about the time of Bencraft's death, he offered him a comedy that he had written some fifteen years earlier. "Mr Beard told him that he was engaged for the next season, but that in the following, if it was found agreeable, he would willingly receive it. Under this condition of its being acted, Dr Shebbeare submitted his manuscript play to the manager, and waited till the beginning of September 1766, when the second season approached without hearing of his piece or enquiring after it". One can only feel that this manuscript was a time-bomb, ticking away in some dusty cupboard to which it had been consigned by Beard, in the same manner that he had seen Rich deal with such things. When Shebbeare enquired after his play, in a letter dated September 2, Beard replied:

"Sir, Being but just returned to Hampton, from a visit in Buckinghamshire, I did not receive the favour of yours of the 2nd instant till last night, to which I am sorry it is not in my power to send you an immediate satisfactory answer. In ten days, or a fortnight, I shall be in town, when you may depend on seeing or hearing from,
Sir, yours etc.   J. Beard"[133]

Shebbeare then started to play semantic games with Beard. He purported to read the line "it is not in my power to send you an immediate satisfactory answer" as "I shall

---

[132] Tobias Smollett, 'Roderick Random', London 1748, vol. 2, pp. 297-8
[133] Correspondence from the *Gentleman's Magazine*, March 1767, pp. 124-6

soon inform you that your piece will be received, though I cannot give you that information now". In order to be able to twist the meaning to this extent he implied that he understood the word 'satisfactory' to mean 'agreeable' rather than 'decisive'.

Beard wrote his second letter on October 1:

"Sir, I am truly concerned that I am obliged to make the comedy you left in my hands accompany this letter; but the friends I am obliged to consult in affairs of this kind (as I am answerable to a whole family for the good or ill success of the theatre) advise that it should not be performed. Their objections are, that the plot is too simple, and the incidents far too few to gratify the general taste, at present. They add, that the improbability of such contrivances being carried on by a counterfeit nobleman, at so public a place as Bristol Wells, would render the performance very hazardous; and it would be greatly augmented by the many sarcasms throughout the piece on trade and nobility, strikingly nervous as the expressions, and naturally easy as the other parts of the dialogue are. If there has been too much delay in my conduct, I must beg you to impute it, good sir, to the disagreeable reluctance with which I return any gentleman's work…I am really much concerned to be reduced to it, and hope… you will be so kind to charge your disappointment on the care and duty I owe (as agent) to a whole family; not on the choice or liking of
Your most obedient humble servant,   J. Beard"

This should have been the end of the matter. At a similar point in his correspondence with Garrick, after his play had received strong criticism, Shebbeare had capitulated. Now he sensed weakness in the ultra-courteous tone that Beard had adopted. He warmed to his task, and wrote back a day later telling Beard that "had I been present at the reading of this piece, as we agreed I *should* be, every objection of your friends had been fairly obviated". Beard had had enough of Shebbeare by now, and wrote back with icy formality a month later, on October 3:

"Sir, The variety of affairs wherein I am concerned … will not afford leisure to enter into a more critical examination of your comedy, or to support a longer argumentation on particulars… I must beg your acceptance of this final answer: the piece you have offered will by no means answer our purposes, and therefore cannot be done… If you are severe enough again to arraign my delay, I repeat, that I am very sorry for it; but it is a fate which (through the great numbers of various performances offered to us, and the constant urgency of business to take up my time) must unavoidably attend many. Had I power to send a more pleasing answer to you, believe me, it would be much more agreeable, Sir, to
Your humble servant,   J. Beard"

But Shebbeare was not done yet. His final letter is too long to quote in full, but can be found in Appendix 4. It is a repository of spite, and venom of such hideous strength that it makes very uncomfortable reading to anyone who has gained a true estimate of Beard's character from the preceding pages of this biography. The ultimate insult - apart from those personal ones launched at his increasing deafness, his relatives, his character and his management - was to have the collected correspondence published. But publish Shebbeare did. The *Gentleman's Magazine* of March 1767 carried the full text of Beard's letters, but only summarised Shebbeare's own ripostes. And then, just when London society was tired of this 'non' story, out came the publication of the complete 'Letters which have passed between John Beard Esq. Manager of Covent Garden Theatre, and John Shebbeare M.D.' But this was a duplicitous move, because in it he included a new, long, final rambling 'apologia' for his actions, that had never been sent to Beard. [134]

Beard must have been even more determined to leave the artistic world's limelight on reading this vitriolic letter. As it was one that he had never had a chance to see in advance, and which must have been penned especially for the publication, it was beneath his dignity to honour it with a reply. The letter had not been included in the March issue of the *Gentleman's Magazine*, where it would surely have caused shock and outrage. In it Shebbeare showed his true colours. But publishing it must have been a two-edged sword, because the public could now gauge the true quality of his character. Where Beard's letters are unfailingly polite and courteous, (as has been shown in the above extracts), Shebbeare's final letter is one long stream of invective, from which I shall quote sparingly:

"...However satisfactory these reasons for declining your duty may appear to you, they are none to me, who am neither concerned nor embarrassed, and have full leisure to pursue you...

...You ought to be qualified to judge on the subject which is criticised... From hence, sir, if you are not qualified to decide on the merits of a theatrical performance, you are in the same predicament respecting the judges who are proper for such an undertaking. And indeed the truth of this observation is evinced by you, and your judges: they, in their criticisms, betray the insufficiency of their understandings, and you of your own in submitting to them...

...I am induced to believe that this *family* (of which you speak in your second letter) may at once be both the *friends* and the *able judges* of which you have spoken: and then they will consist of two old women, an High German Page, and a woollen-draper, of whom the two last are acknowledged to be *by far* the best judges of theatrical productions[135]... And you, Sir, emancipated from the servility of being obliged to obey the will of others, shall be exalted to the glorious state of exerting your own bias. And more particularly, as you have lost your hearing, to your care and duty the music shall be committed...

...But as I am fond, on all proper occasions, to become your apologist, I am persuaded that as in consequence of the decay of your organs of hearing, you deviate into disagreement with the music of the orchestra; so, in like manner, that it is from a decline in memory that you wander into discord of facts in your relation of them...

...Such being the altered state of your faculties, I cannot avoid most sincerely to bewail the misfortune of the public, who are thus cruelly deprived of that man, for surely no-one will presume to say that he is the same with the honest and good-natured Johnny Beard, who before the fatal day on which he was suddenly seized with a fit of management that affected his head, was universally esteemed to sing

---

[134] Printed for G. Kearsley, in Ludgate Street, 1767

[135] Priscilla Rich and Beard's wife Charlotte may be the 'two old women'; Sarah Rich was married to George Voelcker, a Page at Court; and Mary Rich had been married to Mr Morris, a woollen merchant. Henrietta, Bencraft's widow, appears not to be mentioned unless she is intended as one of 'the old women'.

both in tune and in time; and to deliver his relations with politeness and consistency. For these reasons, and because I am apprehensive you may not yield a due attention to my advice, I could wish your *able judges* would *once*, at least, become your *faithful friends*; and prevail on you neither to sing any more songs to the public, nor to give any more relations of things in letters which may be given to them…

…My reasons for coinciding with you in opinion respecting your purposes, are that they seem expressly designed to delude the town with sing-song, Coronation, and Pantomime; at once to corrupt the public taste and pervert the true ends of theatrical exhibitions…" [136]

Tate Wilkinson makes a very telling defence of Beard's predicament, and one that he should have perhaps put into print himself, when he writes:

"… As to Gentlemen writers of genius being excluded from having their works produced, I cannot think the injustice alleged is by any means founded on truth or equity; for I never can believe, even tho' many good plays were to be sunk in oblivion, but that some of them would again visit the world in print, to gratify the author's pride and reputation, and by such means prove how indifferent managers were to merit.   …I cannot think any projector existing would be at great expense to produce a piece that creates confusion in the theatre, damnation to the author, and if persisted in, he excludes the possibility of crowded houses, besides being well abused in every public print in the bargain." [137]

BEARD AS MANAGER: PART 3, 1766 – 1767

On a happier note, we can learn a good deal about the efficient way that Beard handled the theatre's finances in 1766-7, as The *Account Book* for that season fortuitously survives. [138] As the editors of 'The London Stage' succinctly put it: "During Rich's time a regular sum was deducted nightly for the Rich account (£6 in 1760-61) and in addition he withdrew large sums (up to £800) on many occasions. No such deductions or withdrawals appear in this last season of Beard's management". [139] Beard appears to have been as scrupulously honest with the Rich consortium's money as he was careful of their property rights at the time of the riot. He was conscientious and careful, but not skilled at handling volatile situations; preferring to trust to people's good nature or reasonableness. In the case of both Fitzpatrick and Shebbeare he misjudged the lengths to which these hotheads were prepared to go, in order to force their will on him.

The accounts reveal the day-to-day running of the theatre in all its complexity. For example, it cost £2 2s to get a new play licensed by the Lord Chamberlain. The payment to the local Watch (18th century police) was an annual £12 10s. The Scavenger's rate (18th century dustmen) was £2 1s 8d per half year, the Poor rate was £15 12s 6d per half year, and the Land Tax was £37 10s. Fresh water came from the New River at £10 15s 4d per half year.

---

[136] For the full text – see Appendix 4
[137] Tate Wilkinson, 'The Wandering Patentee', York 1795, vol. 4, pp. 126-7
[138] BM Add MS Egerton 2272
[139] 'The London Stage', Part 4, vol. 2, p. 1183

Various tradesmen presented regular bills. Candles and coal were of utmost importance in lighting and heating the house: '4 pounds of Spermeceti candles 7s'; 'paid Barratt (wax chandler) as per bill, £156'; 'paid Jones, coal merchant, £104 15s'. Mr Cooper, the printer, who produced the playbills, was paid regular amounts, ranging from £39 to £41 16s.

The fruit-sellers inside the theatre had to pay a regular amount for the privilege of plying their trade: 'from Condell for Fruit Rent, £20'. An interesting entry is the evidence that refreshments were available back-stage to the performers: 'Bill for wine at the Practises last season, £1 17s 1d'; 'Wardrobe Dinners, £3 5s 5d'.

Then there were the payments for props, costumes, and extra performers: '20 sets of clothing, £169 9s 1d'; 'Thompson for 2 wigs in *Dr Faustus*, £4 5s'; 'Samuel Norman for 4 Grand State Chairs, £63'; John Sutherland for playing bagpipes in *Midas*, 15s'; 'Isaac Wheatland for side drum in *The Female Archer*, 9s'; 'Mr Rayner for Bows and Arrows in M La Riviere's dance [*The Female Archer*], £1 2s'; 'Joseph Stevens, music porter, £1 16s'.

Not only did the theatre use the press to advertise their forthcoming attractions, but they were also prepared to pay for the insertion of promotional articles, as can be seen by the entry in the accounts for a 'Paragraph of the Pantomime in the *Ledger and Gazetteer*, 6s'. This was paid out on November 8 1766 to publicise the pantomime *Harlequin Dr Faustus* that was premiered on November 18.

Beard did not salt away a nightly amount as Rich had done, but instead he built up a handsome profit for the theatre. By January 1 1767 the accounts show a profitable balance of £5365 19s 4d for the operation of the season so far. This would prove to be a major asset when the theatre and its Patent were put up for sale a few months later.

But during his final year it is evident that he cut back on performing. The deafness which had afflicted him sporadically for the whole of his life was becoming worse. Possibly with an eye to his future retirement he began to offload some of his roles onto other performers. Between September and December he never performed more than seven times a month. Squibb took over the role of 'Chasseur Royal' in *The Royal Chace*; either Mattocks or Squibb took over his part in Purcell's 'Solemn Hymn' in *The Royal Convert*; and he did not give himself anything to sing or play in either of the autumn's main afterpieces *The Coronation* (a repeat of the 1761 hit) and the pantomime *Harlequin Dr Faustus*.

The first new all-sung mainpiece this season was an English translation of Niccolo Piccini's opera *La Buona Figliuola*. Entitled *The Accomplished Maid* this was premiered on December 3. Beard was not in the cast. Mattocks and Dibdin had the leading juvenile male roles; but it looks as though the part intended for Beard ('Sir John Lofty') was taken at the last moment by DuBellamy, a singer who had recently joined the company.[140] He was to prove useful as Mattocks was ill for a period this autumn. DuBellamy's debut in the role of 'Young Meadows' on November 12 1766 looks like a case of the understudy going on, since Mattocks was back in the cast the next time it was performed (January 21 1767). DuBellamy was

---

[140] DuBellamy joined the company with his wife, the actress Mrs DuBellamy, in November. His first role was in *Love in a Village* on November 12. Then he was in the cast of *Harlequin Dr Faustus*.

given certain other solo moments, such as the song in *The Conscious Lovers* on December 9 and Beard's part in the *Romeo and Juliet* music.

Beard restricted himself to his usual affable roles in *The Maid of the Mill, Love in a Village, Thomas and Sally,* and gave one performance a month of Macheath in *The Beggar's Opera*. But he was also busy with Shebbeare, and handling other more succesful authors. The first of the season's new plays was Arthur Murphy's new play *The School for Guardians*, which was premiered on January 10 1767. With this work Beard seems to have been moving in an original and interesting new direction, that would lead eventually to the glorious comedies of manners of Richard Brinsley Sheridan. Murphy's plot has some of the same ingredients as Sheridan's great plays *The Rivals* and *The School for Scandal*. It is loosely based on Moliere's *School for Wives*, although some hints are borrowed from earlier Restoration comedies like Wycherley's *The Country Wife* (of 1675). The second new mainpiece was by his close friend Thomas Hull, who was now entrusted with a full length play, after writing two earlier farces. Dibdin is not very complimentary about it:

"Hull, whose various merits as author, actor, and manager, have long been known to the public, produced *The Perplexities*; a comedy that deserved its title, for there never was so perplexed a plot... Beard sung, spoke, and with his usual philanthropy did everything else in his power to serve his friend".[141]

Beard gave the *Prologue* every night, and allowed it a run of nine nights so that Hull could make his full fee. Sylas Neville's diary entry for February 5 1767 reads: "saw the comedy of *The Perplexities*. Beard spoke the Prologue". But it appears that he both sang <u>and</u> spoke the text, as Dibdin implies. Shebbeare, in the preface to his pamphlet, quotes some lines from the Prologue, and also indicates that Beard sang them:

> "Wherefore, I thus entreat, with due submission,
> Between the Bard and me you'd make Decision.
> The whole now on your arbitration waits".

> *Prologue to the PERPLEXITIES, sung by Mr Beard* [142]

The full text[143] reveals, in fact, that Beard made a feature of his lack of experience at speaking verse, and humorously expressed a preference for singing:

> "I speak a Prologue! – what strange whim, I wonder
> Could lead the author into such a blunder? –
> I asked the man as much – but he (poor devil!)
> Fancied a manager might make you civil.
> "Garrick (says he) can with a prologue tame
> The critic's rage – Why can't you do the same?"
> Because (quoth I) the case is different quite;
> Garrick, you know, can prologues speak, and write;
> If like that Roscius I could write and speech it,
> I might command applause, and not beseech it.

---

[141] Charles Dibdin, 'A Complete History of the English Stage', London, 1797, vol. 5, p. 291
[142] J. Shebbeare, 'Letters which have passed between John Beard... and John Shebbeare', London 1767
[143] shown in Appendix 6

But, sure, for one who, all his live-long days
Has dealt in crochets, minims, and sol-fas,
A singer, to stand forth in wit's defence,
And plead 'gainst sound the solemn cause of sense;
Persuade an audience that a play has merit,
Without a single air to give it spirit;
'Tis so much out of character - so wrong -
No prologue, Sir, for me - unless in song.
....

And this is the way, Mr Author,
To trick a plain muse up with art,
In modish fal-lals you must clothe her,
And warm a cold critic's hard heart.
With a fal-lal-lal, etc.
Wherefore I thus entreat, with due submission,
Between the Bard and me you'd make decision.
....

The whole now on your arbitration we rest,
And prologues henceforward shall surely be drest
In what mode soever your taste shall like best –
Which none of us dare deny.
For, howe'er cruel critics and wildings may sneer,
That at times, I alas! Somewhat dunny appear,
If to you, my best friends, I e'er turn my deaf ear,
May your indulgence deny.
Then for his sake and mine (for we're both in a fright)
Till a treat of more goût shall your palates delight,
Let a poor humble comedy please you tonight;
Which surely you will not deny.

One can imagine that Beard sang the text in italics to some well-known refrain. It is also interesting to see him referring to his deafness as publicly as he does here. Shebbeare used it to cruel effect in his final letter published one month later in the March edition of the *Gentleman's Magazine*. Perhaps it was this very admission in the *Prologue* which drew his attention to the singer's infirmity.

Beard's final new addition to the repertoire was another pastiche opera with a text by Bickerstaffe: *Love in the City*. Dibdin had collaborated on this too, and had contributed two finales and a handful of songs. Fiske thinks that the libretto was Bickerstaffe's masterpiece, with an intriguing plot and "dialogue full of life". But in his estimation it was ahead of its time: "it was the originality of the setting that sunk the opera". It certainly sounds as though a large portion of the audience would have been delighted to see a world populated only by working-class Londoners, "the chief of them being a grocer and his son and daughter. The grocer's brother-in-law is in coal. Priscilla Tomboy, described as a Creole from Jamaica, has been placed in the Grocer's house to be educated, and she has a black servant, Quasheba, whom she treats with disdain".[144]

---

[144] Roger Fiske, 'English Theatre Music in the Eighteenth Century', Oxford, 1973, p. 336-7

But the audience in the Pit and Boxes wasn't so keen to see this class made the heroes of a mainpiece, even though they had been accepting them (and worse) in *The Beggar's Opera* for forty years. A critical poem was printed in the Public Advertiser on March 5: [145]

To the Author of *Love in the City*

If e'er again thy Muse engage
To laugh at Folly on the Stage,
Let Cockneys 'scape the stroke
Since 'tis with Men of Sense a Rule
That of all Fools, the Bow-Bell Fool
Can least endure a Joke.

Benjamin Victor reports frankly that "this performance met with an unfavourable reception, the audience expecting better entertainment from the author of *The Maid of the Mill*."[146] To a modern eye the story looks extremely original - as well as adding the word 'Tomboy' to our language. Priscilla Tomboy is a high-spirited character. In Dibdin's Act 2 Finale she even gets involve in a street fight - for which he wrote music that he later referred to as 'The Boxing Trio'. After a paltry four performances, in which Bickerstaffe only took the receipts of the third night (£68 18s) the piece was taken off. It had a later existence in a shortened version - *The Romp* - which was played as an afterpiece. From 1785 onwards this version became popular whenever Priscilla Tomboy was played by Mrs Jordan. Bickerstaffe learned the hard way that the current Covent Garden audience preferred to see civilised Gentry in their comic operas. He returned to that theme in his next collaboration with Dibdin. This was *Lionel and Clarissa* - a work which Beard had commissioned some years previously, but which wasn't finished before he sold the Theatre. It was premiered on February 25 1768, and was one of the first successes for the theatre's new management.

For several years it appears that Beard did not take a Benefit Night whilst he was acting as Manager. There is no evidence in the playbills that he took one in the spring of 1763, 1764 or 1765. But in his last year of management he took two. He must have foreseen that his retirement was looming. On December 1 1766 he was given the privilege of a 'clear' benefit, at which he was able to take the entire proceeds, without any deductions for the night's charges. This means that the Theatre actually gave him a £64 5s bonus, as this sum represented the day-to-day running costs that it was obliged to pay out. The amount which his performance in *The Maid of the Mill* cleared was £234 14s 6d - one of the highest sums he had ever taken on a Benefit Night. His second Benefit Night came in the Spring benefit season of 1767, and was the first of the Covent Garden series. For once, and once only, he took precedence ahead of the 'straight' actors Woodward, Shuter, Smith and Ross. The total taken at the box office was even higher that night: £262 17s. Maybe word had got around that it was his last ever Benefit Night, and all his fans turned out. The theatre must have been incredibly full to have taken such a sum. Pedicord has estimated that the theatre could not have held more than 1,335 people

---

[145] quoted in 'The London Stage', Part 4, vol. 2, p. 1224
[146] B. Victor, 'The History of the Theatres of London', 1771

when it was first built, and that it had not been enlarged at this time.[147] Other estimates, such as the one in the 'Survey of London', put the total capacity at about 1,400.[148] At full capacity the box-office return would have been c.£200. Beard's total, being £62 17s higher than that, is an incredible achievement. But because he reverted to having the usual charges of £64 5s deducted, his total take-home pay this time was £198 12s.

Beard continued to perform about seven times a month in the new year. Speaking, or singing the Prologue to Hull's *The Perplexities* added another nine not very demanding nights. But he extricated himself from some of the Oratorio season this year. Vernon was the tenor in Handel's *Esther* on March 6 and may have taken part in others, such as *Israel in Egypt* on March 13 and *Deborah* on March 11. Without any programmes to confirm or refute it, we must assume that this was the last season in which Beard sang *Samson* (March 18), *Judas Maccabaeus* (March 20 & April 1), and *Messiah* (April 8 & 10). He did not sing the *Messiah* at the Foundling Hospital on April 29, and it seems likely that his cancellation was at short notice, as his part had to be hurriedly divided between the other performers.

At the later Benefit Nights there was a scramble amongst the younger singers to try out some of the parts that they knew Beard was going to have to give up. The most valuable one, of course, was 'Macheath'. *The Beggar's Opera* was never out of the theatre's repertoire. Both Mattocks and Squibb did the role at their benefits; but next season it passed on to Mattocks, the more experienced of the two. Dibdin and DuBellamy both did the 'Sailor' in *Thomas and Sally* at their benefits; but this role passed on to DuBellamy next year. For this - and other - reasons Dibdin transferred to Drury Lane. Beard himself gave a last performance of his favourite roles at the end of the season. His last *Thomas and Sally* took place on April 20, followed by his last *Jovial Crew* on May 2. He joined in the fun of *Midas* one more time on May 11; and he finished his 33-year career with *The Maid of the Mill* on May 15; *The Beggar's Opera* on May 16 [149]; and *Love in a Village* on May 23. This amazing run of performances at the very end of the season makes one wonder just how bad his hearing had grown. One can understand that he was running his career down throughout the 1766-7 season; but he was obviously determined to make it through to the very end. The comments of his loyal following[150] never make any reference to failing powers:

> In all his songs the admirable BEARD
> Is fully understood as well as heard;
> To vitiated taste he gives offence,
> By making sound an echo to the sense.
> Continue, BEARD, the knowing few to please,
> Who all applaud your elegance and ease.[151]

---

[147] Harry W. Pedicord, 'The Theatrical Public in the time of Garrick', New York, 1954, p. 5
The 'London Stage' Pt 4 gives a different estimate, and suggests that the Boxes could hold 729, the Pit 357, the 1st Gallery 700, and the 2nd Gallery 384 = 2170. Their estimate for a sell-out is a box-office return of £320.
[148] Survey of London, vol. xxxv, The Athlone Press, University of London, G.L.C. 1970, p. 75
[149] This was the auspicious occasion when a *pianoforte* was first played in a performance at Covent Garden
[150] See also the poem "Dear good Sir, be serious and give us reason" on page 372
[151] 'The Rational Rosciad' by F- B- L- , London 1767, p. 32

After his retirement other writers praised his performance in these terms:

- "Baker does Beard's part in *Midas*. His not acting is a great loss to the public, as he was inimitable in some things".[152]
- "Went to see *The Maid of the Mill* played for the first time at Drury Lane. Bannister is the best Giles I have seen since Beard left the stage".[153]
- "Giles (in *The Maid of the Mill*) is an extreme well-drawn rural character, and Mr Beard did that honest, unaffected simplicity which distinguishes him, particular justice. His humour was natural, forcible, and intelligible. The farmer has never been quite himself since that very excellent singing actor left the stage".[154]
- "Mr Beard was, as a vocal performer, the best actor of songs I ever remember."[155]
- "Of Hawthorn in *Love in a Village*, we may say that he died with [the departure of] that truly intelligent English singer".[156]
- "Beard was a singer of great excellence. His voice was sound, male, powerful and extensive. His tones were natural and he had flexibility enough to execute any passages however difficult, which task indeed frequently fell to his lot in some of Handel's Oratorios. But, with these qualifications: where the feelings were most roused, he was, of course, the most excellent. If he failed at all it was in acquired taste, which I will venture to pronounce was a most fortunate circumstance for him; for I never knew an instance where acquired taste did not destroy natural expression; a quality self-evidently as much preferable to the other as nature is to art. Oh there be singers that I have listened to, and heard others applaud, aye, and encore too, that have so soared, so sunk, and so cantabileed, that one would have thought some Ventriloquist had made singers, and not made them well, they imitated braying so abominably. Beard was the reverse of this: besides, he was very valuable as an actor. In *The Jovial Crew*, *Love in a Village*, *Comus*, and *Artaxerxes*, he gave proof of this in a degree scarcely inferior to anybody... Beard was at home everywhere."[157]

Beard's last performance was as 'Hawthorn' in *Love in a Village*, and we can see him caught for ever in that flamboyant role in Zoffany's painting [see p. 223]. Subsequent prints that were produced from it extracted the single character of Beard. There is one thing remarkable about the picture that has not yet been mentioned. At his feet there is a dog. This was a real dog called Phillis. The story is delightful, and speaks volumes about Beard. If animals liked him - and there is evidence that he kept several cats - then there are many who will say that there must have been something special about him. For animals do not make mistakes.

"On the morning of the first rehearsal of *Love in a Village*, as Beard, who had been studying the part of 'Hawthorn' entered Covent Garden Theatre, he was followed by

---

[152] Silas Neville's m/s Diary entry for November 27th 1767
[153] Silas Neville's m/s Diary entry for March 31st 1769
[154] Francis Gentleman, 'The Dramatic Censor', York, 1770, vol. 2, p. 117
[155] Tate Wilkinson, 'Memoir of his own life', York, 1790, vol. IV, pp. 149-50
[156] Francis Gentleman, 'The Dramatic Censor', York, 1770, vol. 2, p. 169
[157] C. Dibdin, 'A Complete History of the English Stage', London, 1797, vol. 5, p. 362ff

a pretty little stray female spaniel, which so fondly attached herself to him, that instead of driving her from his heels, he retained her, and made her his characteristic attendant in that opera. Her new master grew very fond of her, and kept her a long while; and when she died, she was lamented not only by Beard himself, but by all the members of the Beef-Steak Club, of which that celebrated singer was one. At one of their meetings the winning qualities of the deceased companion of 'Hawthorn' happening to become the theme of conversation, it was agreed that each member should try his hand at an epitaph for their former favourite. Among those produced was the following, written by the ingenious and esteemed John Walton, author of the well-known Ballad of *Ned and Nell*, and other admired poetical pieces:

Epitaph on Phillis

Beneath this turf a female lies,
That once the boast of fame was;
Have patience, reader, if thou'rt wise:
You'll then learn what her name was.

In days of youth, (be censure blind),
To men she would be creeping;
When 'mongst the many, one prov'd kind,
And took her into keeping.

Then to the Stage she bent her way,
Where none applauded more was;
She gained new lovers every day,
But constant still to one was.

By players, poets, Peers, addressed,
Nor bribe nor flatt'ry moved her;
And though by all the men caressed,
Yet all the women loved her.

Some kind remembrance then bestow
Upon the peaceful sleeper;
Her name was *Phillis* you must know,
And *Hawthorn* was her keeper!"[158]

The rehearsals for *Love in a Village* must have started in November 1762, as the first night was on December 8. It would be good to know whether Phillis was still in the cast with Beard on May 23 1767 when he took his final bow. There may be a diary entry somewhere that will tell us more; but as yet I have not been able to trace any.

It is usually recommended to actors that they should never act with children or animals. Beard managed to cope with the situation with his customary dignity. If Zoffany's painting is to be believed, Phillis looks very well-behaved indeed.

---

[158] Thomas Busby, 'Concert Room and Orchestra Anecdotes', 1825, vol. 3, p. 159. Another copy of this poem is to be found in 'Anne Mathew's Commonplace Book', m/s M.a.144, p. 71 in the Folger Shakespeare Library, Washington, USA, where it is attributed to Dr William Kenrick

"The Miller of Dee" sung by Beard in "Love in a Village"

CHAPTER 12
THE PROFESSIONAL LIFE OF AN ACTOR

CONTRACTS

Beard's first contract at a London theatre was a three-year contract with Charles Fleetwood, at Drury Lane in 1737. We know this, because - many years later - when Beard was encouraging the young Charles Dibdin at the beginning of his career, he suggested that he would take him on for three years at an increasing yearly salary, and: "…if I approved it, order an article to be prepared for three, four, and five pounds a week [*i.e. increasing annually*], which, he assured me, were the terms on which he commenced his own career".[1]

For the way that such an 'article' (or contract) would have been worded we can refer to an agreement drawn up at the same theatre, some years later, by David Garrick:

Agreement with Mrs Abington. May 5th, 1774

"It is agreed this day between Mrs Abington and Mr Garrick, that the former shall be engaged to him and Mr Lacy patentees of the Theatre Royal in Drury Lane for three years from this date, or three acting seasons, at the sum of twelve pounds a week with a Benefit, and sixty pounds for clothes."

Fees had gone up in the interim and Mrs Abington's £12 per week represents what was offered to one of the top artists of her day: - she was fourth in the artistic 'pecking order' at Drury Lane. Some fourteen years earlier Tate Wilkinson recalled in his 'Memoirs of his own Life' that John Rich had offered him £6 per week for 3 years, and a Benefit, at Covent Garden in 1761, and that he had turned it down. Beard was on the Covent Garden books at this time, and we can see from the Theatre Accounts for 1760-1 (BM Egerton ms 2271) that he was earning £7 per week as that theatre's seventh highest earner.[2]

For another example of a contract, of the sort that Beard himself would be drawing up with playwrights and composers in his managerial years, the following document survives from Garrick's time at Drury Lane. Beard's own agreement with Isaac Bickerstaffe (now preserved at the Folger Shakespeare Library) is very similar, and can be consulted in Chapter 11, p. 213.

Memorandum 22nd August 1766 [3]

"It is agreed between David Garrick Esq. and Mr Michael Arne that Mr Arne shall compose the music of a new Dramatic Entertainment called *Cymon*, and as compensation for ye same shall be intitled to and receive one third part of the profits of the first three nights[4] which the author shall take for his own Benefits."

---

[1] Charles Dibdin, 'The Professional Life of Charles Dibdin', vol. 1, 1803, p.46
[2] Miss Macklin was earning £1 13s 4d per day; Sparks & Smith £1 8s per day; Mrs Ward £1 6s 8d; Shuter & Ross £1 6s 6d. Beard was 7th in the pecking order with £1 3s 4d x 6 days = £7. London Stage, Part 4, pp 815-6
[3] W. b. 481; Folger Shakespeare Library, Washington, USA
[4] usually the 3rd, 6th, & 9th

BEARD'S SALARY AT THE THEATRE

For his first 9 days performances at Covent Garden in 1746 Beard was paid £7 10s.[5] At a daily rate of 16s 8d this means that his weekly wage had not risen above the £5 that he had been receiving at Drury Lane in 1740. His Benefit night still brought him in a colossal amount which virtually doubled his year's salary. On the 26th March 1747 he received £94 15s from sales at the door, and £102 9s from tickets sold in advance. Out of this total of £197 4s he had to pay the house-charges of £60 (see *House Charges* p. 264 for an explanation of these) which left him with a profit of £137 4s.

His later weekly earnings are well set out in the 1760 Covent Garden accounts. In addition to his annual salary of £150 as manager of the theatre, he was receiving £210 as the highest-paid singer, which was equivalent to £7 per week or £1 3s 4d per day. This was the highest that his regular wages would ever rise. He was not the highest paid performer at Covent Garden, however, as several actors and actresses commanded higher sums. Ross, Sparks, Shuter and Smith were all on £250 per annum; and Miss Macklin received £300 per annum.

Thus we can see that he began his career as a contracted artist in 1737 with a weekly salary of £3, rising to £5 by 1739. It remained at this level until his 11-year contract with Garrick, which commenced in 1748, when it may well have risen to £6. For the whole of his last period at Covent Garden he was on £7 a week, and - with the exception of the 1766-7 season, did not take a Benefit during his managerial years of 1763-5.

STOPPAGES OF PAY

An artist's pay could be 'stopped' for various reasons, ranging from misdemeanours like missing rehearsals, or refusing to play a role (which carried known fines), to deductions as a result of the theatres being closed. Beard, and all of his Covent Garden colleagues, suffered in 1761 when John Rich deducted nineteen nights of salary from their earnings because of the theatre-closure forced on them by King George II's death. Out of his annual salary of £210 he had £22 5s 9d 'stopped'.

Mrs Clive complained to Garrick in a petulant letter of 1765 about the 'stoppages' in her pay. It appears that 2 guineas were deducted for missing several rehearsals and refusing to play one of her regular roles when called upon to do so:

October 14th, 1765 "You gave Mrs Cibber £600 for playing sixty nights, and £300 to me for playing a hundred and eighty, out of which I can make it appear it cost me £100 in necessaries for the stage; sure you need not want to take anything from it. ...In regard to the affair of *The Devil to Pay*, I sent my compliments to the managers by the Prompter, at the beginning of the season, to beg that it might not be done till the weather was cool, as the quickness of the shift [quick-change] puts me into a flurry, which gives me a violent swimming in my head."[6]

These stoppages are sometimes referred to as 'forfeits' and can occasionally be found itemised in the theatre accounts.[7] Most of the amounts deducted were on a sliding scale, dependent on the artist's salary. For missing a rehearsal, after being

---

[5] 'The London Stage', Part 3, p. 1299

[6] Garrick 'Letters', pp. 203-4

[7] In the Season 1776-7 Covent Garden's total of 'forfeits' was £12 14s. 8d. London Stage, Part 5, p. cii

properly summoned to it, the lowest earners would forfeit 6d. for each scene, or 2s. if they were absent for a whole rehearsal. Refusal to accept a part, or to play a part that was also in the person's repertoire (as with Mrs Clive, above) exacted a larger sum. For Mrs Clive it may have been 2 guineas; but later in the century it rose to £5, and finally, in 1798, to £30.[8] Other misdemeanours that carried 'forfeits' were wilful absence from the theatre on a performing day, and feigning illness.

CONCERT FEES

It is impossible to tell how much Beard earned for his performances with Handel. He is not mentioned in Handel's bank account when, on May 4 1745, £210 was paid to Miss Robinson and £400 to Sig. Francesina.[9] There had been 16 performances in all during the season. If these amounts represent the total that Handel owed these singers, and if they had sung on every night, then they would have earned about 12 guineas and 24 guineas respectively per performance. One other contemporary guide to the amounts that were being paid to Beard's colleagues can be found in the Foundling Hospital accounts for the 1754 and 1758 *Messiah* performances. The fees for these performances ranged from Frasi's 6 guineas and Miss Frederick's 4 guineas, to Wass' and Champness' half fee of 1½ guineas each for sharing the bass arias. This financial picture is somewhat complicated by the fact that in 1751, when Beard first sang at the Foundling Hospital, he returned 2 guineas to the charity.[10] In subsequent years he always took no fee.

So we must assume that he could have earned as much as Miss Robinson's 12 guinea fee in 1745, or taken as little as the 2 guineas that he handed back in 1751. But that sum is more likely to represent only a proportion of what he had earned. His normal fee could well have been in the 6 guinea area that Frasi could command. At that period Beard's reputation was as great as Frasi's: - they visited The Three Choirs Festival together in 1757, when she was paid 50 guineas and they ran up joint expenses of £46 5s 9d.[11] If her 50 guinea payment included Beard's fee as well, then they would have both earned 25 guineas; - which seems more in line with what one might expect them to earn from a series of 3 prestigious concerts. This would have given them around 8 guineas a concert.

The Harris family baulked at paying Frasi 40 guineas to sing at their Salisbury Festival in 1757, and obtained Catherine Fourmantel for far less.[12] How much less is not known; but William Hayes thought that he could acquire good soloists for around 5 guineas a performance (plus accommodation at a good inn), when he was involved with the oratorio performances at Church-Langton in this period.[13]

If Beard could command between 6 and 8 guineas, then in 1745 he would have earned little more than half of what we know that Miss Robinson was paid. Can we deduce from this that Handel's female soloists were more of a draw, and could therefore command higher fees? If the comments in contemporary diaries and letters are anything to go by, this was certainly the case. One can look in vain for

[8] London Stage, Part 5, p. cii
[9] on 4th & 11th May 1745. Deutsch *Handel a Documentary Biography* p. 618-9
[10] 1st May 1751 "Mr Smith had returned him, for the benefit of the Charity, two guineas returned by Mr Beard" Burrows *Handel's performances of 'Messiah': the evidence of the conducting score* ML 56 p.330
[11] Anthony Boden *Three Choirs: A History of the Festival*, Alan Sutton 1992, p. 28
[12] Burrows & Dunhill, 'Music and Theatre in Handel's World', Oxford, 2002, p. 326
[13] William Hayes, 'Anecdotes of the Five Musick-Meetings ...at Church-Langton", Oxford, 1768

reports of Beard's singing - even of title roles - but frequently find reports like this: "I was yesterday to hear *Semele*; it is a delightful piece of music. Francesina is extremely improved, her notes more distinct, and there is something in her running-divisions that is quite surprizing."[14] And again: "On Tuesday last I went to hear *Deborah* performed... We have a woman here, a Mrs Storer, who has a very sweet and clear voice... Dubourg manages her so well in his manner of accompanying her, as to make her singing very agreeable."[15]

If only Mrs Delany had written about Beard in this manner we should have had at least one contemporary account of what he sounded like at this stage of his career. He was nearly thirty and at the height of his powers. It is a great shame that both she, the Earls of Egmont, Radnor and Shaftesbury, and members of the Harris circle only ever mentioned him in their letters when he was below par.

ETIQUETTE AT ORATORIO PERFORMANCES

Sir John Hawkins gives us a clear idea of what the usual concert dress was for performances of oratorios, when he states that the advantages of these performances in the theatre were that "no costly scenery was required, nor dresses for the performers, other than a suit of black, with which all persons that appeared in public were supposed to be provided." He then goes on to say that he is surprised that "neither the singers in the oratorio, nor their hearers, make any distinction in their dress between Lent and a season of festivity".[16]

At the earliest oratorio performances that Handel gave in London, in 1732, this custom had already been established. The anonymous writer of "*See and seem blind*" writes of "Senesino, Strada, Bertolli and Turner Robinson in their own habits".[17] By the time that Beard joined them on the concert platform in his first London oratorios (*Esther*, March 1735) the custom had presumably become one of wearing formal clothes that were black in colour. This has more or less remained a constant feature of oratorio performances for male singers down to our own day. According to The European Magazine 'the chorus singers paid that attention to their attire that rendered the stage respectable'.[18]

The lay-out of the theatre at oratorio performances remained constant throughout the eighteenth century. The arrangement of the musicians at the 1727 Coronation in a tiered formation was the original inspiration for the tiered structure that was built for Covent Garden, and which can be seen in pictures of the auditorium arranged for oratorios.[19] The position of the soloists right down at the front, behind a low enclosing wall, is also clearly shown.

In order to improve the acoustics further it appears that the theatre's wing-space was sometimes closed off, leaving the performing area more akin to a box with three sides. That may be what is implied by the description in a newspaper report that "the wings to the side scenes are removed for a complete screen".[20] Although the habit of taking curtain calls was not yet truly established, there are reports - such as this one - of some important people coming to the front of the stage

---

[14] Mrs Delany, February 11th 1743, quoted in Deutsch *Handel a Documentary Biography* p. 582

[15] Mrs Delany, January 25th 1746, quoted in Deutsch *Handel a Documentary Biography* p. 629

[16] John Hawkins, 'History of the Science and Practice of Music', Book 20, chapter CXCIII, (p.889)

[17] Deutsch, op. cit. p. 301

[18] *The European Magazine*, March 1794, p. 236

[19] Survey of London, vol. xxxv, University of London, GLC, 1970, plate 47a

[20] *The Thespian Magazine*, March 1794, p. 127

to acknowledge the applause. William Coxe writes of the blind Handel that "...It was a most affecting spectacle to see the venerable musician, whose efforts has charmed the ear of a discerning public, led by the hand to the front of the stage, to make an obeisance of acknowledgment to his enraptured audience".[21]

ETIQUETTE IN THE THEATRE

Theatrical curtain-calls as we know them today did not begin to be a regular custom until Edmund Kean began the practice in 1818. In Beard's time applause was frequent and spontaneous throughout the entire dramatic performance. Applause would not only accompany single speeches, but also single lines. For a singer, this would mean that not only whole songs would be applauded (and often encored) but individual verses as well. These frequent bursts of admiration compensated for the absence of a final curtain call in the modern manner. Occasionally the playwright or composer (who would otherwise have remained unseen by the audience) would be called forward to take a bow. Didelot, the choreographer of a new Ballet, was "called forward and paid the tribute due to original and inventive talents" as reported by a newspaper of the time.[22]

Actors would have bowed frequently to the audience. At the beginning of each season the actor was applauded on his or her first appearance (as still happens in Pantomimes today when the star is a well-loved 'personality') "in return for which he makes his grateful obeisance".[23] The speakers of Prologues and Epilogues, and the person who announced a change of performer or the next day's play either bowed or curtsied. During his managerial days at Covent Garden Beard would have appeared before the public in this manner on many, varied, occasions.

[21] William Coxe, 'Anecdotes of G.F. Handel and J.C. Smith', London, 1799, p. 25
[22] The Morning Chronicle, June 3rd 1796
[23] The London Stage, Part 5, p. xciii

One can see him coming forward to address the audience in the print "Fitzgiggo" [see p. 234] with his tricorn hat in his hand, and already beginning to make his obeisance. James Boaden also reports that, at their final exit of the season, leading performers "made the three established curtsies (or bows) to the right and left sides of the house first, and then, in the front of the stage, to the general mass of the people".[24]

BENEFIT NIGHTS

As we have seen, an actor knew from his contract whether he had been granted a Benefit. These performances happened in a block, towards the end of the season, and were highly prized. The higher your ranking in the company (according to salary) the earlier your Benefit would be. As the earlier Benefits were more remunerative, there was plenty of jostling for dates among the high-earning stars. Some behaved in a very prima donna-ish manner, as can be learned from an exchange between Garrick and Mrs Frances Abington. As a result of this tempestuous lady's demand for a better day than the one she had originally chosen, Garrick was drawn into a legal wrangle with her. In a letter of March 1 1776 to his legal Counsel he outlined Mrs Abington's standing in his company:

> "Mrs Abington is engaged as a performer for the season at a salary and a Benefit night. Benefits are generally fixed according to the rank of the performer, and that rank is determined by the rate of salary. The highest salary has the first choice of day, and so on. Mrs Abington stands in the fourth rank of eminence; ..."

When Mrs Abington tried to change her Benefit to a different date Garrick replied:

> "I am directed by the Managers to acquaint you that, conformable to your choice of Saturday the 16th of March for your Benefit, that day was immediately allotted, and is kept for the purpose; and you will consequently name your play, that it may be got ready, and other matters prepared in proper time.
> It may be right to inform you that, in consequence of your choice of that day, all others have been settled and fixed for the other subsequent performers, and that there is no other day vacant till Easter."

As this looked like going all the way to Court to be settled, Garrick took legal advice. His Counsel's opinion was that "...if she declines a Benefit on that night, the managers may give a play on their own account, without any danger of being responsible to her for the profits.[25]

HOUSE CHARGES

The arrangement with the management for normal benefits was that the artist kept all of the box-office takings, after fixed deductions had been made. The amount varied over time, but was to cover all the expenses of mounting the show (heating and lighting being of the utmost importance) as well as paying the theatre's running

---

[24] James Boaden, 'Memoirs of the Life of John Philip Kemble', London, 1825, vol.2, p.194-5
[25] Garrick 'Letters', p. 140

costs (salaries for all of the staff, publicity in the daily bills and in the papers etc.) From 1747, when the first detailed figures are available at Drury Lane, Beard was paying charges of £60. By 1749 these had risen to £63; and that is the sum that Covent Garden deducted when he moved to that theatre in 1759. In order to lessen the charge it was possible for the artist to provide some of the articles that were on the list themselves. Thus, on March 24 1760 the Covent Garden accounts show that 'Beard found his own wax candles': and was presumably not charged for using the ones normally provided by the theatre.

On this particular night Beard brought in a huge amount at the box office. His normal 'take' at Drury Lane had been around £200; but Covent Garden was a bigger theatre with a bigger potential 'gross'. Tate Wilkinson states that "...In 1750, two hundred pounds before the curtain, at Covent Garden, was judged an amazing sum...."[26] At his 1760 Benefit Beard grossed £375 1s. After deduction of the £63 charges that still left him with his biggest ever total of £312 1s. The figures for all of his other Benefit nights (where the accounts survive) can be found in Appendix 2.

There were various ways of endeavouring to get a good 'house' and Beard seems to have been consistently successful throughout his career. Getting a good date was risky, as external matters might affect the audience's willingness to attend. The day of a race-meeting could badly affect attendance, as could rival theatrical offerings - including the Italian Opera at the King's Theatre Haymarket. Saturday was considered a bad day to choose, as there were often Balls, Masquerades and private banquets which would take away the more elegant members of society.

Considerable time and expense was devoted to making a performer's friends and supporters aware of the artist's impending date. A notice in the newspaper was obligatory; but the drawn-out process of calling on potential members of the audience and selling tickets face to face was also an essential part of the process. Kitty Clive gives us a good insight into the workings of the theatre in her farce *The Rehearsal, or, Bays in Petticoats*. In Act 2 she makes fun of herself by having the prompter, Richard Cross, rush out from the wings to say to Mrs Hazard, who has arrived to see a rehearsal of her new play, "Madam, Mrs Clive has sent word that she can't possibly wait on you this morning [to rehearse] as she's obliged to go to some Ladies about her Benefit. But you may depend on her being very perfect, and ready to perform it whenever you please".

Beard went one better by taking his tickets to large numbers of potential buyers and wooing them in song. As he was frequently found singing at City dinners, and at gatherings of Masons (according to Charles Dibdin), he was able to do very good business there. He even managed to sell handfuls of tickets to rich Jewish merchants, who - on account of the location of their businesses in the City - were not regularly in the habit of going to the Covent Garden area for their recreation. Dibdin sets the scene by talking, first, of himself:

"It was in these societies [Masonics etc.] that I was introduced to make a Benefit, as it is called, but I never could buckle to handing about the tickets; though it was certainly, by no means, considered as a disreputable practice. There is a whimsical story told of different performers who were at a public dinner with their tickets in their pockets; and, as often as a song was sung, the tickets were handed round. Beard and Lowe being of the party, the rest, of course, had but very little custom.

[26] Tate Wilkinson, 'Memoirs of his own life', York, 1790, vol. 4, p.123-4

"Dere they come," said a Jew, " - that Shonny Beard and Tommy Lowe, to sell the ticket, and dey come here and sing the song and tell the story, and make dam fool themself."

To return to the story of the tickets, the toast was given, and the president vociferated, "Gentlemen, I knock down Mr Beard for a song". The song over, "Mr Beard," said a gentleman, "please to set me down for a box that will hold nine. There are two guineas and a half, and half a crown". "Thank you sir". "Mr Beard, I'll beg the favour of your toast". "Success to Trade, gentlemen!" "Who do you call upon, sir?" - "I call, sir, upon Mr Lowe, '*The Early Horn*', if you please, sir." "Bravo! When is your benefit fixed?" - "Here is a bill". "I thank you, sir". "Please give to me six box tickets, and change of a guinea and a half". In short, this traffic went regularly on, the articles falling, at every bidding, like a French auction."

Which ever approach the artist took to selling their tickets, the idea was to get as many as possible into the expensive boxes. When there was a danger that the boxes would not hold all of the anticipated audience who had either bought, or put their names down for these prime seats, the capacity was enlarged. At the beginning of Beard's career this was done by building an additional seating area on the stage itself. In 1740 his advertisements stated that 'Part of the Stage will be form'd into Side-Boxes'. In 1742 the comfort of these high payers was taken into further consideration with the statement that 'Servants will be allowed to keep places on the stage, which will be carefully inclosed to prevent the ladies from taking cold.' By 1747 things were getting even more elaborate when the advertisement pronounced that 'The amphitheatre used on the Stage at Benefits will be enclosed and divided into distinct Boxes, with a ceiling and illuminated.'

The other way that the artist could get more tickets sold at the highest price was to turn the pit area into an extension of the boxes themselves. There is some difference of opinion as to whether the front of the boxes could be physically detached, and thus enlarged. Apparently there is evidence in the Theatre Royal, Bristol, that this could be done.[27] The area thus cleared was railed off from the rest of the severe, backless, benches that remained in the pit, allowing more comfortable and spacious seating to be temporarily installed.

When this was going to be done the advertisements announced "Part of the Pit laid into the Boxes". The number of rows of the pit that were removed varied, and were normally itemised, as it was a matter of great pride to the artists. At their respective Benefits at Drury Lane in 1745 Garrick had 5 rows of the pit railed off and Peg Woffington had 6. At Beard's 1737 Benefit (on April 22) two rows of the Pit were laid into the Boxes. By 1760, when the custom of building seating on the stage was no longer regularly happening, it seems that the whole of the pit could be sold at Box prices. At Mrs Clive's farewell Benefit at Drury Lane in 1769 the whole of the Pit was laid into the Boxes, as Beard's had been in 1760 and 1761 when his advertisements announced 'Pit and Boxes laid together at 5s'.

---

[27] "Something analagous can be seen to this day at the Theatre Royal, Bristol, built in 1766, where the present main entrance to the stalls is down a few steps from the circle (the old box tier), a box front having been removed at some time or other". St Vincent Troubridge, 'The Benefit System in the British Theatre', The Society for Theatre Research, London, 1967, p. 150

A special kind of Benefit was reserved for eminent artists, and used sparingly. This was the 'clear' Benefit, and it was the supreme desideratum. As Troubridge says: "not only did it result in a substantial increase in gain to the beneficiary, but it was the hall-mark of stardom. Its attainment was achieved by a nice equation between the importance and drawing power of the leading player, his or her business capacity, and the astuteness of the manager against whom that capacity was pitted".[28] At a 'clear' Benefit the management did not deduct the nightly charges. Mrs Cibber normally only signed a contract that gave her a clear benefit; and Mrs Clive was mortified to have lost hers after an uninterrupted nine years, when she crept back into the Drury Lane fold after seceding to Covent Garden in the 1743 dispute between the actors and Charles Fleetwood. Beard was only granted one, clear of charges, in his very last season. But, as we can see that he refrained from taking any Benefit at all during the years 1763-5, his co-manager Priscilla Rich must have felt that the honour was well earned. His 'clear' Benefit took place at an unusual time of the year, on December 1 1766. An item in the Account Book for December 15 states: "Paid Mr Beard the total amount of the house on the 1st inst. As per agreement £234 14s 6d." The total receipts for that day are shown in the Account Book as £234 14s 6d.

At a Benefit the artist was entitled to choose the entire programme - subject to vetting by the management. Actors used the occasion to show off their very best roles in the main-piece; and they prevailed on their colleagues in the vocal and ballet departments to produce the best after-piece to go with it. It was a time for great originality, and one or other of the pieces could be new or highly original. Mrs Clive, Garrick and Thomas Hull (among others) used it as an opportunity to try out their own plays.[29] Charles Dibdin was encouraged by Beard to put on his first theatre piece - the serenata *The Shepherd's Artifice* - at his Benefit. William Havard sometimes used his Benefit to produce an Ode that he had persuaded a composer to set to music for him. Thus, on April 1 1756 Beard sang a 'New Anniversary Ode in Commemoration of Shakespeare', with music by Boyce, at Havard's Drury Lane Benefit. This had been inspired by a visit to Stratford, long before Garrick had thought of making such a visit. In a letter to Beard's wife Henrietta he wrote to say how moved he had been by visiting Shakespeare's grave, where he had penned these lines 'almost extempore':

> These lines I dedicate to Shakespeare's name
> Not to add lustre to his deathless Fame;
> But that I think, all Mankind who admire,
> Who honour, who feel the Muse's fire;
> Should to this darling Son of Nature bow,
> And pay that rev'rence which I offer now.[30]

Other actors sometimes chose to resurrect an old play at their Benefit, or one that had not been seen in the theatre for a long time. Mrs Hamilton chose a really old

---

[28] St Vincent Troubridge, 'The Benefit System in the British Theatre', The Society for Theatre Research, London, 1967, p. 21
[29] Mrs Clive's *The Rehearsal, or Bays in Petticoats* was first performed at her Benefit on March 15th 1750. Garrick's *Lethe* was first performed at Henry Giffard's Benefit on April 15th 1740. A revised version 'with a new scene by Garrick' was performed at Mrs Clive's Benefit on March 27th 1756. Hull began his series of new farces and plays at Covent Garden with *The Absent Man*, at his 1764 Benefit.
[30] William Havard, 'Jeu d'esprit', N. a. 2, Folger Shakespeare Library, Washington, USA

piece *The Villagers* in 1756. It was a lucky choice, since John Beard - one of the cast that night - remembered it some years later as a suitable piece for Isaac Bickerstaff to adapt. The resulting *Love in a Village* was one of the great successes of Beard's time as a Manager.

It was also possible for lesser actors to use the Benefit night as a glorified audition, by taking on roles that would normally be the preserve of others. In Beard's case the role which he 'possessed' in the theatre, and which was his most valuable asset, was Macheath in *The Beggar's Opera*. He played it four times as the main-piece at his Benefits: in 1738, 1743, 1745 & 1760. During his career many other actors attempted the part at their own Benefits; and there was a race on as soon as it was known that Beard was to retire from the stage. At the 1767 Benefit Season two of his colleagues tried out the role (Mattocks and Squibb), and one of them proved up to the job and inherited it at Covent Garden (Mattocks). Other favourite main-pieces that Beard chose for his Benefits were Milton's *Comus* (with music by Arne), which was performed in 1742 and 1747; and the new ballad operas for which he was responsible: *The Maid of the Mill* (1766) and *Love in a Village* (1767). During his years at Drury Lane with Garrick he refrained from appearing in the main-piece. This was an astute move, as he was able to persuade Garrick himself to perform his very best roles for him in the main-pieces on 10 occasions between 1750 and 1759. Beard himself then performed one of his good roles in the after-piece, such as *The Chaplet* or *The Devil to Pay*; or else performed his best songs and cantatas in the intervals.

There was also scope for some party-pieces and humorous items. Comic actors such as Samuel Foote, Henry Woodward and Ned Shuter had a large stock of 'music-hall' turns that were enormously popular[31]. (Music Hall acts would eventually grow out of these into an art form of their own, and into theatres of their own, in the next century.) Beard had a few similar tricks up his sleeve, and was known for his naval songs in costume. 1740 was the first year that he performed 'A Song in the Character of a Sea-Captain of an English Man-of-War upon the taking of Porto Bello' at his Benefit. In 1745 the Prince and Princess of Wales and Prince George (later King George III) saw the 'Song made on the famous Sea-fight at La Hogue, sung by Beard in the character of a sailor'. At the 1755 Benefit there was '*Rule Britannia* and *Britons Strike Home* sung in character by Beard, accompanied with a chorus' in between the acts. In 1761 and 1762 Garrick helped Beard, even though he had transferred to the rival theatre, by providing a '*Medley Epilogue*, written by Garrick to be sung by Beard' for his Benefit night's entertainment.

REHEARSALS

From Mrs Clive's farce *The Rehearsal, or Bays in Petticoats* we learn many intriguing details about how rehearsals in the theatre operated during Beard's career. In the first scene, when 'Mrs Hazard' is getting ready to attend the rehearsal of her play, her admirer 'Witling' says: "Why, 'tis almost ten". A few pages later her servant 'Tom' enters to say: "Madam, your Chair has been waiting a great while; 'tis after ten, above half an hour." On arrival at the theatre 'Mrs Hazard' asks the

---

[31] On March 26th 1761 Shuter performed his comic version of *The Cries of London*, followed by 'the Origin, Nature and Progress of the Order of British Bucks, with the whimsical behaviour of Choice Spirits, and Mons. Thurot's Trip to Carrickfergus'. On March 25th 1756 he had performed 'Hippisley's Drunken Man'.

prompter: "But pray, Mr Cross, get everybody ready; is the music [i.e. *the orchestra*] come?" Cross, playing himself as the prompter, answers: "Yes, Madam, the music has been here this half hour... Mr Beard and Miss Thomas are gone to dress" - from which we can deduce that the morning rehearsals started at 10am. But this rehearsal was also going to be the final rehearsal, with the actors, like Beard and Miss Thomas, in costume, as is made apparent a few lines later. Mrs Hazard, answering the question "When does your farce come out" [i.e. *open*] answers: "Why, some time next week; this is to be the last rehearsal: and the managers have promised they shall all be dressed [in costume], that we may see exactly what effect it will have."[32]

Later in the century the situation remained very much the same, when Susannah Burney attended an opera rehearsal with her father Charles Burney (either a 'pre-dress rehearsal' or a 'stage and orchestra' rehearsal) in order to catch a glimpse of the castrato who had currently taken her fancy. In the following extract from her letter we can see that: a) the theatre was not heated during morning rehearsals; b) the performers were able to 'mark' their roles (i.e. save their voices by not singing out fully - just as happens these days); c) they could pass easily between the stage area and the pit, in order to greet friends who had been admitted; d) the leader of the orchestra was in charge of the music, and fulfilled the role taken, these days, by the conductor.

"We went into the pit, where there were two or three people. ...All the singers acted as *maestro* during their own songs. ...Madame Le Brun's husband [the oboist Ludwig August Lebrun], who looks a conceited fop, gave the time etc. when she sung. ...In the second act Pacchierotti sings a song of Handel's, "Return, oh God of Hosts" from *Samson*. It is, in its solemn and antique style a fine song. Pacchierotti expressed it like an angel, but, keeping himself I trust in reserve for the time of public performance, was too chaste, and too *retenue*, a fault of which he is indeed not often guilty. ...However, he sung so much *a sotto voce* that it was not very easy to form a judgement concerning him in it. He has a pretty rondeau in the last act, which he likewise whispered. At first we had seated ourselves in a very obscure part of the pit, but when Pacchierotti began his cavatina ...we moved nearer the orchestra. By this means Mr Burney [her father] was soon espied by many who knew him in the band. Cramer [the leader] bowed in the most respectful polite manner. ...He is so mild, so gentlemanlike in his manner of speaking to the band, that it is evident he quite suffers when anything goes wrong. The wind instruments were all out of tune. ...At last he called out in ...his foreign accent, "Gentlemen - you are not in tune at all!" "It's a very sharp morning, sir," said one of them. "We shall do better another time." ...Pacchierotti, whose song was then playing, then went and whispered something to Cramer, who in consequence of it, called to the bassoon player by his name, and desired he would omit playing that passage. "Yes, sir, to be sure I will," cried the dolt. ...We had approached the orchestra very gently during Pacchierotti's cavatina; presently after it the weather was so cold that he gave two or three jumps to warm himself. During this ...he caught our eyes, and almost while he was yet *en l'air* took off his hat, laughing and bowing. "Il fait froid," said he, to excuse his exhibition I suppose; "très froid en verité". As soon as the duet which ends the act was over ...I missed Pacchierotti on the stage, and presently heard his voice behind me. "How does Miss Burney do?" said he... ...In this pretty manner did he sit with us

[32] Mrs C. Clive, 'The Rehearsal, or Bays in Petticoats', London, 1753, p. 12

till recalled to the stage to sing, and indeed the time he spent with us was more agreeably passed by me than any other during which he was not singing. ...There will be another rehearsal Monday, but though we may go to it free gratis, for nothing at all, our dear fastidious sister thinks it not worth while to come to it."[33]

Charles Dibdin gives us another insight into the workings of the theatre when he describes the first rehearsal of a new ballad opera at Covent Garden in his novel "The Younger Brother". It is a colourful depiction, sketched with lively sarcasm, in which he describes people he knew well, such as the manager and patentee, the *prima donna* (possibly Charlotte Pinto, *née* Brent), and a foreign orchestral leader (Karl Friedrich Baumgarten, the first violinist). Beard - unlike the manager shown here (who is most likely to be his successor George Colman) - had given Dibdin plenty of encouragement as an author and composer in his early days[34], and mounted a performance of his first theatre-piece, *The Shepherd's Artifice*, in May 1764. The information that this passage conveys is helpful to an understanding of the everyday life of a performer, however, and shows that rehearsals took place in parts of the theatre other than on the stage itself. The scenario in this extract progresses from a rehearsal room to 'the music room' or orchestral rehearsal room, which was situated in the basement at Covent Garden.

"A morning for the first rehearsal was appointed. The day came, the words were read, during which some of the actors ...yawned at particular passages. These were afterwards to be objected against by the manager, which Charles [the author] anticipated, by taking him aside, and telling him ...that every passage at which the performers had so ill acted the part of yawners should remain, without the smallest alteration. ...The patentee was certainly nettled enough at this spirited conduct of our hero. He however thought proper to suppress what he felt, and they proceeded to the music room, where everything was ready for a repetition of the music. ...He was, however, as badly off, for he found the principal singer in high words with the manager, because the puppy of a composer had truly thought proper to restrict her in her cadences. What did he mean by such insolence? Had anybody ever attempted to point out to a mistress of her profession any limits to her cadenza?

"Madam," said Charles, "...those who sing for me shall sing what I have written, and nothing else. It is my music, and not yours, I choose to give to the world. ...Singing is become a vehicle to convey everything that is extraordinary, and nothing that is pleasing."

The manager made some trifling apology, and desired the repetition might begin. Many of the songs were now performed, to every one of which its respective singer was suffered to make some ignorant objection. At length they came to a sort of bravura song, in the midst of which the leader of the band laid down his fiddle, with an exclamation of "Oh my Gad, my Gad! I vome play dis". "What is the matter now?" said the manager. "Sir," cried the enraged fiddler, "it is no good, no raight, no arminny." He then proceeded to a string of reasoning, which, as it was unintelligible to every hearer, so it must be of course to every reader..."[35]

---

[33] Oliver Strunk, 'Source Readings in Music History', London, 1981, pp. 1000-4

[34] "This propensity Beard very kindly encouraged; and, after he had seen some specimens of songs and other things which I had written and set to music, he advised me to try my hand at something for the stage..." Charles Dibdin, 'The Professional Life of Mr Dibdin', London, 1803, vol. 2, p. 29

[35] Charles Dibdin, 'The Younger Brother', London, 1793, pp. 126-30

Dibdin based this last incident on a real-life situation that had befallen him earlier in his career, when : "Simpson, the hautboy-player[36], and some other persons, persuaded Beard, that my music in *Love in the City* would discredit his theatre; and that, in particular, the overture and a song beginning "Ah! why, my dear" were written contrary to the rules of harmony."

Dibdin took the music to Arne, who "pronounced the whole business a scandalous attempt to ruin the reputation of a young man. ...In consequence of the Doctor's equitable and spirited decision, my music was restored, and performed with success."[37]

Another mention of rehearsals at Covent Garden in Beard's time reveals that new pieces were given a rehearsal period of at least two weeks. Tate Wilkinson makes this clear when, writing about the difficulties he encountered when trying to stage Samuel Foote's play *The Minor* at Covent Garden, he says "we, from various obstacles, could not get it decently done on the stage in less than a fortnight, as other pieces were preparing, such as Macklin's new comedy *The Married Libertine*, his *Love-a-la-Mode*; and Mr Beard and Miss Brent were rehearsing Dr Arne's new opera of *Thomas and Sally*."[38]

Beard and Miss Brent had also rehearsed for a fortnight in 1759, when they were preparing the revival of *The Beggar's Opera*, with new orchestrations by Arne. This opened on October 10, and the previous fortnight, from the beginning of the season, had been taken over entirely by rehearsals. Other plays received less time. With such a vast repertoire, and with no long runs yet occurring regularly, there would always be two or three rehearsals happening simultaneously in various rooms at the theatre. William Powell the prompter kept a complete record of the rehearsals at Drury Lane in the last years of the century. Theatrical practice had not changed much during this period, and Powell can give us a good idea of the customs in Beard's own time. For a new play by Richard Cumberland he noted full rehearsals took place on three days, and rehearsals with smaller groups of actors on a further six days. The rehearsals commenced on April 24, and the first performance was exactly a fortnight later on May 8.[39]

Powell's records show that, at Drury Lane in his day, up to four plays could be rehearsed during the morning period of 10am - 2pm. As might have been expected, he records two major rehearsals taking place simultaneously, one on stage, and another in the rehearsal room. After this the actors went to eat, and the stage was prepared for the evening performance. As the public was admitted at 5pm, and sometimes even earlier on special Benefit nights, or to ease the crowding at the entrances, there was only a turn-round period of three hours for the stage staff to prepare the scenery and props for the two evening shows. Sometimes these would not have been performed for many weeks. The front-of-house also had to be prepared - and sometimes heated - and all the different kinds of candles had to be placed in the chandeliers and girandoles.

---

[36] Also the conductor of the band at Covent Garden. Information from: Richard Cumberland, 'Memoirs of Richard Cumberland', London, 1806, republished New York, 1969, p. 131

[37] Charles Dibdin, 'The Professional Life of Mr Dibdin', London, 1803, vol. 2, p. 55-6

[38] Tate Wilkinson, 'Memoirs of his own Life', York 1790, republished London & New Jersey, 1998, p. 168

[39] The London Stage, Part 5, p. cxlv

On Saturdays the actors collected their weekly pay from the Treasury at the conclusion of the rehearsals. The Covent Garden Treasury is shown on Dumont's engraving of the ground-plan as placed in the front of house, behind the corridor that gives access to the Boxes, where it is designated 'Chambre de la Thrésorerie'.[40] It was at this point in the week that the select members of the *Sublime Society of Beefsteaks* went aloft to their 'noble room at the top of the theatre' for their well-earned meal. The table-cloth was customarily 'removed at half-an-hour after three', and drinking went on until the time for the evening show arrived.

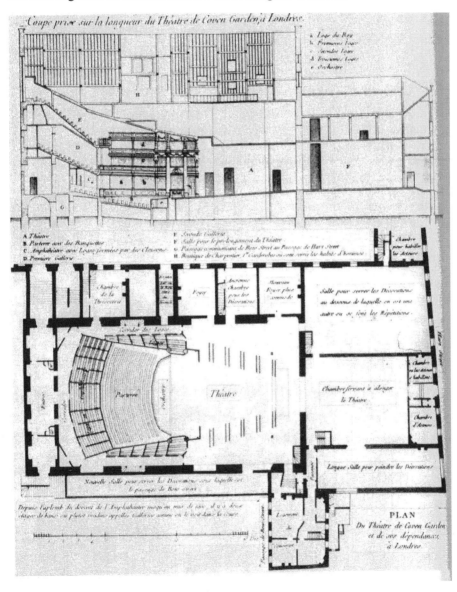

---

[40] The description is in French as the book was the work of Gabriel-Martin Dumont, and published in France in 1774 as "Parallele de Plans des Plus Belles Salles de Spectacles d'Italie et de France". See: *Survey of London* vol. XXXV, The Athlone Press, University of London, 1970, pp. 86-8 and Plate 40.

THE THEATRE BACKSTAGE

The theatre was a hive of activity every day. From the 1760 Covent Garden accounts (when Beard was manager) one can see that there were 31 actors on the books, 21 actresses, 8 singers, 24 dancers, 3 prompters, and 21 in the orchestra. In addition there were 3 painters, 31 front-of-house staff, 26 dressers, 8 charwomen, a lampman, a sweeper, a candleman and 6 bill-stickers. An amount of £2 10s was paid daily to the 'scenemen' backstage, but no clue is given to the number that were required to make the changes of scenery happen smoothly and effectively. As the men's dressers were paid 1s per night and the ladies' dressers 1s 6d, and the bill-stickers received 2s, it is likely that their pay would have never been much above these levels. The humblest actor received 2s 6d. So, at a generous 2s per night, it is likely that there were as many as 20 scene-shifters backstage. How they all fitted in is a mystery. The Ground-plans do not reveal the building as being vast: quite the reverse.

In the engraving (published in 1774) of the Covent Garden theatre that Beard knew for the whole of his working life[41] there seems to be a great shortage of the kind of rooms that make life bearable in the theatre for such different groups of workers. The backstage staff presumably made use of the two rooms at the very back of the theatre (*Salle pour serrer les decorations*) either side of the Green Room (*Chambre servant à alonger le Theatre*). There are only two small dressing rooms for the actors and actresses leading off the back of the Green Room, and one tiny space that might have been a lavatory, and a further dressing room at the very rear of the larger scene-dock. Three larger rooms to the side of the stage (*Foyer, Ancienne Chambre pour les decorations, Nouveau Foyer plus commode*) must have served as principal dressing rooms. This plan does not show the other levels of the theatre, served by the six or so staircases, where further accommodation must have been available for a plethora of dressers, house-servants, and charwomen etc. The plan, however, does refer to a rehearsal room beneath the large scenery-dock (*au dessous de laquelle en est une autre ou se font les Répétitions*), which was the music room described earlier - a room large enough to hold an orchestra, actors and soloists. This is shown in a later plan, dating from 1791. Presumably there were further rooms, and store-rooms, on this level too. The plans drawn up in 1791, after a small amount of remodelling had taken place in the theatre's interior, but not backstage, show a complex set of cellars that are designated for the storage of candles, lamps, stage-props, as well as further dressing rooms, a rest room for the musicians, and a music library.[42] The *Beef-steak Club* was known to keep a fine wine-cellar in the basement. It was one of the notable losses (along with the fine organ used at oratorio performances that Handel had left John Rich in his will) when the theatre burned down in 1808.

In his capacity as manager John Beard would have had the use of Rich's house as his office. Priscilla Rich, John's widow, was presumably still residing here in the house which was situated beside and adjoining the theatre in Hart Street (now renamed as Floral Street).This would have been one of the houses on the right of the view of the theatre shown overleaf. The large window at the very top of all the buildings may well have illuminated the painting-room, which was the 'noble room' where the beef-steaks were cooked and consumed on Saturday afternoons.

---

[41] Plate 40 of *Survey of London* vol. XXXV, The Athlone Press, University of London, 1970
[42] Plate 43b of *Survey of London* vol. XXXV, The Athlone Press, University of London, 1970

The Covent Garden site seen from Bow Street, and showing the Hart Street facade

THE SUMMER MONTHS

The original purpose of the actor's Benefit must have been to provide a means of gaining enough funds to tide them over until the start of the new season. Thus the Benefits were taken towards the end of each season, in March, April and sometimes May, when the prospect of three months without work (June, July and August) was looming large. In practice, this period provided an opportunity for the actors to seek work elsewhere. Mostly they decamped to the provinces, where theatres were beginning to spring up and were now offering Summer seasons. Among the earliest provincial theatres to be built were those at Bath, Bristol, Norwich and York (all before 1740). There was a big increase in the second half of the century, with smaller towns like Newcastle, Richmond in Yorkshire and Margate acquiring buildings. Liverpool and Manchester were not far behind; and elsewhere in the Kingdom there were flourishing theatres in Dublin and Edinburgh providing other opportunities for good London-based actors.

Just before the beginning of the autumn season there were two major Fairs in London where groups of actors set up booths and performed lightweight plays, farces and satires. These took place at Southwark, and at St Bartholomew Fair in Smithfield. Hogarth has given us an idea of what they might have looked like in his engraving 'Southwark Fair' of 1734[43] in which actors, and their rickety, collapsing stage feature prominently. Beard may have needed to pick up work at these 'ad hoc' events early in his career. He may have been at Hallam's Booth in August 1737, and is quite probably the 'Board'[44] mentioned as singing the Roving Shepherd in *The Country Wedding* at Pinkethman's Booth at the Bartholomew Fair in August 1738.

[43] Plate 27, 'Engravings by Hogarth', edited Shesgreen, Dover Publications New York, 1973
[44] The name 'Beard' is occasionally misprinted as Board, and once even as 'Brand' (!), because of the 18th Century handwriting style in which a copper-plate 'e' looks remarkably similar to an 'o', viz. ϴ

His wedding to Henrietta in 1739, and his imagined financial 'prospects', meant that he did not need to work on the fringes of the Patent Theatres for the next few years. Only in 1741, when he finally realised that marriage to Henrietta was not going to be his 'meal-ticket for life' did he need to pick up similar scraps of work at 'The New Wells, Goodman Fields'. His engagement as a singer in the pantomime *The Spanish Husband, or, Harlequin at Portobello* in April 1741 was born out of a desperation for work. This was eventually resolved when he was re-engaged at Drury Lane in the autumn of that year.

John Beard did not traipse around the lesser theatrical venues very much during his career, as so many of his colleagues did. The only definite record of him playing outside London was when he visited the fledgling Richmond Theatre to play his famous role of 'Macheath' alongside his friends Havard, Bencraft and Dunstall in a performance of *The Beggar's Opera* on Saturday September 27 1746. He was more fortunate than most, as he fell on his feet when Ranelagh Gardens opened in April 1745 and appointed him to be their resident male vocalist. He remained at the gardens, singing on a regular basis two or three evenings a week, until at least 1762.

For Beard there was another opportunity to earn money away from London when the Music Festivals that were growing up in the Cathedral cities began to expand their activities and improve their artistic standards. As Beard's reputation was so closely associated with Handel's oratorios, which were the staple fare of these Festivals, he found himself being one of the first London soloists to be invited to the Three Choirs Festival. He made his first definite visit there in August 1755. Daniel Lysons noted in his History of the Three Choirs Festival[45] that there was an advertisement in the local paper (the 'Worcester Journal') that "the additional expense in preparing the oratorio *Samson*, and the larger demands of the London performers make it absolutely necessary to raise the price of the concert tickets from half-a-crown to three shillings".

Other festivals soon followed the trend of inviting singers who had worked with Handel to come and join them in their performances of his oratorios. Oxford played host to Beard in July 1756, and Birmingham in September 1760, when Aris's 'Birmingham Gazette' reported that the conductor, Mr Hobbs, had "spared no trouble in procuring the first Performers that are to be had".[46] Beard was involved there in performances of the three most popular of all Handel's oratorios: *Messiah*, *Samson*, and *Judas Maccabaeus*. Records do not show whether Beard sang for his Chapel Royal colleague, Professor John Randall, in Cambridge. But performances of the same three oratorios took place between 1759 and 1765 under Randall's direction. Only in 1765 is it clear that the tenor soloist on that occasion was Joseph Vernon; leaving the possibility that Beard might have taken part in one or more of the other earlier performances.

ILLNESS AND ABSENCE

If an actor was ill, or unavailable for any reason, they were not paid. This could lead to hardship, and was one of the reasons that Thomas Hull and Beard set up the Covent Garden Theatrical Fund in 1765. Beard himself suffered intermittent health problems. The main one was a hearing problem, which came and went in the early

---

[45] D. Lysons, 'History of the Origin and Progress of the Meeting of the Three Choirs...', Gloucester, 1812, p. 20
[46] RMA Research Chronicle no. 8, 1966

years of his career, but caused alarm to Handel and his supporters, as has been shown in earlier chapters. It eventually forced Beard to retire from the stage in 1767; though he had been canny enough to combine this departure with the sale of the theatre to a new consortium for the handsome sum of £60,000.

In the earlier period it is clear that the loss of income through illness was a major blow. When he was robbed and beaten (we would say 'mugged') on his way home from the theatre on January 16 1750 Beard was off work until the 23rd. He missed performances on the 18th and 19th, when his part was taken by Master Mattocks. The Winston MS Accounts show that he was lent £21 by the treasurer to tide him over this difficult period.[47]

Illnesses which have always adversely affected singers and actors are coughs, colds and throat problems. Beard succumbed, just like everyone else. In the Cross/Hopkins Diaries[48] for 1750 we read:

Sat 15 Dec.   *Mr Beard hoarse, Mr Garrick made apology - but he sang very well*
Mon 17 Dec.   *Mr Beard ill*
Sat 22 Dec.   *'Robin Hood' was stop'd in ye run by Mr Beard's sickness*

On some occasions it is clear that the weather was to blame, as when, in February 1740, Handel's *Acis and Galatea* was put off on the 4th, and again on the 7th "in consideration of the weather continuing so cold". It was then delayed further on the 14th - "two chief singers [one of whom must have been Beard] being taken ill".[49]

There is no knowing why Beard was absent from the theatre on other occasions. In certain years he started his activities late in the season. In 1743, for instance, he appeared for the first time with the Covent Garden company (having transferred from Drury Lane at the end of the previous season) on November 25. In 1746 he began as late as December 11. In 1747 he was ready a little earlier - but not at the very beginning of the season - and commenced with the *Beggar's Opera* on October 31. As he would have had to manage without his salary in these periods, the reasons for these absences must have been compelling. But whether they were as a result of illness, domestic issues relating to the schooling of his step-daughter Barbara, or visits to his Devon-based family, will never be known. Leading actresses, such as Mrs Cibber and George Anne Bellamy, often delayed their first appearances in the season until November, by which time they knew that the flower of London's society would have made their way back to London from their country estates. But this was just snobbishness. The early part of the season (September to the beginning of November) was regarded as a time for repeating old repertoire whilst the new was being prepared. There were very few first performances during this time - although it was occasionally the 'silly season' when the two main theatres vied with each other by mounting the same repertoire, such as *Romeo and Juliet* in October 1750.

During Beard's eleven years at Drury Lane with Garrick he never again started the season late. On one occasion, in 1757, he performed in *The Beggar's Opera* on the first night of the season (September 10) and then persuaded Garrick to give him leave of absence for a week, so that he could visit the Three Choirs Festival in Gloucester for performances on September 14, 15, and 16. But he only

---

[47] Winston MS, 1744-1752, T. a. 55 (7), Folger Shakespeare Library, Washington, USA
[48] Cross/Hopkins Diaries, W. a. 104 (1) (2) (3), Folger Shakespeare Library, Washington, USA
[49] reports in the *London Daily Post* for 6.2.1740 & 14.2.1740

missed one Drury Lane performance, when his role of 'Joe' in *The King and the Miller of Mansfield* was taken for that night only by Atkins. By the 22nd he was back in London, and performing his character role in Foote's *The Englishman in Paris*. This regularity at the opening of the season implies that Beard's delayed return in the years 1743, 1746 and 1747 is most likely to have been as a result of domestic issues in his first marriage.

When Beard was married to Charlotte in the 1760s it is clear from Havard's poem "For Mr and Mrs Beard upon the same Occasion" [the birthday of John Rich Esq.] that they were both suffering from ill-health:

> For see (to sad disease a prey)
> Can aught we sing, or aught we say
> Remove the deep-felt pain?
> Goddess Hygeia! ever fair
> Attend in pity to our prayer.
> This pair to health restore.
> … While the dim Torch of Life decays,
> Grant them contented, painless Days,
> And (if not Pleasure) Ease!

Although Beard's hearing was getting progressively worse in this period Havard's comments about 'deep-felt pain' seem to be referring to something else. In Beard's letters of the 1780s there is reference to Charlotte suffering from a "severe Attack of the Gravel", and "the painful return" of his own "stranguary complaint". These two complaints are problems of the kidneys, bladder and passing of urine. Charlotte's father, John Rich, had died of "an attack of the gravel" in 1761. Contemporary medical treatises describe *the Gravel* as a disease characterised by small stones which are formed in the kidneys, passed along to the bladder, and expelled with the urine. *Stranguary* is similar: there was a restricted urine flow attended with pain, which may have been caused by bladder stones. Nicholas Culpeper (1616-54) in his 'The English Physitian' of 1652 prescribed "Prickly Asparagus or Sperage" for the complaint; as, "boyled in white Wine, [it] provoketh Urin being stopped, and is good against the stranguary or difficulty of making water; it expelleth the gravel and stone out of the kidneys, and helpeth pains in the reins".[50]

John Graunt (1620-1674) in his 'Observations on the Bills of Mortality'[51] says: "Now the *Stone,* and *Stranguary,* are diseases, which most men know, that feel them, unless it be in some few cases, where (as I have heard *Physicians* say) a *Stone* is held up by the *Filmes* of the *Bladder,* and so kept from grating, or offending it." As with the other big illness of the eighteenth century, gout, one of the reasons for this complaint was undoubtedly due to the amount of port and wine that was consumed.[52] Beard's membership of so many London clubs would have ensured that he had maintained a high intake of these liquids.

---

[50] Nicholas Culpeper, 'The English physitian: or an astrologo-physical discourse of the vulgar herbs of this nation', London, 1652.

[51] Rictor Norton, 'Early Eighteenth-Century Newspaper Reports: A Sourcebook, "Bills of Mortality"', December 19th 2001

[52] One of the books in Beard's library, which had been bought during his marriage to Henrietta, was Thomas Thompson's "An historical, critical and practical treatise of the gout".

CHAPTER 13
RETIREMENT

A HOME IN HAMPTON-ON-THAMES

After John Rich's death, the sale of Covent Garden theatre was always an imminent possibility. His will had stipulated that his widow Priscilla had the right to dispose of it when there was a favourable opportunity, and that she should divide the proceeds equally between herself and the four daughters of his second marriage. Until that time came she was to manage the theatre jointly with John Beard. There was certainly a rumour that it was on the market as early as 1766. Garrick, who kept his ear very close to the ground, got wind of the sale as early as one whole year before it was finally sealed. He wrote to George Colman - without realising that his co-manager was the one who was secretly setting up the deal himself - from Hampton on July 15 1766: "...Beard and co. are going (positively) to sell their Patent etc. for £60,000 - but Mum - we have not yet discovered ye Purchasers. When I know you shall know."[1]

The purchase was completed a year later on July 1 1767. Garrick must have had quite a shock when he learned how devious Colman had been. He had formed a consortium with Thomas Harris, John Rutherford and the actor George Powell to raise the necessary £60,000.

Before his retirement it appears that Beard had already bought a property in Hampton, Middlesex. One of his letters to John Shebbeare states "...Being but just returned to Hampton ...I did not receive the favour of yours ...till last night, to which I am sorry it is not in my power to send you an immediate satisfactory answer. In ten days, or a fortnight, I shall be in town..." There are also references in Garrick's letters to Beard travelling to and from Hampton at this period, and performing little chores for him.[2] This was also occasionally reciprocated, as on the occasion when Garrick wrote to Sir George Hay in 1776, and said that "he could not withstand the solicitations of his old friend Beard to send him the enclos'd letter."[3] For the first couple of years of retirement Beard and Charlotte retained the property in St Martin's Lane, and came up to town frequently.[4] Hampton was well connected with the centre of London: there were regular coaches from Holborn and Fleet Street, which travelled via Isleworth or Hounslow, Twickenham and Teddington. There was the occasional danger of encountering highwaymen of course. Hounslow Heath was a notorious spot for them. But Kitty Clive wrote to Garrick to tell of an encounter much closer to home in 1776: "I have been robbed and murdered coming from Kingston, Jimmy [her brother] and I in a postchey [postchaise] at half past nine, just by Teddington Church. I only lost a little silver and my senses, for one of them came into the carriage with a great horsepistol to 'sarch' me for my watch, but I had not it with me".[5]

---

[1] 'The Letters of David Garrick', ed. Little & Kahrl, London, 1963, vol. 2, p. 522

[2] "Perhaps Warwick is not yet set out for Hampton – if Jeremy could catch him at Mr Beard's, he'll stay...." Garrick's m/s letters, February 1767, Folger Shakespeare Library, W. b. 492.
The favour was returned when Garrick promised to deliver a letter to Beard from the Countess Spencer.

[3] 'The Letters of David Garrick', ed. Little & Kahrl, London, 1963, vol. 3, p. 1105

[4] Beard's name continues in the Rates Lists (at the Westminster Archives) until 1769.

[5] quoted in Sheaf & Howe, 'Hampton and Teddington Past', Historical Publications Ltd, London1995 p. 26

So it is more probable that the Beards ran their own carriage after their permanent removal to Hampton. The villa which he built, known as 'Rose Hill', had a carriage house and stabling, and Beard writes in one of his letters of 'expecting the coach at every moment'. He must have used it frequently to make the journey into town in the early years of his retirement. For Beard never lost touch with his friends at the Beefsteak Club, at the Brotherhood of Free and Accepted Masons, or at his other clubs. He regularly attended the Benefit Concerts and Plays for the Decayed Musicians Fund and the Covent Garden Actor's Fund.

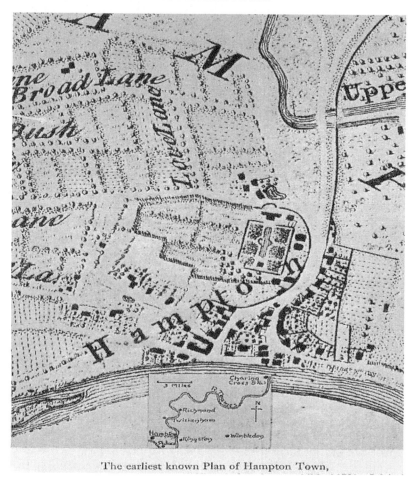

The earliest known Plan of Hampton Town,

Map of Hampton in 1754

Beard and his wife retired in comfort, on the proceeds of Charlotte's portion of the sale of the Covent Garden patent (£12,000), to a villa near David Garrick. Their first house seems to have been known as 'Perkins Land'. Mr Beard is shown as its owner in the Overseers Accounts (1767-1773) with a requirement to pay £2 4s per year into the town's 'Poor Fund'. As the earliest surviving record is from May 1767, before his retirement, this supports the theory that he had already acquired a property in the pretty Thames-side village as a second home. In this he was following in the footsteps of his fellow theatre managers David Garrick, who had lived at Hampton

280

House since 1754, and Thomas Rosoman, the owner of Sadler's Wells Theatre, who had retired to Jessamine House in Thames Street, and lived there until his death in 1782. Beard is recorded in the village as early as 1765, when he attended a Parishioners' Meeting. There is a distinct possibility that this original property was bought as both an investment and as a home for his mother, Mrs Ann Beard. She was certainly living with him at the time of her death in March 1782.

After a few years this property proved too small for the family, especially as Beard and his wife frequently played host to various younger family members. His nieces may have come up from Devon for 'finishing' and turning into young ladies. In 1769 Charlotte's sister Sarah died, leaving two young daughters: Sarah Melosina, aged 8, and Sophia Henrietta aged 6.[6] When their father, George Voelcker also died a year later, the Beards took the girls in, and brought them up as their own. By the time they joined the Beard household in 1770 a larger house had been acquired. In a letter of 1785 Beard mentions 'our damsels' and 'my dearest three' (the girls would have then been aged 24 and 22) being about to go out with his wife visiting neighbours in their coach. Between 1770 and Beard's mother's death in 1782 there would have been four ladies of widely varying ages, plus Beard himself, living in the home he had named 'Rose Hill'.

'Rose Hill' today

The Hampton Manor Books show that Beard had purchased three acres of land, known as White Post Close and lying between the present day Upper Sunbury Road and Oldfield Road, from David Garrick in 1768,[7] in order to build this villa. The land adjoined the estate he was to acquire six years later when he extended his grounds. In 1774 he purchased a further messuage from John and Susanna Cope

---

[6] Sarah was born 11th August 1761 & Sophia on 4th March 1763
[7] Manor Books (Court Rolls) of the Honor and Manor of Hampton, March 4th 1768

Freeman, together with a 1 acre plot in Westfield.[8] At this time the extensive rear kitchen garden must have been added on to the property, which reached northwards to an area known as Gander Goose Green[9] (close to the present-day Hampton Railway station). An old damaged plan of the estate made a century later (below) shows the whole site, with its approach from the Hampton to Sunbury turnpike at the bottom right-hand corner, and formal gardens to the front - which in Beard's day had an uninterrupted view towards the River Thames and Platt's Eyot. At the rear there was a more parklike garden, with shady walks extending down to the orchards and kitchen gardens. An elaborate system of pipework, that fed various fountains and ponds, was uncovered in the grounds during restorations in the 20th century. It appears that John Beard had at last created for himself the tranquil sylvan scene that he had sung about in the summer months of the previous thirty years. He had turned the grounds of his delightful villa into a private Pleasure Gardens of his own!

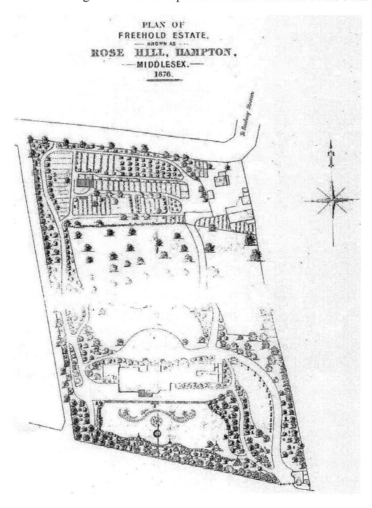

PLAN OF
FREEHOLD ESTATE,
KNOWN AS
ROSE HILL, HAMPTON,
MIDDLESEX.
1876.

---

[8] Manor Books, April 28th 1774, LR 3/44/1 fol 169.
[9] In 1731 the Manor Court Books called it "Wheatley's Green"; but by 1790 it was referred to as "a certain green formerly called Wheatley's and now Gander Goose Green". Henry Ripley, 'The History and Topography of Hampton-on-Thames', London, 1884.

In his will he singled out things that were to be left to Charlotte "for her own sole use and benefit". After a fairly unremarkable list of "all my plate linen china household furniture pictures prints books live and dead stock and all other goods chattels and effects" there is a further reference to "the garden tools and implements and seats in the garden", which must indicate that they had both taken a great deal of interest in horticulture.

The area where they lived was a good place if you were interested in having a garden full of fruit, vegetables and flowers. Hampton was the nursery-lands of the capital. As late as the end of the 20th century there were market gardens all over the area. In the eighteenth century there were famous commercial nurseries at Hammersmith and Brompton; and William Aiton established a 9-acre nursery on the wastelands of Hounslow Heath. All were within easy reach of Hampton. Some of the century's best work on the study of plants was done at the Chelsea Physick Garden, where Beard may occasionally have been able to meet Philip Miller (1691-1771), the writer whose influence was felt far beyond the confines of Chelsea, and whose famous '*Gardeners Dictionary containing the methods of cultivating the kitchen, fruit and flower garden, as also, the physick garden, wilderness, conservatory and vineyard'*, first published in 1731, ran into eight editions in his own lifetime. From the plans of the grounds there is no way that one can infer what the planting was at Rose Hill, beyond saying that there was scope for a typical mid-century arrangement of formal walks, well wooded edges to the site, and evidence of shrubberies near the house. Many new plants were arriving in the country from far afield at this period. Beard could have learned something of them from the work of the RSA. But he would surely have preferred the traditional plants that he had been used to at Ranelagh and Vauxhall Gardens. In his *Observations on Modern Gardening* (1770) Thomas Whately described what Beard and his wife might have been aiming to achieve:

"...the buildings are not the only ornament of the walk; it is shut out from the country by a thick and lofty hedgerow, which is enriched with woodbine, jessamine and every odoriferous plant. ...A path, generally of sand and gravel, is conducted in a waving line ... and the turf on either hand is diversified with little groups of shrubs, or firs, or of the smallest trees, and often with beds of flowers ... in some parts carried between larger clumps of evergreens, thickets of deciduous shrubs or still more considerable open plantations".[10]

At the bottom of their grounds the kitchen garden and orchard were laid out in neat patterns. The plan may indicate buildings in this part of the grounds, and these would most probably have been greenhouses and heated houses for growing exotic fruits. Such large grounds would have required a staff of gardeners. The buildings in the top right-hand corner on the plan may well be such servants' accommodation.

Time has not been kind to John and Charlotte's pride and joy. The view from their principal rooms at the front of the house across to Platt's Eyot in the Thames was blotted out by the Southwark & Vauxhall Water Company in the mid 19th century, when they built huge pumping stations on the water meadows between the Upper and Lower Sunbury Roads and filled the rest of the area with reservoirs. The town had become home to three waterworks by 1855 - The Grand Junction, the

---

[10] quoted in : Penelope Hobhouse, 'Gardening through the ages', New York, London etc, 1992

Southwark & Vauxhall, and the West Middlesex, who merged in 1903 to become the Metropolitan Water Board. The rectangular reservoir just south of the Upper Sunbury Road is still called the Grand Junction Reservoir.

The London and South Western Railway (Shepperton branchline) came to Hampton in 1864, and just skirted the northern edge of the Rose Hill grounds. When the house was sold by a Major P. Lambart in 1902 it was acquired by Hampton District Council for its council offices. The kitchen gardens and park to the north of the house were sacrificed to the construction of ugly, cheap, council housing (referred to in the original plans as 'workers cottages'). The road names are now all that recall the days of its late-eighteenth century glory: Beard's Hill and Rosehill.

The house remains, and is now a public library. Inside, despite the functional alterations that have ripped most of the heart out of the building, there is still occasional evidence of a glamorous past. A couple of elegant pillars adorn the oval entrance hall, and the principal rooms have fine cornices. The carriage house and stables can still be detected in the remodelling of the western wing. The frontage, with the old carriage drive climbing up steeply from the Upper Sunbury Road past a small lodge or gatehouse, remains much as it was, with evidence of a formal terrace containing the fountains whose pipework has been recently rediscovered.

I came to the library here when I was a Hampton resident in the 1970s; and it was the sight of this house, coupled with my love of the Handel oratorios that Beard had been the first to sing, that enthused me to learn everything that I could about its first owner, with the long term view of eventually writing his biography.

John Beard in old age

FRIENDS AND NEIGHBOURS

Hampton, Twickenham and Richmond were the playground of the 18th century London suburbs. The area was one in which it was possible to participate in many recreations. The river was used for regattas, for pleasure boats and for fishing - as can be seen in an old print of the waterfront made in Beard's time.

Over the ferry at Hampton was the large meadow, Molesey Hurst, on which Hurst Park race-course would eventually be built. At this time it was used for informal race meetings, which were more of a fair, and which took place twice a year in June and September, with sideshows, amusements and prize-fighting as well as horse racing. It was called the Cockney Derby because it was a commoner's event, unlike the more fashionable Epsom Derby. Molesey Hurst was also one of the earliest sites in the country for cricket. The *Daily Courant* reported a match there in 1723 between the Gentlemen of London and the Gentlemen of Surrey. There is a painting of just such a match at Molesey Hurst in the 1760s hanging in the Long Room at Lords. In the background the river, St Mary's Church, Garrick's Villa, and the Temple to Shakespeare are all clearly visible.

In 1758 the Hurst was also the location for one of the first games of golf played in England, when the Rev. Alexander Carlyle, John Hume and Parson Black visited David Garrick and played golf on the other side of the river, directly opposite his villa.

Garrick's Villa

So this was a favoured retirement area for a whole host of Musicians, Actors, Painters and Writers who had 'made it good'. Not only did the theatre managers Garrick, Rosoman and Beard retire here, but also ordinary actors like Robert Baddeley,[11] and Dennis Delane. Kitty Clive retired to a small cottage next to Horace Walpole's Strawberry Hill in 1769 - two years after Beard. Her house was called Little Strawberry Hill, though Walpole wittily nicknamed it 'Clive-den'. Here, in a charming building fronting onto the River Thames she lived with her brother, the actor James Raftor who had been a colleague of Beard's throughout his Drury Lane career, and who had understudied him in the 1740 season. Walpole delighted in Kitty's company and wrote that "I have lately planted the green lane, that leads from her garden to the common: 'Well', said she, 'when it is done, what shall we call it?' - 'Why', said I, 'what would you call it but Drury Lane'."

Beard was therefore surrounded by old friends and colleagues. In one of his letters of August 1785 we learn that he was going out to visit "my old friend and flame Kitty Clive, Miss Pope (with all her amiabilities about her) and her flimsy jimsy-pimsy Rafter, the avow'd Favourite of every venerable Twickenham Tabby, who has a taste for Scandal and Quadrille".[12] In this comprehensive list he sums up his feelings about all of Kitty's domestic circle: there is affection for Kitty herself, and respect for her good friend, the actress Jane Pope; and we learn that James Raftor was rather timid and effete, but not as 'catty' as the old tabby - Walpole himself! Walpole, it will be remembered, scarcely ever had a good word to say for

---

[11] see Chapter 6
[12] British Library Egerton Manuscripts, (Collections relating to Musicians 1578 – 1860), Eg 2159 f. 56

Beard's performances. On one occasion he used the adjective 'tolerable', but often Beard was not singled out at all but referred to along with the other cast members.[13] One could not say that Walpole was his fan!

At this time Beard would have been well aware that the Waldegraves had enjoyed great success at Court. James, the second Earl (and his erstwhile brother-in-law) had been a personal friend of Walpole's; and James' widow - Walpole's niece Maria - was now married to King George III's brother, the Duke of Gloucester.[14] So, relations between Beard and this neighbour may have been rather more stiff and formal than they were with his theatrical colleagues. But, if the mention of Quadrille[15] in the above letter implies that Beard was going out to play cards with Kitty Clive, Walpole may have been one of the party, as this was his preferred way of spending his evenings. He was an avid gossip, and loved to hear theatrical anecdotes in his old age, when (as he said of himself) he was "...an old gouty man that live in my armchair and can't tell how the world passes".[16]

It was to be one of the last times that Beard would see his dear colleague Kitty, with whom he had enjoyed so many successes - in Handel oratorios, in *The Beggar's Opera*, and in trifling afterpieces like *The Devil to Pay, Bays in Petticoats* and *Lethe* - as she died only four months later on December 6 1785. The actress Jane Pope wrote these lines as an Epitaph:

'Her generous heart to all her friends was known'.

Beard had known her for fifty years, and the loss of this good neighbour and colleague must have been sadly felt.

There were other losses too. All his friends and colleagues were dying. William Hayes, for whom he had sung at Oxford and the Three Choirs Festival, and whose son had replaced him as tenor soloist in his final Foundling Hospital *Messiah,* had died in 1777. Of the composers that Beard had championed, Arne, who had a home in Thames Ditton, had gone in 1778, and Boyce in 1779. John Stanley succeeded Boyce as Master of the King's Musick and died in 1786. J. C. Smith outlived Beard by four years, and lived long enough to meet Joseph Haydn, when the Viennese composer visited Bath in 1794. But, as we have seen in Chapter 9, they were not to meet at the Handel Commemoration in 1784, when Smith felt too frail to travel. In 1779 Garrick had died, and been given a splendid funeral at Westminster Abbey on February 1. In George Carter's painting *The Apotheosis of Garrick* seventeen costumed actors watch as Garrick is born aloft by two angels. They include contemporary stars like Mrs Abington, Mrs Yates, and Mr King; but the only one of Beard's circle to be portrayed is his friend Thomas Hull. The painting was shown at the Royal Academy in 1784 when Horace Walpole described it as 'Ridiculous and Bad'.[17]

---

[13] "Garrick has produced a detestable English Opera [J.C Smith's *The Fairies*] which ...is sung by some cast singers, two Italians and a French girl, and the Chapel boys." Horace Walpole, letter of February 23rd 1755

[14] The secret marriage had been whispered to have taken place as early as 1766; but the King was not informed until 1772 when the Duchess was pregnant.

[15] This four-handed adaptation of the classic game of *Ombre* was developed in France in the early 18th century. It spread rapidly to become one of the great European games for about a hundred years. In England, however, it was soon rivalled by the newly refined game of *Whist*, with which it eventually had to contend for popularity.

[16] quoted in: Timothy Mowl, 'Horace Walpole', London, 1996, p. 169

[17] quoted in: 'Every Look Speaks – Portraits of David Garrick', Holburne Museum of Art, Bath, 2003, p. 86-7

Amongst his closest actor-friends William Havard and John Dunstall both died in 1778. Beard was very upset by Dunstall's death, as he confided in a letter to Thomas Hull; and he agreed to write the Epitaph for his tombstone. A few years later he was mortified to find that his name had been included on it. In another letter to Thomas and Maria Hull he wrote "it seems my name is inscribed in too large characters on Dunstall's tombstone, and truth I think so too: but they place it to the Acc^t of your brother Johnny's ineffable vanity ... but you know as well as I, I gave no direction to have my name appear at all, much less in letters as long as my leg". [18] It is typical of Beard, the joker from the Beefsteak Club, to include a little wit in the closing lines of his tribute:

> Tried and approved by a discerning age,
> His name shall grace the Annals of the stage,
> Whilst Truth which most he loved, shall tell,
> Thro' every Scene of Life he acted well.
> Go, gentle reader, go, - and if you can,
> Live like this upright, downright Honest Man. [19]

His relationship with Havard had soured as a result of Beard's suspicions that Havard could have warned him that there was going to be a riot at Covent Garden in 1763. Havard's letter to Beard about this will be found in Appendix 4. However, it does not seem to have achieved the intended rapprochement, as Havard omitted to leave Beard - the man he had called his 'brother' in so many letters - any memento at all on his death. He made several small bequests to actors in his will - £20 to the widow of Michael Stoppelaer, another singer/actor, and a mourning ring 'as a token of old respect and ffriendship' to David Garrick: - but nothing similar to his very dearest friend of all. It is sad - especially as it is through the intimate letters and poems in Havard's manuscript 'Jeu d'esprit' that it has been possible to fill in so many details of Beard's private life.

Beard's Chapel Royal colleague Samuel Howard, who had often written Ballads for him, died in 1782; and Thomas Lowe, his arch-rival in the singing stakes, died in sorry circumstances in 1783. Lowe had tried to copy Beard's success, and for many years their careers appeared virtually interchangeable. When Beard entered into management at Covent Garden in the 1760s Lowe tried to do the same thing by taking on the management of Marylebone Gardens. He took on the lease from John Trusler in 1763, at a yearly rental of £170, for a period of fourteen years. But within four years he was bankrupt, claiming that he had lost £2000 in his first three seasons. After struggling on as a paid employee, Lowe retired from the management in 1769 and sold out to Beard's friend and protégé Samuel Arnold. Thereafter Lowe sang at any Gardens that would have him - Finch's Grotto, Ottesley Pool - until the new manager at Sadler's Wells, Tom King, gave him a professional home there for the last eleven years of his life.

There had been a rumour that Beard was going to take over Marylebone Gardens in May 1755. [20] He must have watched Lowe's attempt with interest. But ultimately he would have been relieved to have escaped the problems of recurrent

---

[18] letter of August 18th 1785. British Library Egerton Manuscripts, Eg 2159 f. 56
[19] letter of January 12th 1779. British Library Egerton Manuscripts, Eg 2159 f. 52 (1779)
[20] see: Mollie Sands, 'The Eighteenth-Century Pleasure Gardens of Marylebone 1737-1777', The Society for Theatre Research, London, 1987, p. 33

bad weather and bad approach roads that made these gardens less successful than the competition. There was always a danger of meeting a highwayman or footpad in the dark fields if you walked to Marylebone; and if you went in a carriage you could easily get stuck at the muddy corner known as Nibbs Pound. Not for nothing did John Gay make these gardens the haunt of the very highwayman, 'Macheath', that both Lowe and Beard played so many times on the London stage. Although *The Beggar's Opera* glamourises the gardens, the reality of making them attractive to London Society was less easy to achieve. Firework displays by Signor Torré were a draw in the 1770s, and Fanny Burney's heroine 'Evelina' hears a good concert there and is terrified by the fireworks in her novel of the same name. But the clientele did not come in sufficient numbers, or pay enough when they were there. Sylas Neville recorded in his diary: "At 6 went to Marybone Gardens, a place of the kind of Ranelagh - but not so elegant nor frequented by good company - indeed much indifferent company resort to both".[21]

Another of Beard's tenor colleagues in the theatre had been Joseph Vernon. They had often been together in performances of *The Chaplet*, before Vernon married Jane Poitier without gaining the necessary consents and thereby incurring the audience's wrath. After the marriage was annulled he spent some years in the wilderness before returning to the theatre and joining Beard in J. C. Smith's opera *The Tempest*. During the 1760s and 1770s he was at Drury Lane in all of Beard's old parts, and became a notable 'Macheath' in *The Beggar's Opera*. He predeceased Beard in March 1782, having given his last performances in October 1781.

Fortunately for Beard he was good at making friends. As the old ones drifted out of his life[22] there was a younger generation ready to keep him up-to-date with the musical scene in the capital. At this time his friendship with Thomas Hull kept him in touch with what was going on at Covent Garden under the management of Colman and Harris, and, more importantly, with the fortunes of the Theatrical Fund which he and Hull had set up (see Chapter 6). Thomas Hull became increasingly important at Covent Garden when he bought Colman's share of the Patent in 1774. From then on he was Harris's premiere manager. Beard had already encouraged Hull's attempts as a playwright during his managerial years. It is most probable that he would have been seen in the audience to support his further offerings. They included: *The Royal Merchant*, with music by Thomas Linley, in December 1767; *Henry II, or the Fall of Rosamond*, 1773; *Edward and Eleonora* (a revision of James Thomson's play) 1775; and *True Blue, or The Press Gang*, 1776. When Hull revised Arthur Murphy's ten-year-old comedy *The School for Guardians* in 1777 he took a leaf out of Sheridan's book, and like *The Duenna*, which had been a 'hit' since 1775, he added musical numbers by Arne and called it *Love Finds the Way*. Hull and his actress wife Anna Maria Morrison always remained good friends with Beard and Charlotte, and some of their correspondence still survives.[23]

Charles Wesley was a visitor to Hampton in 1771[24], and Samuel Arnold and Thomas Dupuis who were regular visitors, brought the latest musical gossip. As both of these were ex-choristers of the Chapel Royal they had a lot in common. Both

---

[21] entry for June 8th, 1767, quoted in: Simon McVeigh, 'Concert Life in London from Mozart to Haydn', Cambridge, 1993, p. 43. The takings at Marylebone Gardens for a 3-week period in 1774 are shown on pp. 175-6

[22] Alexander Reid, Surgeon of Chelsea Royal Hospital, died in 1789

[23] British Library Egerton Manuscripts, (Collections relating to Musicians 1578 – 1860), Eg 2159 f. 56

[24] Letter of 25 February 1771 in the John Rylands Library, Manchester

Arnold and Dupuis may have been treble soloists in the Handel oratorios with Beard during their years in the choir, or in the performances of Court Odes by William Boyce. On October 21 1785 they organised a dinner in London ostensibly to celebrate the deceased Bernard Gates' 100th birthday. But, as was shown in Chapter 1, this was almost certainly laid on to celebrate Beard's own 70th birthday.

In 1790 they dropped in on Beard as they were passing by, together with Messrs J.W. Callcott and Hudson, and told him about the recent establishment of the Glee Club.[25] In other correspondence with Samuel Arnold, Beard talks about his customary free Season Ticket to the oratorios, which he wants to dedicate in 1786 to 'my dear friends Mr and Mrs Hewetson'[26]. Elsewhere he is concerned for the welfare of two musicians' widows: Mrs Jones (the widow of a cellist whose Benefit night Beard had sometimes sung at) and Mrs Lampe (the widow of the composer John Frederick Lampe), who were deriving benefits from the Fund for Decayed Musicians, but were being advised to apply to the Theatrical Fund as well. Beard's humane response was to turn a blind eye to the fact that this was contrary to the regulations, where they "would lose by one what [they] gained by the other". He advised them to keep mum about having two pensions, as the Theatrical fund "will rejoice in every addition to her ease and comfort, tho' they cannot alter their laws".

There were local friends as well. Beard was living in retirement in Hampton for twenty-four years. Who they were will never be fully known. But he obviously made a very favourable impression on people. The vicar of St. Mary's Parish Church, the Rev. Abraham Blackborne,[27] who he would have got to know well as a regular member of the congregation, made a touching entry into the parish records when Beard died. Recording his funeral in the 1791 register he wrote:

John Beard Esq. in y[e] Vault (*Eheu*) buried Feb[y]: 12th

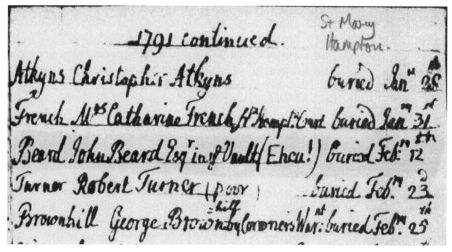

---

[25] Percy Scholes, 'The Great Dr. Burney', Oxford, 1948, Vol. 2, p. 119

[26] This name has been transliterated inaccurately as 'Howatson' in H.D. Johnstone, 'Treasure Trove in Gloucester: a Grangerized copy of the 1895 edition of Daniel Lysons' History of the Three Choirs Festival', RMA Research Chronicle 31, 1998, p. 49. A 'Richard Hewetson' was married to Susanna Burton in St Martin-in-the-Fields on May 12th 1764, during the time that Beard and Charlotte lived in St Martin's Lane.

[27] F.C.E. Atkins, 'A Short Guide to the Parish Church of St. Mary the Virgin, Hampton', Hampton, 1996, p. 16

That solitary word *Eheu,* which occurs nowhere else in this register, is evidence of a little personal emotion welling up on the part of the vicar. Here he is recording more than a mere burial: he is recording the passing of a good friend. *Eheu* is the Latin for '*Alas!*' Other friends that Beard mentions in his letter of 1785 are a "Mr and Mrs Chace", who were coming to visit him in a few days time; and "Capt. Groce and Mrs Bayntun etc" that he is just going out to visit in Richmond. Captain Grose [*recte*] was a famous antiquarian, who had compiled a 'Dictionary of the Vernacular' and was a friend of the painter Zoffany.

Mrs Bayntun is not so easy to identify, but may be the mother of Captain (later Admiral) Henry William Bayntun, (1766-1840) who commanded the *Leviathan* at the Battle of Trafalgar. There is also a reference to a Mrs Huddy. She may have been the widow of the actor Philip Huddy; and if so was most likely to have been receiving financial assistance from the Covent Garden Actors' Fund. In this case the visit would have been a courtesy call.

Two other important friends are named as co-executors of his 1786 will: Richard Hewetson, a 'lace-maker' (who received his complimentary oratorio tickets in 1786) and John Bellamy, a 'silk mercer'. Both are named as being "of the Parish of St Paul's Covent Garden". Research has not revealed much more about them yet, but they may either have been old Masonic friends of Beard's, or friends of Charlotte's through her tailoring connections.[28] But they certainly belong to the group which is so well evoked in E. Rimbault's memorable appreciation of Beard's retirement years:

"He spent his latter years in ease and affluence, in the society of many respectable friends, whom he had gained by his estimable qualities and agreeable talents".[29]

LOCAL ACTIVITIES

As a distinguished resident of Hampton, Beard was invited onto the Committees of many local campaigns. It seems that he was always happy to say yes. Thus, we find him being appointed a trustee for the sale of the Bell Inn, which was a parish property. He was also chosen as one of the 72 trustees of the Hampton to Staines turnpike - the road that passed his front door. This happened as the result of an Act of Parliament, brought in on April 10 1774, "...for amending, widening, and keeping in repair the Road from the Guide-Post at the West End of the Town of Hampton, over Sunbury Common to the Town of Staines, in the County of Middlesex"[30] - a distance of six and a half miles. The qualification for the trustees was to be in possession of an estate of £50 p.a. or £1000 by value, and the long list also included Lancelot (Capability) Brown, David Garrick and Lord North. The toll-house at the Hampton end was at the foot of Beard's drive, at the west end of the town, where it can still be seen.

Also in 1774 the local grammar school put itself on a stronger footing by instituting the Jones Trust. Captain John Jones had left a large bequest to the school in 1692. The income from this had originally paid the wages of a schoolmaster (less

---

[28] John Bellamy was commemorated in St Paul's Covent Garden on his death in September 1794 by the members of 'The Whig Club, of which he was the Father [i.e. the Founder]'. The Whig Club, instituted in May 1784, was composed of "men who solemnly pledge themselves to support the constitution of this country, according to the principles established at the Glorious Revolution".

[29] Dr. E. Rimbault; quoted in Daniel Lysons, 'History of ... the Three Choirs ...', Gloucester, 1812

[30] 13 George III Cap 105

£36 to provide pensions for six 'aged and poore' local men). But, after a half-share in Nando's Coffee House in Fleet Street was added to the Trust funds, it was reorganised to include a governing body of eleven trustees.[31] Once again these included the foremost residents of the town: David Garrick, John Beard, and the Rt. Hon. Frederick North 'commonly called Lord North'. Lord North lived in Bushy House from 1771 until his death in 1792. Thus the three principal residents supervised the school's transformation from a small class held in the Vestry to a Grammar School with new premises in a large schoolroom added to the north side of the chancel of St Mary's Church.[32]

THE BEARD AND RICH FAMILIES AND RELATIONS

In his retirement John Beard would have been able to show more active interest in the family of his brother William, in Kenton, Devon. They were important to him, as we can see by the bequests he made in his will. He may have been able to develop a relationship with his nieces by inviting them to stay with him in London, and learn the fashionable airs and graces under his kindly tutelage, whilst he was still singing and acting in the theatre. Exeter was within easy reach of London by stage-coach. These vehicles travelled frequently up the new turnpike roads that had been constructed in the mid-century. The route from Exeter to London was via the towns of Ilminster, Ilchester and Wincanton. A faster route would have been via Taunton and Bath. Thus, if Elizabeth and Ann had come to London as young ladies, approximately aged between (say) 18 or 20, they would have arrived in c.1753 and c.1759 respectively, whilst Beard was living with Charlotte in St Martin's Lane. Thomasin, being born rather later in 1748 would have come up in about 1766. There is also the niece Harriet, who married William Crawford, and is the daughter of Beard's other, shadowy, brother known as 'Major' Beard. Beard left them all a bequest of £100 each in his will. Ann had died in 1772, just a few months before her father, William.[33] It may be because of the great sadness that Beard displayed on the loss of this niece that William Havard penned the 'Epitaph on the Death of Miss Anna Beard'.

Both of the deaths that occurred in 1772 may have caused Beard and Charlotte to travel down to Kenton, where, close to the church tower in the churchyard of the Parish Church, there is a fine tomb in a prominent position, containing the remains of William's wife Thomasin Bickford and several of her children who had died young. Two of these were named John, in honour of their uncle, but only lived for a few years.[34] Their eldest son, Beard's nephew William, also named his eldest son John at the christening at Kenton in October 1773. That this William was fond of his uncle and aunt is shown both by this act, and by the fact that he had named his eldest daughter Charlotte two years earlier in 1771. Young William followed in his father's footsteps in Kenton by working for William Courtenay, the Earl of Devon.[35] His wedding in 1769 might have been a sufficiently

---

[31] Sheaf & Howe, 'Hampton and Teddington Past', Historical Publications Ltd, London, 1995, p. 83

[32] For further information on Hampton Grammar School see: Bernard Gartside, 'A Brief History of Hampton School, 1557 – 1957'.

[33] Anna was buried on 9/4/1772; and William on 7/8/1772. Another child, Richard, had been buried on 1/2/1771.

[34] John, christened 22/2/1737; buried 23/5/1740; and John, christened 2/11/1740; buried 25/4/1741

[35] Sir William Courtenay, 1st Viscount, was born in St James' Street in the parish of St Martin-in-the-Fields on February 11th 1709. He died on December 19th 1761 at Bath, and was buried at Powderham. His

important event to warrant a trip to Devon. If our John - the singer - had attended this, it might have been the last time that he saw his brother, the elder William, alive. John's brother, William (the elder), was born in 1712 according to his simple, weathered, tombstone, beside the imposing table-tomb containing his wife and children. He figures in the extant Powderham Castle records several times, and is paid for training up apprentices in the 'Servant Ledger' of 1771. In 1771 and 1772 'Old Mr Beard' - sometimes referred to as 'Farmer Beard' - was paid three times for supplying bricks. At his wedding in 1733 he was described as a 'husbandman'. By 1740 there are records of him having an apprentice; and he is now described as a 'yeoman'. He was obviously going up in the world. Other records show him acting as a land-agent on behalf of the Courtenay family, and training up further apprentices. A feature in the Powderham Castle grounds is known today as Beard's Folly; but whether it refers to John's brother or to his nephew cannot now be determined.

William's son and heir, 'young Mr Beard', was paid wages of 27 guineas a year at Powderham, commencing 10th October 1766. This was improved to £40 a year at Christmas 1782. He received £20 in the will of 'the late Lord Courtenay' (the 2nd Viscount) in 1788 and was discharged from service on March 25th 1793, aged 59, with a payment of £87 6s 4d. It appears that he was a trusted servant of the Courtenay family for more than 27 years.

Kenton was regarded as a pleasant place to live, if we are to believe the poet and original 'blue-stocking' Benjamin Stillingfleet. In 1768 a relative of his - someone that the Beard family would get to know well - was appointed to the Vicarage of Kenton. In a letter Stillingfleet wrote to him:

"Dear William ... you will have infinitely more enjoyment at Kenton than you can possibly have in London. You and your brother together may certainly keep a horse: you love riding and shooting, and you may have leave for the last from Lord Courtenay; besides, you will be but eighteen miles from Exeter, where you may now and then go for a few days by way of amusement."[36]

A regular visitor to Powderham Castle, who painted portraits of the Courtenay family which still hang on its walls, was Thomas Hudson (1701-79).[37] He was an Exeter-born painter who lived for a while in Red Lion Square when John Beard was also resident there. From the mid-1740s to the mid-1750s, he was the leading fashionable portrait painter in London, rivalled only by Allan Ramsay. Hudson went into semi-retirement in the late 1750s and then lived near Beard in a house in Cross Deep, Twickenham, a little upstream from Pope's Villa. He painted John Beard at least twice, including the famous portrait with the singer wearing his red 'Macheath' coat, which can be dated to about 1743.[38] With all of these connections, through family and friends, and with his reputation as a star of Drury Lane and Covent Garden theatres going before him, it would not be surprising to learn that Beard was entertained at the castle by the Earl on his visits to Kenton. There is a portrait by

---

son Sir William the 2nd Viscount, was born on October 30th 1742 in the parish of St James, Westminster, and died on December 14th 1788. His son, also William, the 3rd Viscount, was born at Powderham on July 30th 1768, and died in 1835.

[36] 'Literary Life and select works of Benjamin Stillingfleet', London, 1811, vol. 1, p. 187

[37] including a family group of Sir William Courtenay of Powderham, created 1st Viscount 1762, his wife Lady Frances Finch, their children and their dogs. Shown on p. 3 of the Guidebook to Powderham Castle

[38] Now at the Foundling Museum, London, where it hangs on the Grand Staircase.

Hudson of an unknown eighteenth century gentleman in an embroidered coat in the First Library. He bears a striking resemblance to John Beard. It would be nice to think that this was his brother William, and that they sat for their portraits together. But the Courtenay family can cast little light on the matter.[39]

Charlotte Beard lived much nearer her relations, and must have seen them more regularly. Her father had brought up his four daughters at his country house in Cowley, near Uxbridge, in the same County of Middlesex that they were now living in. His house had formerly been the property of the famous actor Barton Booth, and Hogarth painted a group portrait of the family at Cowley at some time before 1731 - though its whereabouts cannot now be established. The Rich family tomb, in which her father lay with his second wife - and her mother - Amy, was nearby in the churchyard of St John the Baptist, Hillingdon. Charlotte's sister Sarah and husband George Voelcker were buried there in 1769 and 1770 respectively. As we have seen, Beard and Charlotte brought up their two orphaned daughters, Sarah Melosina and Sophia Henrietta, thereafter as their own. Charlotte's sisters Henrietta (Bencraft) and Mary (Morris) were also living nearby; and so the progress of their children could be monitored from Rose Hill.

James Morris, first husband to Charlotte's sister Mary, was also buried in the tomb in 1767. Mary had three children from her first marriage, James, Mary and Elizabeth, and remarried John Horsley in 1768. She died before 1815, but her husband was still alive then at High Beech in Essex. The Rich family tomb was opened again in 1783 to receive the body of Priscilla, John Rich's third wife and Charlotte's stepmother. Until her death it would have been easy to keep in touch with Priscilla, living as she did with her brother Edward Wilford, Covent Garden theatre's former Treasurer, in Chelsea. Henrietta Bencraft is referred to in Priscilla's will as living in Hillingdon. She was buried in the tomb in 1812 after a long life of eighty-five years. And, finally, Harriet Bencraft - her unmarried daughter - was buried there in 1837, although time has very nearly erased her inscription. The earlier inscriptions, which are on all four sides, are still perfectly legible and have been protected by the large trees nearby.

The Rich family tomb today

[39] see p. 5 of the Guidebook. It is listed at Powderham as "possibly Admiral Boscowen" (1711-61).

John Beard's lengthy retirement from the theatre came at a stimulating time in the arts. Britain was not at the forefront of musical innovation, which was being driven forward much faster in Europe. But the 'galant' style of Carl Stamitz and J. C. Bach, and the 'classical' style of Haydn's symphonic music, were to take a firm root in public taste in these years. Beard died just before Haydn's two important visits to London. His retirement years also coincided with the entire period of Mozart's remarkable life. The two of them died, in fact, in the same year. At the moment that Beard retired, in May 1767, the eleven-year-old Mozart had barely begun to write any of his masterpieces. His very first opera, *Apollo et Hyacinthus*, was given its premiere on May 13 1767 in Salzburg. Every other remarkable composition was to be written during the long years of Beard's retirement.

The theatre in London, however, was a place of much more originality at this time. Had Beard remained at the helm in Covent Garden for a few more years, he would have been able to take some credit for the remarkable premiere of Richard Brinsley Sheridan's first play, *The Rivals*, at that theatre in 1775. Nevertheless, watching from the sidelines, he would have taken pleasure in the success of the collaboration between Sheridan and his brother-in-law the composer Thomas Linley, whose comic opera *The Duenna* (1775) was another strong musical piece in the mould of the works that Beard had encouraged Bickerstaffe and Arne to write a decade earlier. This became the most successful piece at Covent Garden for the rest of the century, receiving 75 performances in the 1775-6 season alone.[40] At Garrick's retirement in 1776 Sheridan bought a share in Drury Lane, and produced all of his subsequent plays, including *The School for Scandal* (1777) at that theatre. Beard could take some credit for foreseeing this interest in comedies of manners with his encouragement of Arthur Murphy's *No one's enemy but his Own,* and *What we must all come to* (both on January 9 1764), and *The School for Guardians* (January 10 1767) at Covent Garden.[41]

But Beard's true innovation was to turn the theatre into a house which would be renowned for the performance of English Opera. During his retirement we know that he went to a performance of Stephen Storace's *The Haunted Tower* (1789), and heard the music of this star pupil of Mozart who had recently returned home. At the same period Beard would have been able to hear the other singers who had returned to England after success in the premiere of Mozart's *The Marriage of Figaro:* Michael Kelly and Nancy Storace. Nancy, Stephen's sister, who had been a prima donna in Vienna for the four years 1783-7, became the soprano most in demand in London in the late 1780s and 1790s when she and Kelly "raised vocal standards to a level unprecedented at the playhouses".[42] She replaced Elizabeth Linley, Thomas Linley's sister, in the estimation of the public. Elizabeth had been

---

[40] "Lumping the playhouses together and starting in the summer of 1776, *The London Stage* (Part 5) shows that of the twelve most performed main-pieces six were operas, four were plays by Shakespeare, and two were modern plays. If the season 1775-6 were included, *The Duenna* would move up to second place". Fiske, 'English Theatre Music in the Eighteenth Century', Oxford, 1973, p. 412

[41] "The unpopularity of Murphy's politics has disguised from many critics the talent as a writer of unsentimental comedies that ought to have earned him comparison with Goldsmith and Sheridan". 'The Wordsworth Companion to Literature in English', ed. I. Ousby, Cambridge, 1988, reprinted Ware, Hertfordshire, 1994, p. 653

[42] Fiske, 'Nancy Storace', in *The New Grove Dictionary of Music and Musicians*, London, 1980, vol. 18, p.182

forced to retire from a distinguished career in the theatre and the music Festivals after her marriage to Sheridan. Beard would have known her voice well. She made her London debut in Thomas Hull's *The Fairy Favour*, in his final season, on January 31 1767; and sang at the London oratorio seasons and at the Three Choirs Festivals between 1769 and 1773. In 1773 she withdrew from public life, in order to please her new husband, with whom she had eloped to France; thus depriving the British public of hearing her in her husband's later works, such as *The Duenna*.

Before this there had been another significant loss at Covent Garden when Dibdin and Bickerstaffe transferred to Drury Lane one year after Beard's retirement, and produced their successful *Lionel and Clarissa* and *The Padlock* there in 1768. But William Shield revived Covent Garden's fortunes as a nursery for English opera composers in the 1780s, beginning with *Rosina* (a work much indebted to *Love in a Village*) in 1782. This work, from which the attractive quasi-folksong 'The Ploughboy' comes, established Shield overnight. He was to remain at Covent Garden as the undisputed master-composer of English opera until he quarrelled with the management in 1791, the year of Beard's death.

VISITS TO LONDON CONCERTS

Although the deafness which had periodically afflicted him all his life eventually obliged Beard to stop singing at the age of 51, he kept in touch with the London music scene during the twenty-four years of his retirement. There are reports of him attending theatrical performances and the Handel Commemoration in Westminster Abbey, as well as private concerts at the homes of the Sharp family, and the Wesley family. These were among several musical families of the time who held concerts in their own homes. William, James and Granville Sharp were capable amateur musicians who hosted private soirees at home in the winter, and on their boat on the Thames during the summer. They kept a record of the people attending, and Beard signed in as a guest for an evening of Glees on January 25 1776.[43]

Beard and his wife Charlotte also visited the Wesley's to hear their prodigiously talented sons. In 1763 Beard gave the 6-year-old Charles Wesley (1757-1834) a copy of the 1739 edition of Scarlatti's '*30 Essercizi*'. This had been his wedding gift to his first wife Henrietta. The frontispiece, by Jacopo Amigoni, is full of Jacobite references,[44] and would have appealed to her at the time of their 1739 wedding. It is now in the Sibley Library, in Rochester N.Y. and is inscribed 'Charles Wesley 1763. Gift of Mr Beard'. All of the reference works refer to Charles Wesley's love of Scarlatti and other old composers like Corelli and Geminiani. One wonders whether this was fostered at a very early age by Beard's gift. Jane Clark regards this 1738 volume, with its finely engraved notation, to be "the most beautiful example of eighteenth-century music printing".[45] Charles obviously made great use of this fine and very personal gift, which Beard felt able to offer him ten years after the death of his Jacobite first wife. When the Wesley concerts were given at their house in Chesterfield Street, Mayfair, the programmes were devoted in equal proportions to music by the Wesley boys [Charles, and Samuel (1766-1837)] and to baroque works by Handel, Geminiani, Scarlatti and Corelli, played by the young

[43] Brian Crosby, 'The Musical Activities of the Sharp Family', RMA Research Chronicle 34, 2001 p. 86
[44] for a full explanation of the Jacobite symbolism contained in the frontispiece see: Jane Clark, 'Farinelli as Queen of the Night', *Eighteenth Century Music*, Cambridge, 2005, pp. 321 - 333
[45] Jane Clark, 'Farinelli as Queen of the Night', *Eighteenth Century Music*, Cambridge, 2005, p. 321

virtuosos (Charles on the keyboards and Samuel on the violin) and a small instrumental ensemble of a string quartet and 2 horns.[46] Their father, the Rev. Charles Wesley recorded the names of the subscribers, as the Sharps did, and the repertoire that they performed. Between 30 and 50 people were able to be seated in their room, and paid three guineas for a series of seven concerts.[47] Beard must have mentioned the young Charles' precocious talent to his musical friends, because Boyce began to teach him composition, Stanley and Arnold allowed him in to hear their oratorio rehearsals and Kelway taught him the organ at St Martin-in-the-Fields.

As has been shown in an earlier chapter Charles Burney mentions Beard in his 1785 'Account of the Musical Performances ...in Commemoration of Handel'[48] as one of the few musicians still alive who had worked with Handel. Beard is most likely to have taken the opportunity to support this noble occasion - which was in aid of the Fund for Decayed Musicians (soon to be renamed the Royal Society of Musicians) - and which featured Arnold and Dupuis as Joah Bates' sub-conductors. Beard continued his support of the annual concerts promoted by the Society as both 'Benefactor and Subscriber' from at least 1785 until 1790, attending whenever his illness would allow him to travel up to London.[49] When he heard the tenor Samuel Harrison sing 'Oft on a plat of rising ground' from *L'Allegro ed Il Penseroso*[50] he was overheard to remark afterwards: "*I* never sung it half so well."[51]

He was particularly keen to attend concerts by the rising generation of new tenors. He certainly heard Michael Kelly in 1789, less than two years before his death. In his "Reminiscences" Kelly writes:

"This season I received a most flattering mark of attention from Mr John Beard, the celebrated English tenor singer. He did me the honour to come from his house at Hampton (as he told me) to hear me sing 'Spirit of my sainted sire', in *The Haunted Tower*.[52] He sat in the Drury Lane orchestra box, with his trumpet to his ear, for he was very deaf; and after the opera was over came upon the stage to me, and was pleased to express himself in terms of high approbation. I confess such a tribute from such a man was gratifying in the extreme."[53]

His warm friendship with Samuel Arnold, (described in a letter of 1786 as "our beloved Dr Arnold"[54]) continued to the end, the last known visit being as late as August 1790. It is a distinct possibility that Arnold regularly consulted Beard's library when he was producing his Handel edition. It may help to explain one final mystery surrounding Beard's relationship with Handel's music.

---

[46] Johnstone & Fiske, The Blackwell History of Music in Britain, 'The Eighteenth Century', Oxford, 1990, p.235

[47] The British Library has a copy made from the original by Eliza Wesley in 1894: Add. MS 35017.

[48] Charles Burney, *An Account of the Musical Performances in Commemoration of Handel,* London 1785

[49] see the relevant Programme Books in the British Library, ref. RM5b2-7

[50] I have traced performances from newspaper advertisements to May 8th & 22nd 1789 & March 3rd 1790.

[51] Laetitia Matilda Hawkins, *Anecdotes of Sir John Hawkins*, 1822, vol. 1 p.13

[52] a full-length opera by Stephen Storace to a text by James Cobb, premiered at Drury Lane on November 24th, 1789. There were 84 performances in the first two seasons, and Kelly sang the role of 'Lord William', with Nancy Storace as 'Adela' and Mr Bannister junior as 'Edward'. This aria comes in Act 3 of the opera.

[53] Michael Kelly, *Reminiscences* ed. Roger Fiske, O.U.P. London 1975, p. 169

[54] Letter to Dr Samuel Arnold, dated 9th March 1786, in : H. Diack Johnstone, 'Treasure Trove in Gloucester: a Grangerized copy of the 1895 edition of Daniel Lysons' History of the Three Choirs Festival', RMA Research Chronicle 31, 1998, p. 49

John Beard is buried in the Parish Church of St Mary the Virgin, Hampton, in Middlesex. I went there in search of his memorial tablet. The church that Beard worshipped in was completely rebuilt in 1829. But the vault, containing his remains, was not disturbed. The memorials were all re-sited within the new church; and since the church guide[55] contained a reference to Beard's being in the "North Aisle, north wall" I expected to find it easily. I was curious to see if there would be a score of music sculpted on it; and if so, what music might have been selected. I was expecting it to be a Handelian quotation, much in the manner that the fine memorial to Handel in Westminster Abbey displays a page of "I know that my Redeemer liveth". At some stage, however, an organ was placed at the end of the North Aisle completely hiding the marble Memorial. In order to reach it I had to climb through the organ pipes. It was dark and dirty back there, and I could only dimly make out the inscription:

> How vain the monumental praise
> Our partial friends devise!
> While trophies o'er our dust they raise
> Poetic fictions rise.
> Say, what avails, if good or bad
> I now am represented:
> If happily the faults I had
> Sincerely were repented.
> A friend, a wife, or both in one,
> By Love, by Time endear'd,
> Shall banish falsehood from the Stone
> That covers her JOHN BEARD.
>
> He died the 4th of February 1791
> Aged 74 years

This curiously inapposite verse,[56] with its strange emphasis on 'faults' and 'falsehood', (none of which seems particularly applicable to Beard's life), has not seen the light of day for more than a hundred years.[57] Nor has the musical extract which - yes! - is sculpted on the pages of an open music book below. This portion of the tablet was so dark and filthy that I had to take a kind of 'brass-rubbing' of it. When I studied the results by daylight I was surprised to see that the text was a verse of the 'Te Deum':

---

[55] F.C.E Atkins *A short guide to the Parish Church of St Mary the Virgin, Hampton*, Hampton, 1996
[56] A more appropriate one, from the Gentleman's Magazine in Feb. 1791, is shown in Appendix 6
[57] The guidebook says that the organ was "reconstructed in 1901". It is not known whether that was the point at which the memorial was hidden.

The music looked Handelian, and further study proved that it was bars 15 - 35 of the Bass aria, No. 8, in the *Dettingen* Te Deum [HWV 283] which had been composed in July 1743. The first performance was given on Sunday November 27 in a service at the Chapel Royal to celebrate the King's safe return. Mr Abbot, according to pencillings in the score, was the singer of this aria. Another singer mentioned in the score is Bernard Gates, who sang the solo in no. 7 'Thou art the King of Glory'. Beard's name is not found, although he was free on both this date and on the three dates when it was given a public rehearsal in the Chapel Royal.[58] He could also have attended a further public rehearsal that Burrows indicates might have taken place on Friday November 25, so long as it took place in the daytime.[59] In the evening he was singing at Covent Garden as 'Lovemore' in *The Lottery*. Burrows feels that he might have been "one of the 'extraordinary Performers'" mentioned in the Lord Chamberlain's records as having been paid for taking part in the service on November 27.[60] He had certainly taken his usual solo role in the Ode '*Of fields! Of forts! and floods!*' that Greene had written and conducted a week earlier for the King's birthday. An additional reason that could support the theory that Beard did, indeed, sing the small amount of solo tenor music in the *Te Deum* is the fact that the Chapel Royal's principal solo tenor, James Chelsum, (who is mentioned as one of the soloists, along with Beard, in the report of the 1740 wedding music) had died in August.[61] When Handel was composing the work, commencing on July 17, he may have assumed that this useful tenor would be able to cope with the small amount of solo music in nos. 2 & 11. Beard may well have been his late replacement.

But none of that helps explain why the music of movement no. 8 is on Beard's memorial stone. It is an aria that he never sang. The text can hardly have any particular significance on its own merits. Beard had married twice: there were no surviving children from either partnership. The only explanation that I can come up with is as follows: it may be fanciful and completely unsubstantiated - and completely unscholarly - but may be the nearest that we can get to explaining the anomaly...

I imagine that Beard told his second wife Charlotte countless times how he had been 'discovered' as a Chapel Royal chorister by Handel. She would have known how intimately his subsequent career had been tied up with Handel's. All of this would have led, very logically, to her choosing some of Handel's music to put on the memorial to her husband. There were many wonderful arias that she could have chosen. If the text were to be as relevant as the one on Handel's own memorial then some of Beard's greatest 'hits' would be immediately ruled out. "Where'er you walk" and "Love in her eyes sits playing" are certainly too secular. "Sound an alarm", "Why does the God of Israel sleep", "Waft her angels", "Thou shalt dash

---

[58] 26th September, 9th and 18th November

[59] Burrows *Handel and the English Chapel Royal*, Oxford 2005, p. 387

[60] Burrows *Handel and the English Chapel Royal*, Oxford 2005, p. 389 & 615

[61] "…the toll also included James Chelsum (died August 1743)" ibid. p. 389

them" - and any other tenor aria in Messiah - do not have the right eulogistic 'feel' for a memorial stone. As nothing obvious presented itself to Charlotte she must have fallen back on another plan. I have rejected the idea that the *Te Deum* music was chosen at random, since the choice of text - *When thou tookest upon thee to deliver man : thou didst not abhor the Virgin's womb* - must have immediately rendered it unsuitable. So she must have chosen something from a piece that her husband had let her know was particularly special to him.

Handel set the *Te Deum* five times. The one that was best known was the *Utrecht* Te Deum, [HWV 278] composed back in 1713. It was one of Handel's most frequently performed sacred works and would have been performed several times during Beard's years in the Chapel Royal choir.[62] However other versions had entered the Chapel Royal repertoire at other times: the 'Caroline' Te Deum [HWV 280] 1714 revised 1722, and the 'A major' Te Deum [HWV 282] c. 1726 - a partial reworking of the 'Cannons' Te Deum [HWV 281] of 1717. All of them had solos for the verse *"When thou tookest upon thee to deliver Man"*, which were normally given to the alto soloist. Handel was particularly careful to write these for the particular voices of Richard Elford and, later, Francis Hughes. But the short verse, no. 4, in the *Utrecht* Te Deum could also have been sung by a high tenor.[63] Perhaps this is the setting which meant so much to Beard: perhaps he had sung it during his final years in the choir, either as an alto when his voice was getting deeper, or as a tenor in the period between Easter and October 1734 when he probably remained in the choir as a tenor deputy.

If this theory is right, then Charlotte simply put the wrong musical text on the memorial! Perhaps she chose a volume entitled *Te Deum* from the bookshelf and took the wrong one. Perhaps it was the only one left on the shelf. It would not have been extraordinary if others had been lent to Samuel Arnold at an earlier stage, when he was preparing his Handel edition, leaving her little to choose from. John Beard was one of the 381 subscribers to this edition, the first volume of which appeared in 1787. However, Arnold's interest in this major project, together with another one to produce a compendious 'Songs of Handel Compleat', dates back some five years earlier and was to last until 1797. Thus all of his recorded visits to the Beard household fall within this period of activity. His editions of the various *Te Deum* settings are very early issues in the series, whose publication order was: *Athaliah*, *Theodora*, *Messiah*, 'Caroline' Te Deum, 'Cannons' Te Deum, 'Utrecht' Te Deum, 'Dettingen' Te Deum, Jubilate, 'A major' Te Deum, *Sosarme* etc.[64] Perhaps some of the borrowed scores had remained in his possession. But it is good to know that Handel and Beard are united on the hidden memorial. Now is the time to try and get it repositioned within the church, where it can be seen once again.

EPILOGUE

It was said that Hampton became known as the 'town of the widows' in the early nineteenth century, when its principal houses were all inhabited by widows.[65] There was the widow of David Garrick (the actor's nephew) at The Cedars; Garrick's own

---

[62] February 25th 1731, February 17th 1732, February 1st 1733, February 19th (with reh. on the 16th) 1734.
[63] shown as "Alto solo [or Tenor]" in Watkins Shaw's edition for Novello Handel Edition, 1968
[64] J. Coopersmith *The first Gesamtausgabe: Dr Arnold's Edition of Handel's Works* Notes, 1947 p. 285
[65] G.D. Heath, 'Hampton in the 19th Century', Twickenham Local History Society, Paper no. 27, 1973, p.4

widow, Eva Maria, at Hampton House who outlived Charlotte Beard by several years, dying in 1822 aged 99, after 43 years as a widow; Mrs Greg at Spring Grove; Mrs Hare at Barham House; Mrs Gouldsmith and Mrs Glover, the widows of prosperous London merchants, in large houses in Church Street - and Charlotte Beard at Rose Hill. Charlotte continued to live in the house after Beard's death, with the two Voelcker daughters. On August 15 1792, she was a witness at the marriage in the Parish Church of the eldest, Sarah, to the Rev. Thomas Bowen. The younger, Sophia, remained unmarried and died at Hampton in 1799. These two daughters had inherited their mother's share of the Covent Garden patent, and had therefore always been well provided for. One assumes that it is for this reason that they received no mention in Beard's Will. Indeed, it is only from the Will of Sophia Voelcker[66] that we learn of this episode in Beard's life. After the usual preamble, this starts off: "...I give and bequeath unto my dear Aunt Mrs Charlotte Beard the sum of £1000 3% Consolidated Bank Annuities as a small but sincere acknowledgment of my affection and gratitude for her kind tender and uncommon care of me from my early infancy..."

Charlotte died in Hampton in 1818, at the age of 91, after 27 years of widowhood. She was buried alongside her husband in the Parish Church on September 4.[67] From her Will[68] one can see that she was able to maintain a comfortable life-style until her death. She left bequests to 3 domestic servants and a gardener, as well as other named Hampton residents. The bulk of her estate was divided between all her surviving nieces and nephews, including Charlotte Mary Baird (James Bencraft's grand-daughter), who was living with her in 1818.[69] However, she did not make specific provisions for the disposal of Rose Hill. And it turned out there was a problem. According to the rules of the Manorial Court of Hampton, the property still belonged to John Beard - the title had never been transferred to her.

A Court was held on October 8 1818 [70] when "the first proclamation was made for the Person or Persons entitled to the Copyhold Estate whereof Charlotte Beard lately died seized to come into Court and take admittance thereto otherwise the same would be seized into the hands of the Lord for want of a Tenant but no one came [sic]".

One of her Executors was Beard's nephew, John. Presumably, at this moment, he was hurrying up from Devon. However, he had arrived a fortnight later, when a special Court was held on October 24. This John Beard declared that all the Executors of Beard's 1791 Will were now dead, but that he was the son of one of them [not true - Beard's brother, William, was never one of his Executors]. The Court accepted his statement, nonetheless, and temporarily transferred the title of Rose Hill to him. Meanwhile, the property had already been advertised for sale by auction[71] and a buyer found: the new owner, who purchased the property for 3400 guineas, was confirmed by the Court as Edward Strettell.

---

[66] Nat. Arch: PROB11/1334

[67] Apparently the fees for her burial were not received until 1820. [Document of G .W.Heath at Hampton Library]

[68] Nat. Arch: PROB11/1609

[69] In 1819, Charlotte Mary Baird married the lawyer William Wightman who had been a witness to Charlotte Beard's Will. She was not Beard's niece, as is stated in Ripley's 'History of Hampton', but a great-niece (of Charlotte).The Wightmans were still living in Hampton at the time of the 1851 census.

[70] Manorial Court of Hampton, Ref: CRES 5/283 (Nat. Arch.)

[71] Advertisement in 'The Times' newspaper: 18th September 1818

The author at Rose Hill in front of the blue plaque.

BEARD'S EPITAPH IN *THE GENTLEMAN'S MAGAZINE*

Satire be dumb! Nor dream the scenic art
Must spoil the morals and corrupt the heart.
Here lies JOHN BEARD: confess, with pensive pause,
His modesty was great as our applause.
Whence had that voice such magic to control?
'Twas but the echo of a well tun'd soul:
Thro' life, his morals and his music ran
In symphony and spoke the virtuous man.
Go, gentle harmonist, our hopes approve,
To meet, and hear thy sacred songs above:
When taught by thee, the stage of life well trod,
We rise to raptures round the throne of God.

Ob. Feb. 5th 1791, Aetatis suae, 75

A later occupier of the house was William Ewart, the promoter of public libraries, who is commemorated, together with Beard, on the blue plaque fixed to the entrance

CHAPTER 14
BEARD'S VOCAL LEGACY

HIS MUSIC LIBRARY

Apart from the score of Scarlatti's '*30 Essercizi*' which Beard gave to the young Charles Wesley in 1763 it has not been easy to identify other music that he owned.[1] As I suggest (above) some of his Handel scores and manuscripts may have passed into Samuel Arnold's keeping when the latter was preparing his famous Handel edition in the 1780s and 1790s. Beard subscribed to the edition, as is revealed by the list of subscribers found tucked into one of the Library of Congress copies.[2] Samuel Arnold's library was sold at auction in May 1803.[3]

The parts from which Beard sang Boyce's *Court Odes* are all in the Bodleian Library, and so must have been gathered in after the performances by a tidy-minded composer. A part bearing Beard's name is included in the set of *Messiah* material presented to the Foundling Hospital under the terms of Handel's will in 1759. But the tenor solo copy does not appear to have been sung from, leading to the supposition that Beard continued to use his old copy for subsequent performances in the 1760s.

A copy that does contain evidence of having been used in performance is his copy of the tenor music in *The Foundling Hospital Anthem* (described earlier, in Chapter 6), which is now in the Library of the Royal College of Music (RCM 2254). Equally interesting is another manuscript at the Royal College of Music, which may well be Beard's own scrap-book of theatre music for a particular year's performances. This is a miscellaneous collection of music (RCM 2232) which has so far confused music scholars. Roger Fiske says: "harder to date is MS 2232 in London's Royal College of Music" before admitting that he cannot make sense of the strange mixture of music for plays and operas.[4] However, the volume makes a lot more sense if it is seen as a collection of material useful to one particular person, at one particular time. Who could that person be?

A perusal of the music contained in the volume shows that it does not now contain precisely what is shown in the index, as some pages containing music for a certain *Oedipus* have been removed. What this music might have been is not clear, as the only performances of *Oedipus* that I have traced were three performances at Covent Garden in January 1755, when the Dryden play was advertised as 'not acted in 12 years'. Without these pages the first page of the volume is now numbered as page 21. But the volume does contain the following:

a) *Macbeth* music

> Heckat air: 'O what a dainty Pleasure's this to sail in the Air'
> Music when the cauldron is discovered
> Heckat: 'Black Spirits and white, red Spirits and grey'

---

[1] Harry Diack Johnstone has kindly supplied me with a list of the music publications to which Beard subscribed.
[2] M3.H21, Copy 1 – see J.M. Coopersmith *The first Gesamtausgabe: Dr Arnold's Edition of Handel's Works* Notes, 1947 p. 282: "...Of those who actually knew Handel, the best-known are John Beard, Charles Burney..."
[3] J.M. Coopersmith *The first Gesamtausgabe: Dr Arnold's Edition of Handel's Works* Notes, 1947 p. 286, f/n 32
[4] R. Fiske, 'English Theatre Music in the Eighteenth Century', Oxford, 1973, p. 116

b) Overture to *The Fair Penitent*

c) The Address to Sleep, sung by Mr Beard in the Tragedy of *Tamerlane*

d) The Music in *Lethe*
> Song: 'Ye mortals whom Fancies and Trouble perplex'
> Song for the 'Fine Lady': 'The card invites, in crowds we fly'
> Sung by Mr Beard in *Lethe*: 'Come mortals, come, come follow me'

e) The music in *The Provok'd Husband*
> Song: for 'Miss Jenny'
> Song: 'What tho' they call me Country Lass'

f) *The Devil to Pay*
> Song for 'Jobson'
> Song for 'Butler'
> Song for Sir John Loverule: 'Ye Gods ye gave to me a wife'
> Song for Sir John Loverule: 'Of all states in Life so various'
> Song for Lady Loverule: 'Tell me no more of this or that'
> Song for Sir John Loverule: 'Grant me ye Pow'rs but this request'
> Song for Nell: 'My swelling heart now leaps with joy'
> Song for Conjuror: 'My little Spirits now appear'
> Chorus of Spirits: 'All this we will with care perform'
> Song for Sir John Loverule: 'The Early Horn'
> > *in full-score for Horn, Violin 1 & 2, Viola, Bass*
> Song for Jobson: 'Of all the Trades from East to West'
> Song for Jobson: 'I'll into my Stall, 'tis broad day now'
> Song for Nell: 'Though late I was a Cobler's Wife'
> Song for Nell: 'Ladies with an artful grace'
> Song for Nell: 'Oh charming cunning man, thou hast been wond'rous kind'
> Duet for Sir John/Nell: 'Was ever Man possest of so sweet, so kind a Wife'
> Song for Lady Loverule: 'Let every face with Smiles appear'

The interest in this volume lies principally in the complete music for Beard's most frequently performed afterpiece - *The Devil to Pay*. The music for the song which he famously inserted into it in 1736, 'The Early Horn,' is unusually given in full-score - unlike the rest of the music. The only pieces of music which would not have involved Beard as a performer are:
> b) the Overture to *The Fair Penitent*
> e) the 2 songs in *The Provok'd Husband.*
Otherwise all of the music would have helped him in rehearsal, and on two occasions (c & d) he is named as the performer. Of course, this could be a keyboard player's part, though the full-score of 'The Early Horn' might suggest otherwise. There is so much tenor music in it that it seems more likely that it belonged to a performer who played these roles. In the period in question there are only two possibilities: Beard and Lowe. *Lethe* was performed by Beard in April 1740, and again in January 1749 when Garrick revived it at Drury Lane. The other works were all in the Drury Lane 1748-9 and 1754-5 repertoires, whilst Beard was on contract at the theatre there, viz:

<u>Drury Lane 1748-9</u>

The Devil to Pay commencing 20 September 1748
The Provok'd Husband commencing 1 October 1748
The Fair Penitent commencing 22 October 1748
Macbeth 28 October 1748
Tamerlane 4 & 5 November 1748
Lethe commencing 2 January 1749

<u>Drury Lane 1754-5</u>

The Devil to Pay commencing 19 September 1754
Macbeth 24 September 1754
Lethe commencing 15 October 1754
Tamerlane 4 November 1754
The Fair Penitent commencing 6 November 1754
The Provok'd Husband 6 May 1755

Thomas Lowe was not in any performance of *Lethe* until it entered the Covent
Garden repertoire on October 2 1759, proving that the book could not have been
used at Covent Garden <u>before</u> that date. On October 2 it was most likely to have
been Lowe who played Beard's part as - although Beard was now working at Covent
Garden too - it is clear that he didn't make his first appearance with the company
until October 10, when he appeared in the new production of *The Beggar's Opera*
with Miss Charlotte Brent. However, there were no performances of *The Fair
Penitent* this season.

<u>Covent Garden 1759-60</u>

The Devil to Pay commencing 24 September 1759
The Provok'd Husband commencing 1 October 1759
Lethe commencing 2 October 1759 – probably with Thomas Lowe as 'Mercury'
Tamerlane 5 November 1759
Macbeth 17 April 1760
[The Fair Penitent] no performance this season

So, the likelihood of this being a volume that Beard could have used, rather than
Thomas Lowe, is quite high.

BEARD THE SINGER

Garrick wrote feelingly of the fact that an actor's artistry dies with him, and is not
long remembered thereafter:

> But he who struts his hour upon the stage,
> Can scarce extend his fame to half an age;
> Nor Pen, nor Pencil, can the actor save;
> The Art, and Artist, share one common grave.[5]

---

[5] quoted in Benjamin Victor, 'The History of the Theatres of London...', 1771

The same is equally true of singers. But the music which Beard sang does live on. Some is forgotten, but the best of it is performed as much - if not more - than it was in his own day.

The music which is forgotten today is the ephemeral corpus of 'popular' ballads, which was the eighteenth century equivalent of 'pop' music today. I imagine that the best part of ours will be equally forgotten in two hundred years time (if not sooner). Beard earned a living singing these songs, but would have been the first to admit that their life expectancy was extremely limited. There are occasional songs which have survived down to our age. Elizabeth Poston made a pretty arrangement of William Boyce's ballad 'By thy banks, gentle Stour'[6] in the 1950s, which is still performed today. She also resurrected other ballads that Beard may or may not have sung at the Pleasure Gardens, such as William Defesch's 'Polly of the Plain' and Michael Arne's 'The Lass with the delicate air'. Facsimile editions of eighteenth century song albums, such as Bickham's *The Musical Entertainer*, Thomas Arne's *Lyric Harmony* and *Vocal Melody*, and Boyce's *Lyra Britannica* make it possible to study - and recreate - these ephemeral works today.[7]

Elizabeth Poston was also one of the first editors to recognise the beauty of Boyce's serenata *Solomon*, before it was revived by the Early Music Movement in the 1980s. Her versions of the soprano air 'Tell me lovely shepherd' and the duet 'Together let us range' have been useful songs for young singers for fifty years or more. Other editors to rekindle interest in the music of this period are Ella Ivimey, who made useful arrangements of Pleasure Gardens songs, such as Michael Arne's 'Invitation to Ranelagh' (1948); and Maurice Bevan, who resurrected some of the lost cantatas of John Stanley and Thomas Arne in the late 1950s. Publishers have kept some of this music in print, mainly for teaching purposes; and we must be thankful for Schott's 'Voice and Recorder' series, and Stainer and Bell's slim volumes of 'English Solo Song', for preserving other music that Beard was the first to perform.[8]

The songs that were performed in the plays at Drury Lane and Covent Garden are largely forgotten, with the exception of Arne's songs for David Garrick's Shakespeare productions. These have not only survived, but have passed into a unique area of repertoire known as *Traditional Songs*. Arne would have been surprised to have found his tunes equated with 'folksong'; but he would have been delighted to know that the songs that John Beard sang as Amiens, in *As You Like It*, ('Blow, blow thou Winter Wind', 'Under the Greenwood Tree', and 'When Daisies pied'), and as Lorenzo in *The Merchant of Venice* ('Tell me where is fancy bred') were still being sung and loved two hundred and fifty years later. Most children of the mid-twentieth century would have sung these, as well as the songs from *The Tempest* ('Where the bee sucks' and 'Come unto these yellow sands') at some stage during their school days. Arne's songs for Milton's *Comus* and the *Masque of Alfred* never went entirely out of fashion either; the tenor arias 'Not on Beds of fading Flowers' and 'Now Phoebus sinketh in the West' and the mezzo aria 'Come calm content' were available in late Victorian editions, long before the Baroque revival stimulated interest in these works once again.

---

[6] from Lyra Britannica, London, 1747, where the text is "On thy banks, gentle Stour".
[7] *Music for London Entertainment 1660-1800*, Macnutt, Tunbridge Wells, 1985, has produced many of these.
[8] for example: 'Georgian Songs', and volumes devoted to Arne and Boyce.

Arne has not been so successful where his serious operas, such as *Artaxerxes*, are concerned. This work is surely due for a revival, now that there are counter-tenors sufficiently able to undertake the two castrato roles of 'Artaxerxes' and 'Arbaces' in it. Hyperion Records has led the way with a 1995 recording, in which Beard's fine aria "Behold, on Lethe's dismal Strand" can be heard once again.[9] But there are two further airs of Arne's which will never fade from the repertoire, and with which Beard was closely involved from the outset: 'Rule Britannia' (from the masque of *Alfred*); and 'The National Anthem', which he performed as 'God bless our noble King, / God save great George our King' in the first performance at Drury Lane Theatre on September 28 1745.

The after-pieces which kept Beard so busy in the theatre have supplied very few tunes that have remained in the repertoire. But Pantomimes did rather better: Boyce's 'Heart of Oak' from *Harlequin's Invasion* (1759) has remained as a traditional tune beloved by military bands, even long after Garrick's words have been forgotten. Another traditional song which was first sung onstage by Beard was 'The Miller of Dee' from *Love in a Village* (1762). Although the tune was old (it occurs in *The Devil to Pay* and other ballad operas as 'The Budgeon is a fine Trade'), the words are presumably by Isaac Bickerstaffe. The song became lastingly popular, and even got anthologised in the National Song Book.

Of course, the work which has survived best of all down to our day is *The Beggar's Opera*. This work by John Gay, with popular tunes arranged and orchestrated by Johann Christoph Pepusch, arose as a satire on the British political scene at the end of Robert Walpole's administration, but proved remarkably hardy. In fact, it was never out of fashion during Beard's life, even when its initial relevance had been long forgotten. But every age has altered and re-interpreted it to their own taste. Beard himself was involved in the first major overhaul, when he invited Arne to re-orchestrate it in a more contemporary 'galant' style for the famous 1759 Covent Garden production in which he starred with Charlotte Brent, and which broke box-office records by running for 40 nights. At the beginning of the 20th century Frederick Austin had a similar success with his operetta-style of orchestral arrangements, in the production first seen at the Lyric Theatre Hammersmith in 1920 (transferring to the Kingsway Theatre in 1922) produced by Nigel Playfair and conducted by Eugene Goossens. He himself performed the principal role of 'Macheath', which he had now turned into a baritone role. Benjamin Britten turned it back into a tenor one for Peter Pears in 1948, and realised the traditional airs in his own distinctive style. Kurt Weill and Bertolt Brecht had gone even further in 1928 when they completely reinterpreted the story as a satire on the corruption of 1920s Germany in *Die Dreigroschenoper* (*The Threepenny Opera*).

All of this music reveals Beard as an easy communicator, with a gift for putting the text across naturally and convincingly. But it does not reveal much more about the quality of his voice, other than that he had a flexible and wide range. The song which he himself composed, *Cross Purposes*[10], takes him up to a high B natural once in every verse. The songs in *The Devil to Pay,* which he performed as many times - if not more - than *The Beggar's Opera*, demand a compass of very nearly 2 octaves in the Air 'Of all Comforts I miscarry'd', taking him from a low C up to a high B flat.

---

[9] Volume 33 of their *English Orpheus* series, CDA67051/2
[10] See page 163

It is Handel's Oratorios which give us the clearest idea of what Beard's voice was capable of performing. Boyce and Greene wrote equally well for him in their Court Odes, but these pieces are not known at all today, and are unlikely to be revived. Boyce's *Solomon* is becoming better-known as a result of a fine 1989 recording for Hyperion Records. The aria from Boyce's *Secular Masque*, 'The Sword within the Scabbard keep', known as 'The Song of Momus to Mars', which was successfully performed by Beard at Boyce's Doctorate in Cambridge as well as at Drury Lane, re-emerged in 20th century song albums as a Baritone aria. His musical after-pieces, *The Chaplet* and *The Shepherd's Lottery*, are still awaiting rediscovery, and new performing editions. The Dirge in *Romeo and Juliet*, and the Masque *Peleus and Thetis* are in the process of being rediscovered, and can now be heard in a 1996 recording by Opera Restor'd.[11] Maurice Greene's solo music is still little-known, although his cantatas, his song collection *The Chaplet* (1738), and his settings for voice and keyboard of *Spenser's Amoretti* (1739) would be welcome additions to the modern-day tenor's repertoire.

So it is to Handel that we must turn to learn about Beard's voice, and to discover how its tessitura, its flexibility, and its tonal quality has informed all music for the tenor voice that has been modelled on the Handel format, such as Haydn's two great oratorios *The Creation* and *The Seasons*, and - later still - the oratorios of Mendelssohn.

Handel quickly realised what the nineteen-year-old Beard was capable of singing, and wrote music for him that must have fitted his voice like a glove. After requiring him to sing an aria adapted from a castrato show-stopper (in *Parnasso in Festa)* in the Wedding Anthem *Sing unto God* (1736), he never demanded such elaborate coloratura from him again:

Much of the original pitch is retained in the hurried arrangement, rendering this aria a not very satisfactory mutation into a tenor piece.[12] Realising that this kind of vocal writing would not work down an octave at Beard's pitch, he was careful to write a more controlled 'fioritura' for him in future *Allegro* movements. There are still many vocal runs in these later arias: one only has to think of 'Every Valley', 'The Enemy said: I will pursue', and 'Why does the God of Israel sleep' to remember that Beard must have had a flexible voice. But vocal lines such as this passage from *Sing unto God,* with its extraordinarily long phrases, consistently high tessitura, and rapid passage-work, never occur later in music specifically designed for Beard's voice.

---

[11] Hyperion Records CDA66935
[12] However I myself had success with it in concerts with The London Bach Society, conductor Paul Steinitz, which were the first performances in modern times, & subsequently recorded on *EMI* Record CSD 3741 in 1973.

In contrast, the first oratorio to have been specifically conceived with him in mind - *Alexander's Feast* in February 1736 when he was aged 21 - has attractive vocal runs that are designed to illustrate the text and further the mood of the music rather than show off the voice:

The Prin-ces ap - plaud with a fu - rious joy, the Prin-ces ap - plaud,_____ with a fu - rious joy,

John Hawkins had been right when he talked of Beard having a 'firm voice' which was capable of 'an articulate utterance of the words, and a just expression of the melody'. These are features which are particularly noticeable in the music Handel wrote for him. He was capable of more than what Burney wrote about his rival Thomas Lowe: that he could only be safely trusted with a ballad. Some of the most effective music which Handel was to write for Beard was extremely 'firm' and military in nature. *Judas Maccabaeus* is full of such numbers, and 'Sound an Alarm' and 'Call forth thy Powers' are some of the finest. But as early as 1739 this style of aria was provided for Beard in the *Ode on St Cecilia's Day*:

The trum-pet's loud clang-our ex - cites us to arms, ex - cites us to arms, to arms, to arms, the trum - pet's loud clang - our ex - cites us to arms, with shrill notes of____ an - ger____ and____ mor - tal____ a - larms,_____

The variety of aria types which Handel wrote for Beard in these early years was extremely wide, ranging from extrovert *Allegro* numbers like these, to simple and sensitive melodic numbers. *Saul*, which was premiered at the time of his first wedding in January 1739, contains this lovely *Largo* for Beard's character of 'Jonathan':

Sin not, O King, a - gainst the Youth, who ne'er___ of - fend - ed___ you: Think, to his loy - al - ty___ and truth what great____ re - wards___ are___ due!

Handel also wrote charming *Sicilianos* for him. *L'Allegro ed il Penseroso* (1740) contains one of the best of them. Possibly as a result of Arne's recent success with the music for Milton's *Comus* (1738) Handel turned to an easy Vauxhall-song style himself for many of the airs in this setting of Milton. 'Let me wander not unseen' was to remain in Beard's repertoire to the very end of his career, since a version of it, set to Bickerstaffe's new words, was inserted into the ballad opera *Love in a Village*. In May 1767 this work was to be Beard's swansong in the theatre.

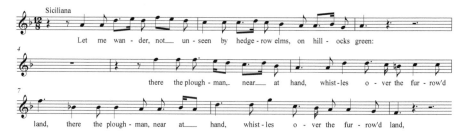

In addition to these lilting melodies, set in compound time, Beard was also given some fine slow movements in common time. This group of arias includes some of the best known of Handel's arias for the tenor voice, such as 'Total eclipse' (*Samson* 1743), 'Where'er you walk' (*Semele* 1744), and 'Waft her Angels' (*Jephtha* 1752).

At the end of the oratorios in which Beard had been entrusted with the title role Handel often wrote a different kind of *Andante* aria: one of great emotional depth, and with a finely controlled mood set to music with long arching phrases. 'Thus when the Sun' (*Samson* 1743), 'With honour let desert be crown'd' (*Judas Maccabaeus* 1747) and 'For ever blessed be thy holy name' (*Jephtha* 1752) are such numbers, in which the hero considers the whole sequence of events that have just unfolded. They reveal the greatness of Handel's skill and soundness of his theatrical judgement; but also show that he believed Beard was equipped to do them justice:

The aria 'For ever blessed' is the last aria for Beard's character in Handel's last, completely original, oratorio. Thus it could be the last new piece which he wrote for the singer. It is a simple melody, set well within his comfortable range of low C to high A, and, within its modest length of 18 bars, points the way ahead with remarkable foresight to the style of Mendelssohn's tenor arias in *St Paul* and *Elijah*:

310

The final and most remarkable body of music that Handel was inspired to create by Beard's highly charged singing was the dramatic accompanied recitative or *accompagnato*. These dynamic movements carry the drama forward with music that is immensely responsive to the changing nature of the text. They vary from being heightened *recitativo secco* to being mini-scenes with an ever-changing arioso feel. In movements such as 'My griefs for this' (*Samson*), 'So will'd my father, now at rest' (*Judas Maccabaeus*), and 'Ah, whither is she gone, unhappy fair?' (*Semele*), Handel pushed the conventions of baroque opera further forward towards the through-composed, monodic operas of the nineteenth century. The finest of them all is 'Deeper and deeper still' (*Jephtha*) which charts a wide range of emotions in its restless harmonic and rhythmic shifts; and which is a striking psychological study of a man - literally - at his wits' end:

This passage reveals, yet again, that Beard possessed a strong, thrilling top to his voice. This is confirmed by other contemporary sources, including Charles Burney. Handel, it will be seen, always saved the high notes for the musical climax - as here at "that lash me into madness". He did not squander the high notes unnecessarily; and in this his vocal writing differs from that of his contemporary J.S. Bach, whose tenor soloists floated their high notes, and could sing arias with a higher overall tessitura than these of Handel. One only has to think of the tessitura of such arias as 'Benedictus' (*B Minor Mass*) and 'Erwäge' (*Johannes Passion*) and - in the following extract - 'Ach, schlage doch bald' (*Cantata 95*) to realise that Handel was writing for a different, more theatrical, voice.

Handel had not always had tenors like this. In fact, there is evidence that the tenors that he first encountered in England, at Cannons, the palace of James Brydges, Duke of Chandos, sang with a tessitura that ran up from the tenor range into the falsetto of the counter-tenor one. The Chapel Royal records of the day do not always specify whether a singer was truly a tenor or a countertenor. For example, Thomas Bell shared a place as 'Countertenor' at the Chapel Royal with Thomas Gethin, who was clearly a tenor.[13] Richard Elford's name appears in a Tenor partbook of the period,

---

[13] Burrows, 'Handel and the Chapel Royal', Oxford, 2005, p. 579

but he sang the Alto solos in Croft's *Odes,* and in Handel's *Utrecht* Jubilate and *Caroline* Te Deum.[14] This flexible voice is shown most clearly in Handel's original version of *Acis and Galatea,* whose choruses (sung one to a part by the soloists) require three tenors capable of singing in an extended falsetto range.

This was a voice that had been known to Purcell at the end of the seventeenth century, and for which he had composed in works like *The Fairy Queen.* It lingered longer on the mainland of Europe. Much of the solo writing by the French court composers Rameau, Mondonville and Boismortier makes the same vocal demands. For example, the role of 'Don Quichotte' in Boismortier's *Don Quichotte chez la Duchesse*[15] (1743), which was written for the singer Bérard, lies somewhere between the countertenor range and that of a very high tenor:

But this is clearly not written for the sort of voice that John Beard had. However, French music continued to require tenors capable of singing music that remained this high, and in the nineteenth century a new generation of composers required the same facility. Rossini is the best known one to take his French tenors up stratospherically high. But other contemporary composers, such as Meyerbeer and Auber, used this range, which was best displayed by the singer Adolphe Nourrit (1802-39). He created roles in *Moise, La Muette de Portici, Count Ory, Guillaume Tell, Robert le Diable, La Juive* and *Les Huguenots* between 1827 and 1836.

Beard, by contrast, had a solid middle and lower register to his voice. His arias frequently demonstrate that this had an almost 'baritonal' quality to it. The fact that his theatrical roles included so many 'hearty' characters - which we, today, would associate with the baritone repertoire - such as soldiers, sailors, highwaymen and squires, leads to the assumption that his middle-range was as full and solid as his top was bright and ringing. Just one example will suffice to demonstrate this: and it is taken once again from his greatest Handel role, 'Jephtha', whose six arias and ten recitatives (*secco* and *accompagnato*) cover the widest range of moods that Handel ever wrote for a character in his oratorios:

[14] Burrows, 'Handel and the Chapel Royal', Oxford, 2005, p. 583-4
[15] J.Bodin de Boismortier 'Don Quichotte chez la Duchesse', ed. Roger Blanchard, Paris, 1971, pp. 46-7

THE MESSIAH

The most lasting testimonial to Beard's vocal skill is the tenor music in the greatest of all Handel's oratorios, *Messiah*, which was written for his voice in 1741. He did not take part in the premiere in Dublin on April 13 1742, as we have seen in earlier chapters; but he did give the London premiere on March 23 1743. In Dublin the local tenor soloist, James Bailey, was not sufficiently able to sing the aria 'Thou shalt dash them', so Handel wrote a substitute recitative which was sung, on this occasion only, by William Lamb.[16] The original tenor music underwent very little alteration once it entered Beard's repertoire, and many scholars have remarked on the fact that, whereas Handel recomposed the solo music for his soprano, contralto/castrato, and bass soloists, the most significant alteration he made to the tenor arias was to delete one bar of orchestral music in the opening and closing ritornellos of 'Every Valley'.[17] Such was his confidence in Beard's performance that he gave him the soprano aria 'Rejoice greatly' to sing on an occasion when a sudden crisis with his sopranos demanded that it was reallocated. He also added a short aria for him, 'Their sound is gone out', when he restructured the middle of Part 2 in around 1743.[18] At some stage, possibly in the mid-1750s, the alto/tenor duet 'O Death, where is thy sting' was reduced from 41 bars long to 24 by means of a simple, internal cut. This was probably occasioned by the need to shorten the work to suit the London theatre audience.[19]

Beard's contribution to the 30 performances of *Messiah* that he gave with Handel between 1743 - 59 only varied in accordance with the number of soprano soloists Handel had engaged. When there was only one performer he sang all of the music which was originally composed for the tenor voice. When there were two, the second soprano robbed him of 'He was cut off' and 'But thou didst not leave his soul in Hell' which, as can be seen by the fact that they are written in the manuscript in the tenor clef, were originally intended for a male singer.[20]

The arias and *accompagnatos* reveal that Beard's strengths were once again uppermost in Handel's mind when he was composing the music in the summer of 1741. He wrote *Messiah* and *Samson* in one famous stretch, from August 22 to October 29. As Beard was chosen for the title role in *Samson* it is clear that Handel wrote the *Messiah* music for the same tenor voice. Handel used Beard's sturdy delivery of extrovert text, and ability to create a mood, by giving him the opening vocal music. 'Comfort ye' is a dramatic accompanied recitative or *accompagnato* in the manner of 'Deeper and deeper still', although the emotion is not so personal or highly charged. However, it concludes with an arresting pronouncement of Isaiah's prophecy which would have made his audience sit up and pay attention:

---

[16] "It can be clearly seen that it was a matter of a makeshift never required again". Jens Peter Larsen, 'Handel's Messiah, origins, composition, sources', London 1957, republished New York, 1972, p. 238. See also: Watkins Shaw, 'A Textual and Historical Companion to Handel's Messiah', Novello, Sevenoaks, 1965, p. 110-1

[17] Jens Peter Larsen, *op. cit.*, p. 216

[18] Jens Peter Larsen, 'Handel's Messiah, origins, composition, sources', London 1957, republished New York, 1972, p. 233; and Watkins Shaw, 'A Textual and Historical Companion to Handel's Messiah', Novello, Sevenoaks, 1965, p. 113-4

[19] Larsen suggests that it may have been made "at a very early date – perhaps having in mind the less competent Dublin soloists. ...It can hardly be doubted that [Handel] used the shortened form in his last years". *op. cit.* p. 240

[20] Jens Peter Larsen, *op. cit.*, p. 226-7

The aria 'Every Valley', as has already been mentioned, is an *Allegro* movement featuring many shapely vocal runs. The highest note is G sharp: well within Beard's limits. It is reached via a leap, in a section of vocal writing which is descriptive of "crooked ways" being "made straight":

The next music for the tenor, in Part 2, is an *accompagnato*, 'All they that see him laugh him to scorn', in which the strings' dotted rhythm is descriptive of the lashes at Jesus' scourging, but in the line of recitative lying above this the tenor is simply required to sing firmly. Then come the four Passiontide movements, 'Thy rebuke', 'Behold and see', 'He was cut off' and 'But thou didst not leave his soul in Hell', which give the singer the biggest opportunity in the work to convey a changing pattern of moods. These begin with a deep sympathy for the 'suffering servant', and build with confidence to a major-key acceptance that the sufferings were undergone to save us all from corruption. The tempo moves forward correspondingly from Largo to Andante larghetto; and the second and fourth numbers are in the style of the *Andante* arias (mentioned earlier) which contain music of great emotional depth, in which the finely controlled mood is set to melodies with long arching phrases:

The highest note for the tenor has still only risen to a G sharp by this point. Handel reserved the top A - the highest note that he gives to Beard in the oratorios - for the extrovert aria, with highly effective short runs, that is the nearest thing to a 'Rage' aria that the tenor gets in this work. 'Thou shalt break them' contains only two written top A's (though there is scope for a third in an optional final cadence at bar 65) which are approached by a leap, in the same manner that Handel approaches them in 'military' arias like 'Sound an alarm' (*Judas Maccabaeus*) and 'Sharp violins proclaim' (*Ode on St Cecilia's Day*):

Apart from the duet in Part 3, and some *secco* recitatives, that is all the music that Handel provided for the tenor soloist in *Messiah*. But he must have been happy in his choice of soloist as Beard only failed to sing the work for him on two occasions (apart from the Dublin premiere), when his private circumstances prevented him.

It was his voice that dictated the way that Handel would write these arias. Tenors that have come after him must have had cause to thank Beard for having had such a useful range, with a flexibility which is functional rather than showy, and with an ability to supply some effective top notes at climactic moments. Haydn, who heard Handel's oratorios in London in the 1790s wrote for a voice like this as the singers that he heard - Thomas Norris and Samuel Harrison - were Beard's immediate successors. Mendelssohn seems to have developed his tenor arias from Handel movements like 'For ever blessed be thy holy name' (*Jephtha*) rather than from the Bach arias that he had got to know through his revival of the *Matthäus Passion* - even though Elijah's Bass aria, "It is enough', is clearly modelled on Bach's 'Es ist vollbracht'.

As Mollie Sands has said, "English tenors should regard John Beard as their patron saint, the founder of their race. It was Mr Handel who first put tenors on the musical map, and John Beard was Handel's first tenor".[21]

---

[21] Mollie Sands, 'Invitation to Ranelagh', London, 1946, p. 50

APPENDIX 1

WORKS THAT BEARD SANG FOR HANDEL: 1734 - 1747

ORATORIO	*OPERA*
1734	*Il Pastor Fido* (Silvio)
	Ariadne in Creta (Alceste)
1735	*Ariodante* (Lurcanio)
Esther (Habdonah)	
Deborah (Sisera)	
Athaliah (Mathan)	
	Alcina (Oronte)
1736 *Alexander's Feast* (Tenor solos)	
Acis and Galatea (Acis)	
Esther (Habdonah)	
Wedding Anthem 'Sing unto God' HWV 263)	
	Ariodante (Lurcanio)
	Atalanta (Amintas)
	Alcina (Oronte)
	Poro (Alessandro)
1737	*Arminio* (Varo)
	Partenope (Emilio)
	Giustino (Vitaliano)
Alexander's Feast (Tenor solos)	
Il Trionfo del Tempo e della Verita (Piacere)	
Esther (Habdonah)	
	Berenice (Fabio)
	Alcina (Oronte)
1738 excerpts from *Deborah* ('Oratorio' at King's Theatre Haymarket)	
1739 *Saul* (Jonathan)	
Alexander's Feast (Tenor solos)	
Il Trionfo del Tempo e della Verita (Piacere)	
Israel in Egypt (Tenor solos)	
Alexander's Feast + *St. Cecilia's Day Ode* (Tenor solos)	
Acis and Galatea (Acis) + *St. Cecilia's Day Ode* (Tenor solos)	
	Jupiter in Argos (Arete ?)
1740 *Acis and Galatea* (Acis) + *St. Cecilia's Day Ode* (Tenor solos)	
L'Allegro ,il Penseroso ed il Moderato (Tenor solos)	
Esther (Ahasuerus)	
Israel in Egypt (Tenor solos)	
Wedding Anthem 'Pasticcio' of HWV 262 + HWV 263	
1743 *Samson* (Samson)	
L'Allegro ,il Penseroso + *St. Cecilia's Day Ode* (Tenor solos)	
Messiah	
1744 *Semele* (Jupiter)	
Samson (Samson)	
Joseph and his Brethren (Judah & Simeon)	
1745 *Hercules* (Hyllus)	
Samson (Samson)	

Saul (Jonathan)
Joseph and his Brethren (Judah & Simeon)
Belshazzar (Belshazzar)
Messiah
1746 *Occasional Oratorio* (Tenor solos)
1747 *Occasional Oratorio* (Tenor solos)
Joseph and his Brethren (Judah & Simeon)
Judas Maccabaeus (Judas)

HANDEL WORKS WITH NO PART FOR BEARD: 1734-7
1737   *Il Parnasso in Festa*
                                             Didone Abbandonata
                                             Faramondo
                                             Alessandro Severo
                                             Serse
1741   *Deidamia*

BEARD'S ABSENCE FROM HANDEL'S DUBLIN SEASON: 1741-2

Beard did not perform these works during Handel's Dublin season, although they were conceived with his voice in mind, and Jennens suggests that Handel was expecting him there:
1742   *Messiah* (1st version)   *Imeneo* ('Hymen')

BEARD'S ABSENCE FROM HANDEL'S ORATORIOS: 1748-50

It is curious that Beard should have been unavailable to Handel in these years. Handel always had a good relationship with theatre managers, and usually managed to obtain the singers he required: "I think I can obtain Mr Rich's permission… since so obligingly he gave leave to Mr Beard and Mr Reinhold".[1] In 1748 Beard was on the roster at Covent Garden, so he had the night off whenever Handel had his oratorio performances. He was also free on Handel's performing nights in 1749-50 A breakdown of his work schedule in these years is shown in Chapter 4, pp 102-106.

THE WORKS THAT BEARD SANG FOR HANDEL: 1751-9

1751   ? *Esther* (Ahasuerus) March 15 [*Winton Dean can't decide between Beard & Lowe*] [2]
           ? *Judas Maccabaeus* (Judas) March 20 [*No evidence - Winton Dean can't decide*] [3]
           Messiah (tenor solo) April 18; May 16 (at Foundling Hospital) [4]
1752   *Joshua* (Joshua) Feb 14, 19
           Hercules (Hyllus) Feb 21
           Jephtha (Jephtha) Feb 26, 28, March 4
           Samson (Samson) March 6, 11, 13, 18, 20
           Messiah (tenor solo) March 25, 26; April 9 (at Foundling Hospital)

---

[1] Handel to Jennens, 9th June 1744: Deutsch, pp. 590-1
[2] "The new part was adapted for Lowe, but there is some doubt whether he sang it: one of the airs ('Tune your harps') was sung by Beard in public a month later, and another ('Jehovah crowned') was attributed to Beard in Walsh's contemporary edition of the songs." Dean *Handel's Dramatic Oratorios and Masques*, p. 213
[3] "It is not possible to distinguish all the casts" Dean *Handel's Dramatic Oratorios and Masques*, p. 472
[4] "... for the Benefit of the Charity two guineas [were] returned by Mr Beard"

1753 *Alexander's Feast* (tenor solo) March 9, 14
The Choice of Hercules (Attendant on Pleasure) March 9, 14
Jephtha (Jephtha) March 16, 21
Judas Maccabaeus (Judas) March 23, 30
Samson (Samson) April 4, 6, 11,
Messiah (tenor solo) April 13; May 1 (at Foundling Hospital)
Foundling Hospital Anthem (tenor solo) April 16 (at Foundling Hospital)
1754 *Alexander Balus* (Jonathan) March 1, 6
Deborah (Sisera) March 8, 13
Saul (Jonathan) March 15, 20
Joshua (Joshua) March 22
Judas Maccabaeus (Judas) March 27, April 3
Samson (Samson) March 29
Messiah (tenor solo) April 5; May 15 (at Foundling Hospital)
1755 *Alexander's Feast* (tenor solo) Feb 14, 19
The Choice of Hercules (Attendant on Pleasure) Feb 14, 19
L'Allegro ed Il Penseroso + Song for St Cecilia's Day (tenor solo) Feb 21
Samson (Samson) Feb 26, March 7
Joseph and his Brethren (Simeon and Judah) Feb 28
Theodora (Septimius) March 5
Judas Maccabaeus (Judas) March 12, 14
Messiah (tenor solo) March 19, 21; May 1 (at Foundling Hospital)
1756 *Athaliah* (Mathan) March 5, 10, 12
Israel in Egypt (tenor solo) March 17, 24
Deborah (Sisera) March 19
Judas Maccabaeus (Judas) March 26, 31
Jephtha (Jephtha) April 2
Messiah (tenor solo) April 7, 9; May 19 (at Foundling Hospital)
1757 *Esther* (Ahasuerus) Feb 25, March 2
Israel in Egypt (tenor solo) March 4
Joseph and his Brethren (Simeon and Judah) March 9
The Triumph of Time and Truth (Pleasure) March 11, 16, 18, 23
Judas Maccabaeus (Judas) March 25
Messiah (tenor solo) March 30, April 1; May 5 (at Foundling Hospital)
1758 *The Triumph of Time and Truth* (Pleasure) Feb 10, 15
Belshazzar (Belshazzar) Feb 22
Israel in Egypt (tenor solo) Feb 24
Jephtha (Jephtha) March 1
Judas Maccabaeus (Judas) March 3, 8
Messiah (tenor solo) March 10, 15, 17; April 27 (at Foundling Hospital)
1759 *Solomon* (Zadok) March 2, 7
Susanna (First Elder) March 9
Samson (Samson) March 14, 16, 21
Judas Maccabaeus (Judas) March 23, 28
Messiah (tenor solo) March 30, April 4, 6

Handel dies on April 14th 1759

BEARD'S PERFORMANCES AT THE FOUNDLING HOSPITAL: 1759-1767

These were conducted by J.C. Smith

May 3rd, 1759	Messiah (1st performance after Handel's death)
May 24th, 1759,	Concert in memory of Handel, including the *Foundling Hospital Anthem*
May 2nd, 1760	Messiah
April 24th, 1761	Messiah
May 5th, 1762	Messiah
April 29th, 1763	Messiah
May 8th, 1764	Messiah
April 2nd, 1765	Messiah
April 15th, 1766	Messiah
April 29th, 1767	Messiah *Beard withdraws. The tenor solos are divided between the other soloists. The castrato Gaetano Guarducci sings most of the arias. Mr Hayes sings some recitatives and the Duet. Mr Clarke also sings some music. Hayes was the soloist in the period 1768-1771.*[5]

ORATORIO AT COVENT GARDEN (UNDER BEARD'S MANAGEMENT) AFTER HANDEL'S DEATH

These were managed by J. C. Smith and John Stanley

Total	Title	Total	Title
	HANDEL WORKS		**J. C. SMITH WORKS**
17	Judas Maccabaeus	3	Paradise Lost
16	Messiah	1	Rebecca
13	Samson		
7	Alexander's Feast		**JOHN STANLEY WORK**
4	Acis & Galatea		
4	Deborah	2	Zimri
3	Israel in Egypt		
2	Theodora		
2	L'Allegro ed Il Penseroso		**PASTICHE WORKS**
1 [2]	The Occasional Oratorio [2nd performance cancelled]		
1	The Triumph of Time and Truth		
1	Semele	2	Nabal
1	Jephtha	1	Israel in Babylon
1	Solomon	1	The Cure of Saul
1	Esther		
74		10	

---

[5] see also: Donald Burrows 'Handel and the Foundling Hospital', *Music and Letters*, July 1977, p. 283-4

APPENDIX 2

JOHN BEARD'S THEATRICAL CAREER: HIS BENEFIT NIGHTS

1ˢᵗ Benefit Thurs 8 April 1736 Hickford's Room   *address unknown*
Vocal and Instrumental music. The vocal by Beard. Solo on the violin by Festing.

1ˢᵀ CONTRACT AT COVENT GARDEN

2nd Benefit Fri 22 April 1737 Covent Garden   *address unknown*
The Provok'd Wife + The Country House
Singing: II A new Cantata by Beard; III *Chanson a Boire* by Leveridge & Salway
IV by Beard. End of afterpiece: *Since times are so bad* (Purcell) by Leveridge &
Salway
Benefit Beard. Two rows of the Pit will be laid into boxes

3-YEAR CONTRACT AT DRURY LANE FOR CHARLES FLEETWOOD

3rd Benefit Thurs 27 April 1738 Drury Lane address unknown
The Beggar's Opera (Macheath = Beard, Polly = Mrs Clive, Lucy = Mrs Pritchard,
Peachum = Macklin) + The Devil to Pay – "*The Early Horn*" introduced into Berad's part. Benefit Beard

4th Benefit Tues 3 April 1739 Drury Lane   *New North Street, Red Lion Square*
Love for Love + The Devil to Pay (Sir John (with *The Early Horn*) Beard; Lady Loverule = Mrs
Pritchard, Nell = Mrs Clive). Singing: II Would you taste the noontide air (from Comus) by Beard;
IV by desire, Oh Happy Pair (out of *Alexander's Feast*). Benefit Beard. Tickets at Beard's house

5th Benefit Wed 9 April 1740 Drury Lane   *New North Street, Red Lion Square*
The Constant Couple + The Devil to Pay
Singing: II See from the silent Groves by Beard; IV by particular desire, a Song in the Character of a Sea-
Captain (the Captain of an English Man-of-War upon the taking of Porto Bello) by Beard
Benefit Beard. [Part of the Stage will be form'd into Side-Boxes] Tickets at Beard's house

SABBATICAL YEAR 1740-41

FURTHER 2-YEAR CONTRACT AT DRURY LANE FOR FLEETWOOD

6th Benefit Sat 1 April 1742 Drury Lane   *Red Lyon Street, near Lamb's Conduit*
Comus (with additional arias from Handel's L'Allegro) + The Mock Doctor
Benefit Beard. Tickets and places to be had at Beard's lodgings…and of Bradshaw at the Kings Arms etc.
Servants will be allowed to keep places on the stage, which will be carefully inclosed to prevent the ladies
from taking cold.
Receipts £207

7th Benefit Tues 22 March 1743 Drury Lane   lodgings on North side of Red Lion Sq
The Beggar's Opera (Macheath = Beard, Polly = Mrs Clive, Lucy = Mrs Pritchard,) + The School Boy.
By Command of their Royal Highnesses the Prince and Princess of Wales.
Benefit Beard. Tickets and Places to be had at Beard's lodgings… also to be had of Hobson at the Stage
Door. Stage will be form'd into Side-Boxes.
Receipts ?

2nd CONTRACT AT COVENT GARDEN (5 YEARS)

8th Benefit Wed 28 March 1744 Covent Garden   *House in Red Lion Square*
The Old Batchelor + Damon and Phillida (Damon = Beard, Phillida = Mrs Clive) (in which characters
will be introduced the favourite Duetto in *Solomon*, composed by Dr Boyce) / Singing: II New Song by
Handel, sung by Beard; IV To Arms & Britons strike home by Leveridge, Beard, Reinhold, etc. Benefit
Beard. By Command a Ballad Opera not acted these 3 years [*recte* last perf. 30 Nov. 1742].
Amphitheatre on Stage. Send servants by three. Tickets to be had of Beard…
By Command of their Royal Highnesses the Prince and Princess of Wales.

9th Benefit Thurs 28 March 1745 Covent Garden   *House in Red Lion Square*
The Beggar's Opera (Macheath = Beard, Polly = Mrs Clive, Lucy = Mrs Pritchard)
Singing: By particular Desire, the Song made on the famous Sea-fight at La Hogue, sung by Beard in the
character of a sailor. Benefit Beard.
**By Command of their Royal Highnesses the Prince and Princess of Wales,
Prince George, Prince Edward, and the Lady Augusta.**
Tickets of Beard… and of Page at the Stage Door

10th Benefit Mon 17 March 1746 Covent Garden   *House in Red Lion Square*
The Conscious Lovers, in Act II a new Ballad by Beard + Phebe (Hunter = Beard, Phebe = Mrs Dunstall,
Tippet = Mrs Hippisley). Singing: Song of Diana, from Dryden's '*Secular Masque*' set by Boyce; by
Particular Desire, A French Song by Beard. Benefit Beard. [Ladies to send Servants early to keep places
to prevent mistakes.] Tickets at his house…

11th Benefit Thurs 26 March 1747 Covent Garden   *House in Red Lion Square*
Comus (Bacchanal = Beard) + The Lying Valet. Benefit for Beard. The amphitheatre used on the Stage at
Benefits will be enclosed and divided into distinct Boxes, with a ceiling and illuminated.
Send Servants by three. Tickets of Beard at his house …
Receipts: ready money £94 15s + £102 9s from tickets = £197 4s, Charges £60

12th Benefit Mon 21 March 1748 Covent Garden   *House in Red Lion Square*
Merry Wives of Windsor (Falstaff = Bridgwater, Ford = Ryan, Bardolph = Dunstall, Anne Page = Mrs
Storer, Caius = Stoppelaer) + Venus and Adonis (Venus = Mrs Lampe, Adonis = Mrs Storer, Mars =
Beard) Afterpiece: A Masque of Music, reviv'd, in two Interludes, perform'd at the end of the 3rd and 5th
Acts. Written by Colley Cibber. Servants will be allowed to keep places on the Stage, which (for the
better accommodation of the Ladies) will be form'd into an Amphitheatre, illuminated and enclos'd, as at
an Oratorio…Tickets for Boxes and Stage to be had of Beard at his house… and of Page at the Stage
Door. Ladies desired to send servants to keep Places by three o'clock (*General Advertiser*)

3rd PERIOD AT DRURY LANE (11 YEARS) WITH GARRICK.

13th Benefit Wed 29 March 1749 Drury Lane   *Tickets from Hobson at Stage Door*
Hamlet (Hamlet = Barry; Ophelia = Mrs Cibber, 1st time) + Tit for Tat (+ Woodward, 'One Dish of his
own Chocolate'- a mimickry upon Mr Foote "receiv'd with uncommon applause" [General Advertiser]) /
Singing by Beard. Receipts £275 (Cross) / House charges £63 (Powell)
5 rows of Pit laid into boxes, and on the stage; which for the better accommodation of the Ladies will be
enclos'd and form'd into Front and Side Boxes. Tickets and Places of Hobson at the Stage Door.

14th Benefit Sat 24 March 1750 Drury Lane   *New North Street, Red Lion Square*
The Suspicious Husband (Ranger = Garrick, Frankly = Havard) + The Chaplet (Damon = Beard, +
Master Mattocks, Miss Norris, Mrs Clive). Benefit for Beard. Part of Pit will be rail'd into Boxes, where
servants may keep Places and on the Stage. Tickets to be had of Beard at his house… and of Hobson at
the Stage Door. Receipts: from cash £67 12s + £132 13s in tickets = £200 5s / Receipts: £205 (Cross) /
House charges £63 (Treasurer's Book)

15th Benefit Wed 10 April 1751 Drury Lane   *North Street, Red Lion Square*

The Stratagem (Archer = Garrick, Mrs Sullen = Mrs Pritchard, Aimwell = Havard) / The Devil to Pay
(Loverule = Beard, Nell = Mrs Clive) Singing: *A Cantata* set by Dr Boyce, sung by Beard.
End of the Cantata: the *Parody* of Shakespeare's Stages of Life, by Garrick* [see appendix 8]. Last time
of performing the mainpiece this season. Benefit for Beard. No Part of Pit will be rail'd into the Boxes.
Servants allow'd to keep places on the Stage. Tickets and Places to be had of Beard at his house … and at
the Stage Door. Tickets deliver'd out for the 21st March will be taken.
*[Wed 20th March: 'This morning we were surpris'd with the unhappy news, that Frederick Prince of
Wales Dy'd the Night before between ten and eleven – Mr Beard's benefit was to be on Thursday & many
of ye Bills were posted before we heard of this Accident – the Bills were immediately torn down, and the
House shut up before my Ld. Chamberlain sent orders for doing so It is said our having permission to
open so soon, before the Prince was Bury'd, was on account of the Actors Benefits depending'. (Cross)]*
Receipts £200 (Cross) / House charges [£63]

16th Benefit Sat 21 March 1752 Drury Lane   *lodgings, Russel Street, Covent Gdn*

The Inconstant (Duretete = Garrick, Bissarre = Mrs Clive) + A Duke and no Duke (Trappolin =
Woodward) / Singing: II *A New Cantata* (compos'd by Mr Arne), sung by Beard; III Singing – Master
Vernon; 1V *The Incantation Song* in Dryden's *Indian Queen* (composed by Purcell) sung by Beard.
Benefit for Beard. Afterpiece: By Particular Desire. Part of Pit will be rail'd into Boxes. Ladies send
servants by 3 o'clock. Doors open at half past three. Tickets at Mr Beard's lodgings … Last till Holidays.
Receipts £250 (Cross) / House charges [£63]

17th Benefit Tues 27 March 1753 Drury Lane   *lodgings, Russel Street, Covent Gdn*

The Suspicious Husband (Ranger = Garrick, Clarinda = Mrs Pritchard) + The Double Disappointment
(Loveless = Master Vernon), Isabel = Miss Norris) / Singing: I *Cymon and Iphigenia*, a Cantata compos'd
by Mr Arne, sung by Beard; II *The School of Anacreon*, a New Cantata compos'd by Mr Arne, sung by
Beard; IV (By Desire), *The Lass of the Mill*, sung by Beard, accompany'd on the *Harp* by Mr Parry;
Music. III a piece on the *Welch Harp*, by Parry.
Benefit for Beard. Tickets of Beard … and at the Stage Door.
Receipts £260 (Cross) / House charges [£63]

18th Benefit Thurs 28th March 1754 Drury Lane   *Mrs Coleman's, in East St,*
                                               Red Lyon Square

The Fair Penitent (Lothario = Garrick, Calista = Mrs Cibber) + The Devil to Pay (Loverule = Beard,
Nell = Mrs Clive) / Singing: I *Rise Glory*, in the Opera *Rosamond* by Arne, sung by Beard; II A Song by
Miss Thomas; III (By Desire) A Ballad by Beard; IV A Pastoral Dialogue compos'd by Arne, sung by
Miss Thomas and Beard. Benefit for Beard. Afterpiece by Particular Desire.
Tickets at Mr Beard's lodgings … and at the Stage Door. Part of Pit laid into Boxes.
Receipts £280 (Cross) / House charges [£63]

19th Benefit Wed 2nd April 1755 Drury Lane   *Mrs Coleman's, in East St,*
                                               Red Lyon Square

The Stratagem (Archer = Garrick, Mrs Sullen = Mrs Pritchard) + Miss in her Teens (Fribble = Yates,
Flash = Woodward) / Singing: II *A New Cantata* by Beard; III *Hooly and Fairly* by Desire, by Beard; V
Rule Britannia and *Britons Strike Home* sung in character by Beard, accompanied with a chorus; Music.
IV a Piece upon the *Harp* by Parry / Dancing: all concluding with Hornpipe by Mathews etc. Benefit for
Mr Beard. Afterpiece: By Desire.
Tickets of Beard … and at the Stage Door.
Receipts £300 (Cross) / House charges [£63]

20th Benefit Tues 30th March 1756 Drury Lane   *at Mrs Lane's, next door to Old*
                                    Slaughter's Coffee House, St Martin's Lane

The Mistake (Don Carlos = Garrick, + Woodward, Mrs Clive, Mrs Bennet, Mrs Pritchard) + Britannia
((David Mallet & Arne) Mars & Boatswain = Beard) / Prologue spoken by Garrick in character of a sailor
/ Singing: By Beard. II By Desire *Cymon and Iphigenia*; III *A Tale of a Cock and a Bull*; IV Genius of
England
Benefit for Beard. Part of Pit laid into boxes
Receipts £287 (Cross) / House charges [£63]

21st Benefit Thurs 31 March 1757 Drury Lane   *next door to Old Slaughter's*
Coffee House,

Every Man in his Humour (Kitely = Garrick) + The Englishman in Paris (Buck = Foote, with the
Original *Prologue*, by Desire - Foote) / Singing: I *The Country Wedding* by Beard; II *The Bonny Broom*
by Miss Young; III *Sir Watkins Delight*, on the Harp, by Parry; IV *The Toast* by Beard;
V A Duetto, *When Phoebus the top of the Hills does Adorn* by Beard and Miss Young.
Benefit for Mr Beard. Part of Pit will be laid into Boxes, etc.
Receipts £350 (Cross) / House charges [£63]

22nd Benefit Wed 29 March 1758 Drury Lane   *next door to Old Slaughter's*
Coffee House, St Martin's Lane

The Suspicious Husband (Ranger = Garrick, Clarinda = Mrs Pritchard) + Catharine and Petruchio
(Catharine = Mrs Clive, Woodward = Petruchio) / Singing: by Beard and Champness; A Piece on the
Harp by Mr Evans. Benefit for Beard. Tickets of Beard … and of Varney at stage door. Part of Pit will be
laid into Boxes. Amphitheatre on stage.
Receipts £280 (Cross) / House charges [£63]

23rd Benefit Thurs 29 March 1759 Drury Lane   ?

The Busy Body (Marplot = Garrick, Charles = Havard, Patch = Mrs Clive) + The Lying Valet / Singing:
I *A New Ballad* by Beard; II *The Goldfinch* by Miss Young; III *A Bacchanalian Song*, compos'd by Dr
Boyce, sung by Beard; V *A New Comic Dialogue* compos'd by Dr Boyce and sung in character by Beard
and Miss Young. Benefit for Beard. Pit laid into boxes. Amphitheatre on stage.
Receipts £280 (Cross) / House charges [£63 Winston MS 8]

A play at Drury Lane Theatre

3rd CONTRACT AT COVENT GARDEN (8 YEARS), AS CO-MANAGER

24th Benefit Mon 24 March 1760 Covent Garden   *house next Old Slaughter's,*
St Martin's Lane

The Beggar's Opera (Macheath = Beard, Ben Budge = Bencraft, Lucy = Miss Young, Polly = Miss
Brent) + The Country House (Lucca = Dunstall, Janno = Shuter)/ Dancing: *Country Dance* by Characters
of the Opera; *A Hornpipe* by Miss Dawson; A New Dance call'd *The Shepherdess* by Miss Wilford etc.
Benefit for Beard. Mainpiece by Particular Desire; Last time of performing it this season. Afterpiece: Not
Acted these two years. Pit and Boxes laid together at 5s. First Gallery 2s. Upper Gallery 1s. Stage 5s.
Those who have places either in the Boxes or Pit are requested to come thro the Box-Lobby, as at an
Oratorio; and to send their servants to keep places by 3 o'clock.   Tickets to be had of Mr Beard
...and of Mr Sarjant at the Stage Door where places for the Boxes may be taken.
Receipts: £129 1s + £246 from tickets (Boxes and Pit 984).
Total income £375 1s / Charges £63. [Beard found his own wax candles]

25th Benefit Sat 14 March 1761 Covent Garden   *house next Old Slaughter's,*

The Jovial Crew (Hearty = Beard, Randal = Dunstall, Justice Clack = Shuter, Rachel = Miss Brent) +
Love a-la-Mode (Sir Archy = Macklin, + Barrington, Shuter, Dunstall, Cresswell, Miss Macklin)
Entertainment: *Medley Epilogue*, written by Garrick to be sung by Beard. Benefit for Beard. Last time of
performing till Easter Holidays. Pit and boxes to be laid together. Several of Mr Beard's Friends being
pre-engaged for Monday 23rd March, advertised for his Benefit, and Mr Rich having kindly given him
Saturday 14th, he humbly hopes (the shortness of the Time not permitting him to wait on his Friends as
usual) those Ladies and Gentlemen who desire to favour him with their presence, will be pleased to send
for their tickets and places, to his House next Old Slaughter's Coffee House in St Martin's Lane.
Receipts: £100 2s 6d plus £206 15s from tickets [= £306 17s 6d] (Boxes and Pit 827) (Account Book).
Charges: £63 (Account Book)

26th Benefit Tues 30th March 1762 Covent Garden   ?

The Miser (Miser = Shuter, Clerimont = Hull, etc) + The Dragon of Wantley (Moor of Moor Hall =
Beard + Shuter, Mrs Vernon, Miss Brent, The Dragon = The Giant) / Entertainment: *A Medley Epilogue*
(with alterations), written by Garrick, sung by Beard / Dancing: The Pedlar Trick'd. Benefit for Beard.
Ladies desired to send servants by 3 o'clock. Music for the afterpiece by John Fredrick Lampe.
Receipts: ?

1763 No Benefit Night, Covent Garden,   *No building on stage this year*

Order of benefits: Woodward, Smith, Mrs Ward, Shuter, Miss Brent, Ross, Dyer, [Arne}, Sparks…

1764 No Benefit Night, Covent Garden,   No persons admitted behind the scenes

Order of benefits: Woodward, Miss Poitier, Ross, Smith, Shuter, Walker, Miss Brent, Mrs Ward…

1765 No Benefit Night, Covent Garden,   None admitted behind Scenes

Order of benefits: Woodward, Smith, Shuter, Ross, Miss Poitier, Mrs Bellamy, Mrs Ward, Sparks...

1766 27th Benefit Monday 1 December 1766, Covent Garden,   "Beard's Night"

The Maid of the Mill (Giles = Beard, Sir Harry = Shuter, Lord Aimworth = Mattocks, Mervin = Baker,
Fairfield = Gibson, Ralph = Dibdin, Fanny = Miss Poitier, Patty = Mrs Pinto, Theodosia = Mrs Mattocks)
+ The Citizen (Citizen = Woodward, Old Philpot = Shuter, Sir Jasper = Dunstall).
Mainpiece: by Particular Desire. Mr Beard's Night. [This was a "clear" benefit night, as indicated by an
item in the Account Book for 15th December: "Paid Mr Beard the total amount of the house on the 1st
inst. As per agreement £234 14s 6d."]
Receipts: £234 14s 6d (Account Book)

1766 Order of benefits: Woodward, Smith, Shuter, Ross, Miss Brent, Mrs Bellamy, Miss Macklin...

28th Benefit Monday 16 March 1767 Covent Garden,   "Beard's Night"

Love in a Village (Hawthorn = Beard, Woodcock = Shuter, Sir William Meadows = Bennet, Young
Meadows = Mattocks, Eustace = Dyer, Hodge = Dunstall, Margery = Mrs Baker, Deborah Woodcock =
Mrs Walker, Lucinda = Mrs Mattocks, Rosetta = Mrs Pinto, late Miss Brent) +
The Citizen (Citizen = Woodward, + Dunstall, Shuter, etc) / Dancing: The Female Archer (Miss Wilford).
Mainpiece by Particular Desire. Beard's Night.
Receipts: £262 17s. (Account Book) Charges £64 5s. Balance to Beard £198 12s (Account Book)

"Got but a bad place in the 2s Gallery at Covent Garden where I saw *Love in a
Village* with the *Citizen*… At the end of Act 2, we had the dance of the *Female
Archer*, by Mad. LaRiviere, Miss Wilford, etc with Miss Pope of the other house.
Ought to be particularly encouraged because she is virtuous. Mr Elliot has sold her
to Cumberland." (Neville MS Diary)

1767 Order of benefits: *Beard*, Woodward, Smith, Shuter, Ross, Mrs Pinto (formerly Miss Brent), Mrs
Bellamy, Mrs Mattocks, Miss Macklin…

OTHER BENEFIT NIGHTS

RANELAGH GARDENS

From an undated letter of William Havard to John Beard: "...*I have been favoured with two letters from honest Ben Read* [6]: *in one of them he acquaints me that the Ranelagh managers are dispos'd to offer you a Benefit*".[7]   It is not known how early these Benefit Nights started, but they certainly took place on:

Date	Principal work
June 14 1758	Handel, *Acis and Galatea*
June 13 1759	Handel, *L'Allegro ed il Penseroso*
June 11 1760	Handel, *L'Allegro ed il Penseroso*
June 12 1761	Arne, *The Judgement of Paris*
June ? 1762	Beard sang: '*A Medley*, written by David Garrick'[8]

THE LONG ROOM, WELL WALK, HAMPSTEAD

"For Dorman's friends". Joseph Dorman, the poet and author of the popular ballad opera *The Woman of Taste: or the Yorkshire Lady* (otherwise known as *The Female Rake*) of 1735, lived in Hampstead, and died there in February 1754. He organised an annual concert for the last years of his life;and his son, Ridley, a Drury Lane violinist, carried on, with Beard still as soloist, until 1761.

Date	Principal work
August 1 1750	Boyce *Cantata*
August 24 1751	
August 15 1752	
? 1753	
August 31 1754	
August 23 1755	Boyce, *Solomon*
? 1756	
? 1757	
? 1758	
August 1 1759	Handel, *Acis and Galatea*
August 25 1760	Boyce, *The Secular Masque* [9]
August 17 1761	Sig. de Giardini, violin; with vocals by Frasi and Beard.

---

[6] Ben Read was one of Beard's circle of friends, and became a member of the Beefsteak Club on April 15th 1758. See also the cartoon drawing of him on p.324

[7] Letter from Havard to J.B. Esq. m/s N. a. 2. pp 97-99. Folger Shakespeare Library, Washington, USA

[8] mentioned in a List of Garrick's poems; see also Tate Wilkinson, 'The Wandering Patentee', 1795, vol. 4, p. 267: "I gave a *Medley* which Mr Garrick himself had wrote for Mr Beard. He designed it first as a compliment to Mr Beard for his Ranelagh Benefit, but after that he altered it for the playhouse..."

[9] Programme booklet at the Folger Shakespeare Library: PR 3291 M53 Cage; and also at the London Theatre Museum.

APPENDIX 3

LIST OF COURT ODES PERFORMED BY JOHN BEARD

1734

It is not known at what point Beard commenced his long relationship with the tenor solos in these Odes. In a petition of 1757 he stated that he had been employed in performing them for 24 years, which would imply that he began in the year 1733, whilst still a Chapel Royal chorister. October 28 1734, therefore, seems a more likely starting point. Counting that year as number 1 he would indeed have sung Odes for 24 years by 1757.

Birthday, Oct 28	Again the joyous morn	Greene / Cibber

1735

McGuinness states that "in the extant Odes from 1735 to 1740, of the two soloists employed – the tenor, Beard, who bore the chief burden, and the soprano, a boy from the Chapel Royal – it was the tenor who received the plums. The opening solo 'Come lovely Virgin, Fair-ey'd Peace', 1736, is one such song".[10]

New Year	Happy Britain! raise thy voice	Greene / Cibber
Birthday, Oct 28	Monarch of Musick	Greene / Cibber
Performed Oct 30		Bodleian Mus. d. 33, d. 34

1736

New Year	Ye smiling Seasons, sing the day	Greene / Cibber
Birthday, Oct 28	Come lovely virgin, Fair-ey'd Peace	Greene / Cibber
Performed Oct 30		Bodleian Mus. d. 38

1737

New Year	Grateful Britons! grace the day	Greene / Cibber
		Bodleian Mus. d. 37
Birthday, Oct 28	Come, fair embracing sisters, come	Greene / Cibber

1738

New Year	*No Ode performed on account of death of Queen Caroline on Nov. 20 1737*	
Birthday, Oct 28	*An Ode was "performed before his Majesty in the Great Council Chamber at St. James's" as usual, but no more is known about it.*	

1739

New Year	Refulgent God! with radiant smiles	Greene / Cibber
Birthday, Oct 28	'Twas on the glorious morn	Greene / Cibber
		Bodleian Mus. d. 39

1740

New Year	With sounds that suit the Monarch's ear	Greene / Cibber
		Bodleian Mus. d. 40
Birthday, Oct 28	*Beard was not a performer as he had temporarily left the Stage*	

1741

New Year	*Beard was not a performer. He returned as a soloist at New Year 1742*	
Birthday, Oct 28	*Beard was not a performer. He returned as a soloist at New Year 1742*	

---

[10] Rosamond McGuinness, 'English Court Odes 1660-1820', Oxford, 1971, p. 203

1742

New Year	To mend the World and bless Mankind	Greene / Cibber
Birthday, Oct 28	While ambition flies to arms	Greene / Cibber

1743

New Year	Glory! what art thou, dazzling fire!	Greene / Cibber
Birthday, Oct 28	Of fields! of forts! and floods!	Greene / Cibber

1744

New Year	*'The Ode is put off on account of a Council... in the Great Council Chamber'*	
Birthday, Oct 28	Again on Caesar's natal day	Greene / Cibber

1745

New Year	In vain the Muse with grateful lays	Greene / Cibber RCM MS. 229
Birthday, Oct 28	Sacred to song and mirth	Greene / Cibber Bodleian Mus. d. 35, f. 2

1746

McGuinness states that "the tenor at the beginning of the Ode for January [1746] ... received a solo which was considerably better than average. ...Greene thought sufficiently highly of the Bass aria 'Thus while roaring cannon' from the 1745 ode ...to use it again briefly in Jan. 1746 for the tenor solo 'O'er Fields, o'er floods he wings his way'.[11]

New Year	While European arm'd Allies	Greene / Cibber Bodleian Mus. d. 35, f. 33
Birthday, Oct 28	'Tis done! The turmoil's past!	Greene / Cibber Bodleian Mus. d. 35, f. 61

1747

New Year	Swift as the circling sun	Greene / Cibber Bodleian Mus. d. 35, f. 96
Birthday, Oct 28	When Man from Paradise remov'd	Greene / Cibber

1748

New Year	When Truth the nether world explored	Greene / Cibber
Birthday, Oct 28	Could fervent vows this day prolong	Greene / Cibber

1749

New Year	*The Ode was not performed because it was a Sunday*	
Birthday, Oct 28	When Glory with a painful eye	Greene / Cibber

1750

New Year	While votive Lays awake the Year	Greene / Cibber
Birthday, Oct 28	Great Patriot Prince of race sublime	Greene / Cibber

1751

New Year	Glory! where art thou, goddess, where?	Greene / Cibber
Birthday, Oct 28	To Caesar thus blithe Albion sings	Greene / Cibber

1752

New Year	*No Ode on account of death of the Queen of Denmark on Dec. 8th 1751*	
Birthday, Oct 28	Great Patriot Prince of race sublime	Greene / Cibber

---

[11] Rosamond McGuinness, 'English Court Odes 1660-1820', Oxford, 1971, p. 204-5

1753

New Year   What Warrior King   Greene / Cibber
Birthday, Oct 28 *The Ode was not performed because it was a Sunday*

1754

New Year   Hail! hail! auspicious rising year   Greene / Cibber
Birthday, Oct 28 When Glory with refulgent wings   Greene / Cibber

1755

New Year   As Rome of old, for Halcion days   Greene / Cibber
Birthday, Oct 28 Pierian sisters hail the morn   Boyce / Cibber

> Bodleian Mus. d. 11, f. 1   Mus. Sch. d. 298

T. accompanied Recitative   'Such were in Edward's days our Sires'
T. aria *Allegro* C maj.   'For Realms so rul'd'
Singers: Mr Baildon, Mr Beard, Mr Savage, Mr Wass

1756

New Year   Hail! hail! auspicious day   Boyce / Cibber

> Bodleian Mus. Sch. d. 300

T. Recitative   'Such is the praise by Britain paid'
T. aria 3/8 G maj.   'Annual aids when Senates grant'
This aria goes up regularly to a high G, and the lowest note is E.
Singers: Mr Beard, Mr Savage, Mr Wass

Birthday, Oct 28 When Caesar's natal day   Boyce / Cibber

> Bodleian Mus. d. 11, f. 57   Mus. Sch. d. 299

A.T.B. Solo Trio
T. Recitative   'What once has been, again may be'
T. aria *Allegro assai* D maj. 'Refulgent thus in Caesar's line'
This aria has long melismas, and a bravura passage going up to a top A, held for 5 beats.
Singers: Mr Baildon, Mr Beard, Mr Savage, Mr Wass

1757

New Year   While Britain in her Monarch blest   Boyce / Cibber

> Bodleian Mus. Sch. d. 301

T. Recitative   'While Britain, in her Monarch blest'
T. aria *Allegro* 6/8 G maj.   'Rude and rural though our lays'
This aria has a martial feel, and goes repeatedly up to a high A in an arpeggio phrase.
T.B.B. Solo trio   'What happier days could Heav'n ordain'
Singers: Treble solo, Mr Baildon, Mr Beard, Mr Savage, Mr Wass

Birthday, Oct 28 Rejoice, ye Britons, hail the day!   Boyce / Cibber

> Bodleian Mus. Sch. d. 302

T. aria *Andante Vivace* C maj.   'So mild, so sweet is Caesar's sway'
This aria goes up briefly to a high A twice, and down to a low C.
T. Recitative   'So when Apollo sings'
A.T.B.B. Solo Quartet   'Ah! late and glorious may he go'
Singers: Mr Baildon, Mr Beard, Mr Savage, Mr Wass

1758

New Year   Behold the Circle forms! Prepare!   Boyce / Cibber

> Bodleian Mus. Sch. d. 303

T. Recitative   'Turn, turn we now our Annals o're'
T. aria *Allegro assai* B flat maj. 'Our rights, our Laws, our Liberty'
This aria has many Handelian runs, going up to A flat, and down to low D.
Singers: Mr Baildon, Mr Beard, Mr Savage, & an unnamed Bass (replacing Mr Wass)

Birthday, Oct 28   When Othbert left th'Italian plain   **Boyce / Whitehead**

Bodleian Mus. Sch. d. 304 / RCM MS. 95, f. 1

T. Recit, a continuation of B. Recit 'Proceed, nor cast one ling'ring look behind'

T. Air / Recit 3/4 C maj. 'By those who toil for Virtue's meed': *Larghetto, Recit, Allegro*, etc

This is a scena, forced upon the composer because of the new Poet Laureate's rambling style. Cibber had written verses specifically conceived for treatment as arias. Whitehead's verse is prolix, and rambling, with many changes of mood. Boyce responds by writing in a variety of arioso and recitative formats.

Singers: Mr [Baildon deleted] Cowper, Mr Beard, Mr Savage, Mr Wass

1759

New Year   Ye guardian Powers, to whose command   **Boyce / Whitehead**

Bodleian Mus. Sch. d. 305 / RCM MS. 95, f. 27

T. Recit	'Ye guardian Powers, to whose command'
T. aria *Moderato* C maj.	'Angelic bands, where'er ye rove'
T. aria *Allegro* (continuation)	'Avert each ill, each bliss improve'
T. Recit (continuation)	'Yet Oh, where'er deserting Freedom's isle'

Beard has written in several pencil annotations, reminding him of the instrumental cues in this complex movement, which, once again, is full of changes of mood, time signature, key, and aria / recit format.

Singers: Mr Baildon, Mr Beard, Mr Savage, Mr Wass

Birthday, Oct 28   Begin the Song   **Boyce / Whitehead**

Bodleian Mus. Sch. d. 306 / RCM MS. 95, f. 47

T. aria *Allegro* 3/4 G maj.   'But what are wreaths in battle won?'

This is written as a conventional aria, suggesting that Boyce had persuaded Whitehead to write verse that would be easier to set to music. It is certainly no easier to understand than some of his previous verse. This is the sort of recalcitrant material that Boyce had to transform into something singable for Beard:

> 'But what are wreaths in battle won?
> And what the tribute of Amaze,
> Which Man too oft, mistaking, pays
> To the vain idol shrine of false renown?
> The noblest wreaths the Monarch wears
> Are those his virtuous rule demands,
> Unstain'd by widows' or by orphans' tears,
> And woven by his Subjects' hands.'

The final line is given a Handelian feel with a melisma on the first syllable of '*woven*' and takes in a top A.

T.B. Verse, D maj.   'Comets may rise and wonder mark their way'

Singers: Mr Baildon, Mr Beard, Mr Savage, Mr Wass

1760

New Year   Again the sun's revolving sphere   **Boyce / Whitehead**

Bodleian Mus. Sch. d. 307 / RCM MS. 95, f. 72

T. Recit	'Again the sun's revolving sphere'
T. aria *Larghetto* B flat maj.	'Suspended high in memory's fane'
T. aria (continuation)	'From the first blush of Orient day'
T.B. Duet 6/8	'Each month exerts a rival claim'
T. Recit	'Around thy Genius waiting stands'
T. aria *Larghetto*	'O grant a portion of thy praise'

This time there were no counter-tenor soloists, so Beard had an even larger role than usual. The Duet with the new Bass (Mr Cox - who in June 1762 was also given a Tenor 2 solo) was developed into considerable length. Unusually in this Ode there was only one chorus, for S A.

Singers: Mr Beard, Mr Cox, Mr Savage

Birthday   *No Ode – George II died on 25th October; George III, b. June 4th 1738, now King*

1761

New Year	Still must the Muse, indignant, hear	Boyce / Whitehead

Bodleian Mus. Sch. d. 308

T.B.B. Trio   'For alien sorrows heaves her gen'rous breast'
T. aria *Allegro* E flat maj.   'Thee, Glory, thee, thee, Glory'
This aria is heroic in tone, in a style that Beard had been performing at the theatre and for Handel throughout his career. It goes up to thrilling high G, and down to low E flat. This is the tessitura of martial arias like Handel's 'The Princes applaud' and 'Love sounds the alarm'.
T. Recit   'And who is he, of regal mien'
T. aria *Allegro assai* C maj.   'Another George!'
T. aria *Allegro* 3/8 D maj.   'Oh, if the muse aright divine'
Singers: Countertenor (unnamed), Mr Beard, Mr Cox, Mr Savage

Birthday, June 4	'Twas at the nectar'd feast of Jove	Boyce / Whitehead

Bodleian Mus. Sch. d. 309

Duet A maj.   'In vain ye tempt, ye specious harms'
T. Recit   'Oh call'd by Heav'n to fill that awful throne'
T. aria *Allegro* 6/8 D maj.   'The fairest wreaths already won'
Verse, 4 voices 6/8 D maj.   'Oh think what thou alone canst give'
Singers: Treble solo 1, Treble solo 2, Mr Cooper, Mr Beard, Mr Cox, Mr Savage

1762

New Year	God of Slaughter, quit the scene	Boyce / Whitehead

Bodleian Mus. Sch. d. 310

T. Recit   'You too, ye British dames, may share'
T. aria *Moderato* G maj. 3/4   'From the Baltic shore'
T. recit / *Allegro* / recit   'When the fierce female tyrant of the North'
T. aria *Moderato* A maj.   'She gave her treasur'd tribute to the brave'
T. recit   'We want them not'
T / B recit   'Yet, Oh ye fair'
T.B. Duet   'The royal dame would plead her dear adopted country'
Another long rambling Ode, in which Boyce found it difficult to make a distinction between aria, arioso, and recitative. Written in a hasty hand, Beard has not even bothered to make any corrections when the text is unclear or orthographically incorrect. This is the Ode that Baron Kielmansegge heard, and thought "not badly done".
Singers: Treble solo 1, Treble solo 2, Mr Cooper, Mr Beard, Mr Cox, Mr Savage

Birthday, June 4	Go, Flora	Boyce / Whitehead

Bodleian Mus. Sch. d. 311

T. arioso *Pomposo*   'O Goddess of connubial love'
T. aria D maj.   'Goddess of connubial love'
This is written, once again, as a conventional aria, suggesting that Boyce had reminded Whitehead to write verse that would be easier to set to music.
Singers: Treble solo, unnamed countertenor solo, Mr Beard, Mr Cox (tenor 2), Mr Savage

1763

New Year	At length th'imperious Lord of War	Boyce / Whitehead

Bodleian Mus. Sch. d. 312

T. arioso *Vivace* G maj.   'Th'attendant Graces gird her round'
T. recit.   'Be to less happy realms resigned'
T. aria *Allegro* A maj.   'O teach us, delegates of Heav'n'
T. recit.   'Future subjects, future kings shall bless the fair example'
Singers: Treble solo, Mr Cooper, Mr Beard, Mr Cox, Mr Savage

Birthday, June 4	Common births, like common things	Boyce / Whitehead

Bodleian Mus. Sch. d. 313

T. aria 3/8 F maj.   'Common births, like common things'
T. recit   'Born for millions, Monarchs rise'
T. aria *Vivace* 2/4 F maj.   ''Tis not our King's alone, 'tis Britain's natal morn'

T.B. duet B flat maj.   'Happy those whom truth sincere'
T. & Chorus *Allegro*   'Such may Britain find her Kings'
Singers: Treble solo, Mr Cooper, Mr Beard, Mr Savage

1764

New Year   *The Ode was not performed because it was a Sunday*
Birthday, June 4   To wedded Love, ye Nations bow   Boyce / Whitehead
                                                Bodleian Mus. Sch. d. 314

A.T. Duet, 6/8 C maj.   'To wedded Love, ye Nations bow'
T. aria *Spirituoso*   'Heartfelt joys - domestic Treasures'
T. recit.   'On private Virtue's solid base'
T. '*Nervous*'   'The man must make the Monarch great'
T. aria *Allegro ma non troppo*   'From taintless roots the flowers must rise'

The instruction 'nervous' has been put into the part by a different hand to the copyist's, probably by Beard himself. The final aria develops into an extended movement with Chorus. It is clear that Beard was frequently being entrusted with both opening and closing these Odes. As there was no Bass soloist this time, Beard had a larger part to play in this Ode.
Singers: Treble solo, Mr Cooper, Mr Beard

1765

New Year   Sacred to thee   Boyce / Whitehead
                                                Bodleian Mus. Sch. d. 315

Duet, 6/8 C maj.   'Whate'er the frozen Poles provide'
T. recit. *Larghetto*   'When Spain's proud pendants wav'd in Western skies'
"   *Allegro*   'Daring mortals, whither tend these vain pursuits'
"   *Larghetto*   'These sacred waves no keel shall rend'
"   *Allegro*   'Yes, yes, proceed and conquer too'
T. aria *Vivace* G maj.   'Nor Betis', nor Iberus' stream'
T. aria *Allegro* D maj.   'A chosen race, to Freedom dear'

Once again Beard's final aria becomes the final Chorus - to the same text.
Singers: Treble solo, Mr Cooper, Mr Beard, Mr Savage

Birthday, June 4   Hail to the rosy morn   Boyce / Whitehead
                                                Bodleian Mus. Sch. d. 316

T. recit.   'And shall the British lyre be mute'
T. aria *Larghetto* C maj. 3/4   'To Him we pour the grateful lay'
T. aria *Spirituoso* G maj. 3/8   'Fled are all the ghastly train, writhing pain'

Once again Beard's lively last aria becomes the final Chorus. Its text celebrates the King's recovery from the first significant bout of his mystery illness, which had prevented him attending any more than one of Handel's Oratorios that year at Covent Garden. He only managed to hear Beard as 'Judas Maccabaeus' on February 22nd.
Singers: Treble solo 1, Treble solo 2, Mr Cooper, Mr Beard

1766

New Year   *No Ode was performed on account of death of Prince Frederick William on Dec. 29 1765*
Birthday, June 4   Hail to the man   Boyce / Whitehead
                                                Bodleian Mus. Sch. d. 318

T. aria / arioso / recit   'So Edward fought on Cressy's bleeding plain'
D maj. – F maj. – D maj.   [see page 185 for the full text, and its changes of tempo etc]

Singers: Treble, Contratenor, Tenor - No names are given on the Solo Parts, but the Chorus Parts have the instruction: 'Air by Mr Beard, ending "But sung the truths you feel"', proving that he was still a performer.

1767

New Year   When first the rude, o'er-peopled, North   Boyce / Whitehead
                                                Bodleian Mus. Sch. d. 317

T. recit / Chorus / recit D maj.   'Thus George and Britain bless Mankind'
T. aria *Allegro* F maj.   'From foreign strands new subjects come'
T. recit   'Away ye Barks, the favouring wind springs from the East'

T. aria *Spirituoso* C maj. 3/8   'Britannia from each rocky height'

There are two top As in the Allegro aria, proving that Boyce was still confident that the top of Beard's voice was strong and could cope with the tessitura, despite knowing that he was about to retire from the Stage for good.

Singers: Principal Treble solo, Mr Cooper, Mr Beard

John Beard gives his last performance at Covent Garden on May 23rd, and retires from the Stage

Birthday, June 4   Friend to the poor   Boyce / Whitehead

Bodleian Mus. Sch. d. 319

T. recit. *Allegro* C maj.   'Then George arose; his feeling heart Inspired the Nation'
T. aria 2/4 B flat maj.   'And Justice tho' the sword she drew'
T. *Moderato*   'Yes, Mercy triumphed; Mercy shone confest'

The *Moderato* section contains a pencilled trill mark, in Beard's hand. It is curious that Beard's role in the Odes was not made significantly easier now by involving a Bass soloist, or another 2nd Tenor soloist, as in other years.

Singers: Treble solo 1, Treble solo 2, Countertenor [no name], Mr Beard

1768

New Year   Let the voice of music breathe   Boyce / Whitehead

Bodleian Mus. Sch. d. 320

T. recit.   'Poets should be Prophets too'
T. aria *Vivace* 6/8 C maj.   'Plenty in his train attends'
  "   *Allegro*   'No more shall George whose parent breast'
Duet   'And heartfelt Ease, whose glow within'
T. solo & Chorus   'But grateful Mirth, whose decent bounds'

Singers: Principal Treble solo, Mr Cowper, Mr Beard

This was absolutely the last time Beard sang in public. Boyce didn't write music that made any concessions to his age or lack of recent singing experience. The compass of his arias was still average for a normal tenor voice, taking him as high as top G, and as low as the tenor's low E. The final text which he sang was very suitable for a modest man, whose life was decent and honourable, and who had been known for his geniality and good humour. It runs:

> *'But grateful Mirth, whose decent bounds / No riot swells - no fear confounds -*
> *And heartfelt Ease, whose glow within / Exalts Contentment's modest mien*
> *In ev'ry face shall smile confest, / And in his people's joy the Monarch too be blest'.*

The King may have met Beard in later years. The most obvious occasion would have been at the 1784 Handel Commemoration. He kept in touch with the outside world by reading the daily newspapers. Fanny Burney found this remarkable. She was present at Windsor with Mrs Delany on December 19 1785 when the King entered their drawing-room for a casual chat, and remarked "...that he found by the newspapers that Mrs Clive was dead. ...This led on to more players. ...Then Mrs Siddons took her turn, and with the warmest praise. "I am enthusiast for her," cried the King, "quite an enthusiast. I think there was never any player in my time so excellent - not Garrick himself; I own it!" [12]

If only there had been a diary writer like Fanny Burney around twenty years earlier to remark on the King's tastes whilst Beard was at the height of his powers! But it is good to know that he was aware of actors after their retirement. Perhaps he read of Beard's own death in the papers in January 1791, when the unique Royal Pension that he had provided to the singer as *Vocal Performer in Extraordinary to His Majesty* finally came to an end.

---

[12] 'Fanny Burney's Diary', The Folio Society, 1961, pp. 146-7

APPENDIX 4
BEARD'S PUBLIC AND PRIVATE CORRESPONDENCE

THE 1763 COVENT GARDEN RIOT

BEARD'S LETTER TO THE *PUBLIC ADVERTISER*, March 1ˢᵗ & 3rd 1763.

The Case concerning the late Disturbance at COVENT-GARDEN THEATRE, *fairly stated and submitted to the Sense of the* PUBLIC *in* GENERAL.

As the Opposition to FULL-PRICE at *Drury Lane Theatre* was first founded upon the Pretence of its having been exacted on unjustified Occasions, it was imagined, that let what would be the Event of that Dispute, the MANAGERS of *Covent Garden* ought in no sort to be affected by it, as no such Complaint had ever been pretended against them; yet, when Mr *Garrick* thought proper to waive his private Advantage, for the sake of the public Peace, it was deemed necessary for the same laudable Purpose, to perform such Pieces only for the present at Covent Garden, as could by no means bring the point, which had been so lately and so violently agitated, into immediate Debate again, and even 'Latter Account'[13] was taken to *Love in a Village*.

When the Opera of ARTAXERXES was revived (a piece as distinct from the common Course of Business as even an ORATORIO itself) it was generally understood, the Peculiarity of the Performance, together with the apparent extraordinary Expence attending it, would sufficiently exempt it from the Limitations which had been prescribed at the other Theatre; accordingly it was advertised in the same Manner it had ever been, at FULL PRICES.

Mr Beard received some private Hints the Evening before the intended Representation, tho' not till after the Bill was sent to the Press, that an Opposition was intended by some particular persons, but flattered himself that the Candour and Justice of the PUBLIC *in* GENERAL would distinguish in a case so particularly circumstanced; and when he was called upon the Stage, would have humbly offered such Reasons, as had they been calmly and dispassionately heard, might possibly have prevented the Violence which ensued. In this he was constantly prevented by an incessant and clamorous Demand of a general and decisive YES or NO.

As MANAGER only, and TRUSTEE for other *Proprietors*[14], he thought himself totally unimpowered to resign up their Rights by so sudden and concise a Conveyance; and as the Point in Dispute was an essential Matter of *Property*,

---

[13] '*Latter Account*' – short for 'the latter account of it' - was the contemporary way of expressing that Half-Price tickets would be available. *Love in a Village* had been advertised at Full Prices on the first night, December 8ᵗʰ 1762. Beard is therefore explaining that, in the light of the Drury Lane riot, he had discontinued the 'Full Price only' stipulation on *Love in a Village*. It was performed without an afterpiece. This dispensation was not of as much value as it would have been, if an afterpiece had been played. Therefore, as we see in paragraph 7, a demand of this nature had been made.

[14] The *proprietors* were John Rich's widow Priscilla, and his four surviving daughters Henrietta, Charlotte (Beard's wife), Mary and Sarah. Beard was co-manager with Priscilla, who was something of a 'sleeping partner' in the running of the business.

conceiv'd their concurrence absolutely necessary to any Determination on his Part, which at this juncture was impossible to be obtained.

In this difficult Situation, where *Acquiescence* subjected him to a Breach of that Trust which had been reposed in him, and *Refusal* exposed him to Insult and Displeasure, his submitting rather to the *latter* than be guilty of the *former*, it is hoped will be deemed an Offence not altogether worthy so severe a Resentment.

However unfortunately he may have incurred the Imputation of *Insolence*, *Obstinacy*, or at least *Imprudence*, in not immediately submitting to the Demands proposed; yet when it is considered, that these Demands were enforced by *Part* of the Audience only, and that he had then great Reason to believe such Submission would be very far from producing the salutary Effect of *Theatrical Tranquillity*, he may not perhaps be judged so blameable.

Mr Beard had at that Time received several anonymous Threatening Letters and Notices concerning many other Branches of what they called Reformation. – He was ordered by *one* to add a *Farce* to LOVE *in a* VILLAGE, or the House should be pulled about his Ears. – By *another*, he was commanded to put a Stop to the farther Representation of that *Opera*, upon the Penalty of enforcing his Compliance, by a Riot the next Night of Performance; and very lately received certain Information of Meetings which have already been held, and an Association forming, to reduce the *Prices* at the Theatre to what they were forty Years since, - though it is *notorious* the Expence of Theatrical Entertainments are more than doubled. – For these Reasons: He looked upon the Occasion of the *present Disturbance* only as a Prelude to *future Violence*; as the *first*, not the *last* Salutation of this Extraordinary Kind, to be expected; and apprehended that too easy an Acquiescence might possibly prove rather *Encouragement* than *Prevention*.

Nevertheless, in Gratitude for the many Favours and Indulgencies received from *the* PUBLICK, and from an earnest Desire to promote that Order and Decorum so essential in all Public Assemblies, the *Proprietors* have now jointly authorized Mr BEARD to declare, that they shall think themselves equally bound with the *Managers* of the other *Theatre*, to an Observance of those Limitations which *they* have agreed to.

Mr BEARD, tho' sensible how unworthy an Object his Character is, for the *Attention* of the PUBLICK, yet hopes his Zeal to have it appear in a fair Light, will not be deemed Impertinence, and therefore begs leave to mention one Occurrence that relates particularly to himself. It has been industriously reported, that both before and after Mr Garrick's Submission to the *Point* in *Dispute*, he himself had expressly promised to give it up likewise, but has now insolently dared to resume a Right, which he had already disclaimed. How incapable Mr BEARD is of such a Conduct, he flatters himself those who know him will testify: To those who do not, it may not be unnecessary solemnly to declare, that so far from ever making *such* a *promise*, he constantly insisted, that it neither was in his *Power* or *Intention* to comply with the Demand.

JOHN BEARD

BEARD'S LETTER TO THE *PUBLIC ADVERTISER*, February 25th 1763
regarding the costs of Artaxerxes

Whereas a very unjustifiable disturbance happened last night at this theatre; the managers think it incumbent on them to acquaint the Publick that when the Opera of *Artaxerxes* was in rehearsal it was determined that no expence should be spared to render the performance as elegant as the nature of so peculiar an Entertainment would admit. This desire occasioned so considerable an increase of the nightly charge 'twas thought by many disinterested persons would justify additional prices; but to avoid giving the least umbrage, and in gratitude for the Public indulgence on other occasions, no such advance was attempted. When it is known that the extraordinary nightly expence attending this performance amounts to upwards of *Fifty Pounds* it is humbly apprehended no persons of justice and candour will think the Full Price an exorbitant gratification for such unusual disbursements. The Management therefore flatter themselves that a resolution to oppose the arbitrary and illegal demands of a particular set of persons, contrary to the general sense of audience, will not be deemed arrogant or unreasonable, especially when those demands are enforced by means subversive to Private Property, and in violation of that decorum which is due to all public assemblies.

JOHN BEARD, WILLIAM HAVARD AND THE RIOT

John Beard had his suspicions that his good friend William Havard had prior knowledge of the impending riot and failed to warn him about it. He seems to have thought that Havard actually knew Thaddeus Fitzpatrick and his followers (the *Junto*), and was privy to their deliberations. It appears to have subsequently soured their long friendship, since Havard failed to mention Beard in his will, and did not leave him money for a mourning-ring, as he did to his other theatrical colleagues.

The draft of the following letter, which we have to assume was sent to Beard, is in Havard's m/s scrap-book of poems, letters, speeches and writings, known as '*Jeu d'esprit*'.[15] It was certainly penned after 1767, when Beard ceased to be manager of Covent Garden, and possibly after September 1768 when Havard retired from the stage. Thus at least five years had elapsed since the 1763 riot before Havard tried to set the record straight.

WILLIAM HAVARD'S M/S LETTER TO JOHN BEARD (post 1768)

'I never thought that Johnny Beard would have received a letter from me, the sole contents of which must be a vindication of my Character from the imputation of Breach of Friendship and Good Faith ... But so it seems I am circumstanced – the knowledge of which has but lately reached, and greatly distresses, me.

Your coolness to me arises (by this information) from a suggestion of my having been privy, and in the consultations of the *Junto*, which was the occasion of much damage done to Covent Garden Theatre, while you were one of its managers.

---

[15] Folger Shakespeare Library, Washington, USA; m/s N.a.2

Before I proceed in my justification, I will first apply to your feelings as a friend; and to your sentiments of me as a man: - These two powerful Advocates were (formerly) of my side of the question. Let me add another, which, tho' a political one, hath its weight: -

I belonged to another Theatre; nor is it probable that one, so circumstanced (let friendship be out of the question) could have been guilty (for 'guilty' I will call it) of the charge laid against me, and which, I am sorry to find, you have adopted.

'Tis fruitless to call to mind, and yet I will not avoid the Recollection, how long – how pleasing – and I hoped, how unalterable an Affection did once subsist betwixt us two …
How happy I was in the enjoyment of it whilst it did continue – and how unalterable it is yet with me, tho' it has now had the misfortune of being now under the Damp of your Unkindness.

After this preamble, read my Justification:-

I never knew of this intended attack upon your House, till after you yourself, and all our Bedford-Members were acquainted with it: - for, if you remember, after you had been above stairs with the Party (where you dissented in opinion from them) you came down to the Bedford Club.[16]

That night, being engag'd in the City, I was not at the Club, and did not know any thing intended before, or what was done afterwards, till the day following, and then as Coffee-House news only.

Still further to strengthen my justification I solemnly declare, I never knew of any intentions of the kind; neither did I meet, or see any of the persons upon the occasion: - and I believe, upon recollection it will recur to your own reason (my attachment to you being so very well known) that I must have been the last person that they would have chosen to consult with upon such an occasion.

Had I known your suspicions of me sooner, the matter should not have remained so long unexplained. But how could I think that a friend would open his ear to

---

[16] The *Bedford Coffee House* was attached to the property of Covent Garden Theatre, as was the *Shakespeare's Head* tavern. These two were the meeting place for actors and their friends. There was obviously a Club in an upstairs room at the Bedford to which both Beard and Havard belonged. Beard had presumably been 'upstairs' at the Theatre (in his office?) discussing the matter of 'Full-Price' admissions to *Artaxerxes* with the 'Party'. Could this have been the consortium of Proprietors? If so, it seems as though he was out of step with them.
According to his protestation that 'As MANAGER only, and TRUSTEE for other *Proprietors,* he thought himself totally unimpowered to resign up their Rights by so sudden and concise a Conveyance' he implies that no prior discussion had taken place, and that the riot had taken him by surprise. His excuse is even lamer in the light of his prior knowledge of 'certain Information of Meetings which have already been held, and an Association forming, to reduce the *Prices* at the Theatre'. It is clear that the proprietors were forewarned.
This is the closest we will ever get to knowing whether it was Beard, or the Proprietors, that held out for 'Full Price' only; thus courting the disaster that they were well aware of. In his letter to the Public Advertiser of 1st March Beard lets slip that he "received some private Hints the Evening before the intended Representation, tho' not till after the Bill was sent to the Press, that an Opposition was intended by some particular persons."

accusations against me, when he should have defended me upon the principles of his own heart?

By the way – the want of explanations in friendships has been the loss of many – and, methinks, I have more pride about me than to let the world see, that a connection, so firmly built as ours seemed to be (and indeed I believe was) should be destroyed by suppositions which have no foundation in reality.

To conclude: I once more assure you that I was totally unacquainted with the transaction till it was publicly known – so help me God! – And, in the security of an honest conscience, declare that I never wished for, or connived at, any injury to you: but that I shall (in spite of misrepresentations) ever be

Your most affectionate friend,   W. H.'

THE BEARD / SHEBBEARE CORRESPONDENCE

John Shebbeare was Joseph Pittard (1709-88). Famous for having received a pension from King George III at the same time as Samuel Johnson, on which occasion it was said that the King had pensioned both a He-bear and a She-bear. William Mason (1725-97), in the 'Heroic Epistle to Sir William Chambers' links the names of Shebbeare and Johnson together as sharers in the favours of George III:

> "Witness, ye chosen train,
> Who breathe the sweets of his Saturnian reign:
> Witness, ye Hills, ye Johnsons, Scots, Shebbeares,
> Hark to my call, for some of you have ears".

Mason also wrote the *Epistle to Dr. Shebbeare*, in 1777. Shebbeare wrote a savage critique of Garrick's acting ('Observations on Mr Garrick's Acting') in 1758 which cannot have endeared him to Drury Lane's manager – to whom he had also sent a play for consideration.

SHEBBEARE'S FIRST LETTER

"Sir,   London, Sept. 2nd, 1766

About this time two years, when I waited upon you, and offered to your acceptance a Comedy, you informed me that you was engaged for the succeeding season, but that in the following, if it was found agreeable, you would willingly receive it. In consequence of this it was immediately sent for your perusal. Since that time two seasons have elapsed, and I have received no answer from you. After so long a detention in your hands, I should think myself guilty of injustice to your good character, by entertaining the smallest thought that it will not be played the ensuing winter, and as the theatric season is now approaching, I should be much obliged, if you will acquaint me at what time you think it may most conveniently be given to the public.

I am you very humble servant,   J. Shebbeare"

THE ANSWER

"Sir,   Hampton, Sept. 7th, 1766
Being but just returned to Hampton, from a visit in Buckinghamshire, I did not receive the favour of your's of the 2nd instant till last night, to which I am sorry it is not in my power to send you an immediate *satisfactory* answer. In ten days, or a fortnight, I shall be in town, when you may depend on seeing or hearing from,
Sir, your most humble servant,   J. Beard"

The following letter was sent in consequence of the promise in the preceding.

"Sir,   October 1st, 1766
I am truly concerned that I am obliged to make the Comedy you left in my hands accompany this letter; but the friends I am obliged to consult in affairs of this kind (*as I am answerable to a whole family for the good or ill success of the theatre*) advise that it should not be performed. Their objections are, that the plot is too simple, and the incidents far too few to gratify the general taste, at present. - They add, that the improbability of such contrivances being carried on by a counterfeit nobleman, at so public a place as Bristol Wells, would render the performance very hazardous; and it would be greatly augmented by the many sarcasms throughout the piece on trade and nobility, strikingly nervous as the expressions, and naturally easy as the other parts of the dialogue are. - If there has appeared too much delay in my conduct, I must beg you to impute it, good Sir, to the disagreeable reluctance with which I return any gentleman's work of genius, and particularly one that comes under the sanction of a name so well known, and justly admired in the literary province as your's. I am really much concerned to be reduced to it, and hope, in justice, you will be so kind to charge your disappointment on the care and duty I owe (as agent) to a whole family; not on the choice or liking of
Your most obedient humble servant,   J. Beard"

THE ANSWER to the two preceding letters.

"Sir,   October 2nd, 1766
After so long a detention of the Comedy, I know not whether I am more surprized at the apology which you have made for the sending it back, than at the reasons which you assign for the not accepting it. I shall therefore attempt to shew the insufficiency of the latter, and I flatter myself that, when you have considered what I herein transmit you, I shall have no occasion to explain my sentiments on the former.

The first objection of your friends is, that *the plot is too simple and the incidents far too few, to gratify the general taste at the present.* In answer to this, I know no better method, than that of appealing to a comparison of this Comedy with others which are played; and when you have shewn me a number of them in which the incidents are more numerous, diversified and interesting, and the unravelling the whole more natural, unborrowed and unforeseen, I will pay obedience to the criticisms of your friends.

Your next objection is, that *the impossibility of such contrivances being carried on by a counterfeit nobleman, at so public a place as Bristol Wells, would render the performance very hazardous.* In this place, I imagine, by the word *performance*, you mean the success would be rendered hazardous by the scene of action: and this hazard I apprehend would be the case, wherever it can be placed; and is in common to all situations, and to all new exhibitions on the theatre. By the term, impossible, I fancy you mean improbable; and that you found this improbability on the place being public, and therefore improper to be chosen by the persons who attempt to carry on their intended deceit.

This opinion of *your friends* appears to have arisen from inattention to that rule by which they ought to have judged. They seem to have pronounced this impossibility, from a consideration of things, according to their own characters, and not of those which are delineated in the play. It is probable indeed, that they might not have selected such a scene for the transacting an imposition; but certainly there is nothing improbable, that those who have chosen it in the comedy, would have done the same in real life. Public places are, and ever have been, the scenes of such adventurers, and for this reason, among many others, because the presumption of appearing in them imparts a great degree of credibility to their fictitious characters: a circumstance which ought to have determined the character of Subtle,[17] knowing in mankind, hackneyed in imposture, of a superior cunning which contemns little objects, and driven to such expedients which are only to be accomplished in such frequented places, to have determined on such a public situation. And certainly Wilding and Lucy, who are under his direction, are such from their age and inexperience, who naturally acquiesce with the judgement of Subtle in this instance.

But let it be supposed these theatrical personages have mistaken the proper place for carrying on their design; is it any thing unusual, that those, who thro' wrong judgement have adopted fictitious characters, should err in chusing their scene of action? Were there no mistaken opinions in the conduct of men, I fancy comedy would find but few subjects for her exhibitions. Besides, this judgement tends to the disappointment of their designs, and to expose those vices and follies, which are not susceptible of it in other places; which is the object intended by the piece. Hence it appears, that the selecting this scene is in every view consentaneous [*sic*] to the characters which I have drawn, and the ends which are proposed; that your friends have judged without a just rule, and determined on fallacious principles; and consequently the common hazard to which all new performances are subject is not encreased [*sic*] by this scene of action.

I come now to your last objection, that *the hazard is augmented by the many sarcasms throughout the piece, on trade and nobility.* This indeed is a curious remark of your friends; since the sarcasms, as they call them, are neither on trade nor on nobility, but on the vices and follies which sometimes attend them. And though your friends, in their censure, seem to conceive that these vices and follies are the very same things with merchants and noblemen, and therefore not to be touched, I am of a different opinion; and am persuaded, that whatever is reprehensible in either rank, is the becoming object of comedy, and may be delineated without the least disparagement either of nobility or commerce. For if degrees of wealth and title are to preclude the inquisition of the comic muse, and impart a sanction to vice and

---

[17] Shebbeare has chosen to give this character the same name as the alchemist in Ben Jonson's *The Alchemist.*

folly, who are to be the objects of her satire? Is the public to be entertained with the adventures of none but highwaymen and beggars?[18]

Besides, Sir, your friends do me injustice in not observing, that there are, in this piece, the characters of a real nobleman of untainted honour, and of absolute use to the *dénouement* of the whole; and a merchant, of singular integrity: how then have I been improperly sarcastical on nobility and trade? Do your friends imagine that commerce and peerage are insusceptible of vice and folly? or that such objects should not be treated with that satire, which they call sarcasm? Satire in such cases has seldom encreased the hazard of success. Tameness and insipidity, and not excess of satire, have been the complaints against the new comedies which have been latterly exhibited.

From what I have said, you will plainly perceive that, had I been indulged with being present at the reading this piece, as we agreed I should be, every objection of your friends had been fairly obviated. Wherefore, since this is now the case, though you have been determined by their opinions to reject, I doubt not but in consequence of this refutation of them, and in justice, you will be induced to acquaint me with your change of sentiments.

Permit me to add also, that though the criticisms of your friends had proved unanswerable, since they so highly applaud the other parts of this Comedy, by much the more essential, they would still be unequal to a justification of your returning it: because nothing is more easy than changing the scene, and taking the sting from satire; and few plays, I believe, have been offered to a Manager, against which the objections have been so few and ill grounded.

I shall not at present animadvert on the long detention of this Play, the manner of apologising for that particular, and the sending it back; nor on the other circumstances of your letter. I shall only observe, on your declaring *yourself answerable to a whole family for the good or ill success of the theatre*, that if you are responsible to them as Manager, you are in like manner responsible to the public also; and that if a single family, which receives the profits, be entitled to your precaution, that no piece be injudiciously undertaken; the whole public, which pays the money, have an equal right, that nothing which deserves acceptance should be refused. Wherefore, as every objection, which your friends have afforded you, is fairly refused, and the other requisites of a comedy are acknowledged to be in this, I am persuaded you will recall your interdict, and give me no reason to complain that Mr Beard has ill used me. I am Your humble servant,   J. Shebbeare"
P.S. Be pleased to favour me with an answer.

THE ANSWER to the preceding letter.

"Sir,   October 3rd, 1766
The variety of affairs, wherein I am concerned and embarrassed, will not afford leisure to enter into a more critical examination of your Comedy, or to support a longer argumentation on particulars.

---

[18] a reference to *The Beggar's Opera* in which Beard frequently starred as 'Macheath'

Submitting my single opinion to those of several able judges, and being by my situation obliged to be biassed by the will of others, much more than my own, I must beg your acceptance of this final answer: The piece you have offered will by no means answer our purposes, and therefore cannot be done.

I again repeat my concern that I must return any gentleman's production on his hands, but I cannot avoid it.

If you are severe enough again to arraign my delay, I repeat, that I am very sorry for it; but it is a fate, which (through the great numbers of various performances offered to us, and the constant urgency of business to take up my time) must unavoidably attend many.

Had I power to send a more pleasing answer to you, believe me, it would be much more agreeable to, Sir, Your humble servant,   J. Beard"

THE ANSWER to the preceding letter.

"Sir,   October 10th, 1766
If any thing could have added to the illiberality with which you have already treated me, it is the cavalier manner in which you have replied to my last letter. For through the tinsel of your civility it is perfectly discerned, either that you cannot invalidate the evidence of what I have offered, and have therefore declined the attempt; or that you think me undeserving your farther notice. A treatment which becomes you not to give, nor me to receive with acquiescence. It seems as if you expected to escape from this dilemma, in which too you will be mistaken, by declaring that your *concerns and embarrassments* will not afford you leisure to enter into a more critical examination of my Comedy, or support a longer argumentation on particulars. Of the number of affairs, in which you are now concerned, I cannot determine; but I can plainly see that your embarrassments will not be diminished by the method which you have taken to be freed from them; and however satisfactory these reasons for declining your duty, for such it is, may appear to you, they are none to me, who am neither concerned nor embarrassed, and have full leisure to pursue you.

Should such an *argumentation of particulars*, in which it has been proved you have made no use of arguments, be received as an apology for your *present* conduct, in what manner will it palliate the *past*; your having detained the Comedy two years, without having once considered it; and now returning it, because you have not at *this time* leisure to afford it a more critical examination? Have the two theatrical vacations, which have passed since you received this piece, been so replete with *concerns and embarrassments*, that they could not afford you leisure to attend to *that care and duty* which, by your situation as manager, you owe the public, of entertaining them with new performances; and that justice which is due to writers, of not returning these performances, till after an ample examination, and on reasonable objections they are found improper for the stage? This intended excuse of your's therefore, so totally void of all justification, should not have been offered by you, nor can it be accepted by me, till one of us at least has renounced all pretensions to common sense and good manners.

The next stroke of *argumentation* which you offer in your defence is, *that of having submitted your single opinion to those of several able judges, and being by your situation obliged to be biassed by the will of others much more than your own*. If those *able judges* be the same persons whom you denominate your *friends*, in the preceding letter, surely no man has ever had less foundation, than yourself, for this change of appellation, nor than they, for this distinction of abilities. Is it not adorning the indigent with stars, who have no coats on which to sew them? Do such critics deserve the name of able? and where you could get several of them, I am at a loss to guess. Were their names known, you would have no less reluctance to be seen in their company, than Sir John Falstaff had against marching with his scare-crows through Coventry; for the intellectual marks of your able judges are not less disgraceful, than the bodily [*sic*] of the plump knight's rag-o'-muffins, and yet they serve to fill a pit as well as better.

Do their abilities consist in their discernment of characters; of the motives on which they proceed, or of those places which ought to be selected for their scene of action? Can the apprehension of being discovered at a public place, be an objection to the choice of it by Subtle, who ought, in consequence of his character, to know that this very circumstance of it's being improbable, which naturally occurs to a diminutive deceiver, is the very reason why a more enlarged and exalted cunning should prefer it. For if it be unlikely, in the general opinion, that men of supposititious [*sic*] characters should repair to such places as are generally imagined to accelerate their discovery, does not their daring to be present at them add the greatest verisimilitude, of their being in reality what they presume to represent, and extinguish almost every spark of suspicion? have they not just reason to select them?.....

.....After all, Sir, if you have really submitted your single opinion to the *abilities* of your *judges*, the politeness of the above remark must be assigned to them: but of this you must decide among yourselves. I only wish that a due remuneration may fall on the proper person. Should the latter be the case, I own it is an unwarrantable submission in you, since, in order to decide of *their abilities* in criticism, and to submit to their decrees, *you* ought to be qualified to judge on the subject which is criticised. I fancy no man will be allowed to be a proper judge of the abilities of those who pretend to understand painting, unless he can form a judgement of the pictures also on which their judgement has been made. I apprehend the decisions of the judge are to be compared with the objects of them; and the degrees of their abilities to be determined from the comparison. From hence, sir, if you are not qualified to decide on the merits of a theatrical performance, you are in the same predicament respecting the judges who are proper for such an undertaking. And indeed the truth of this observation is evinced by you, and your judges: *they*, in their criticisms, betray the insufficiency of *their* understandings, and *you* of *your* own in submitting to them.

If these gentlemen believe themselves to be the able judges which you represent them; and free from the embarrassments and concerns in which you are engaged, oblige me with the favour of a meeting with them. And to this, if they are convinced their remarks are right, they can have no just objection: more particularly as I promise inviolably to conceal their names if they chuse it. In this conference, then, they can support the criticisms which they have made. I will as chearfully acknowledge their superiority, and my defects; and as willingly recede from all pretensions to the reception of the play, and even from all complaints of your disingenuous usage in detaining it so long unnoticed, as they or you can desire. But if I am not indulged with this equitable request, I must consider them either as men ashamed of their critical reflections, or as conscious of their having been influenced by sinister motives, and therefore skulking in the obscurity of not being known, in order to perpetrate what they dare not attempt to justify in the light of their proper persons.

And on this occasion it may not be amiss for you to recollect, that at no very great distance of time, and probably in consequence of your submission to the same *able judges*, when you altered the usual prices at the theatre, you were reduced to the no very pleasing condition of publickly apologizing for the offence, and retracting the cause of it. Wherefore, as a friend, and probably a truer than your able judges, I just take the liberty of hinting it possible, that something similar to that which has already intervened on the subject of the price, may again prove to be the event of your precluding an entertainment.[19]   So much being said on your judges, I come now to consider those persons by whose *will*, you say, you are obliged to be *biassed*: and these, I presume, are the *family* of which you speak in your second letter. And in this place, on a reconsideration of the matter, I am induced to believe that this *family* may at once be both the *friends* and the *able judges* of which you have spoken: and then they will consist of two old women, an High German Page, and a woollen-draper, of whom the two last are acknowledged to be *by far* the best judges of theatrical productions[20] ....

....And you, Sir, emancipated from the servility of being obliged to obey the will of others, shall be exalted to the glorious state of exerting your own, and of running according to your own bias. And more particularly, as you have lost your hearing, to *your care and duty* the music shall be committed; for as I value myself on the ability of my judgement, in this distribution of departments, as much as I do that of your *able judges* on my Comedy, I would not have it suggested that you are more defective in qualifications for your employment than your two brothers, who are so specifically adapted to the perfect discharge of the *cares and duties* which are assigned them.

...But as I am fond, on all proper occasions, as you may observe, to become your apologist, I am persuaded that as in consequence of the decay of your organs of hearing, you deviate into disagreement with the music of the orchestra; so, in like manner, that it is from a decline in memory that you wander into discord of facts in your relation of them. And in this place I do expect you will acknowledge my kindness in freeing you from this *embarrassment and concern*, since your accounts would seem to be otherwise irreconcilable. Such being the altered state of your faculties, I cannot avoid most sincerely to bewail the misfortune of the public, who are thus cruelly deprived of that man, for surely no-one will presume to say that he is the same with the honest and good-natured Johnny Beard, who before the fatal day on which he was suddenly seized with a fit of management that affected his head, was universally esteemed to sing both in tune and in time; and to deliver his relations with politeness and consistency. For these reasons, and because I am apprehensive you may not yield a due attention to my advice, I could wish your *able judges* would *once*, at least, become your *faithful friends*; and prevail on you neither

---

[19] Shebbeare appears to be hinting that he could provoke a further riot if his play were not performed.

[20] Priscilla Rich and Beard's wife Charlotte may be the 'two old women'; Sarah Rich was married to George Voelcker, a Page at Court; and Mary Rich had been married to Mr Morris, a woollen merchant. Henrietta, Bencraft's widow, appears not to be mentioned unless she is intended as one of 'the old women'.

to sing any more songs to the public, nor to give any more relations of things in letters which may be given to them....

Having advanced thus far, I am come to that passage, in which you so cavalierly tell me, that *the piece which you have returned will by no means answer your purposes, and therefore cannot be done*: and indeed as in this declaration consists the whole strength of your argumentation I agree with you, and candidly confess that it will not answer your purposes; but I am not, at the same time, persuaded that on that account it ought not to be *done*.

My reasons for coinciding with you in opinion respecting your purposes, are that they seem expressly designed to delude the town with sing-song, Coronation, and Pantomime; at once to corrupt the public taste and pervert the true ends of theatrical exhibitions. In this manner the means of turning vice and folly into ridicule, and of rendering them contemptible, more particularly in those whose examples are the most prevalent, are purposely precluded; and the heart is prevented from melting into acts of human kindness, and from being incensed with horror against cruelty and oppression in favour of virtue in distress.

Not only are these the purposes you are suspected of pursuing. Do you not depreciate all new compositions of rational amusement; and deter those men of letters, who have a true sensation of the liberal pride of writing well, from attempting to exercise their talents on dramatic subjects? can such men acquiesce with the disingenuous usage and preposterous decisions, which they are convinced they shall receive from you, your friends, your family, and your judge? And all this you presume to act through fear the town may be reclaimed from their present pursuit of futile, if not pernicious entertainments, by the representation of good sense and just satire. In this manner, with playing and vamping old plays, reviving *Squire's of Alsatia*,[21] and converting old opera's into new, of which not a few in decency ought to be exploded, whilst you are supinely indulged with acquiring an annual revenue, of not so little as a clear ten thousand pounds, by the works of dead authors, you are ungratefully depressing the merits of the living, and precluding them from the benefit of third nights,[22] which would then travel from your to their pockets: and these are more than suspected reasons, that by every means you endeavour to prevent the reception of new plays. Nor are they withheld from these advantages alone, the remuneration of the public applause, which to men of ingenuity and learning, is infinitely more endearing than pecuniary reward is by the same means impracticable to be given or received....

....If the *care and duty* which you owe your *little family*, who are gorged with riches, superside [*sic*] that *care and duty* which are due to the *large family* of the public who enrich them, and they approve your conduct, I am satisfied on that head. But believe me, Mr Beard, I am not to be charmed by sweet words; not even when they are put into sweet verse by your *friend*,[23] set to sweet music by Dr Arne, and sweetly sung by yourself. And I am persuaded you will think it no degradation of your excellence, when I prefer the melody of your voice, and your skill in singing, to the exquisiteness of your judgement in theatric pieces: because the whole nation

---

[21] Thomas Shadwell's *The Squire of Alsatia* (1688) was revived at Covent Garden on Nov. 18 1763.

[22] Authors of new plays received the takings of the 3rd, 6th and 9th night

[23] Tom Hull, whose Prologue to his play *The Perplexities* Beard spoke and sung in Jan. & Feb. 1767.

have confessed your title to the former, and you yourself have disclaimed it to the latter....

....And now, Sir, after all that has been said, should your implicit submission to your *able judges, your obligation to be biassed by your family, your care and duty for their interest, the disagreeable reluctance of returning the play*, and all the sweet compliments to the bargain, be accepted as an apology for you, as Manager of the theatre, yet as master of the ceremonies at Ham[p]stead, how will you exculpate yourself for this breach of politeness, and for the contempt with which you have treated me? Perhaps you may answer, that you was then John Beard, the singer and servant of the Patentee, and now that you are John Beard, Esq: Patentee, Manager, and Master of the Players, and that, as manners and men too change with circumstances, you lay claim to that plea, in vindication of your conduct. General as the precedent may be, and satisfactory as you may conceive it in your favour, I cannot accept your last letter as your final answer..........

....It is in consequence of these considerations, and not your unpoliteness, that I am chiefly induced to the permitting the publication of the letters which have passed between us on this subject .... and now, Sir, I attend *a second final* answer.
I am, your humble servant,   J. Shebbeare" [24]

MISCELLANEOUS CORRESPONDENCE

to Tom Hull Esq. (of Martlet Court, Bow St., Covent Garden, London)[25]

a letter referring to the death of John Dunstall (1717-1778),Beard's actor & singer friend: a performer at Goodman's Fields from 1740 and Covent Garden from 1744 until his death, who was buried St Paul's Covent Garden on January 8ᵗʰ 1779, with an Epitaph by Beard.

Dear Tom,   Rose Hill, Old New Years Day (i.e. Jan. 12ᵗʰ) 1779
The loss of poor Dunstall affects me exceedingly. He was as just, as honest, as sincere a Man as ever liv'd: the bluntness of his Address, serv'd only as a Foil; to every social Virtue, which he possest in the most eminent degree; whatever he said or did, was from the Heart; He ate heartily, drank heartily, laugh'd heartily, and lov'd *with all his Heart*: it may be truly said of *Jack*, as of *Paul*, "He knew no Guile".

Who ever heard him depreciate an *absent* Enemy, or flatter a *present* Friend? Oh no - his Bosom was too full of the noblest feelings of Humanity, to leave room for the little polite Arts of Deceit or Cunning: he had great theatrical Merit, was indefatigable in his Business, an Honour to his Profession, and as far as his Power extended, a Friend to Mankind; He honour'd, he succour'd Merit in Rags,[26] and despis'd unfeeling Arrogance, tho' in the gilded Chariot of a Manger. Such are my real thoughts of Honest Jack: He is the subject of my Meditations in my Garden, my Parlour, my Bed: and if this sketch of his character appears tolerable in black

---

[24] Publication of the complete 'Letters which have passed between John Beard Esq. Manager of Covent Garden Theatre, and John Shebbeare M.D.'

[25] from: British Library Egerton Manuscripts (Collections relating to Musicians 1578-1860) Eg 2159 f. 52 (1779)

[26] word unclear, but probably referring to his charity towards the poor (in 'rags').

and white, it is because the Outline is Just. we were nearly of the same age, and no wonder I indulge these serious Reflexions on *The Man of Worth*, and pay this little tribute of an

Epitaph
To the ever respectable Memory
of
John Dunstall Comedian
who died Jan[ry] 1779 in the 62nd year of his Age

A Man by Nature open, warm, sincere;
(whose Heart scarce Death could cool) lies buried here.
Unpolish'd Manners, rough as the Northern Wind,
But half conceal'd, a gentle, gen'rous Mind:
Firm in his *own* Distress - at Others' Woe
His manly Heart would melt, - the Tear would flow;
Belov'd from Youth to Age, by Old and Young,
Tho' Flatt'ry ne'er disgrac'd his honest Tongue[27]:
Tried, and approv'd, by a discerning Age,
His name shall grace the Annals of the stage,
Whilst *Truth* which most he lov'd, shall tell[28],
Thro' every Scene of Life, he acted well.
Go gentle Reader, go, ------- and if you can,
Live like this *upright,* downright <u>Honest</u> <u>Man</u>.

Dear Tom, <u>You know</u> I do not pretend to write, but <u>I know</u> you are my Friend, and by that tie are bound to endure, and to conceal my weaknesses. and am sure will forgive the attempt, for the sake of the Motive. <u>Live,</u> and be <u>happy</u> my dear Tom, that I may be <u>happy</u> whilst I <u>live</u>: and tell dear Maria, that except yourself, there is no man <u>living</u> loves honours and esteems her more than   J[no]: Beard
     My Charlotte bids me add all that's kind from her, to Both, a thousand loves to dear Emmy, and tell her I will not lose my Xmas kisses.

to Maria Hull Esq. (of Duke's Court, Bow St., Covent Garden, London)[29]

a letter inviting Tom Hull's wife Maria to visit Beard and his wife Charlotte at Hampton, whilst her husband is busy with the preparations for the new Covent Garden season; referring to unkind comments that Beard's own name had been inscribed on Dunstall's memorial tablet; and describing the visits Beard is about to make to neighbours and local friends – including Kitty Clive and James Raftor in their house, Little Strawberry Hill, Twickenham, next door to Horace Walpole.

Rose Hill, 18th Aug. 1785

"What horrid silence thus invades our Ears"? (as the King of Brentford says.[30]) Well as I love dumb things,[31] the taciturnity of your Pen, begins to be alarmingly painful: Maria's love for her Rosehillian Friends, sets her far above the poor and proud etiquette of, Who wrote last? not that you have any Claim to that Shadow of a

---

[27] This line later became: 'Tho' servile flattery ne'er disgrac'd his tongue': see Appendix 6
[28] This line later became: 'Whilst <u>Truth</u> which most he lov'd, shall boldly tell': see Appendix 6
[29] British Library Egerton Manuscripts (Collections relating to Musicians 1578-1860) Eg 2159 f. 56
[30] a character in a comedy in which Beard regularly played. The line is a version of Dryden's:
An horrid stillness first invades the ear,/ And in that silence we the tempest fear. 'Astraea Redux', 1.7
[31] Beard had a dog called 'Phillis' and several cats

Plea, for your Charly[32] wrote to you last Friday. Write then directly, and d'ye hear? be sure you begin with the two prettiest monosyllables alive viz: *All Well*. An Old Dog (poor Johnny) without Teeth cannot grow a Sheeps Head (Maria) but adszoundlikins, if we do not hear from you soon, I will so mumble you when we meet, I'll make you rememember [*sic*] me 'till you learn to go to Bed at One, and rise at Nine. I have had a sweet letter from Tom,[33] Charly told you so. I do not expect him to write often to me, I know he has other Fish to fry[34]; but I expected frequent Accounts of his Welfare, from a Hand we love, and a Pen we admire as much as his own.[35] Pray Madam have you any serious Thoughts of revisiting Rose-Hill? I can easily conceive your Aversion to a Stage-Coach (tho' you are an Honour to the Drama[36]) but as Mr & Mrs Chace have flatter'd us with the Hopes of a Visit, why not creep into a corner of their Carriage? If so, be kind enough to let us know when, for fear we should be gone abroad already, as we are almost daily repaying Visits of Civility, to Richmond, Twickenham etc. etc. and one of Friendship is worth 5000 of Ceremony.

The Ides of Aug[t] are past, and if you do not come soon, adieu to all our fair and friendly Hopes, for when Tom returns, not his Majesty's eight creams would be able to draw you in his State Coach from Dukes Court[37] to Hampton.

Do you know Maria, the tenderhearted critics have vext my righteous Spirit exceedingly? they have - it seems my Name is inscribed in too large Characters on Dunstall's tombstone, and truth I think so too: but they place it to the Acc[t] of your Brother Johnny's ineffable Vanity: I own I am proud of witnessing the worth of poor Dunny, but you know as well as I, I gave no Direction to have my Name appear at all, much less in Letters as long as my leg. 'Tis very certain I never tho[ught] of gaining a great name, by scribbling a little Epitaph, at best the weak Effusion of strong Friendship: and therefore safe in my own Integrity, let me say with Prior,[38] or somebody prior to him, faith I don't know who –

Let them censure, what care I?
The Herd of Critics I defie

and there's an end of the matter. Richmond Hoy! I expect the Coach at every Moment, to carry us to Capt Groce, Mrs Bayatun etc. Tomorrow our Damsels take another Flight to Mrs Huddy; whither we follow them on Saturday, to meet my old Friend and Flame Kitty Clive, Miss Pope[39] (with all her Amiabilities about her) and flimsy jimsy-pimsy Rafter,[40] the avow'd Favourite of every venerable Twickenham Tabby,[41] who has a Taste for Scandal and Quadrille. The Coach is at the door - the dearest loves of my dearest 3 [42] attend you - Adieu   J[no]: Beard

---

[32] i.e. Charlotte

[33] presumably her husband Tom Hull (1728-1808)

[34] The second half of August would have been a busy time for the theatre managers, preparing casts and repertoire for the season which started in early September.

[35] a reference to Hull's ability as a Poet and Dramatist

[36] Maria (1727-1805) had been a successful actress as Anna Maria Morrison until her retirement in 1775

[37] In 1779 the Hulls had lived at Martlet Court. Duke's Court was nearby and parallel with it, and also ran between Bow Street and Drury Lane. Perhaps they had moved there between the writing of these two letters.

[38] Matthew Prior (1664-1721)

[39] the actress Jane Pope (1742-1818), who kept up a long correspondence with Kitty (now at the Folger Library)

[40] James Raftor (? pre-1711 – 1790), Kitty Clive's sister, who lived with her at Little Strawberry Hill

[41] Horace Walpole (1717-97) who this year – 1785 – published his *Essay on Modern Gardening*

[42] Charlotte and her orphaned nieces Sarah Melosina and Sophia Henrietta Voelcker

to Dr Samuel Arnold (of Great Pulteney Street, Golden Square, London)[43]

a letter obliquely referring to Arnold's success at the 1784 Handel Commemoration concerts at Westminster Abbey; thanking him for the honour done to him by the members of the Chapel Royal choir at the recent Dinner given on October 21st 1785 (possibly on the occasion of his 70th birthday); a response to Mrs Lampe and Mrs Jones' request for help from the Actors' Fund <u>*as well as*</u> *the Musicians' Fund; and a reference to the recent illness of George Colman (the elder) 1732-94, joint patentee of Covent Garden Theatre since Beard's retirement in 1767.*

My ever dear Friend   Rose Hill 1st Dec. 1785

I have a little million of notices to thank you for the kindest and most elegant of letters: and *first, & all first,* for the assurance of your dear little woman's miraculous recovery and return, to repay you for all that anxiety, which only the best of hearts could feel, and which no tongues nor pen could describe. May your long and mutual sufferings be rewarded with long and mutual happiness! May your future success be equal to your merit, and your name engrav'd in the rolls of honour, close by the immortal Handel![44] And may every friend to every virtue, love and esteem you as I do! Will we pay our respects to Mr Arnold? Yes *greedily,* the very first time we go to London, but when that will be, God only knows: for at this present writing .I have a most painful return of my stranguary complaint,[45] and unless call'd by unexpected business, shall hardly think of revisiting the Capital on this side of C[hris]^tmas – what you and Dupuis can mean by offering so much incense to a *leaden calf* of your own creating, I know not; for I think you would scorn to prostitute your praise to *one of gold,* tho' cast by Arch-B^p Aaron, or the Pope of Canterbury himself: that I have been fortunate beyond my deserts or expectation I own; but be assur'd I should heartily despise myself (and so would you) could I ever be guilty of affecting the least superiority over the humblest of my school-mates, excepting only the painful pre-eminence of age; and to *that alone* I ascribe the extreme kindness of my brethren on the happy 21st of October; kindness that has kept my heart warm ever since, and will, as long as my (somewhat impaired) memory lasts. But how shall I thank you for your goodness to poor Mrs Jones! Indeed she is worthy your humane endeavours to serve her, and if you succeed, as I think you must, the whole merit and reward is your own. You seem'd to wish I would draw her petition: I am a stranger to the usual form, and therefore thought it might be better to address the Society as [per] enclos'd, for it would have been too hard a tax on her modest merit to proclaim her own praise, or respect her distress in a petition from herself. Nevertheless my dear friend, if there is any, the least impropriety in my mode of application, I beg you will kindly commit it to the flames, and take the trouble of applying to the Governors in the most eligible manner. Mrs Jones and Mrs Lampe[46] should have a strict charge not to open their lips to any one, concerning any benefit she may derive from the Musical Fund, as by the laws of the Theatrical Institution, she would lose by *one,* what she gained by the *other* – but of this I am *perfectly assured,* that unless she divulges it *herself,* the humane Theatrical Committee, in consideration of her merits and misfortunes, so far from noticing it from the information of others, will

---

[43] from: Harvard Theatre Library – Autographs: Musical & Dramatic Vol. 1 (TS990.1F)

[44] an oblique reference to Arnold's involvement in the 1784 Handel Commemoration concerts at Westminster Abbey

[45] see footnote on p. 278

[46] Mrs Lampe and Mrs Jones had both been on the Covent Garden payroll as singers during Beard's time as manager; Mrs Lampe was already there when Beard arrived in 1759, and Mrs Jones joined the company in 1762.

rejoice in every addition to her ease and comfort, tho' they cannot alter their laws. No tongue can tell my sufferings for three or four days past, they are so frequent, so violent, they almost take from me the power of assuring you that I am most truly, your ever oblig'd, grateful, and affectionate   J[no]: Beard

In the midst of my pains, my heart rejoices in the recovery of Coleman; thank you for your kind information: I am assur'd he is daily benefitted by the Richmond air – why the little man did not know how much he was belov'd, I'm sure I did not know how much I lov'd him – tho' <u>fath & soll</u> ['faith and soul'] he has paid too dearly for the experience. My best of nurses and her nieces[47] join me in all that's very kind to you & dear Mrs Arnold.

NB – if you should adopt my address and petition for Mrs Jones, be so good to fill up the chasm left for Mr Jones's P[tion] [Petition] name – which I cannot recollect.

to Dr Samuel Arnold (of Great Pulteney Street, Golden Square, London)[48]

> *a letter telling of a two week visit to Chelsea; with a request for two complimentary season tickets, as in previous years, for the 1786 Oratorio season; a response (as before) to Mrs Jones' request for help from the Actors' Fund, and Thomas Sanders Dupuis' efforts on behalf of a certain Mr Luther, a fellow Mason; and containing information requested by Charles Burney for his life of Dr. William Boyce in his 'A General History of Music', published subsequently in 1789.*

Rose Hill 9th March 1786

After a Fortnight's Absence, on a visit to Chelsea,[49] I Yesterday return'd to this our serene abode, and to make my Wellcome Home doubly agreeable, found two Epistles from our beloved Dr. Arnold: 'tis true they were rather under the middle Size, but like your Self contain'd the *multum in parvo*. When we left this Place, we had promis'd our Selves the pleasure of Seeing (or at worst enquiring of you the Health of) Mrs Arnold & Family; but not to mention our being Frost-bound, my poor Charlotte had a severe Attack of the Gravel, which has not yet thought fit to take its final leave, tho' thank Heaven she is greatly mended. I thank you most kindly and sincerely for enrolling us in the number of your select Friends. Mr Linley[50] had during the whole time he was concern'd in the Oratorios,[51] indulged me with a Return Ticket, for two into any Part of the House; in the following Form –

> *Oratorio's for the Year 1785 –*
> *Admit Two into any Part of the House*
> *and return this Ticket to Bearer*   Tho[s.] Linley

and I was happy in dedicating it to my dear Friends Mr and Mrs Hewetson;[52] on the approach of the present Season I wrote to the worthy Linley for a renewal of the obliging Priviledge, but rec[d:] no Answer till the day before I left Chelsea, when I found my poor Friend was retir'd into the Country for the Recovery of his Health. I

---

[47] Charlotte's orphaned nieces Sarah Melosina and Sophia Henrietta Voelcker

[48] from: H.D. Johnstone, 'Treasure Trove in Gloucester: a Grangerized copy of the 1895 edition of Daniel Lysons' History of the Three Choirs Festival', RMA Research Chronicle 31, 1998, p. 49

[49] Charlotte's stepmother, Priscilla Rich, lived in Chelsea until her death in 1783. Her brother Edward Wilford continued to live there until his death on July 17th 1789. He left Beard £10 in his will. Beard's friend, and doctor, Alexander Reid lived at the Royal Hospital, Chelsea until his death in 1788. So Beard could have been visiting either of these two; and was probably receiving medical advice for Charlotte's complaint at the same time.

[50] From this year Thomas Linley, senior (1733-95) was running the Oratorio season jointly with Arnold.

[51] i.e. since 1774

[52] for Richard Hewetson (spelled Howatson in 'Treasure Trove in Gloucester') see page 264

requested the Favour of foolish Tom [Hull][53] to explain my Wishes to you, which I suppose either his or your Engagem[ts:] of more consequence have prevented his doing. If you think fit to indulge me for the remainder of the (I most earnestly hope successful) Season, be so good [as] to enclose it to Mrs Hewetson, and you will oblige me beyond the Power of Words to express. How then shall I tell you my Feelings for your Goodness to poor Mrs Jones! I certainly grow very foolish in my old Age, for I could not read your success in her Favor without a gush of Tears, but they were Tears of Joy and Gratitude: I grow envious too, for I almost grudg'd you the sweet Fruits of your Benevolence: I am glad however I do not know the two dissentient Voices, for I would not go out of the World with hatred in my Heart. I am in a pack of Troubles on Acc[t.] of worthy Brother Dupuis – he kindly wrote me Word of his Success for Bro[r.] Luther, and I return'd an immediate Answer, which, as I have lost his Address, I directed to Him in Park Lane, Hyde Park Corner, and as I am doubtful of the Place of his Residence, much fear my Letter may have miscarried. Will you be so kind when you next see him, to say, What did not occur to me when I wrote that I believe the Rev[d.] Mr Fitzherbert, and the Rev[d.] Mr Moses Wight[54] can furnish Dr. Burney with most of the leading Incidents in the blameless Life of the amiable Dr. Boyce, for if I am not greatly mistaken, they both were his intimate Friends to the Time of his Death. If dear Mrs Arnold is in Town, present her with the united Loves of Charlotte & John Beard, if not, keep it warm in your Heart till you see Her, as warm as the Constant Wishes, Esteem, and Affection, of your ever oblig'd   J[no]: Beard

Our Lasses[55] join in [sending] best Love

To the Royal Society of Musicians and particularly To the Governors of the Fund for the Releif of decay'd Musicians and their Familys[56]

Gentlemen, It is with infinite satisfaction I hear that the late increase of your Capital has enabled you to make a more comfortable Provision for such Widows of our deceased Brethren, as are under the Circumstances of claiming Relief from so benevolent, and now so happy and permanent an Establishment. The Society's Book will inform you, that the late Mr Charles Jones was a worthy Member of our Community, attended all the prescribed Dutys, and paid his Subscriptions to the time of his Death; notwithstanding his Widow was precluded from reaping any Benefit from the Fund, by a then (but now no longer) necessary Law; as from the Time of her dismission from the Theatre in Covent Garden, She has received £30 p Ann[.m] from the Theatrical Fund. But Gentlemen, permit me to acquaint you, that her State of Health has been so deplorable, so hopeless, that after paying for her Lodging, and her Apothecary's Bills, there could be very little left, to purchase Food and Raiment... Was it not for the unremitting Tenderness [of] Mrs Lampe, and the occasional Kindness of [a] few other friends... she must inevitably have perished: ...yet, through all her Sufferings, She is never heard to mumur or complain... The unsullied Reputation of the poor patient Sufferer... renders her a still more worthy Object of your kind Consideration. ...I am with all due Respect and Esteem, Gentlemen, your much oblig'd humble Servant   J[no]: Beard

---

[53] Thomas Hull the actor and Beard's friend was, by now, acting Manager at Covent Garden.
[54] William Fitzherbert (1715-97) & Moses Wight (1701-95) were both minor canons of St. Paul's Cathedral & priests at the Chapel Royal; both, like Beard, subscribed to publications of Boyce's music.
[55] Charlotte's orphaned nieces Sarah Melosina and Sophia Henrietta Voelcker
[56] Document held in the Gerald Coke Handel Collection at the Foundling Museum, London

APPENDIX 5
BALLADS, SONGS AND CANTATAS

The miscellaneous songs and ballads that Beard sang so successfully during his career, divide up into various types and groups, depending on the venue he was performing in, and the nature of the entertainment provided there. The music that he sang covers the entire range of vocal music being composed in the middle of the eighteenth century - from elaborate *Cantatas* to lightweight, ephemeral ballads.

It must be remembered that he was one of the original 'cross-over' artists - to use a modern term. Thus, some of his audience might have known him only for the trifles that he sang at the Pleasure Gardens: the forerunners of the modern pop-song. Others, who visited the select music clubs that were springing up in the City at this time, such as the Castle Concerts and the Academy of Vocal Musick, would have thought of him as an interpreter of serious and high-minded cantatas and oratorios: the equivalent of today's 'high-brow classical' music. There was also an emerging audience for what we would think of as normal 'classical' concerts at the various music rooms - Hickford's Room and the Great Room, Dean Street - where Beard was a frequent visitor.[57] The theatre-going public would have seen him as the star of some much-loved ballad operas such as *The Beggar's Opera*, *The Devil to Pay* and *The Maid of the Mill*; which were the 'musicals' of their day.

In any one week Beard would have slipped effortlessly from one style to the other – and even on the very same day. In the 1750s it was not unusual for him to perform Handel's *Messiah* at noon, a serious play with incidental music at 6pm, and a farcical ballad-opera at 9pm. When consulting the following lists of different vocal pieces that were in his repertoire it will be good to remember that they were nearly all written for him; and that they jostled alongside each other in his performance diary. For ease of identification I have divided them up, perhaps rather loosely, into:

- Cantatas / Oratorios performed at London's Music Clubs and concert halls
- Patriotic Songs sung as *Interval Music* at the theatres
- Other songs, ballads and duets sung as *Interval Music* at the theatres
- Ballads sung at the Pleasure Gardens, such as *Ranelagh Gardens*

There were certainly occasions when these divisions broke down, as - for example - on the occasions when Ranelagh offered more serious entertainment, or the theatres let him sing a trifling ballad that was currently a favourite with the public. Beard was a typical 'Nanki-poo' (as in W.S. Gilbert's comic creation) and had a song for every occasion:

> *A wand'ring minstrel I -*
> *A thing of shreds and patches,*
> *Of ballads, songs and snatches,*
> *And dreamy lullaby!*
> *My catalogue is long,*
> *Through every passion ranging;*
> *And to your humours changing*
> *I tune my supple song!*[58]

---

[57] I am indebted to Simon McVeigh for the useful information that I have derived from his 'Calendar of London Concerts 1750 – 1800', Goldsmiths College, University of London.
[58] Gilbert & Sullivan, 'The Mikado', 1885, solo and chorus 'A Wandering Minstrel I'.

**Cantatas, Oratorios, and excerpts from them, sung at
London's Music Clubs, Theatres, and concert halls**

<u>Decayed Musicians Fund Benefit Concert</u>   <u>Various Venues: mainly King's Theatre</u>

April 10 1745	Handel 'Total Eclipse' (*Samson*)
	Handel 'Why does the God of Israel sleep' (*Samson*)
	Handel 'The flocks shall leave the mountains' (*Acis & Galatea*)
April 16 1751	Handel 'Why does the God of Israel sleep' (*Samson*)
	Handel 'Tune your harps' (*Esther*)
March 23 1752	Handel 'Through the land so lovely blooming' (*Athalia*)
	Handel 'The trumpet's loud clangour' (*St Cecilia Ode*)
	Handel 'Love in her eyes' (*Acis & Galatea*)
	Handel 'The flocks shall leave the mountains' (*Acis & Galatea*)
April 30 1753	Maurice Greene 'O lovely Fair' & 'Faithful Youth'
	Handel 'The flocks shall leave the mountains' (*Acis & Galatea*)
Feb. 28 1754	Handel 'Endless Pleasure' (*Semele*)
	Nicolo Pasquali 'O 'Tis Elysium All', (Cantata '*Celia*')
Feb. 17 1755	Arne Cantata '*Cymon & Iphigenia*'
April 5 1756	*Beard may have withdrawn: his name disappears from the advertisements*
Feb. 2 1759	Arne role of 'Alfred' (*Alfred*)
March 12 1761	Samuel Howard 'When Bacchus, jolly God'

<u>Lock Hospital Benefit</u>   <u>Various Venues</u>

April 22 1752	Purcell 'Ye twice ten hundred Deities' (*The Indian Queen*)
	Handel 'Through the land so lovely blooming' (*Athalia*)
	Unknown composer 'Beneath this' (Cantata)
	Handel 'The flocks shall leave the mountains' (*Acis & Galatea*)
May 7ᵗ 1753	Handel *Judas Maccabaeus*
May 23 1754	Handel *L'Allegro ed il Penseroso* + *St Cecilia Ode*
May 4 1759	Handel unspecified arias
May 18 1762	Sacred Music from Handel Oratorios
April 15 1763	Avison & Giardini *Ruth*
Feb. 29 1764	Arne *Judith*
Feb. 13 1765	Avison & Giardini *Ruth*
	Beard may have withdrawn from this and been replaced by Vernon

<u>The Smallpox Hospital</u>

March 3 1753	Handel *Alexander's Feast* (conductor John Stanley)

<u>The Westminster Hospital</u>

April 10 1755	Songs (for the Feast Day Celebrations)
May 15 1755	Songs (at St. Anne's Church, Westminster)

<u>The Middlesex Hospital</u>

April 26 1758	Handel *Anthems* (at St. Anne's Church, Westminster)

City of London, Lying-In Hospital for Married Women, Benefit

May 12 1753 Arne role of 'Alfred' (*Alfred*)
May 16 1759 Handel unspecified arias (at St. Andrew's Church, Holborn)

Great Room Dean Street

March 5 1753 Handel arias from *Samson* (Benefit for John George Freake)
Feb. 22 1754 Barbandt 'Psalm 51' + oratorio excerpts
Feb. 1 1757 Handel *L'Allegro ed il Penseroso* (Benefit for Mrs Pontifex)
March 31 1758 Handel *Acis and Galatea* (Benefit for Mrs Abegg)
April 1 1758 Handel *Acis and Galatea* (Benefit for a Widow in great distress)
March 1 1759 Handel *L'Allegro ed il Penseroso*

Crown Tavern, Academy of Ancient Musick

January 18 1739 Handel *Alexander's Feast* (Tenor solos)

Crown Tavern, St Cecilian Society

October 21 1755 Handel *Acis and Galatea* (Acis)
October 28 1755 Handel *Acis and Galatea* (Acis)

The Crown and Anchor

March 21 1744 Defesch *Love and Friendship*

The Devil Tavern, Apollo Society

April 16 1736 Boyce *David's Lamentation over Saul and Jonathan*

King's Theatre Haymarket

April 29 1745 Cantata by Stanley (Benefit for Mrs Robinson)
April 25 1754 Handel *L'Allegro ed il Penseroso* (Benefit for Frasi)

Little (New)Theatre Haymarket

April 6 1749 Handel *Acis and Galatea* (Benefit for Frasi)
April 23 1751 Handel 'Happy Pair'(*Alexander'sFeast*((Benefit for J. Snow)
       + Handel Trio (*Acis & Galatea*)
April 2 1753 Handel *Acis and Galatea* (Benefit for Frasi)
May 2 1757 Handel *Acis and Galatea* (Benefit for Jonathan Snow)

Castle Tavern, Castle Music Society Concerts

April 5 1749 Handel *Acis and Galatea*
May 3 1749 Handel *Esther* (conductor John Stanley)
March 16 1751 Handel *Samson*
October 23 1751 Handel *Acis and Galatea*
January 20 1752 *unknown*
January 27 1752 *unknown*

*Castle Music Society, at Haberdasher's Hall**

Oct. 19 1757	Pasquali, 'O 'Tis Elysium All', (Cantata '*Celia*')
	+ Howard, 'Ye cheerful Virgins'& 'When Bacchus, jolly God'
Dec. 21 1757	Handel, 'Comfort Ye' & 'Every Valley' (*Messiah*)
	+ Arne, 'The Woodlark whistles thro' the Grove' (*Eliza*)
	+ Boyce, Duet 'Thou soft invader of the Soul' (*Solomon*)
Feb. 16 1758	Arne, Cantata 'Frolic and free'
	+ Purcell, 'Ye twice ten hundred deities' (*The Indian Queen*)

* Beard may have taken part in more of these Concerts. The programmes are extant for the first, ninth, and fifteenth nights only of the 1757-8 season. "The printed programmes provide important information about the Society. They confirm that the evening's music was divided into two parts. More importantly, the choice of music and the calibre of soloists such as Beard and Frasi disclose the tone and the standard the society sought to achieve".[59]

Drury Lane

March 28 1750	Boyce, *Solomon* (Benefit for Jones)
April 11 1750	Sacred Music (Benefit for Geminiani)
March 4 1763	*The Cure of Saul* (Handel 'Pasticcio' by Dr. Brown)
	(Benefit for Colleges in Philadelphia & New York)
April 27 1763	*The Cure of Saul* (Handel 'Pasticcio' by Dr. Brown)
	(Benefit for Colleges in Philadelphia & New York)

Hickford's Room

April 8 1736	Songs, for his Benefit. Beard's 1st Benefit Concert
April 20 1736	Songs (Benefit for Rowland) *possibly delayed until May 10 1736*
April 21 1749	Handel *Acis and Galatea* (Benefit for Miss Oldmixon)
April 30 1751	Songs (Benefit for Marianne Davies aged 7)

Hickford's Room: J.C. Smith's Season of 1740

Jan. 4, 11, 18, 25	J.C. Smith *Rosalinda*
February 1, 8	J.C. Smith *Rosalinda*
April 18	J.C. Smith *Rosalinda*
Feb. 22, 29	J.C. Smith *David's Lamentation over Saul and Jonathan*
March 7, 27	J.C. Smith *David's Lamentation over Saul and Jonathan*
April 2, 11, 25	J.C. Smith *David's Lamentation over Saul and Jonathan*

The Long Room, Hampstead

Sept. 21 1745   Benefit for Thomas Roseingrave
and see:
Appendix 2 (p. 325) for Beard's Benefit Concerts here every August from 1750-61

---

[59] Brian Cosby *RMA Research Chronicle 34*

Patriotic Songs sung as *Interval Music* at the theatres

Composer	Title	*1st recorded performance*

War of Jenkins's Ear   *1739- 42*   &   *War of the Austrian Succession*   *1740-48*

Purcell	To Arms *(Bonduca)*	CG 24.10.39
Purcell	Britons strike home *(Bonduca)*	"
Handel	Nel Pugnar *(Arianna in Creta)*	CG 25. 3. 40
John Frederick Lampe	A Song in the character of a Captain of an English "	
	Man-of-War upon the Taking of Porto Bello	
	('Come my lads, with souls befitting')	
Richard Leveridge	Black-eyed Susan	CG 26.4.40
	('All in the dawn the fleet was moored') Text by John Gay	

The Jacobite Rebellion   *1744-6*

Purcell	Genius of England (*Don Quixote*)	CG 8.3.44
Handel	The Trumpet's loud clangour (*StCecilia Ode*) CG 17.4.44	
arr. Thomas Arne	God bless our noble King (*National Anthem*) DL 28.9.45	
John Frederick Lampe	A New Occasional Song	CG 11.10.45
Handel	A New Occasional Ballad	CG 3.12.45
	(*possibly*: Handel 'Stand round, my brave boys')	
Handel	God save the King (from 'Zadok the Priest') CG 28.12.45	
John Frederick Lampe	The English Hero's Welcome Home	CG 8.1.46
Handel	Trio from *Acis and Galatea*	CG 25.1.46
arr. Pepusch	Over the hills and far away	CG 7.2.46
	(*with new text*: 'He that is forced to go and fight')	
Handel	Occasional Song on the defeat of the Rebels CG 25.4.46	
	(*possibly*: Handel 'From scourging Rebellion')	
Michael Festing	Britannia sees brave William shine	CG ? 1746
	(*A Song in honour of the Duke of Cumberland*)	
Michael Festing	Loyal Song 'From barren Caledonian lands' CG ? 1746	
	(*in praise of the Duke of Cumberland*)	

The Seven Years' War   *1756 - 63*

Thomas Arne	Rule Britannia	DL 2.4.55
Purcell	Britons strike home *(Bonduca)*	"
?	A New Song, in the character of a Sailor	DL 7.10.55
William Boyce	Heart of Oak (Text by David Garrick)	CG 23.4.61

Other songs, ballads and duets sung as Interval Music at the theatres

Composer	_Title_	_1st recorded performance_

Composer	Title	1st recorded performance
Henry Purcell	The Opinion of the Ancients (Duet)	CG 12.4.36
"	Mad Bess ('From silent shades')	CG 10.3.37
"	Let Caesar & Urania live (Duet)	CG 14.3.37
	(from: 'Sound the trumpet, beat the drum')	
"	From rosy bowers (_Don Quixote_)	"
"	Celia has a thousand charms (_Rival Sisters_)	CG 26.3.37
"	Mad Dialogue (Duet)	CG 30.11.38
"	Mad Tom (_in character_)	DL 10.12.41
"	Mad Bess ('From silent shades') (_in character_)	CG 21.4.48
"	The Incantation Song (_The Indian Queen_)	DL 21.3.52
	(_presumably_ 'Ye twice ten hundred deities')	
"	Sing all ye Muses (_Don Quixote_) (Duet)	DL 7.5.57
"	A Solemn Hymn (sung in '_The Royal Convert_')	CG 15.11.62

Samuel Howard	As I saw fair Clara (duet) poem by R. Steele	CG 15.3.37
	(_possibly_ 'A Song designed for the play _The Conscious Lovers_')	
?	Mr Cowley's 'Swallow'	CG 18.4.37
?	A new Trumpet song	CG 25.4.37
?	A Cantata accompanied by Trumpets	CG 28.4.37
?	The Lady's Lamentation for the loss of Senesino	CG 2.5.37
?	A new English Cantata	CG 18.10.37
?	J'aime la Liberté	CG 17.4.38
John Ernest Galliard	The Early Horn	CG 3.5.38
?	The Life of a Beau	CG 13..5.38
J.C. Pepusch	See from the silent Groves Alexis flies	CG 17..5.38
?	Celia that I once was blest	CG 6.1.39
G.F. Handel	O Happy Pair (_Alexander's Feast_)	CG 3.4.39
Thomas Arne	Would you taste the noontide air (_Comus_)	"
?	The Protestation	CG 11.5.39
?	On, on, my dear Brethren (_A Masonic Song_)	CG 15.5.39
?	Thus mighty Eastern Kings	"
Thomas Arne	Cantata	CG 25.4.40
Thomas Arne	Rise, Glory, rise (_Rosamond_)	DL 24.10.41
Thomas Arne	Was ever Nymph like Rosamond (_Rosamond_)	DL 8.12.41
?	Song with French Horns	DL 17.2.42
John Stanley	Cantata	DL 20.3.42
Turlough O'Carolan	Bumper 'Squire Jones ('Ye good fellows all')	DL 29.3.42
?	Singing in Italian	DL 5.4.42
G.F. Handel	Let me wander not unseen (_L'Allegro_)	DL 6.4.42
G.F. Handel	Sweet bird (_Il Penseroso_)	DL 21.4.42
G.F. Handel	Hark, the little warbling choir	DL 8.10.42
	(_presumably_ 'Hush, ye pretty warbling choir' _Acis and Galatea_)	
Thomas Arne	Distracted I turn (_The Judgement of Paris_)	DL 19.10.42
Samuel Howard	Stella and Flavia every hour	DL 6.4.43
William Boyce	A New Song	DL 11.5.43
William Boyce	Together let us rove (duet) _Solomon_	DL 28.3.44
G.F. Handel	A New Song	DL 28.3.44
?	A Bacchanalian two-part song	DL 7.4.44
?	Cantata	CG 24.4.44
Jonathan Martin	To thee, O gentle Sleep (_Tamerlane_)	CG 5.11.44
?	Cantata	CG 28.11.44
John Frederick Lampe	What d'ye call it	CG 4.4.45
Scotch ballad	We're gaily yet (_The Provok'd Wife_)	DL 1.5.45
William Boyce	Song of Diana (_Secular Masque_)	CG 13.3.46
	'With horns and with hounds'	

John Stanley	Cantata VII 'Who'll buy a Heart'(*12 Cantatas*)	CG 24.4.47
John Stanley	Cantata III 'Whilst others barter'(*12 Cantatas*)	CG 8.3.48
	'*in the character of Anacreon*'	
Maurice Greene	Go lovely rose	CG 28.3.48
?	The famous Song of '92' *(Fair Quaker of Deal)*	CG 13.4.48
	[*possibly* 'How little do the Landmen know']	
Maurice Greene	Go rose, my Chloe's bosom Grace	CG 27.4.48
?	A Scotch Cantata	DL 6.10.48
?	Singing instead of the Scotch Cantata	DL 2.1.49
Thomas Arne	A New Cantata	DL 21.3.52
William Boyce	Cantata	DL 25.4.52
Thomas Arne	Cantata 'Cymon and Iphigenia'	DL 27.3.53
Thomas Arne	Cantata I 'The School of Anacreon'	"
Michael Festing	The Lass of the Mill, 'Who has e'er been at Baldock'	"
?	Cantata proper to the play (*The Refusal*)	DL 20.12.53
?	A favourite French Air	DL 19.3.54
	[*possibly* 'Lison dormoit dans un boccage']	
Thomas Arne	A Pastoral Dialogue (Duet)	DL 29.3.54
?	A New Ballad	DL 2.5.54
?	Mary Scot	DL 10.5.54
?	A Scots Cantata	"
? (Scottish song)	Hooly and Fairly	"
	('Oh! gin my wife wad drink hooly and fairly')	
('new set')	To thee, O gentle Sleep (*Tamerlane*)	DL 4.11.54
Thomas Arne	Rule Britannia	DL 2.4.55
?	A New Cantata	"
?	A Tale of a Cock and a Bull:	
	'To take in good part, the squeeze of the hand'	DL 30.3.56
William Boyce	An Ode in Commemoration of Shakespeare	DL 1.4.56
?	The Country Wedding:'a Song from Roger & Joan'	DL 31.3.57
?	The Toast	"
?	When Phoebus the top of the Hills does adorn (Duet)	"
?	A New Ballad	DL 29.3.59
William Boyce	A Bacchanalian Song	"
William Boyce	A New Comic Dialogue (Duet) 'in character'	"
	= probably 'Dialogue of Johnny and Kate'	DL 2.4.59
William Boyce	An Ode in honour of the Anti-Gallicans	DL 16.5.59
?	A *Medley Epilogue* written by Garrick	CG 14.3.61
Thomas Arne	A Pastoral Dialogue (Duet) (*Arcadian Nuptials*)	CG 19.1.64

ALBUMS CONTAINING RANELAGH SONGS FROM BEARD'S TIME

from 'Eighteenth Century (1701-1790) cheap-print Finding Aid'
Dicey & Marshall Catalogue

The Chanter: or the merry companion. In two parts: being a choice collection of the most favourite songs, lately sung at both the Theatres Royal ... and all the publick gardens, by Mr Beard, Mr Lowe etc. London, 1753 Ref: ESTCT 187939

A choice collection of all the songs, sung this season, at Vauxhall, Ranelagh, Marybone Gadrens, Sadlers Wells, etc. by Mr Beard, Mr Lowe, Miss Brent, Miss Catley, Miss Plenius, Miss Young, Miss Poitier etc, London 1765 Ref: ESTCN 15063

The entertaining companion, or, merry songster's delight: being, a choice collection of all the songs sung this and last season at both the Theatres, Sadlers Wells, Ranelagh, Vauxhall, and Marybone Gardens. By Mr Beard, Mr Lowe etc. Southwark [1766?] Ref: ESTCT 106285 x

The Songster's Delight: being a choice collection of all the songs, sung this season, at Vauxhall, Ranelagh, Sadlers Wells etc. by Mr Beard, Mr Lowe, Mrs Vincent, Mrs Stevenson, Miss Young, etc. London [?] Ref: ESTCT 155689

Albums of Ranelagh Songs from the British Library Integrated Catalogue

Michael Christian Festing: A Collection of English Cantatas and Songs. Sung by Mr Beard at Ranelagh House [1750] B Lib. H.1652.T.(19.)

Michael Christian Festing: Six English Songs and a Dialogue with a Duet sung at Ranelagh House by Mr Beard and Mrs Storer [1749] B Lib. Cup.401.k.8.

George Berg: A Collection of New English Songs sung by Mr Beard & Miss Formentell at Ranelagh ...Book II [1757] B Lib. G.359.(2.)

George Berg: A Collection of New English Songs sung by Mr Beard & Miss Formentell at Ranelagh ...Book VI [1759] B Lib. G.806.g.(5.)

William Bates: A Collection of New English Songs sung by Mr Beard & Miss Young at Ranelagh [c.1760] B Lib. H.1660.dd.(1.)

Thomas Arne: Vocal Melody, Books I – IV. An entire new collection of English Songs and a Cantata sung at Vauxhall, Ranelagh and Marybon-Gardens [1746-52] B Lib. G.321.(2.)

Michael Arne: A favourite Collection of English Songs. Sung by Mr Beard & Miss Young etc. at the Public Gardens [1757] B Lib G.234.a.

A favourite Collection of English Songs. Sung by Mr Beard & Miss Young etc. at Ranelagh Gardens [1757] B Lib. H.2815.a.(14.)

A favourite Collection of English Songs. Sung by Mr Beard & Miss Young etc. at Ranelagh Gardens [1758] B Lib. H.1652.w.(23.)

Single Ranelagh Songs from the British Library Integrated Catalogue

Cross Purposes. 'Tom loves Mary passing well'. Sung and composed by Mr Beard at Ranelagh [1748] *The words imitated from Moschus* B Lib. I. 539.(157.)

Fairest creature, thou'rt so charming. (Music by Renatus Harris, words by John Beard) c. 1735 B Lib. I. 530.(66.)

The Musical Hodge Podge. 'An old woman clothed in grey'. Compiled by Henry Carey. c.1735 B Lib. G. 306.(60.)

As Jamie gang'd blithe his way. B Lib. H.1994.b.(4.)

As Jockey was walking one Midsummer Morn. B Lib. G.306.(63.)

Fair Hebe I left with a cautious design. (Words by Viscount Cantelupe) B Lib. G. 305.(270.)

The Gamester's Song (Music by James Oswald, words by David Garrick) [1756] B Lib P.P.5438

Give us Glasses, my Wench [1755] B Lib P.P.5439

I made love to Kate [1759[B Lib. P.P.5439

The Lass of the Mill [c.1740] (Music by Michael Christian Festing) B Lib. G. 313.(101.)

The Non-pareil [1745?] (Music by William Boyce) B Lib. H.1994.c.(14.)

Oh what had I ado for to marry, 'Hooly and Fairly' [1745?] B Lib. G. 310.(224.)

Orpheus and Eurydice [1740?] (Music by William Boyce) B Lib. G. 305.(127.)

Robin's Complaint (Music by James Oswald, words by Lord Binning) [1745?] B Lib. G. 307.(162.)

The Sun was sleeping in the Main [1755] B Lib. P.P.5439

Susan's Complaint (Music by James Oswald) [1745?] B Lib. G. 306.(80.)

That Jenny's my Friend [1754] (Words by E. Moore) B Lib. P.P.5439

To take in good part the squeeze of the hand, A Cock & Bull song. [1757] B Lib. P.P.5439

When first by fond Damon, Flavella was seen. [1760?] B Lib. I. 530.(174.)

With early Horn salute the Morn (music by Galliard) [1737?] B Lib. G. 313.(137.)

The World in disguise: or Masks all. 1749. B Lib. 1482.EE.6.

Ye Belles and ye Flirts. Address'd to the Ladies. [c.1750] B Lib. H.1652.vv.(2.)

Ye Chearful Virgins have ye seen. 'Myrtilla'. [1760?] (Music by S. Howard) B Lib. H.1994.a.(35.)

Ye medley of mortals. 'The Masquerade Song' [1749] B Lib. P.P.5439

Ye true honest Britons [1757] B Lib. P.P.5439

Ye Virgins who do listen.'The unnatural Parent, or the Virgin's last resolve' [1752] B Lib. P.P.5439

Young Hobbinol, the blithest Swain. 'Hobbinol' [1751] (Music by R. Davies) B Lib. P.P.5439

Songs from Plays at DL or CG in the British Library Integrated Catalogue

As blyth as the Linnet sings (*Robin Hood*) Music by Charles Burney	G.306.(65.)
The Beer Drinking Briton (*Harlequin Mercury*) Music by Thomas Arne	P.P.5438
By the gayly circling Glass (*Comus*) Music by Thomas Arne	G.306.(233.)
The Chace is o'er, and on the Plain (?*C.G.*) Music by Samuel Howard	G.312.(16.)
Distracted I turn (*The Judgement of Paris*) Music by Thomas Arne	G.316.d.(101.)
Hence with cares, complaints and frowning (*Love in a Village*) W. Boyce	H.1601.u.(139)
How little do the Landmen know (*The Fair Quaker of Deal*)	P.P.5439
I'll sing you a song that shall suit you (*Robin Hood*) Charles Burney	G.303.(66.)
In story we're told (*The Fair*)	P.P.5439
My Dolly was the fairest thing [Handel's 'Let me wander not unseen'](*Love in a Village*) G.310.(122.)	
Not on Beds of fading Flowers (*Comus*) Music by Thomas Arne	G.809.ww.(2.)
Now Phoebus sinketh in the West (*Comus*) Music by Thomas Arne	G.305.(112.)
The Sun from the East tips the mountains (*Apollo & Daphne*)	I.530.(5.)
The Tars of old England (*The Reprisal*)	H.1994.(54.)
There was a jolly Miller once (*Love in a Village*) Music by Thomas Arne	H.1601.u.(20.)
Th'happy news at length is come (*Thomas and Sally*) Music by T. Arne	P.P.5441
Thy Father away! (*Artaxerxes*) Music by Thomas Arne	G.312.(187.)

To an Arbor of Woodbine (*Robin Hood*) Charles Burney	G.312.(74.)	
Tom's Return (*Thomas and Sally*) Music by Thomas Arne	P.P.5439	
Under the Rose (*Love in a Village*) Music by Thomas Arne	H.1994.a.(207.)	
We're gaily yet (*The Provok'd Wife*)	I.530.(170.)	
We've fought, we have conquer'd (*Eliza*) Music by Thomas Arne	H.1601.a.(104)	
We've fought, we have conquer'd (*Alfred*) Music by Thomas Arne?	G.313.(250)	
What cheer my honest mess-mates (*The Fair*)	P.P.5441	
When Glory invites, what Briton so mean (*The Fair*)	P.P.5441	
Women when they gain a Heart (*Robin Good-fellow*) Music by S. Howard	G.313.(132.)	
The World is a well furnish'd Table (*Love in a Village*) Music by T. Arne	H.1601.u.(25.)	

THE CANTATAS OF BOYCE, ARNE, STANLEY & PASQUALI

Some of the finest concert music that was written in the 18th century for the tenor voice was the collection of Cantatas by leading composers such as Boyce, Arne and John Stanley. These were chamber pieces, which circulated in elegantly published editions. But their first performances had often been given by John Beard, whose voice was the one that the composers had in mind, at his concerts at Hickford's Rooms, for the Castle Concert series, at Ranelagh, and in the intervals at the principal London theatres.

In the lists given above it will be seen that certain cantatas were frequently performed by him, and became personal favourites of the singer. Amongst these we find:

Thomas Arne	Cantata 'Cymon and Iphigenia'	Drury Lane 27.3.53
Thomas Arne	Cantata 'The School of Anacreon'	"
Thomas Arne	Cantata 'Frolic and free'	Castle Concerts 16.2.58
William Boyce	Cantata	Drury Lane 25.4.52
Niccolo Pasquali	Cantata 'Celia' ('O 'Tis Elysium All')	King's Theatre 28.2.54
John Stanley	Cantata	Drury Lane 20.3.42
John Stanley	Cantata	King's Theatre 29.4.45
John Stanley	Cantata 7 'Who'll buy a Heart'	Covent Garden 24.4.47
John Stanley	Cantata 3 'Whilst others barter'	Covent Garden 8.3.48

John Potter, in his 'Observations', makes the case for this important body of music:

"Boyce's]music] has a number of beautiful strokes of genius; in fine, it is elegant and sublime. It stares the Italians in the face and asks them, with what justice they can claim the art of beautiful modulation alone? How delicate are the airs, ...how charming the melody! Can anything be more so? Really it is almost impossible.

The compositions of Dr Arne are much admir'd, and are deserving the kind reception they meet from the public. He is a composer of some taste and merit, and has oblig'd the world with many pleasing performances. In the song way he is great, his accompaniments are sprightly and elegant. He may justly be reckoned among the number of our first rank composers.

The ingenious Mr Stanley is a person of great merit, and it would be a kind of ingratitude not to pay that respect and justice which is due to his great abilities, both as a composer and a player. His elegant cantatas breathe the spirit of true taste and delicacy; such a pure simplicity of subject, so finely carried on, and so strongly affecting; plainly show the hand of a masterly genius."[60]

---

[60] John Potter, 'Observations on the present state of Music and Musicians', London, 1763

APPENDIX 6
POETRY RELEVANT TO BEARD'S CAREER

GARRICK'S Parody of *Shakespeare's Stages of Life,* performed at Beard's benefit on Wednesday 10th April 1751 at Drury Lane Theatre.

AN EPILOGUE – by DAVID GARRICK [61]

As half-bred curs, when they have beat their foe
Will snarl, and give one snap before they go;
As Game-Cocks too, (true symbols of a wit)
Will still sparr on, till they have left the Pit;
So our old Bard, tho' he has lashed you sore,
In this his Piece, must give you one lick more.

  That all the Town's a Farce, He says and swears,
And all the Men and Women merely Players!
Prompted by Folly, Interest or Art,
Each Actor in his life plays many a Part,
Ill-suited to his Head, and foreign to his Heart.

  And first, the Politition [sic] – deep in Port,
He hums – and haws – and – hiccups 'gainst the Court,
Swears Virtue should revive, were he the Head –
Reels home, beats Spouse, and tumbles into bed.

  The Doctor next, with sapient Wig and Lip,
Will feel your Pulse, nod, hem, write, take the tip;
So he plays his Part. Then the Ladies see,
Rising at noon; - they sip one dish of Tea,
Then range the City round, and scarcely stop,
Seeking the Bubble fashion, Shop by Shop;
All night 'tis Rout and joy. 'Towards Morn they flag,
Creeping like Snails unwillingly from Brag.

  Then come the tender, well surtouted Beaux,
Mewling and puking, with each wind that blows;
In silken Hose too wide, they trip the Ground,
And their sweet voices whistle in the sound.

  The Statesman next, to shew [h]is Patriot Care,
With crop'd-ear'd Bob, flapt Hat, sits high in Air,
The Legislator of a Chaise and Pair.

  The Connoisseur comes last, muff'd like a Bear,
Full of strange Phrase, and in his paper'd Hair;
He'll judge, dispute, decide, paint, dance and sing,
Sans eyes, sans Ears, sans Taste, sans every Thing.

---

[61] from "A Collection of Prologues and Epilogues and other miscellaneous verses written by David Garrick", Folger Shakespeare Library, Washington, USA. ms Folger: W.b. 467 ff. 25-6. First used on Saturday 16th March 1751 for "*A Lick at the Town*" at Henry Woodward's Benefit, at Drury Lane Theatre.

**GARRICK'S Prologue to *The Fairies,* written and spoken by Garrick
on Monday February 3rd 1755 at Drury Lane Theatre.**
[Version from *The Gentleman's Magazine*, February 1755]

PROLOGUE – by DAVID GARRICK

Three nights ago I heard a Tête a Tête
Which fix'd, at once, our English opera's fate:
One was a youth born here, but flush from Rome.
The other born abroad, but here his home;
And first the English foreigner began,
Who thus address'd the foreign Englishman:
An English Opera! 'Tis not to be borne;
I both my Country and their Music scorn:
Oh, damn their *Ally Croakers,*[62] and their *Early Horn.*[63]
Signor si – bat sons – wors recitativo[64]*:*
Il tutto, è bestiale e cativo,
This said I made my exit, full of terrors!
And now ask mercy, for the following errors:
  Excuse us first, for foolishly supposing,
Your countryman could please you in composing;
An op'ra too! – play'd by an English band,
Wrote in a language which you understand. -
I dare not say "who" wrote it – I could tell ye,
To soften matters – Signor Shakespearelli:
This awkward Drama – (I confess th'offence)
Is guilty too of Poetry and Sense.
Our last mischance, and worse than all the rest,
Which turns the whole Performance to a Jest:
Our singers are all well, and all will do their best.

But why would this rash fool, this Englishman,
Attempt an Op'ra? 'Tis the strangest Plan!
  Struck with the wonders of his Master's Art,
Whose sacred Dramas shake and melt the heart,
Whose Heaven-born strains the coldest Breast inspire,
Whose Chorus-Thunder sets the Soul on Fire!
Inflam'd, astonish'd! at those magic Airs,
When *Samson* groans, and frantic *Saul* despairs;
The Pupil wrote – his Work is now before ye,
And waits your stamp of Infamy or Glory!
  Yet, ere his errors and his faults are known,
He says, those faults, those errors, are his own;
If through the clouds appear some glimm'ring rays,
They're sparks he caught from his great Master's blaze! [65]

---

[62] This tune is credited to Larry Grogan, an Irish piper, who wrote it circa 1725. It is said to be based on the rejection of a gentleman's suit by Alicia Croker. In 1753 it was sung in "The Englishman in Paris." It has mistakenly been credited to Samuel Foote, who wrote the play.

[63] Beard's first 'hit' in the theatre: see chapter 2

[64] i.e. "bad songs, worse recitativo"

A MEDLEY
WRITTEN BY DAVID GARRICK, AND FIRST SUNG BY
MR BEARD AT RANELAGH, 1762, ON HIS BENEFIT NIGHT [66]

MEDLEY SONG

Your bounty and you,
Can everything do,
You teach my poor singing to feel-a; *[repeat]*
You tune up my throat,
You swell every NOTE,
From gamut below up to e-la. *[repeat]*

You make me rejoice,
Both in heart and in voice,
Your smiles do my courage so steel-a; *[repeat]*
That your ears I will rack,
I'll stretch till I CRACK,
From gamut below up to e-la. *[repeat]*

SONG II *Tune – Nancy Dawson*

Physic and law have a stated price,
Money you give, and they give you advice,
All is so pretty, so charming, and nice,
And thus they return your favour: *[repeat]*

I can only thankful be
You can have nothing at all from me,
But a squeez'd-up seat, and a dish of my tea,
And an olio of speeches and quavers. *[repeat]*

SONG III *Tune – Britons strike home*

Fiddlers strike up,
Assist, assist my humble strum; *[repeat]*
Scrape, sound and record,
Scrape, sound and record, *[repeat]*
My cheerful thanks
In grateful song.

SONG IV *Tune – I love Sue*

For I love you, and you love me,
And whilst I try to sing,
And you touch the string,
My tweedledum's happy with your tweedledee.

SONG V *Tune – Dumb, Dumb, Dumb*

Now if you think I'm wrong,
In all I've said or sung,
And wish that poor I had been dumb, dumb, dumb.

[65] Compare with m/s W. b. 467, p.40, Folger Shakespeare Library, Washington, USA
[66] from: Tate Wilkinson, 'The Wandering Patentee', 1795, vol. 4, pp. 261 - 7

Tho' the fish is in the net,
Yet I shall fume and fret,
And tho' I have caught you, be glum, glum, glum.

I therefore beg and pray,
That nothing you will say,
Lest others next year should not come, come, come.

For if like you they're taught,
They'll not like you be caught,
And therefore, I pray you all, mum, mum, mum.

SONG VI *Tune – Trolly-lo*

There was a man, and married he would be,
Sing trolly, lolly, lolly, lolly, lo,
He got him a wife, but they could not agree,
Ho, ho! did he so, did he so, did he so.

But here they do come, and here they do agree,
Sing trolly, lolly, lolly, lolly, lo,
For they can't abide themselves, the company, nor me,
Ho, ho! let 'em go, let 'em go, let 'em go.

SONG VII

Fain would I please you all,
But that can never be,
Could I please nine in ten,
Why that's enough for me:
Wits cry they're squeez'd, and rail,
And cry, O fye, for shame!
But were you all in my place,
Why, you would do the same.

SONG VIII *Tune – Down, Derry Down*

May each wish as he ought that Great Britain may thrive,
That freedom and friendship may faction survive;
On sea and on shore, as we have, may we shine,
And this year *sixty-two* equal fam'd *fifty-nine* [67]
Derry down, down, derry down.

Still guided by justice, may commerce increase,
As we have glorious made war, may we glorious make peace;
O gant, ye kind powers, freedom's throne long to sit on
Our young patriot king, who boasts he's a Briton.
Derry down, down, derry down.

THE END

---

[67] *Alluding to Lord Hawke's complete victory over the French, 1759* [Tate Wilkinson's original footnote]

Prologue to the Benefit Play, May 13th 1766, for the Advancement of the Theatrical Fund, instituted at Covent Garden Theatre. Written by Mr Hull.

[Benefit towards the Increase of a Fund, establish'd by the Performers of the Theatre Royal Covent Garden for the support of Decayed Actors and their Families. This Fund, having been begun by voluntary contributions among the performers, improved by a proportionable Weekly Deuction on their salaries, and intended as a reciprocal Provision for them, their widows and children, in sickness and infirmity, it is humbly hoped an appeal to the Generosity of the Public will not be taken amiss.]

PROLOGUE – by THOMAS HULL [68]

Brief, and uncertain as the tinsell'd Pow'r
That decks our transient Monarchs of an hour,
Are Youth's gay Pleasures, and its gaudiest Pride.
Wisely to use our moments, and provide
Some solid comforts for declining Age
Is the theme of Wisdom's letter'd rage.

The toiling Ant, whom wond'rous instinct trains
In thrifty lore, provides with cheerful pains,
While yet the Fruits of bounteous Summer last,
A frugal hoard for Winter's snug repast.

We humbly imitate such prudent care,
And from a present Good a portion spare
For Life's chill season, while to you we owe
That our Hopes blossom, and our Harvest grow.

When the enfeebled Frame no longer glows
With mimic Agonies and fancied Woes,
But with'ring Age appears with all his train
Of unfeigned Miseries and real Pain:

When the full voice, that wont in frantic heat,
Bid this high roof th'empassion'd notes repeat,
"Turning again, thro' Time's impairing Round,
To childish treble, whistles in the sound".

Each sinew slacken'd, ev'ry nerve unstrung,
While falt'ring Accents tremble on the tongue:
How will Remembrance, o'er the frugal meal,
Your timely Care in speechless Rapture feel!
How praise the prudent Thrift of wealthier hours,
And bless each hand that made such Blessings ours!

---

[68] *The Jester's Magazine* or, *The Monthly Merry-Maker*, for May 1766, p. 241. British Library: RB.23. a. 10509

Prologue to 'The Perplexities'
by Thomas Hull (1767)[69]

Sung and spoken by John Beard - 'Mr Beard enters hastily'
"I speak a Prologue! – what strange whim, I wonder
Could lead the author into such a blunder? –
I asked the man as much – but he (poor devil!)
Fancied a manager might make you civil.

"Garrick (says he) can with a prologue tame
The critic's rage – Why can't you do the same?"
Because (quoth I) the case is different quite;
Garrick, you know, can prologues speak, and write;
If like that Roscius I could write and speech it,
I might command applause, and not beseech it.

But, sure, for one who, all his live-long days
Has dealt in crochets, minims, and sol-fas,
A singer, to stand forth in wit's defence,
And plead 'gainst sound the solemn cause of sense;
Persuade an audience that a play has merit,
Without a single air to give it spirit;
'Tis so much out of character – so wrong –
No prologue, Sir, for me – unless in song.

The same (quoth I) you poets reap,
And all your gains, are owing,
To sounds that even measure keep,
And stanzas smoothly flowing;

But me the lyre would better suit
Than verses of Apollo;
The fiddle, hautboy, horn, or flute
I'm always used to follow.

"Sir (says he) you'll mar
My verse and meaning too" –
Sir, must I turn fool,
To humour such as you?

I'll sing it if you please –
"Sing! cries he, in a huff,
Of you and your sol-fa's
The town has had enough". –

Oh! then I bounc'd and swore –
Was I much to blame?
Had you been in my place
Why you'd have done the same.

---

[69] The Gentleman's Magazine, February 1767, p. 87

If for old-fashioned tunes he's not too nice,
I'd give him fifty of 'em in a trice,
With words more fitted to his purpose here,
Than all the rhymes he'd jingle in a year.
He challeng'd me to shew a single sample
Of what I bragg'd – I did – as for example! -

The scene is prepar'd, the critics are met,
The judges all rang'd – a terrible show!
Ere trials begin the Prologue's a debt.
A debt on demand – so take what we owe.

And this is the way, Mr Author,
To trick a plain muse up with art,
In modish fal-lals you must clothe her,
And warm a cold critic's hard heart.
With a fal-lal-lal, etc.

Wherefore I thus entreat, with due submission,
Between the Bard and me you'd make decision.
The whole now on your arbitration we rest,
And Prologues henceforward shall surely be drest
In what mode soever your taste shall like best –
Which none of us dare deny.

For, howe'er cruel critics and wildings may sneer,
That at times, I, alas! somewhat dunny appear,
If to you, my best friends, I e'er turn my deaf ear,
May your indulgence deny.

Then for his sake and mine (for we're both in a fright)
Till a treat of more goût shall your palates delight,
Let a poor humble comedy please you tonight;
Which surely you will not deny.

Thomas Hull

EPITAPH UPON THE DEATH OF Mr. W[illiam] GIBSON
by William Havard [70]

However prais'd or censur'd on the Stage,
(As it is hard to please this Critic Age)
Yet in one Part not Roscius could excel
My worthy friend – the Part of living well.
A life well acted form'd his even play,
Where all the Virtues regularly lay:
Each Act, each Scene did to the moral tend –
[and*] the world gives its plaudit at the end.　　　*deleted
He died August 1771

EPITAPH ON MR. HAVARD COMEDIAN
by David Garrick [71]

Havard from sorrow rests beneath this stone;
An honest man – beloved as soon as known;
Howe'er defective in the mimic art,
In real life he justly played the part!
The noblest character he acted well,
And Heaven applauded – when the curtain fell.
He died 20th February, 1778

William Havard

EPITAPH TO THE EVER RESPECTABLE MEMORY
OF JOHN DUNSTALL COMEDIAN
by John Beard [72]

A man by nature open, warm, sincere;
(Whose heart scarce Death could cool) lies buried here.
Unpolished manners, rough as the northern wind,

---

[70] Folger Shakespeare Library, 'Jeu d'esprit', N. a. 2. f. (164)
[71] 'A collection of Epitaphs and Monumental Inscriptions..." London, 1806, Vol. 2, p.4
[72] British Library, Egerton Manuscripts, EG 2159 f. 52 (1779); and and 'A collection of Epitaphs and Monumental Inscriptions..." London, 1806, Vol. 2, p. 83

But half conceal'd a gentle, gen'rous mind;
Firm in his own distress – at others' woe
His manly heart would melt, - his tear would flow;
Belov'd from Youth to Age, by old and young,
Tho' servile flattery ne'er disgrac'd his tongue.
Tried, and approv'd, by a judicious age,
His name shall grace the Annals of the Stage;
While Truth, which most he lov'd, shall boldly tell
Thro' every Scene of Life he acted well.
Go, gentle reader, go, - and if you can,
Live like this upright, downright Honest Man.
He died January 1779 in the 62nd year of his age

JOHN BEARD'S EPITAPH

presumed to have been written by Thomas Hull [73]
but actually by Dr. Cousens, Rector of St. Gregory, Old Fish St.

Satire be dumb! Nor dream the scenic art
Must spoil the morals and corrupt the heart.
Here lies JOHN BEARD: confess, with pensive pause,
His modesty was great as our applause.
Whence had that voice such magic to control?
'Twas but the echo of a well tun'd soul:
Thro' life, his morals and his music ran
In symphony and spoke the virtuous man.
Go, gentle harmonist, our hopes approve,
To meet, and hear thy sacred songs above:
When taught by thee, the stage of life well trod,
We rise to raptures round the throne of God.
Ob. Feb. 5th 1791, Aetatis suae, 75

JOHN BEARD'S EPITAPH

on his Memorial in the Parish Church of St Mary the Virgin, Hampton

How vain the monumental praise
Our partial friends devise!
While trophies o'er our dust they raise
Poetic fictions rise.
Say, what avails, if good or bad
I now am represented:
If happily the faults I had
Sincerely were repented.
A friend, a wife, or both in one,
By Love, by Time endear'd,
Shall banish falsehood from the Stone
That covers her John Beard.
He died the 4th of February 1791 Aged 74 years

---

[73] in *The Gentleman's Magazine*, February 1791; and 'A collection of Epitaphs and Monumental Inscriptions..." London, 1806, Vol. 2, p. 184.

18th Century Poetry mentioning John Beard

from: The Beau's Lament for the loss of Farinelli
by Henry Carey (c. 1738)

Come, never lament for a singer, said I,
Can't English performers his absence supply?
There's *Beard* and there's Salway, and smart Kitty Clive,
The pleasantest, merriest mortal alive.

from: Horace Satire III
translated by Thomas Neville M.A. (1758)

A fault there is, for which the tuneful herd,
Are fam'd, from *Farinelli* down to *Beard*.
Press them, you'd think they never would sing more;
Unask'd, no hints can teach them to give o'er.
In this one point TIGELLIO would offend,
Alike inflexible to foe and friend.
A fav'rite air no eloquence could buy;
Not AMORET could win him to comply:
Let him alone, or catch him in the vein,
He'd trill, and warble in eternal strain.

from 'The Fribbleriad'
by David Garrick (1761)

There is a place upon a hill,
Where cits of pleasure take their fill,
Where hautboys scream and fiddles squeak,
To sweat the ditto once a week;
Where joy of late, unmixed with noise
Of romping girls and drunken boys –
Where decency, sweet maid, appeared,
And in her hand brought *Johnny Beard*.

from: The Rational Rosciad
by F- B- L- , (1767)

In all his songs the admirable *Beard*
Is fully understood as well as heard;
To vitiated taste he gives offence,
By making sound an echo to the sense.
Continue, *Beard*, the knowing few to please,
Who all applaud your elegance and ease.

Ode by Earl Nugent
extract from 'The New Foundling Hospital for Wit' (1784)

What clamour's here about a dame
Who, for her pleasure, barters fame!
As if 'twere strange or new,
That ladies should themselves disgrace,
Or one of the Milesian race,
A widow should pursue.

She's better sure than *Scudamore*
Who while a Duchess, play'd the whore,
As all the world has heard;
Wiser than *Lady Harriet* too,
Whose foolish match made such a do,
And ruin'd her and *Beard*.

Upon the new Performances exhibited at the two Theatres this Winter
excerpt from 'The Gentleman's Magazine' for the year 1767, page 42

... *Beard* for a while seem'd much afraid,
'Till he brought *Th'Accomplish'd Maid*[74]:
At whom, old Slyboots, General G[arric]k,
Push'd, with his bouncing *Earl of Warwick*[75].
But such a Maid, and such an Earl!
A flimsy bully, piss-tail girl!
Take 'em, thou ghost of *Edmund Curl*.
But now have at your eyes and ears;
The high-puff'd *Cymon*[76] next appears:
Earth, heav'n, and hell, are all united,
The upper gall'ry so delighted!
They sing, they dance, they sink, they fly!
For scenes, shew, dresses, all defy:
And then the wit and humour – stay –
We'll talk of them another day;
With both, the *School for Guardians*[77] stor'd,
You'd sware 'twas written by a Lord:
So fine the wit, so fine the plot,
You have 'em, and you have 'em not:
The plot and wit make such a pother,
You cannot see the one for t'other:
Tis M[urph]y now, and now Moliere:
'Tis, 'tis neither, English, French,
And all to serve a pretty wench...

---

[74] *The Accomplished Maid*, a 'new comic opera' by Niccolo Piccini, was premiered at Covent Garden on December 3 1766, with further performances on December 4, 15, 17, 18, 22, & January 9, 14, 16.
[75] *The Earl of Warwick*, a tragedy by Dr. Franklin was premiered at Drury Lane on December 13 1766.
[76] *Cymon,* a Romance by Garrick with music by Michael Arne, opened at Drury Lane on January 2 1767.
[77] *The School for Guardians,* a play by Arthur Murphy derived from Molière, opened at Covent Garden on January 10 1767, with further performances on January 12, 13, 15, 17, & February 18.

Elegiac Verses on the death of the late Manager of Covent Garden John Rich [78]

To the Editor of Lloyd's Evening Post, 1761

<u>Columbine</u>
Ah me! what cloud o'er Covent Garden spreads,
Threatening to burst in thunder o'er our heads!
...For *Rich* is dead. ...Adieu the mimic scene!
And all the tricks of fav'rite Harlequin!

<u>Pantaloon</u>
...Alas! our champion in the dust is laid,
And Pantomimes shall yield to Shakespeare's shade.
                                    ...I've heard
That Shakespeare's Shade will be revived by *Beard*;
And see, the magic Droll is put to flight!
While Tragedy, her poignard waves in sight;
And sock-invested Comedy, with pride,
Shines through the scene, our follies to deride...

From the PUBLIC ADVERTISER: Tuesday 26 May 1767

A second familiar EPISTLE to JOHN BEARD, Esq; on the disposal of the Patent, and his Declaration of retiring into the Country, to live the Year round: By the Writer of the First [epistle].

Dear good Sir, be serious, and give us reason,
Why fly from your State, - are you jealous of Treason?
I think as to that there's no Cause for a Doubt,
If they love you *within* as we love you without;
Though all Men in Power have *some*, we confess,
Of Enemies, ne'er had a Manager less:
It therefore of Consequence cannot be so –
Doth your Deafness increase on you? – *West* answers No.
And *Wild* tells the World (*Wild*, tho' poor is sincere)
That if *John* and he whisper, you readily hear;
If this be the Case then, permit me to say,
'Tis ungrateful, ungenerous, stealing away;
Away from a Public so oft you have try'd,
And that ne'er undefended abandoned your Side;
That if still you'd continue, would still you protect;
Yet if all we say to you work no Effect,
And tho' reigning so long, you'll needs abdicate now,
Your Glories yield up for a Cot and a Cow;
In spite of Persuasion, resign thus and fell us,
Ere yet you march off, be so kind, Sir, to tell us,

---

[78] taken from the *Winston* M/S, Y. d. 23 (168); Folger Shakespeare Library, Washington, USA

When in *Comus* his Rout you no longer appear,
Who the gay, circling Glass shall triumphantly bear?
For whom in sweet Thrills shall fair *Polly* complain,
Or whom on the Heath shall *Matt* ride with again?
When *Hawthorn's* departed with Dog and with Gun,
Who nearer than Hampton can match us with one?
Or when our old *Giles* can no longer be found,
Shall the Mill not stand still, tho' the Millers go round?
The Summer you'll pass as most other Folks do,
Who have fortunes, Good-humours, and Spirits like you:
But the Horrors of Winter, say, how will you bear,
Who talk of retiring the Round of the Year?
Consider, when done with the Hurries of Life,
You'll have naught to amuse you except a good Wife;
When the Weather permits, you may hunt and may shoot,
May drink with the 'Squire – kiss Madam to boot;
May Gammon the Parson, or sing him a Song,
And be happy (if so you can) as the Day's long.
But the bliss that occasions some Hearts to o'erflow,
May be loath'd and detested by others we know;
As vary our Faces, e'en vary our Minds, –
Whilst Dick prefers Courtiers – Tom dotes upon Hinds.
And so, if not fond of the Pleasures I spoke,
Your flight to the Country is all a mere joke.
What a Life for a Man, who, perpetually gay,
The Gloom of December converted to May!
For a Man, who, at home or abroad, was employ'd
In a round of Fatigues, which Fatigues he enjoy'd.
Such Persons of Providence ne'er were designed,
Like Hermits, to skulk from the rest of Man kind:
Do, pr'ythee, think better on't – let me be heard –
You'll shorten your Days by't – what says Mrs Beard?
If my Reasoning's right, so pronounc'd from her Lip,
I shall honour the Standish wherein that I dip,
You'll take her advice, and be sav'd from the Hip.

This poem refers to some of Beard's most famous roles in *Comus*, *The Beggar's Opera*, *Love in a Village* and *The Maid of the Mill*. His contemporaries may have been aware of the significance of the names *West*, *Wild* and *John*. A footnote in the original print refers to them as his "surgeon", "barber" and "servant", in that order.

Beard did prefer to take early retirement, and used his 24 years as a resident of Hampton to enjoy being with his extended family, and using position in local society to get involved in many local matters (as shown in Chapter 13). The touching comment by the Vicar in the parish register of Deaths ("Eheu") suggests that he knew Beard well: perhaps they had indeed played Backgammon together!

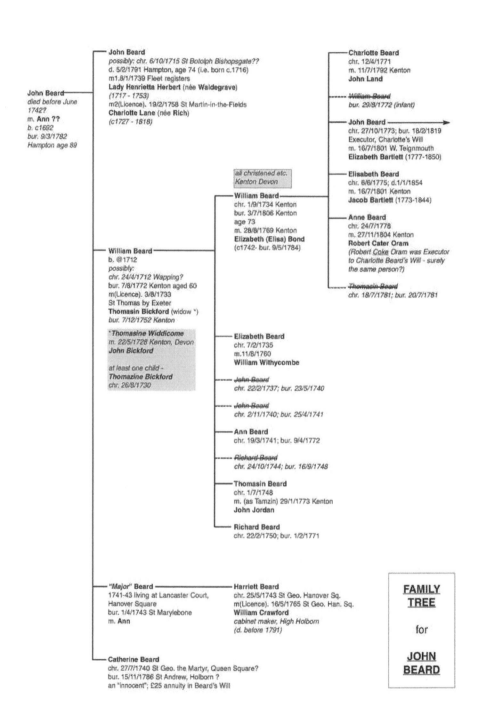

John Beard
died before June
1742?
m. Ann ??
b. c1692
bur. 9/3/1782
Hampton age 89

John Beard
possibly: chr. 6/10/1715 St Botolph Bishopsgate??
d. 5/2/1791 Hampton, age 74 (i.e. born c.1716)
m1.8/1/1739 Fleet registers
Lady Henrietta Herbert (née Waldegrave)
(1717 - 1753)
m2(Licence). 19/2/1758 St Martin-in-the-Fields
Charlotte Lane (née Rich)
(c1727 - 1818)

all christened etc.
Kenton Devon

William Beard
chr. 1/9/1734 Kenton
bur. 3/7/1806 Kenton
age 73
m. 28/8/1769 Kenton
Elizabeth (Elisa) Bond
(c1742- bur. 9/5/1784)

William Beard
b. @1712
possibly:
chr. 24/4/1712 Wapping?
bur. 7/8/1772 Kenton aged 60
m(Licence). 3/8/1733
St Thomas by Exeter
Thomasin Bickford (widow ")
bur. 7/12/1752 Kenton

"Thomasine Widdicome
m. 22/5/1728 Kenton, Devon
John Bickford

at least one child -
Thomazine Bickford
chr. 26/8/1730

Charlotte Beard
chr. 12/4/1771
m. 11/7/1792 Kenton
John Land

~~William Beard~~
bur. 29/8/1772 (infant)

John Beard →
chr. 27/10/1773; bur. 18/2/1819
Executor, Charlotte's Will
m. 16/7/1801 W. Teignmouth
Elizabeth Bartlett (1777-1850)

Elisabeth Beard
chr. 6/6/1775; d.1/1/1854
m. 16/7/1801 Kenton
Jacob Bartlett (1773-1844)

Anne Beard
chr. 24/7/1778
m. 27/11/1804 Kenton
Robert Cater Oram
(Robert Coke Oram was Executor
to Charlotte Beard's Will - surely
the same person?)

~~Thomasin Beard~~
chr. 18/7/1781; bur. 20/7/1781

Elizabeth Beard
chr. 7/2/1735
m.11/8/1760
William Withycombe

~~John Beard~~
chr. 22/2/1737; bur. 23/5/1740

~~John Beard~~
chr. 2/11/1740; bur. 25/4/1741

Ann Beard
chr. 19/3/1741; bur. 9/4/1772

~~Richard Beard~~
chr. 24/10/1744; bur. 16/9/1748

Thomasin Beard
chr. 1/7/1748
m. (as Tamzin) 29/1/1773 Kenton
John Jordan

Richard Beard
chr. 22/2/1750; bur. 1/2/1771

"Major" Beard
1741-43 living at Lancaster Court,
Hanover Square
bur. 1/4/1743 St Marylebone
m. Ann

Harriett Beard
chr. 25/5/1743 St Geo. Hanover Sq.
m(Licence). 16/5/1765 St Geo. Han. Sq.
William Crawford
cabinet maker, High Holborn
(d. before 1791)

Catherine Beard
chr. 27/7/1740 St Geo. the Martyr, Queen Square?
bur. 15/11/1786 St Andrew, Holborn ?
an "innocent"; £25 annuity in Beard's Will

> **FAMILY
> TREE**
>
> for
>
> **JOHN
> BEARD**

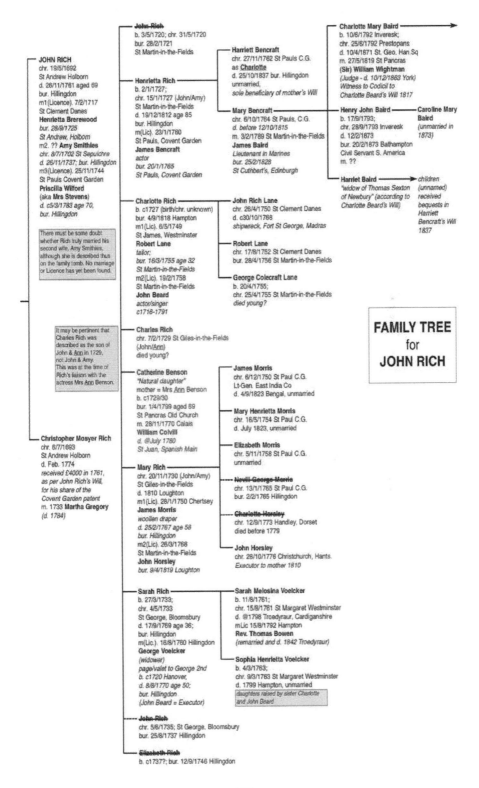

JOHN RICH
chr. 19/5/1692
St Andrew Holborn
d. 26/11/1761 aged 69
bur. Hillingdon
m1(Licence). 7/2/1717
St Clement Danes
Henrietta Brerewood
bur. 28/8/1725
St Andrew, Holborn
m2. ?? **Amy Smithies**
chr. 8/7/1702 St Sepulchre
d. 26/11/1737; bur. Hillingdon
m3(Licence). 25/11/1744
St Pauls Covent Garden
Priscilla Wilford
(aka Mrs Stevens)
d. c5/3/1783 age 70,
bur. Hillingdon

There must be some doubt
whether Rich truly married his
second wife, Amy Smithies,
although she is described thus
on the family tomb. No marriage
or Licence has yet been found.

It may be pertinent that
Charles Rich was
described as the son of
John & Ann in 1729,
not John & Amy.
This was at the time of
Rich's liaison with the
actress Mrs Ann Benson.

Christopher Mosyer Rich
chr. 6/7/1693
St Andrew Holborn
d. Feb. 1774
received £4000 in 1761,
as per John Rich's Will,
for his share of the
Covent Garden patent
m. 1733 **Martha Gregory**
(d. 1784)

John Rich
b. 3/5/1720; chr. 31/5/1720
bur. 28/2/1721
St Martin-in-the-Fields

Henrietta Rich
b. 2/1/1727;
chr. 15/1/1727 (John/Amy)
St Martin-in-the-Fields
d. 19/12/1812 age 85
bur. Hillingdon
m(Lic). 23/1/1760
St Pauls, Covent Garden
James Bencraft
actor
bur. 20/1/1765
St Pauls, Covent Garden

Charlotte Rich
b. c1727 (birth/chr. unknown)
bur. 4/9/1818 Hampton
m1(Lic). 6/5/1749
St James, Westminster
Robert Lane
tailor;
bur. 16/3/1755 age 32
St Martin-in-the-Fields
m2(Lic). 19/2/1758
St Martin-in-the-Fields
John Beard
actor/singer
c1716-1791

Charles Rich
chr. 7/2/1729 St Giles-in-the-Fields
(John/Ann)
died young?

Catherine Benson
"Natural daughter"
mother = Mrs Ann Benson
b. c1729/30
bur. 1/4/1799 aged 69
St Pancras Old Church
m. 28/11/1770 Calais
William Colvill
d. @July 1780
St Juan, Spanish Main

Mary Rich
chr. 20/11/1730 (John/Amy)
St Giles-in-the-Fields
d. 1810 Loughton
m1(Lic). 28/1/1750 Chertsey
James Morris
woollen draper
d. 25/2/1767 age 58
bur. Hillingdon
m2(Lic). 26/3/1768
St Martin-in-the-Fields
John Horsley
bur. 9/4/1819 Loughton

Sarah Rich
b. 27/3/1733;
chr. 4/5/1733
St George, Bloomsbury
d. 17/9/1769 age 36;
bur. Hillingdon
m(Lic). 16/8/1760 Hillingdon
George Voelcker
(widower)
page/valet to George 2nd
b. c1720 Hanover,
d. 8/8/1770 age 50;
bur. Hillingdon
(John Beard = Executor)

John Rich
chr. 5/6/1735; St George, Bloomsbury
bur. 25/8/1737 Hillingdon

Elizabeth Rich
b. c1737?; bur. 12/9/1746 Hillingdon

Harriett Bencraft
chr. 27/11/1762 St Pauls C.G.
as **Charlotte**
d. 25/10/1837 bur. Hillingdon
unmarried,
sole beneficiary of mother's Will

Mary Bencraft
chr. 6/10/1764 St Pauls. C.G.
d. before 12/10/1815
m. 3/2/1789 St Martin-in-the-Fields
James Baird
Lieutenant in Marines
bur. 25/2/1828
St Cuthbert's, Edinburgh

John Rich Lane
chr. 26/4/1750 St Clement Danes
d. c30/10/1788
shipwreck, Fort St George, Madras

Robert Lane
chr. 17/8/1752 St Clement Danes
bur. 28/4/1756 St Martin-in-the-Fields

George Colecraft Lane
b. 20/4/1755;
chr. 25/4/1755 St Martin-in-the-Fields
died young?

James Morris
chr. 6/12/1750 St Paul C.G.
Lt-Gen. East India Co
d. 4/9/1823 Bengal, unmarried

Mary Henrietta Morris
chr. 16/5/1754 St Paul C.G.
d. July 1823, unmarried

Elizabeth Morris
chr. 5/11/1758 St Paul C.G.
unmarried

Nevill George Merrie
chr. 13/1/1765 St Paul C.G.
bur. 2/2/1765 Hillingdon

Charlotte Horsley
chr. 12/9/1773 Handley, Dorset
died before 1779

John Horsley
chr. 28/10/1776 Christchurch, Hants.
Executor to mother 1810

Sarah Melosina Voelcker
b. 11/8/1761;
chr. 15/8/1761 St Margaret Westminster
d. @1798 Troedyraur, Cardiganshire
mLic 15/8/1792 Hampton
Rev. Thomas Bowen
(remarried and d. 1842 Troedyraur)

Sophia Henrietta Voelcker
b. 4/3/1763;
chr. 9/3/1763 St Margaret Westminster
d. 1799 Hampton, unmarried
daughters raised by sister Charlotte
and John Beard

Charlotte Mary Baird
b. 10/6/1792 Inveresk;
chr. 25/6/1792 Prestonpans
d. 10/4/1871 St. Geo. Han.Sq
m. 27/5/1819 St Pancras
(Sir) William Wightman
(Judge - d. 10/12/1863 York)
Witness to Codicil to
Charlotte Beard's Will 1817

Henry John Baird
b. 17/9/1793;
chr. 28/9/1793 Inveresk
d. 12/2/1873
bur. 20/2/1873 Bathampton
Civil Servant S. America
m. ??

Harriet Baird
"widow of Thomas Sexton
of Newbury" (according to
Charlotte Beard's Will)

Caroline Mary Baird
(unmarried in
1873)

children
(unnamed)
received
bequests in
Harriett
Bencraft's Will
1837

FAMILY TREE
for
JOHN RICH

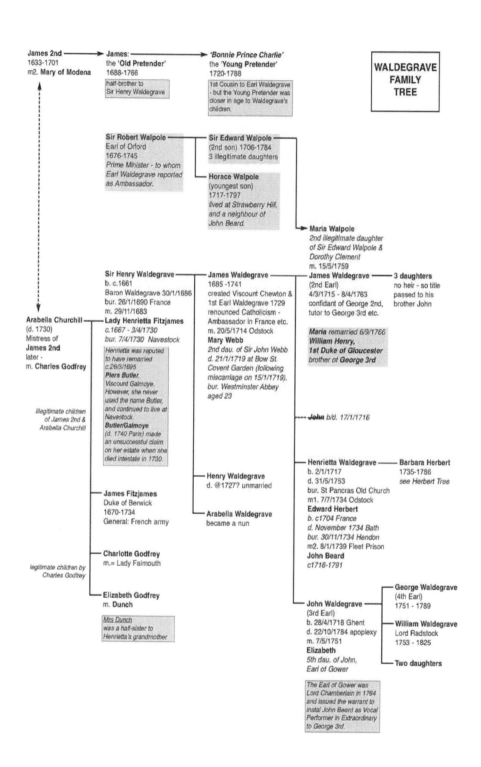

James 2nd
1633-1701
m2. Mary of Modena

James:
the 'Old Pretender'
1688-1766

half-brother to
Sir Henry Waldegrave

'Bonnie Prince Charlie'
the 'Young Pretender'
1720-1788

1st Cousin to Earl Waldegrave
- but the Young Pretender was
closer in age to Waldegrave's
children.

Sir Robert Walpole
Earl of Orford
1676-1745
Prime Minister - to whom
Earl Waldegrave reported
as Ambassador.

Sir Edward Walpole
(2nd son) 1706-1784
3 illegitimate daughters

Horace Walpole
(youngest son)
1717-1797
lived at Strawberry Hill,
and a neighbour of
John Beard.

Maria Walpole
2nd illegitimate daughter
of Sir Edward Walpole &
Dorothy Clement
m. 15/5/1759

Arabella Churchill
(d. 1730)
Mistress of
James 2nd
later -
m. Charles Godfrey

Sir Henry Waldegrave
b. c.1661
Baron Waldegrave 30/1/1686
bur. 26/1/1890 France
m. 29/11/1683
Lady Henrietta Fitzjames
c.1667 - 3/4/1730
bur. 7/4/1730 Navestock

Henrietta was reputed
to have remarried
c.26/3/1695
Piers Butler,
Viscount Galmoye.
However, she never
used the name Butler,
and continued to live at
Navestock.
Butler/Galmoye
(d. 1740 Paris) made
an unsuccessful claim
on her estate when she
died intestate in 1730.

James Waldegrave
1685 -1741
created Viscount Chewton &
1st Earl Waldegrave 1729
renounced Catholicism -
Ambassador in France etc.
m. 20/5/1714 Odstock
Mary Webb
2nd dau. of Sir John Webb
d. 21/1/1719 at Bow St.
Covent Garden (following
miscarriage on 15/1/1719).
bur. Westminster Abbey
aged 23

James Waldegrave
(2nd Earl)
4/3/1715 - 8/4/1763
confidant of George 2nd,
tutor to George 3rd etc.

Maria remarried 6/9/1766
William Henry,
1st Duke of Gloucester
brother of George 3rd

3 daughters
no heir - so title
passed to his
brother John

illegitimate children
of James 2nd &
Arabella Churchill

John b/d. 17/1/1716

Henry Waldegrave
d. @1727? unmarried

James Fitzjames
Duke of Berwick
1670-1734
General: French army

Arabella Waldegrave
became a nun

Henrietta Waldegrave
b. 2/1/1717
d. 31/5/1753
bur. St Pancras Old Church
m1. 7/7/1734 Odstock
Edward Herbert
b. c1704 France
d. November 1734 Bath
bur. 30/11/1734 Hendon
m2. 8/1/1739 Fleet Prison
John Beard
c1716-1791

Barbara Herbert
1735-1786
see Herbert Tree

legitimate children by
Charles Godfrey

Charlotte Godfrey
m.= Lady Falmouth

Elizabeth Godfrey
m. Dunch

Mrs Dunch
was a half-sister to
Henrietta's grandmother

John Waldegrave
(3rd Earl)
b. 28/4/1718 Ghent
d. 22/10/1784 apoplexy
m. 7/5/1751
Elizabeth
5th dau. of John,
Earl of Gower

George Waldegrave
(4th Earl)
1751 - 1789

William Waldegrave
Lord Radstock
1753 - 1825

Two daughters

The Earl of Gower was
Lord Chamberlain in 1764
and issued the warrant to
instal John Beard as Vocal
Performer in Extraordinary
to George 3rd.

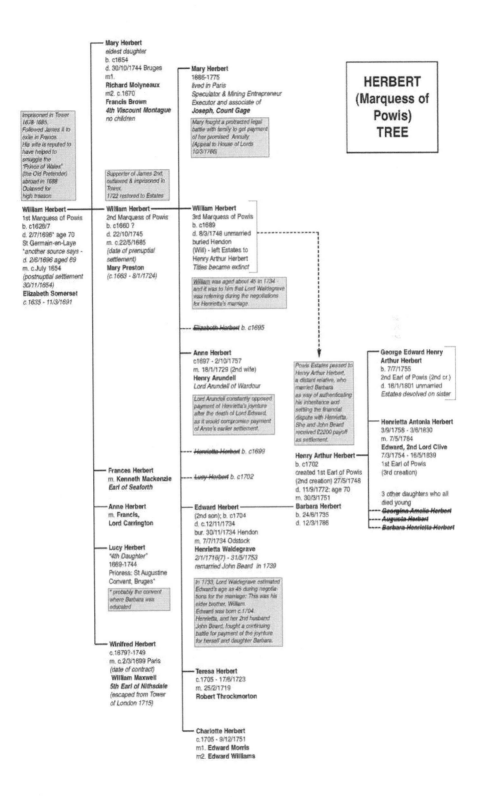

Mary Herbert
eldest daughter
b. c1654
d. 30/10/1744 Bruges
m1.
Richard Molyneaux
m2. c.1670
Francis Brown
4th Viscount Montague
no children

Mary Herbert
1686-1775
lived in Paris
Speculator & Mining Entrepreneur
Executor and associate of
Joseph, Count Gage

Mary fought a protracted legal
battle with family to get payment
of her promised Annuity
(Appeal to House of Lords
10/3/1766)

**HERBERT
(Marquess of
Powis)
TREE**

Imprisoned in Tower
1678-1685.
Followed James II to
exile in France.
He wife is reputed to
have helped to
smuggle the
"Prince of Wales"
(the Old Pretender)
abroad in 1688
Outlawed for
high treason

Supporter of James 2nd,
outlawed & imprisoned in
Tower.
1722 restored to Estates

William Herbert
1st Marquess of Powis
b. c1626/7
d. 2/7/1696* age 70
St Germain-en-Laye
*another source says -
d. 2/6/1696 aged 69
m. c.July 1654
(postnuptial settlement
30/11/1654)
Elizabeth Somerset
c.1635 - 11/3/1691

William Herbert
2nd Marquess of Powis
b. c1660 ?
d. 22/10/1745
m. c.22/5/1685
(date of prenuptial
settlement)
Mary Preston
(c.1663 - 8/1/1724)

William Herbert
3rd Marquess of Powis
b. c1689
d. 8/3/1748 unmarried
buried Hendon
(Will) - left Estates to
Henry Arthur Herbert
Titles became extinct

William was aged about 45 in 1734 -
and it was to him that Lord Waldegrave
was referring during the negotiations
for Henrietta's marriage.

~~Elizabeth Herbert~~ b. c1695

Anne Herbert
c1697 - 2/10/1757
m. 18/1/1729 (2nd wife)
Henry Arundell
Lord Arundell of Wardour

Lord Arundell constantly opposed
payment of Henrietta's jointure
after the death of Lord Edward,
as it would compromise payment
of Anne's earlier settlement.

~~Henrietta Herbert~~ b. c1699

~~Lucy Herbert~~ b. c1702

Powis Estates passed to
Henry Arthur Herbert,
a distant relative, who
married Barbara
as way of authenticating
his inheritance and
settling the financial
dispute with Henrietta.
She and John Beard
received £2200 payoff
as settlement.

**George Edward Henry
Arthur Herbert**
b. 7/7/1755
2nd Earl of Powis (2nd cr.)
d. 16/1/1801 unmarried
Estates devolved on sister

Henrietta Antonia Herbert
3/9/1758 - 3/6/1830
m. 7/5/1784
Edward, 2nd Lord Clive
7/3/1754 - 16/5/1839
1st Earl of Powis
(3rd creation)

3 other daughters who all
died young
~~Georgina Amelia Herbert~~
~~Augusta Herbert~~
~~Barbara Henrietta Herbert~~

Henry Arthur Herbert
b. c1702
created 1st Earl of Powis
(2nd creation) 27/5/1748
d. 11/9/1772: age 70
m. 30/3/1751

Frances Herbert
m. **Kenneth Mackenzie**
Earl of Seaforth

Anne Herbert
m. **Francis,
Lord Carrington**

Edward Herbert
(2nd son); b. c1704
d. c.12/11/1734
bur. 30/11/1734 Hendon
m. 7/7/1734 Odstock
Henrietta Waldegrave
2/1/1716(?) - 31/5/1753
remarried John Beard in 1739

In 1733, Lord Waldegrave estimated
Edward's age as 45 during negotiations for the marriage: This was his
elder brother, William.
Edward was born c.1704.
Henrietta, and her 2nd husband
John Beard, fought a continuing
battle for payment of the jointure
for herself and daughter Barbara.

Barbara Herbert
b. 24/6/1735
d. 12/3/1786

Lucy Herbert
"4th Daughter"
1669-1744
Prioress: St Augustine
Convent, Bruges*

* probably the convent
where Barbara was
educated

Winifred Herbert
c.1679?-1749
m. c.2/3/1699 Paris
(date of contract)
William Maxwell
5th Earl of Nithsdale
(escaped from Tower
of London 1715)

Teresa Herbert
c.1705 - 17/6/1723
m. 25/2/1719
Robert Throckmorton

Charlotte Herbert
c.1705 - 9/12/1751
m1. **Edward Morris**
m2. **Edward Williams**

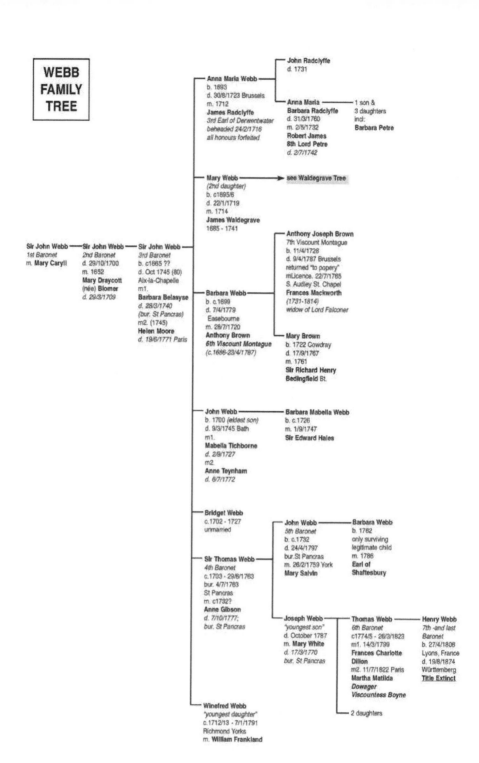

WEBB FAMILY TREE

Sir John Webb
1st Baronet
m. **Mary Caryll**

Sir John Webb
2nd Baronet
d. 29/10/1700
m. 1652
Mary Draycott
(née) Blomer
d. 29/3/1709

Sir John Webb
3rd Baronet
b. c1665 ??
d. Oct 1745 (80)
Aix-la-Chapelle
m1.
Barbara Belasyse
d. 28/3/1740
(bur. St Pancras)
m2. (1745)
Helen Moore
d. 19/6/1771 Paris

Anna Maria Webb
b. 1693
d. 30/8/1723 Brussels
m. 1712
James Radclyffe
3rd Earl of Derwentwater
beheaded 24/2/1716
all honours forfeited

John Radclyffe
d. 1731

**Anna Maria
Barbara Radclyffe**
d. 31/3/1760
m. 2/5/1732
**Robert James
8th Lord Petre**
d. 2/7/1742

— 1 son &
3 daughters
incl:
Barbara Petre

Mary Webb
(2nd daughter)
b. c1895/6
d. 22/1/1719
m. 1714
James Waldegrave
1685 - 1741

→ see Waldegrave Tree

Barbara Webb
b. c1699
d. 7/4/1779
Easebourne
m. 26/7/1720
Anthony Brown
6th Viscount Montague
(c.1686-23/4/1787)

Anthony Joseph Brown
7th Viscount Montague
b. 11/4/1728
d. 9/4/1787 Brussels
returned "to popery"
mLicence. 22/7/1765
S. Audley St. Chapel
Frances Mackworth
(1731-1814)
widow of Lord Falconer

Mary Brown
b. 1722 Cowdray
d. 17/9/1767
m. 1761
**Sir Richard Henry
Bedingfield** Bt.

John Webb
b. 1700 (eldest son)
d. 9/3/1745 Bath
m1.
Mabella Tichborne
d. 2/9/1727
m2.
Anne Teynham
d. 6/7/1772

Barbara Mabella Webb
b. c.1726
m. 1/9/1747
Sir Edward Hales

Bridget Webb
c.1702 - 1727
unmarried

Sir Thomas Webb
4th Baronet
c.1703 - 29/6/1763
bur. 4/7/1763
St Pancras
m. c1732?
Anne Gibson
d. 7/10/1777;
bur. St Pancras

John Webb
5th Baronet
b. c.1732
d. 24/4/1797
bur.St Pancras
m. 26/2/1759 York
Mary Salvin

Barbara Webb
b. 1762
only surviving
legitimate child
m. 1786
**Earl of
Shaftesbury**

Joseph Webb
"youngest son"
d. October 1787
m. **Mary White**
d. 17/3/1770
bur. St Pancras

Thomas Webb
6th Baronet
c1774/5 - 26/3/1823
m1. 14/3/1799
**Frances Charlotte
Dillon**
m2. 11/7/1822 Paris
**Martha Matilda
Dowager
Viscountess Boyne**

Henry Webb
*7th -and last
Baronet*
b. 27/4/1806
Lyons, France
d. 19/8/1874
Württemberg
Title Extinct

— 2 daughters

Winefred Webb
"youngest daughter"
c.1712/13 - 7/1/1791
Richmond Yorks
m. **William Frankland**

BIBLIOGRAPHY

'A Catalogue of the Pictures in the Garrick Club', London, 1936

'A collection of Epitaphs and Monumental Inscriptions…to which is prefixed An Essay on Epitaphs by Dr Johnson', London, 1806

'A Dialogue in the Shades, between the celebrated Mrs Cibber, and the no less celebrated Mrs Woffington', London, 1766

Allen, Brian, 'Francis Hayman', Yale University Press, New Haven and London, 1987

Allen, Robert J., 'The Clubs of Augustan London', Harvard University Press, Cambridge, USA, 1933

Angelo, Henry, 'Reminiscences…', London, 1828

Armstrong, John, 'Marriage, an Ode', London, 1764

Arne, Thomas A., 'Lyric Harmony', *Music for London Entertainment 1660-1800*, series F vol. 2, Macnutt, Tunbridge Wells, 1985

Arnold, Walter, 'The Life and Death of the Sublime Society of Beefsteaks', London, 1871

Ashbee & Harley, 'The Cheque Books of the Chapel Royal', Aldershot, 2000

Ashbee, Andrew, 'Records of English Court Music', Snodland, c. 1986

Atkins, F.C.E., 'A Short Guide to the Parish Church of St. Mary the Virgin, Hampton', Hampton, 1996

Baker, David E., 'Biographia Dramatica', London, 1812

Baker, John, 'The Diary of John Baker', ed. Philip Yorke, London, 1931

Baldwin, David, 'The Chapel Royal Ancient and Modern', London 1990

Barlow, Jeremy, 'The Enraged Musician', London 2005

Barlow, J., & Joncus, B., eds, 'The Stage's Glory, John Rich (1692-1761)', University of Delaware Press, Newark, 2011

Bartlett, Ian, and Bruce, Robert J., 'William Boyce's "Solomon"', *Music & Letters* 61, 1980

Bartlett, Ian, 'Boyce and Early English Oratorio', *The Musical Times* 120, 1979

Beard, John, 'The Case concerning the late disturbance at Covent-Garden Theatre fairly stated…', London, 1763

Beare, George, 'George Beare, eminent Face Painter *fl.* 1743-9', Exhibition Catalogue, Pallant House, Chichester, 1989

Beechey, Gwilym, 'Memoirs of Dr William Boyce', *The Musical Quarterly* 57, 1971

Bellamy, George Anne, 'An Apology for the Life of George Anne Bellamy', 5 volumes, London, 1785

Bennett, William, 'An unpublished letter of Thomas Arne', *The Monthly Musical Record* 64, 1934

Bickham, George, 'The Musical Entertainer', London, 1737, reissued in facsimile by The Sudbrook Press, Buckinghamshire

Bindman, David, 'Hogarth', London, 1981 reprinted 2003

Boaden, James, 'Memoirs of the Life of John Philip Kemble', London, 1825

Boden, Anthony, 'Three Choirs: A History of the Festival', Alan Sutton, Stroud Glos., 1992

Body & Gallop, 'The Coaching Era', Fiducia Press, Bristol, 2003

Boismortier, J. Bodin de, 'Don Quichotte chez la Duchesse', ed. Roger Blanchard, Paris, 1971

Boswell, James, 'Life of Johnson', London, 1799, ed. G.B. Hill, rev. L.F. Powell, Oxford, 1934

Boswell, James, 'London Journal 1762-3', ed. Frederick A. Pottle, Heinemann, London, 1950

Boyce, William, 'Lyra Britannica', *Music for London Entertainment 1660-1800*, series F vol. 3, Macnutt, Tunbridge Wells, 1985

Boyce, William, 'Three Birthday Odes for Prince George', *Music for London Entertainment 1660-1800*, series F vol. 4, London, 1989

Boyce, William, 'The Shepherd's Lottery', *Music for London Entertainment 1660-1800*, series C vol. 4, London, 1990

Brooke, John, 'King George III', London, 1972

Brownlow, John, 'Memoranda or Chronicles of the Foundling Hospital', London, 1847

Brownsmith, John, 'The Dramatic Timepiece…', London, 1767

Brownsmith, John, 'The Theatrical Alphabet…', London, 1767

Bruce, Robert J., 'William Boyce: Some Manuscript Recoveries', *Music & Letters* 55, 1974

Brumwell and Speck, 'Cassell's Companion to Eighteenth Century Britain', London, 2001

Burden, Michael, 'The Independent Masque 1700-1800', *RMA Research Chronicle* 28, 1995

Burke, John, & others, 'A Genealogical and Heraldic Dictionary of the Peerage…' (*Burke's Peerage*), various edns.

Burn, J. S., 'The Fleet Registers, comprising the History of the Fleet Marriages…', London, 1833

Burney, Charles, 'A General History of Music', London, 1789, reprinted ed. Frank Mercer, London 1935, & N.Y. 1957

Burney, Charles, 'An Account of the Musical Performances … in honour of Handel', London, 1785

Burney, Fanny, 'Fanny Burney's Diary', *The Folio Society*, London, 1961

Burney, Fanny, 'Evelina', Oxford, 1968, reprinted 1982 etc.

Burney, Fanny, 'The Early Diary of Frances Burney', ed. Annie R. Ellis, Bell, 1907

Burnim, Kalman A., 'David Garrick Director', Southern Illinois University Press, Carbondale and Edwardsville, 1961

Burrows Donald, & Dunhill, Rosemary,eds., 'Music and Theatre in Handel's World', Oxford, 2002

Burrows, Donald, 'Handel & the Foundling Hospital', *Music & Letters* 58, 1977

Burrows, Donald, 'Handel's Peace Anthem', *The Musical Times 114*, 1973

Burrows, Donald, 'The Autographs and early copies of Messiah: Some further thoughts', *Music & Letters 66*, 1985

Burrows, Donald, 'Handel and the 1727 Coronation', *Musical Times* 118 (1977)

Burrows, Donald, 'Handel and the English Chapel Royal', Oxford, 2005

Burrows, Donald, 'Handel', Oxford, 1994

Burrows, Donald, 'Handel's performances of 'Messiah': the evidence of the conducting score', *Music & Letters* 56, 1975

Burrows, Donald, 'Mr Harris's Score: a new look at the 'Mathews' manuscript of Handel's 'Messiah", *Music & Letters* 86, 2005

Burrows, Donald, 'Thomas Gethin: a Handel tenor', *Musical Times* 116 (1975)

Busby, Thomas, 'Concert Room and Orchestra Anecdotes', 3 vols., London, 1825

Carpenter, Adrian, 'William Croft's church music', *The Musical Times* 112, 1971

Chamberlayne, John, 'Magnae Britanniae Notitia...', 22nd-38th Editions, London, 1708-55

Charke, Charlotte, 'A Narrative of the Life of Mrs Charlotte Charke...', London, 1755

Chetwood, William, 'A General History of the Stage from its Origin to the Present Time', London, 1749

Churchill, Charles, 'Genuine Memoirs of Mr Charles Churchill...', London, 1765

Churchill, Charles, 'The Rosciad', Dublin, 1761, & London, 1763

Clark, Jane, 'Farinelli as Queen of the Night', *Eighteenth Century Music*, Cambridge, 2005

Clayton, Antony, 'London's Coffee Houses: a stimulating story', Historical Publications, London, 2003

Clive, Catherine, 'The Rehearsal: or Bays in Petticoats', London, 1753

Coffey, Charles, 'The Devil to Pay, or, the Wives Metamorphosed', London, 1748

Coke and Borg, 'Vauxhall Gardens, a history', New Haven & London, 2011

Colman, George, 'Some particulars of the life of the late George Colman...', London, 1795

Cooke, William, 'Memoirs of Charles Macklin', London, 1804

Coopersmith, J.M., 'The first Gesamtausgabe: Dr Arnold's Edition of Handel's Works', *Notes*, 1947

Coxe, William, 'Anecdotes of G.F. Handel and J.C. Smith...', London, 1799

Cradock, J., 'Literary and Miscellaneous Memoirs', London, 1826

Craske, Matthew, 'William Hogarth', Tate Publishing, London, 2000

Crewson, Richard, 'Apollo's Swan and Lyre', London, 2000

Crosby, Brian, 'The Musical Activities of the Sharp family', *RMA Research Chronicle 34*, 2001

Cudworth, Charles, 'Boyce and Arne: 'The Generation of 1710", *Music & Letters* 41, 1960

Cudworth, Charles, 'Handel, a biography with a survey of books, editions & recordings', London, 1972

Culpeper, Nicholas, 'The English physitian: an astrologo-physical discourse of the vulgar herbs of this nation', London, 1652

Cumberland, Richard, 'Memoirs', London, 1806

Cummings, W.H., 'Dr Arne and Rule, Britannia', London, 1912

Cummings, W.H., 'God save the King', Novello, London, 1902

Davies, Thomas, 'Dramatic Miscellanies', 3 vols., London, 1784; reprinted AMS Press, 1973

Davies, Thomas, 'Memoirs of the Life of David Garrick, Esq.', London, 1780; and London, 1808

Dean, Winton & Knapp, J. Merrill, 'Handel's Operas 1704-1726', Oxford, 1987

Dean, Winton, 'Handel and the Opera Seria', Oxford, 1970

Dean, Winton, 'Handel's Dramatic Oratorios and Masques', London, 1959

Delany, Mary, 'The Autobiography and Correspondence of Mary Delany', 6 vols., ed. Lady Llanover, London, 1861-2

Deutsch, Otto, 'Handel, a Documentary Biography', London, 1955

Dewes, Simon, 'Mrs Delany', London, 1940

Dibdin, Charles, 'A Complete History of the English Stage', 5 vols., London, 1797-1800

Dibdin, Charles, 'The Younger Brother', London, 1793

Dibdin, Charles, 'The Professional Life of Mr Dibdin, written by himself', 4 vols., London, 1803

Dibdin, Thomas, 'Reminiscences of Thomas Dibdin', London, 1827

Dictionary of National Biography, various edns.

Drogheda (Lord), Davison & Wheatcroft, 'The Covent Garden Album: 250 years of Theatre, Opera and Ballet', London, 1981

Edwards, Edward, 'Anecdotes of Painters...', London, 1808

Erickson, Carolly, 'Bonnie Prince Charlie, a biography', Bury St. Edmunds Suffolk, 1993

'Every Look Speaks – Portraits of David Garrick', Holburne Museum of Art, Bath, 2003

Festing, Michael, '6 songs & a dialogue with a Duet, sung at Ranelagh House by Mr Beard & Mrs Storer', London, 1748

Fiske, Roger, 'Boyce's Operas', *The Musical Times* 111, 1970

Fiske, Roger, 'English Theatre Music in the Eighteenth Century', Oxford, 1973

Fitzgerald, Percy, 'The Life of David Garrick', London, 1868 & 1899

Fitzpatrick, T., 'An Enquiry into ...a certain Popular Performer ...with an introduction to D[avi]d G[arric]k', London, 1760

Flower, Newman, 'Handel', London, 1923, revised edition 1959

Freeman, T. M., 'Dramatic Representations of British Soldiers and Sailors on the London Stage, 1660-1800', Lewiston N.Y., 1995

Friedlander, Arthur M., 'Two Patriotic Songs by Handel', *Musical Times*, May 1925

Frost, Tony, 'The Cantatas of John Stanley (1713-86)', *Music & Letters* 53, 1972

Garrick, David, 'The Fribbleriad', London, 1761

Garrick, David, "David Garrick: selected verse", ed. J.D. Hainsworth, Armidale, Australia, 1981

Garrick, David, 'Some unpublished correspondence of David Garrick', ed. George Pierce Baker, Boston, Mass., 1907

Garrick, David, 'The letters of David Garrick', vol. 2, ed. Little and Kahrl, OUP, London, 1963

Garrick, David, "The private correspondence of David Garrick', ed. James Boaden, London, 1835

Gartside, Bernard, 'A Brief History of Hampton School, 1557 – 1957',

Gay, John, 'The Beggar's Opera', Dover, New York, 1973

Gay, John, 'The Beggar's Opera', ed. Edgar V. Roberts, University of Nebraska Press, London, 1968 reprinted 1973 etc.

Gay, John, 'The Beggar's Opera', King's Music, Huntingdon, Cambs., c. 1990 [facsimile]

Gay, John, 'The Beggar's Opera', with Introduction by John Hampden, London, 1928, reprinted 1962

Genest, John, 'Some account of the English Stage ...1660 – 1830', 10 vols., Bath, 1832

Gentleman, Francis, 'The Dramatic Censor', London, 1770

Goldsmith, Oliver, 'Collected Works', ed. Friedman, Oxford, 1966

Goldsmith, Oliver, 'The Bee and other Essays', Oxford, 1914

Goldsmith, Oliver, 'The Bee', no. VIII, London, 1759

Greene, Maurice, 'Spenser's Amoretti...', London, 1739

Hailey, Elma, 'The Brietzcke Diary, 1759-65', *Notes & Queries*, 28 April 1951, 18 August 1951

Halsband, Robert, 'Mr Beard', Covent Garden Theatre '*About the House*', vol. 3 no. 2, 1971

Halsband, Robert, 'Sublime Steaks', Covent Garden Theatre '*About the House*', vol. 3 no. 10, 1971

Halsband, Robert, 'The Noble Lady and the Player', *History Today*, July 1968

'Hampstead: Social and Cultural Activities', A History of the County of Middlesex: Volume 9: *Hampstead*, Paddington, 1989

'Handel and the Fitzwilliam', Fitzwilliam Museum, Cambridge, 1974

'Handel House Museum companion', ed. Jacqueline Riding, London, 2001

Handel, G.F., 'Acis and Galatea', ed. Wilhelm Weismann, *Peters Edition*, Frankfurt, Leipzig, London, New York, 19??

Handel, G.F., 'Alexander's Feast', ed. Donald Burrows, *Novello Handel Edition*, London, 1982

Handel, G.F., 'Athaliah', ed. Chrysander, *Handel Gesellschaft 5*, Leipzig, 1859

Handel, G.F., 'Belshazzar', ed. Donald Burrows, *Novello Handel Edition*, London, 1993

Handel, G.F., 'Das Alexander-Fest', ed. Konrad Ameln, *Bärenreiter*, Kassel, Basel, London, N.Y., 1955

Handel, G.F., 'Dettingen Te Deum', ed. Chrysander, *Handel Gesellschaft* 25, Leipzig, Bergdorf-bei-Hamburg

Handel, G.F., 'Foundling Hospital Anthem', ed. Chrysander, *Handel Gesellschaft 36,* Leipzig, 1872

Handel, G.F., 'Four Coronation Anthems', ed. Clifford Bartlett, Oxford, 1988

Handel, G.F., 'Il Pastor Fido', ed. Chrysander, *Handel Gesellschaft 59 & 84,* Leipzig, Bergdorf-bei-Hamburg 1890

Handel, G.F., 'Imeneo', ed. Donald Burrows, *Hallische Händel-Ausgabe*, Bärenreiter, 2002

Handel, G.F., 'Israel in Egypt', ed. Chrysander, *Handel Gesellschaft* 16, Leipzig,

Handel, G.F., 'Jephtha', ed. Caspar Neher & Günther Rennert, *Bärenreiter*, Kassel, Basel, London, New York, 1961

Handel, G.F., 'Judas Maccabaeus', ed. Merlin Channon, *Novello Handel Edition*, London, 1998

Handel, G.F., 'L'Allegro ed il Penseroso', ed. Chrysander, *Handel Gesellschaft* 6, Leipzig

Handel, G.F., 'Messiah', ed. Arnold Schering & Kurt Soldan, *Peters Edition*, Frankfurt, Leipzig, London, New York, 1939 & 1967

Handel, G.F., 'Messiah', ed. Clifford Bartlett, Oxford, 1988

Handel, G.F., 'Messiah', ed. Watkins Shaw, *Novello Handel Edition*, London, 1959

Handel, G.F., 'Occasional Oratorio', ed. Chrysander, *Handel Gesellschaft* 43, Leipzig, Bergdorf-bei-Hamburg

Handel, G.F., 'Samson', ed. Donald Burrows, *Novello Handel Edition*, London, 2005

Handel, G.F., 'Saul', ed. Percy M. Young, *Bärenreiter*, Kassel, Basel, London, New York, 1968

Handel, G.F., 'Sing unto God', ed. Paul Steinitz, Oxford, 1971

Handel, G.F., 'The Ways of Zion do mourn', ed. Watkins Shaw, *Novello Handel Edition*, London, 1979

Handel, G.F., 'Theodora', ed. Günther Weissenborn, Zen-on, Japan, 1971

Handel, G.F., 'This is the day which the Lord hath made', ed. Chrysander, *Handel Gesellschaft 36*, Leipzig, 1872

Handel, G.F., 'Utrecht Te Deum', ed. Watkins Shaw, *Novello Handel Edition*, London, 1969

'Handel's Conducting Score of Messiah, reproduced in facsimile...', *Royal Musical Association*, Scolar Press, London, 1974

Harley, John, 'Music at the English Court in the 18th & 19th centuries' *Music & Letters* 50, 1969

Harman, Claire, 'Fanny Burney, a Biography', London, 2000

Hartmann, Cyril H., 'Enchanting Bellamy', London, 1956

Havard, William, 'Jeu d'esprit', m/s, Folger Shakespeare Library, Washington, USA

Hawkins, John, 'A General History of the Science and Practice of Music', London, 1776

Hawkins, Laetitia Matilda, 'Anecdotes, Biographical sketches and Memoirs', London, 1822

Hawkins, Laetitia Matilda, 'Memoirs, Anecdotes, Facts and Opinions...', 2 vols., London, 1824

Hayden, Ruth, 'Mrs Delany: her life and her flowers', The British Museum Press, London, 1980

Hayes, David A. 'East of Bloomsbury: streets, buildings and former residents', *Camden History Society*, 1998

Hayes, William, 'Anecdotes of the Five Music-Meetings ...at Church Leighton', Oxford, 1768

Heath, G.D., 'Hampton in the 19th Century', *Twickenham Local History Society*, 1973

Heath, G.D., 'The Chapel Royal at Hampton Court', *Twickenham Local History Society*, 1979

Herber, Mark D., 'Clandestine Marriages in the Chapel and Rules of the Fleet Prison 1680-1754', London, 2001

Hickman, Katie, 'Courtesans', London, 2003

Highfill, Burnim, Langhans, 'A Biographical Dictionary of Actors, Actresses, Musicians, Dancers, Managers & other stage personnel in London, 1660-1800', Southern Illinois University Press, Carbondale & Edwardsville, 1973

Hilton, Lisa, 'Mistress Peachum's Pleasure: the life of Lavinia, Duchess of Bolton', London, 2005

Hirsch, Paul, 'Dr Arnold's Handel Edition (1787-1797)', *The Music Review*, May 1947

Hoare, Sir Richard Colt, 'History of Modern Wiltshire', vol. 3, London, 1835

Hobhouse, Penelope, 'Gardening through the ages', New York & London, 1992

Hogarth, George, 'Memoir of Charles Dibdin...', London, 1842

Hogwood, Christopher & Luckett, Richard, eds., *Music in Eighteenth Century England*, Cambridge, 1983

Hogwood, Christopher, 'Handel', London, 1984

Hoskins, Robert H.B., 'Dr Samuel Arnold (1740-1802) an historical assessment', University of Auckland (Thesis), 1981

Hunt, John Dixon, 'Vauxhall and London's Garden Theatres', Cambridge, 1985

Hyde, Ralph, 'The A to Z of Georgian London', Harry Margary & Guildhall Library, London, 1981

Jackson, William, (of Exeter) 'Observations on the Present State of Music in London', London, 1971

Jenkins, Neil, 'Mighty Diverting', Illustrated talk given on Radio 3, 1975. [Text at London Museum]

Jenkins, Neil, 'John Beard: the Tenor voice that inspired Handel', *Göttinger Händel-Beiträge*, 12, pp. 197-216, Göttingen, 2008

Jenkins, Terry, 'The life of Lady Henrietta Herbert née Waldegrave', *Montgomeryshire Collections* 94 2006, pp. 103-129

Johnson, Samuel, 'Lives of the English Poets', ed. G.B. Hill, Oxford, 1905

Johnstone, H. Diack, 'Handel at Oxford in 1733', *Early Music*, May 2003

Johnstone, H. Diack, 'Treasure Trove in Gloucester...', *RMA Research Chronicle* 31, 1998

Joncus, B., & Barlow, J., eds, 'The Stage's Glory, John Rich (1692-1761)', University of Delaware Press, Newark, 2011

Keates, Jonathan, 'Handel: the man and his music', London, 1985

Kelly, Michael, 'Reminiscences', ed. Roger Fiske, O.U.P., London, 1975

Kendall, Alan, 'Garrick, a biography', London, 1985

Kidson, Frank, 'The Nurseries of English Song', *The Musical Times* 63, 1922

Kielmansegge, Count Frederick, 'Diary of a Journey to London in the years 1761-2', London, 1902

Klima, Slava, Bowers, Garry & Grant, 'Memoirs of Dr Charles Burney, 1726-1769', Univ. of Nebraska, Lincoln & London, 1988

Knapp, J. Merrill, 'A Forgotten Chapter in English 18th Century Opera', *Music & Letters* 42, 1961

Knapp, Mary, 'Checklist of Vesre by David Garrick', Univ. of Virginia Press, 1955

Larsen, Jens Peter, 'Handel's Messiah: Origins - Composition - Sources', London 1957 & N.Y. 1972

Letters of David Garrick and Georgiana Countess Spencer', ed. Earl Spencer & Christopher Dobson, Cambridge, 1960

Lewis, Peter E., 'Fielding's Burlesque Drama: its place in the tradition', Edinburgh University Press, c.1987

Lillywhite, Bryant, 'London Coffee Houses: a Reference Book...', London, 1963

Lloyd, Robert, 'To George Colman Esq: a familiar Epistle', London, 1761

Lockman, John, 'Rosalinda, A Musical Drama ...An Enquiry into the Rise and Progress of Operas and Oratorios', London, 1740

Lonsdale, Roger, 'Dr Charles Burney', London, 1965

Luckett, Richard, 'Handel's Messiah, a celebration', London, 1992

Lysons, Daniel, 'History and Progress of the ... Three Choirs Festival', Gloucester, 1812

Maddison, R., 'An Examination of the Oratorios which have been performed this season at Covent Garden Theatre', London, 1763

Mander and Mitchenson, 'Guide to the Maugham Collection of Theatrical Paintings', National Theatre, London, 1980

Mann, Alfred, 'Handel's successor: notes on J.C. Smith the younger', *Music in Eighteenth Century England*, Cambridge, 1983

Matthews, Betty, 'The Royal Society of Musicians of Great Britain: List of Members 1738-1984', London, 1985

McGuiness, Rosamond, 'English Court Odes 1660-1820', Oxford, 1971

McGuinness, Rosamond, 'The Music Business in Early Eighteenth-Century London', *The Quarterly Journal of Social Affairs*, 1985

McKillop, Alan Dugald, 'Bonnell Thornton's Burlesque Ode', *Notes and Queries*, 23rd July 1949

McVeigh, Simon, 'Calendar of London Concerts advertised in the London daily press', Goldsmiths College, Univ. of London, 2003 -

McVeigh, Simon, 'Concert life in London from Mozart to Haydn', Cambridge, 1993

McVeigh, Simon, 'Music and Lock Hospital in the 18th Century', *The Musical Times* 129, 1988

'Memoirs of Dr. Charles Burney', ed. Klima, Slava, Bowers, Garry & Grant, University of Nebraska Press, 1988

Montagu, Lady Mary Wortley, 'The complete letters of Lady Mary Wortley Montague', ed. Robert Halsband, Oxford, 1966

Moritz, Carl Philip,'Journeys of a German in England in 1782', ed. & trans. R. Nettel, London, 1965

Mowl, Timothy, 'Horace Walpole', London, 1996

'*Music for London Entertainment 1660-1800*', Macnutt, Tunbridge Wells, 1985

Myers, Robert Manson, 'Anna Seward: An Eighteenth Century Handelian', Williamsburg, 1947

Myers, Robert Manson, 'Handel, Dryden, Milton. Being a series of Observations...', London, 1956

Myers, Robert Manson, 'Mrs Delany: an 18th century Handelian', *The Musical Quarterly* 32, 1946

Nash, Mary, 'The Provoked Wife. The life and times of Susannah Cibber', London, 1977

Neville, Sylas, 'The Diary of Sylas Neville', ed. B. Cozens-Hardy, London, 1950

Neville, Thomas, 'Mr Neville's Imitations of Horace', London, 1758

'New Grove Dictionary of Music', ed. Stanley Sadie, London, 1980

'New Grove Dictionary of Opera', ed. Stanley Sadie, London, 1992

Nichols and Wray, 'A History of the Foundling Hospital', London 1935

Norton, Rictor, 'Early Eighteenth-Century Newspaper Reports: A Sourcebook, "Bills of Mortality"', December 19th 2001

Oulton, Walley C., 'A History of the Theatres of London from 1771-1795', 2 vols., London, 1796

Page, E.R., 'George Colman the elder', New York, 1935

Parkinson, John A., 'An index to the Vocal Works of Thomas Augustine Arne...', Detroit, 1972

Pasquali, Nicolo, '12 English Songs in score', London, 1750

Pearce, Charles E., 'Polly Peachum', London, 1913

Pears, Peter, 'Handel's Favorite Tenor', Aldeburgh Festival Programme Book, pp. 5-6, 1976

Pedicord, Harry W., 'By Their Majesties' Command', *The Society for Theatre Research*, London, 1991

Pedicord, Harry W., 'The Theatrical Public in the time of Garrick', Southern Illinois Press, Carbondale, Illinois, 1954

Phillips, Hugh, 'Mid-Georgian London', London, 1964

Picard, Liza, 'Dr Johnson's London', London, 2000

Pine, Edward, 'The Westminster Abbey Singers', London, 1953

Porter, Roy, 'Enlightenment', London, 2000

'Posthumous Letters addressed to Francis Colman and George Colman the elder etc.', London, 1820

Postle, Martin, 'Thomas Gainsborough', Tate Publishing, London, 2002

Potter, John, 'Observations on the Present State of Music and Musicians', London, 1762

Potter, John, 'Theatrical Review', 2 vols., London, 1772

'Powderham Castle', the Guidebook, Exeter, c. 2000

'Powis Castle', The National Trust Guidebook, c.2000

Price, Cecil, 'Theatre in the age of Garrick', Oxford, 1973

Purcell, Henry, 'Don Quixote', *Music for London Entertainment 1660-1800*, series A vol. 2, Macnutt, Tunbridge Wells, 1984

Range, Matthias, 'William Boyce's anthem for the Wedding of King George III', *The Musical Times*, Summer 2006

Reilly, Joan, 'The Theatre Royal, Richmond Green, 1765-1884', *Journal of the Richmond Local History Society* no.9, 1988

Riding, Jacqueline, 'The Purest Benevolence: Handel and the Foundling Hospital', *Handel House Trust*, c.2001

Rimbault, E.F., ed., 'The Old Cheque-Book …of the Chapel Royal from 1561-1744', *Camden Society* N.S.3., 1872

Rimbault, Edward, 'Charles Dibdin as a writer', *Music & Letters*, April 1938

Ripley, Henry, 'The History and Topography of Hampton-on-Thames', London, 1885

RMA Research Chronicle no. 5, 1965, Salisbury Festivals

RMA Research Chronicle no. 6, 1966, Cambridge Festivals

RMA Research Chronicle no. 8, 1966, Birmingham Festivals

Robbins Landon, H.C., 'Handel and his World', London, 1984

Rogers, Ben, 'Beef and Liberty', London, 2003

'Rose Hill, Hampton', *Local History Notes*, Richmond upon Thames Local Studies Collection, c. 2000

Rosenthal, Harold, 'Covent Garden: Memories and Traditions', London, 1976

Rubenhold, Hallie, 'The Covent Garden Ladies', Stroud Glos., 2005

Sadie, Stanley and Hicks, Anthony, 'Handel Tercentenary Collection', *RMA Association*, Basingstoke & London, 1987

Sadie, Stanley, 'Handel', London, 1962

Sanders, L.G.D., 'The Festival of the Sons of the Clergy, 1655-1955', The Musical Times 97, 1956

Sands, Mollie, 'The Eighteenth-Century Pleasure Gardens of Marylebone 1737-1777', *The Society for Theatre Research*, 1987

Sands, Mollie, 'The problem of Teraminta', *Music & Letters* 33, 1952

Sands, Mollie, 'Invitation to Ranelagh, 1742-1803', London, 1946

Scholes, Percy A., 'George the Third as Music Lover', *The Musical Quarterly* 28, 1942

Scholes, Percy A., 'The Great Dr Burney', Oxford, 1948

Scholes, Percy A., 'God save the Queen', Oxford, London, 1954

Shapiro, A.H., 'Drama of an infinitely superior nature: Handel's early English Oratorios…', *Music & Letters* 74, 1993

Sheaf & Howe, 'Hampton and Teddington Past', Historical Publications Ltd, London, 1995

Shebbeare, John, (Joseph Pittard), 'Observations on Mr Garrick's Acting', London, 1758

Shebbeare, John, (Joseph Pittard), 'Letters which have passed between John Beard… and John Shebbeare', London, 1767

Shebbeare, John, (Joseph Pittard), 'Letters on the English Nation, by Batista Angeloni, a Jesuit resident in London', London, 1755

Shesgreen, Sean, ed., 'Engravings by Hogarth', New York, 1973

Simon, Jacob, ed., 'Handel: a celebration of his Life and Times', National Portrait Gallery, London, 1985

Smith, Helen R., 'David Garrick', The British Library, London, 1979

Smith, Ruth, 'Handel's Oratorios and Eighteenth Century Thought', Cambridge, 1995

Smith, Ruth, 'The achievements of Charles Jennens, 1700-1773', *Music & Letters* 70, 1989

Smith, William C., 'A Handelian's Notebook', London, 1965

Smith, William C., 'George III, Handel, and Mainwaring', *The Musical Times* 65, 1924

Smither, Howard, 'A History of the Oratorio', 4 vols., Univ. of North Carolina Press, Chapel Hill, 1977

Smollett, Tobias, 'Roderick Random', London, 1748

Smollett, Tobias, 'The Expedition of Humphrey Clinker', London, 1771

Smollett, Tobias, 'Sir Launcelot Greaves', London, 1762

Sobel, Dava, 'Longitude', London, 1995

Stein, Elizabeth, 'David Garrick, Dramatist', New York, 1938

Stillingfleet, Benjamin, 'Literary Life and select works of Benjamin Stillingfleet', London, 1811

Strunk, Oliver, 'Source Readings in Music History', London, 1981

Summerson, John, 'Georgian London', Yale University Press, New Haven and London, 1945 repr. 2003

'Survey of London', vol. xxxv, The Athlone Press, University of London, G.L.C., 1970

'The Blackwell History of Music in Britain', *The Eighteenth Century*, ed. Johnstone & Fiske, Oxford, 1990

'The Cambridge Companion to Handel', ed. Donald Burrows, Cambridge, 1997

'The correspondence of Gio. Giacomo Zamboni', *RMA Research Chronicle* 24, 1991

'The Foundling Museum', London, 2004

'The Gentleman's Magazine', various dates

'The London Stage 1660-1800', Part 3, 2 vols., ed. Arthur Scouten, Carbondale, Illinois, 1961

'The London Stage 1660-1800', Part 4, 3 vols., ed. George Winchester Stone, Carbondale, Illinois, 1962

'The London Stage 1660-1800', Part 5, 3 vols., ed. C.B. Hogan, Carbondale, Illinois, 1968

'The New Foundling Hospital for Wit', Pt. 1-4, London, 1768-71; & New Edition in 6 vols, London, 1784

'The New Oxford History of Music', *Concert Music 1630-1750*, ed. Gerald Abraham, Oxford, 1986

'The New Oxford History of Music', *The Age of Enlightenment 1745-1790*, ed. Wellesz & Sternfeld, Oxford, 1973

'The Rational Rosciad' by F- B- L- , London, 1767

'The *Revels* History of Drama in English', vol. 5, 1660-1750, ed. T.W. Craik, London, 1976

'The *Revels* History of Drama in English', vol. 6, 1750-1880, ed. C. Leech & T.W. Craik, London, 1975

'The Stuffed Owl; an anthology of bad verse…', ed. Wyndham Lewis & Charles James Lee, London & Toronto, 1930

'The Wordsworth Companion to Literature in English', ed. I. Ousby, Cambridge, 1988, reprinted Ware, Hertfordshire, 1994

'Theatrical Disquisitions, or, a Review of the late Riot at Drury Lane Theatre…', London, 1763

Thorold, Peter, 'The London Rich: the creation of a great City…', London, 1999

'Three Original letters to a Friend …on the cause and manner of the late Riot at …Drury Lane', London, 1763

Timbs, John, 'Clubs and Clublife in London', London, 1873

Timbs, John, 'Curiosities of London', London, 1867

Troubridge, St. Vincent, 'The Benefit System in the British Theatre', *Society for Theatre Research*, London, 1967

Vaughan, William, 'British Painting The Golden Age', London, 1999

Vickers, Brian, ed., 'Shakespeare: the Critical Heritage', vol. 4 (1753-65) & 5 (1765-74), London, 1979

Vickers, D., ed., 'Handel', Farnham, 2011

Victor, Benjamin, 'The History of the Theatres of London from 1760 to the present time', London, 1771

Waldegrave, Lady Mary Hermione, 'Waldegrave Family History', private publication, 1975

Waldegrave, the 13th Earl, The Private Papers of the Waldegrave Family, Chewton Mendip

Waldegrave, the 1st Earl, 'Letters to Lord Waldegrave, private and domestic, 1732-40', Chewton Mendip

Waldegrave, the 1st Earl, 'The French correspondence of James, 1st Earl Waldegrave', ed. Rex A. Barrell, Lampeter, c. 1996

Waldegrave, the 2nd Earl, 'The Memoirs and Speeches of James, 2nd Earl Waldegrave', ed. J.C.D. Clark, Cambridge, 1988

Walpole, Horace, 'Horace Walpole's correspondence with Sir Horace Mann', ed. Lewis, Smith & Lam, Yale University Press, 1954

Walpole, Horace, 'The Letters of Horace Walpole', ed. Mrs Paget Toynbee, Oxford, 1903-5

Watkins Shaw, Harold, 'A Textual and Historical companion to Handel's Messiah', Novello, Sevenoaks Kent, 1965

Watkins Shaw, Harold, 'The Story of Handel's Messiah', Novello, London, 1963

Watkins Shaw, Harold, 'The Succession of Organists', Oxford, 1991

Wedd, Kit, 'The Foundling Museum', The Foundling Museum, London, 2004

Wilkinson, Tate, 'Memoirs of his own Life…', 4 vols., York, 1790

Wilkinson, Tate, 'The Wandering Patentee…', York, 1795

Williams, C.F. Abdy, 'A short Historical Account of the Degrees in Music at Oxford and Cambridge…', London, 1893

Williams, C.F. Abdy, 'Handel', London, 1901

Woodforde, Rev. James, 'The Diary of a Country Parson', London, 1992

Wollenberg, Susan, 'Music at Oxford in the Eighteenth & Nineteenth Centuries', Oxford, 2001

Wollenberg, Susan, 'The Oxford exercises in the 18th century', *Early Music*, November 2000

Woodiwiss, Audrey, 'The History of Covent Garden…', London, 1980

Wright, Geoffrey N., 'Turnpike Roads', Shire Publications, Princes Risborough, Bucks., 1997

Wroth, Warwick, 'The London Pleasure Gardens of the 18th Century', London, 1896, reprinted 1979

Wyn Jones, D., ed., 'Music in Eighteenth Century Britain', Aldershot, 2000

Wyndham, Henry S., 'The annals of Covent Garden Theatre', London, 1906

Yorke, Philip C., ed., 'The Diary of John Baker… 1751-1778…', London, 1931

Young, Percy M., 'Handel', London, 1947

Zöllner, Eva, 'English Oratorio after Handel: The London Oratorio Series & its repertory 1760-1800', Marburg, 2002

INDEX